D0323832

JFK

—AND—

VIETNAM

DECEPTION, INTRIGUE, AND THE STRUGGLE FOR POWER

John M. Newman

WARNER BOOKS

A Time Warner Company

Copyright © 1992 by John M. Newman
All rights reserved.

Warner Books, Inc., 1271 Avenue of the Americas, New York, NY
10020

 A Time Warner Company

Printed in the United States of America
First printing: February 1992
10 9 8 7 6 5 4 3 2 1

Library of Congress Cataloging-in-Publication Data

Newman, John M.
    JFK and Vietnam : deception, intrigue, and the struggle for power
/ John M. Newman.
        p.   cm.
    Includes bibliographical references and index.
    ISBN 0-446-51678-3
    1. Vietnamese Conflict, 1961–1975—United States.   2. United
States—Politics and government—1961–1963.   3. Kennedy, John F.,
(John Fitzgerald), 1917–1963.   I. Title.
DS558.N49   1992
959.704'3373—dc20   91-37711
                                                            CIP

Book design by Giorgetta Bell McRee

To those who served,
and their families.

ACKNOWLEDGMENTS

As an academic who has for twenty-five years studied and taught East Asian history, and as a military man with many East Asian assignments, this subject would appear to be one with which I should be comfortable. That did not turn out to be the case. Although the material was often electrifying, it was just as often depressing, tragic, and frightening. There were times when I worried whether I should go forward with it. I took solace in the works of other active-duty Army officers who are also scholars in this field. Among them, Andrew Krepinevich's *The Army and Vietnam* and Charles Parker's *Vietnam: Strategy for a Stalemate* were particularly inspiring for their courage in handling controversial theses with bold candor.

My own military background should not be construed in any way to mean that the views in this work represent those of the Army, the Department of Defense, or any government organization. Also I would like to say—because I am so often asked about it—that never in the more than ten years of working on this subject (or at any other time in my eighteen years of service) has the Army or anyone in my chain of command criticized me for pursuing this subject or in any way attempted to influence me against it. My experience has been quite the contrary, and I thank them now for their encouragement and trust.

To those who helped early on and throughout the process of putting this account together, like George Allen, Bill Benedict, Don Blascak, Jim

Drummond, Roland Dutton, Sam Dowling, Hal Ford, Jimmy Harris, Jerry King, Daniel Porter, I thank them all from the bottom of my heart. Much of this work would not have been possible without the benefit of their insights and their willingness to share what, in some instances, were painful recollections. For some, it was their wish that young soldiers and officers learn what happened during the early years of the Vietnam War in the hope that this might help prevent any repeat of their unsavory experience. My thanks go also to the many other former Army advisors and intelligence specialists whose contributions were useful to this work. To McGeorge Bundy, William Bundy, Walt Rostow, and especially Bill Colby, I thank them for the time they gave from their busy schedules for interviews.

For documents I am indebted to the Army's Center for Military History in Washington and Carlisle Barracks, Pennsylvania, for their untiring help in the declassification of documents—long overdue but for which there has never been enough manpower to make the effort. They will shortly be, along with the taped interviews and transcripts, at the John F. Kennedy Library where future historians and researchers may use them. Special thanks go to Army historian Vince Demma, whose help and advice were indispensable. To the staffs at the Kennedy and Johnson libraries I am deeply indebted for their prompt, efficient, and extensive assistance with the documents, especially to William Johnson at the Kennedy Library for all of the services he provided.

John Bardi, Don Blascak, Dan Ellsberg, David Lifton, and Peter Dale Scott read early versions of either the entire manuscript or major portions of it. They provided useful criticisms, insights, and sound advice. David, who has long been a source of encouragement, gave liberally from his own time to offer comments and criticisms. To Patricia Lambert, who painstakingly and efficiently edited the entire work, provided written and verbal improvements to the text on technical and conceptual points, and who, in general, treated every sentence with loving care, I am especially grateful. Pat's contribution was enormous and this work is far more readable as a result of her efforts. My thanks go also to Susan Suffes, Senior Editor at Warner Books, for her helpful feedback, and also to Fred Chase, whose thorough copy editing helped not only the text but also the source notes—for which serious researchers will be appreciative. I am also grateful for the help given by Oliver Stone and Alex Ho in finding this publisher, and appreciative of Oliver's genuine and continuing interest in research on the Vietnam War.

What prompted this endeavor and sustained me through it all is the academic side of my life. Dr. Richard Thornton of George Washington University has been my teacher, advisor, and friend for the last twenty-five years; he always provided unfailing support and wise counsel. To

Jiyul Kim and Charles Hooper I am indebted for the kind of friendship and encouragement that only someone who is very nearly in the same shoes that you are can give. To the fifteen majors in my staff group at the Command and General Staff College (CGSC) who put up with my tribulations and eagerly discussed the implications of the shared experiences in this work as they pertain to counterinsurgency, they should be able to see how the discussions in our classroom often emerge in these pages.

To my wife and children, with whom I have spent too little time in the course of this project, please forgive me. Future historians are indebted to Alexandra, Mary Sue, and John, whose little hands did so much work to help sort and stamp the 15,000 pages of documents so that they may be easily found, used, and cited. Special credit should be given to my oldest daughter, Alexandra, who did an amazing amount of work on documents and helped on special research topics.

It goes without saying, all the contributions aside, I alone accept responsibility for any shortcomings in this work. In some ways it would have been easier to sit on this material for several more years, to wait for the declassification of more documents, to do more research, fine-tuning, and polishing. It is my hope that in publishing this work now others will have access to the material earlier, and that the attention of many people will make the process of reconstructing the history of the Vietnam War a better one.

CONTENTS

FOREWORD

by John Bardi

Who cares? Why bother? What does this have to do with me? Even if I were interested, I can't get involved—and I don't have the time! Sound familiar? It ought to. It is the sound of citizenship in America. But perhaps this soundscape is beginning to change; and if so, then John Newman's book is a melody for a new song of citizenship.

Certainly this book seems destined to create an impact. Based on much new material, including interviews conducted by the author and documents, newly declassified, it is the most exhaustive study to date of the early years of our involvement in Vietnam. The main conclusion of the book—that while publicly proclaiming a continuing commitment (to appease the right) and a modest withdrawal (to appease the left), Kennedy was actually secretly planning to withdraw from Vietnam as soon as he was reelected—should stimulate major reexamination not only of the war but of the Kennedy presidency as well.

Yet in spite of all the impressive scholarship, this is not a book for the specialist alone. After all, American myth and self-image are involved here, and the writing is up to the pedigree of the tale. Like a storyteller on a roll, John Newman writes with factual clarity *and* high dramatic intensity. If these events could speak in their own voice, this is the sound they would make.

The result is an American tragedy of Shakespearean scope and power.

Reading this book is like watching that tragedy being acted on stage before us. As we turn the pages we want to scream our warnings out loud.

Too, there is a Shakespearean cast of characters here—honest soldiers, officials who endlessly engage in intrigue and deception, gullible citizens, Far Eastern feudal potentates . . . right up to the tragic hero himself, President Kennedy. And if we are all touched with the dross of our earthly natures, then some of us seem to be more touched than others. Thus do the villains emerge: the unscrupulous schemer, Edward "Iago" Lansdale, the shocking manipulator, General "Macbeth" Taylor, and the almost interchangeable dissemblers, the MACV "Rosencrantz and Guildenstern" leaders. And everywhere in the background are soldiers in the lower ranks, unaware that their valiant and often heroic efforts are merely urinations into the howling wind of a storm of deception and betrayal.

Of course, the central character—the Hamlet of the entire tragedy—is President Kennedy. Thinking hard ("to be or not to be" involved) and finding himself being systematically deceived, he ends up engaging in an elaborate deception himself. The result is that, even this many years past, we are still confused and uncertain. Was he a great man fighting as best he could against "something rotten," or was he too full of pride to notice that he was becoming the very thing he was fighting against?

But that is another book. This book is sufficient unto itself. And happily, the author does not seem to be operating from a political subtext. Indeed, the political lessons of this study are simple: politicians should tell the truth about policy, soldiers should stay out of politics, and intelligence analysts should never, ever allow their data to be corrupted. Perhaps reading this book will help to bring these lessons home. If so, then in the spirit of Kennedy's famous inaugural lines, John Newman will have delivered a large part of what *he* can do for his country.

JFK
AND
VIETNAM

The web of our life is of a mingled yarn, good and ill together; our virtues would be proud if our faults whipped them not, and our crimes would despair if they were not cherished by our virtues.

Shakespeare
All's Well That Ends Well

PART I

LOSS OF INNOCENCE

PROLOGUE

HOOK, LINE, AND SINKER

"This is the worst one we've got, isn't it?" President Kennedy said, as he looked up at Walt Rostow with a worried expression on his face. "You know, Eisenhower never mentioned it. He talked at length about Laos, but never uttered the word Vietnam."[1] It was only six days after the inauguration, and Kennedy had just finished reading a report on Vietnam. Rostow, his specialist on Southeast Asia in the National Security Council,[2] had given it to Kennedy and insisted he read every word. Rostow described it as "an extremely vivid and well written account of a place that was going to hell in a hack."[3] In between the well-crafted lines of this report, however, was an ulterior motive: its author, Edward Lansdale, wanted to be the Ambassador to South Vietnam.

Lansdale, then an Air Force general working in the Office of Special Operations for the Secretary of Defense, had a long history of experience in covert operations and was a recognized expert on Vietnam. An advertising specialist before joining the OSS (the precursor of the CIA) in World War II, then the Army, and eventually the Air Force, Lansdale had served in Vietnam during the Eisenhower administration and contributed in a major way to the birth and subsequent development of South Vietnam. In the process he became a close personal friend of South Vietnamese President Ngo Dinh Diem. In the Eisenhower period, Lansdale had worked in the Saigon Military Mission, but he had powerful allies in the CIA, and his professional patron was the agency's Director, Allen Dulles.[4]

Lansdale even owed his promotion to Brigadier General to Dulles, who had intervened with Air Force Chief of Staff Curtis LeMay to bring it about.

In January 1961 Lansdale returned from a fact-finding trip to Vietnam, where the communists, who had launched a serious guerrilla campaign two years earlier, had made impressive gains. His report said the Viet Cong goal was to take over South Vietnam in 1961, and that they were much closer to accomplishing this objective than he had realized from the reports he had read in Washington.[5] While in Vietnam, Lansdale was shocked when he saw intelligence maps of the estimated situation, and he reported that Diem "held similar grim views."[6]

The extent of the area controlled by the Viet Cong was particularly disturbing. They had the initiative, Lansdale said, and, excluding Saigon, control over most of the region "from the jungled foothills of the High Plateau north of Saigon all the way south down to the Gulf of Siam." This was Vietnam's "bread-basket," he pointed out, "where most of its rubber and rice are grown." If the Viet Cong succeeded, Lansdale warned, the rest of Southeast Asia would be "easy pickings for our enemy," because the toughest pro-American force in that region would be gone. Lansdale had a solution for this dire problem: the U.S. needed to show strong support for President Diem and make changes in U.S. personnel, including the replacement of Ambassador Elbridge Durbrow. Durbrow, he said, was not considered a friend by the Vietnamese because they believed he sympathized with an attempted coup, staged in November 1960, against Diem.

A bespectacled, gravel-voiced career Foreign Service Officer with a "combative and peppery nature" and a vocabulary fit for a barroom, Durbrow had many years of diplomatic experience in the Soviet Union and had been serving as the American Ambassador in Vietnam since March 1957. Unlike his predecessor, Durbrow asserted his authority as head of the mission, which led to problems with the Chief of the Military Assistance and Advisory Group (MAAG), Lieutenant General Samuel T. ("Hangin' Sam") Williams, who liked to run the MAAG independently of the Embassy. The two often ended up in shouting matches during Country Team meetings.[7] Durbrow, or "Durbie" as his State Department colleagues called him, eventually ran afoul of Diem, who did not take kindly to the American Ambassador's attempt, in September 1960, to superimpose the American system of legislative controls and checks and balances on South Vietnam's government.[8]

Two days after Kennedy read the Lansdale report, the General was invited to attend a meeting in the President's office.[9] Present were Vice President Johnson, Secretary of State Dean Rusk, Secretary of Defense Robert McNamara, Chairman of the Joint Chiefs of Staff Lyman Lemnitzer, and CIA Director Dulles. The meeting, called to discuss Cuba, was expanded to include Vietnam due to the President's "keen interest" in the Lansdale report.[10] After the CIA briefing on the Cuban invasion plan, Assistant Secretary of State for the Far East J. Graham Parsons and Lansdale joined the meeting. The President greeted Lansdale and complimented him on his report.[11] Kennedy, motioning to Rusk, then asked Lansdale, "Has the Secretary here mentioned that I wanted you to be Ambassador to Vietnam?"[12] Lansdale replied that it would be an honor.

Before receiving Lansdale's presentation, Kennedy decided to hear a briefing on the Counterinsurgency Plan (CIP) for Vietnam. Ambassador Durbrow had recently forwarded the CIP from Vietnam, and Parsons was there to explain its contents to the President. The CIP boiled down to two key elements. The first was more U.S. military aid for a 20,000-man increase to Diem's army. The second was a requirement tying this aid to reforms by Diem. These included streamlining his civil and military chains of command; instituting an economic planning system; and democratic reforms, such as allowing the formation of political parties and village elections.

Kennedy questioned whether the military measures in the CIP were sufficient to achieve the stated goal of permitting Saigon to move onto the offensive. No one offered a clear answer. He then asked if the real problem was one of "politics and morale," but this important question, too, went unanswered.[13] Kennedy ordered McGeorge Bundy, his Assistant for National Security Affairs, to promptly see that a task force, similar to the one on Cuba, be set up for Vietnam.[14] Twice the President expressed interest in South Vietnamese guerrilla operations against the North Vietnamese.[15] "We must be better off in three months than we are now," Kennedy declared.

This poorly focused and superficial discussion of the CIP, especially its linkage of U.S. aid to political reforms, would return to haunt American Vietnam policy. For no one told Kennedy of the poisonous waters that spawned this linkage: that Ambassador Durbrow, objecting to the enlargement of the South Vietnamese Army, came up with the idea of reforms as a quid pro quo compromise. Furthermore, no one questioned how Diem might react to them. Yet the CIP assumed that Diem's ability to resist the communist threat depended, in large part, on their success. Nor did anyone tell Kennedy these reforms were, in fact, anathema to Diem, and that Ambassador Durbrow (who knew this) anticipated that Diem might have to be forced to implement them.[16]

Vietnam had been added to the agenda at the last moment and the principals were poorly prepared to deal with the subject. Parsons privately thought the CIP was inadequate, and later revealed he had made a deliberate but veiled attempt to portray it that way, but the President and "others present" didn't get what he was driving at.[17]

Considering his close relationship with Diem, Lansdale might have mentioned Diem's distaste for Durbrow's prescription for democracy in South Vietnam. Instead, Lansdale's focus was self-serving and his comments designed to persuade Kennedy to appoint him the new Ambassador.[18] Lansdale had already begun his lobbying effort in his written report, which advocated "an unusual man" be sent to Vietnam—one who, because of his understanding, could influence people. The report emphasized the need to "get close to the Vietnamese," touted Diem's confidence in the CIA and the MAAG, and stressed Diem's distrust of certain "Americans" in the Foreign Service, a not-too-subtle dig at Durbrow. At the meeting Lansdale continued jabbing at Durbrow, reiterating to Kennedy that Diem felt Durbrow and others were not fully behind him, and suspected the Ambassador favored the coup rebels.

Kennedy asked if a letter or gesture would help rebuild Diem's morale, and Lansdale replied that it "would help a great deal." Lansdale's charges against Durbrow, however, put Secretary of State Rusk on the spot, sealing the Ambassador's fate. Rusk reacted by pointing out that U.S. diplomats "were caught between pressing Diem to do things he did not wish to do and the need to convey to him American support." Nonetheless he conceded that Durbrow "should be relieved in the near future."[19]

Neither Lansdale's presentation nor Parsons' briefing on the CIP told the whole story. Kennedy was not given, and he failed to demand, an explanation of why American aid was to be inextricably linked to reforms; nor did he ask how important these reforms were to the overall success of the program, and what alternatives should be considered if Diem refused to carry them out. Such a discussion would have revealed deep divisions in his administration on fundamental issues in Vietnam policy. These divisions remained concealed, and a few days later Kennedy took his first step toward a deeper American commitment to Vietnam. Alarmed by Lansdale's Vietnam trip report, Kennedy impulsively grasped for the first solutions within reach: Lansdale *and* the CIP. Ironically, Lansdale would facilitate Diem's effort to undermine the reforms mandated by the CIP and, as a result, American policy would become bogged down for the next three months. Moreover, the hidden fissures in Kennedy's administration and the conflict over what to do about Diem formed a slowly growing cancer that would end with Diem's assassination three years later.

Diem's tragic end affected no one more deeply than Lansdale, who could not have foreseen this outcome on that first triumphant day in Kennedy's office. That day Kennedy had been immediately attracted to Lansdale, perhaps because both men had similar qualities: energy, fresh ideas, directness, and self-confidence in the face of adversity. Far from being put off by the dark side of America's most celebrated covert operator, the President was fascinated by Lansdale's James Bond mystique. The one thing Kennedy made up his mind to do right away was to remove Ambassador Durbrow and replace him with Lansdale. That hasty, pivotal decision to admit Lansdale into the inner sanctum of power was a choice that Kennedy alone made. The President had bit hard and took the bait, hook, line, and sinker.

NOTES

1. W.W. Rostow, *The Diffusion of Power: An Essay in Recent History* (New York: Macmillan, 1972), p. 265.

2. W.W. Rostow, interview with Richard Neustadt, April 11, 1964, JFK Library, Oral History Collection, p. 44.

McGeorge Bundy was Kennedy's Special Assistant for National Security Affairs, but Walt Rostow was responsible for Vietnam and Laos in the NSC and reported directly to the President. Robert Johnson and Robert Komer were Rostow's assistants on the Far East.

Rostow, in the interview, in choosing between January 26 and February 2 for the date he gave the Lansdale report to Kennedy, wrongly chose February 2. We know that McGeorge Bundy noted the President's reaction to the report on January 27, and of the President's remark to Lansdale himself about the report during the January 28 meeting. See Department of State, *Foreign Relations of the United States, 1961–1963: Vietnam* (Washington, D.C.: U.S. Government Printing Office, 1988), vol. 1, p. 13 (hereafter referred to as *State History*).

3. Rostow, interview with Richard Neustadt, April, 11, 1964, p. 44.

4. The role of Allen Dulles and Secretary of State John Foster Dulles in Lansdale's career is suggested by Lansdale's own work, *In the Midst of Wars* (New York: Harper and Row, 1972), pp. 343–45.

5. For the full text see Department of Defense, *United States–Vietnam Relations, 1945–1967 [The Pentagon Papers]* (Washington, D.C.: U.S. Government Printing Office, 1971), Book 11, pp. 1–13 (hereafter referred to as *PP*, DOD ed.).

6. In fact, a December 4, 1960, MAAG map depicting areas controlled by the Viet Cong is extant (although it is deteriorating). JFK Library, NSF, Agencies-MAAG, Document 65a, Red Area Map,

7. Ronald H. Spector, *Advice and Support. The Early Years, the U.S. Army in Vietnam* (Washington, D.C.: U.S. Government Printing Office, 1983), p. 276.

8. William Colby, *Lost Victory* (Chicago: Contemporary Books, 1989), pp. 74–75.

9. The only record of this meeting currently available is Rostow's memo to McGeorge Bundy two days after; JFK Library, NSF Country File, Vietnam, Box 193, January 30, 1961.

10. This is according to a January 27 McGeorge Bundy memo to Dulles, Rusk, and McNamara; *State History,* 1961, p. 13, n. 1.

11. *State History,* 1961, Document 3, pp. 13–15.

12. David Halberstam, *The Best and the Brightest,* (New York: Random House, 1972), p. 128.

13. Someone, probably Chief of Staff Lemnitzer, answered that most of the GVN forces were "pinned" on the front against 300,000 North Vietnamese forces, the idea being that more than politics and morale were involved. While it may have been true that more than politics was involved, most of the GVN forces were certainly not on the border.

14. In a conversation with McNamara and Rostow afterward, Rusk expressed "anxiety" that "these task forces might obtrude the normal workings of the government." McNamara replied that "for crisis situations such measures would have to be accepted." See Rostow memo to McGeorge Bundy, January 30, 1961, in *State History,* 1961, Document 4, pp. 16–19.

15. In the first instance Kennedy asked whether such operations were possible. Dulles replied that only four teams of eight men each existed, and that they were only being used in the south for harassment. Dulles also cryptically noted, "The CIA had other notions about offensive operations." In the second instance, Kennedy "stated he wants guerrillas to operate in the north and asked what the situation there was."

16. See full text of Durbrow's January 4, 1961, cable in *PP,* DOD ed., Book 10, p. 1,359. See also Senator Mike Gravel, ed., *The Pentagon Papers: History of United States Decision Making on Vietnam* (Boston: Beacon Press, 1971), vol. 2, p. 25 (hereafter referred to as *PP,* Gravel ed.). Lansdale had hinted at differences of opinion by saying the CIP had been written in the Defense Department and then sent to Saigon for coordination, but this vagary was not pursued.

17. J. Graham Parsons, interview with Dennis J. O'Brian, August 22, 1969, JFK Library, Oral History Collection, p. 22. In this interview, Parsons incorrectly dated this White House meeting as having taken place on January 21 or 22.

18. Deputy Assistant Secretary of Defense William Bundy later (in his unpublished manuscript) recalled it had been easy to see that "Lansdale hoped that he himself might be picked" as the new Ambassador. William Bundy, unpublished manuscript, p. 3-32.

19. Summary Record of a Meeting, The White House, Washington, January 28, 1961, 10 A.M.–12:15 P.M., drafted and initialed by J. Graham Parsons, in *State History,* 1961, Document 3, p. 15. The Rostow record of the meeting does not include Rusk's comment that Durbrow should be relieved. Since Durbrow was approaching four years of service as Ambassador, Parsons' version is probably correct. Note also that Parsons' "Record Summary" says "Rusk suggested, and the President agreed" that the Vietnam task force be established. This contradicts Rostow's record that Kennedy proposed it and Rusk expressed misgivings about it afterward to McNamara and others. On this point, Parsons' version seems suspect.

CHAPTER ONE

STRAIGHT TO THE BRINK OVER LAOS

THE "LAOS NEUTRALIZATION GAMBIT"

The day before John F. Kennedy was inaugurated, he got a surprising piece of advice from the outgoing President. Eisenhower told him that Laos was the key to all of Southeast Asia, and if Laos fell the U.S. would have to "write off the whole area."[1] Laos, a small landlocked country in the middle of the Southeast Asian peninsula, straddles both Thailand and South Vietnam. Because of this location its fall posed a threat to Thailand and, especially, South Vietnam. Laos would have to be defended, Eisenhower said, even if the U.S. had to do it without help from its allies. Neutralization was out of the question. "It would be fatal," Eisenhower told Kennedy, "for us to permit Communists to insert themselves into the Laotian government." Kennedy, however, had his own ideas. During his first press conference he declared Laos should be an "independent" country free of domination by either side.[2] Unfortunately, Kennedy's vision would never be realized, and the unfolding deterioration in that country would become the primary foreign policy focus of the new administration prior to the Bay of Pigs fiasco. Eventually, communist domination of key Laotian terrain would open the door wide for infiltration into South Vietnam.

By early February it looked as though Eisenhower's concerns had been justified: the military situation in Laos was critical. Supplied by an ongoing Soviet airlift, the communist Pathet Lao already held the strategic Plain of Jars. The U.S.-backed forces, commanded by General Nosavan Phoumi, were dangerously dispersed defending the approaches to Vientiane, Luang Prabang, and the southern panhandle (see map #1 in insert). Kennedy ordered the formation of a Laos Task Force and asked for daily reports. Rusk delivered the initial task force plan to the White House meeting on February 7, 1961. It had three basic elements: 1) the King of Laos would declare Laos neutral; 2) General Phoumi would conduct an offensive against the communist Pathet Lao and capture the Plain of Jars in central Laos to strengthen the negotiating position of the government; and 3) the Southeast Asian Treaty Organization (SEATO) would carry out supporting moves, including the deployment of a U.S. military unit to Thailand.[3] There was a broad consensus among Kennedy's advisors that the communists had to be stopped by force before a genuinely neutral Laos could exist, and that the U.S. should intervene militarily "if necessary."[4] A neutral Laos in which the Pathet Lao held the upper hand militarily posed the larger strategic problem of communist control of the Ho Chi Minh Trail, which would give them logistical access to Vietnam, Cambodia, and Thailand. Thus the plan called for defeating the Pathet Lao *and* declaring Laos neutral.

Kennedy had to do something, and, on the surface, this plan looked good. It did not commit the U.S. to anything and it would leave the pro-American Phoumi forces in a militarily advantageous position, a position which could facilitate the introduction of U.S. forces, if necessary. The real crux of the plan was Phoumi's offensive, and the Task Force recommended the plan because the U.S. intelligence community assured the members that Phoumi's forces would have little trouble defeating the Pathet Lao. This assessment was based on a Special National Intelligence Estimate (SNIE), which predicted Phoumi's American-trained and financed forces would win against the Pathet Lao.[5] This estimate relied largely upon the input of two Army officers working in the office under the Army Assistant Chief of Staff for Intelligence (ACSI),[6] particularly the Chief of the Indochina Desk, who had recently returned from attaché duty in Laos.

At this point, however, an unusual and unfortunate sequence of events unfolded. The Laos estimate was drafted at a low level of classification because the Air Force representative in the coordination process did not have certain security clearances. Officers in another ACSI office, the North Vietnam Desk, had intelligence of a higher classification that refuted the thesis that Phoumi could win. These officers went to the final coordination meeting, intending to clear the room of those without the right clearances and, using their information, turn the estimate around. Their plan, one of them recalls, was thwarted by the SNIE's drafter, who denied their request to clear the room. Consequently, the CIA published the estimate in its original form; and based on this "military" advice—that there were limited North Vietnamese forces in Laos and that Phoumi could take the Plain of Jars in three weeks—Kennedy approved the Laos Task Force plan.[7]

Of course, Kennedy was unaware of the critical information showing Phoumi might well lose. This intelligence lapse was tragic. It led directly to a strategy that failed, a failure that narrowed the available policy options and moved the U.S. to the brink of war in Southeast Asia.

When Kennedy approved the "Laos neutralization gambit,"[8] as Rostow called the plan, he excluded the provision for a deployment of U.S. troops to Thailand. As a result, U.S. forces were not in a position to help Phoumi when the plan went awry. Within three weeks of the plan's adoption, the Pathet Lao consolidated their hold on the Plain of Jars. Admiral Felt warned that the volume of the "commie supply effort" was greater than needed for defense, raising the specter of a communist offensive, and concluded: "It needs to be repeated again and again that the only way to save Laos now is by successful military action."[9] Phoumi's offensive never materialized, and on March 6, in a vicious offensive of their own, the Pathet Lao destroyed a large portion of his forces. "Phoumi's troops broke and ran," Roger Hilsman, Director of the State Department's Bureau of Intelligence and Research, later said of the battle.[10] Rostow reported it to Kennedy this way: "without much of a fight, our boys fell back, apparently beyond the crucial crossroads."[11] These crossroads opened the approaches to Vientiane, Luang Prabang, and, more importantly, to the Mekong Valley and South Vietnam. The new administration's policy in Southeast Asia was headed for deep trouble.

OPERATION MILLPOND

The failure of the initial administration plan in Laos was upsetting to the President. According to Schlesinger, the Phoumi fiasco "confirmed Kennedy's impression of Phoumi's singular incompetence," and he decided then that Laos must have a coalition government.[12] The failure of the "neutralization gambit," then, was actually the catalyst that moved Kennedy beyond the *ideal* of an externally neutral Laos toward the *concrete* internal prescription of a coalition government. However, even though the inclination of Kennedy's thinking was toward a political solution, that of the bureaucracy that served under him was just the opposite.

With few exceptions State and Defense department officials felt the situation could not be saved by pursuing a nonmilitary political strategy.[13] The Laos Task Force considered a variety of measures to "maintain a minimum military position" from which to negotiate neutralization, but concluded "none of these seemed promising."[14] Chester Bowles, Under Secretary of State, objected to a military solution on the grounds that the Chinese would not permit an American presence in Laos. The Joint Chiefs countered that military measures were available to cope with this.[15] Their idea was to put U.S. forces into South Vietnam and advance west to block any Chinese incursion through the mountains of Laos and, if necessary, to resort to the extreme measure of using nuclear weapons. It is difficult to imagine that sort of proposal today, but it was not atypical of the cold war mentality that characterized those days.

General Phoumi's failure had clearly sent Laos planning back to the drawing board. Rostow acknowledged as much when he wrote to Kennedy, "our initial dispositions with respect to Laos, both diplomatically and militarily, have not succeeded, and we enter a new phase."[16] Despite the President's inclination toward a political solution, the communist advance on the ground posed a grave dilemma. Even though Kennedy wanted to negotiate neutralization, says his aide, Theodore Sorensen, he was "determined not to start negotiations until the fighting stopped."[17] Hilsman recalled the problem in this way:

> The only possible incentive for the Communists to go to the negotiating table was fear of an American intervention. And on this there could be no bluff. The United States had to be determined to intervene if necessary. This in turn meant that public statements and private communications about our determination had to be backed up with concrete movements of American troops.[18]

Moving American forces was something Kennedy was willing to do.

To decide how to proceed, a key strategy meeting was held on March 9. At the meeting the Laos Task Force recommended Operation Millpond, a "seventeen-step escalation ladder" beginning with military advisors, moving to token units and then on to deploying a massive force. The task force, however, was more disposed to the use of American forces than the President.[19] Although Kennedy gave the go-ahead to preparations for a military buildup, he emphasized to all present that he had not given the final "go" signal.[20]

Nevertheless, one of the measures he approved did put American servicemen on the ground in Laos. McNamara assigned this measure "the highest priority." It transferred Marine (H-34) helicopters for CIA-directed (White Star) U.S. Army Special Forces advisory operations there.[21]

Half of the helicopter crews were Marines, and the rest were Army and Navy personnel. Three hundred U.S. Marines were deployed to Udorn, Thailand, for maintenance. Before they arrived from the *Bennington* on March 28, the communists launched yet another offensive.[22] The communists, it appeared, did not take Washington seriously.

"60,000 SOLDIERS, AIR COVER AND EVEN NUCLEAR WEAPONS, OR ELSE STAY OUT"

As preparations for military actions proceeded, Kennedy still worked for a diplomatic solution. At his March 15 press conference, he said, "It is our hope from all of these negotiations will come a genuinely independent and neutral Laos, which is the master of its own fate."[23] During the last weeks of March, these overtures failed,[24] and the pro-American Laotians were in full retreat while the Pathet Lao continued to add to the territory under their control. Such a total collapse of the American position prompted work on yet another plan for intervention, this one prepared in the State Department.[25] The plan was to put 26,000 troops, half of them Asian and half of them American, into Laos "merely to hold certain key centers for diplomatic bargaining purposes, not to conquer the country. They would shoot only if shot at." Meanwhile, on March 19 the Commander-in-Chief, Pacific (CINCPAC), ordered Joint Task Force 116 and its supporting forces on alert. On March 20 Marine Major General Weller was ordered to assemble and activate the command on Okinawa, and the order was given for most of the U.S. Seventh Fleet to concentrate in the South China Sea.[26] At the end of two days (March 21–22) of NSC meetings, a divided and disorganized administration was moving inexorably toward war.

At the first meeting Rostow clashed with the Joint Chiefs. He argued for the introduction of a small number of U.S. combat forces into the Mekong Valley, not to fight the Pathet Lao, but to deter them and provide a bargaining chip for an international conference.[27] The JCS opposed Rostow's plan, "drawing a lurid picture of an all-out communist response, with thousands of Viet Minh [North Vietnamese communists] pouring into Laos and the ultimate possibility of war with China."[28] Rostow was furious. He later criticized the Chiefs' military advice and contended that "They were wrong about Communist logistical capabilities which they grossly overrated."[29] The Joint Chiefs were not opposed to intervention: the issue was *limited versus large-scale* intervention. By raising the specter of Vietnamese or Chinese involvement, the Joint Chiefs were opposing *limited intervention*. The JCS position was "all or nothing: either go in on a large scale, with 60,000 soldiers, air cover and even nuclear weapons, or else stay out."[30]

Even though nothing was resolved at this first NSC meeting, at the end of the day CINCPAC ordered U.S. forces to "a readiness state just short of the condition where intervention was deemed imminent." For a second day the debate dragged on. According to Hilsman, "over and over again the discussion each time came to the same dead ends"[31]: if Laos were abandoned, the communists would mount pressure against Thailand, Cambodia, and South Vietnam; on the other hand, any attempt to push out the communists with less than an all-out commitment could lead to another Korean-style bloodletting; and any large-scale intervention or use of nuclear weapons ran the risk of starting World War III.

In the end, Kennedy decided to send a clear signal of American determination to the communists. Three aircraft carriers with 1,400 Marines aboard steamed toward the South China Sea; 150 Marines rushed to Udorn, Thailand (near the Laos border), and another 2,600 made ready on Okinawa. On the evening of March 23, the President held a press conference to underscore these deployments. He said, "if in the past there has been any possible ground for misunderstanding of our desire for a truly neutral Laos, there should be none now."[32] Since the previous December 13, Soviet planes "have been conspicuous in a large-scale airlift into the battle area," he said, along with "combat specialists" from North Vietnam, and "it is this new dimension of externally supported warfare that creates the present grave problem."

The three U.S. aircraft carriers formed Task Force 77 200 miles off of Da Nang to provide air support for anticipated operations in Laos. Air support was also provided from Sangley Point in the Philippines, and two Marine fighter squadrons (VMF-312 and VMF-154) were transferred from Naval Air Station, Atsugi, Japan, to join the Marine fighter squadron (VMA-212) already at Cubi Point in the Philippines. Forces from other parts of the Pacific, the 1st Marine Brigade and elements of the 4th Marines and Marine Aircraft Group 13 were loaded up and set sail for Okinawa. Refueling and other logistical operations necessary to sustain the force converging off the coast of Vietnam were complete by March 24. According to the Navy history of the Vietnam War:

> This movement of naval forces to Southeast Asia reflected the Navy's increased readiness to project forces ashore. It was a harbinger of deployments that occurred later in the Vietnam War. . . . The fleet and its embarked forces again stood ready to implement national policy in Southeast Asia.[33]

Although the scale was smaller, the pace of the buildup was as swift as that for Operation Desert Shield thirty years later.

Between March 26 and April 1, a joint British-American diplomatic initiative calling for a peace conference appeared to gain Soviet agreement;[34] but on April 4, a Soviet broadcast complicated the situation by making an unacceptable demand. Moscow wanted agreement on holding a conference prior to any cease-fire.[35] The chances for a political solution seemed to be fading.

Meanwhile, to consolidate command and control of the large military forces preparing to intervene in Laos, a new commander was put in charge. On April 7, Army Lieutenant General Paul D. Harkins, the Deputy Commander-in-Chief, U.S. Army Pacific, established an overall headquarters on Okinawa. Joint Task Force 116 was deactivated and most of its staff transferred to his new command.[36] As the British and Russians haggled over the cease-fire, and the Pathet Lao continued to make gains on the ground, Harkins waited for the green light from Washington. As he described it:

> I had a marine brigade and an air wing and we were in the Philippines already. All the planes were lined up on the runway, but nobody ever knew about it, and we had five thousand men there. I'd go to the club at night and play bridge in civilian clothes, of course, and nobody knew that I was [a] lieutenant general and sitting there ready to invade Laos.[37]

Back in Washington Kennedy delayed making a final decision as another crisis in a different part of the world moved to center stage. Operation Zapata, the planned overthrow of Castro, scheduled for April 17, was only ten days away. Its disastrous outcome would have an unpredictable and profound effect on U.S. policy toward Southeast Asia.

ONLY LBJ SUPPORTED BURKE

When the news of the final failure of the Cuban operation reached Washington on April 20, the attempt to obtain a cease-fire in Laos had been stalled for three weeks while the Pathet Lao continued to take territory. On that day Kennedy quietly upgraded the American military effort in Laos to a Military Assistance Advisory Group (MAAG) and ordered all U.S. soldiers in Laos, who had been keeping a low profile by wearing civilian clothes, to put on their uniforms. This *appeared* to bear fruit, as Moscow finally agreed, on April 24, to a cease-fire. The Pathet Lao, however, realizing a cease-fire was fast approaching, attacked in force, "as if to overrun the country before the cease-fire could take effect."[38]

At midnight on April 25, the new MAAG Chief in Laos reported a desperate "plea" from Phoumi for U.S. B-26 air strikes. The MAAG Chief said Phoumi's forces were "on the ropes" and that the air strikes—backed up by U.S. or SEATO intervention—were the only way to stop the Pathet Lao from seizing all of the towns held by Phoumi.[39] Nine hours later, the U.S. Ambassador in Laos, Winthrop Brown, reported the fall of Muong Sai and requested authorization for the air strikes. Brown said he realized such action would "torpedo" the cease-fire negotiations and "most likely involve immediate intervention" of U.S. and SEATO forces, but he knew of no other way to stop the communists.[40]

A cabinet meeting on April 26 groped for a course of action.[41] Admiral Arleigh Burke, Chief of Naval Operations, attended and, feeling that a decision to intervene would "shortly" be given, told the Navy to "preposition the fleet with embarked marines."[42] At 10:00 P.M. the JCS sent out a worldwide "general advisory," saying the situation in Laos had "become exceedingly grave," and ordering CINCPAC to be prepared to stop Chinese intervention, strike intermediate bases in North Vietnam, and, if necessary, strike bases in China that could support operations against Laos.[43] CINCPAC ordered Lieutenant General Harkins to ready his commands, deploy a battalion of the 3rd Marines forward at Cubi Point, and move a battalion of the 9th Marines (involved in training exercises off Borneo) to a position off the tip of South Vietnam. U.S. Navy ships from all over the Pacific were ordered to head for Southeast Asia.[44] At Camp Courtney, Okinawa, Joint Task Force 116 and its air component were redesignated "SEATO Field Forces" and readied for action.[45]

April 27 was a day of "prolonged crisis meetings"[46] on Laos, which were eventually expanded to include eight senators and seven congressmen. "The President was under great pressure," concerned that Vientiane would fall in hours, and feeling a conference would be pointless if the Pathet Lao captured all of the key areas.[47] Admiral Burke sat in for Lemnitzer, Chairman of the Joint Chiefs of Staff, and, in a strange briefing on military options, argued that the U.S. would either lose Southeast Asia without a war, or be forced to fight a long one and use nuclear weapons. He urged SEATO Plan 5—the deployment of a large SEATO force to both Laos and South Vietnam that would defend Southeast Asia from a base centered on the Mekong River. He then startled those present by saying "this was not enough." He believed more troops were needed, but pointed out that strategic reserves were too low to deploy enough men to win without resorting to nuclear warfare.

The Army Chief of Staff, General George Decker, and the Marine Corps Commandant, General David Shoup, interjected that due to limitations of U.S. airlift and Laotian airfields, only 1,000 men per day could be put on the ground in Laos. This was too few to defend the capital and the forces themselves would be vulnerable.[48] These remarks, while sound, were unexpected and seemed to undercut Burke's proposal. It was hard, says Schlesinger, "to make out what the Chiefs were trying to say."[49] Secretary McNamara turned the discussion into a free-for-all with the comment that perhaps it was too late to intervene because these U.S. forces might be "driven out."[50]

The reactions of others listening to the Chiefs' proposals were similarly confused, especially those of the State Department. Bowles, sitting in for Rusk, argued that SEATO Plan 5 would trigger a Chinese intervention, but U. Alexis Johnson, Deputy Under Secretary of State for Political Affairs, contended the best way to avoid war was "to be seen as ready to use force." This "was a tougher line than Bowles had taken," Johnson said later, "but I knew that Rusk agreed with me."[51] Completing the procession of disparate recommendations made to the President in this meeting, Rostow said he still favored a limited troop deployment to Thailand as a show of force, a view supported by Ambassador-at-Large Averell Harriman and Admiral Lemnitzer, who were then traveling together in Laos.[52]

The real problem was the seeming incoherence of the Joint Chiefs' position, which evoked an image, U. Alexis Johnson recalls, of a small, beleaguered band of American troops stuck on an airstrip in Laos while the President contemplated using nuclear weapons against China to rescue them.[53] The JCS, writes Charles Stevenson, a scholar who interviewed most of those who attended the meeting, "were not really concerned" about a war with China; but, he adds:

> Their plans in case of Chinese intervention, however, were quite frightening. These called for the seizure of Hainan Island, which was defended by three Chinese divisions, deployment of 250,000 U.S. troops to South Vietnam, followed by operations across North Vietnam into Laos to block Chinese intrusions. If these U.S. forces were in danger of being overrun, the Chiefs expected to use nuclear weapons.[54]

Rostow later said of the Chiefs' advice, "I never saw a worse performance by our military" and told Schlesinger it was the worst White House meeting of the entire Kennedy Administration.[55]

What happened next was pregnant in its implications for what was to come later in the Vietnam war. In an unusual move, Vice President

Johnson created an opportunity for the Chiefs to regroup and more clearly state their views: he proposed that each of them separately put their ideas into writing.[56] Kennedy agreed, and then broadened the meeting to include the congressional leaders, with Admiral Burke addressing this group. Burke ardently advocated fighting in Laos regardless of the difficulties or the possibilities of escalation and the use of nuclear weapons. He asked:

> if we do not fight in Laos, will we fight in Thailand where the situation will be the same sometime in the future as it is now in Laos? Will we fight in Vietnam? Where will we fight? Where do we hold? Where do we draw the line?[57]

After this passionate plea for intervention, the President asked for the views of those present and encountered virtually unanimous opposition to sending in U.S. forces. Only one person in the room spoke out in support of Admiral Burke's proposal: Vice President Johnson.[58] "He said he thought I had something," Burke recalls of LBJ that day, "but that was because he spoke first, perhaps. . . . I've been grateful to him ever since. . . . I lost that battle, and I lost it completely."[59] He remembers thinking afterward "a lot of people are going to die in this country sometime in the future if this thing is allowed to go by." And Burke did not give up:

> . . . I went back [that same day]. I wrote a memorandum to the President, and you just don't send a memorandum over to the President: You take it over. And I got thrown out . . . the President said, "This is settled."

In the NSC meeting Kennedy had deferred a final decision on intervention in Laos. Burke, however, now knew better than anyone what the Navy history of the war would later conclude: "The decision not to intervene had, in effect, been made."[60] Burke cabled Admiral Felt (CINCPAC): "I am afraid that we may not execute [in Laos]."[61]

The chaotic Laos meeting of April 27 and, in particular, the intense Kennedy-Burke exchange afterward, gave rise to a rapid series of reappraisals and reversals of judgment on Vietnam policy that opened a breach between the President and the Chiefs. That breach would widen to a chasm by the end of the year. As things stood in late April, the Chiefs still hoped that Kennedy would intervene if the circumstances were right. Although futile, this hope was fueled as much by Kennedy's procrastination as by the Vice President's support.

Vietnam seemed the place. The time seemed right. And Kennedy himself had brought the issue to a head during the April 27 meeting. For reasons that will soon become apparent, Bowles had tried to delay consideration of a report just completed by the Vietnam Task Force with the following remarks:

> Still we have made many mistakes in Southeast Asia—one of them in trying to turn Laotians into Turks. We need to delay in acting on the [Vietnam] paper in order to study the problem even though from a superficial look at it the paper appears to be good.[62]

Kennedy, irritated by the jab at Laos policy, pushed Bowles' delaying tactic aside. There would be an NSC meeting in two days on the Vietnam report, the President said. This was the same day the President was to make his final decision on Laos.

Admiral Burke saw the opening—U.S. forces were still poised for intervention. There was no time to lose. The Laos operation had only been shot down because of poor logistics, he cabled Felt on April 27, a problem that did not exist in Vietnam and Thailand.[63] Then he divulged what he hoped would happen: "We may land about 5,000 Marines in Vietnam and an equal number of Army and Air Force troops in Thailand." The problem now was the Vietnam Task Force report. It had no provision for putting U.S. troops into Vietnam. But there was still time to change it. That is precisely what happened.

A LAOS ANNEX FOR THE VIETNAM REPORT

The next day the Pentagon amended the basic Vietnam report by including a Laos Annex "which went far beyond the modest military proposals in the original."[64] The new ingredient was a major U.S. troop commitment for training purposes in Vietnam, prompted by the anticipated political settlement in Laos. The U.S. troop commitment to South Vietnam proposed in the final version of this Annex was 3,600 men, including the deployment from Okinawa to Nha Trang of 400 men in the 1st Special Forces Group and two divisional training commands of 1,600 men each at Kontum and Ban Me Thuot.[65] Three days later this proposed deployment for training purposes was changed to unilateral U.S. intervention with combat troops.

The Laos Annex to the Vietnam report was the opening salvo of a drive initiated by the JCS to intervene in Vietnam, an effort born within hours of the Pentagon's realization that Kennedy was not going to intervene in

Laos. The person who inserted the key words committing U.S. troops to Vietnam was Edward Lansdale.

NOTES

1. See *PP*, DOD ed., Book 10, pp. 1,360–64, for a record of Eisenhower's recommendations to JFK on Laos.

2. *Public Papers of the Presidents of the United States: John F. Kennedy, 1961–63* (Washington, D.C.: U.S. Government Printing Office, 1962), vol. 1, p. 8 (hereafter referred to as *Public Papers*). The date of this press conference was January 25. Both Chester Bowles (then the Under Secretary of State) and Arthur Schlesinger state that before his inauguration, Kennedy had already decided neutralization was the only practical answer in Laos. See Chester Bowles, *Promises to Keep* (New York: Harper and Row, 1971), p. 394. Schlesinger adds, "But he knew the matter was not that simple any longer. For the effort had been made, American prestige was deeply involved, and extrication would not be easy." Arthur Schlesinger, *A Thousand Days* (New York: Fawcett, 1965), p. 307.

3. Rusk memo to JFK, undated but from the first week of February 1961, JFK Library, POF Country File, Laos.

4. Bowles, *Promises to Keep*, p. 394. Bowles says he did not agree with this consensus.

5. The account given here is based on the recollection of two Army officers working in ACSI at the time, George Allen and Bill Benedict, the latter officer having attended the final drafting session. It was also Benedict who led an unsuccessful attempt to insert a more pessimistic view based on the intelligence held in his office. George Allen and Bill Benedict, joint interview with the author, July, 21 1988.

6. Ed Sorensen and Jim Creighton. Creighton was the Chief of the Indochina Section, South Asia Branch, Eastern Division, Directorate of Foreign Intelligence, ACSI, and had been a former attaché in Laos. Their view was probably colored by self-serving reports from Army officers training Phoumi's forces in Laos.

7. Rostow, interview with Richard Neustadt, April 11, 1964, p. 46: "The official military position was: Phoumi says he can do it in five days. We think it will take three weeks." See also Schlesinger, *A Thousand Days*, p. 308: "Our military experts assured Kennedy this would lead to the speedy recapture of the Plain of Jars."

8. Rostow memo to JFK, February 23, 1961, JFK Library, POF, O'Donnell, Box 64a, Document 5a, p. 2.

9. Harry Felt, Msg, CP 012300Z, Mar 1961; quoted in Edward Marolda and Oscar Fitzgerald, *The United States Navy and the Vietnam Conflict* (Washington, D.C.:

U.S. Government Printing Office, 1986) p. 60 (hereafter referred to as *USN and the Vietnam Conflict*).

10. Roger Hilsman, *To Move a Nation* (New York: Doubleday, 1967), p. 127. Rostow was less kind in his interview with Richard Neustadt (p. 46): "Then, early in March, the Communists pulled up a couple of mortars; let fly; and the Laos bugged out." Harriman told of a briefing he received from an American officer who said, "Only a few months ago, the Laotians used to retreat without their weapons; now they take their weapons with them when they run away." See Chester Cooper, *The Lost Crusade* (New York: Dodd, Mead, 1970), p. 171.

11. Rostow memo to JFK, March 7, 1961, JFK Library, NSF, Regional Security SEA, Box 223/231.

12. Schlesinger, *A Thousand Days*, p. 308.

13. Bowles, *Promises to Keep*, p. 395.

14. This was according to a March 7, 1961, memo from Rostow to Kennedy; JFK Library, NSF, Regional Security, SEA, Box 223/231.

15. Bowles, *Promises to Keep*, pp. 395–96.

16. Rostow memo to JFK, March 9, 1961, JFK Library, POF Country File, Laos, Box 1.

17. Sorensen, Theodore, *Kennedy* (New York: Harper & Row, 1965), p. 642.

18. Hilsman, *To Move a Nation*, p. 131.

19. Charles A. Stevenson, *The End of Nowhere: American Policy Toward Laos Since 1954* (Boston: Beacon Press, 1972), p. 142.

20. Sorensen, *Kennedy*, p. 643.

21. *USN and the Vietnam Conflict*, p. 60.

22. Ibid., p. 61.

23. Kennedy, *Public Papers*, 1961, p. 83.

24. Efforts to get the Soviets to cease the airlift were unsuccessful, the key meeting probably being Rusk's March 18 talk with Soviet Foreign Minister Gromyko. See William Gibbons, *The U.S. Government and the Vietnam War* (Princeton: University Press, 1986), vol. 2, p. 20.

25. Rostow memo to JFK, March 17, 1961, JFK Library, POF Staff Memos File, Box 64A.

26. *USN and the Vietnam Conflict*, p. 61.

27. Schlesinger, *A Thousand Days*, p. 310.

28. Ibid.

29. Rostow, interview with Richard Neustadt, April 11, 1964, p. 46.

30. Schlesinger, *A Thousand Days*, p. 310. Many senior officers felt the U.S. should never again fight a limited (non-nuclear) ground war in Asia (as in Korea), a view so often expressed that its adherents became known as the "Never Again Club." Hilsman reports the Never Again Club was not a unanimous view among the military: "many . . . were also convinced that the alternatives [to a limited ground war]—either a very big war or the abandonment of Asia—would be worse." Unfortunately, Hilsman does not identify who, in his view, these officers were. See *To Move a Nation*, p. 129. Although on this occasion Lemnitzer opposed limited intervention in Laos, he would reverse his position and support just such an intervention only six weeks later. In fact, there were considerable differences of opinion among

the Chiefs on the desirable level of intervention and the likelihood of a Chinese response, differences that would crystalize and surface several weeks later. However, these differences were unknown to the President during the March 21–22 White House meetings.

31. Hilsman, *To Move a Nation*, pp. 129–30.

32. Kennedy, *Public Papers*, 1961, p. 214.

33. *USN and the Vietnam Conflict*, p. 62.

34. On March 26, Kennedy met with British Prime Minister Harold Macmillan in Florida to seek support should the use of force become necessary. He told Macmillan he had in mind a limited force of four to five battalions to hold Vientiane and other key positions. Macmillan later said Kennedy was not anxious to use force and that he was sympathetic with the President's need to demonstrate that the U.S. would not be "pushed out" of Laos. Macmillan agreed to participate (with cabinet approval) in the "appearance" of resistance. See Harold Macmillan, *Pointing the Way, 1959–1961* (New York: Harper and Row, 1972), pp. 333–35. A much needed break came on April 1, when Khrushchev responded favorably to a British proposal to revive the International Control Commission (ICC) for Laos and to prepare for a peace conference.

35. Hilsman, *To Move a Nation*, p. 133.

36. *USN and the Vietnam Conflict*, p. 63.

37. Paul D. Harkins, interview with Ted Gittinger, November 10, 1981, LBJ Library, Oral History Collection, p. I-4. See also Harkins interview with Jacob B. Couch, Jr., April 28, 1974, U.S. Army Military History Research Collection, Carlisle Barracks. pp. 47–48. General I.D. White retired as the United States Army Pacific (USARPAC) commander on April 1, 1961, and was replaced by General Collins on April 4. Harkins was then ordered to Okinawa to "pick up the Task Force and be ready to invade Laos." Harkins claims he had enough airlift to "take the whole Task Force and Brigade and staff right to Laos in one lift." Shortly thereafter, "It got hotter and hotter and I was sent to the Philippines with my Task Force and we were stationed at Clark Field" (Harkins, interview with Couch).

38. Schlesinger, *A Thousand Days*, p. 315.

39. CHMAAG Vientiane, Laos, to CINCPAC, April 26, 1961, LBJ Library, VP Security File, Box 4.

40. Ambassador Brown (Laos), to Rusk, cable No. 1943, April 26, 1961, LBJ Library, VP Security File, Box 4.

41. U. Alexis Johnson, *Right Hand of Power* (Englewood Cliffs, N.J.: Prentice-Hall, 1984), p. 322. The subsequent JCS advisory might have been the result of such a meeting, but there is no record of it and none of the memoirs of the period mention an NSC meeting on April 26 except U. Alexis Johnson's. If there was a meeting in the White House, it was probably a hasty discussion of the night's cable traffic, and it may have considered the agenda and participants for the larger meetings of the following day.

42. *USN and the Vietnam Conflict*, p. 66. Later that afternoon, CINCPAC sent a message to the JCS requesting the authorization for such prepositioning moves, which the JCS immediately granted. See Gareth Porter, *Vietnam: The Definitive Documentation of Human Decisions* (Stanfordville, NY: Earl M. Coleman Enterprises, 1979), vol. 2, pp. 95–96. These were probably in connection with implementation of SEATO Plan 5, but the paragraph in the JCS response that gave CINPAC specifics is still classified. Researchers should note that this is the message referred to in *PP*, Gravel ed., vol. 2, p. 42, but that was not printed.

43. *PP*, Gravel ed., vol. 2, p. 42.

44. *USN and the Vietnam Conflict*, pp. 67–68.

45. Robert Futrell and Martin Blumenson, *The United States Air Force in Southeast Asia: The Advisory Years to 1965* (Washington, D.C.: U.S. Government Printing Office, 1981), p. 64 (hereafter referred to as *Air Force History*).

46. *PP*, Gravel ed., vol. 2, p. 42.

47. U. Alexis Johnson, *Right Hand of Power*, pp. 322–23.

48. *USN and the Vietnam Conflict*, p. 69. Sustainment was equally vexing: of the 3,279 STONS (short tons) required daily during the first three days of the operation, only 1,766 could be transported, and only 778 of the daily required 1,053 for the next five days.

49. Schlesinger, *A Thousand Days*, p. 315.

50. *USN and the Vietnam Conflict*, pp. 69–71.

51. U. Alexis Johnson, *Right Hand of Power*, p. 324.

52. *Congressional History*, vol. 2, p. 26; and Schlesinger, *A Thousand Days*, p. 316.

53. U. Alexis Johnson, *Right Hand of Power*, p. 323.

54. Stevenson, *The End of Nowhere*, pp. 301–2, n. 60. This extraordinary plan Stevenson attributes to a confidential source. However, it is not unlike the position that General LeMay argued for the following day (see below).

55. Rostow interview with Richard Neustadt, April 11, 1964, p. 46; Schlesinger, *A Thousand Days*, p. 315.

56. Schlesinger, *A Thousand Days*, p. 315.

57. *USN and the Vietnam Conflict*, pp. 71–72.

58. Stevenson, *The End of Nowhere*, p. 152. Here Stevenson's source was an interview with Admiral Burke. Burke makes that same claim in his oral history, interview with Joseph O'Connor, January 20, 1967, JFK Library, Oral History Collection.

59. Burke, interview with Joseph O'Connor, January 20, 1967, pp. 35–36.

60. *USN and the Vietnam Conflict*, p. 72.

61. Ibid.

62. Burke, memo for record after the meeting, *State History*, 1961, Document 36, pp. 82–83.

63. *USN and the Vietnam Conflict*, p. 72.

64. *PP*, Gravel ed., vol. 2, p. 40.

65. See the final Black draft of the Laos annex in *PP*, DOD ed., Book 11, p. 61.

CHAPTER TWO

LANSDALE:
"LONE WOLF AND OPERATOR"

LANSDALE AND DIEM

On December 29, 1960, Edward Lansdale was on his way to visit Vietnam. At the airport Hilton Inn in San Francisco, he dashed a letter off to his old friend General "Hangin' Sam" Williams—just retired from the Army—who had last served as the U.S. MAAG Chief in Vietnam. Lansdale could only squeeze in twelve days in Saigon, he wrote to Williams, but, "Even so, our mutual Foreign Service friends are howling that I shouldn't visit, and if I do, it should only be for a week. To hell with them."[1] He had prepared well for his reunion with Diem. Among his luggage was a large, cumbersome item he had sent a colleague to find only days before. It was an $800 one-piece, hand-carved mahogany desk top from an exclusive store in Washington, D.C. At Lansdale's insistence a plaque had been added with the inscription "To the Father of his Country, Ngo Dinh Diem."

Lansdale had been instrumental in Diem's rise to power, but now his regime was besieged with troubles: he was increasingly unpopular; the American Ambassador was pressuring for reforms he felt he could not accept; there was constant talk of a coup among the military; and the Viet Cong were overrunning the countryside. The religious background of Diem's family did not fit well with the predominantly Buddhist population of Vietnam. Under the influence of Portuguese missionaries, Diem's ancestors had converted to Christianity during the seventeenth century, and he had been educated in a French Catholic school.[2] His early political rise through the ranks of Vietnam's provincial government was interrupted in 1933 when he criticized French control of the government, resigned under pressure, and left for the United States. During his sojourn there he met many influential Americans, including Francis Cardinal Spellman, Justice William Douglas, and Senators Mike Mansfield and John Kennedy. Diem lobbied the Eisenhower administration in vain to oppose French colonialism in Vietnam, and then departed for France where, strangely enough, he made the connection with the person who would propel him to power: Vietnamese Emperor Bao Dai.

Originally a puppet installed by the Japanese, Bao Dai was then in self-imposed exile and, finding Diem's American connections useful in countering the French, named Diem his Prime Minister. Consequently, Diem returned to his homeland in 1954 to take over the government in South Vietnam, and inherited the political arrangement imposed by the Geneva Accords after the French defeat: a continuing French presence in the south until nationwide elections in 1956 to unify the country. This strange Catholic-French-Japanese imperial mixture of Diem's background afforded him no political base whatsoever, and his quest for power led him to default on the elections and simply replace the French with an American presence, a plan that, in the growing tensions of the cold war, found sufficient support in Washington to enable it to happen.

Secretary of State John Foster Dulles wanted to train Diem's army and harness it to the emerging American defense structure in East Asia, and the argument—advanced by influential politicians like Senator Mansfield—that Diem was the only man who could lead South Vietnam swayed President Eisenhower into going along. It is ironic that the Joint Chiefs, though they would later reverse their position, were initially cool to this plan; they were wary because Diem lacked a stable government, and only reluctantly went along with the Dulles plan, which was implemented by the first U.S. Ambassador, Donald Heath. As the American commitment to South Vietnam hardened, Diem's position eroded, and it was in this situation that the skills of Edward Lansdale came into play.

Lansdale had actually arrived in South Vietnam a month before Diem, and had already set up an extensive covert network to sabotage the residual communist infrastructure left over from the period of the war against the French. This network was probably the key asset Lansdale used to help thwart a 1954 coup attempt by some South Vietnamese generals against Diem, and it would prove valuable in protecting Diem from the noncommunist opposition that was rapidly building. Lansdale also played a major role in the movement of Catholic refugees into the south from

North Vietnam, whose elite members Diem installed in all the key military and political posts in the country. Lansdale played the crucial role again in 1955, helping Diem put down yet another attempted coup by the military—this time backed by Diem's former patron, Emperor Bao Dai. Lansdale's advertising techniques were instrumental in a referendum that deposed the old Emperor.

By 1957 Diem, now the chief of state, had used his power to subdue the dissenting religious sects and smash the Viet Minh cells in the Mekong Delta, accomplishments which led Eisenhower to hail Diem as the "miracle man" of Asia. Supremely confident in his own invincibility, Diem allowed his government to turn into a complete oligarchy in which the rampant nepotism of his brothers, relatives, and a few wealthy landowners completely alienated the educated urban middle class. Lansdale, who had left the country, was not on hand to help when this situation reached crisis proportions and the communist insurgency—spurred by new Soviet assistance to Hanoi—regenerated. Diem's sagging image led to pressure from Washington for elections to defuse the growing noncommunist antipathy toward the regime, elections that Diem held—and blatantly rigged—in August 1959. This produced, in April 1960, demands for reforms from the country's most distinguished nationalists and former cabinet members, but Diem simply closed down the opposition newspapers and began incarcerating his political opponents. Diem's resistance to Durbrow's demands for reform, as well as the fact that Diem was channeling most of the U.S. financial aid into the coffers of his military and police forces, led the Ambassador to recommend a change of leadership in Saigon.[3] An attempted coup in November 1960 failed, as those previously had, but the apparent sympathy of Durbrow and others in Saigon for the plotters left Diem's relationship with Washington deeply fractured at a time when the insurgency was getting out of control. This was the situation in December 1960 when Lansdale came back to have a look and assess the damage.

"GIVING EVERYONE HELL"

When the trip was over Lansdale wrote another letter to Williams, and said his talks with Diem were just like old times and that "we both enjoyed ourselves."[4] He told the former MAAG Chief the talks had provided him with "a lot of ammunition to fire" at the State Department officials who had pictured Diem as an autocratic dictator, and added, "I've been giving everyone hell for the past week, in every form I could think of." He said his report to the Secretary of Defense included a number of constructive political moves for the State Department, which "I hope keeps their busy little hands doing something useful for a change and out of mischief."

Lansdale's report was destined to go beyond Secretary McNamara; and its underlying objective succeeded on January 28 when Kennedy decided to relieve Ambassador Durbrow. That had been Lansdale's goal all along. Things got serious right after Kennedy's election, recalls a Lansdale colleague; after that, "There wasn't enough Lansdale could say wrong about Durbrow."[5] Following his command performance in the White House on January 28, Lansdale, confident he would soon be sitting in Durbrow's chair in Saigon, returned to his office "jubilant," and boasted, "I'm going back to Vietnam in a higher assignment."[6]

While Lansdale was exulting over his victory at his Pentagon office, across town at the State Department Secretary Rusk and his Assistant for Far Eastern Affairs, J. Graham Parsons, were mulling over the question of just exactly who Lansdale really was.[7] In a discussion that same evening, Parsons informed Rusk that Lansdale was not a "team player" and that he particularly resented Foreign Service officials. Rusk also learned about Lansdale's covert credentials for the first time. The character of the all-knowing political manipulator, Colonel Hillindale, in the novel *The Ugly American* was based on Lansdale, Parsons explained. Lansdale served ably in the Philippines, and was close to Diem in Vietnam; he was a "lone wolf," Parsons said, "tagged as [an] operator." Rusk interrupted him. "How tagged?" he asked. What Parsons said to Rusk about Lansdale's shady reputation is unknown. His reply is still classified. This tag, however, would certainly be borne out in the events which followed.

PLOTS, CARROTS, AND COUPS

A few days before his fateful appointment with President Kennedy, Lansdale received from his old friend General Williams even stronger ammunition that he could use against Ambassador Durbrow. Williams sent him a copy of an anonymous letter, written by someone still working in the MAAG in Saigon, which contained an intimate view of a divided American Mission in Vietnam and extraordinary details of plotting by the Ambassador against President Diem.[8]

Durbrow's relations with Diem had steadily deteriorated to the point that he is "practically Persona non Grata," the letter began. Only recently Lieutenant General Lionel McGarr (MAAG Chief in Saigon) had been subjected to a "long tirade" from Diem about Durbrow, the author said, adding, "I would say it was the worst yet." Durbrow had decided to use Diem's request for an increase in his army "so he can dangle it in front of Diem's nose" in order to extract reforms; but this tactic had run aground during the last days of the Eisenhower administration, when Secretary of State Christian Herter personally ordered Durbrow not to "dangle that carrot."

The letter imputed deep antipathy toward Diem on the part of the Ambassador, who, upon hearing for the first time of Diem's request for 20,000 more troops, said he would rather "see Vietnam go down the drain" than give in to Diem. The letter further accused Durbrow of seeking Diem's overthrow:

> [Durbrow] has actually recommended and urged that we "plot" openly to overthrow the present government and to look around for another man. We had to rebut all this garbage and I will say that the Chief [General McGarr] gave a good rebuttal. All I can say is what kind of people are running our government that can allow such things [to] go on—and I am sure they know what is going on.

As if to explain how it *might* be possible that the U.S. government was not well informed, the anonymous author said that he had seen reports going to Washington which were slanted or "downright lies."

The letter writer took Durbrow's coup plotting seriously, and gave an astonishing account of the Ambassador's role in the August 1960 coup. He said: "There was so much skullduggery going on with the striped pants boys [CIA and State] that I hardly know where to begin." Durbrow was "delighted" with the coup attempt, the letter charged, adding that, even though it would be denied, "There is positive proof that some of his boys were with the rebels and helping them out." The letter accused these men of shifting the blame to McGarr when they were discovered by Diem's men in the act. Two of them "were caught red-handed" helping in the rebel command post, and, when asked what they were doing, replied, "They were working for General McGarr." Because of this little perfidy, the letter said McGarr had some "tall explaining to do after it was over," and concluded, pointing the finger at the real culprit, "They were there with the blessing of the top man [Durbrow]."

No wonder Williams, who was an old enemy of Durbrow when Williams had been the MAAG Chief, and who knew Lansdale's report would be read by high officials in Washington, relayed this anonymous letter to him. Arriving in Lansdale's hands just before his meeting with Kennedy, this letter could only have strengthened his determination to attack Durbrow. Moreover, it must have impressed on Lansdale the fact that Durbrow would continue to be a dangerous element in the Saigon equation until he was physically out of the country. Lansdale decided that Diem must do something to disarm Durbrow, and Lansdale came up with a plan to do just that.

Other accounts suggest a less active role by Durbrow in the coup,[9] but, at the very least, this anonymous letter reveals the political mine field in the American mission in Saigon inherited by Kennedy from the Eisenhower administration. Lacking unity of command, purpose, and objective, U.S. Vietnam policy cried out for clarification and firm leadership from the new President. Instead, the situation had only become more complicated by the contradiction inherent in Kennedy's first two decisions on Vietnam. Even though moved enough by General Lansdale and his Vietnam report to fire Durbrow, Kennedy nevertheless approved the CIP with its linkage between aid and reforms. The confusion surrounding the change in American administrations gave Diem much to worry about; but help was on its way. Only two days after the meeting at which Kennedy decided to approve the CIP, a letter was written to Diem revealing the highly classified proceedings of that session.[10] Included was a list of the officials in the new administration considered friendly toward Diem. The source of this sensitive and invaluable information was Diem's friend Edward Lansdale.

Lansdale informed Diem that his heart would have been warmed if he had heard the NSC conversation. Diem and Lansdale had undoubtedly discussed the contents of Lansdale's Vietnam report, and he was now able to divulge to Diem Kennedy's keen interest in it. He assured Diem he could count on Kennedy, and said Diem had "friends" in Washington and Americans "trying to help you" in Saigon. He identified Allen Dulles (Director of the CIA), Lemnitzer (Chairman of the Joint Chiefs of Staff), and Admiral Burke (Chief of Naval Operations) in Washington, and in Saigon, William Colby (CIA Station Chief in Saigon) and General McGarr (MAAG Chief). Lansdale also laid out the arguments that Diem's enemies in Washington would use against him in "private" talks as word spread about Kennedy's favorable reaction to Lansdale's report.

Lansdale warned that many people in Washington, just like many people in Asia, were "watching you right now to see what you will do next." He then proposed an ingenious plan designed specifically to make such critics "close their mouths." The scheme, which had two parts, was designed to turn the tables and dangle the carrot of reforms before Durbrow's nose. In the first step Diem was to announce the government reorganization he was already working on, and then broadcast a talk with military commanders and province chiefs to "rouse spirits now, the way

Winston Churchill did for Britain at a dark hour."[11] The aim, of course, was to shut Durbrow up by making him think Diem was genuinely moving toward reform.

The second step would be a secret meeting in which the military leaders and province chiefs would speak their minds. General McGarr and CIA Station Chief Colby, Lansdale said, should "attend this meeting and take notes." Besides permitting some of Diem's potential opposition to let off steam, this provision would exclude Durbrow and allow Diem's—and Lansdale's—friends to develop intelligence on key provincial and military leaders. Diem should have been pleasantly surprised by Lansdale's letter, for now, armed with an update on his friends and enemies and a plan of attack, it would be easy to sabotage Durbrow and the reforms in the CIP.

McGarr was already busy quashing opposition to Diem within the MAAG. On January 30, McGarr called his staff and senior advisors together and criticized those "rumors" about corruption, nepotism, favoritism, political dogmatism, and interference in military matters that end with the statement that Diem "must go" to save Vietnam.[12] McGarr instructed his officers that these rumors were based on the "Communist technique of half truths and insinuations" and not supported by hard facts. Due to human nature, he said, these rumors had been further spread by "certain elements" of the U.S. community in Vietnam and added, threateningly, that even U.S. military personnel were "not entirely immune to this questionable pastime." He warned all MAAG personnel to refrain from giving credence, "tacit or openly," to these rumors. It would appear to be more than just coincidence that McGarr was placing what amounted to a muzzle on the MAAG only two days after the Lansdale-Kennedy meeting. And, as shall be seen, the coordination between Lansdale and McGarr was just beginning.

DURBROW'S LAST DUEL WITH DIEM

There is no formal record of State telling Durbrow that he would be moving on, but surely a quiet word was passed to him or a phone call made to soften the blow. For the sake of appearances the Ambassador was allowed to stay on until June. So Durbrow still had a platform from which to attack Diem and strike back at Lansdale for doing him in at the White House meeting. Three days after that meeting Durbrow sent a cable to Washington opposing Lansdale's suggestion for a clear U.S. statement of support for Diem.[13] While this was worth doing when appropriate, he said, such a statement was "dubious" for the time being.

He argued that any assertion of U.S. support for Diem should be limited to a "greeting" by Kennedy.[14] Durbrow then hinted there could be another coup attempt, warning that if Diem continued to resist reforms, "his survival will be problematical."[15]

On February 3 a joint State-Defense departments message, signed by Rusk, informed Durbrow that the CIP had been approved and spelled out how he should negotiate it with Diem.[16] The instructions given were both unrealistic and cavalier, reflecting a continuing lack of understanding at the senior level in Washington of the unworkable nature of the CIP. Durbrow was told to make it clear to Diem that the new U.S. aid was only for 1961 and that future money would depend on reform, and to work out an agreeable version of the CIP within two weeks. If Diem failed to cooperate Durbrow was to provide recommendations that could include a "suspension" of U.S. aid. This must have been music to Durbrow's ears. He was now free to turn up the pressure on Diem.

Before Durbrow could make his next move, however, Diem preempted him by executing Lansdale's mouth-closing plan. On February 6 Diem held a press conference and staged a show along the lines laid out in Lansdale's letter. Diem announced a series of reforms to decentralize governmental powers and improve democratic institutions and village administration. Confused, Durbrow sent an upbeat cable to Washington summarizing his view of the event.[17] He said Diem did a good public relations job and added that, though Diem's speech had positive and negative aspects, its overall tone was "encouraging." Though it lacked any immediate concession such as village council elections, Durbrow called Diem's program "substantial" and "in the direction we have been urging."

Just as Lansdale had foreseen, Diem's diversion hamstrung Durbrow, depriving him of a solid case for recommending a halt in U.S. aid during the subsequent lengthy and unfruitful negotiations. The scheme hatched by Lansdale and implemented skillfully by Diem now enabled Diem and McGarr to work independently of the isolated American Ambassador. Diem, who surely knew Durbrow was going to be relieved, was not about to make political concessions to a lame-duck Ambassador, and was content to simply stonewall Durbrow until his departure for Washington in June. It did not take long for Durbrow to catch on to Diem's game. The blinders came off as soon as Durbrow presented Diem with the CIP on February 13.

Durbrow was surprised when Diem reacted by immediately objecting to the requirement that Saigon had to share the costs associated with the force increase. Diem brushed this off with the excuse that he did not know where he could find the money.[18] Then he cunningly played on the Ambassador's bent for democracy, arguing that the new troops were needed immediately to protect installations and people from communist

attacks during the coming elections. When Durbrow mentioned the
two-week negotiation period, Diem's Secretary of State, Nguyen Dinh
Thuan, replied he would study the plan carefully and discuss it with
Durbrow "soonest." In the cable he sent afterward, Durbrow, sensing
trouble, said he was not very hopeful the government would move that
fast.

A week went by and Durbrow could only report another rebuff by
Thuan, who claimed he had not yet had a chance to study the plan
carefully.[19] By March 8 Durbrow had run out of patience, and complained
in a angry cable that, despite his repeated advice to the contrary, Diem
still had not cooperated and would not act decisively unless he was "highly
pressured" to do so.[20] Durbrow then made an unusual request of Rusk.
The Ambassador said if there was no appreciable success by the time they
met at the SEATO meeting in Bangkok at the end of March, he wanted
personal instructions from the Secretary to "lay before Diem" in order to
force a decision. It was Durbrow's last hope and it proved to be a futile
one.

Meanwhile, on March 3 General McGarr sent a strongly worded letter
to the Pentagon blasting State's idea of withholding aid for noncompli-
ance with reforms.[21] He warned against being "stampeded" into such an
action, and said it could weaken South Vietnamese military actions, allow
further Viet Cong successes, be dangerous to the U.S position in Southeast Asia, and could run counter to Kennedy's announced intention to
hold Vietnam. Washington leaders "will probably wish to reconsider the
possible withholding of such aid as contrary to our President's policy,"
McGarr announced with characteristic bombast. This would not be the
last time he would marshall the President to his side.

General McGarr, now working at complete cross purposes to Durbrow,
began to move on implementing military aspects of the CIP despite the
lack of progress on reforms. This naturally animated the Ambassador. On
March 16 he grumbled that McGarr had made an "oral agreement" with
Thuan on the military part of the program and was "quietly" ordering
equipment for the 20,000-man increase to Diem's army.[22] Durbrow had
immediately demanded to see Diem to discuss the requirement for reforms, but the most Durbrow could muster from Diem was an empty
promise that he would do "as best he could."

Durbrow's last gasp occurred at the SEATO conference (March 29) in
Bangkok, where he pleaded with Rusk to lay down the law to Diem.
Durbrow not only failed to win Rusk over, but had to sit passively and
watch while Thuan presented to Rusk Diem's case against implementing
the reforms.[23] In reply, Rusk gave only a token defense of the U.S. desire
for a comprehensive CIP package. Durbrow's humiliation was complete
when Rusk told Thuan the U.S. administration was trying to speed up

"procedures and decisions," and invited Thuan to take up these problems with the incoming Ambassador, a man, he said, "who will be very understanding." Rusk's reply was a clear signal to Diem that Washington had abandoned Durbrow. Diem appeared to have triumphed. But had he? At that very moment, someone in Washington was building the case for the very contingency Durbrow had forecast: a coup against Diem.

"THEY WANT TO HAVE A COUP"

In the final moments of Durbrow's crumbling initiative to discipline Diem, someone in the State Department tried to get the U.S. intelligence community to sign up to the idea that a coup was a possible solution. At 10:00 A.M. on the 28th of March, an office under the Army Assistant Chief of Staff for Intelligence (ACSI) in the Pentagon received a call from the Office of National Estimates at the CIA.[24] CIA informed ACSI that a Special National Intelligence Estimate (SNIE), on the "Prospects in South Vietnam," was ready for final coordination. A draft of the SNIE would be sent to ACSI by 10:30, and the final coordination meeting on the SNIE would be held at CIA at 1:00 that afternoon. When the draft SNIE arrived, the ACSI analyst who received it, Bill Benedict, was shocked at its contents and quickly found his boss to tell him someone "wanted to throw Diem out." Both men went immediately to the ACSI himself, General Alva Fitch.

Major Benedict, a respected analyst with Southeast Asian experience, told the General, "They want to have a coup in Vietnam, and I don't think it's in the Army's best interest that this should happen." Fitch immediately agreed. He called the Chief of the Estimates Division into his office and told him to "get over there and kill this thing." The Army went to the coordination meeting and opposed that portion of the estimate dealing with the coup. According to Benedict, the drafter "just went into orbit, but that opened the door." Others joined in, and "so we wound up with a SNIE that says we can't win with him, but we sure in hell will lose without him."

This early examination by the intelligence community of what impact a coup against Diem would have on U.S. interests in Vietnam was a harbinger of things to come. Although those who argued it would be good for U.S. interests failed this time, they would succeed two years later. According to Benedict, the person pushing this thesis was the Director of the State Department's Bureau of Intelligence and Research, Roger Hilsman. Perhaps it was a coincidence that someone at State, if indeed it was Hilsman, pushed such a controversial and far-reaching idea while the Secretary of State was out of town. The fact is that precisely the same coincidence would occur in 1963, when coup plotting would lead to Diem's assassination.

LANSDALE'S SHIFTING FORTUNES

Diem was not the only person who found his fortunes buffeted by the uncertainties of the early days of the Kennedy administration. Although Durbrow was leaving and, for the moment at least, Diem was free of American pressure for reforms, his friend Lansdale would not be coming to Vietnam as the new Ambassador. Sometime during February or early March Kennedy changed his mind about Lansdale. What prompted this is unclear. We do know that Lansdale was unpopular in Washington. Even his nominal boss, Deputy Secretary of Defense Roswell Gilpatric, described him as "in the dog house" with both the Defense and State departments.[25] The Pentagon brass disliked his ties with the CIA and, according to Hilsman, McNamara was persuaded by the Pentagon's apprehension.[26] Still others think it was Rusk who played the key role.[27]

Lansdale himself has only added to the confusion. In a February 14 letter to Hangin' Sam Williams, Lansdale reported that Kennedy had inquired "if Dean Rusk had spoken to me yet about my becoming Ambassador," and added that Kennedy wanted him in this post.[28] Lansdale then told Williams he had been trying to "wriggle" out of the appointment. Given what we know about the extent of Lansdale's efforts to become the Ambassador, this letter may indicate that by the middle of February he already knew he was out of the running. The true sequence of events leading Kennedy to change his mind about Lansdale has likely disappeared forever. Such a murky trail is typical of the life of Lansdale, who would probably turn in his grave if any question about him could be easily answered.

Whatever the reason, the flamboyant Lansdale had lost this round. Kennedy settled on Frederick E. Nolting, an affable career Foreign Service Officer with no Vietnam experience, which was actually an asset. He had no ties to any Vietnamese leaders or generals that could make Diem suspicious. Consequently, Nolting was ideal for the job of restoring close relations with Saigon. Who pulled Nolting's name out of the hat is also unclear, but Nolting suspects it was Rusk.[29]

In Washington it was obvious that Vietnam policy had stalled and would have to be overhauled. As Kennedy's top Vietnam advisor in the NSC, Rostow's recommendations shaped this process. He fired the opening salvo in a March 29 memo to Kennedy, saying it was urgent to get properly organized to launch an effective "counter-offensive" in Vietnam.[30] Rostow summed it up in this way:

> We must somehow bring to bear our unexploited counter-guerrilla assets on the Vietnam problem: armed helicopters; other Research and Development possibilities; our Special Forces units. It is somehow wrong to be developing these capabilities but not applying them in a crucial active theater. In Knute Rockne's old phrase, we are not saving them for the Junior Prom.

As candid as these lines appear in sounding the bugle charge, the fact is that in this and his subsequent memos something was missing. They lacked certain important details of the behind-the-scenes maneuvering that would escalate and peak in the subsequent months. Perhaps Rostow was unaware of these details; another possibility is that Rostow was a supporter of Lansdale. In either case, the President was not well informed.

In his March 29 memo Rostow suggested a Diem visit to Washington or a visit to Vietnam by Vice President Johnson, and advised Kennedy to get General McGarr together with Nolting in Washington and issue them "fresh instructions." This would enable them to start "this new phase as a team." Rostow said McNamara had some "ideas" on how to organize this team. As it turned out, so did Rostow. His memo recommended appointing someone to "backstop" Nolting and McGarr full-time in Washington and, citing the "military component in the problem," suggested Lansdale.[31]

Rostow quickly changed his mind about who the "backstop" man should be. In an April 3 memo to Kennedy he reiterated that a fresh review of Vietnam policy was "urgently" needed, and that a "first class operational officer" be put in charge at the Washington end.[32] McNamara agrees, he said, "and I suspect Mr. Rusk has returned in a mood which will incline him to agree." Surprisingly, he no longer recommended Lansdale for this position, saying, "Although General Lansdale should figure prominently in the Washington enterprise, it would be best if the full-time Washington commander of the Vietnam Task Force came from State." Someone at State, possibly Bowles, who had been in charge while Rusk was at the SEATO conference, apparently caused Rostow to back off of Lansdale. The "Washington enterprise" would become the Vietnam Task Force, an entity Kennedy had called for back in January at the first Vietnam meeting, and Lansdale would not be in charge. Or so it seemed at that point.

On April 12, Rostow again wrote to Kennedy: "I believe we must turn to gearing up the whole Vietnam operation."[33] This time Rostow listed nine items to take up at "an early high level meeting," the first of which was still the appointment of a "first-rate back-stop man in Washington." Rostow made no comment at all on who should head up the task force, saying only that McNamara, "as well as your staff, believes this [appointment] to be essential."[34] It is likely that Rostow was also discussing the question with Pentagon officials. His invocation of McNamara, along with his failure to repeat his earlier advice that State head up the task force, suggest that Rostow now favored a Defense Department person for the job. He had not, however, abandoned Lansdale.

LANSDALE: JUDGE, JURY, AND EXECUTIONER

The following day Rostow met with Lansdale, and showed him a copy of the April 12 memo to Kennedy.[35] Apprised of what the President had been reading on the matter, Lansdale proceeded back to the Pentagon, where he hatched his most incredible plan yet to capture the emerging Vietnam policy apparatus. The surviving evidence of this plan is a lengthy paper, written immediately following Lansdale's April 13 session with Rostow. This unsigned document was "certainly," say the authors of *The Pentagon Papers*, penned "by Lansdale."[36]

The document called for a presidential directive to form a Vietnam Task Force and laid out a program of action for the task force to recommend to the President.[37] Initially, the task force would: 1) submit a statement of U.S. goals and plans; 2) select a special three-man staff to accompany the Ambassador to Vietnam; and 3) bring the four of them together in Washington and present them to Kennedy for his instructions. Since Lansdale had already spelled out these goals in this same paper, as well as the tasks and "immediate steps" to achieve each of them, he had, in effect, already completed the work of the task force. Lansdale intended to give the members of the task force only a few days to rubber-stamp his plan. If approved by the President, the structure and sequence of the program would deliver real control over Vietnam policy into Lansdale's hands.

To control the plan itself, Lansdale counted on being appointed the Operations Officer.[38] To control the plan's initial implementation, he planned on being in the three-man group that would accompany Nolting to Vietnam.[39] Afterward Lansdale would resume control of the task force in Washington to "supervise and coordinate the activities of every agency carrying out operations pursuant to the plan" until the problem in Vietnam was solved. In other words, Lansdale had devised a plan under which his own powers would be so sweeping that he would be able to dictate any upcoming changes in Vietnam policy.

It seems unlikely that Lansdale would have been so audacious unless he was being encouraged by someone. But who? Two items point to Rostow. One is the way he kept the door open by urging Kennedy that Lansdale should still "figure prominently" in the "enterprise." The other is the effort he made to place Lansdale on the ground in Vietnam during the crucial phase of implementation. Resistance to this idea was to be expected. For what Lansdale—and presumably Rostow—knew, and the State Department rightly feared, was that the Lansdale-Diem link would overshadow both the new Ambassador and the others in the group.

Finding a means, or excuse, for getting Lansdale to Vietnam was the first order of business. Another reckless blast from Durbrow gave Rostow and Lansdale a golden opportunity to do just that. The episode began with a conversation between journalist Joseph Alsop and Diem during which Diem criticized the Americans for not properly backing him. Alsop relayed Diem's comments to the Ambassador, who, predictably, flew off the handle. On April 12 an angry Durbrow fired off a cable asking that State send him instructions directing that unless Diem began implementing the CIP, the U.S. would not provide funds for the 20,000-man force increase.[40] Always alert for a new opportunity, Lansdale latched on to Durbrow's demand and used it for his own ends.

Lansdale telephoned Rostow's office and said Alsop's use of "the needle" had put Durbrow into "a state of shock."[41] Durbrow, Lansdale said, was involved in a personality clash with Diem, and it would be a mistake to let the Ambassador "lay down the law" to Diem. Lansdale had a better idea: he should go to Vietnam. He would be willing to accompany Rostow and McNamara or Gilpatric on a "quick visit" for Kennedy to come up with a course of action. Rostow encouraged the idea by sending a memo to Kennedy seconding and elaborating on this, Lansdale's latest strategem.[42]

Rostow told Kennedy that Durbrow had reacted with excessive force and that it would be unwise to instruct Durbrow to deliver such an ultimatum. The incident, Rostow said, underlined the "extreme urgency" of starting up with "new faces," and added that a visit to the field by a "Washington team" was called for. "I gather that McNamara would like to go himself," Rostow said, stretching the truth a bit, "or send Gilpatric with Lansdale." While conceding that Nolting was the right choice, Rostow asserted that Lansdale would have been a good Ambassador; and even though he would not be going in that capacity, Rostow made the case forcefully for a Lansdale trip:

> But I am sure we must find a way to send Lansdale for a visit to
> Vietnam soon in a way that will strengthen Nolting's hand—not
> weaken it. This is wholly possible.

While Rostow presented this idea as if it would be to Nolting's benefit,
the proposition was dubious at best, and it seems doubtful that Nolting
would have agreed. The immediate upshot of the "needle" incident was
inconclusive: Durbrow did not get to deliver his ultimatum to Diem and
the issue of a Lansdale trip was still up in the air.

A few days later, Lansdale's fortunes seemed to skyrocket. Although
the April 20 cabinet meeting that discussed the task force plan is still
classified, when it was over the President had ordered the formation of
the task force with Gilpatric as its Director, and, not surprisingly, Lansdale
as the Operations Officer. Gilpatric was given one week to appraise the
situation in Vietnam and recommend a program of action to the President.[43] Such a short schedule was precisely what Lansdale wanted; it
helped him railroad his plan through the new task force.

At the group's first meeting on April 24,[44] great pains were taken to
make it clear to those present, which included the new American Ambassador, Frederick Nolting, that Lansdale was going to Vietnam. The scene
played this way: Gilpatric opened the proceedings by announcing that
Lansdale would accompany Lyndon Johnson on his trip to Vietnam. This
was not enough for Lansdale, who could not resist the temptation to add
another trip to his itinerary—after all, the "needle" incident and his "quick
visit" idea had not yet been decided upon. So he simply announced that
he would also be making a "side visit" to Vietnam "to support the Task
Force efforts in the field." Just in case anyone in the room had doubts,
General McGarr piled on with the comment that Diem wanted to see
Lansdale and "would like him to stay in Vietnam as long as possible."

McGarr then reported on the situation in Vietnam and used the opportunity to take a few jabs at Durbrow, who was not present. McGarr
complained that he had not been able to get his views through to his
own superiors because of Durbrow's insistence that the MAAG reported
through the Ambassador, and he then insinuated that Durbrow had been
holding up the war effort. McGarr reported grim news about the battlefield situation,[45] and used it to argue that the military problem had to be
solved first, before moving ahead in psychological, economic, and "other"
areas, a veiled reference to Durbrow's reforms.

Gilpatric announced that Lansdale would draw up the plan for presentation to Kennedy, and Lansdale handed out a draft "Presidential Task
Force Program," containing various tasks of a national plan very similar
to those in Lansdale's proposal.[46] He had purposely omitted from this
draft those details which would assure his control of the policy apparatus,

but those details *would* be in the version going to the President. Although the group "agreed" to meet on the 26th to finalize the program, this meeting never took place.[47] The version sent to the White House on April 27 was the original Lansdale plan.[48]

The U.S. objective, it said, was to prevent communist domination in South Vietnam. To do this the plan proposed to accelerate and add to the existing CIP, but with one major difference: those portions agreed to by South Vietnam would now be "implemented as rapidly as possible." In other words, U.S. military support had finally been decoupled from the requirement for democratic reforms. Its many pages of actions emphasized stabilizing the countryside instead of pressing Diem on political and administrative reforms. The military measures slightly exceeded those in the CIP: whereas the CIP would pay for *most* of the Vietnamese forces, the new plan proposed to pay for *all* of them.

As far as implementing the new program, the details were spelled out in the last paragraph. Those organizational details, kept hidden from the task force members at the April 24 meeting, which were the crux of Lansdale's plan, now showed up in the final sentence of the report. It said: "In carrying out his duties while in the field, the Operations Officer of the Task Force will cooperate with and will have the full support of the Ambassador and the Country Team."[49] To emphasize this point, Gilpatric included the following paragraph in a cover memo to the President:

> . . . Brigadier General E.G. Lansdale, USAF, who has been designated Operations Officer for the Task Force, will proceed to Vietnam immediately after the program receives Presidential approval. Following on-the-spot discussions with U.S. and Vietnamese officials, he will forward to the Director of the Task Force specific recommendations for action in support of the attached program.[50]

Confident that Kennedy would agree with this program, Lansdale, with Gilpatric's approval, already had sent several messages to many of his old colleagues asking them to join up with him in Saigon during the first week of May. Lansdale's confidence, however, was misplaced.

LANSDALE SWITCHES HORSES

Lansdale had no idea that he was about to be cut off at the knees. On McNamara's copy of the task force report above the sentence saying

Lansdale would proceed to Vietnam, the Secretary wrote the following: "will proceed to Vietnam when requested by the Ambassador."[51] Indeed, Lansdale's official role in Vietnam policy was about to disappear entirely. The reason for McNamara's marginalia was a bold move by Secretary Rusk. Lansdale himself did not learn of the details until 1963. In a letter to his friend Hangin' Sam, he described Rusk's intercession:

> I was knocked out of position to influence decisions on [Vietnam] in 1961. . . . Strangely enough . . . our little VN task force . . . had prompted Dean Rusk to tender his resignation to Kennedy if I were to be kept on this task. We sure must have scared these folks.[52]

Forced to choose between Lansdale and his Secretary of State, Kennedy dumped Lansdale.

By April 27 Lansdale knew his influence on Vietnam policy within the Kennedy administration was, for all practical purposes, finished. At best he would be called upon to offer advice about the obstreperous behavior of Diem, whose own stock was slipping steadily in Washington. April 27, 1961, then, was a watershed day in the history of U.S. policy in Southeast Asia: it was on this day that Admiral Burke sent his message alerting Admiral Felt that Kennedy would not "execute" in Laos. As previously discussed, this decision gave rise to a rapid series of reappraisals and reversals of judgment on Vietnam policy. And sometime during the night or early the next day, someone in the Pentagon inserted a major change in the Vietnam Task Force report.

The change was slipped into a Laos Annex and attached to the report.[53] This Laos Annex was redrafted two times between the end of the chaotic White House meeting on April 27 and its appearance the next day. Consequently, there were three versions. The new ingredient, a major U.S. troop commitment for Vietnam, was not in the first version written by Gilpatric's aide, Colonel Black. It was inserted in the second version and retained in the third and final report. The second version, which is the first document to recommend a U.S. troop commitment to Vietnam during the Kennedy administration, was written by General Edward Lansdale.

Interestingly, this recommendation for a troop commitment, which would shortly turn into a recommendation for unilateral U.S. intervention, ran contrary to Lansdale's own views, which favored social programs and psychological measures. It is one of the ironies of the war that his original ideas were better suited to the situation in Vietnam than those of most Westerners, and certainly more appropriate than the idea of fighting the insurgency by sending in a large American ground combat force. Lansdale coined the term "civic action" for programs whose design and application focused on the ideology and psychology of the people. He believed that economic programs must increase the self-reliance of the people, that military aid should go only to forces whose objective was protecting the people, and that the war itself should be based on a strategy of "directing psychological blows" to the enemy's leadership.[54] This could be done in Vietnam, Lansdale thought, by giving the people security and a "political basis of action."[55] This political action, he felt, "should be the implementing of Vietnamese governmental policy by Vietnamese force commanders, aided by Vietnamese psychological warfare units." It was an ambitious and unorthodox approach to counterinsurgency and one that would never be implemented.

Somewhere along the way Lansdale had become emotionally and psychologically attached to Vietnam—and obsessed by the notion that if only he had the chance he could still save the country. Diem did not follow Lansdale's civic action prescription, but Lansdale's friendship and loyalty to him clouded Lansdale's vision and he grew ever more committed to preserving Diem. In the final analysis, however, the South Vietnamese leader became, more than anything else, a vehicle through which Lansdale could continue to play a key role, because he was the only person in the Kennedy administration that Diem trusted. Lansdale had hoped he could make Diem see the problem the Lansdale way. In his efforts to do so, Lansdale turned into his own worst enemy, relying on the instincts of the "lone wolf and operator" he had become, and alienating key officials as he indulged in the plotting and scheming of which he had become a master.

By the end of April 1961 Lansdale recognized that his dream of bringing Diem around had already eluded his grasp and it was only a matter of time before Diem would be pushed aside. The obsession with Vietnam remained, however, and the star rising on the policy horizon—despite Kennedy's reluctance—was American intervention; and Lansdale, driven by his overriding ambition, reached out for it. For Lansdale, being removed from influence by Kennedy was a heartbreaking experience. Under the circumstances, then, it is perhaps not surprising that Lansdale wrote the first document urging a large U.S. troop commitment to Vietnam. He was embracing more powerful patrons, those who would have their way in the end. Lansdale, the civic action advocate, had changed horses, and when the troops finally arrived in early 1965, he would be there with them.

NOTES

1. Lansdale to Williams, December 29, 1960, Hoover Institution, Williams Papers, Box 20.

2. A more detailed but still unburdensome description of Diem's background can be found in Stanley Karnow, *Vietnam: A History* (New York: Viking, 1983), pp. 213–39, from which much of this account was taken.

3. Colby, *Lost Victory*, p. 107.

4. Lansdale to Williams, January 17, 1961, Hoover Institution, Williams Papers, Box 20.

5. The colleague was Air Force Colonel Fletcher Prouty; Prouty interview with John Newman, June 26, 1991.

6. Ibid.

7. "Notes on a Meeting Between the Secretary of State and the Assistant Secretary of State for Far Eastern Affairs" (Parsons), Washington, January 28, 1961, 6:47 P.M., *State History*, 1961, Document 5, pp. 19–20.

8. The letter's author and recipient (a former MAAG officer now working in the U.S.) are still unidentified. General Williams mailed the extracts used here to Lansdale on January 19, 1961. Hoover Institution, Lansdale Papers, Box 42. The original letter from the unidentified MAAG individual was dated January 1, 1961. Williams, in his letter to Lansdale, said, "I know the person who wrote the letter and consider him absolutely reliable. Whether or not what he wrote is true or not I don't know, but I do know that he thought it was true or he would not have written it. Added to what you have picked up it may give you some background interest."

9. See, for example, William Rust, *Kennedy in Vietnam: American Vietnam Policy, 1960–1963* (New York: Charles Scribner's Sons, 1985), p. 11.

10. Lansdale to Diem, January 30, 1961, in *State History*, 1961, Document 6, pp. 20–23.

11. The Churchill analogy would be used again by Vice President Johnson in May 1961.

12. Remarks by Chief of the Military Assistance Advisory Groups in Vietnam (McGarr), Saigon, January 30, 1961, in *State History*, 1961, Document 7, pp. 24–25.

13. Saigon Embassy to State No. 1329, January 31, 1961, in *State History*, Document 8, pp. 25–28.

14. One reason Durbrow offered was so as not to have it appear the U.S. was showing favoritism in the upcoming South Vietnamese elections, but this was not the main reason. Durbrow complained that Diem had done little more than say he was giving "active consideration" to the "certain liberalizing reforms" the Embassy had been pressing him to adopt, and that much time had been lost since the coup attempt of the previous November. Therefore, he said, a clear statement of support "might further convince him we have no alternative but to support him no matter what he does," and "induce him to further procrastinate from taking the necessary actions I am convinced he must do."

15. Durbrow had already built a coup contingency into the inherent logic of the CIP. The CIP said: "*at the present time* the Diem government offers the best hope for defeating the Viet Cong" (emphasis added). See *PP*, Gravel ed., vol. 2, p. 25 (emphasis added by the *PP* authors). The text can also be seen in *State History*, 1961, Document 1, pp. 1–12; the assumptions are on p. 7. This assumption, when combined with the next assumption immediately following it in the CIP—that Diem had the potential to cope "if necessary corrective measures are taken"—implied that, conversely, if Diem did not take these actions, he would not offer the best hope against the Viet Cong. Durbrow now recommended the U.S. do everything possible to get Diem to "plant the seeds of democracy," while at the same time use its influence to warn the non-communist opposition elements that "any effort *on their part* to pull a coup" might lead to a communist takeover. Durbrow said he had already "instructed all key members of various agency staffs" in Vietnam to "make clear we oppose any coup *which would only enhance prospects of Communist takeover.*"

16. "Joint State-Defense-ISA Message," signed by Rusk, to U.S. Embassy Saigon, February 3, 1961, in *PP*, DOD ed., Book 11, pp. 14–16.

17. Embassy Saigon to State, No. 1351, February 8, 1961, in *State History*, 1961, Document 10, pp. 29–30.

18. Durbrow cable to State, February 13, 1961, in *State History*, 1961, pp. 31–32.

19. Embassy Saigon to State, No. 1391, February 22, 1961; see *State History*, 1961, p. 37, n. 2.

20. See *State History*, 1961, p. 42, n. 4.

21. The letter, to General Palmer, is in *State History*, 1961, Document 17, pp. 43–44.

22. Embassy Saigon cable to State No. 1466, March 16, 1961, in *State History*, 1961, Document 20, pp. 47–51.

23. The record of the conversation is printed in *State History*, 1961, Document 21, pp. 52–57. Thuan told Rusk that few foreigners realized the Viet Cong had occupied South Vietnam's entire countryside prior to 1954. During this time they indoctrinated a large part of the population and afterward kidnapped much of the youth for the move north, he said, so that many of the Viet Cong soldiers are husbands, brothers, or sons of the people in the countryside, and are able to exert strong pressure on the people to collaborate with them. Noting that the communists had changed their tactics from subversion to all-out guerrilla terrorism and increased infiltration of trained cadres from the north, Thuan said, "Diem cannot put into effect all the democratic freedoms, but as the Viet Cong threat diminishes and the people become educated and more sophisticated democracy can make progress."

24. Bill Benedict took the call for ACSI; the caller from the Office of National Estimates (ONE) was Abbot Smith, the drafter. This reconstruction is based upon my interviews with Benedict on June 6 and July 21, 1988, and a joint interview with Benedict and George Allen on July 21, 1988.

25. Roswell Gilpatric, interview with Dennis J. O'Brian, May 5, 1970, JFK Library, Oral History Collection.

26. Hilsman, *To Move a Nation*, p. 419.

27. Rust, *Kennedy in Vietnam*, p. 27. See also J. Graham Parsons, interview with Dennis J. O'Brian, August 22, 1969, JFK Library, Oral History Collection.

28. Lansdale letter to Williams, February 14, 1961, Hoover Institution, Williams Papers, Box 20.

29. Frederick E. Nolting, *From Trust to Tragedy* (New York: Praeger, 1988), p. 11.

30. Rostow memo to JFK, March 29, 1961, JFK Library, POF, O'Donnell, Box 64A.

31. "If State wants the job," Rostow said, "the man must be first class and freed from other duties."

32. Rostow memo to JFK, April 3, 1961, JFK Library, NSF, Country File, Vietnam, Box 193. This was a cover memo to the ineffectual responses to Kennedy's NSAM on guerrilla operations against the North, but its focus was clearly on the need for a person to head up the Vietnam effort in Washington.

33. Rostow memo to JFK, April 12, 1961, JFK Library, NSF, Country File, Vietnam, Box 193.

34. It is possible that McNamara wanted the head of the task force to come from the Defense Department, but there is no documentary evidence for this. The real purpose of Rostow's assertion with respect to McNamara and "your staff" was to give the impression of a building consensus for the task force.

35. *PP*, Gravel ed., vol. 2, p. 34.

36. Ibid., p. 35.

37. The full text is in *PP*, DOD ed., Book 11, pp. 22–35. Although the Lansdale paper is dated April 19, the authors of *The Pentagon Papers* rightly argue that it "must have been prepared some days earlier" due to the April 21 suspense concerning the task force report to Kennedy. They guess that it must have been "about the time of Lansdale's discussion with Rostow on the 13th." This estimate seems sound; if it was earlier, it could not have preceded Rostow's April 3 cover memo (on the CIA/DOD responses to NSAM-28). This is because of the appearance of the title "Vietnam Task Force" and Rostow's backing away from naming Lansdale as its head on that date. Prior to April 3, the paper would have been inconsistent with Rostow's March 29 proposal to name Lansdale for the job.

38. This is clear from Gilpatric's April 17, 1961, memo and enclosures to the State Department. See JFK Library, NSF, Country File, Vietnam, Box 193.

39. This is clear from the first paragraph under "Immediate Steps" in the paper.

40. For portions of this cable, see *State History*, 1961, p. 72, n. 2.

41. A record of the April 14, 1961, phone call is at the JFK Library, NSF, Country File, Vietnam, Box 193. Lansdale's call was for Rostow. Fortunately, Rostow was not in, and as a result, a lengthy note was left for Rostow that we can read today and that offers valuable insight into Lansdale's actions at this time.

42. Rostow memo to JFK, April 15, 1961; see *State History*, 1961, Document 30, pp. 72–73.

43. See McNamara's April 20, 1961, memo to JFK, JFK Library, NSF, Country File, Vietnam, Box 193. This memo gave Gilpatric an April 28 reporting date to JFK. See also McNamara's April 20, 1961, instruction to Gilpatric, LBJ Library, VP Security File, Box 10. This memo, written later in the day, gave Gilpatric until April 27 to report to JFK.

44. From a State Department set of notes on the proceedings of the April 24 Task Force meeting, in *State History*, 1961, Document 33, pp. 77–80.

45. He said only 42 percent of the country was under GVN control, and that ninety of the ARVN's 120 battalions were fully committed, many having been in continuous operations for one to two years without training. The force increase was needed simply for rotation and training purposes.

46. A copy of the program passed out at the April 24 meeting is in *State History*, 1961, Document 32, pp. 74–77.

47. The agreement on the April 26 meeting is from the State notes of the meeting, but the authors of *The Pentagon Papers* note that "present files do not show whether there was another full meeting" before the paper was sent to the President on the 27th; see *PP*, Gravel ed., vol. 2, p. 35. McGarr was addressing the Cuba Study Group at Taylor's request on the 26th; see Maxwell Taylor, *Swords and Plowshares* (New York: Norton, 1972), p. 221. The *State History*, 1961, documents similarly do not indicate that a meeting on the 26th took place.

48. Dated April 26, this, the first draft, can be found in *PP*, DOD ed., Book 11, pp. 42–57. It was also called, inappropriately, the "Gilpatric Plan" or the "Gilpatric report."

49. *PP*, DOD ed., Book 11, p. 56.

50. Ibid., p. 42.

51. Ibid., p. 38.

52. Lansdale letter to Williams, October 10, 1964, Hoover Institution, Williams Papers, Box 20.

53. *PP*, Gravel ed., vol. 2, p. 40.

54. See Lansdale, *In the Midst of Wars*, pp. 369–73.

55. Lansdale Vietnam trip report, January 17, 1961, *PP*, DOD ed., Book 11, p. 11.

CHAPTER THREE

THE STRUGGLE OVER U.S. TROOPS ERUPTS

VIETNAM POLICY: THREE MONTHS OF GRIDLOCK

Kennedy's advisors had not served him well during the first three months of his presidency. This was demonstrated most dramatically in the Cuban debacle, but the same was true with respect to the problems in Southeast Asia. It has been seen how the confused and desperate attempt to cope with the deterioration in Laos failed, leaving the administration, by late April 1961, in need of a much clearer definition of its policy on Vietnam. Kennedy's advisors proved no better able to handle this task, and were even more divided by the policy that emerged in the end. So far one part of the story that led to this impasse has been described in detail; before proceeding to the decisions of early May it is necessary to trace the outline of the broader struggle that produced them.

On the heels of the January 28 approval of the CIP, Kennedy made two other decisions. First he directed that more emphasis be placed on how to deal with guerrilla wars.[1] His interest in counterguerrilla warfare in Southeast Asia was undoubtedly heightened by Khrushchev's bellicose speech on January 6, 1961, promising Soviet support for "wars of national liberation"—which specifically mentioned Vietnam. At an NSC meeting on February 1, Kennedy issued National Security Action Memorandum

(NSAM) 2, which ordered the Secretary of Defense to examine ways to put emphasis on developing counterguerrilla forces.[2] Despite this directive, the executive branch was slow to respond, and Rostow recalled that his job, from his first talk with Kennedy after the inauguration, was not merely to follow Laos and Vietnam, but to "help the President get the Pentagon and the whole town to take guerrilla warfare seriously."[3]

The second decision reflected Kennedy's concern that the CIP contained no immediate military measures to turn around the quickly deteriorating situation in South Vietnam. A report attached to the CIP had assured Kennedy that, if the plan's provisions were carried out, victory was just eighteen months away.[4] Unimpressed, the President penned on this cover memo the sardonic question "Why so little?"[5] On February 5, he issued NSAM-12 to Chief of Staff Lemnitzer asking if South Vietnamese forces could be more effectively distributed for counterguerrilla activities.[6] The President's message was clear: to get cracking "immediately" instead of waiting for the proposed increase in South Vietnamese forces to take effect.

As the weeks rolled by and the developing crisis in Laos moved the U.S. to the verge of war, the power struggle between Ambassador Durbrow and President Diem brought the CIP and Vietnam policy in general to a grinding halt. Kennedy grew impatient but, perhaps because the situation in Laos demanded so much of his time and attention, he at first failed to grasp the true dimensions of the problem. In addition, the Washington bureaucracy was lethargic. Kennedy's January 28 instruction to form a Vietnam task force was shelved for almost three months; the task force would not be created until late April. The response to Kennedy's NSAM-2 on developing counterguerrilla measures was equally slow.[7]

Kennedy began prodding the bureaucracy to pick up steam at a February 23 NSC meeting when he expressed dissatisfaction with American progress in developing a worldwide counterinsurgency capability. These remarks moved Chief of Naval Operations Admiral Burke to say this in a cable to Admiral Felt (CINCPAC): "There is going to be an awful lot of guerrilla warfare training by U.S. forces all over [the] world, I'll betcha."[8] Moreover, Kennedy had inquired about South Vietnamese operations against North Vietnam and six weeks had passed without result. Kennedy reiterated his interest in this question by issuing NSAM-28 on March 9, directing the CIA and the Defense Department to report what actions might be taken "in view of the President's instruction that we make every possible effort to launch guerrilla operations in Viet-Minh [North Vietnam] territory."[9]

Beyond this, however, Kennedy did not pay much attention to Vietnam at this point. As then Assistant Secretary of Defense Gilpatric later recalled:

The President seemed to me to be at times rather irked or distracted at having to focus his attention on Vietnam, as opposed to the problems of the Atlantic Alliance; the relations with the Soviet Union; and this kind of competitive contest with Khrushchev— which fascinated him, and occupied a good deal of his thinking and time.[10]

The President's own level of interest, then, may have contributed to the lumbering nature of the Vietnam policy apparatus.

Below the level of the President, the principal impediments to U.S. Vietnam policy during the first three months of the Kennedy administration were the internecine skirmishing between Diem and Durbrow in Saigon and the power struggle between Lansdale and the State Department in Washington. In addition, the continuing disunity of the American Mission in Saigon doomed whatever chance Durbrow, already weakened by his lame-duck status, might have had to get Diem to cooperate. At the same time, in Washington, the competition between Lansdale and the State Department added to the confusion and denied Durbrow the support he so badly needed.

The interconnections of these power struggles make them difficult to untangle and resolve. The strings tying Lansdale to Diem played a role in both conflicts, and Kennedy's early decision to appoint Lansdale to replace Ambassador Durbrow had a result Kennedy had not foreseen. Encouraged by Lansdale, Diem became all the more intractable and proceeded to torpedo the CIP. State cables directing Durbrow to turn up the pressure on Diem had similarly negative results, only encouraging the Ambassador's intransigence and prolonging the agony that ensued.

The first break in the deadlock came in the latter part of February, when the State Department succeeded in derailing the Lansdale appointment, and Kennedy decided on Nolting instead. This change simplified the lines of struggle, leaving Diem and Durbrow to quibble to the bitter end in Saigon, and Lansdale's attention focused on seizing control of the apparatus from Washington. It became apparent that there would be no progress in Saigon while Durbrow was on the scene, and Kennedy soon became impatient and moved up Nolting's arrival date from June to early May. Rusk's signal of cooperation to Diem at the end of March (at the SEATO Conference in Bangkok) finally resolved the conflict in Saigon.

Flailing away all the way up to his last month on the job, Durbrow continued to make a minor nuisance of himself, a factor that Lansdale attempted unsuccessfully to exploit in Washington as his struggle with the State Department reached its climax at the end of April. By the time Rusk took the bull by the horns and confronted Kennedy, resolving the conflict as he should have in the beginning, three precious months had passed. In that time the Viet Cong had continued to expand their military forces and their political infrastructure while the Americans had squandered away valuable time squabbling with the Vietnamese and among themselves.

Lansdale's bid to capture the Washington policy apparatus reached its climax on April 27, a week after the failure in Cuba. That week was a busy one. For one thing the moment of truth had arrived for a decision on intervention in Laos. On the same day that Lansdale's plan went down in a stinging defeat at the hands of Rusk and Kennedy, the stormy NSC meeting left Admiral Burke—and others who were pushing for intervention—with the impression that Kennedy would decide against it. Yet Kennedy had officially deferred a final decision, and an NSC meeting scheduled for April 29 would give the JCS one more chance. In accordance with Vice President Johnson's suggestion, each of the Chiefs would have the opportunity to present their "detailed views" on intervention in Laos.

Prior to the NSC session, however, the Chiefs first met with McNamara, Rusk, Robert Kennedy, Bowles, U. Alexis Johnson, and other State Department officials for a brainstorming session on certain questions posed by the President.[11] Looking over the minutes of that meeting thirty years later is an unsettling experience. The repeated references to the use of nuclear weapons leave one with an eerie, surrealistic feeling, not because generals were considering nuclear scenarios—which is, after all, part of their job—but because of the wholly inappropriate context in which the use of such weapons was discussed, apparently without any reservations.

The record of this meeting provides an indelible baseline for determining the views of the national leadership at that time on the monumental issue of sending American soldiers into war. It reveals the true background of the debate, which immediately followed, on the introduction of U.S. combat troops to Vietnam. In fact, the drive for intervention in Vietnam was only forty-eight hours old when this meeting took place. Above all else, this record leaves the reader with the unforgettable image of a President pitted against his own advisors and the bureaucracy that served under him.

THE APRIL 29 CONSENSUS

All participants in the brainstorming session foresaw dire consequences to the loss of Laos. McNamara said, "We would have to attack the DRV [North Vietnam] if we gave up Laos." Rusk argued that if a cease-fire was "not brought about quickly" it would be necessary to implement

SEATO Plan 5. Admiral Burke stated flatly that the loss of Laos would require the deployment of U.S. forces to Thailand *and* Vietnam, and that the U.S. "would have to throw in enough to win—perhaps the 'works.'" The thing to do now, he said, was "to land and hold as much as we can and make clear we were not going to be pushed out of Southeast Asia." Air Force Chief of Staff General LeMay said a cease-fire was impossible without "military action." He favored SEATO Plan 5 backed up by air support, and argued this would produce a cease-fire without a Chinese response. Marine Corps Commandant Shoup stated that bombing with B-26s before landing the troops would make it "possible to obtain a cease-fire and get the panhandle of Laos." Army Chief of Staff General Decker stated, "We should have [gone in] last August [1960]." He now urged that troops be put in Thailand and Vietnam to see if this would pressure the communists into a cease-fire in Laos.[12] The only one of the Chiefs not present, the Chairman, General Lemnitzer—in Laos at the time— "endorsed the case" for a "limited commitment."[13]

McNamara worried that U.S. forces would be vulnerable to sabotage, attack by guerrillas, and Chinese air strikes, but Burke, LeMay, and even Rusk felt intervention was still feasible. In the end, McNamara said, "The situation was worsening by the hour and that if we were going to commit ourselves, then we must do so sooner rather than later." Rusk wanted to put troops in Vientiane and seize the Laotian panhandle as well. Shoup wanted to bomb the Pathet Lao, land troops, *and then* secure a cease-fire and the Laotian panhandle. Burke wanted to take Vientiane airport initially, and then land and hold as much as possible. Decker wanted to put troops in Thailand and Vietnam and then invade Laos if a cease-fire was not obtained. LeMay wanted SEATO Plan 5, air strikes, *and war with China as well*, saying, "We should go to work on China itself and let Chiang [President of Taiwan] take Hainan Island."

The issue of whether intervention would trigger a Chinese response found the group evenly divided. The lengthy discussion on this point boiled down to this: McNamara, Burke, Decker, and Bowles, in varying degrees, all felt U.S. intervention could very easily trigger a Chinese response and the consequent need to resort to nuclear weapons. Rusk, Bohlen, and LeMay felt U.S. intervention would not trigger a Chinese response, although LeMay, as noted, wanted to "go to work on China" anyway.

On the general question of intervention in Southeast Asia, the record of this extraordinary session shows that Kennedy's principal civilian and military advisors:

- were sharply divided on what form this intervention should take and on whether it would trigger a Chinese response;

- differed somewhat on the significance of the loss of Laos; and
- were nearly unanimous in advocating U.S. intervention in Laos.

It also reveals the "all or nothing" argument of the JCS was not, as is often thought, a tactic to avoid a limited war. On the contrary, they wanted to intervene, and wanted to do so with the assurance that, if necessary, they could use nuclear weapons. Despite the consensus among most of Kennedy's top advisors that intervention was necessary, there was no such consensus on the President's most basic questions: What form should it take? What would the Chinese reaction be? And, where would it lead to in the end?

THE APRIL 29 NSC MEETING

Most of the participants went straight from the brainstorming session into the NSC meeting.[14] Originally scheduled to look only at the Vietnam report, the agenda was broadened to include a discussion of Laos.[15] Surprisingly, this Laos discussion has to date escaped historical scrutiny: it has never been commented on in any work covering this period.[16] This is unfortunate, for that day the NSC examined issues of great national importance. There *is* a surviving draft record of this meeting, located in the Vice Presidential Security Files of the Lyndon Baines Johnson Library. This record states that the Council examined "considerations involved in the various alternative courses of action" in Laos.[17] As a consequence of this discussion, the President made a momentous decision. He agreed to "undertake certain military and diplomatic measures" before the next NSC meeting on May 1.

While we still do not know their exact content, we may reasonably surmise what these measures were from a JCS message to CINCPAC immediately after the meeting.[18] This message directed CINCPAC to prepare plans for moving two brigade-sized forces of 5,000 men each to Udorn, Thailand, and Da Nang, Vietnam, with "all arms and appropriate air elements." Only U.S. forces were involved but the State Department was "taking action to explore" whether these troops could be given a "SEATO cover." The message also reported that no decision had been reached "today" on implementing SEATO Plan 5; that they expected a decision on the Thailand deployment on May 1, and a decision on the Vietnam deployment even later due to the ongoing negotiations in Geneva.

What Kennedy had authorized was *preparations* to move two brigades and associated combat support elements into position for a unilateral U.S. intervention in Laos under a SEATO cover. The campaign plan appeared to include ground offensives along multiple axes, one from Thailand, to be decided on by May 1, and the other from Vietnam, to be decided after a justification for breaking the 1954 Geneva Accords was formulated. From the foregoing, it is obvious that Kennedy had indeed agreed to *threaten* intervention in Laos. But Kennedy's plan, says his aide, Theodore Sorensen, "combined bluff with real determination in proportions he made known to *no one*."[19] Apparently Kennedy kept even his closest advisors in the dark about his ultimate intentions.

In the meeting McNamara rightly pointed out that if the decision was to intervene it had to be done right away. The situation was deteriorating so rapidly that each passing day meant a higher price in American lives in the event of intervention. Rusk too argued for a quick decision. He followed up with a memo the next day in which he said that if a cease-fire was not achieved within forty-eight hours, he advised the implementation of SEATO Plan 5 or a deployment of SEATO forces into Thailand to be ready for a move into Laos.[20] Even if a cease-fire was achieved, Rusk said, the U.S. goal at the conference table should be a "mixed up Laos"— the more fractured the better. Rusk predicted that a coalition government would "tend to become a Communist satellite," and argued that "even partition would be a better outcome than unity under leadership responsive to the Communists."

THE MAY 1 NSC MEETING AND BEYOND

By the time the May 1 NSC meeting finally convened, the "realities of Laos," as Rusk called them, had produced an overwhelming sentiment among Kennedy's advisors for intervention there.[21] A force of 10,000 men was ready for action, and the views of the Joint Chiefs were again delivered to the President in writing. Whereas on April 27 the Chiefs had appeared confused about going into Laos, they now left no doubt about their unity. McGeorge Bundy wrote in a note to Kennedy that "it's not at all clear why they are now unanimous."[22] Sorensen says there were still "splits" in the Chiefs' written responses, but the majority "appeared to favor the landing of American troops in Thailand, South Vietnam and the government-held portions of the Laotian panhandle."[23]

Chastened by the Bay of Pigs, however, Kennedy was now far more skeptical of the Chiefs' recommendations. According to Sorensen, Kennedy "began asking questions he had not asked before about military operations in Laos." The Chiefs were no more successful in explaining their proposals than they had been four days earlier, and proceeded to crumble under Kennedy's detailed questioning. He raised the most basic military issues about their campaign plan, and their answers seem incomprehensible in retrospect. How many airstrips in Laos? the President asked. Only *two* was the answer; and these were only usable during daylight and good weather and were always vulnerable to attack. If the communists attacked and "we didn't use nuclear weapons," Kennedy asked, "would we have to retreat or surrender in the face of an all-out Chinese intervention? That answer was affirmative." "If we put more forces in Laos, he asked, would that weaken our reserves for action in Berlin or elsewhere? The answer was again in the affirmative."[24] Kennedy sat in "stunned silence" as he heard that the dispatch of even 10,000 men to Southeast Asia would denude American strategic reserves.[25] The meeting was "unforgettable for all present," says Rostow. There was no order or consensus: "It was chaos."[26]

The deployment to Thailand, anticipated in the JCS message to CINC-PAC, did not occur. Kennedy decided to defer "final decisions" pending "further developments in the cease-fire negotiations."[27] He was "prepared under certain conditions to deploy U.S. forces to Thailand," and directed the Chiefs to prepare a presentation for the following day on the "military implications of various measures that might be undertaken in Laos, Thailand, and other countries of Southeast Asia." This was little more than a placebo, a tactic Kennedy often used: to avoid flatly turning down a proposal from the Chiefs, he would send them away with instructions to do a study and get back to him on it.

On May 1 Kennedy, through McNamara, asked Admiral Burke if the Marine battalion afloat off Bangkok was ready, and Burke replied they were and could be in Bangkok in twelve hours.[28] However, at the subsequent May 2 meeting there was still no decision to intervene. Kennedy directed only that contingency planning be continued "in the light of the rapidly deteriorating situation," and instructed Rusk and McNamara to promptly send him a joint recommendation on U.S. action in Laos.[29] Again, Kennedy's actions would lead to nothing more than a study and a recommendation, but the forces continued to build for intervention. On May 2 CINCPACFLT ordered the ship *Bon Homme Richard* to leave Hawaii for the Western Pacific, and also ordered a battalion of the 5th Marines to head for Okinawa.

That same day Harriman and Lemnitzer, who had just arrived in Vietnam from Laos, met with Diem. "Laos must be saved at all costs," Diem pleaded, otherwise Vietnam would become "untenable" and open to massive infiltration or invasion.[30] Diem warned that North Vietnamese forces were already advancing on Southern Laos and would take the area adjacent to South Vietnam "unless SEATO acted rapidly." Without SEATO action, he said, the North Vietnamese, under the guise of the Pathet Lao, would take over so much territory that they would never voluntarily leave and there would then be no chance for a neutral Laos. Diem advocated using Chinese nationalist troops in Vietnam with the U.S. Air Force and Seventh Fleet bolstering the "depleted" forces on Taiwan. Citing captured documents, Diem complained that 2,000 Viet Cong had infiltrated into the south since the previous December, and the troop increase for his army as well as more naval craft were desperately needed to protect Vietnam's long frontier and coast line. Lemnitzer assured Diem the U.S. "would do everything in its power" to help Vietnam fight the communists.

Diem's appeal for U.S. intervention in Laos would not reach Washington until May 4. By this time the issue was truly dead in the White House. The time had passed for intervention in Laos. The work of the NSC meeting the following day was focused solely on "salvaging" something from the Laos negotiations. The feeling of most present was that the chance for doing even this "was slim indeed."[31] The only option left was to find some concrete way to reassure Vietnam and Thailand of America's continuing support. A vice presidential trip, which had been under consideration for some time, seemed an appropriate way to do this.

As the U.S. military buildup came to a halt, Laotian forces on the ground, which had been anticipating the arrival of U.S. troops, retreated to defensive positions. South Vietnamese troops entered Laos to provide fallback positions for the Laotian garrison retreating from Tchepone in the middle of the panhandle.[32] The communists, who began stalling again on the cease-fire, were now in control of the key terrain ensuring unhindered infiltration into South Vietnam.

"THANK GOD THE BAY OF PIGS HAPPENED"

A key factor in Kennedy's decision not to intervene in Laos was his growing alienation with the Joint Chiefs resulting from the abortive Cuban invasion. At an April 21 breakfast meeting attended by Rusk, McGeorge Bundy, and others, Kennedy, who had been reading stories in the morning papers about who was to blame for the Bay of Pigs, commented "acidly" that the Chiefs were not mentioned, which meant the stories had been leaked by the Pentagon.[33] That same day retired Army Chief of Staff Maxwell Taylor, who had been forced out of the government for criticizing the Eisenhower administration's emphasis on strategic weapons, received a call from the President. Kennedy said he was in "deep trouble," and asked Taylor to come to the White House to talk about it. Taylor later wrote of his experience the following day:

> I was ushered into the Oval Room and there met Kennedy, Vice President Johnson, and McGeorge Bundy along with a few other officials who drifted in and out. I sensed an air which I had known in my military past—that of a command post which had been overrun. There were some glazed eyes, subdued voices, and slow speech that I remembered observing in commanders routed at the Battle of the Bulge or recovering from the shock of their first action.[34]

This passage dramatically illustrates the painful aftermath of the Cuban blunder; it was an experience Kennedy would never forget. The alienation between the President and the Chiefs carried over into the debate on Laos, and was deepened by Kennedy's refusal to intervene there.

Kennedy looked upon the Cuban failure as a lesson well learned. On May 3 he told Schlesinger:

> "If it hadn't been for Cuba, we might be about to intervene in Laos." Waving a sheaf of cables from Lemnitzer, he added, "I might have taken this advice seriously."[35]

Sorensen later had a nearly identical experience with Kennedy:

> "Thank God the Bay of Pigs happened when it did," he would say to me in September. . . . "Otherwise we'd be in Laos by now—and that would be a hundred times worse."[36]

His suspicions raised by the Cuban experience, Kennedy took a closer look at the Laos problem and was "appalled," says Schlesinger, "at the sketchy nature of American military planning for Laos—the lack of detail and the unanswered questions."[37]

Kennedy's growing antipathy toward the Joint Chiefs was matched by their growing irritation with him. General LeMay was particularly unhappy. As Robert Futrell, in *The United States Air Force in Southeast Asia*, explains:

> Part of the difficulties in dealing with a possible use of force, General LeMay believed, was due to President Kennedy's procedural habits and tendencies. The President seemed to depend on ad hoc committees in lieu of the Joint Chiefs, leading to vetoes, stalling, lengthy discussions, and too many people "in the act and making decisions

in areas where they weren't competent." This approach to policy, LeMay believed, failed to recognize that "going to war is a very serious business and once you make [the] decision that you're going to do that, then you ought to be prepared to do just that."[38]

Lemnitzer similarly "deplored the tendency of the U.S. government to waste time in quibbling over policy."[39]

This picture of a President pitted against his military advisors is an unpleasant one, for a commander-in-chief must have confidence in the generals under him and rely on their professional judgments if the national security mechanism is to perform correctly or at all. Unfortunately for American policy in Vietnam, this mechanism broke down completely at the very time when crucial advice and decisions were necessary. Three months had already passed with the U.S. Vietnam apparatus virtually prostrate, while the Viet Cong relentlessly built up their forces and increased the area under their control. The situation was indeed a somber one as the President pondered what to do about Vietnam.

THE CHIEFS URGE INTERVENTION IN VIETNAM

When the Vietnam report, along with the U.S. troop commitment in the Laos Annex, came to Kennedy on April 29, he had simply ignored the Annex. He was in no mood to make any final decisions then. When Lansdale and Gilpatric reissued the Task Force Report on May 1, with the April 28 Annex still included, the concept of *unilateral* U.S. intervention had been introduced. As pointed out in the previous chapter, although the U.S. troop commitments were still described as solely for training, this revision was clearly headed in the direction of intervention. When the subject of combat troops was brought up at the May 5 NSC meeting,[40] however, Rusk effectively killed the proposal by arguing it would torpedo the upcoming Laos conference.

By that time Lansdale had lost control of the Vietnam Task Force, as Kennedy had directed the State Department to run it. Lansdale was still offered a role, but, embittered, he now advised Gilpatric that Defense should stay "completely out" of the directorship of the task force. Having a Defense officer or himself in a position of "partial influence" would only provide State with a "scapegoat to share the blame when we have a flop," Lansdale complained.[41] He did not intend to play second string to anyone in the State Department, and was content, for the time being, to watch the debate over intervention in Vietnam from the sidelines.

The twin failures of Cuba and Laos gave the Kennedy administration's foreign policy track record a black eye; and the rapidity with which the Pentagon now sought to place the forces that had been destined for Laos into South Vietnam instead caught Kennedy at a particularly vulnerable moment. For the fiasco at the Bay of Pigs had raised questions about Kennedy's resolve against communism, a situation only exacerbated by his decision against intervention in Laos. He was under great pressure to make a stand somewhere.

On May 6 the Vietnam Task Force issued its report.[42] The impact of State's takeover of this final version was to soften the U.S. troop commitment implied in the earlier Defense version. The explicit recommendation in the Defense Department's draft that the U.S. make clear its determination to intervene unilaterally, if this were necessary, was dropped.[43] The report noted that in preparation for a possible commitment of combat troops to Vietnam that "might result from an NSC decision following discussions between Vice President Johnson and President Diem," the Defense Department was studying the required size and composition of such a force. Possible actions being considered included deployment of two U.S. battle groups with necessary command and logistics units, an engineer battalion, a CINCPAC naval component for coastal patrol, and a CINCPAC air component to provide close air support for South Vietnamese troops. Accordingly, on May 8 Deputy Secretary of Defense Gilpatric sent a memo to the Chiefs asking for their views and those of CINCPAC on the advisability of sending forces and on the size and composition of them.[44]

That same day Lemnitzer, still in East Asia, sent a real barn-burner of a cable to the Pentagon.[45] Lemnitzer said it appeared the "unhappy sequence of events in Laos" was being repeated, adding this "can only mean the loss of Vietnam." In a scathing indictment of the President's cautious approach to the communist threat in Southeast Asia, Lemnitzer argued the problem in simple terms:

> does the U.S. intend to take the necessary military action now to defeat the Viet Cong threat or do we intend to quibble for weeks and months over details of general policy . . . while Vietnam slowly but surely goes down the drain of Communism as North Vietnam and a large portion of Laos have gone to date?

This cable was a dramatic illustration of the Chiefs' anger over the failure to intervene in Laos and their determination to do so in Vietnam.

On May 10 the JCS put their views on the record.[46] On that date they delivered a resolute and emphatic recommendation for sending U.S. combat troops to Vietnam. This unique and startling memo deserves a detailed examination here. The Chiefs now argued that if the administration decided to keep Southeast Asia out of the communist "sphere," U.S. forces "should be deployed immediately" to South Vietnam, so that they would not be subjected to the kind of combat situation existing in Laos. The Chiefs recommended that a decision to "deploy suitable forces" be made.

The memo went on to list the specific purposes for intervention in Vietnam: to provide a deterrent against North Vietnamese or Chinese aggression; the assumption of some of the South Vietnamese Army's static defense duties, releasing them to concentrate on counterinsurgency actions; training South Vietnamese forces; providing a "nucleus" for additional U.S. or SEATO operations in Southeast Asia; and finally to show firmness "and our intent to all Asian nations." The Chiefs' plan for intervention took into account Felt's concerns about the operational flexibility of U.S. forces already in the Pacific, and said the troops would come from the U.S. so as not to tax the capabilities of CINCPAC. In order to accomplish their plan the Chiefs recommended:

> President Diem be *encouraged to request* that the United States fulfill its SEATO obligation, in view of the new threat now posed by the Laotian situation, by immediate deployment of appropriate U.S. forces to South Vietnam;

> Upon receipt of this request, suitable forces could be immediately deployed to South Vietnam in order to accomplish the above-mentioned purpose. Details of size and composition of these forces must include the views of both CINCPAC and CHMAAG which are not yet available. [emphasis added]

This memo was the first of many the Chiefs would send to Kennedy in 1961 arguing the case for massive U.S. intervention in Vietnam. One very important element that it did not overlook was the necessity of getting Diem to request U.S. forces. As shall be seen, this problem would be dealt with soon.

The same day the JCS views were sent to the White House, Admiral Burke cabled Felt that intervention was the only way to avoid a repeat of the U.S. performance in Laos.[47] Burke's cable noted, "Where there are no U.S. troops in place, there is no will to send them when the going gets tough." He felt strongly that only a few units were needed for this purpose, because making a decision to reinforce them "is more easily taken" than the decision to commit them in the first place. He explained how this had worked in Laos: "We have missed the boat in Laos by not having [a] foot in [the] door."

Burke's cable prompted Admiral Felt to come up with his recommendation on what U.S. forces were required in South Vietnam. He sent out a cable the next day saying he supported the JCS decision, particularly since, as he now understood the Chiefs' thinking, it would mean additional forces from the U.S. being assigned to his command.[48] Within a few days, Felt sent a more specific recommendation to the Pentagon saying these troops should include one Army infantry division with its logistical support; eight B-57s for border surveillance and close air support; four F-102s for air defense; and a few reconnaissance aircraft. Felt also wanted General McGarr's title to be changed to "Commander, U.S. Forces Vietnam," putting him in charge of, under CINCPAC, all U.S. forces there.[49]

The 10th of May, then, was a landmark day in the history of the Vietnam War: it was the first time the Chiefs went on record unequivocally for putting U.S. combat troops into Vietnam. In addition, two other related events occurred that day that have been overlooked completely by major works on the war. Lansdale, in a memo to Gilpatric, weighed in with his "personal views" on the matter and sided with the Chiefs.[50] Lansdale was now an ardent supporter of intervention in Vietnam. He argued that the loss of Vietnam would place the entire defense line of the Western Pacific and Indian Ocean in "great jeopardy," and that "every other nation in the world will question the effectiveness of U.S. military doctrine, organization, equipment and training against Communist methods." To deal with this threat, he advocated sending U.S. combat forces to Vietnam as a deterrent force like those employed in Germany. These forces, he concluded, should include a "hard core" capable of defending itself "in foreseeable combat until reinforced as required in a contingency," and other elements to help in local public works "to make the U.S. military presence a welcome one with the local population."

The other event occurred in Saigon, where Lansdale's ally General McGarr launched a most unusual plan. It began with a curious cable to CINCPAC that had the tone of an advertising campaign—something quite out of character for McGarr. McGarr had something to sell, and to legitimize his pitch he invoked the name of President Kennedy. He even went so far as to suggest a unity of viewpoint between the President and the Chairman of the Joint Chiefs of Staff on Vietnam policy. McGarr said: "President Kennedy and General Lemnitzer have repeatedly stated Vietnam is not to go behind the Bamboo Curtain," and that with this in mind he was conducting two studies.[51]

McGarr's linkage of Lemnitzer and Kennedy seems especially odd in light of Lemnitzer's unrestrained assault on Kennedy's policy unleashed only two days earlier. Clearly when he crafted this cable, accuracy was not McGarr's priority. Invoking Kennedy's name up front was a tactic to package and sell his two new studies. The studies themselves raise other questions. Only one of them was described in detail and from both key information was withheld. Of the study he described, McGarr said that it concerned new U.S. forces necessary to "insure effective implementation [of] those military courses of action approved by [the] President." It showed an immediate requirement for 156 more men, and a further increase of 272 phased over a three-month period. "Subsequent additional personnel are envisioned," McGarr said, but he was "not prepared at this time to submit specific needs." Interestingly, he would put these needs in writing immediately after a discussion with Diem and Vice President Johnson two days later. The "additional personnel" envisioned would be 16,000 U.S. combat troops.

Of the other study McGarr said only that it was being made to determine the required South Vietnamese force structure assuming that "Laos goes Communist or Communist inclined." This sentence was a bit curious, since a good bit of Laotian territory—especially that close to South Vietnam's borders—was already communist or communist inclined. McGarr didn't have these figures on hand either; but again, he would come up with them just two days later. The "required" force would entail nearly doubling the size of the South Vietnamese Army from 150,000 to 280,000 men.[52]

Events soon to unfold would cast a new light on McGarr's strange communiqué. As will soon be seen, McGarr, assisted from Washington by the unseen hand of Lansdale, was preparing for a vice presidential trip to Saigon. The situation would be tricky and revolve around President Diem. He could be expected to be most grateful to have his army doubled at U.S. expense. The question was, how would he react to the 16,000 U.S. combat troops? Lyndon Johnson's trip had not yet been officially announced; that prerogative Kennedy had retained for himself. He too was preparing for the Vice President's trip, and in an equally unusual way.

The day after Johnson would leave for Vietnam, Kennedy would call together his National Security Council and issue NSAM-52. While its full contents will be discussed later, two items are worth mentioning now. NSAM-52 approved the Vietnam Task Force report but *altered* the report's recommendation that the Defense Department study the size and composition of U.S. forces that might be deployed to Vietnam by placing that study under the "guidance" of the new Task Force Director, the State Department's Sterling Cottrell.[53] More importantly, NSAM-52 *removed* the sentence that stated that such a deployment of U.S. forces to Vietnam could result from "an NSC decision following discussions between Vice President Johnson and President Diem."

Why did Kennedy remove this important sentence from the NSAM— only hours before Johnson's first scheduled talk with Diem? This curious deletion has so far escaped historical scrutiny, and one can only wonder if it suggests that the President was concerned about what the Vice President was up to in Saigon. Such a concern, as it turned out, would have been justified.

NOTES

1. At the January 28 meeting, CIA Director Dulles urged that "counter-guerrilla forces" should be strengthened before organizing the new 20,000-man increase in regular Vietnamese forces. He said the MAAG "had no adequate provision for paramilitary forces" and that there was "no clear authority in Washington" on the matter.

2. NSAM-2, February 3, 1961, *PP*, DOD ed., Book 11, p. 17.

3. Rostow, interview with Richard Neustadt, April 11, 1964, p. 45.

4. Schlesinger, *A Thousand Days*, p. 500.

5. Congressional Research Service, interview with Elbridge Durbrow, October 25, 1978.

6. NSAM-12, February 6, 1961, in *State History*, 1961, Document 9, p. 29. See also the draft version, Kennedy memo to Lemnitzer, February 5, 1961, JFK Library, NSF, Regional Security, SEA, Box 128A. Someone had said during the January 28 White House meeting that a "high proportion" of ARVN was "pinned on the front" facing North Vietnam. There is no record of a reply by Lemnitzer, probably because GVN forces were not concentrated on the border (see n. 9). So in NSAM-12, Kennedy asked Lemnitzer: "Are there troops stationed along the border who could be made available for this activity?" The Vietnamese Army had 150,000 men and "we are planning to add 20,000 more," the NSAM said, while "the guerrillas number from 7,000 to 15,000."

7. At a February 22 planning meeting, Richard Bissell (Special Assistant for Planning and Coordination, CIA) was finally given the task of organizing a study on deterring guerrilla warfare to include its application in Vietnam.

8. The CNO 240133Z FEB 1961 message to Felt is quoted in *USN and the Vietnam Conflict*, p. 100.

9. NSAM-28, March 9, 1961, *PP*, DOD ed., Book 11, p. 18.

10. NBC News White Paper, "Death of Diem," December 22, 1971, Part 1.

11. Memorandum of Conversation, April 29, 1961, *PP*, DOD ed., Book 11, pp. 62–66.

12. Army General Decker's comment that a conventional war was unwinnable, and "if we go in" it would mean bombing Hanoi and China and perhaps using nuclear weapons, has led some observers to surmise that the Joint Chiefs were not in favor of intervention. This interpretation is obviously misinformed, as the minutes of this meeting make abundantly clear. Lemnitzer, Burke, Shoup, and LeMay all clearly favored intervention, and so did Decker.

13. Schlesinger, *A Thousand Days*, p. 316. Schlesinger says the "military" did not want to put troops in unless "they could send at least 140,000 men armed with tactical nuclear weapons."

14. Robert Kennedy, McNamara, Gilpatric, Burke, Rusk, Bowles, and Steeves did, while Decker, LeMay, and Shoup did not. McGarr, Nolting, and Young were added.

15. This was not unexpected, for on the 28th Burris informed Vice President Johnson that Laos was expected to be added to the agenda. See Burris memo to LBJ, April 28, 1961, LBJ Library, VP Security File, Box 4.

16. This is true for all of the works cited in this book, a bibliography that is fairly exhaustive. The only work that even acknowledges an NSC meeting took place on April 29 is the *State History*, but it states, "No record of the discussion at the Council meeting has been found." See *State History*, 1961, Document 40 ("editorial note"), p. 88.

17. "Draft Record of Actions" of the 480th NSC meeting, April 29, 1961, LBJ Library, VP Security File, Box 4.

18. *PP*, Gravel ed., vol. 2, p. 41. The authors state: "Classified records available for this study do not explain this alert. But the public memoirs indirectly refer to it, and as would be expected, the alert was intended as a threat to intervene in Laos if the communists failed to go through with the cease-fire which was to precede the Geneva Conference."

19. Sorensen, *Kennedy*, p. 646.

20. Rusk memo to JFK, April 30, 1961, JFK Library, POF, Country File, Laos, Box 121

21. One notable opponent was Senator Mansfield, who wrote a lengthy letter to Kennedy on May 1 arguing against intervention. Mansfield warned Kennedy the U.S. public reaction to a neutral government in Laos would be mild compared to a pro-U.S. government "kept in power with American blood and treasure." See Mansfield letter to Kennedy, May 1, 1961, *Declassified Documents*, 1978, 208C.

22. Bundy note to JFK, JFK Library, POF, Country File, Laos, Box 121.

23. Sorensen, *Kennedy*, pp. 644–45.

24. Ibid, p. 645.

25. Stevenson, *The End of Nowhere*, p. 135.

26. Rostow, interview with Richard Neustadt, April 11, 1964.

27. NSC "Record of Actions" for the 481st NSC meeting, May 1, 1961, LBJ Library, VP Security File, Box 4.

28. *USN and the Vietnam Conflict*, p. 72.

29. NSC "Draft Record of Actions" for the 482nd NSC meeting, May 2, 1961, LBJ Library, VP Security File, Box 4.

30. Harriman Cable to Kennedy, May 4, 1961, *Declassified Documents*, 1975, 318b; the meeting, however, took place on May 2, 1961. See *State History*, 1961, Document 41, pp. 89–91, especially p. 89, n. 2.

31. *PP*, Gravel ed., vol. 2, p. 9.

32. CIA Central Intelligence Bulletin, May 6, 1961, *Declassified Documents*, 1986, 3096.

33. Peter Wyden, *Bay of Pigs* (New York: Simon and Schuster, 1979), pp. 304–5.

34. Taylor, *Swords and Plowshares*, p. 180.

35. Schlesinger, *A Thousand Days*, p. 316.

36. Sorensen, *Kennedy*, p. 644.

37. Schlesinger, *A Thousand Days*, p. 315.

38. *Air Force History*, p. 65.

39. Ibid., p. 69.

40. This account of the meeting is based upon the notes taken by Admiral Burke at the meeting, and from a (May 9) McNamara memo to the service secretaries afterward. See *State History*, 1961, Document 46, p. 125, and p. 115, n. 3 respectively.

41. *PP*, Gravel ed., vol. 2, p. 44.

42. *PP*, DOD ed., Book 11, pp. 138–54. Other than what it said on the combat troops issue, there were no other surprises or major changes in the final report.

43. *PP*, Gravel ed., vol. 2, p. 44.

44. *PP*, DOD ed., Book 11, p. 131.

45. Lemnitzer cable to JCS, May 8, 1961, in *State History*, 1961, Document 47, pp. 126–28. Lemnitzer specifically asked that his cable be passed to McNamara, Gilpatric, Wheeler, and Bonesteel.

46. *PP*, Gravel ed., vol. 2, pp. 48–49. The memo was sent to the White House on May 10, and a copy sent to Lyndon Johnson, on his way to Vietnam, via cable on May 11.

47. *USN and the Vietnam Conflict*, p. 108.

48. Ibid., pp. 108–9.

49. *Air Force History*, p. 69.

50. Lansdale memo to Gilpatric, May 10, 1961, JFK Library, NSF, Regional Security SEA, Box 223/231.

51. McGarr cable to Felt, May 10, 1961, in *State History*, 1961, Document 50, pp. 129–31.

52. MAAG-V, Staff Study, Requisite RVNAF Force Structure, May 18, 1961, Army Center for Military History, Washington, D.C.

53. Cottrell had served as Political Advisor to CINCPAC until April 1961.

PART II

TAKING CHARGE

CHAPTER FOUR

LBJ IN SAIGON

"LBJ might have been freewheeling out there."
—**William Colby,**
December 29, 1987

THE LEAK

On May 9 Lyndon Johnson was in New York at a labor function, and before leaving the city he was surprised to hear that he would be going to Vietnam that day. "He heard it on the radio," recalls Air Force Colonel Howard Burris. Someone had leaked the story to the press and Johnson was angry. There had long been talk in the White House about an LBJ Vietnam trip, and it had even been mentioned in a presidential press conference, but to get the news that way burned him up. Besides, LBJ didn't want to go anyway. "He came back to the White House and told Kennedy he wasn't going to go," Burris says.

Burris, who first met LBJ in the 1930s, and was his Military Representative, vividly recalls the confrontation between Johnson and Kennedy that day:

> I remember, I was sitting there against the wall in the NSC meeting listening to all this screaming taking place. Kennedy said he wanted Johnson to go and Johnson just refused. Kennedy said, "You're going tonight and the Foreign Service and [McGeorge] Bundy will brief you."[1]

There was nothing Johnson could do about it; like it or not he was going to Saigon. Burris recounts what happened then:

> Johnson went out and just got stoned. He came back and went to sleep on his couch and finally let the Foreign Service guys in. I think one or two were Assistant Secretaries.

One of them was the Assistant Secretary of State for Public Affairs, Carl Rowan. Also present were representatives from the Defense Department and the CIA. What happened next was memorable. Rowan remembers Johnson began the meeting by railing about the leaking of the story to the press. "I want you State Department folks to know that I think you're a bunch of little puppy dogs, leaking on every hydrant."[2] Johnson continued in the same vein:

> I tell you, you just write down the name of the reporter who wrote that goddam story, and you wait a few weeks and you're gonna see that reporter write something nice about the leaker because the reporter's got to pay that guy off, and I can tell you I'm waiting to see if there's a nice profile about old Chester Bowles, 'cause I think he's the one who leaked the story about my trip.

Johnson was blaming the Under Secretary of State, the number two man in the Department. "I sat there in astonishment," Rowan says, "absolutely certain that the leak came not from Chester Bowles but from the President of the United States."

Johnson was still in a rage when the plane left Washington. "We got on the plane that night," Burris says, "and there was this briefing book with all the inputs from the various agencies and so forth." He gave it to LBJ, who looked at it for no more than a minute, and said, "Howard, if you give me any of this State Department crap again I'll throw you off this plane."[3] This rebuke was mild compared to what lay ahead in the Far East. Rowan says Johnson was drinking a lot in those days, and the more he drank the meaner he got, and verbally abused his staff "in ways I found hard to believe." Yet when sober or in a good mood, Rowan says, he spoke with greater eloquence on the needs of poor nations and injustice in America "than any individual I ever knew in my life."[4] Indeed Johnson was a man full of conflict and contradiction, traits that would manifest themselves fully during this trip and in his report afterward, and, eventually, to the misfortune of the country and the world, in the course of the Vietnam War.

At 6:40 P.M. on May 11 Johnson's plane landed in Saigon. Johnson, accompanied by President Kennedy's sister, Jean, and brother-in-law, Stephen Smith, proceeded to the official government guest house, Gia Long Palace, and then on to a dinner hosted by Ambassador Nolting at the rooftop restaurant of Saigon's Caravelle Hotel.[5] Kennedy had added his own family members to the official party to impress on Diem the earnestness with which he desired to improve the fractured relationship between America and South Vietnam. Having them along, however, was a constant irritant to Johnson. Throughout the trip Johnson "talked over and over about the fact that he had not been born rich like the Kennedys," and complained that he had not gone to Harvard but to a "little crappy Texas college," Rowan wrote later, commenting, "Johnson had one of the greatest inferiority complexes I ever saw in a high-level public official."[6]

JOHNSON'S FIRST MEETING WITH DIEM

Johnson's meeting with Diem began the next morning at 8:00 A.M. Beforehand Johnson had received a cable from CINCPAC with the precedence "OPERATIONAL IMMEDIATE," a priority reserved for the most important and time-sensitive messages.[7] It was a top secret message from the Joint Chiefs, relayed via CINCPAC to General McGarr in Saigon with Vice President Johnson listed as the sole "INFO ADDRESSEE." No copy was sent to Ambassador Nolting nor anywhere else in the Pacific theater. The message was a verbatim transcript of the JCS recommendation to McNamara that Diem be "encouraged to request" U.S. combat troops. When the cable went through CINCPAC, Admiral Felt added that McNamara was aware of but had "not as yet" approved it.

Johnson barely had time to digest the contents of the cable before going to the palace for his talk with Diem. During this initial meeting Johnson avoided the subject of combat troops raised in the cable, confining the discussion to the points contained in a letter Kennedy had asked him to deliver to Diem. After the appropriate introductions, Johnson handed the letter to Diem, who sat down at his desk and read it over carefully, while Johnson sat back and watched. The letter contained several specific proposals for a joint effort by both countries to step up the campaign against the communists,[8] and only briefly alluded to the political reforms of the CIP. It mentioned neither U.S. combat troops nor a defense treaty.

Diem reacted to it by telling Johnson that he had problems financing the 20,000-man increase in his army and also that reforms had to be appropriate to Vietnam, an underdeveloped country threatened by communist subversion.[9] LBJ then did something that would disappoint Kennedy's staff when they found out about it later:[10] he committed the U.S. to provide equipment (helicopters and armored personnel carriers) for the 20,000-man increase without extracting in return any commitment from Diem on local financing. Diem must have felt good at this point. "He was tickled as hell," Johnson said the following day.[11] Little wonder. Johnson had just given in on what for months had been a major stumbling block between Washington and Saigon.

The rest of the meeting went like clockwork. Diem "responded, one by one, to President Kennedy's proposals," Johnson recalled, "and in less than three hours we had agreed on all of them."[12] When it was over, Johnson had another surprise in store. He urged the Vietnamese President to send a "letter of reply" to Kennedy "as early as possible," and to put in this letter a detailed list of Vietnam's most urgent needs as he saw them. This massaged Diem's mandarin ego,[13] and he happily agreed to what looked like more largesse without strings from Washington. The timing of the letter's arrival would be critical to what Johnson might say in the report he would deliver after his Asian trip. He therefore asked Diem to send the letter *before* his scheduled return to Washington.[14]

Johnson's invitation for Diem to write a letter to Kennedy with a shopping list in it was a digression that had not been planned in Washington. It would not be the last one either, for Johnson was about to take a major detour.

THE CHURCHILL OF ASIA

Later in the morning LBJ delivered a rousing speech to the South Vietnamese National Assembly that Nolting described as the "high point" of the Vietnam trip.[15] The speech, written by Carl Rowan and Johnson aide Horace Busby the night before, was based partly on what Johnson wanted to say but more on what cables from Washington directed he should say.[16] Reading from the approved statement, Johnson promised that the U.S. was ready to immediately help expand the South Vietnamese Army and meet Vietnam's educational, rural development, and new industrial and long-range economic needs.[17] Then he added a few words of his own:

> I informed your Vice President that the United States stands ready to assist in meeting the grave situation which confronts you. I have

gone into detail with your President. There are many things the
United States is willing to do.[18]

With more meetings still ahead, this last sentence might have been a hint
to Diem that there was still something important left—beyond the details
of their first talk—to discuss.

At this point in the trip a change occurred in Johnson's approach to
the press. Things had not gone well with the media and it was Johnson's
own fault. He had acted precipitously after an incident a few days earlier
in Bangkok. For no apparent reason, Johnson had insulted Rowan during
a press conference by calling him a "dummy"; Rowan shot back that "who
the dummy is will be determined by how the questions are answered"
and later, in private, threatened to take the first plane back to Washington.
Johnson told Rowan he would not be insulting him anymore because he
would not be seeing reporters anymore.[19]

That decision changed during his first morning in Vietnam. For some
reason, Johnson decided to make up. Rowan was astonished when, in the
middle of lunch, Johnson telephoned to say he was willing to talk to the
reporters. Moreover, he wanted to do so immediately; so Rowan and a
State Department colleague rounded up a contingent of reporters and
went to LBJ's room. Rowan went in and told Johnson the reporters were
waiting. "Hell, bring 'em on in," Johnson replied, sitting on his bed in
his underwear. Rowan claims "there followed the only press conference
that, to my knowledge, a senior American official held in his skivvies."[20]

This unusual press conference was only the beginning of the public
spectacle that Johnson had suddenly decided to act out. In Saigon streets
his "plunging into crowds despite security precautions" delighted and
moved the people, said a cable from Saigon.[21] At the evening reception
hosted by Diem, Johnson promised that America would stand "shoulder
to shoulder" with the South Vietnamese in their fight against communism,
and he praised Diem as the "Churchill of Asia." This accolade could not
have been more flattering to the diminutive Diem. It was as if Johnson
"were endorsing county sheriffs in a Texas election campaign," Stanley
Karnow, then a reporter, recalled of LBJ's performance.[22]

One of Kennedy's goals for the trip was to bolster Diem's confidence
and reassure him of American support. Johnson's comments to the press,
his antics in the streets, and his buttering up of Diem at the banquet
more than fulfilled that part of his mission. Concealed behind Johnson's
ebullient behavior, however, lay a venturesome plan. His next meeting
with Diem was scheduled to take place after the banquet and Johnson
was paving the way for that session. He would use it to carry out the
suggestion contained in the top secret cable from the Joint Chiefs.

THE TALK ABOUT TROOPS

At their first session Johnson had been holding something back, but so had Diem. "I knew Diem was a hard bargainer and a proud man," Johnson later said of him, "and I expected differences on more than one issue."[23] The foreplay ended at the no-holds-barred second round of talks that evening, with Ambassador Nolting and General McGarr also present.

Diem opened the discussion with an attack on the U.S weak suit— Laos, which was being overrun by the communists as Kennedy pursued negotiations for neutralization. Diem insinuated that the polite but "timid" Laotians felt abandoned by the U.S.[24] Charging that the U.S. Ambassador to Laos had discouraged the Laotians on every occasion where they tried to "undertake positive action," Diem said the Laotian government had wanted to ask for the U.S. Ambassador's recall many times but had not done so because of "timidity." Diem then laid down his hand: he said he needed an increase in his army of 120,000 men over and above its current level of 150,000. This was, incredibly, 100,000 more than the 20,000 then under discussion with the U.S. Moreover, Diem indicated that he could not afford to pay for it.

Johnson responded by attacking Diem's weak suit, asking why 150,000 South Vietnamese soldiers could not deal with a Viet Cong force that numbered only 10,000. Then Johnson laid down his own hand: how about introducing U.S. combat troops to do the job? Diem replied that he did not want U.S. troops to fight in his country except in the case of overt aggression against South Vietnam; but he did want an increase in U.S. training personnel.[25]

In retrospect, what followed next seems too coincidental not to have been planned, and in it is the hint of Edward Lansdale's hand. General McGarr immediately asked Diem if he would accept the introduction of U.S. combat troops "for direct training purposes."[26] With no argument, nor comment whatsoever, Diem agreed. It was almost as though he knew beforehand how this part of the conversation would unfold. McGarr had conveniently provided Johnson and Diem with a compromise on the troop issue, one that parallels precisely the formula Lansdale had inserted on April 27 into the Vietnam Task Force report.

What the Chiefs really wanted, of course, was to put U.S. combat troops into Vietnam. To do this they needed Diem's approval. The question was, how to get it? If there was one person who knew how Diem's mind worked and could come up with a way, that person was Lansdale. Certainly Diem and his generals did not themselves originate the idea of a further 100,000-man increase in the South Vietnamese Army. They arrived at the figure by working it out with General McGarr sometime *before Johnson arrived.* Diem, in his second letter to Kennedy, confirmed that this figure had been worked out with McGarr.[27] Since McGarr, in his curious "Bamboo Curtain" cable about his two "studies," which was sent only two days earlier, claimed he didn't yet have this figure, either McGarr had purposely withheld it then or had arrived at it sometime during the forty-eight-hour period before Johnson's arrival.

If McGarr provided the 100,000-man figure to Diem before Johnson's arrival, isn't it reasonable to assume that McGarr also discussed with Diem the idea of using U.S. combat troops? Lansdale's draft of the Laos Annex had already said these combat troops were required as trainers for the projected increase in the South Vietnamese Army. Would McGarr have mentioned the one without the other? We know Lansdale's report and McGarr's study were coordinated because they both used an identical figure for the U.S. troops: 16,000 men. Lansdale knew Diem was a tough negotiator and would demand something in return. In Lansdale's May 10 memo we find the seed for the deal now arranged with Diem: U.S. combat troops under the rubric of training in return for a big increase in the size of Diem's army. The size of this increase, more than 100,000 new soldiers, though unrealistic on the Washington end, was a sugar-coated lure in Saigon.

The linchpin in the plan was the role of the Vice President. Why did Johnson wait to pop the big question on Diem until General McGarr was present? Again, consider the scenario. Diem asked for his increase, which Johnson did not reject; and then Johnson put U.S. combat troops into the equation, to which McGarr then added the fig leaf of training. Did Johnson know what McGarr was up to? Johnson's aide Colonel Burris did. "I remember about McGarr saying the troops were for training," Burris recalls, "but it was really just under the *guise* of training."[28]

The training mission of these forces was indeed a "guise," designed to make the quid pro quo more desirable. The authors of *The Pentagon Papers* rightly point out that the training mission for these combat units was little more than a device for getting Diem to accept them, and that Diem thought it was a concession desired by Washington, the price tag for the large increase in the South Vietnamese Army he was asking the U.S. to pay for.[29]

There is no proof that Johnson was rehearsed for the combat troops discussion, but the idea is hard to rule out. Adding to the intrigue is the fact that Colonel Burris was specifically instructed, by persons he calls "the boys in the woodwork," not to discuss the combat troops issue with his own boss, Vice President Johnson.[30] But why? "I was not authorized to," Burris says, because "Diem was a marked man," and someone who should not be dealt with on this issue. That dark remark, made thirty years later, is disturbing to say the least; from it this much is clear—while we don't know if someone rehearsed Johnson there is no doubt that someone rehearsed Burris. This raises some troubling questions: Who was giving orders to the Vice President's aide? And why?[31] The answers to both these questions remain elusive but the evidence suggests an anti-Diem bias and an effort from some quarter to influence the discussion of U.S. combat troops. For the person to whom Johnson would most likely turn for advice on this issue would have been his Military Advisor, Colonel Burris.[32]

News of another—possibly related—part of the intrigue involves the role played by McGarr. That role was crucial since the formula to which Diem agreed required McGarr's presence at the meeting. Yet Ambassador Nolting, or someone on his staff, tried to keep him out. When the list of those attending was published in the Embassy, McGarr's name was missing. McGarr sent word to Thuan, who informed Diem, and the issue was settled when Diem demanded McGarr's presence. News of this entire episode wound up in Lansdale's hands before Johnson's return to Washington.[33]

What does this all mean? A pattern seems to suggest itself here: someone tried to curtail military advice to the Vice President, and General McGarr's name was removed from a list. Both acts involved military officers and one, perhaps both, related directly to the troops issue. Were these two acts connected? Did someone in the Embassy have access to the top secret cable the Chiefs sent to Johnson? Did someone figure out the script beforehand and attempt to rewrite it?

Another possibility about such a script—if one existed at all—is that it may have been designed to afford LBJ plausible denial afterward. Johnson would be able to say he had asked Diem if he wanted U.S. combat troops and the answer was no. Of course, while this statement would be technically correct, it would only be a part of the truth. Moreover, separating this one question and Diem's response to it from the full context of the conversation made the exchange misleading. Omitting the rest of the discussion would be convenient for Johnson, allowing him to conceal any agreement that might be reached and his role in brokering it should the President disapprove.

Script or no script, the nuances of the Johnson-Diem conversation are, of course, beyond reach. There can be no question, however, that more than a Diem no to U.S. combat troops took place that night—far more. Unfortunately, this important episode has thus far been lost in the dustbin of history—with a little help, it would appear, from careless scholarship. As a result, erroneous interpretations have arisen, which claim not only that Diem said no to U.S. combat troops, but that Kennedy,[34] or the "White House,"[35] gave "explicit instructions" or "charged" Johnson to bring the subject up in the first place. The effect of these misguided claims is to paint Kennedy as a hawk on Vietnam.

George Kahin's book *Intervention*, for example, in an attempt to prove Kennedy's "attraction" to the idea of sending combat troops to Vietnam, erroneously cites *The Pentagon Papers* as evidence that Kennedy "charged" Johnson with asking Diem about combat troops.[36] *The Pentagon Papers*, of course, says nothing of the sort, and such faulty sourcing has only served to confound the problem that arises from the neglect of the fact that Johnson carried out the Joint Chiefs' proposal, *and* that Diem agreed to the troop formula offered during that conversation.

Moreover, in a May 5 press conference Kennedy actually had pulled back from saying that Johnson should raise this issue. His comment, in response to a question on combat troops, was somewhat confused:

> The question of troops is a matter—the matter of what we are going to do to assist Vietnam to obtain its independence is a matter under consideration. There [are] a good many [issues] which I think can most usefully wait until we have had consultations with the government, which up to the present time—which will be one of the matters which Vice President Johnson will deal with; the problem of consultations with the Government of Vietnam as to what further steps could most usefully be taken.[37]

Was this an order for Johnson to ask about combat troops? Hardly. On the contrary, as far as what Johnson would be raising in his consultations with Diem, it is clear that the President shifted the issue from combat troops to "what we are going to do to assist Vietnam."

This much we can be sure of: Kennedy did not have an "attraction" for sending combat troops to Vietnam and he did not "charge" Johnson to go there and ask Diem about it. Our understanding of what happened during the trip is limited because we have no transcripts of the conversations. While it is reasonable that we may never understand exactly what took place during the late-night discussion between Johnson and Diem, it is curious that someone who was right there in the room didn't understand either.

THE MIDNIGHT COMPROMISE

The new Ambassador, Frederick (Fritz) Nolting, did not grasp what was happening. In all fairness it should be pointed out that Nolting was handicapped by his lack of Asian experience and the fact that the meeting took place on his third day of work. Still, he heard what was said but he thought Diem did not understand what McGarr meant by "U.S. combat units fully equipped for fighting, but which would be used for training Vietnamese armed forces."[38] Of course, subsequent events would prove Nolting wrong. For in less than a month Diem would request—in the letter Johnson asked him to send—American forces using, with a slight modification, the Lansdale-McGarr formula.

Following this second Johnson-Diem talk, a late-night session in Nolting's office took place during which the Ambassador quarreled with the Vice President. At issue was Johnson's suggestion that Diem send an early letter to Kennedy; according to William Colby, who was there, Nolting did not want this letter to go out.[39] Why did the Ambassador wait until midnight to voice his objection? The answer lies in the sequence in which Johnson presented his suggestions to Diem that day. During the morning meeting, Johnson got Diem to agree to put a shopping list in a letter to Kennedy. At the evening meeting, as a result of the discussion, U.S. combat troops were added to that list, and Nolting was strongly opposed to U.S. combat troops in Vietnam.[40]

Since Nolting felt Diem misunderstood McGarr's request, Nolting demanded that a clarification on that point be obtained from Diem prior to his sending the letter to Kennedy. The argument that night in the Ambassador's office produced a compromise, the immediate terms of which can be deduced from a cable Nolting sent three days afterward.[41] Two letters would be sent instead of one—an initial letter without substance, and a detailed one after the clarification was received. It is likely the three men also agreed to keep the entire issue of combat troops quiet until Diem responded to the clarification request. Nolting remained silent on it for six full days, and when he finally talked about it—under pressure from the State Department for information—he still had not gotten the clarification.[42]

Despite the apparent success of the negotiations, LBJ was uncertain of Diem's reaction to him. He was still thinking it over the next morning in his room when Carl Rowan showed up to talk about press coverage.[43] "I don't know about this fellow, Diem," Johnson said. "I tried to get knee-to-knee and belly-to-belly so he wouldn't misunderstand me, but I don't know if I got to him." As Diem's subsequent actions would show, Johnson had nothing to worry about.

The following day, prior to his departure for the Philippines, Johnson paid a twenty-minute farewell visit to Diem. He informed Diem that he would be a "strong supporter of Vietnam in Washington."[44] Then apparently in keeping with the compromise reached with Nolting the previous night, Johnson now asked Diem for two letters instead of one. The first letter should be a "brief" response to Kennedy's letter, more of a simple acknowledgment than anything else. The second one, Johnson continued, should be a "follow-up letter" timed to arrive in Washington by the time he got back. This would be a "substantive letter," detailing Diem's views on "additional assistance" that Vietnam will "really need" to stop the communists. Johnson suggested that Diem include in this letter his request for the additional 100,000-man increase in his army. Nolting's various accounts of this final Johnson-Diem meeting do not indicate whether Johnson also said this letter should contain a request for U.S. combat troops as a training force. Most likely Johnson did not bring the issue up. To have mentioned it that morning would have closed the door on any chance for Johnson to disassociate himself from the deal if the reaction to it in the White House was unfavorable. As it turned out, Kennedy's reaction to it was exactly that.

THE FIRST LETTER

As promised, Diem's first letter, dated May 15, arrived before Johnson returned to Washington. In it Diem agreed with the proposals in Kennedy's letter, delivered by LBJ, and added that Johnson had "graciously" asked for his own suggestions as to Vietnam's most urgent needs. "I was most deeply gratified by this gracious gesture by your distinguished Vice President," Diem gushed, "particularly as we have not become accustomed to being asked for our own views as to our needs." This dig was not missed in Washington. In the margin next to this sentence on Kennedy's copy of the letter someone wrote "touche!"[45]

Diem turned the screw further by alluding to the collapse of the U.S. position in Laos. He called attention to Vietnam's "long and vulnerable" borders with Laos, and said "recent" developments there underscored his "grave concern" for Vietnam's security. Now facing the "very real possibility" of communist forces pressing simultaneously from North Vietnam, Laos, and Cambodia, Diem said he was making an urgent determination of the "needs to save our country," and added, "I know I can count on the material support from your great country which will be so essential to achieving final victory." Diem concluded:

> I was deeply gratified at Vice President Johnson's assurances that our needs will be given careful consideration in Washington. An estimate of these needs as we see them will accordingly be furnished to you in a second letter which I shall write in about a week.

But what would these "needs" be? Would he tell Kennedy of the agreement reached with Johnson and McGarr? Diem's second letter would become the subject of intense interest in Washington long before its arrival.

Nolting's initial cables did not advise Washington of McGarr's maneuver on combat troops, Diem's acquiescence, or Nolting's own (wrong) interpretation of the exchange. Nolting would not forward this information until a week later on May 18, one day before a crucial NSC meeting that will shortly be discussed.[46] By that time the State Department was clamoring for information about what had gone on in Saigon during the Johnson trip. Much had happened in Washington while Johnson was away, events that would trouble him in Bermuda where he wrote his report for the President.

NOTES

1. Howard Burris, interview with the author, June 29, 1991.
2. Carl Rowan, *Breaking Barriers* (Boston: Little, Brown, 1991), p. 182.
3. Burris, interview with the author, June 29, 1991.
4. Rowan, *Breaking Barriers*, p. 182.
5. *State History*, 1961, Document 53 (Editorial Note), p. 135.
6. Rowan, *Breaking Barriers*, p. 196.
7. JCS cable 995614, May 11, 1961, LBJ Library, VP Security File, Box 10.
8. *PP*, DOD ed., Book 11, pp. 132–35. It proposed: an increase in MAAG personnel; MAAG advice to the Self Defense Corps; U.S. support for the entire Civil Guard Force of 68,000; U.S. support for a Vietnamese Junk Force; sending "certain military specialists" to help in public works projects; U.S. Special Forces to train South Vietnam's Special Forces; a combat development test center; a team of economic experts to work out a financial plan for this increased joint effort; joint consideration of going beyond the 20,000-man increase in ARVN; and developing more effective anti-infiltration measures.
9. Nolting cable to State, May 13, 1961, in *State History*, 1961, Document 54, pp. 136–38.
10. Robert Johnson memo to Rostow, June 15, 1961, JFK Library, NSF, Country File, Vietnam, Box 193.
11. Rowan, *Breaking Barriers*, p. 188.
12. Lyndon Johnson, *The Vantage Point* (New York: Holt, Rinehart and Winston of Canada, 1971), p. 54.

13. As Diem later explained to Kennedy in his initial letter of reply, he was not accustomed to being asked for his own views by the Americans.

14. Nolting cable to State, May 13, 1961, in *State History*, 1961, Document 54, p. 137.

15. Crockett cable to Bowles at State, No. 1735, May 13, 1961, *Declassified Documents*, 1982, 2727.

16. Rowan, *Breaking Barriers*, p. 186.

17. For a summary see Facts on File, *South Vietnam: U.S.-Communist Confrontation in Southeast Asia, 1961–1965* (New York: Facts on File, 1966), vol. 1, p. 20.

18. Rowan, *Breaking Barriers*, pp. 187–88.

19. Ibid., p. 184.

20. Ibid., pp. 185–86.

21. Crockett cable to Bowles at State, No. 1735, May 13, 1961, *Declassified Documents*, 1982, 2727.

22. Karnow, *Vietnam*, p. 250.

23. Lyndon Johnson, *The Vantage Point*, p. 54.

24. For the first among several of Nolting's accounts of this conversation, see his May 15 cable (No. 1743) to State, JFK Library, NSF, Country File, Vietnam, Box 193.

25. Up to this point, my reconstruction of the second round of talks is from the May 15 Nolting cable.

26. Strangely, Nolting's initial May 15 cable to State failed to say anything about the McGarr maneuver, and reported only Diem's answer to Johnson's question that U.S. troops were only needed in case of overt aggression. For details of the episode, a careful analysis of Nolting's May 18 cable (JFK Library, NSF, Country File, Vietnam, Box 193 and *PP*, Gravel ed., vol. 2, pp. 65–68) is necessary. Researchers should beware, however, that both accounts are inaccurate: Nolting misread Diem, and the authors of *The Pentagon Papers* did not have access to at least Nolting's May 18 cable, and possibly others as well. Lacking the May 18 cable, the authors could not have known about McGarr's agreement to a clarification (discussed below), and this is probably why they were unable to see the connection to the two-letter compromise (also discussed below) reached that evening. The authors were also unaware of the argument between Johnson and Nolting over the letter (also discussed below).

27. Diem letter to Kennedy, June 9, 1961, JFK Library, NSF, Country File, Vietnam, Box 193.

28. Burris, interview with the author, June 29, 1991.

29. *PP*, Gravel ed., vol. 2: see p. 66 on training as a "device," and p. 67 on Diem's agreement to such forces as a concession.

30. Burris, interviews with the author, May 8, 1991, and June 29, 1991.

31. In the interviews, Burris declined to go into the matter further.

32. But Burris did not go with LBJ to the meeting: "I was not at that meeting after the banquet. We just went over to the Majestic [Hotel], just to the bar and had fun, but I was not at the meeting after dinner." Burris, interview with the author, May 8, 1991.

33. General Williams letter to Lansdale, May 23, 1961, Hoover Institution, Lansdale Papers, Box 42.

34. George Kahin, *Intervention: How America Became Involved in Vietnam* (Garden City, NY: Anchor/Doubleday, 1987), p. 133.

35. Gibbons, *The U.S. Government and the Vietnam War*, vol. 2, p. 42.

36. Kahin, *Intervention*, p. 133. Kahin cites page 54 in the Gravel edition of the *Pentagon Papers*. Unhappily for Mr. Kahin, page 54 says nothing about any Kennedy instructions to LBJ—and nothing about Kennedy at all. In fact on page 55 it says only that "Johnson brought up the possibility" and that "we do not know what, if anything, Johnson was authorized to say if Diem had reacted affirmatively."

37. Kennedy, *Public Papers*, 1961, p. 356.

38. Nolting cable to State, May 18, 1961, JFK Library, NSF, Country File, Vietnam, Box 193.

39. The source and participant is William Colby. This account was furnished to the author in a December 29, 1987, interview with the former CIA Director.

40. Colby, interview with the author, December 28, 1990.

41. Nolting cable to State No. 1744, May 15, 1961, in *State History*, 1961, Document 55, p. 139.

42. Nolting cable to State, No. 1767, May 18, 1961, JFK Library, NSF, Country File, Vietnam, Box 193. On this same day, Lansdale would write about the details of the LBJ-Diem-McGarr discussion of U.S. combat troops. See Chapter Five.

43. Rowan, *Breaking Barriers*, p. 188.

44. *State History*, 1961, Document 55, p. 139.

45. Diem letter to Kennedy, May 15, 1961, JFK Library, NSF, Country File, Vietnam, Box 193. The marginalia was probably Rostow's or Kennedy's.

46. Nolting cable to State, May 18, 1961, JFK Library, NSF, Country File, Vietnam, Box 193.

CHAPTER FIVE

JFK IN WASHINGTON

NSAM-52

When Vice President Johnson met for the first time with Diem in Saigon, President Kennedy had, a few hours before, concluded a meeting with his Security Council in Washington to finalize the course for American policy in Vietnam. Recorded and issued that day in National Security Action Memorandum (NSAM) 52,[1] his decisions had enormous consequences for the war effort and they would not be revised until the end of the year. The main work before the NSC that day was to consider the final Vietnam Task Force report, but the principal issue facing the President was whether to commit U.S. combat troops to the defense of South Vietnam. The previous day (May 10), the Joint Chiefs had made an emphatic appeal for such forces, and, at their request, this plea was sent directly to the Security Council.[2] In it, the Chiefs also asked that Diem be encouraged to request U.S. forces, and on the evening of May 12 in Saigon (which would have been late on May 11 in Washington due to the time differential), LBJ, Diem, and McGarr worked out a formula by which the Joint Chiefs' request might be arranged.

Of course when the NSC meeting convened, on May 11, Kennedy and his advisors had no idea that a formula for sending U.S. combat troops to Vietnam was about to be worked out in Saigon. Moreover, Kennedy cut those paragraphs of the task force report that discussed sending such troops from the NSAM he issued that day. The most significant item in NSAM-52 was its first provision, namely, the approval of the U.S. objective: to prevent communist domination of South Vietnam. The implications of this decision were far-reaching, for Kennedy embraced this objective knowing that in South Vietnam the communists were very close to, if not already in, a dominant position.[3] In so doing, he took his most substantial step yet toward deepening American involvement in the war. At the same time, the excision of those lines that discussed sending combat troops was also an important decision, and an early indication of Kennedy's aversion to the use of combat troops in Vietnam.

Kennedy also approved the task force report's concept of operations: to create a viable democratic Vietnam by initiating military, political, economic, psychological, and covert actions on an "accelerated" basis. That this concept went beyond the purely military component was appropriate to the challenge in Vietnam. It was also broadly stated, leaving the President virtually free to maneuver as he pleased in carrying it out. The objective of preventing communist domination, however, was so simply and clearly stated that major Viet Cong gains would leave the President no alternative but to take strong military action.

The military recommendations of the task force were divided into three sections: a) military actions already approved at the April 29 NSC meeting;[4] b) additional military actions necessary because of the new threat along South Vietnam's border with Laos; and c) a Defense Department study of U.S. forces to be deployed to South Vietnam "which might result from an NSC decision following discussions between Vice President Johnson and President Diem." In constructing NSAM-52, Kennedy reaffirmed the April 29 decisions—item a—and approved the new measures—item b. The NSAM specifically identified the page numbers—four and five—of the Task Force report pertaining to item b in order to avoid any confusion with item c. Item c, as written, was dropped.

Kennedy knew his Laos decisions were responsible for the increased threat to South Vietnam and he was willing to pay for the consequences with a new aid package. That was covered in item b and included an increase in the number of U.S. personnel assigned to the MAAG: a new six-man element to help with border surveillance; a Combat Development Test Center; fourteen Americans to increase public works projects; and a 400-man Special Forces Group at Nha Trang for training Vietnamese Special Forces. In addition, the JCS, CINCPAC, and MAAG were to assess the "military utility" of another 30,000-man increase to the South Vietnamese army, which would bring the total to 200,000.

Kennedy's decisions in NSAM-52, then, were both sweeping and significant. The objective of American Vietnam policy was now nothing less than preventing what appeared to be just around the corner—communist domination. Moreover, the new aid package had 400 Special Forces troops on their way, as trainers to be sure but, nonetheless, *on their way*. Still, NSAM-52 fell well short of what the Joint Chiefs were asking for: a major commitment of U.S. combat forces to Vietnam. While turning down what the Chiefs wanted, Kennedy had nevertheless significantly increased the American stake in Vietnam. Perhaps because he felt uncertain about this momentous step, Kennedy built into it an opportunity to change his mind. He issued NSAM-52, "Subject to amendments or revisions which he may wish to make" at the following, May 19, meeting. This gave the President and his advisors eight days to reconsider these decisions.

This provision for reassessment in NSAM-52 provokes the following question: if the President felt that the weight of these decisions was so great that a period of reexamination was called for, why limit it to just eight days? After all, the stakes were high. In analyzing this question two facts clamor for attention. First, all of Kennedy's top advisors were present when NSAM-52 was issued except one: Lyndon Johnson. Not only was he absent, but the mission that he was carrying out at that very moment in Saigon could well affect any amendments or revisions the President might wish to make. This introduces another question: why close off the review period on the 19th, four days before the Vice President's scheduled return? The only reasonable conclusion one can draw is that President Kennedy purposely planned the timing of NSAM-52 and its scheduled review to exclude the Vice President.

Second, if excluding Lyndon Johnson was deliberate, the dropping of item c from the military measures Kennedy approved that day takes on added significance. Kennedy had no quarrel with a Defense Department study that was included in that item. On the contrary, studies were becoming a favorite stalling tactic of his. In this instance, he directed that Defense make a "full examination" of the size and kind of forces necessary "in the case of a possible commitment of U.S forces to Vietnam."[5] What Kennedy found most objectionable in the wording of item c was its provision that a commitment might result from *an NSC decision following the LBJ-Diem talks*. It was this language that Kennedy deftly excised.

Did Kennedy know what Johnson was up to in Vietnam? It is impossible to say, but by ensuring that Johnson and whatever arrangements he might make with Diem would play no role in NSAM-52, Kennedy effectively countered, by accident or design, the plan that was unfolding simultaneously in Saigon to strike a deal with Diem for the introduction of U.S. combat troops. The task force report's provision for two U.S. "battle groups" (16,000 troops) to form two "divisional training areas," and the formula worked out with Diem for their deployment, would not come to pass. Four hundred U.S. Special Forces troops for training Vietnamese Special Forces was as far as Kennedy was prepared to go.

LATE NEWS FROM SAIGON

An official communiqué released at the end of Johnson's trip signaled Diem's agreement to the proposals in the Kennedy letter that Johnson had delivered. This cleared the way for implementing some of the specific provisions of NSAM-52. The first contingent of thirty U.S. Special Forces personnel, flown from Fort Bragg,[6] along with new Army Security Agency units and many other U.S. military personnel (none of them combat troops), were already waiting at Clark Air Base in the Philippines for the green light to proceed to Vietnam. Secretary of State Rusk gave it the day after Johnson left Saigon. On May 14, while preparing for the opening of the Laos Conference in Geneva, Rusk cabled Nolting that the "units described en route now at Clark Base" should "proceed as expeditiously as possible," adding only that he wanted to avoid the arrival of several aircraft at once so that the "movement not appear flagrant or ostentatious."[7]

The combat troops issue was still not closed as long as the review period for NSAM-52 was in effect; and whatever Kennedy's reasons were for initiating it—and Kennedy kept his reasons to himself—the Joint Chiefs looked upon the review as an opportunity to again make their case for the introduction of U.S. combat troops into Vietnam. Meanwhile, Bowles and others at the State Department opposed to the idea of combat troops still had no inkling of what Johnson and Diem had discussed in Saigon, and could only guess what the Pentagon position might be at the review.

With only a week to go, time was short. In an effort to find out what Defense had in mind, State's Sterling Cottrell, who now chaired the Vietnam Task Force, asked its members to submit to the May 17 meeting any views they intended to express at the review.[8] When the time came, however, the Defense representative was silent on the Pentagon's plans while the State Department representative gave away State's position by attacking the provision of NSAM-52 that would serve as a diplomatic basis for a U.S. troop commitment to Vietnam.[9] This, of course, put State at a disadvantage.

Understandably, as the May 19 review approached, there was a great demand for information about what was going on in Saigon. The missing piece of the puzzle from State's point of view was a specific account of the discussion among Johnson, Diem, and McGarr on combat troops.

Finally, in Saigon, Nolting responded to the wave of cables from the State Department requesting information.[10] At first he claimed that, since the requests had arrived late or were garbled in transmission, he was not in a position to "make any extensive substantive comments prior to the May 19 NSC meeting." To State's relief, on the day before the review, he did provide a fuller account of the Johnson-Diem meeting on the night of May 12.[11] From this cable the State Department at last learned about Diem's acceptance of the Lansdale-McGarr formula for U.S. combat troops in Vietnam.[12]

In the meantime, McGarr and Lansdale, with Diem's cooperation, were moving quickly to exploit the opening created by the Vice President's talks with Diem. They coordinated a plan to send South Vietnamese Secretary of State Thuan to Washington with the second letter as soon as possible. The idea was for Thuan to arrive with the combat troops request *before* the Vice President's return, and for the Joint Chiefs to submit a proposal for these U.S. forces at the same time. The degree to which Diem worked with McGarr and excluded Ambassador Nolting is attested to by the fact that Lansdale, in Washington, already knew about the proposed Thuan trip on May 18, while Nolting, in Saigon, would not learn of it until the next day.[13]

McGarr and Lansdale moved simultaneously to leave their opponents no reaction time, both submitting proposals the day before the review. In his, McGarr requested 16,000 U.S. combat troops be sent to Vietnam to train South Vietnamese divisions, and if Diem would not accept this, McGarr said he would settle for 10,000 men.[14] McGarr's request was timed perfectly to coincide with Lansdale's memo to Gilpatric and a JCS request to McNamara the same day. In his memo to Gilpatric, Lansdale passed on the latest CINCPAC view: one U.S. infantry division should be sent to the central highlands, "reinforced with Army Aviation, Engineers, Artillery, etc."[15] Lansdale easily dispensed with Diem's initial negative response on combat troops with a quote from Nolting, saying the Ambassador himself had said Diem would welcome "as many U.S. military personnel as needed for training and advising Vietnamese forces." Then Lansdale reported what he had heard from McGarr in Saigon: that while Diem did not want U.S. combat troops to fight in Vietnam, he would accept "U.S. combat forces as trainers for the Vietnamese forces at any time." For their part, the JCS restated their recommendation of May 10 that U.S. combat troops should be sent to Vietnam.[16]

This entire episode moved the authors of *The Pentagon Papers* to conclude that Lansdale, McGarr, and the Joint Chiefs "were primarily interested in getting U.S. combat units into Vietnam, with the training mission as a possible device for getting Diem to accept them."[17] This conclusion appears justified by the facts. Moreover, Lansdale and McGarr had tactically outmaneuvered their opponents at State by engineering Diem's approval of a formula for introducing troops during the Johnson-Diem discussion while the Ambassador unwittingly looked on. But even with Diem's agreement, their larger strategy still depended on approval from the White House, and on May 19 their plans went up in smoke.

MAY 19—THE REVIEW

The record of the May 19 review of NSAM-52 is still classified. The only reference to the exact contents of NSC Action No. 2428, which resulted from it, is a footnote in the Department of State's history: "At its meeting on May 19, the National Security Council noted that National Security Action Memorandum No. 52 required no revision."[18] We do know that a draft record of the meeting's actions, which is still classified, was circulated to the participants for comments on May 22.[19] We know also that Kennedy must have approved the final "Presidential Program for Vietnam," which was disseminated the day after the meeting.

Without access to the minutes we can only guess at how the discussion progressed. However, since Kennedy did not authorize any revision of NSAM-52 we can reasonably surmise that the Pentagon proposal for combat troops was either blocked from the agenda or dealt with and disapproved. Either way, this was a resounding defeat for the Chiefs. Moreover, the final Presidential Program sent by cable to Saigon the next day dropped any reference to the Pentagon *study* about sending combat troops.[20] Only the paragraph providing that the State Department look at the diplomatic setting for such a troop deployment remained. Otherwise, there were no other changes in the NSAM-52 version of the final Task Force report that now became the Presidential Program for Vietnam.

It is very likely that the idea of a new bilateral military arrangement was discussed and shot down. Bowles, acting for Rusk, evidently carried through on State's threat to show Kennedy a cable preempting the start of any negotiations. There is no doubt that the treaty idea was defeated, either during the meeting or shortly afterward: Bowles immediately sent Nolting a terse two-line cable saying, "Negotiations authorized for a new bilateral arrangement with [South Vietnam] should not be initiated until further notice."[21]

Meanwhile Johnson's two letters scheme also ran afoul at the White House. Sometime late on the morning of the review, the State Department received word from Nolting that Diem wanted to send Thuan to

Washington with a second letter.[22] The contents of Nolting's cable suggest the Ambassador had finally caught on and wanted to disrupt the scheme. For even though he had been present when Johnson specifically asked that the second letter arrive in Washington before his own return, Nolting now suggested that Thuan's trip take place in mid-June. Since Nolting knew Johnson would return on May 24, he also knew that a mid-June Thuan trip would ruin the Vice President's plan.

Chester Bowles had already heard—from Nolting on May 17—the story of the LBJ-Diem-McGarr discussion and this new cable from the Ambassador now made it possible for Bowles to see what McGarr and Diem were up to. Opposition was marshaled, and sometime on the day of the NSC meeting the idea of a quick Thuan visit was defeated, and with it any chance for the second Diem letter to arrive before the Vice President's return. The next morning Bowles cabled Washington's go-ahead to Nolting's proposal, indicating June 12–16 as the best window for Secretary of State Thuan to call on Kennedy and Johnson.[23] A careful scrutiny of Bowles' cable suggests he probably tipped off the White House that the second Diem letter would contain the shopping list Johnson had invited Diem to send. As a result, Diem's emissary, Thuan, was going to get a cold reception in Washington. Bowles said he had a "tentative" yes for a personal call on Kennedy by Thuan during his stay, but told Nolting not to let Thuan know because the President could not be committed in advance.

In advance of what? The reluctance to confirm these arrangements was surely due to the controversy surrounding the Johnson-Diem discussion and the resulting uncertainty about the contents of the letter Thuan would be bringing from Diem. Everyone wanted to know—*before* Thuan arrived—what would be in that letter. Bowles asked Nolting to get a copy and send it to State to permit "prior staffing" and "better handling" of Thuan. Nolting failed in this mission, but as the implications of the Johnson-Diem deal became clearer, State's initial hesitancy about the Thuan visit hardened. On May 23 State sent a blunt message for Thuan. Since Diem might expect Thuan to come home with the "bacon," the cable said, Nolting should make it clear that Thuan would not "reap a harvest in Washington."[24]

In an intriguing footnote to the May 19 review, the issue of an authorization to study the question of combat troops immediately resurfaced. It would appear that Bowles had played the crucial role in engineering its deletion from the original Presidential Program cabled to Saigon on May 20. The study was quickly reinstated in the program. On May 23, Rusk, now back in the saddle at the State Department, sent Nolting a terse cable, instructing him to insert a new paragraph in the program. It read:

"A full examination will be made of the size and composition of forces which would be desirable in the case of possible commitment of U.S. forces to Vietnam."[25]

Rusk may have been pressured by the Pentagon but, if his remarks at the April 29 brainstorming session are any guide, he was sympathetic to the idea of intervention anyway. The authors of *The Pentagon Papers*, however, read more into this on-again off-again sequence. They remark, "We seem to be seeing here a pattern" where "someone or other is frequently promoting the idea of sending U.S. combat units." They point out that this precise sequence will occur again in June and November when the record seems to move toward a decision to send combat troops, or a decision in principle, so long as Diem can be persuaded to accept them. They state:

> But no decision is ever reached. The record never shows the President himself as the controlling figure. In June, there does not seem to be any record of what happened, at least in the files available to this study. In May, and, as we will see, in November, the President conveniently receives a revised draft of the recommendations which no longer requires him to commit himself.[26]

If this analysis is correct, the implication is that Kennedy was just as clever as Lansdale in reading his opponents and just as slippery in countering their moves, sometimes before they were even made.

The early period of Kennedy's administration, which was marked by a certain impulsive innocence about his decisions and character judgments, was over. The President was finally catching on to the agendas of his subordinates and, where they conflicted with his own, he now seemed able to neutralize them. At least as far as Vietnam policy is concerned, it appears that Kennedy was taking charge. That this was the case became apparent to the Vice President before he returned to Washington.

THE BERMUDA TRIANGLE

At the end of his trip Johnson spent three difficult days in Bermuda writing his report, attempting to triangulate his views with those of the President and the Joint Chiefs—and these were choppy waters to navigate in. "After a lot of backing and filling and changing directions totally," Colonel Burris recalls of this effort, "the recommendation that was going to the press was . . . do not get bogged down, Mr. President, in a land war in Southeast Asia."[27] But was this not inconsistent with LBJ's asking Diem if he wanted combat troops? The answer, of course, is yes; the explanation for this inconsistency lies in the dilemma that had developed for Johnson prior to his return.

Johnson's principal quandary was this: the formula worked out with Diem for the insertion of combat troops had been completely superseded by events in Washington while he was away. Both NSAM-52, and the review Kennedy conducted of it, had dashed, for the time being, any hopes the Joint Chiefs had for putting combat forces into Vietnam. This fact alone made those days in Bermuda trying: "It was confusing, just so much back and forth," Burris says, "Up and down, up and down, do we get in, do we get out."[28] What made matters more difficult was the second letter Johnson had asked Diem to write. The Vice President himself had suggested to Diem that he add the request for the 100,000-man additional increase in the South Vietnamese Army to the shopping list. Would Diem also include the other half of the quid pro quo—a request for U.S. combat troops to train this new force?

This unanswered question had already led to State Department queries about the contents of the letter. "The thing was fuzzy, and Johnson didn't really want to get involved in Vietnam," Burris claims, "but the Joint Chiefs wanted Diem to say he wanted us in." Johnson's personal views will be returned to shortly, but the point here is that, because the situation was awkward for Diem too, he was stalling. Johnson had hoped Diem would make the first move, but Diem was now waiting to see what Johnson would do, adding another concern to his predicament.[29] There were so many pressures on him: What would be in Diem's letter? What would the Chiefs say? What would his friends in the Senate say? And, finally, what would the President say? Johnson had little time to decide what to do—and, most importantly, how to get himself off the hook on the issue of combat troops.

In crafting his report Johnson also had to contend with submissions from his least favorite people—State Department types. Understandably, this produced some contradictory and inconsistent passages among the different parts of the report. In the end, however, Johnson chose to distance himself from the combat troops idea while simultaneously advocating a commitment that might well require they be sent in the future. Diem had said no when Johnson first raised the subject of combat troops. So Johnson decided to report only that part of the discussion while hiding the more important fact that Diem had agreed—in his very next sentence—to U.S. combat troops using McGarr's training formula.

Three separate documents relating to Johnson's written report have survived, but only one is clearly dominated by the tone, style, colloquial expressions, and analogies suggestive of Lyndon Johnson.[30] It is most useful to discuss the contents of that version in the order that Johnson arranged it. His trip had been "illuminating far beyond my expectations," Johnson began, but he added that he only wanted to offer "perspective" instead of proposing details for U.S. policy. He wasted no words in going straight to the "recent developments"—meaning Kennedy's decision to pursue a neutral solution through negotiation—in Laos, which had created, he said, a "deep and long lasting impact" of doubt and concern over U.S. intentions among all of the leaders he had visited. No amount of success at Geneva would ever erase this, he said, and these leaders did not want their fate negotiated by other countries. They would accept the U.S. making "the best of a bad bargain" on Laos, but, Johnson said: "Their charity extends no further."

Johnson cautioned that though his mission had arrested the decline of Asian confidence in America, it had not restored "any confidence already lost." Asian leaders made it clear that American deeds had to follow words—and soon. "We didn't buy time," Johnson said, "we were given it." Johnson was clearly painting the problem in Southeast Asia as *an American failure*. "If these men I saw at your request were bankers," Johnson said, making the matter more personal, "I would know—without even bothering to ask—that there would be no further extension on my note." Since American money was being extended to Asian countries, not the reverse, it is worth examining what Johnson was driving at with this catchy analogy. He was telling Kennedy that he was responsible for the collapse in Southeast Asia, and that the leaders there would not forgive any more mistakes. It was a harsh pronouncement, if not an implied condemnation, and one can only wonder what Kennedy thought as he read it.

Turning to his own actions with Diem, Johnson said he had made no commitments "beyond those authorized in your letters." This was not true on financing for the increase in Diem's army, which Kennedy would soon find out. However, Johnson's comment most likely referred to U.S. combat troops since this was the only major issue that lay outside Kennedy's letter. With respect to his personal thoughts, Johnson said the trip had "sharpened and deepened" the convictions he had taken to Asia with him. Then he presented his first and most basic conclusion in this startling pronouncement:

> The battle against Communism must be joined in Southeast Asia with strength and determination to achieve success there—or the United States, inevitably, must surrender the Pacific and take up our defenses on our own shores.

These were exceedingly strong words, and probably reflect Johnson's honest belief. Is it possible that he already understood the argument between the competing concepts of forward presence and disengagement that would dominate the beginning of the next decade? Or was he expressing the mind-set of a man who, like many of his contemporaries, was shaped by the events that flowed from Munich, where appeasement led to the prolonged and bloody Second World War? Whatever his underlying thoughts, Johnson told Kennedy that the struggle did not have to be lost. British and French indecisiveness left no alternative to United States leadership in Southeast Asia, he declared. In Vietnam, Diem was the key. "The country can be saved," he said, but added, "we must decide whether to support Diem—or let Vietnam fall."

Johnson then finessed the ticklish problem of U.S. combat troops by saying this might have to be faced at "some point." Asian leaders do not want them "at this time," he said, "other than on training missions." Combat troops were not required or desirable but this did not mean an open communist attack would not bring calls for them. Johnson then cleverly avoided a definitive statement on troops by framing the question as a choice between U.S. support or complete disengagement. For the present, he argued, the time had arrived for "the basic decision," whether to help these countries or "throw in the towel and pull back our defenses to San Francisco and a 'Fortress of America' concept." But this decision, he told Kennedy,

> must be made with the full knowledge that at some point we may be faced with the further decision of whether we commit major United States forces to the area or cut our losses and withdraw. . . .

The U.S. would have to remain the master of this decision, Johnson said, and he recommended a "clear-cut and strong program of action."

In an attachment to his report, Johnson spelled out the price of failing to follow through: "The failure to act vigorously to stop the killing now in Vietnam may well be paid for later with the lives of Americans all over Asia."[31] Again, these were strong words; they make clear the formula Johnson was proposing: no combat troops now, but an unequivocal commitment that might mean sending them in the future. The stronger and quicker that the U.S. acted now, he was saying, would mean fewer American deaths in the end.

From this statement it seems clear that Johnson would support sending combat troops at some point in the future *if necessary*, but there remains the question of Burris' claim that his boss was opposed to getting tied down in Vietnam. In that regard, Burris' own recollections are enlightening: "My feelings are that when Johnson said let's not get bogged down in that land war . . . I don't think he had a really deep perception and comprehension of what the whole scene was about."[32] This observation may be close to the truth; if so, it tells us a great deal about Johnson's views at this early stage of the war: they were rooted in the superficial politics of Washington, not in the underlying realities of the situation in Vietnam. Johnson had supported the Chiefs on intervention in Laos, and that initiative had been soundly squashed by Kennedy. In putting forward his Vietnam report Johnson was now trying to please the Chiefs without alienating Kennedy, and without tying the albatross of intervention around his own neck.

As might be expected, the final product of LBJ's efforts in Bermuda was an amalgamation of inputs from the State Department, passages to placate the advocates of intervention, and strands of his own, perhaps, superficial thinking. Despite its multifaceted nature and all the strong words, its recommendations did not step over the line: no combat troops were needed for now. By the time Johnson delivered the final version of his lengthy written report to Kennedy on May 24, it had already been "cleared and approved by the White House itself."[33]

This confusing collage of ideas and recommendations would be unacceptable to the hawks in Congress and Johnson knew that when he delivered his report to them. His ties to Congress were anchored in years of personal experience and associations. So testifying before these men must have been particularly painful for him. Just four weeks earlier in front of sixteen of their members he had advocated sending U.S. combat troops into Laos. Now the message he was delivering seemed to be on a different track: no U.S. troops were necessary in Vietnam. Confronting him were some ardent interventionists, among them, Senator Thomas Dodd, who had lobbied Johnson during his trip. The morning he left Saigon Johnson received a cable from Dodd complaining that American standing was "at an all time low in Asia" because of the Bay of Pigs fiasco.[34] The Asian people questioned American determination and willingness to stand by their friends, he said, and because of American inaction now believed Chinese propaganda that America was a paper tiger. Dodd appealed to Johnson:

> We must restore their faith in us, in our intentions, in our integrity, our *loyalty to our* friends, we must not write Laos off and need not do so. Passive surrender of Laos after all our brave talk will imperil Vietnam and Cambodia and will result in eventual collapse of SEATO. I earnestly and deeply believe America is in [its] most critical period in history. You and the President can and must get the United States back on the right road. You have a fateful and historic opportunity to do so. Generations of free men will honor you for it. [emphasis in original]

This was strong medicine, designed to strike at the heart of Kennedy's failure to achieve a truly neutral Laos, and an implied warning to Johnson that he was viewed as being on the same "wrong road" as Kennedy.

What Dodd and his colleagues thought of the Vice President mattered a great deal to him, and he had planned for his trip to be a catalyst in winning congressional support for the war effort in Vietnam. Nolting's cables disclose that Johnson "repeatedly stressed" to Diem the "necessity of having adequate evidence to convince Congress it should vote additional aid funds" to Vietnam.[35] These cables also suggest that Johnson gave Diem the impression that aid *over and above* that promised in Kennedy's letter would be forthcoming if he had sufficient evidence to place before the U.S. Congress.[36] When Johnson testified before that body, however, he had no such evidence for them, and no bold new program to announce.

The record of his testimony reveals that the experience was an ordeal for Johnson. During his May 25 questioning before the Senate Foreign Relations Committee, Johnson said he was very "depressed" about Laos and that nothing would come out of the conference in Geneva. The Russians, he said, "are going to bust it up, and I think that the communists will practically have it."[37] Senator Dodd chimed in that a drama "which may toll the death knell" for the U.S. and Western civilization was unfolding in Southeast Asia, and said if a "truly free" Laos without the communists did not come from the conference the U.S. should commit its prestige and resources "to achieve an independent Laos by force of arms."

Congressman Paul Findley said Johnson's statement that U.S. combat troops were not needed at the time was "an invitation to trouble.[38] Findley advocated publicly offering combat troops to Vietnam because they would be the most effective deterrent against aggression. War might be avoided if the U.S. committed combat troops before communist action, he argued, whereas committing them "midstream" might trigger a large war. Vietnam would be another Laos, he predicted, adding, "We will be forced to send combat forces to a war already in progress, or once more be identified with failure."

Johnson must have been relieved when this trial was over. If it taught him nothing else, it was a clear indication of what the administration was up against in resisting the calls for intervention. He had his own aspirations for the White House, and getting out of the limelight was the most prudent thing to do. Johnson went underground at this point, and played no further public role in Vietnam policy until he became President. Like Lansdale, he was content, for the time being, to watch from the sidelines.

That was a good place to be when the second letter from Diem arrived in Kennedy's office.

KENNEDY REACTS TO DIEM'S SECOND LETTER

Disappointed by the outcome of Johnson's report, Diem did his best to preserve the situation. He modified the second letter, and then misled Nolting about its contents in order to forestall an attack from State prior to the letter's arrival. He had kept Nolting completely in the dark by withholding the clarification on the issue of U.S. combat troops, and continued to do so until he was certain of the outcome of Johnson's return to Washington.[39] At that point, Diem apparently altered strategy, deciding to include in the letter the request for U.S. troops but to call them "selected elements" of the Armed Forces. Diem then proceeded to give Nolting, through Thuan, his long-awaited clarification, but did not tell him whether or not it would be the second letter.

In his May 27 cable summarizing this talk with Thuan, Nolting relayed Diem's clarification: a "U.S. combat brigade as trainers" was not desirable "at the present time."[40] Instead, Diem proposed two separate increases to American forces: 1,000 more personnel for the MAAG, and "U.S. military personnel in civilian clothes" to train Vietnam's Self Defense Corps.[41] When Nolting pressed for details about the letter, Thuan said it "had not yet taken final shape" and, regarding its contents, mentioned only the request for an additional 100,000-man increase in Diem's army. Thuan had chosen his words carefully, and in a manner that deceived Nolting. The Ambassador could now only assume that if the letter would have any request for U.S. troops at all, it would be for trainers in plain clothes for the Self Defense Corps. The whole plain clothes idea was a ruse, and nothing like it would appear in the letter Kennedy would read three weeks later. In that letter Diem, with a semantic slight of hand, would ask for U.S. forces using the Lansdale-McGarr formula.

The fact that General McGarr, and not Ambassador Nolting, knew what was in the letter Diem's emissary would be carrying was a symbol of Nolting's loss of control over the situation in Saigon. Kennedy decided it was high time to make clear who was in charge of the diplomatic mission. While there may have been instances in other countries of in-fighting and of the military going behind the Ambassador's back, there is no question that the situation was out of control in Saigon. On May 29 Kennedy sent out what amounted to a manifesto to all Embassies in the world leaving no doubt that the Ambassador was "in charge" of the entire mission. He stated further:

> The Mission includes not only the personnel of the Department of State and the Foreign Service, but also the representatives of all other United States agencies which have programs or activities in [specified country].[42]

Kennedy sent copies to all of the departments of the government in Washington as well. His message was duly noted in Saigon: McGarr, too, took up residence on the sidelines, and the intrigues there disappeared—for the time being.

There was still the awkward situation of the second Diem letter, however, and on June 7 the State Department predicted for Kennedy, as best it could, what would be on Diem's shopping list. Kennedy was told the letter might request a 100,000-man increase in the South Vietnamese Army, and was advised to tell Thuan this should be decided after a new Special Financial Group traveled to Vietnam to study the situation.[43] Kennedy ignored this advice. When Thuan arrived in the Oval Office on June 14, he found the President in an unfriendly mood, and irritated with the letter from Diem. There would be—as State had already signaled—no harvest to reap in Washington.

The requests in this second letter[44] far exceeded anything envisioned in previous American aid programs such as the CIP or the new Presidential Program approved in May. After reading Diem's request for the new 100,000-man increase and $175 million to pay for it, Kennedy said that South Vietnam could pay for it themselves. When Thuan responded that they could not, Kennedy told him to go see Senator Everett Dirksen and Senator Bourke Hickenlooper, who, he said, might be useful "in the extremely difficult struggle" to obtain the funds requested by Diem.[45] Kennedy underscored his point by ordering that Diem's letter be immediately given to McNamara, who was testifying before the Senate that day, remarking dryly that this would help the Senate better understand the "magnitude" of what was involved in helping Vietnam. Kennedy did agree that more Americans should be added to the MAAG to train Vietnamese troops, but added that this MAAG increase "should be done quietly without publicly indicating that we did not intend to abide by the Geneva Accords."[46]

Like Lansdale's Vietnam report, Diem's letter tied the new request for a 100,000-man increase in South Vietnam's army, and the U.S. forces for training them, to the threat from Laos.[47] Diem said his generals wanted 16 divisions, but that "our present needs as worked out with General

McGarr" called for 15 divisions. Such an increase, Diem said, would require a "great intensification" of the training program and "considerable expansion" of the MAAG. Then came the crucial sentence on the new U.S. forces for this expansion:

> Such an expansion, in the form of *selected elements* of the American Armed Forces to establish training centers for the Vietnamese Armed Forces, would serve the dual purpose of providing an expression of the United States' determination to halt the tide of communist aggression and of preparing our force in the minimum of time. [emphasis added]

Neither the word "combat" nor "troops" was in the sentence, but "elements" were units or portions of them nonetheless, and the units would have to be infantry.

The authors of *The Pentagon Papers* rightly point out the striking similarity between this sentence in Diem's letter and the language in both Lansdale's Laos Annex to the Vietnam Task Force report and McGarr's expanded version of it.[48] They point out, in particular, Diem's explicit statement that he used McGarr's advice when drafting the proposals, and argue that Diem might have "agreed to put in this request that sounded like what McGarr wanted" as a concession in return for the 100,000-man increase he was asking for. This analysis is correct.[49] Moreover, by the time Thuan arrived with the idea, it was no more than an irritating reminder of LBJ's caper in Saigon. Kennedy and Thuan did not even bother to discuss it.

The entire saga of the second Diem letter—written at the Vice President's request—only added to the fallout from Johnson's trip and further damaged the poor relationship between Kennedy and Johnson. The local currency costs of completing the 20,000-man increase was a sore point too. Thuan had told Rusk in their March meeting in Bangkok that Vietnam would have no problem financing these costs in 1961, but Diem had suspended recruiting after the Johnson trip in May.[50] The day after the Kennedy-Thuan talks, Robert Johnson was still complaining about it to Rostow:

> The Vice President, during his visit to Vietnam, committed the U.S. to provision of the end items for a 20,000 man increase in the armed forces without getting a [South Vietnamese government] commitment as to local financing. . . . They have now refused to undertake recruiting until financing arrangements are worked out.[51]

The feeling was that the Vice President's trip had given Diem the impression that Washington was so worried about the war that he could successfully apply pressure to the U.S.; President Kennedy used his talk with Thuan to disabuse Diem of this notion.

That same evening on board the *Sequoia*, Thuan and Vice President Johnson had a private dinner that included Walt Rostow.[52] If the subject of combat troops came up that night, it is likely that LBJ and Thuan agreed to drop the entire matter. The final McGarr study upon which Diem's letter was based was given a quiet burial. The only surviving copy, not surprisingly, is among the papers of Vice President Johnson.[53] He did not produce it at the time and for good reason. Its very title was embarrassing, "MAAG Response to Vice President Johnson's Request for a Statement of the Requirements to Save Vietnam from Communist Aggression," and would have been another reminder of Johnson's Vietnam escapade.

ENTER: MAXWELL D. TAYLOR

Kennedy's patience with the JCS had already worn thin, and his May 29 manifesto—the proclamation sent to all Embassies—underlining the authority of his Ambassadors, had already severely clipped McGarr's wings in Saigon. The scheme engineered by McGarr, Lansdale, and the JCS, brokered by Johnson, and acquiesced in by Diem was the last straw. In Kennedy's eyes everyone in the Executive Branch who had influenced Southeast Asia policy was suspect. They had let him down. He now turned to someone outside the policy apparatus, someone he thought he could trust: General Maxwell D. Taylor. Taylor recollects:

> My active involvement in Vietnam matters began about mid-June [1961] while I was still working on the Cuba report. I would fix the specific moment as a chance encounter with the President outside the door of his White House office. He was holding in his hands President Diem's letter of June 9 which he passed to me and asked how he should answer it. My effort to provide him an answer was the beginning of an involvement in the Vietnam problem to which I was to commit a large part of my life during the next eight years.[54]

Taylor, along with Rostow, would dominate Vietnam policy for the next five months. Taylor's reign, culminating with a trip to Vietnam in late

October, would, as it turned out, only add fuel to the momentum, already strong among Kennedy's advisors, for intervention in Vietnam. The same would be true of his Cuba report.

Although few people recognized it then or afterward, Taylor's Cuba report would have far-reaching and profound effects on Vietnam policy.[55] As a result of that report, on June 28 Kennedy approved three NSAMs, numbers 55, 56, and 57, which Taylor played a major role in crafting. Taken together, these three documents reaffirmed Kennedy's desire to get moving with the development of counterinsurgency and paramilitary capability and, at the same time, to reorganize agency and departmental responsibilities using the lessons learned from the defeat in Cuba.

The first of the three, NSAM-55,[56] had the distinction of Kennedy's personal signature—most NSAMs were signed by his Security Advisor, McGeorge Bundy—and the additional unique feature of being addressed only to the Chairman of the Joint Chiefs of Staff, General Lemnitzer. Kennedy was angry with Lemnitzer for being poorly informed about the military dimensions of the Cuban operation and, by the time he signed NSAM-55, Kennedy was certain this same weakness had marked Lemnitzer's proposals for the invasion of Laos. Entitled "Relations of the Joint Chiefs of Staff to the President in Cold War Operations," NSAM-55 reflects Kennedy's dour frame of mind. There is no way to describe this NSAM other than an incensed finger-wagging lecture to Lemnitzer.

Kennedy began with a general scolding about giving advice and responding to requests, and added that he expected the Chiefs' advice "to come to me direct and unfiltered." Most of the rest was a didactic sermon on how the Chiefs should present their views in government councils, when to do so, how to do their homework in order to speak with unity, how to broaden themselves to "be more than military men," and so on. The crux of NSAM-55, however, was this: Kennedy charged the Joint Chiefs with responsibility for "defense of the nation in the Cold War" and "dynamic and imaginative leadership . . . of military and paramilitary aspects of Cold War programs." This mandate was *big* news, since cold war paramilitary operations were—up to this moment—the exclusive fiefdom of the CIA. On this point NSAM-55 was more than a memo to Lemnitzer, whom Kennedy would replace with Taylor the following year. It was the opening shot in Kennedy's campaign to curtail the CIA's control over covert paramilitary operations.

NSAM-56 and NSAM-57 flowed from the requirements generated by NSAM-55. NSAM-56[57] was addressed only to the Secretary of Defense, and entitled "Evaluation of Paramilitary Requirements." It called for an inventory of paramilitary assets in the U.S. Armed Forces, a determination of the requirements for indigenous paramilitary forces in various areas of the world and then set the goal—"a plan to meet the deficit"—in each case. Within the Department of Defense, the task of compiling this inventory was given to Lansdale. The result of his work was three papers, issued in Deputy Secretary of Defense Gilpatric's name, which were sent directly to Taylor's office in the White House.[58]

NSAM-57,[59] addressed to State, Defense, and the CIA, was entitled "Responsibility for Paramilitary Operations." This NSAM was important because it spelled out the ramifications and precise definitions lacking in NSAM-55. NSAM-57 decreed that all paramilitary operations had to be presented to the Strategic Resources Group, which would assign the operation to "the department or individual best qualified" to carry it out. The Defense Department would normally run overt paramilitary operations. Only paramilitary operations "wholly covert or disavowable" could be assigned to the CIA, and then only if they were within the "normal capabilities" of the agency. Anytime a covert paramilitary operation required large numbers of people, equipment, or military experience "peculiar to the Armed Services," primary responsibility would rest in the Defense Department, with the CIA in a supporting role.

The consequence of these presidential directives was the first significant chink in the CIA's covert armor since its creation. Walter Bedell Smith, Eisenhower's Under Secretary of State, in his remarks to the 13th meeting of Taylor's Paramilitary Study Group, described this change in these words: "It's time we take the bucket of slop and put another cover on it."[60] What this sarcastic remark meant, of course, was that some of the CIA's larger covert operations should be transferred to the Defense Department. Trying to keep American covert paramilitary actions in Vietnam a secret would indeed be a "bucket of slop," as the Defense Department and the President would find out to their dismay. Among the most important covert programs that would be affected by these decisions was the activity of the U.S. Special Forces in Vietnam. At that time they were under the operational control of the CIA, but in 1962, under the code name Operation Switchback, control over these paramilitary forces would be switched to the Defense Department.

In looking over the long-range implications of these three NSAMs, one cannot help but wonder: Did Taylor know he would be replacing Lemnitzer as Chairman of the JCS when he helped draft NSAM-55? Did he know he was, in effect, writing his own ticket? At the very least, Taylor knew that his role as the President's special advisor on military and intelligence matters would be enhanced by the transfer of some covert CIA functions to the Joint Chiefs.

NOTES

1. *PP*, DOD ed., Book 11, pp. 136–37.

2. Memo for the NSC, May 10, 1961, LBJ Library, VP Security File, Box 4.

3. As noted previously, the MAAG Chief, General McGarr, estimated that "Diem controlled little more than 40 percent of the territory in South Vietnam and that almost 85 percent of his military forces were immobilized by the insurgency." See Maxwell Taylor, *Swords and Plowshares*, p. 221.

4. NSAM-52's reconfirmation of the military actions approved by the April 29 decision included the 20,000-man increase in ARVN; an increase for the Civil Guard from 32,000 to 68,000; a radar surveillance capability in South Vietnam; and assistance for a Vietnamese Junk Force.

5. Kennedy was not as generous to Defense as he might have been, because he tied the hands of the drafters by directing that this study would have to be conducted under the "guidance" of the new Vietnam Task Force Director, State Department's Sterling Cottrell, who was named in the NSAM. Cottrell had served as Political Advisor to CINCPAC until April 1961.

6. Francis Kelly, *Vietnam Studies: U.S. Army Special Forces, 1961–1971* (Washington, D.C.: U.S. Government Printing Office, 1985), p. 5.

7. Rusk cable to Nolting, May 14, 1961, JFK Library, NSF, Country File, Vietnam, Box 193. At the May 15 Vietnam Task Force meeting, Cottrell announced that the Rusk authorization pertained to ninety-three U.S. personnel waiting at Clark Air Base. See Robert Johnson memo to Rostow, May 17, 1961, JFK Library, NSF, County File, Vietnam, Box 193.

8. This occurred at the May 15 meeting of the Vietnam Task Force. There is collateral evidence that Kennedy might have already stacked the deck against the Pentagon, as the following comment from White House staffer Robert Johnson after the May 15 meeting makes clear: I subsequently emphasized to Mr. Cottrell the fact that this Memorandum [NSAM-52] was being scheduled on the agenda for information and that it was intended that the Memorandum should stand and that there would be no discussion of it in the NSC unless an agency had a serious point that it wished to argue in front of the President. See Robert Johnson memo to Rostow, May 17, 1961, JFK Library, NSF, Country File, Vietnam, Box 193.

9. Robert Johnson memo to McGeorge Bundy, May 19, 1961, JFK Library, NSF, Country File, Vietnam, Box 193. The language in question was provision number seven in the NSAM, which authorized Ambassador Nolting to begin negotiations "looking toward a new military bilateral arrangement" with Vietnam. State now wanted to limit the Ambassador's latitude to a "consideration" of negotiations instead of actually beginning them.

10. Nolting cable, May 18, 1961, JFK Library, NSF, Country File, Vietnam, Box 193.

11. "General McGarr and I were present," he said, when Diem told Vice President Johnson he did not want U.S. combat troops to fight but did want a "necessary increase in U.S. training personnel." Nolting continued:

GEN McGarr then asked specifically about introduction [of] U.S. combat units for direct training purposes and understood Diem would agree to this. I did not broach the specific idea with Diem in my talks with him at Dalat, but I think there is possibility Diem might not have completely understood that GEN McGarr had in mind introduction of U.S. combat units fully equipped for fighting, but which would be used for training Vietnamese armed forces. GEN McGarr and I agree on desirability of clarifying this with Diem, which will be done at earliest opportunity. This would of course be important factor in policy recommendation from here.

It was not Diem who misunderstood McGarr, but Nolting. If Nolting did understand from the beginning, then he was using his position to block the combat troops idea. This is a possibility, since Nolting had the chance and purposely did not bring up the subject during his weekend trip with Diem at Dalat. In either case, Nolting's withholding the details of the key exchange prevented State from knowing the details until the day before the final NSC meeting.

12. As a result State softened its position somewhat, deciding at the last minute "not to nit pick the Action Memorandum itself," but instead to show a cable to Kennedy. The cable would say that there might be revisions to details in implementing the NSAM, and that "Nolting should not begin working on a bilateral agreement, pending further consideration and instructions." The net effect, if Kennedy agreed (and he would), would still be to forestall an agreement.

13. Lansdale's memo said that since Diem had not made the combat troops request yet, a firm decision should await the Thuan visit, "since President Diem is sending Nguyen Dinh Thuan . . . to Washington next week to bring us Vietnam's 'definitive military needs.'" In fact Thuan would not come until the second week in June. The dates were not yet set because no one outside of the Pentagon knew about it. The fact that Diem would send his Secretary of State with the infamous second letter was news. That Diem wanted to send Thuan the following week indicates that the plan was still to get the letter there before Johnson arrived on the 24th. The twelve-hour time difference between Washington does not affect this observation, since the earliest Nolting could have learned of it on the 19th would have been 9:00 or 10:00 P.M. EST on the 18th, too late for the Lansdale memo of the 18th. Besides, Lansdale's source was probably McGarr, and he very likely was informed on the 17th or even before.

14. *PP*, Gravel ed., vol. 2, p. 11.

15. Lansdale memo to Gilpatric, May 18, 1961, *PP*, DOD ed., Book 11, pp. 157–58. The CINCPAC recommendation also included some air and naval forces.

16. *PP*, Gravel ed., vol. 2, p. 65.

17. Ibid., p. 66.

18. *State History*, 1961, p. 132, n. 3. This may in fact be its entire contents with respect to Vietnam.

19. NSC memo on Draft Record of Actions, 484th NSC Meeting (May 19, 1961), May 22, 1961, LBJ Library, VP Security File, Box 4.

20. For details, see State cable No. 1423, May 20, 1961, in *State History*, 1961, Document 56, pp. 140–43.

21. Bowles cable to Nolting, May 19, 1961, JFK Library, NSF, Country File, Vietnam, Box 193.

22. Nolting cable to State, May 19, 1961, No. 1771, JFK Library, NSF, Country File, Vietnam, Box 193.

23. State cable to Saigon No. 1421, May 20, 1961, *Declassified Documents*, R/C, p. 780, Document A.

24. See State cable to Saigon No. 1433, May 23, 1961, *Declassified Documents*, RC, 781.

25. Rusk cable to Nolting, May 23, 1961, JFK Library, NSF, Country File, Vietnam, Box 193.

26. *PP*, Gravel ed., vol. 2, p. 68.

27. Burris, interview with the author, May 8, 1991.

28. Ibid., June 29, 1991.

29. In his first, May 15, letter, he said he would send the second letter in a week, i.e., about May 22. But the letter had not arrived and even though McGarr was helping Diem craft the letter's proposals, Thuan was still tight-lipped with Nolting about its contents. So LBJ would have to report to Kennedy before the letter's arrival.

30. If there were other documents, they have been lost. There is a report (see *PP*, DOD ed., Book 11, pp. 159–66) with an attachment (see *State History*, 1961, Document 59, pp. 149–51), and a second, apparently separate report (see *State History*, 1961, Document 60, pp. 152–57). A close analysis of the attachment to the first report and the second report suggests these two documents were written by the State Department with, perhaps, some input from LBJ. The second report, even though saying (to be consistent with LBJ's position of support for Diem) there appeared no alternative to Diem, contains much language critical of Diem and the "efficacy" of his methods, and probably reflects the views of State drafters.

31. *State History*, 1961, Document 59, p. 151. This sentence was very likely insisted on by Johnson.

32. Burris, interview with the author, May 8, 1991.

33. Gibbons, *The U.S. Government and the Vietnam War*, vol. 2, p. 44.

34. Dodd cable to LBJ, May 13, 1961, LBJ Library, VP Security File, Box 40.

35. Nolting cable No. 1748 to State, May 15, 1961, *Declassified Documents*, 1983, 536.

36. Gibbons misses this point, i.e., that aid beyond that discussed in Kennedy's letter might be forthcoming; for example, LBJ had encouraged Diem to put a new request for help to finance a 100,000-man increase in his army into the second letter to Kennedy. See Gibbons, *The U.S. Government and the Vietnam War*, vol. 2, p. 43.

37. Senate Foreign Relations Committee, History Ser., vol. 13, pt. 1, pp. 629–51.

38. *Congressional Record*, vol. 107, p. 8,587.

39. Nolting had questioned Thuan on May 19 about Diem's attitude on the introduction of U.S. combat troops "fully equipped for fighting but which could be used for training Vietnamese armed forces." With the crucial NSC meeting going on in Washington that same day, Thuan answered evasively he "would take the matter up with Diem." (Nolting cable to State, May 24, 1961, JFK Library, NSF, Country

File, Vietnam, Box 193.) On May 24 Nolting sent another cable indicating he had on two occasions since May 19 asked Thuan for a response from Diem on the question of U.S. combat troops. (Nolting cable to State, May 24, 1961, JFK Library, NSF, Country File, Vietnam, Box 193.) Nolting said he "made it clear to Thuan that I was not presenting [a] concrete U.S. proposal," and simply wanted Diem's reaction. Again, since Johnson had not yet reported in Washington, Thuan was still evasive. On both occasions Thuan said Diem had not retracted his positive answer to McGarr on U.S. combat troops, but that Diem was "still thinking about the matter weighing pros and cons."

    40. Nolting cable to State No. 1803, May 27, 1961, JFK Library, NSF, Country File, Vietnam Box 193.

    41. It is a safe bet that this latest change was in fact made on the advice of McGarr, who probably envisioned sending combat units out of uniform. When the letter finally arrived, it was "elements" of the U.S. Armed Forces and their uniforms were back on, but none of this mattered because the scheme was doomed to fail. Kennedy did not bring it up and neither did Thuan.

    42. JFK letter to Ambassadors, May 27, 1961, JFK Library, White House Central Subject Files: Foreign Affairs, Box 29.

    43. State talking paper, attachment to Battle memo to O'Donnell, June 7, 1961, JFK Library, NSF, Country File, Vietnam, Box 193. Headed by Eugene Staley, this group was not scheduled to depart for Vietnam until June 17.

    44. Diem letter to Kennedy, June 9, 1961, JFK Library, NSF, Country File, Vietnam, Box 193.

    45. Record of the Kennedy-Thuan conversation, June 14, 1961, JFK Library, NSF, Country File, Vietnam, Box 193.

    46. The United States was not a signatory to the 1954 Accords, but had been observing some of the provisions anyway; for example, there had been a limit on the number of French troops that could remain in the south, which the United States had already exceeded. The exact ceiling was subject to some technical interpretations, but the line was generally agreed to be around 888.

    47. Diem's letter was very close to what Lansdale had put into the Vietnam Task Force report Laos Annex on April 28. In the letter Diem went further, claiming his lightly defended position along the demilitarized zone "is even today being out-flanked by communist forces which have defeated the Royal Laotian Army garrisons in Tchepone and other cities in southern Laos." He said recent captured documents indicated 2,860 men had infiltrated along Route 9 from Laos into Vietnam.

    48. *PP*, Gravel ed., vol. 2, p. 66.

    49. The authors erred, however, in their analysis of the subtle change Diem added to the McGarr formula. Diem's second letter said the training centers would be for training combat leaders and technical specialists, whereas the previous U.S. proposals said the centers would be for training entire Vietnamese divisions. This change suggests, say the authors, that Diem may have had something different in mind than McGarr when he said "selected elements of the American Armed Forces." This is not true. The authors did not have access to the Nolting cables cited above and were therefore not able to track the changes and analyze their relative proximity to the key NSC meeting and LBJ report in Washington.

50. Nolting cable to State No. 1863, June 9, 1961, in *State History*, 1961, Document 67, pp. 169–71.

51. Robert Johnson memo to Rostow, June 15, 1961, JFK Library, NSF, Country File, Vietnam, Box 193. The memo to Rostow also revealed that Thuan's argument about needing to keep foreign exchange reserves above the $200 million level was specious. As Saigon's foreign reserves grew, it simply "continuously shifted upward its view" of what constituted "adequate" foreign exchange reserves. State informed Nolting during the Thuan visit that analysis showed Saigon had the resources to finance the rest of the 20,000-man increase, but that Diem had deliberately turned an economic issue into a "politico/military" issue in an attempt to place the onus for the slowdown on the U.S. (State cable to Nolting No. 1534, June 16, 1961, in *State History*, 1961, Document 71, pp. 177–78.) State's analysis only confirmed what Saigon already knew and in fact communicated to State two weeks earlier. (Nolting cable to State No. 1837, June 2, 1961, *Declassified Documents*, RC, 784B.) State then authorized Nolting to say the U.S. would throw in $5.1 million, which was about one-third of the amount required to finish paying the local currency costs of the 20,000-man increase.

52. *State History*, 1961, p. 172.

53. MAAG Response to Vice President Johnson's Request for a Statement of the Requirements to Save Vietnam From Communist Aggression, *Declassified Documents*, 1978, 147B. The report was found in the May 1961 portion of the papers of Colonel Burris, Johnson's Military Aide.

54. Maxwell Taylor, *Swords and Plowshares*, p. 221.

55. The most notable exception is Fletcher Prouty, an Air Force Colonel at the time working in the Pentagon. See his book *Secret Team* (Englewood Cliffs, NJ: Prentice-Hall, 1973), pp. 114–21.

56. JFK Library, NSF, Box 330.

57. Ibid.

58. The three papers were: "Defense Resources for Unconventional Warfare"; "Unconventional Warfare Resources—Southeast Asia"; and "Indigenous Paramilitary Forces." See Edward Claflin, *Kennedy Wants to Know* (New York: William Morrow, 1991), p. 69.

59. JFK Library, NSF, Box 330.

60. *Declassified Documents*, 1978, 442A.

CHAPTER SIX

CONSENSUS BUILDS FOR INTERVENTION

THE STALEY MISSION AND NSAM-65

"What do I do about this?" Kennedy asked Taylor, handing his military representative Diem's second letter and then strolling away.[1] Taylor recommended that Kennedy give Diem only an interim reply that would say that while the 20,000-man increase was being implemented the U.S. would study the implications of his request to expand his army beyond this level. Taylor said Kennedy should then consider a pending JCS proposal to further increase Diem's army to 200,000 but withhold a decision on any figure until the President received the Staley report.[2]

In mid-June Kennedy had sent a financial team, headed by Dr. Eugene Staley, to Vietnam to help develop an economic plan.[3] Unfortunately the deteriorating war and conflicting ideas about the optimum size of the South Vietnamese Army had mired the Staley group in discussions on military force levels instead of financial matters. After a month of study, the group returned to Washington and recommended an emergency "Joint Action Program" that included various financial, economic, and social actions.[4] Its major recommendations concerned force levels, and offered the President two alternatives: an increase to 200,000 men, based on the assumption that the existing level of insurgency would continue; or an increase to 278,000 men, based on the assumption of increased communist activity in South Vietnam and effective communist control of Laos. Reaction in Washington to the Staley report was cool. Vice President Johnson's aide, Colonel Burris, reported on August 1 that Staley put more emphasis on augmenting old programs than on implementing them, and had been influenced to a "great degree" by General McGarr, who "favored a massive military buildup."[5] On the same day Robert Johnson wrote to Rostow that the report showed how disorganized Vietnam policy was and said Kennedy "ought to have more adequate background" before responding to the Diem letter.[6]

The perception that the Staley mission was based on an inadequate survey of the situation coincided with Taylor's first major recommendation to the President on Vietnam policy. In a July 27 memo to Kennedy, Taylor had joined with Rostow in framing U.S. policy options in Southeast Asia in this way: 1) disengage as gracefully as possible; 2) find a pretext and, using U.S. force, attack Hanoi; or 3) build up indigenous strength to the extent possible, while preparing to intervene with U.S. forces if "the situation gets out of hand."[7] Only the third was feasible, and it required a fuller review of the situation in Vietnam than that contained in the Staley report.

In a July 28 White House meeting, Kennedy accepted Staley's recommendations but would not commit any precise amounts of money.[8] During the discussion, Rostow advised that any new money commitments should be deferred until a new mission to Southeast Asia could determine whether a solid foundation existed for additional U.S. aid, information, he said, that was "not available in Washington."[9] Kennedy agreed with this and Rostow suggested that Taylor head up a mission for that purpose. Since Harriman's negotiations at Geneva were at a delicate stage, Kennedy thought it imprudent to send his military advisor to Laos, but he still wanted someone "well known to him" to go and check on the situation personally. The discussion then turned to a Taylor visit to Vietnam, but Taylor resisted this suggestion on the grounds that he had too much "unfinished homework" to do in Washington. He wanted to look at the problem first to figure out what "facts need to be checked." The discussion ended inconclusively, with Kennedy asking for a list of questions that a mission to Southeast Asia might answer, and adding that he hoped to have a recommendation "soon" on who would lead such a mission.

There would be no quick decision, and the Staley recommendations were settled, without another high-level visit, in two NSC meetings in early August. In the first one, on August 4, Kennedy said he agreed with the "basic tenets" of the report,[10] and approved an increase in the South Vietnamese Army to 200,000 men pending a further review of the situation to be made on August 11. On that date he issued NSAM-65, which stated specifically that the U.S. would provide equipment and training assistance for an increase in the South Vietnamese Army from 170,000 to 200,000.[11] The NSAM also said that because this force level would probably not be achieved until 1963, consideration of any further increase would have to wait a year.

THE BATTLEFIELD SITUATION

An upsurge in Viet Cong attacks, which became noticeable shortly after the Johnson visit, continued to build into a countrywide offensive during the summer and fall of 1961. On May 14, the day after Johnson left Saigon, the Viet Cong launched a series of attacks in the Saigon-Dalat corridor, and on May 23 they launched a major operation near the northern provincial capital of Hue.[12] The Viet Cong were demonstrating a new boldness in tactics and a much larger force with which to carry them out.[13] For example, a May 23 cable from Ambassador Nolting cited a successful Viet Cong attack in Long An Province in which the Viet Cong attacked a Self Defense Corps outpost and then ambushed the government airborne force sent in to relieve the outpost.[14] Nolting also reported frequent Viet Cong attacks only twenty to forty kilometers northwest of Saigon on Route 1.

South Vietnam's battlefield losses were fast canceling out the force increase being carried out with the new American aid program, the CIP. The May casualty statistics reported in the June 19 Vietnam Task Force report showed total losses were 1.97 to 1 in favor of the South Vietnamese government—but this was not a very encouraging picture.[15] A State Department cable at the end of June stated the monthly average of government soldiers killed and wounded in action was 230 and 800, respectively, for 1961.[16] Thus, about 43 percent, or 430 men per month,[17] of the 6,000 new recruits in 1961 were already battlefield losses! This same cable put Viet Cong strength at 12,000, up significantly since the March estimate of 9,000. This was even worse news. At a time when losses were increasing on both sides due to the escalating war, the Viet Cong were not only expanding, but doing so more rapidly, in absolute and relative terms, than the government forces. The size of the Viet Cong was fast approaching the point where the South Vietnamese Army would be unable to cope with them.

During the Viet Cong offensive in Vietnam, the communists also achieved a stunning victory along the major infiltration route—soon to be called the Ho Chi Minh Trail—in Laos. The communist battle plan in Laos was brilliant. It began under the cover of the Geneva negotiations, and made excellent use of deception to confuse the Americans as to the true objective until it was too late to react effectively. The warring factions in Laos had held their first negotiations on May 11, and when these talks were over enough had been accomplished to put a cease-fire into effect. This cease-fire was the green light for the delegations to proceed in Geneva, and proceed they did that very day. Beginning the next morning, however, and continuing for the next six weeks, the communists seized control of the terrain in southern Laos astride the South Vietnamese border and released a flood of infiltrators that further tipped the balance on the battlefield there.

This campaign opened amidst minor cease-fire violations on both sides, but in southern Laos the increasing pattern of attacks soon secured the airfield at Tchepone, which sits in Laos a little south of the dividing line between North and South Vietnam.[18] These attacks into the southern panhandle of Laos were reported by Thai sources on May 12 and 18, and Vietnamese sources reported on May 18 that Soviet aircraft were actually landing at the Tchepone airfield. By the level and type of activity that followed, it was obvious the Soviet airlift into southern Laos included fresh Viet Cong battalions and their supplies. On May 23 Vietnamese sources reported aggressive reconnaissance and harassing attacks by Viet Cong and Pathet Lao units along Route 9 west of Tchepone, and the next day Laotian sources reported the arrival of two Pathet Lao battalions at Moung Phine, fifteen miles southwest of Tchepone.

The Pathet Lao simultaneously attacked the U.S.-supported Meo position at Padong near the Plain of Jars in north-central Laos. Here they attacked with infantry supported by artillery, which grew in intensity as the days went by. The Padong action was a deception to divert attention from the initial push south from Route 9 in the southern zone. On June 6, with the Pathet Lao on the verge of overrunning Padong, the American representative, Averell Harriman, walked out of the Geneva talks in protest.[19] On June 11, after the communists backed off of Padong, Harriman returned to the conference table, but on that same day the first of two Viet Cong airdrops occurred quietly in the southern zone, the second taking place on June 13. These actions were reported by both Vietnamese and Laotian sources but there was little associated combat, and no disruption of the Geneva talks.

The Americans were still preoccupied with events in the north, and paid little attention when the communists attacked to the south from their base in the Tchepone area, overrunning the junction of trails at Ban Xat on June 13. The central-south zone was then quiet for over a month as the communists resupplied and prepared for the final part of their plan there. In the north the communists continued harassing attacks, sufficient to draw attention, but maintained their overall activity at a level low enough to keep the Americans at the table in Geneva. Suddenly, on July

21, major fighting erupted in the central-south zone. Over the course of the following days, a regimental-sized combined Viet Cong–Pathet Lao force conducted a well-prepared offensive operation, clearing out the entire area surrounding Tchepone, including the trails leading south toward Cambodia and west into Vietnam.[20]

The creation of the "pocket at Tchepone"[21] opened the door wider for Viet Cong units to infiltrate into South Vietnam. During his June talks with Kennedy, Thuan said 2,800 communist troops had entered Vietnam over the previous four months.[22] A July 12 CIA field report indicated that, in June alone, 1,500 troops had infiltrated into South Vietnam.[23] In other words, while keeping American attention focused on northern Laos and the Geneva talks, the communists had doubled their rate of infiltration into South Vietnam. Now, in possession of the airstrip at Tchepone and the trail network to the south and west, the communists could, at a time of their choosing, accelerate infiltration even more. The same CIA report said a covert source in Hanoi stated that 30,000 men, trained in China and the Soviet Union, were "ready" to infiltrate via Laos. They were already in position in Laos, having moved in gradually and avoided combat in order not to draw undue attention to themselves. The noncommunist forces operating in the central-south zone had seen sporadic evidence of this buildup beginning in mid-May. A month later, the cumulative statistics of these low-level sightings was staggering: between May 12 and June 12 alone, the Viet Cong forces sighted in central and southern Laos by South Vietnamese and Laotian patrols—not counting Pathet Lao units—included one regiment, seven separate battalions, seven separate companies, and two combined Viet Cong–Pathet Lao battalions.[24] These reports—by themselves—indicated that approximately 15,000 Viet Cong troops from North Vietnam were sitting in Laos astride the infiltration routes leading into South Vietnam.

The Americans now got interested in a hurry. Concern in Washington about what to do mounted over the summer and fall. A June 19 draft memorandum by Vietnam Task Force Director Cottrell concluded that the only realistic way of blocking the Viet Cong advance through Laos to Vietnam was for Vietnamese and Thai troops to join a Laotian Army effort in southern Laos, backed, if needed, by U.S. forces for "hit and run operations."[25] Cottrell stated that political power alone was no longer sufficient, and warned that unless the U.S. decided then and there to do what "may be necessary" to hold the line against a communist takeover, then "millions of dollars and untold past effort" would go down the drain as this rich rice region was added to the "Sino-Soviet bloc empire." Rostow's assistant, Robert Johnson, reported his surprise at the "apparent unanimity of view that, unless we undertake military action in Laos, it would be virtually impossible to deal effectively with the situation in

Vietnam."[26] Johnson said the Cottrell proposals "raise very directly the question of U.S. intervention in Laos," and added, "I wonder whether it isn't about time to have the NSC and the President review the Laos situation?"

On June 20, Rostow authored a memo to Kennedy arguing the necessity of examining "more explicitly the military and political links between the Laos and Vietnam problems."[27] Rostow said SEATO Plan 5 was no longer the best solution, and recommended a limited intervention in the Laotian panhandle and air strikes against North Vietnam. The next day Rostow wrote another memo to Kennedy warning that the Viet Cong were planning a big push after the Laos conference, regardless of the outcome in Geneva, and that "very substantial Soviet supplies have been moved into Hanoi, not for use in Laos but against Vietnam."[28] The coming Vietnam crisis, Rostow predicted, would likely peak at the same time as the Berlin crisis, and he counseled military planning to account for both. More visible to the American public than Vientiane or Saigon, Berlin was a symbol of Western freedom—an island surrounded in a communist sea. It was also far more likely to touch off a direct U.S.-Soviet conflict.

After Khrushchev insinuated privately to Kennedy, during their June summit, that the West should get out of Berlin, the Soviet leader had made uncompromising public statements and escalated the issue. That administration officials anticipated the worst was still to come is clear from the heavy emphasis on military preparations in a proposal Dean Acheson (former Secretary of State and now an occasional advisor to Kennedy) sent to the President on July 5. At a key meeting on July 8 at Hyannis Port, Kennedy expressed dissatisfaction with such a purely military approach and with how the problem was being handled by his advisors.[29] He told Acheson to work on a "political program"; Rusk to produce a negotiating prospectus; and McNamara to come up with a tough military plan that would "provide the communists time for second thoughts and negotiation before everything billowed up in nuclear war." As the situation deteriorated in Southeast Asia in July and August and the Viet Cong prepared for a fall offensive, the crisis in Berlin mushroomed, keeping the focus of Kennedy's attention riveted there.

The case was still building for intervention in Southeast Asia, however, and Rostow's call for parallel planning on Berlin and Southeast Asia was in fact an attempt to prevent the administration from turning a blind eye toward Laos and Vietnam. He and others, like State's U. Alexis Johnson, made sure this did not happen. In a July 8 memo to Rostow, Johnson agreed that SEATO Plan 5 would not protect the Laos-Vietnam border.[30] He suggested the JCS examine a panhandle operation, and added that General Taylor was working on this same idea. Johnson said a U.S.-

backed panhandle operation followed by the threat of action against North Vietnam should logically follow an expansion of the covert U.S. training program in Laos. Meanwhile, a Special National Intelligence Estimate (SNIE) published on July 5 assessed the consequences of a combined South Vietnamese–Thailand–Royal Laotian government panhandle action involving U.S. troops. One of its principal conclusions was that such an operation would not make the communists more reasonable at the conference table in Geneva.[31] Thus, the intelligence community deprived the Rostow plan of an important supporting argument, namely that strong military action would bring concessions at Geneva. Furthermore, the estimate's conclusions implied that any military action to create a de facto partition of Laos would have to be justified on the grounds of protecting Vietnam despite any potential damage to the Geneva talks that might ensue.

NSAM-80: END OF THE ROSTOW PLAN

Unperturbed by the July SNIE, Rostow lobbied hard for U.S. intervention in Laos. On July 10 he sent U. Alexis Johnson a memo using the precise argument the SNIE had refuted, saying, "I assume we agree that without the other side becoming persuaded we mean business in Southeast Asia, there is unlikely to be a Laos settlement acceptable to us."[32] Rostow discussed his plan with Rusk on July 12, and followed this up with a memo to him on July 13.[33] He told Rusk that SEATO Plan 5 was not an adequate deterrent, and proposed that, if the U.S. did not get help from the U.N., direct unilateral action against North Vietnam was in order. On July 14 Rostow wrote to Kennedy that the twin threats in Berlin and Southeast Asia suggested the desirability of modifying the state of emergency arrangements in effect since World War II, in order to provide a legal basis for stronger defense and other preparations.[34] Taylor, Rostow told Kennedy, had "approved" this memo. On July 18, Rostow met with Taylor and U. Alexis Johnson, during which they discussed the need for clearing out the Tchepone pocket.[35] The idea of "using evidence of North Vietnamese aggression as a foundation for more aggressive limited military action against North Vietnam" was also discussed, a foreshadowing of what was to happen after the Gulf of Tonkin incident in August 1964.

U. Alexis Johnson briefed the "new military alternative" to Kennedy at a July 28 White House meeting.[36] Part one of this plan, said Johnson, was "the capture of southern Laos." The second part, he continued, was "a direct air and naval operation against Haiphong or Hanoi" should North Vietnam intervene in any substantial way. Kennedy was not impressed. His questions exposed the fact that the details of such plans had not been thought through, that there was no "careful" way to take southern Laos, and that it was unclear if action against Hanoi would have the desired effect or even how easy it would be to hold what was taken. Kennedy reminded those present that "earlier" military plans with respect to Laos were based on optimistic estimates "invariably proven false in the event." Kennedy said he was "not persuaded" that the airfields and situation in Southern Laos would allow "any real operation" to save that area, and emphasized that the American people and "many distinguished military leaders" were reluctant to see U.S. troops get involved in that part of the world.

That the gap between the President and his advisors—the military now joined by the civilians—over intervention, which had opened earlier in the year, was steadily increasing, is evident from the rest of this discussion. The advocates of intervention protested that it was somehow different this time, that no decision was being sought now, and pleaded for only an *understanding* that "the President would at some future time have a willingness to decide to intervene if the situation seemed to him to require it." In response to this awkward and hypothetical proposition, the President "made it very plain that he himself is at present very reluctant to go into Laos." His advisors, on the other hand, were very eager to go in. The gap was becoming a gulf, each side just as determined as the other, and equally confident in the soundness of its views.

In an August 1 memo to Kennedy, Rostow and Taylor joined forces and recommended a joint Lao–Thai–South Vietnamese "mopping up" campaign against the Tchepone pocket "stiffened" with U.S. Special Forces advisors under the Laos MAAG; the development of a whole "spectrum" of U.S. actions against North Vietnam; and the sending of a U.S. military mission to South Vietnam no later than the second half of August.[37] At an August 7 NSC meeting Kennedy asked to see plans designed to cover these kinds of actions.[38] Three days later General Lemnitzer told the President that the Chiefs' current planning assumed a "de facto division of Laos" and that their concept of operations was to secure a series of bases in Laos along the Mekong with U.S. and other forces "to release indigenous forces for other military activities."[39] The external (nonindigenous) force included at least one U.S. infantry division and part of a Marine division. After securing the bases in Laos, these forces, commanded by the U.S., would be prepared to mount air and naval operations against North Vietnam.

On August 11, Rostow criticized the Chiefs' plans in a private memo to Kennedy.[40] He argued that the Chiefs' panhandle operation was on too big a scale to "give us what we want," which he said was something larger than a local Laotian operation, but still smaller than SEATO Plan 5. Rostow complained, "We are making piecemeal progress in Southeast Asia planning," and he concluded, "We desperately lack a central mechanism to give the operation pace and coherence." On August 11, Taylor, now in complete synch with Rostow, joined in the criticism, saying in a memo to Kennedy that he was not convinced the plans Lemnitzer briefed were truly feasible militarily.[41] He said there was much work to be done to "tidy up" the situation in Southeast Asia, and complained there was still no Southeast Asia Task Force. "Greater intensity of effort" was needed, he said, and warned, "Time is running out as the dry season in Laos approaches." Taylor concluded: "I do not believe we can afford any further delay in this matter."

Over the two remaining weeks of August, the issue of what to do about Laos came to a head. A task force on Southeast Asia was created, headed by John Steeves of the State Department. The initial paper issued by the task force called for the addition of 2,000 more U.S. Special Forces personnel in Laos, as well as more logistic, air, and naval support. In a critical August 15 review of this report, Rostow's deputy, Robert Johnson, said he thought the U.S. commitment had to be "substantially larger" than this.[42] Curiously, Kennedy urged Rostow to take his vacation "now," and Rostow, concerned that Kennedy would make the final decision during his absence, weighed in with his plan for the President on August 17.[43] As it turned out, Rostow's concerns about what would happen in his absence were totally justified.

In his final report, Rostow proposed a series of moves, the bottom line of which was SEATO intervention and a SEATO field commander on the ground by September 15. "Your decision here is not easy," he told Kennedy. "It involves making an uncertain commitment in cold blood." He compared such a decision with the 1947 Truman Doctrine—to support free peoples who are resisting attempted subjugation by armed minorities or outside pressures. He maintained it was the only way to hold the area in the long run. On August 18, Rostow appealed to Robert Kennedy, saying he had worked on his Laos plan "in greatest intimacy and harmony" with General Taylor.[44] The urgency of it Rostow explained as follows:

> I deeply believe that the way to save Southeast Asia and to minimize the chance of deep U.S. military involvement there is for the President to make a bold decision very soon. The rainy season is over by October 1; and the rains taper off from mid-September.

Having made his case to both the President and his brother in the strongest way he could, Rostow went on vacation.

Kennedy had essentially passed the baton of Vietnam policy to Taylor after the ignominious end to the LBJ Saigon escapade in June. With Rostow gone, Taylor was alone in the driver's seat, but he found a new working ally, State's U. Alexis Johnson, with whom to press forward on Rostow's plan. On August 22, Taylor sent Johnson a memo[45] saying that the objectives in Southeast Asia were clear: minimizing the loss of territory to the communists in Laos; protecting the flanks of South Vietnam and Thailand; and minimizing U.S. military involvement. The problem, Taylor said, was to decide the size of the U.S. military forces required and, once committed, how to disengage these forces. While the overall plan was taking shape, he asked that the responsible governmental agencies get cracking on the details.

Meanwhile, at a key meeting of the Southeast Asia Task Force on August 24, Averell Harriman, who was still negotiating the Laos settlement, effectively killed Rostow's plan. In an August 25 memo to McGeorge Bundy, Robert Johnson described the meeting, which took place in Secretary of State Rusk's office.[46] The memo said John Steeves (Deputy Assistant Secretary of State for Far Eastern Affairs) and Taylor "made a valiant effort" to defend the Rostow plan but to no avail. It was evident, Robert Johnson said, that Rostow's plan "was defeated" at this meeting. McNamara had not accepted the plan either. The task force then devised a new plan: first make "an all-out college try" at the Laos negotiations, recognizing that—if the communists overrun the government forces—"we may completely eliminate the existing meager basis we have for military action in Laos," and should this occur, "we will organize our defense in the area on a different basis." Further "stiffening" of Laotian forces by U.S. advisors was to be done only on a "gingerly basis," while discussions could be held to ensure SEATO Plan 5 was ready to be implemented "if there is an actual rupture in the cease fire."

The new plan was forwarded to Kennedy by Rusk on August 29,[47] and the NSC met that same day to consider it. After some discussion, Kennedy issued his final decision as NSAM-80.[48] Besides increasing photoreconnaissance and U.S. support to the Meos, NSAM-80 had three key provisions: an "intensification" of Harriman's diplomatic efforts in Geneva; an authorization to discuss SEATO Plan 5 with allies as a contingency plan only; and a small increase in U.S. advisors in Laos to a level of 500 men. NSAM-80 therefore represented only a marginal increase in the American commitment to Laos, and was a far cry from the bold move Rostow and Taylor had so "valiantly" fought for.

Even if Kennedy favored intervention in Laos—which he did not— there had been little likelihood of doing so in the month of August, during which the Berlin crisis had reached its climax. At a July 13 NSC meeting Rusk had joined forces with Acheson to argue against negotiations with the Soviet Union until the hour became acute, while Acheson, supported by Vice President Johnson, argued vehemently for a proclamation of national emergency.[49] Kennedy rejected mobilization but in a July 25 televised address he declared, "We cannot and will not permit the communists to drive us out of Berlin, either gradually or by force."[50] He asked Congress to increase appropriations for the Armed Forces and to raise the authorized strength of the Army from 875,000 men to one million; dispatched 90,000 more Air Force and Navy personnel to Europe; and called up selected units from the Reserves. Misjudgment on either side, Kennedy said, "could rain down more devastation in several hours than has been wrought in all the wars of human history."

Khrushchev snapped right back in an August 7 televised speech of his own, and, in a tone "considerably higher-pitched" than Kennedy's, also speculated about the perils of a nuclear holocaust.[51] Just after midnight on August 13, the communists blocked off the streets and began building the Berlin Wall. Kennedy dispatched LBJ to Berlin with the message that the city was an ultimate American commitment, and ordered a U.S. Army armored force of 1,500 men to drive through East Germany to Berlin. At the time, Schlesinger recalls Kennedy, in private, making the following revealing remarks:

> "If Khrushchev wants to rub my nose in the dirt . . . it's all over." But how to convince Khrushchev short of a showdown? "That son of a bitch won't pay any attention to words," the President said bitterly on another occasion. "He has to see you move."[52]

When Khrushchev finally realized Kennedy would not back down, the Soviets backed off and Johnson was on hand to welcome the American tanks as they rolled into Berlin. By the end of the month, the crisis in Europe had passed, but in Southeast Asia it loomed large on the horizon.

VIETNAM: THE INSURGENCY GAINS MOMENTUM

At 1:00 A.M. in the morning on September 18, three Viet Cong battalions attacked Phuoc Vinh, a provincial capital just sixty miles north of Saigon.[53] The communist force easily overran the defending Civil Guard company, and killed forty-two residents in the process. Two South Vietnamese Ranger companies were patrolling in the vicinity, but instead of aiding the beleaguered Civil Guard company, they ran off into the jungle. Their commander later claimed his intent was to "ambush" the Viet Cong when they withdrew. The Viet Cong captured 100 rifles, 6,000 rounds of ammunition, freed 250 suspected Viet Cong prisoners, and staged a "trial" in the marketplace during which they beheaded the province chief and his assistant.

This incident was part of a new and ominous trend against the government in South Vietnam. Throughout the summer and fall of 1961, the pace of the insurgency in South Vietnam increased. A September 13 MAAG brief argued that while the increased Viet Cong activity appeared to be a final push for control, the South Vietnamese Army still had a good chance of containing the communists unless Hanoi provided "massive" assistance.[54] A September 20 MAAG report listed four battalion-sized Viet Cong attacks in northern South Vietnam during the previous three days.[55] It was the first time the Viet Cong had attacked in the northern I Corps area in such magnitude, the report noted; and this attack, coupled with other large VC actions in the III Corps (southern Delta) area, portended an increase in communist activity throughout the country and a move to a new phase in the insurgency. The captured VC had American weapons, the report noted, indicating a possible recent movement of communists into South Vietnam from Laos.

At a Vietnam Task Force meeting on September 22, the military briefer noted that the estimated size of Viet Cong forces adjacent to Laos (outside of the Delta) was over 7,000, more than double their size at the beginning of the year.[56] A September 25 MAAG report recapping increased VC activity in the III Corps area noted that total VC strength was estimated at 17,000, including thirty-one battalions and sixty-three separate companies.[57] The report said two-thirds of these forces were operating in the Delta, and another report noted that this was an increase from 7,000 at the beginning of 1961.[58] Given the ten-to-one ratio required in counterinsurgency operations, the South Vietnamese Army, which was still trying to expand to 170,000, was stretched to its very limit.

The basis for the doctrinal assumption that ten soldiers were necessary to contain one guerrilla centered on the nature of guerrilla warfare itself, in which guerrillas suddenly emerge to conduct hit-and-run operations against government installations and small forces and then blend back into the population. Consequently, large numbers of government troops are tied down in static defense duties while equally large government forces attempt to catch, surround, and defeat smaller guerrilla forces in the field. Actually, Rostow, in response to a question from Kennedy, wrote to him on July 31 that total regular South Vietnamese strength stood at just 142,000 men—about 28,000 less than required to fend off an insurgent force of 17,000 guerrillas.[59]

On October 5, the senior American advisor in the II Corps (central) area, Colonel Wilber Wilson, submitted a report that contradicted the view that the South Vietnamese Army was increasing its effectiveness.[60] Recent operations in the II Corps area, he said, indicated a lack of a "will to fight" on the part of South Vietnamese small-unit commanders. It was not that these soldiers were afraid, but that poor leadership was stultifying the senior noncommissioned officers and junior officers. Colonel Wilson said this problem was "particularly acute." On October 10, the State Department sent a cable to Saigon saying that Washington was "gravely concerned" about the "rapid escalation" of communist actions in Vietnam.[61] If the present volume of infiltration continues, the report went on, SEATO military assistance on a scale adequate to at least reduce the "volume of infiltration" might thus be required. Another State cable of the same date warned that the most important recent development was the large-scale Viet Cong attacks in central Vietnam resulting from both increased infiltration from Laos and a heavy buildup in the local guerrilla forces.[62]

VIETNAM: CONSENSUS FOR U.S. INTERVENTION

The sharp deterioration in the battlefield situation in Vietnam pushed the policy apparatus inexorably toward intervention. A pivotal event was the trip of Brigadier General William Craig, of the Pentagon Joint Staff, to Vietnam in early September. Craig bluntly stated that SEATO Plan 5 had to be immediately implemented, and warned that the future of the U.S. in Southeast Asia was at stake.[63] "It may be too late," he said, unless the U.S. acted immediately. On September 15, Rostow sent a memo to Kennedy explaining the highlights of Craig's report, and added that Hanoi believed "that the end of Stage 2—in Mao's theory of warfare—has arrived; that is, the end of guerrilla warfare and the beginning of open warfare."[64] On September 18, Robert Johnson exhorted Rostow to send Kennedy a full and complete copy of Craig's report, but the main points of Johnson's memo are still classified, as are parts of Craig's.[65]

On September 26 General Taylor informed Kennedy that plans for Southeast Asia were still not ready for presentation.[66] He said two alternatives were in the works: an expanded SEATO Plan 5 in the case of an overt resumption of hostilities in Laos, which he felt unlikely, and a plan for the more likely scenario of "ambiguous communist aggression," meaning constant nibbling away of territory. Unexpectedly, on September

30, Diem transformed the context of the debate on Vietnam policy. Toward the end of a long discussion in Saigon with Ambassador Nolting, Admiral Felt, and General McGarr, Diem asked for a bilateral defense treaty with the U.S. Diem told his surprised American audience that he feared the outcome of the Laos situation and increased communist infiltration into Vietnam. He said he felt the U.S. would not act to help Vietnam under the SEATO treaty because of the negative attitudes of its French and British allies. Nolting reported this turn of events in a cable to Washington on October 1, and offered his own opinion that Diem wanted a more binding commitment from the U.S. than was currently in effect under SEATO because he felt U.S. policy in Laos had exposed his flank.[67]

Diem's request gave the advocates of intervention in Vietnam the opening they needed. The Pentagon study of U.S. forces required in Vietnam had been on hold since the ungraceful end to the Johnson trip the previous June, and Diem's "statement" that these forces were only needed in case of external aggression. Diem's unexpected request for a bilateral treaty, which implied a request for combat troops, provided fresh impetus to the effort to put U.S. combat forces into Vietnam. This opportunity was not lost on Rostow, whose Laos plan had fallen by the boards during his absence. Now back from vacation, he steered the effort for intervention in Southeast Asia away from the waning prospect of Laos toward the increasingly bright prospect of Vietnam.

On October 2, Robert Johnson sent a memo to Rostow describing the current status of the two Laos plans.[68] The expanded SEATO Plan 5 had been approved by the JCS but the Joint Staff still had "nit picks." He said the Joint Chiefs were still examining the "ambiguous aggression" plan, a plan, Johnson said, that "may offer you an opportunity to express your views on the use of U.S. forces to protect the Vietnamese border." Rostow did not wait for the final "ambiguous aggression" Laos formula to surface. He knew the time was ripe and took the initiative. On October 5, he sent a memo to Kennedy saying that McNamara had asked for a delay of the NSC meeting on Vietnam scheduled for that same day.[69] Delaying the meeting was a good idea, Rostow said, "because some solid notions about Vietnam and Laos are beginning to emerge, but require careful political and military staffing." Harriman is to talk with you today about his Laos negotiations, he told the President, and "it is essential that he return to Geneva as soon as possible to resume the dialogue with Pushkin" (the Soviet representative). It could hardly have escaped Rostow's notice that, if the NSC meeting on Vietnam were delayed until after Harriman's departure for Geneva, the wily Harriman would not be hanging around to destroy Rostow's emerging Vietnam plan as Harriman had done to the Laos plan while Rostow was on vacation.

Rostow was now ready to put Laos aside and push full steam ahead on Vietnam. In his October 5 memo to Kennedy he said that Laos planning was "in tolerably good shape"; then he zeroed in on the real target: "But it is now agreed that it is more likely that the other side will concentrate on doing Diem in than on capturing the Mekong Valley during this fighting season." The fact is, no one made this argument prior to Diem's request for a treaty. Rostow now told the President that the U.S. had to move "quite radically" to avoid total defeat in Vietnam. "The sense of this town," he told Kennedy, "is that, with Southern Laos open, Diem simply cannot cope." He also said the South Vietnamese force buildup was going slower than that of the Viet Cong.

All elements of the policy apparatus now converged toward a decision to intervene in Vietnam during the first two weeks of October. At an October 5 luncheon, a group of senior officials, including Rostow, U. Alexis Johnson, and others, concluded that there would be an "unfavorable outcome" in Vietnam without a major change in U.S. policy.[70] Deputy Assistant Secretary of Defense William Bundy's record of the meeting noted that their discussion "helped to trigger Mr. Rostow's proposal for SEATO forces in Vietnam, which is now under urgent JCS consideration." Only Under Secretary of State Bowles challenged the idea of putting U.S. combat forces inside Vietnam. On October 5, he drafted a memo to Kennedy urging a political settlement rather than a military solution.[71] In a cover note to Schlesinger, Bowles noted his memo had produced a "negative reaction" in the State Department. The same day, General Lemnitzer sent the Chiefs' view to McNamara.[72] He said they had examined measures short of U.S. intervention in Southeast Asia for a long time, and "the time is now past where actions short of intervention by outside forces could reverse the rapidly worsening situation." He added that "there was no feasible military alternative of lesser magnitude which will prevent the loss of Laos, South Vietnam and ultimately Southeast Asia."

The Chiefs, who had been recommending SEATO Plan 5—a far larger intervention in Southeast Asia—since early in the year, did not like Rostow's paltry plan for putting U.S. forces inside Vietnam on the Laos border. They were prepared, however, to play along just to get a foot in the door, which, as Burke had noted in April, they had failed to do then. In an October 9 meeting with McNamara and the JCS, William Bundy told the Chiefs that "the proposal to put the forces along the border was made for political reasons."[73] From the notes taken by the Chief of Naval Operations, Admiral George Anderson, there is no question that the Chiefs went along with this but only with the astonishing provision that once the troops actually arrived in Vietnam they would "NOT" be put on the border. That the word "not" was capitalized in Anderson's memo only underscores the unsavory character of this ignoble footnote in the history of the war.

McNamara wanted a "positive recommendation" on intervention in South Vietnam and Anderson obliged: "If we cannot go into Laos, we should go into South Vietnam," he said. McNamara agreed to this and asked for an estimate by October 11 of the "forces needed to eliminate the Viet Cong." When the meeting was over, the JCS put their views in writing.[74] They still preferred SEATO Plan 5, their memo to McNamara said, but if this was "politically unacceptable at this time" they would agree to a 9,600-man SEATO combat force to be deployed in Vietnam, of which 5,000 would be U.S. troops.

An October 10 memo from William Bundy to McNamara argued that it "*is* really now or never if we are to arrest the gains being made by the Viet Cong. . . . On a 70-30 basis, I would myself favor going in," Bundy said.[75] "But if we let, say, a month go by before we move, the odds will slide (both short-term shock effect and long-term chance) down to 60-40, 50-50, and so on." U. Alexis Johnson agreed. That same day he wrote that even if infiltration through Laos was cut off, there was still no assurance that Diem's army "will in the foreseeable future be able to defeat the Viet Cong."[76] He said, "Supplemental military action must be envisaged at the earliest stage that is politically feasible." What he meant by "supplemental military action," of course, was U.S. combat troops. As to the number required, he said, "Three divisions would be a guess." If Johnson's proposals were followed, it would have meant that around 40,000 American soldiers would be going into Vietnam.

The events of September–October mirrored those of April–May in that a concerted move for intervention in Laos was transformed into a concerted move for intervention in Vietnam. What had taken place in between the recurring episodes of this foreboding cycle was the education of John Kennedy. The failure in Cuba, the haranguing by Khrushchev in Vienna, and the tumult of the Berlin crisis had all been parts of this learning process. So were the incessant arguments of his advisors for intervention in Laos and Vietnam, which, by this time, must have seemed no more than a dogmatic litany to Kennedy. The developing crisis in Vietnam served only to magnify the widening gulf between Kennedy and his advisors and add to his impatience with them. He could not afford to procrastinate any longer on his plans to make major personnel changes in the government. These changes, many of which took Washington by surprise, followed an event that surprised and shocked the President: a report written by Maxwell D. Taylor.

NOTES

1. John Taylor, *General Maxwell Taylor* (New York: Doubleday, 1989), p. 248; see also Karnow, *Vietnam*, p. 251.

2. Maxwell Taylor, *Swords and Plowshares*, p. 222.

3. Staley was president of the Stanford Research Institute.

4. For the full text see *PP*, DOD ed., Book 11, pp. 182–226.

5. Burris memo to LBJ, August 1, 1961, LBJ Library, VP Security File, Box 5.

6. JFK Library, NSF, Country File, Vietnam, Box 194.

7. Taylor/Rostow memo to JFK, July 27, 1961, JFK Library, NSF, Regional Security, SEA, Box 223/231.

8. Memorandum of Discussion on Southeast Asia, July 28, 1961, July 31, 1961, JFK Library, NSF, Regional Security, SEA, Box 231A.

9. Maxwell Taylor, *Swords and Plowshares*, pp. 222–23. Taylor confuses some elements of the July 28 meeting with the August 4 meeting, but the minutes of the July 28 meeting and follow-up memoranda make this easy to piece back together.

10. These tenets were: that the military situation was the most critical, that economic and social progress was necessary, and that developing economic self-sufficiency in South Vietnam was a good thing; see *Declassified Documents*, 1981, 590A.

11. NSAM-65, *PP*, DOD ed., Book 11, pp. 241–44.

12. Facts on File, *South Vietnam*, p. 22.

13. Vice President Johnson would report to Kennedy on May 25 that VC strength had reached 12,000, up significantly from the March NIE estimate of 8,000–10,000.

14. Nolting cable to State, May 23, 1961, JFK Library, NSF, Country File, Vietnam, Box 193.

15. Robert Johnson memo to Rostow, June 20, 1961, JFK Library, NSF, Country File, Vietnam, Box 193.

16. State cable to Wolf (in Paris), June 27, 1961, JFK Library, NSF, Country File, Vietnam, Box 193.

17. The May figures were close to another set of 1961 figures submitted by Sterling Cottrell on June 9, 1961 (JFK Library, NSF, Country File, Vietnam, Box 193), which yielded the following 1961 monthly totals for killed and captured GVN forces: Jan—468; Feb—311; Mar—338; Apr—431; May—562. For those interested, the monthly average here is 422, but the figures were growing the last four months in a row.

18. The following account is a reconstruction based upon thirteen CIA field reports from Laos and four telegrams from the U.S. Embassy in Vientiane included as source material in a draft Vietnam Task Force report, June 19, 1961, *Declassified Documents*, 1973, 432C.

19. Stevenson, *The End of Nowhere*, p. 162.

20. "Covert Annex—Laos (11–24 July)" to the Southeast Asia Task Force Status Report, undated but obviously from July 1961, *Declassified Documents*, 1973, 337C.

21. Memo of Taylor, U. Alexis Johnson, and Rostow discussion, July 18, 1961, in *State History*, 1961, Document 98, pp. 231–33.

22. State Department Memorandum of Conversation, June 14, 1961, JFK Library, NSF, Country File, Box 193.

23. CIA field report, July 12, 1961, JFK Library, NSF, Country File, Vietnam, Box 193.

24. "Source material on PL [Pathet Lao] and VC [Viet Cong] activity in South Laos," attached to the task force progress report (draft), June 19, 1961, *Declassified Documents*, 1973, 432C.

25. Task force progress report (draft), June 19, 1961, *Declassified Documents*, 1973, 432C.

26. Robert Johnson memo to Rostow, June 20, 1961, JFK Library, NSF, Country File, Vietnam, Box 193.

27. Rostow memo to Kennedy, June 20, 1961, JFK Library, NSF, Country File, Vietnam, Box 193. It is still classified but we know its thrust from a later July 6 Rostow note to U. Alexis Johnson; see Gibbons, *The U.S. Government and the Vietnam War*, vol. 2, p. 54.

28. Rostow memo to Kennedy, June 21, 1961, *Declassified Documents*, 1981, 644B.

29. For passages from Acheson's report and the Hyannis Port meeting, see Schlesinger, *A Thousand Days*, pp. 360–61.

30. U. Alexis Johnson memo to Rostow, July 8, 1961, JFK Library, NSF, Regional Security, SEA, Box 223/231.

31. Although the SNIE (58-2-61) is still classified, we know this from a later Robert Johnson memo. See Robert Johnson to Rostow, July 26, 1961, JFK Library, NSF, Regional Security, SEA, Box 223/231.

32. Rostow memo to U. Alexis Johnson, July 10, 1961, JFK Library, NSF, Country File, Vietnam, Box 193.

33. Rostow memo to Rusk, July 13, 1961, JFK Library, NSF, Country File, Vietnam, Box 193.

34. Rostow memo to Kennedy, July 14, 1961, JFK Library, NSF, Regional Security, SEA, Box 231A.

35. Memorandum of Conversation, July 18, 1961, JFK Library, Thomson Papers.

36. Memorandum of Discussion on Southeast Asia, July 28, 1961, dated July 31, 1961, JFK Library, NSF, Regional Security, SEA, Box 231A.

37. Rostow-Taylor memo to JFK, August 1, 1961, JFK Library, NSF, Regional Security, SEA, Box 231A.

38. The only way we know of this meeting is from a later Rostow memo. See Rostow memo to JFK, August 11, 1961, JFK Library, NSF, Regional Security, SEA, Box 231A.

39. The current plans were typed up as of August 8, 1961, see "Southeast Asian Contingency Planning Currently Active Within the Joint Staff," August 8, 1961, JFK Library, NSF, Regional Security, SEA, Box 231A. The August 11 Rostow memo above mentions the briefing as having occurred on August 10, and a Taylor memo of the same date identifies Lemnitzer as the briefer, see Taylor memo to Kennedy, August 11, 1961, JFK Library, NSF, Regional Security, SEA, Box 231A.

40. Rostow memo to Kennedy, August 11, 1961, JFK Library, NSF, Regional Security, SEA, Box 231A.

41. Taylor memo to Kennedy, August 11, 1961, JFK Library, NSF, Regional Security, SEA, Box 231A.

42. Robert Johnson memo to Rostow, August 15, 1961, JFK Library, NSF, Regional Security, SEA, Box 231A.

43. Rostow memo to JFK, August 17, 1961, JFK Library, NSF, Regional Security, SEA, Box 231A.

44. Rostow memo to RFK, August 18, 1961, JFK Library, NSF, Regional Security SEA, Box 231A.

45. Taylor memo to U. Alexis Johnson, August 22, 1961, JFK Library, NSF, Regional Security, SEA, Box 231A.

46. Robert Johnson memo to McGeorge Bundy, August 25, 1961, JFK Library, NSF, Regional Security, SEA, Box 231A.

47. Rusk memo to Kennedy, August 29, 1961, JFK Library, NSF, Regional Security, SEA, Box 231A.

48. NSAM-80, *PP*, DOD ed., Book 11, pp. 247–48.

49. Schlesinger, *A Thousand Days*, p. 362.

50. Kennedy, *Public Papers*, 1961, p. 534.

51. Schlesinger, *A Thousand Days*, p. 365.

52. Ibid., p. 363.

53. This account is based on the reconstruction by Rust, *Kennedy in Vietnam*, p. 37.

54. Vietnam brief, September 12, 1961, *Declassified Documents*, 1981, 447B.

55. MAAG report, JFK Library, NSF, Country File, Vietnam, Box 194.

56. Robert Johnson memo to Rostow, September 22, 1961, JFK Library, NSF, Country File, Vietnam, Box 194.

57. CHMAAG, Saigon, to CINCPAC, September 25, 1961, message, *Declassified Documents*, RC, 74C.

58. "Southeast Asia" report, October 4, 1961, JFK Library, NSF, Regional Security, SEA, Box 231A.

59. Rostow memo to Kennedy, July 31, 1961, JFK Library, NSF, Country File, Vietnam, Box 193.

60. Report by Senior Advisor, II Corps, Wilbur Wilson, October 5, 1961.

61. State cable to Saigon, No. 484, October 10, 1961, *Declassified Documents*, RC, 792A.

62. State cable to Saigon, No. 462, October 10, 1961, *Declassified Documents*, RC, 792A.

63. Report, General Craig, September 15, 1961, JFK Library, NSF, Regional Security, SEA, Box 231A.

64. Rostow memo to JFK, September 15, 1961, JFK Library, NSF, Regional Security, SEA, Box 231A.

65. The Craig memo was cited above; for the sanitized Robert Johnson memo of September 18, 1961, see JFK Library, NSF, Regional Security, SEA, Box 231A.

66. Taylor memo to Kennedy, September 26, 1961, JFK Library, NSF, Regional Security, SEA, Box 231A.

67. Saigon cable to State No. 421, October 1, 1961, *Declassified Documents*, RC, 788F.

68. Robert Johnson memo to Rostow, October 2, 1961, JFK Library, NSF, Regional Security, SEA, Box 231A.

69. Rostow memo to Kennedy, October 5, 1961, JFK Library, NSF, Regional Security, SEA, Box 231A.

70. *State History*, 1961, Document 144, p. 321.

71. *State History*, 1961, Document 145, pp. 322–25.

72. *PP*, DOD ed., Book 11, pp. 295–96.

73. See the notes of Admiral Anderson, Chief of Naval Operations, pertaining to this meeting in *State History*, 1961, Document 148, p. 328.

74. See JCS memo to McNamara, *PP*, DOD ed., Book 11, pp. 297–311. The JCS also passed the substance of its memo to McNamara to General Taylor; see JCS to Taylor, October 9, 1961, *Declassified Documents*, RC, 260A.

75. William Bundy memo to McNamara, October 10, 1961, *PP*, DOD ed., Book 11, p. 312.

76. *PP*, DOD ed., Book 2, part IVB.1, p. 78.

CHAPTER SEVEN

TAYLOR TOO

THE FIG LEAF IS REMOVED

By October it was obvious that the battlefield situation in South Vietnam was fast approaching the critical point. Naturally this unfavorable news found its way into the newspapers, which also caught wind of a startling new rumor and printed that too. The rumor was that Diem had made a request for U.S. combat troops. On the surface it appeared this subject had been put to rest. After all, Vice President Johnson reported in May that Diem had said no to them. Of course, if all of the facts had come to light, they would have revealed a different story: that Johnson had concealed Diem's agreement to the terms for such troops and that Kennedy had simply ignored Diem's cryptically worded request for them when it arrived in the second letter.

As a consequence of the masquerade in May and June, the new rumor caught the State Department off guard. A spokesman, who was probably simply telling the truth as he knew it, remarked that he did not know whether South Vietnam had asked for U.S. troops or not. That went straight into print as well, creating the impression of confusion at State and prompting reporters to try to sniff out an angle from Embassy officials in Saigon. On October 9 Ambassador Nolting sent a desperate plea for information to State, saying, "We badly need official guidance" from

Washington on "thinking" about sending U.S. forces to Vietnam.[1] The
answer he received the next day said no decision had been made in
Washington and that Vietnam had made no such request.[2] The resort to
this old standby position that Diem had made no request was naive, and
Diem destroyed it for good two days later. Thuan finally passed on the
unvarnished truth to a startled Nolting: yes, Diem did want U.S. combat
troops, and he wanted them put near the 17th parallel—the "demilitarized" zone—to prevent attacks there and free up his army to deal with
the Viet Cong elsewhere.[3]

The timing of Diem's demarche was no coincidence. The day before,
an important NSC meeting had taken place in Washington in which
Kennedy had staved off yet another recommendation for combat troops
from his advisors and also decided to send General Taylor to Vietnam.
Diem's unequivocal request for U.S. combat troops—minus the fig leaf
of "training"—was perfectly timed to influence the planning and terms
of reference for Taylor's trip. In addition, another new element was added
to the rising chorus for combat troops at this critical juncture: the U.S.
intelligence community published two Special National Intelligence Estimates that buttressed the case for American intervention in Vietnam.

THE OCTOBER 11 NSC MEETING—NSAM-104

The first of these estimates, SNIE 53-2-61, "Bloc Support of the Communist Effort Against the Government of Vietnam," was issued on October
5, and the second, SNIE 10-3-61, "Probable Communist Reactions to
Certain SEATO Undertakings in South Vietnam," was issued the day
before the NSC meeting at which Kennedy released a new NSAM and
made the decision to send Taylor to Vietnam. These intelligence estimates
came at a crucial time—at the very moment when Taylor, Rostow, and
U. Alexis Johnson joined together with the Joint Chiefs of Staff to urge
Kennedy to intervene with conventional forces in Vietnam.

The first SNIE concluded that the insurgency was controlled by Hanoi,
and Hanoi was identified as the "implementing agency" for the communist
bloc.[4] The Viet Cong hard-core forces had grown to 16,000, an increase,
the estimate noted, of 12,000 since April 1960, and 4,000 over the
previous three months. The Viet Cong apparatus, its scope and area of
operations were rapidly expanding, the SNIE said, and more recently
their forces had begun operating in large units and conducting large-scale
attacks. The second SNIE essentially concluded that North Vietnam and
China would not commit large forces to counter the SEATO moves under

consideration.[5] Thus on the eve of the crucial NSC meeting, the U.S. intelligence community painted a critical picture of the situation in South Vietnam and, in effect, gave a green light to intervention there.

The principal business of the October 11 meeting was to hear and consider a major presentation by State's U. Alexis Johnson. His briefing followed the outlines of a proposal for intervention contained in a paper entitled "Concept for Intervention in Vietnam."[6] In the paper Johnson had combined the ideas of Taylor, Rostow, the Southeast Asia Task Force, and the Joint Chiefs, and he now discussed the specifics for Kennedy. The number and type of American troops his plan envisioned sending to Vietnam was close to what the Joint Chiefs had proposed: 11,000 ground combat troops out of a total SEATO force of 22,800. They were to be initially stationed in the north near Pleiku. The timing of this deployment was to be immediate, and the rationale for this urgency—provided in his paper—was that "the costs would be much less than if we wait or go in later, or lose [South Vietnam]."

Kennedy was still opposed to sending U.S. combat troops to Vietnam. Feeling for intervention among his advisors, however, was growing stronger, and so Kennedy decided to defer a final decision and send Taylor out for a close look at the situation. Although the minutes of the meeting have disappeared,[7] notes made by Lemnitzer[8] and Gilpatric,[9] who attended, as well as the text of NSAM-104, which Kennedy issued that day,[10] are sufficient to reconstruct the outlines of what happened.

The President's advisors did not come away empty-handed, for Kennedy did authorize that one Air Force Jungle Jim squadron be sent to Vietnam. This squadron was equipped for bombing and close air support of ground combat troops, but Gilpatric's notes indicate Kennedy directed that it was not to be used for combat. The squadron would serve under the MAAG and its mission would be to train the South Vietnamese Air Force in counterinsurgency tactics. The President also authorized U.S. advisors to go along with South Vietnamese guerrillas on missions inside Laos. These authorizations, along with other measures[11] and the Taylor trip, were incorporated into NSAM-104. In essence, by issuing this NSAM Kennedy significantly increased the U.S. Air Force advisory role in Vietnam and bought some breathing space before facing the ultimate question of sending in American ground forces.

The Taylor mission would be the pivotal event leading to the major decision on Vietnam of Kennedy's presidency. In picking Taylor to lead the mission, Kennedy chose a man whom he judged to be an expert in unconventional warfare, an intellectual who quoted Thucydides,[12] and the one general he thought shared his own views and that he could, therefore, trust to carry out his bidding. Kennedy did not want to send U.S. combat troops to Vietnam and intended to use the Taylor trip not only for elbow room, but also to help strengthen his case against intervening. Diem's sudden request for U.S. combat troops, by removing any obstacle in Saigon, put the onus on Taylor within hours of Kennedy's decision to send him.

KENNEDY PLANTS A STORY

The precise mission that Taylor would carry out became the subject of debate as soon as the October 11 NSC meeting was over. Lemnitzer wrote to McGarr immediately afterward that the mission was to examine the "feasibility and desirability" of U.S. intervention and recommend measures short of intervention. Gilpatric's notes give a different slant: Taylor was to examine the feasibility of the plan for intervention briefed at the NSC meeting as well as plans for intervening with fewer U.S. forces, and explore "other alternatives in lieu of putting any U.S. combat forces into Vietnam." Everyone had their own opinions about what Taylor should examine and recommend. At the bottom of this confusion was a simple conflict: Kennedy's advisors wanted U.S. intervention and he did not. The President, however, had the final say; the NSAM directed Taylor to "examine" the feasibility of intervention, but to "recommend action" short of it.

At an October 13 NSC meeting, Kennedy issued a directive to Taylor outlining the trip's missions. The short history of this directive provides strong evidence that Kennedy and Taylor were already at odds over the trip before it began. Taylor's version of what the President's instructions should be differed significantly from what the President wanted done. The first draft of the directive was written by Taylor himself right after the October 11 NSC meeting.[13] In it Taylor had Kennedy order an examination of current CIA operations, U.S. aid, and command relationships; an evaluation of "what could be accomplished" by intervention; and a look at other forms of "unconventional" American assistance.

By the time of the October 13 NSC meeting, however, Kennedy had completely turned around the directive. His remarks during the meeting and the changes he made to Taylor's draft directive are very revealing.[14] In the discussion Kennedy complained about the "build-up of stories" that the U.S. was contemplating sending combat troops to Vietnam, and said "too much emphasis is being put on this aspect and could well result in a tremendous letdown in Vietnamese morale if they expected such action and we decided otherwise." Kennedy made it clear that publicly Taylor was to be looking at whether an increase in U.S. efforts was called for at all. On a very "close hold" basis, Kennedy said, Taylor would be authorized to give his "most discreet consideration" to the introduction of combat troops, and only, Kennedy insisted, if Taylor deemed such action "absolutely essential."

Kennedy then removed all references in the directive that provided for studying intervention, command relationships, unconventional assistance, and CIA operations. In the place of Taylor's six paragraphs that covered these items, the President inserted three of his own that were markedly different.[15] Two, in particular, deserve attention:

> In your assessment you should bear in mind that the initial responsibility for the effective maintenance of the independence of South Vietnam rests with the people and government of that country. Our efforts must be evaluated, and your recommendations formulated, with this fact in mind.
>
> While the military part of the problem is of great importance in South Vietnam, its political, social, and economic elements are equally significant, and I shall expect your appraisal and your recommendations to take full account of them.

These words make abundantly clear that Kennedy would not look kindly on a recommendation from Taylor that included U.S. combat troops.

The final event in Kennedy's send-off for Taylor concerns an intrigue the President pulled in the press. The episode began at his October 11 press conference, during which he announced that he was sending Taylor to Vietnam. He would be going to talk with Diem and American officials there, Kennedy explained, about "ways in which we can perhaps better assist the Government of Vietnam in meeting this threat to its independence."[16] Predictably, this had drawn harassing questions from reporters. Might not some people interpret the trip as a "confirmation of reports that you intend to send combat troops?" asked one correspondent. Kennedy had replied noncommittally that he would await Taylor's return before deciding "what is best to do." Naturally, the newspapers ignored this and the next day reported flatly that Taylor was going to Vietnam to study the question of combat troops.

These stories upset Kennedy and, when combined with Taylor's unwelcome version of the trip directive, must have heightened Kennedy's fears that Taylor might recommend combat troops. Since Kennedy had already made up his mind against troops, and was not about to get trapped in a public debate that made him appear weak on communism, he devised a plan to avoid this. The first step was his revision, on October 13, of Taylor's terms of reference, a revision that downplayed the issue of U.S. combat troops. The next step Kennedy carried out the following day, when he planted a bogus story in the *New York Times*. The story, probably leaked directly by the President himself, said Taylor was being sent to Vietnam for a wide variety of reasons. Near the end of a long list of them was the question of troops at some indefinite time in the future.[17] That much was true, but the story also included a statement that was not:

> Military leaders at the Pentagon, no less than General Taylor himself are understood to be reluctant to send organized U.S. combat units into Southeast Asia. Pentagon plans for this area stress the importance of countering communist guerrillas with troops from the affected countries, perhaps trained and equipped by the U.S., but not supplanted by U.S. troops.

This was a brilliant stroke. Those closest to policy knew the story was not true and could, without too much difficulty, guess the source. No one was prepared to counter it by leaking the truth—that the Pentagon had proposed sending American combat troops to Vietnam and that the President was opposed to it. The issue all but disappeared from the newspapers. Diem, who had sent Nolting a request for troops the day before the article appeared, did not bring up the subject during Taylor's visit. But it did not forestall Maxwell Taylor from bringing the subject up himself.[18]

THE TAYLOR "MOB" GOES TO SAIGON

"General Taylor would like you to bring a dinner jacket," read a buck slip (an internal office note) attached to Lansdale's trip itinerary.[19] Another buck slip informed Lansdale that Taylor wanted those accompanying him on the trip to be in his office at 5:00 P.M. on Friday, October 13.[20] Lansdale was back in business and on his way to Vietnam. For a moment, as he stared at the note, it would appear that the old covert operator seemed to forget who was in charge of this trip; he began jotting down in the margins wide-ranging instructions to his staff:

—Unconventional warfare
—Prepare black book on what done in past, what should be done in future
—Areas useful for others to look into

1. SVN [South Vietnam]
2. Laos
3. Thailand
4. Phils [Philippines]

Lansdale told a friend he was going along only because McNamara and Gilpatric had insisted, but the truth was that little arm-twisting had been necessary.[21]

At the Friday trip meeting in his office, Taylor made it clear that this was *his* trip and that it would be *his* report when they returned.[22] "I explained to my colleagues that I felt I had a mandate from the President to give him my personal views and recommendations upon return," Taylor recounts, and, anticipating that there would be dissenting views in the group, he invited their opinions but said these would be included in appendices to his own report.[23] Rostow was going along also and would "act as a sort of deputy" on the mission. It would be "a little like two professors going over the outlines for a series of student term papers," Rostow later said, condescendingly.[24]

Lansdale did not fancy himself a student of either Rostow or Taylor. After the meeting in Taylor's office Lansdale wrote about him in rather unflattering terms. "He has a mob going," Lansdale said to his old friend General Hangin' Sam Williams.[25] Then he lamented: "There are times when patriotism is pretty costly, and I think you know my feelings at being part of a big showy deal with a lot of theorists." Lansdale figured only he could make this trip worthwhile. "Maybe I can snatch a few minutes alone with Diem and others, and make it pay off," he told Williams, and added, "and I'll be damned if I'm about to tuck my tail between my legs for anyone."

Taylor and Lansdale crossed swords even before they arrived in Saigon. It was a long flight over the Pacific, time that Taylor used to get organized and establish the pecking order for those on the mission. "Immediately after take off from Andrews Air Force Base," Rostow recounts, "Taylor and I talked at length with each member of the mission."[26] They handed out areas of responsibility like homework assignments to their pupils. The process went smoothly until it came to Lansdale.

Taylor assigned Lansdale a job he knew Lansdale did not believe in. He told Lansdale to look into the possibility and cost of erecting a huge fence to stop infiltration that would run the length of Vietnam's borders with Cambodia and Laos.[27] Then Taylor added insult to injury by informing Lansdale that he would not be among the members allowed to visit with Diem.[28] "Well, I'm an old friend of Diem's," Lansdale shot back. "I can't go to Vietnam without seeing him. I'll probably see him alone. Is there anything you want me to ask him?" This left Taylor's blood boiling, and he refused to discuss the matter further.

When the plane landed in Saigon on October 18, Taylor began a talk with reporters on the tarmac. With Taylor suitably engaged, Diem's personal secretary, who was there to greet the mission, casually approached Lansdale and invited him to the presidential palace for dinner. Lansdale informed Rostow and left the group to spend the evening with Diem. At the same time that Lansdale was heading for the palace and Taylor was talking to reporters, Diem was addressing South Vietnam's National Assembly and proclaiming that the threat from the Viet Cong was so grave it required a declaration of a state of emergency. The trip was off to an interesting start.

"The first evening I was there," Lansdale later said of that evening with Diem, "he looked really down in the dumps—so I told him to go to bed instead of talking with me."[29] Diem declined his old friend's advice but he did have good reason to be depressed: the Viet Cong had expanded from 10,000 to 17,000 during 1961, Laos was becoming a highway for communist infiltration while the Americans negotiated a settlement there, and the Mekong Delta was ravaged by the worst flood in many decades. Most of what discussion did take place that night centered on the possibility of introducing U.S. combat troops to Vietnam.[30] Diem pressed Lansdale for his advice on whether Vietnam should request them, and Lansdale claims he was evasive on the issue. Diem's brother Nhu was present that evening and he answered many of the questions Lansdale put to Diem, a reflection of the power Nhu had gained over his brother since Lansdale's visit the previous January. "It got obnoxious after a time," Lansdale later said in an interview;[31] so he asked Diem which of the two was in charge. Lansdale was shocked and worried that brother Nhu was "taking over the place."

The following day, Diem treated Taylor to his usual long monologue and did not mention U.S. combat troops until the last moment. "I offered Diem the opportunity on several occasions to raise the matter of American troops," Taylor wrote later, but "he avoided the subject until near the end of the interview and then dealt with it with deliberate ambiguity."[32] Taylor's prodding finally paid off, and Diem said it was impossible to contain the Viet Cong with his 150,000-man army and, though he formerly had hoped to cope without foreign troops, increased Viet Cong strength and the situation in Laos had forced him to reexamine his position. Taylor found "a general consensus" among Vietnamese and Americans in Vietnam that U.S. forces were needed quickly. His own "military subcommittee" argued that prompt U.S. intervention was the only way of saving South Vietnam and all of Southeast Asia, while his "political officers" (Sterling Cottrell and William Jorden) felt even this would not be enough to win, and urged a "go slow" in U.S. commitments.

In his final meeting with Diem, Taylor suggested U.S. forces be introduced as a "flood relief task force," a plan Diem enthusiastically agreed with. The introduction of 8,000 U.S. combat forces under a flood relief cover (Taylor did not like to use the word "cover"[33]) became the central piece of the plan he would recommend to Kennedy. Even though this idea was included among various other provisions covering U.S. advisory and support missions and ideas on how to reform and broaden Diem's government, its real significance was unmistakable. Taylor's advance "eyes only" cables to Kennedy barely touched on reforms. They dealt mainly with military matters that, as David Halberstam rightly states, "were extremely conventional in attitude."[34] The contents of these, one from Saigon on October 24 and two more from the Philippines on November 1, are the key to understanding Taylor's report and recommendations. They explained and justified to the President his proposal to send 8,000 combat troops to Vietnam under the cover of a "flood relief task force."[35]

Taylor came back to Kennedy with the same old combat troops solution spruced up with a humanitarian cover. It failed to go beyond the simplistic notion that it was only a question of how much military force was needed to defeat the enemy. Ironically, one of Taylor's findings was that intelligence was poor, but even this did not lead him to pose the more fundamental question: why were the Viet Cong winning? Though few observers have been willing to say so, Taylor's recommendation to send combat troops was, in itself, a major failure—for him personally, and for the Kennedy administration. That failure is a topic that warrants some attention.

The true dimensions of Taylor's failure have seldom been defined, in part because Taylor himself has muddied the record. Many of his later public comments attempted to cover up the combat role of the forces he proposed sending to Vietnam. Appearing on *Meet the Press* in 1968, he denied he had envisioned such a role.[36] "I made no recommendation of that sort," Taylor claimed. "It was very widely reported," a panelist shot back; Taylor then replied:

> I am very sorry to say it is incorrect. The only reference to ground forces which I made was the desirability of sending a task force which could assist in the engineering problems resulting from the great inundation of the Delta. These engineer-type troops would be accompanied by their own self-defensive force.

Later, in a 1971 NBC program on the war, Taylor elaborated on his reasoning for bringing in American troops and "underscoring the flood task" in this way: it would allay South Vietnamese fears that the U.S. was about to "sell Vietnam down the river" like Laos; it was a genuine humanitarian gesture to help with flood relief; and, if the presence of our forces didn't "have the effect that we had expected," then the U.S. could say, "They came . . . repaired the flood damage and then went home."[37]

In that same NBC program Walt Rostow acknowledged that the troops in fact had a secondary purpose "as a reserve force." *In plain English this meant a backup combat force for the South Vietnamese Army.* Was it possible that Taylor did not know his "eyes only" cables to Kennedy had been published in the *New York Times* six months earlier as part of *The Pentagon Papers?* At that time the American reading public could see that, in addition to boosting morale and flood relief work, Taylor himself had three other tasks in mind for these forces:

(c) Conduct such combat operations as are necessary for self-de-
    fense *and for the security of the area in which they are stationed.*
(d) *Provide an emergency reserve to back up the Armed Forces of the
    GVN in the case of a heightened military crisis.*
(e) *Act as an advance party of such additional forces as may be intro-
    duced if CINCPAC or SEATO contingency plans are invoked.*
    [emphasis added][38]

In his cables Taylor further explained the reserve combat role of these troops. He said that, "in general," this should not be against "small-scale guerrilla" forces in the jungle. What he had in mind was far larger: "As a general reserve *they might be thrown into action (with U.S. agreement) against large, formed guerrilla bands which have abandoned the forests for attacks on major targets*" [emphasis added].

Taylor obviously had not expected anyone other than Kennedy and a few other officials—let alone the American public, just ten years later— to be reading this cable. As to the actual extent to which the troops would engage in flood relief work, Taylor said that this would depend upon "further study" of that problem, and added he saw "considerable advantages in playing up this aspect" of their mission. The "possibility of emphasizing the humanitarian mission will wane," Taylor warned, "if we wait long in moving in our forces or in linking our stated purpose with the emergency conditions of the flood." *In other words, Kennedy had better hurry up and send in the combat troops before the flood—and the cover for this deployment—went away.*

Why did Taylor try to hide the fact that he had recommended a combat role for American ground forces in Vietnam? The first part of the answer to this compelling question is what David Halberstam pointed out in 1969: General Taylor failed to live up to his reputation as an intellectual and original thinker, and his report abandoned the concepts of counterinsurgency in favor of conventional warfare, and, with some window dressing, advocated a Korean War–style strategy (a large conventional U.S. force).[39] That Halberstam's bold evaluation is rarely endorsed by others writing on the subject is unfortunate, for in this author's view his analysis is right on target.

During the trip Taylor had assigned his least favorite person, Ed Lansdale, the job of answering this important question: "what unconventional warfare techniques should be considered in coping with [the] VC insurgency?"[40] Lansdale's answer was that the unconventional war effort was "bogged down," and that despite the wealth of ideas, abilities, and equipment, "somehow things simply don't get done effectively enough."[41] Lansdale then revealed his true stripes with the following comment:

> This might remain true despite our sending in more people, new types of weapons, or changing organizational structures. Thus, just adding more of many things, as we are doing at present, doesn't appear to provide the answer we are seeking.

The "spark" the South Vietnamese needed to get on with the work of winning the war, he said, was to place the "right Americans into the right areas of the Vietnamese government to provide operational guidance." This was not the answer Taylor had in mind; the fact is that he liked neither Lansdale nor his recommendations. Taylor later said of him that "he could turn out ideas faster than you could pick them up off the floor, but I was never impressed with their feasibility."[42] The feeling was mutual: "My trip to Saigon with Taylor in the Fall of 1961," Lansdale wrote later, "was a farce, largely."[43]

The second part of the answer as to why Taylor tried to cover up the combat role of the troop commitment he recommended to Kennedy lies in the personal relationship between the two men and the charge Kennedy had given Taylor in the first place. This aspect of the issue has been fouled by accounts that seek to portray Kennedy as a hawk attracted to the idea of sending combat troops to Vietnam. George Kahin seizes on the Taylor trip to portray Kennedy as an interventionist. "In sending out his most hawkish advisors," writes Kahin, "Kennedy presumably expected them to come up with hawkish recommendations, and that is precisely what he got."[44] This misconstrues Kennedy's views and is not an accurate description of what happened. Fortunately for history, Taylor himself admitted— five years before his death—in a 1982 interview with military historian Andrew Krepinevich that he left Washington "knowing the President did not want a recommendation to send forces."[45] Krepinevich, also a military officer, realized the profound significance of Taylor's failure:

while admitting that the "new" Communist strategy of insurgency bypassed the Army's traditional approach to war, Taylor offered all the old prescriptions for the achievement of victory: increased firepower and mobility, more effective search-and-destroy operations, and if all else failed, bombing the source of the trouble (in thought if not in fact), North Vietnam, into capitulation.

William Colby provides this insight: while Taylor's idea of being able to respond flexibly to military contingencies—instead of always relying on nuclear weapons—was a breath of fresh air in Washington, his views on how to respond to an insurgency were nevertheless remarkably conventional.[46]

Kennedy's admiration for Taylor's "flexible response" doctrine led to unfounded conclusions about the General's ability to understand the sort of warfare going on in Southeast Asia, and the President was now paying a high price for his mistake. Taylor made his recommendation to send in American combat troops without a clear understanding of the nature of the insurgency. Most important, Taylor's report did not result in a range of choices for the President that would enable him to take a middle ground between a military and a political approach. In the end, Taylor too— knowing that Kennedy would be opposed to combat troops—threw in his lot with the interventionists. Combined with the intense lobbying from the President's other advisors to respond in a like manner to this crisis, Taylor's proposals left the President more isolated than ever before and under great pressure to intervene in Vietnam.

KENNEDY'S VIETNAM PROGRAM—NSAM-111

When Taylor returned on November 2, Washington was already in an uproar over the report he would make the next day. Kennedy was so shocked by Taylor's recommendation to send 8,000 combat troops to Vietnam that he recalled some copies of the final report.[47] Not even Walter McConaughy, the Assistant Secretary of State for Far Eastern Affairs, was permitted to read it. Because the Taylor report itself was less than explicit about what it called a "hard commitment to the ground," only those with access to the "eyes only" cables—Taylor, Rostow, McNamara, Rusk, and a handful of others—knew the truth.[48] That Taylor had recommended combat troops was a very closely held secret.

Kennedy reacted to the Taylor report by again planting misleading stories. They stated flatly that Kennedy was opposed to sending combat troops to Vietnam and strongly implied that Taylor had not recommended doing so. These stories, Halberstam noted, enhanced Taylor's reputation "and again gave the impression that he was different and better than other generals."[49]

On November 4, according to William Bundy's memoirs, at the very first NSC meeting after Taylor submitted his report, a "long and pointed" discussion ensued that foundered on the following point:

> Almost at once there was dissatisfaction with the half-in, half-out, nature of the "flood relief task force," and a consensus of disbelief that once thus engaged the U.S. could easily decide to pull the force out.[50]

The JCS opposed using military forces for purely psychological purposes, and McNamara argued the U.S. had to decide first whether it wanted to make a "Berlin-type" commitment to Vietnam. U. Alexis Johnson at State had long been advocating intervention; McNamara, Gilpatric, and the JCS at Defense;[51] and McGeorge Bundy,[52] Rostow,[53] Robert Johnson,[54] and Komer[55] at the NSC, all came on board in favor of it. Harriman[56] and Bowles[57] at State, as well as Galbraith, were opposed. Rusk was not against it but had reservations so long as Diem, whom Rusk called "a losing horse," remained in charge.[58]

In the middle of this debate, the U.S. intelligence community reversed itself on the key issue of a communist response to U.S. intervention. Whereas on October 10, SNIE 10-3-61 had argued that there would be no significant response from North Vietnam or China, a new SNIE issued on November 5 argued that U.S. intervention would bring about an offsetting increase in infiltration from North Vietnam, and that bombing North Vietnam would bring about a strong response from China and the Soviet Union.

It is unlikely that this intelligence estimate played a crucial role in Kennedy's final decision. The key NSC meeting took place on November 15, 1961, and featured a caustic and revealing exchange between General Lemnitzer and President Kennedy. It began with the President resisting arguments by Rusk and McNamara in favor of intervention:

> The President asked the Secretary of Defense if he would take action if SEATO did not exist and McNamara replied in the affirmative. The President asked for justification and Lemnitzer replied that the world would be divided in the area of Southeast Asia on the sea, in the air and in communications. He said communist conquest would deal a severe blow to freedom and extend communism to a great portion of the world. The President asked how he could

justify the proposed courses of action in Vietnam while at the same
time ignoring Cuba. General Lemnitzer hastened to add that the
JCS feel that even at this point the United States should go into
Cuba.[59]

This passage is a dramatic illustration of the fact that, for Kennedy, Saigon
was no Berlin. It illuminates the degree to which the President had become
isolated from the cold warriors demanding a similar commitment to Vietnam, and is a reminder of the lingering mutual animosity and grudges
that sprang from the debacle in Cuba.

Kennedy said he would make his decision after he talked with the
Vice President, who was not present, but Kennedy's decision was already made. There were more discussions, more memos, more pleas,
and when Rusk and McNamara saw the writing on the wall, they made
a joint effort to at least get a complete presidential commitment to Vietnam. This effort too was to no avail, and the final version of NSAM-
111, issued on November 22, contained no U.S. combat troops for
Vietnam, and no ultimate American guarantees to save Vietnam from
communism. In their place, Kennedy approved a significant increase in
American advisors and equipment. There Kennedy drew the line. He
would not go beyond it at any time during the rest of his presidency.
The main lesson of this climactic event is this: *Kennedy turned down
combat troops, not when the decision was clouded by ambiguities and contradictions in the reports from the battlefield, but when the battle was unequivocally desperate, when all concerned agreed that Vietnam's fate hung in the
balance, and when his principal advisors told him that vital U.S. interests
in the region and the world were at stake.*

What does this tell us, if anything, about Kennedy's resolve and his
aims in the larger U.S.-Soviet geostrategic struggle? What were his reasons
for rejecting the proposals of his most senior advisors? Kennedy's stand
in Berlin unquestionably demonstrated that he did not lack resolve, as his
stand in the Cuban missile crisis the following year would again make
abundantly clear. If his refusal to intervene was not a question of resolve,
what then? In the November 15 meeting it would appear that Kennedy's
arguments opposing intervention were based less on the inappropriateness
of such a response to the insurgency at hand, and more on his perception
that the American public and the Congress would not support such a
move. To his credit, however, Kennedy did say:

he could make a rather strong case against intervening in an area
10,000 miles away against 16,000 guerrillas with a native army of
200,000, where millions have been spent for years with no success.

While this observation may have gone to the heart of Diem's failure, the simple truth is that Kennedy lacked, as did his principal advisors, a clear understanding of the nature of the Vietnamese society, the nature of the insurgency there, and the reasons why these fundamental questions, if left unanswered, would swallow all the advisors and equipment he could muster to throw at the problem.

Kennedy deepened the American commitment consistently and considerably during 1961 without any adequate discussion of the problem. For the greater part of 1961 the energies of many key players were consumed in the parochial protection of vested interests and outright squabbling and scheming. The American commitment deepened in the process, but the new ideas and aid, which arrived intermittently, were incoherent, applied in an uncoordinated manner, and did little to influence the battlefield situation. The CIA Station Chief at the time, William Colby, has given an incisive and poignant account of this failure:

> I frankly gave more thought and effort to ensuring that the station would receive permission to continue the small—but, I thought, promising—projects we had started than to outlining my fundamental strategy for Vietnam. Unfortunately, this was the attitude of most of the other participants in the process. The result, therefore, was more a laundry list of the desires of the individual agencies involved than a basic review of our situation in Vietnam and of the strategic direction we should take in the future.

Moreover, Colby says of Kennedy:

> He had not articulated any very solid expression of his own ideas or strategy. Consequently, we had produced an agglomeration of the preferences of all the agencies involved, devoid of any strategic concept or inspiration.[60]

The consequence of this haphazard and nearsighted American policy in Vietnam was business as usual in Saigon and the unchecked growth of the insurgency in the countryside. When Kennedy's program—an increase in advisors—finally emerged in unequivocal terms at the end of his first year, the insurgency was probably already beyond the capacity of an advisory approach to check it. About the only thing one could point to that matched the steady growth of the communists in Vietnam was the steady growth in the struggle over Vietnam policy in Washington and Saigon.

THE THANKSGIVING DAY MASSACRE

By the end of November 1961, Kennedy finally got around to the unsavory business of putting people out to pasture. The personnel changes of
November 26 became widely known as the "Thanksgiving Day Massacre."
Their roots went back at least as far as the fallout from the Bay of Pigs
fiasco earlier in the year. The final reorganization carried out at the State
Department and Central Intelligence Agency between November 26 and
29 occurred in the wake of Kennedy's major decision on Vietnam, NSAM-
111, promulgated on November 22, 1961. The underlying dynamic of the
"massacre" was the lack of compliance in the government with Kennedy's
decisions. Sorensen goes so far as to argue that Kennedy was discouraged
with the State Department right from the beginning. It was never clear
to the President, he states, who was in charge, "and why his own policy
line seemed consistently to be altered or evaded."[61] The battle over Vietnam policy in the fall of 1961 was the final catalyst that spurred these
changes. Kennedy designed this restructuring to do more than bring
additional New Frontiersmen into the State Department. Given the deep
division between the President and his advisors over intervention in Vietnam, it was inevitable that some of the key job changes placed officials
who agreed with the President into those assignments with the most
influence over Vietnam policy.

The two major changes at the State Department were the appointments
of George Ball to replace Bowles, in the number two spot as Under
Secretary, and Averell Harriman to take McConaughy's place as Assistant
Secretary of State for Far Eastern Affairs. Ball's former number three
position, the Second Under Secretary of State, was filled by George
McGhee, but for political instead of economic affairs. McGhee's old job,
Chairman of the Department's Policy Planning Council, was slated to be
filled by Rostow after the first of the year. Rostow's deputy, Robert
Johnson, would go with him to State. Brooks Hays replaced Rostow as
the President's Special Assistant, while Frederick Dutton took Hays' old
job at State as Assistant Secretary for Congressional Relations. The move
of Rostow was fortunate for two reasons—his hawkish views were not
shared by the President—and his economic expertise and global perspective could be better used in the Policy Planning Council. This reorganization of the administration left McGeorge Bundy as the lone heavyweight
on Vietnam in the White House.

The removal of Bowles and McConaughy deserves comment. There is
some irony in the fact that Kennedy "liked Bowles, liked most of his ideas
and liked most of his personnel recommendations."[62] The real problem
at State had been the mismatch between McConaughy and U. Alexis

Johnson. With respect to Vietnam policy, McConaughy, as the Assistant Secretary for Far Eastern Affairs, should have overshadowed Johnson, the Deputy Under Secretary for Political Affairs. Just the reverse was the case, however, as the Department's policy initiatives were being driven by Johnson, who, like Rostow, was a leading proponent for introducing combat forces in Vietnam. The problem, then, was one of management, but Kennedy did not want to remove his Secretary of State, Rusk. Bowles' firing was a signal from the President that he wanted better team management at State, and George Ball was the logical choice to replace him. In addition, Ball was acceptable to Kennedy because he too opposed sending U.S. combat troops to Vietnam.

However, the *real news* at State was Harriman's appointment as the Assistant Secretary for Far Eastern Affairs *and* the decision *not* to allow U. Alexis Johnson to move into the number three job vacated by his boss, George Ball. McGhee was moved from the Policy Planning Council to fill this spot—Under Secretary for Political Affairs. McGhee's views against sending combat troops were emphatically delivered in a memo to Rusk the day after his appointment. McGhee warned that sending U.S. combat troops to Vietnam would lead to pressures to attack North Vietnam and from there "into a widening conflict which might be hard to terminate short of an all-out struggle with [Beijing]."[63] The outcome of the Thanksgiving Day Massacre, therefore, was to keep the number two and three slots out of the hands of the interventionists, while, at the same time, bringing in Harriman, whose presence neutralized U. Alexis Johnson.

While Roger Hilsman was left in place as head of State's intelligence organization (INR), the long-anticipated shake-up at the apex of the intelligence community—the CIA—was finally executed. Two days after the "massacre" at the State Department, Kennedy gave a very short speech in the Cabinet Room in the White House at the swearing in of John McCone as the new CIA Director. The firing of Allen Dulles and his deputy, Charles Cabell, was the direct consequence of the Cuban debacle, but McCone's ceremony was timed to coincide with the purge at State, and the President's remarks resonated throughout the CIA. He limited his remarks to just four sentences, and the last one was a clear warning: "We want to welcome you here and to say that you are now living on the bull's-eye, and I welcome you to that spot."[64] The threatening way in which Kennedy likened the CIA to a big target could not have been lost on McCone—or the rest of the agency for that matter.

In the midst of implementing these important personnel moves, Kennedy demanded, on November 27, that someone step forward and take personal responsibility for carrying out his Vietnam policy. The person who emerged that day as Kennedy's point man on the Vietnam War was Robert Strange McNamara.

NOTES

1. Nolting cable to State, No. 457, October 9, 1961, JFK Library, NSF, Country File, Vietnam, Box 194.

2. State cable to Saigon, No. 408, October 10, 1962, *Declassified Documents*, RC, 792C.

3. From an October 13, 1961, Saigon Embassy cable to State, in *PP*, Gravel ed., vol. 2, pp. 651–52.

4. SNIE 53-2-61: "Bloc Support of the Communist Effort Against the Government of Vietnam," *Declassified Documents*, 1978, D141.

5. SNIE 10-3-61: "Probable Communist Reactions to Certain SEATO Undertakings in South Vietnam," *Declassified Documents*, 1984, 95.

6. "Concept for Intervention in Vietnam," October 11, 1961, JFK Library, NSF, Country File, Vietnam, Box 194.

7. *State History*, 1961, p. 343, n. 2.

8. Lemnitzer memo to McGarr, October 11, 1961; see *State History*, 1961, p. 343, n. 2.

9. Glipatric, memo for record, October 11, 1961, *PP*, DOD ed., Book 11, pp. 322–23.

10. NSAM-104, *PP*, DOD ed., Book 11, p. 328.

11. These concerned producing a white paper on North Vietnamese aggression and possible protests to the International Control Commission (ICC) and the United Nations.

12. Halberstam, *The Best and the Brightest*, p. 172.

13. Draft Instructions, as written by Taylor, October 11, 1961, in *State History*, 1961, Document 157, pp. 345–46.

14. The only record we have of the meeting is in an October 13, 1961, message from General Lemnitzer to Admiral Felt; see *State History*, 1961, Document 163, pp. 362–63.

15. For the text see Maxwell Taylor, *Swords and Plowshares*, pp. 225–26.

16. Kennedy, *Public Papers*, 1961, p. 656.

17. *PP*, Gravel ed., vol. 2, p. 82.

18. Ibid.; Karnow, *Vietnam*, p. 251; and Gibbons, *The U.S. Government and the Vietnam War*, vol. 2, p. 71.

19. October 12, 1961, buck slip, "Re attached itinerary," Hoover Institution, Lansdale Papers, Box 36.

20. October 12, 1961, buck slip, "General Taylor's office phoned . . . ," Hoover Institution, Lansdale Papers, Box 36.

21. Lansdale letter to General Williams, October 13, 1961, Hoover Institution, Williams Papers, Box 20.

22. This reconstruction is based on William Rust's account of the meeting; see Rust, *Kennedy in Vietnam*, p. 44.

23. Maxwell Taylor, *Swords and Plowshares*, p. 227.

24. Rostow, *The Diffusion of Power*, p. 274.

25. Lansdale letter to General Williams, October 13, 1961, Hoover Institution, Williams Papers, Box 20.

26. Rostow, *The Diffusion of Power*, p. 274.

27. Halberstam, *The Best and the Brightest*, p. 164.

28. Rust, *Kennedy in Vietnam*, p. 45.

29. Lansdale letter to General Williams, November 28, 1961, Hoover Institution, Williams Papers, Box 20.

30. Rust, *Kennedy in Vietnam*, p. 45.

31. Ibid., p. 46.

32. Maxwell Taylor, *Swords and Plowshares*, p. 232.

33. Robert Johnson memo to McGeorge Bundy, November 1, 1961, JFK Library, NSF, Country File, Vietnam, Box 194.

34. Halberstam, *The Best and the Brightest*, p. 169.

35. For the text of these cables see *PP*, Gravel ed., vol. 2, pp. 85–91. For excerpts of the Taylor report see pp. 93–98. For the entire Taylor report, see JFK Library, NSF, Country File, Vietnam, Box 301.

36. *Meet the Press*, March 31, 1968.

37. NBC News White Paper, "Death of Diem," December 22, 1971, Part 1.

38. *PP*, DOD ed., Book 11, pp. 339–40.

39. Halberstam, *The Best and the Brightest*, pp. 162–79. Actually, Halberstam erred in his first attempt to analyze the report in 1964, and thought Taylor did not recommend combat troops; see Halberstam, *The Making of a Quagmire* (New York: Random House, 1964), p. 67.

40. "Paper Prepared by the Taylor Mission," October 18, 1961, in *State History*, 1961, Document 173, pp. 388–90.

41. Lansdale memo to Taylor, October 23, 1961, in *State History*, 1961, Document 185, pp. 418–20.

42. Rust, *Kennedy in Vietnam*, p. 45.

43. Lansdale letter to Williams, October 10, 1964, Hoover Institution, Williams Papers, Box 20.

44. Kahin, *Intervention*, p. 136.

45. Andrew Krepinevich, *The Army and Vietnam* (Baltimore: Johns Hopkins University Press, 1986) p. 61.

46. Colby, interview with the author, October 29, 1987.

47. Halberstam, *The Best and the Brightest*, p. 169.

48. *PP*, Gravel ed., vol. 2, p. 102.

49. Halberstam, *The Best and the Brightest*, p. 177.

50. William Bundy, unpublished manuscript, pp. 22–23.

51. Memo to JFK signed by McNamara, Gilpatric, and the JCS, November 8, 1961, in *PP*, Gravel ed., vol. 2, pp. 108–9.

52. McGeorge Bundy memo to JFK, November 15, 1961, JFK Library, NSF, Country File, Vietnam, Box 195.

53. Rostow memo to JFK, November 14, 1961, JFK Library, NSF, Country File, Vietnam, Box 195.

54. Robert Johnson memo to Rostow, November 14, 1961, JFK Library, NSF, Country File, Vietnam, Box 195.

55. Komer memo to McGeorge Bundy, October 31, 1961, JFK Library, NSF, Regional Security SEA, Box 231A.

56. Harriman memo to JFK, November 11, 1961, JFK Library, NSF, Country File, Vietnam, Box 195.

57. Bowles, *Promises to Keep* pp. 408–9.

58. *PP*, Gravel ed., vol. 2, p. 105.

59. Notes on National Security Council Meeting 15, November 1961, LBJ Library, VP Security File, Box 4.

60. Colby, *Lost Victory*, pp. 107–13. As the CIA Station Chief in Saigon, he also participated in several of the Washington meetings of late April and early May 1961.

61. Sorensen, *Kennedy*, p. 287.

62. Ibid., p. 288.

63. Memorandum From the Under Secretary-Designate for Political Affairs (McGhee) to the Secretary of State, November 27, 1961, in *State History*, 1961, Document 283, p. 672.

64. Kennedy, remarks at the swearing in of John McCone, Central Intelligence Agency, November 29, 1961, *Public Papers*, 1961, p. 490.

CHAPTER EIGHT

MCNAMARA TAKES CHARGE

"MYSELF AND L"

On November 27 an unusual meeting took place in the White House.[1] It was a meeting on Vietnam, ostensibly arranged by Taylor, with a curious assortment of people in attendance. Allen Dulles, on his last official day as CIA Director, was there, but his replacement, McCone, was not; Lansdale, now in charge of anti-Castro operations—code-named Mongoose—was also in attendance; Agency for International Development Administrator Fowler Hamilton, and Bureau of the Budget Director David Bell were on hand. From the NSC staff there was McGeorge Bundy and Walt Rostow, who was moving on to a different job at State. From State there were Rusk and U. Alexis Johnson, but the new number two and three men—Ball and McGhee—were absent, as were Harriman and Hilsman. From Defense there were three: McNamara, Lemnitzer, and William Bundy. And, finally, there was Taylor himself, whose role as Vietnam architect would disappear as a result of this meeting. The Vice President was not there.

Kennedy was not there yet, and the talk rambled on about the problem of Diem. U. Alexis Johnson said Diem would not accept a sweeping reorganization of his government. State's proposal was to send Lansdale out as "an explainer" of the U.S. position in order to clear things up.

Lansdale wrote to Hangin' Sam the next day that the idea was that the U.S. could not help win the war as long as a "dictator" was in power.[2] Taylor and Rostow claimed this idea wasn't one of theirs, although, Lansdale added, "I'm suspicious." He interpreted the trip proposal in this way: "So, one of the thoughts being ginned up is that I go over as his personal advisor and, presumably, clobber him from up close." Lansdale claimed that in the meeting he "pointed out that this was a duty without any honor and I'd be damned if I'd do that." Lemnitzer's notes of the meeting show that after Lansdale finished talking Rusk suggested Nolting be recalled if the next round of talks with Diem were unproductive. The discussion continued for a moment or two, and then the President entered the room.

Rusk began to recapitulate the conversation up to that point. Uninterested, Kennedy turned to Lansdale. Does "our program make sense?" he asked him. "Yes," Lansdale replied, but there could be misunderstanding about what "should be cleared up," he said, with calculated ambiguity. After a brief question on a report being prepared in State,[3] Kennedy suddenly unloaded his frustration over the lack of support for his Vietnam policy. The rest of the meeting was short and electrifying. "When policy is decided on," Kennedy declared, "people on the spot must support it or get out." Coming after the "massacre" of the previous day, the effect of this comment could not have been lost on those present who still had jobs. The President was not finished; he ordered that there be "wholehearted support" for his decisions, and demanded to know who, at the Defense Department, would personally be responsible for carrying out his Vietnam program.

Those whom Taylor had invited to this meeting had reason to anticipate Kennedy's question. Taylor had sent a memorandum informing them that the President had two questions about the "organization in Washington":

(1) Have State-Defense agreed upon the division of responsibilities for the implementation of the new program?

(2) Whom should the President regard as personally responsible for the effectiveness of the Washington end of this operation? (NOTE: The President wishes a proposal to meet this point, having in mind an individual to be identified with this program as Mr. Kohler has been for Berlin.)[4]

McNamara, prepared, answered the question. "Myself and L," he replied, the "L" referring to Lemnitzer. McNamara was just being kind to Lemnitzer, who would be replaced soon by Taylor as Chairman of the JCS. This exchange is another of the more significant details that have faded with time. In June 1965, when McNamara was asked what he thought about scornful references to "McNamara's War," he answered that in a November 1961 conversation with the President, he had "volunteered to look after the war."[5] Several works on the Vietnam conflict have noted this comment but all have missed the fact that McNamara was responding to a demand Kennedy put to his advisors for personal responsibility, a demand coupled with the explicit threat that anyone who did not support his policy should "get out." The President had, on November 22, set the limits to U.S. participation in the war, and, on November 26, approved a sweeping change of personnel in the government charged with implementing that policy. Finally, in this meeting, he called his top advisors to the White House to discuss what lay ahead and identified the man who would be personally responsible for executing this effort.

At that moment the baton for Vietnam policy had passed from Taylor to McNamara, and the Secretary of Defense had an enormously complicated mess to straighten out. Kennedy's decision to kill the proposal for introducing U.S. combat forces into Vietnam left the bureaucracy that had planned it in disarray. There were many problems ahead, but the two most vexing were Diem—who had been banking on U.S. intervention—and U.S. military arrangements on the ground in Vietnam. These arrangements too had been based on the assumption of U.S. intervention, and some, without authorization from Washington, had already been put in place.

NOLTING'S HEADACHES

For its part, the State Department now had the difficult task of implementing a policy that had not been foreseen, namely, to convince Diem to implement reforms in the absence of a clear-cut American commitment to Vietnam. Nolting cabled Rusk on November 22 that a "very sad and very disappointed" Diem was brooding over the situation. Diem's reaction was relayed through Thuan and then through Nolting to State:

> US asking great concessions of [South Vietnamese government] in realm [of] its sovereignty, in exchange for little additional help; that this is [a] great disappointment after discussions with General Taylor involving, in particular, [the] concept of Delta task force; [and] that Diem seemed to wonder whether US was getting ready to back out of Vietnam as, he suggested, we had done in Laos.[6]

The Taylor plan for combat forces under a flood relief cover had seemed to Diem the only way to both save the country *and* preserve his own political position by avoiding the appearance of massive direct American intervention.

Kennedy's decision was a severe blow to Diem. He had planned to bring together his Cabinet and selected members of the Assembly to discuss what Kennedy would propose after Taylor's return. Diem had consulted with them during the Taylor visit and they were enthusiastic about bringing in U.S. combat forces. Diem now argued that the contrast between the arrangements discussed then and the new U.S. position was "too striking," and said he was hesitant to put the American position— meaning reforms without the assurance of U.S. troops—before his cabinet ministers for fear they would "lose heart."[7]

For the Americans, the prospect of an uncooperative Diem was unsettling. On November 22 three American ships packed full of men and equipment had set sail for Vietnam, and were due to arrive in Saigon at the end of the first week in December. But what if no agreement from Diem had been received by then? Despite warnings that Diem would never implement the proposed reforms, on November 22 NSAM-111 had been finalized and the ships dispatched. One military historian has observed that the reason McNamara approved all of these military moves so quickly is that he assumed Diem would "formally agree later" to the U.S. program.[8] It was developing into a very awkward situation. Nolting began stalling for time in Saigon, saying Diem could not be pushed too fast, while at the November 27 White House meeting Rusk was already talking about recalling Nolting if Diem did not come around immediately. As the three American ships laden with helicopters and 430 U.S. servicemen steamed full ahead toward Vietnam, a first-class diplomatic and public relations dilemma was in the making.

If Diem would not cooperate, the only alternative appeared to be to divert the ships. Accordingly, State had informed Nolting as early as November 25 that the decision on whether ships would proceed directly to Saigon would depend on the outcome of his negotiations with Diem.[9] Even if the Diem problem was solved, final decisions still had to be reached quickly on how to handle the International Control Commission (ICC)[10] and the press. In the interim, the requirements for secrecy left Nolting sitting on a bombshell in Saigon.

Two hours after the November 27 White House meeting at which McNamara took charge of Vietnam policy, Rusk sent a cable to Nolting demanding cooperation from Diem.[11] It directed Nolting to engage in a "frontal effort" to disabuse Diem of his "misinterpretation" of the new U.S. proposals. Rusk listed again all of the "crucial elements" of the required reforms, saying it was "essential" that Diem make some symbolic moves "especially for international and American public opinion," such as putting a friendly labor leader in some government post or letting some political prisoners out of jail. In charging the Ambassador with this unhappy mission, Rusk left no room to wiggle. He told Nolting to "promptly return to Washington" if his discussions were unsatisfactory, and to pass on this warning to Diem. Wringing reforms out of Diem, however, was only one of Nolting's headaches. For Diem was not the only one in Saigon who was caught off guard by Kennedy's November decisions. So was the U.S. Air Force, as Ambassador Nolting found out to his surprise.

The November Kennedy decisions derailed military arrangements that had been anticipated and, in the case of the U.S. Air Force, that had already been confidently implemented. American Farm Gate T-28 and SC-47 (Jungle Jim) aircraft that had begun arriving at Than Son Nhut airport near Saigon as early as November 16 had been placed under a new Air Force command, the 2d ADVON (Advance Echelon).[12] While Farm Gate had a training mission controlled by the MAAG, the Air Force's Pacific Command (PACAF) argued that Farm Gate "had a second mission of combat operations." Since MAAGs are not permitted by law to command operational forces, and the new U.S. combat command—anticipated *prior* to November 22—would take time to put into place, PACAF wanted an advanced echelon of the Pacific 13th Air Force activated in Saigon, and Admiral Felt (CINCPAC) had authorized it.

The American pilots were told they could conduct combat operations *while* training the Vietnamese. This was what General LeMay himself had told the Farm Gate detachment commander, Colonel King.[13] There was no misunderstanding that these arrangements for combat were getting ahead of the game; on the contrary, getting on with the job and letting the paperwork catch up afterward was the idea. This meant, however, that the "appearance" of a new American Air Force combat command in Vietnam would have to be temporarily disguised. This was easily achieved by having the MAAG Air Force Section Chief, Brigadier General Roland Anthis, also function as the commander for the new command—the 2d ADVON. In this latter function, Anthis would not report to General McGarr (MAAG), but directly to PACAF's 13th Air Force.

Anthis took control of four Farm Gate detachments, one of them the 2d ADVON staff itself, *before the Kennedy decisions promulgated in NSAM-111*. Anthis assumed command on November 20, sharing space with the MAAG Air Force section in the Brink Hotel in downtown Saigon. It was an audacious move by PACAF and Admiral Felt, but it should be reemphasized here that they were counting on Kennedy approving a U.S. ground combat role in Vietnam, a role that would require U.S. bombers and close air support to protect the troops. The command arrangements might well have gone unnoticed for some time, except that Anthis made a decision that brought them to light.

Unaware of the turn of events in the White House, General Anthis decided to move 2d ADVON to a location more convenient for controlling his operating units—into a building next to the headquarters of the Vietnamese Air Force on the air base at Tan Son Nhut. His new Vietnamese Air Force neighbors had not heard about any new U.S. Air Force command, and were naturally "puzzled by Anthis' presence."[14] In Anthis' estimation, he commanded all American operational air forces in Vietnam, including Jungle Jim forces, the air control and warning unit, the units scheduled to arrive for defoliant operations, and even some units in Thailand as well. However, in view of the deliberate attempt to avoid the appearance of a new command, his decision to move his headquarters to Tan Son Nhut was surprising. Perhaps even more surprised than the Vietnamese Air Force was the American Ambassador.

The problem for Nolting—and everyone else in Saigon—after November 22, was that he still wasn't sure just *what* had been decided back in Washington. On that day he had sent a long list of items he needed clarified. When he discovered Anthis' new headquarters two days later, Nolting still had not heard back from State, which was, at that very moment, reeling from the "massacre" at the hands of Kennedy. Nolting was angry when he discovered what Anthis was up to—it was at the least both an illegal and presumptuous operation. Yet Nolting was also puzzled and perhaps confused because he had no way of knowing how high up the decision to form 2d ADVON had been made. Consequently, Nolting directed Anthis to delay further expansion of 2d ADVON until clarification was received from Washington.

The explanation for all of the confusion was quite simple: in Washington Kennedy had shattered the plans for American intervention and now Nolting was picking up the pieces in Saigon. He cabled Rusk on November 25 explaining what he had learned "yesterday" from Anthis. He was careful to state that he had no beef with Anthis and that he was not "specifically" objecting to the 2d ADVON, but protested that he found it "incomprehensible" that a new U.S. military headquarters could be established in Vietnam without consulting either himself or the government there.[15] Nolting asked for a "precise understanding" that any "combat or quasi-combat operations" carried out by 2d ADVON be cleared in advance by him. He signed off with the words "please instruct urgently."

When Admiral Felt caught wind of Nolting's protest, he suddenly decided, after a "fresh study," not to call 2d ADVON a new "headquarters," but simply a "facility." He instructed Anthis to return to his MAAG office and "conduct his advance echelon business" through Detachment 7 in

Saigon.[16] This was not an order to cease combat operations, but simply a way to lower visibility. At this point, the story takes an even more remarkable turn. Anthis became obdurate, and simply refused to see the Farm Gate commander in charge of the air strikes, Colonel King, when he asked for clarification. King was seen instead by the 2d ADVON operations officer, who "speculated" that it was unlikely Farm Gate would be cleared even for daylight combat. However, King, who was a long way from Washington, did things his own way:

> King's officers then borrowed several aerial flares from the Vietnamese, pressed an SC-47 into service for improvised flaredrops, and under the illumination made strike passes with their T-28s. Colonel King went back to Saigon and reported that his unit could make night attacks.[17]

All Nolting's actions had produced, then, was a prohibition on American air strikes during daylight. He also tried tattling on Anthis' new organization to the South Vietnamese, but was informed their government had no objection to 2d ADVON.

What happened next is typical of how events on opposite sides of the planet can become entangled as messages literally pass each other en route. Felt instructed General McGarr to calm Nolting down; McGarr waited one day—probably to get the story straight with Anthis—and then met with Nolting on the 28th. Nolting immediately sent a cable to State saying McGarr had explained that 2d ADVON was not a headquarters "at this time" but might be later after "certain" covert operations were authorized. Nolting added he was also told "we may if asked deny publicly and officially" to the South Vietnamese government that any new U.S. command and headquarters had been established in Vietnam.[18] Nolting asked the Department if all of this was correct, and added, perhaps with some irritation, that he would "appreciate" advance notice of plans to initiate "covert operations" using 2d ADVON.

Only hours before Nolting sat down in Saigon to write this cable, Kennedy had delivered his order for people to comply with his policy or get out. It was just two hours after this meeting that Rusk cabled Nolting with a demand for cooperation from Diem, and four minutes after that cable another one was sent to Nolting with the answer to his original November 25 question about 2d ADVON. Nolting was in the process of signing his own cable, acknowledging his understanding of a covert operations role for 2d ADVON, when he was handed both of the cables from State. The one on 2d ADVON directed that "no public information should be volunteered" about it, that McGarr had been told to explain it fully to him (which, of course, had just taken place), that no new command

or headquarters had been authorized, and that the status of 2d ADVON
was "undetermined pending prerequisite high level Washington decisions."[19] After reading this, Nolting tacked an additional line onto his
new cable saying: "Matter satisfactorily resolved." Resolved for the time
being at Nolting's level, perhaps, but not in Washington. The thorny
question of U.S. air strikes, like many others, would now fall on the desk
of Robert McNamara.

The day was not over in Saigon, however, and before long Nolting
was on the wire again with another cable relaying still another of his many
headaches: the approaching American ships.[20] The November 28 issue of
Pacific Stars and Stripes had printed a story saying the Military Sea Transport Service (MSTS) had confirmed that the ships had set sail the previous
Tuesday for Saigon carrying new U.S. troops and helicopters. The MAAG
and Embassy cables about the ships had all been sent at the secret or top
secret level due to the classified nature of the activity and the fact that no
agreement had been reached with Diem. This MSTS confirmation to the
press was a serious security breach at the worst possible time. The MSTS
had also been sending cables about the ships' movements and contents in
the clear. Two had been received by the American Naval attaché in the
Saigon Embassy, the first asking for diplomatic clearance for one of the
ships, the *Core*, to dock and unload in Saigon, and the second one discussing the *Core*'s sailing orders.

Nolting relayed all of this disturbing news to Washington, along with
reassurance that he would not permit the Naval attaché to request clearance from the Vietnamese "until I have been advised that movement of
helicopter companies to South Viet Nam has been finally approved." His
cable prompted a short but emphatic two-sentence cable, sent that same
evening, from the State Department, to all concerned agencies. It read:

> Supercedes all previous messages. Do not give other than routine
> cooperation to correspondents on coverage [of] current military
> activities in Vietnam. [Make] No comment at all on classified activi-
> ties."[21]

The fact was that the men and equipment aboard the approaching ships
were a major breach of the 1954 Geneva Accords, and even though the
U.S. was not technically a signatory to them, the Eisenhower administration had stayed within their terms. Kennedy was naturally nervous about
public knowledge that he was going beyond them.

The year 1961 had been a year of failure for American policy, while
the insurgency expanded and gained momentum. Now American policy
was moving at top speed, trying to make up for lost time, but without

careful attention to the problems of public disclosure and congressional involvement. In the confusion and hectic pace of decision making at this point, a reason always seemed to present itself for withholding this or that action from public view. The ultimate decision to keep the details of U.S. policy classified, however, was Kennedy's alone. These little secrets quickly accumulated and grew, like chambers in a hornet's nest.

By December 4, Nolting had managed to nurse Diem along to the point where he was prepared to offer some form of lip service to the U.S. demands for reform, the details of which Nolting relayed in a memo of understanding to Washington.[22] With the *Core* only a fews days away from Saigon and U.S. preparations for implementing the increased military effort gathering speed in Washington, Rusk decided this was the most that could be squeezed out of Diem. Accordingly, Nolting was informed that, while Diem had not "gone as far as we would like," the text of the memo of understanding was a "sufficient basis upon which to move ahead."[23] Nolting was told to arrange for an exchange of letters between Diem and Kennedy. Diem's letter, a request for increased U.S. aid, was publicly released, along with Kennedy's reply granting it, on December 15.[24] Diem's letter, which did not give any firm commitment for reforms, had actually been written in Washington.[25]

At this time, the State Department also decided how the new program would be justified publicly. The decision, which was cabled to Nolting on December 5, rejected the Ambassador's earlier November 21 proposal to "further develop" the U.S. position on the Geneva Accords, by which he had meant redefining the troops ceiling so that Washington could be "more direct and forthright about increased U.S. military personnel in Vietnam."[26] State told Nolting that a sudden increase in the ceiling from 888 to 3,500 men would cast "serious doubt" on U.S. credibility, "would impress no one and would not redound to our credit."[27] Instead, the new program would be justified on the grounds that Hanoi had first breached the Accords. When the North Vietnamese "end their aggressive acts and resume their observance of [the] Geneva Accords, these measures of support can be terminated," the public would be told. In order to advertise Hanoi's aggression, Rusk held a press conference on December 8 to announce the release of a report entitled "A Threat to the Peace: North Vietnam's Effort to Conquer South Vietnam."[28]

By mid-December, then, the twin problems of public justification and Diem's response to the new Kennedy commitments had been handled— juggled would be a more apt description—to the extent that they no longer posed a threat to proceeding with implementation of the new U.S. program. There remained one final issue to resolve: the new American command structure for Vietnam.

"AHEAD FULL BLAST"

Ambassador Nolting was not the only one who was anxious to know how the terms of NSAM-111 would be translated into actions. By approving that NSAM, Kennedy had authorized immediate actions to "provide such new terms of reference, reorganization and additional personnel for United States military forces as are required for increased United States military assistance" to Vietnam.[29] Actually, the Joint Chiefs had, at McNamara's direction, been working on these actions, particularly the new command arrangements, before NSAM-111 was approved. The NSAM's provisions on the new terms of reference for the military were identical to those of the joint State-Defense memorandum tabled at the key November 11 NSC meeting at which the NSAM was first discussed.[30] *What McNamara and the Joint Chiefs did not know and had not anticipated as that meeting broke up was that the key provision of the joint memorandum—to commit U.S. combat forces to Vietnam—would be disapproved by the President a week later.*

Two days after the November 11 meeting, McNamara, still anticipating a decision to commit U.S. combat forces, had sent Lemnitzer two memos. The first[31] was a general order to press "forward with all possible speed" on all the actions listed in paragraph 3 of the joint memorandum.[32] McNamara now singled out one of these actions for special attention, and it was that action that was the subject of the second memo to Lemnitzer.[33] In it McNamara asked for the "earliest possible" recommendations along with a draft order from the Joint Chiefs on a new command structure for South Vietnam. McNamara wanted a new U.S. commander to assume responsibility for all activities, including intelligence operations, and to "report directly to the JCS and thence to me for all operational purposes." By dropping CINCPAC out of the chain of command, McNamara was attempting to keep control as close to himself as possible. He also solicited personal recommendations from the Chiefs as to who this new commander would be. Finally, the Secretary wanted to know which organization and people in the Joint Staff (under the JCS) would keep tabs on "the operation" for the Chiefs and himself, and directed that they should expect to send reports to the President "on a twice-a-week basis until further notice."

McNamara had asked, "for obvious reasons," that this matter be kept quiet. Preparing for full-fledged intervention in Vietnam and organizing it as a theater of war reporting straight to the Chiefs was a sensitive matter, especially since the President had not yet rendered any decision. He said that he would personally handle the necessary discussions with the State Department. By the time the Joint Chiefs responded to McNamara on

November 22,[34] Kennedy had already shot down the proposal to send U.S. combat troops to Vietnam. Apparently referring to Kennedy's rejection as "current guidance as to the nature of the mission and the magnitude of US forces to be assigned to the new command," the Chiefs ruled out two of the three command structures they had been considering. These two were a unified command under the JCS and a joint task force under the JCS, both of which were tantamount, like McNamara's, to setting up a war theater of operations, structures clearly unwarranted in view of Kennedy's decision.

The JCS proposed the creation of a unified subordinate command under CINCPAC "similar to those already established in Korea, Taiwan and Japan," which would have service component commanders and would be over the existing MAAG. The command's title was to be "United States Forces, Vietnam (USFV)," and the commander's title "COMUS Vietnam." The commander would have "operational" command over all U.S. forces in Vietnam, including the MAAG, and report directly to CINCPAC. He would also be "co-equal" to the U.S. Ambassador as far as his status in country was concerned.

Since Kennedy had ruled out intervention, the JCS proposal meant that the new person in charge would be mainly a titular commander. He would be in direct command of the operational side of the effort—which would now be small—and have only *indirect* command over the principal and far larger advisory effort. Even though subordinate to the new commander, the MAAG Chief would still have direct control over most of the U.S. forces in Vietnam. The JCS appear to have followed McNamara's instructions to keep their plans quiet, as Nolting's November 22 cable, asking what was meant by the new terms of reference, indicates. One person who was informed was Taylor,[35] and he used his knowledge of the situation and his position as Kennedy's closest military advisor to preserve as much authority as possible for the new job. This he did because he expected the assignment to go to his old friend and protégé, General Paul D. Harkins.

Meanwhile, on November 27, McNamara, having just "volunteered" to take care of Vietnam for the President, returned to the Pentagon and laid out a plan of attack in a meeting that night. He cabled this plan to Felt and McGarr the following day.[36] He said the situation in Vietnam was "obviously causing great concern" in Washington, and that he would be keeping "continuous personal contact" with the situation, starting with "a first meeting" at Pacific Command headquarters in Hawaii on December 16. The uncertainty of Diem's position and doubts about his willingness to reform "must not prevent us from going ahead full blast . . . on all possible actions short of [the] large scale introduction of U.S. combat forces." The timing of implementing these actions would be affected by political developments, he said, "but we cannot let this slow down our making all necessary preparations and movements." He had already reached a "series of decisions," which would be sent directly.

OPERATION BEEF-UP

These decisions became known collectively as Operation Beef-Up,[37] a comprehensive package of military actions taken to step up the war effort in South Vietnam. The first Beef-Up report listed every one of these actions along with the status and future required decisions for each. It reveals the extensive nature of the new American equipment and technology sent to Vietnam as well as details on the servicemen who began to arrive in large numbers to operate and maintain the equipment and train the South Vietnamese.

McNamara approved the deployment of the 8th and 57th U.S. Army Light Helicopter Companies, with maintenance detachments, all of which had departed San Francisco on board the *Core* on November 22 and were scheduled to arrive in Saigon on December 10. A third company was alerted for action and expected to be ready by December 15. Each company was equipped with twenty-two helicopters (twenty H-21s and two H-13s in each company).[38] These helicopters would give the South Vietnamese Army a mobility it had not known before and, indeed, the helicopter was destined to play a major role in the war. Fifteen T-28C light aviation Navy planes were put aboard the *Core* to be given temporarily to South Vietnam's Air Force until the arrival of thirty modified T-28B (NOMAD) planes in March 1962. Two U.S. Air Force mobile training teams were formed and expected to arrive in Saigon on December 5 to begin training the Vietnamese to fly and maintain these aircraft. McNamara also approved the provision of nine L-20 light observation aircraft to the South Vietnamese Air Force, and these were expected to be available by January 1.

CINCPAC was already reviewing the need to augment the Pacific Air Force transportation capability with a new unit in South Vietnam,[39] and for air reconnaissance and photography had activated Project Able Mable at Don Muang air base in Thailand on November 11. Able Mable consisted of four RF-101 aircraft flying missions over South Vietnam and Laos, with a photo-processing element in Saigon for the film from the missions over Vietnam. Thought was being given to augmenting the sixty-seven U.S. Air Force servicemen operating the surveillance and height-finding radar at Tan Son Nhut airfield near Saigon with 300 more

USAF personnel, to establish a limited Tactical Air Control System (TACS).[40]

The CIA took the lead in planning actions to improve the political intelligence system. To improve military intelligence several plans were being developed by the JCS. These included a Joint Intelligence Group (JIG) under the Vietnamese Joint General Staff and operated with U.S. guidance; augmentation of Vietnamese intelligence organs and the MAAG intelligence (J-2) section with more people; and the establishment of a separate counterintelligence organization in the South Vietnamese Army.[41]

A series of actions was directed to improve Vietnamese naval planning, operations, logistics, and intelligence, but the emphasis here was on more efficient utilization of available resources. The MAAG was given the lead in these matters, while the JCS accelerated the development of plans for coastal surveillance and control and other U.S. and South Vietnamese naval force requirements. Measures to expedite training and equipping of the Vietnamese Civil Guard (CG) and Self Defense Corps (SDC) were also directed, including new U.S. weapons and equipment and 207 more American advisors.[42]

McNamara approved 734 additional personnel for the MAAG, mostly military advisors, all of whom were to be phased in prior to March 31, 1962.[43] On the matter of the new command structure, however, lips were still sealed in the Pentagon, and the Beef-Up paper only noted that the JCS had submitted recommendations for a new subordinate unified commander. The Beef-Up report listed two actions under the heading "Collateral Actions Pending or Approved." The first was defoliant operations, which, it said, were being considered by the State Department. Some military preparations for defoliation had already been made, including the installation of equipment on Vietnamese aircraft, the delivery of chemicals to Saigon, planning for delivery of more chemicals, and the reconfiguration of six American C-123 aircraft for defoliant operations.[44]

The other "collateral" action was the final deployment of all Jungle Jim aircraft and full utilization of this detachment. As of November 22, eight T-28s and four SC-47s had arrived at Bien Hoa airfield in South Vietnam, while the remaining four RB-26s in Taiwan were being modified, the reason for which has been sanitized from the Beef-Up report now available for use by scholars. Presumably the aircraft were being configured for combat operations of some sort. The report noted that McNamara had approved an advisory and training function for Jungle Jim; that these missions were being executed; that the USAF personnel were in uniform; and that the planes had Vietnamese markings. Their combat role was, of course, a sensitive subject, and a sore one with Ambassador Nolting. It would dominate McNamara's first meeting with his Pacific commanders.

THE FIRST SECDEF CONFERENCE

On December 16, 1961, Secretary McNamara arrived in Honolulu to convene the first of eight SECDEF conferences he would hold on the Vietnam War during the Kennedy presidency. Admiral Felt hosted the meeting in his CINCPAC headquarters at Camp Smith, Honolulu, and William Bundy and General Lemnitzer accompanied McNamara from the Pentagon, while Nolting and General McGarr also flew in from Saigon. That not all was yet in place to permit the new Kennedy program to proceed was evident from the outset early in the morning. Disagreements over agenda item number five, command relationships for the new American military structure, caused this item to be dropped from the formal proceedings.[45] McNamara, Nolting, and Felt met privately to discuss the festering command problem.[46]

At the conference opening, McNamara announced his intention to have these SECDEF conferences once a month for the next three months, and set forth the following three tenets:

c. We have great authority from the President.
d. Money is no object.
e. The one restriction is [that] combat troops will not be introduced.[47]

Point e came through loud and clear. A memo by Felt's Political Advisor, Edwin Martin, who attended, states, "The Secretary at the outset stressed that the primary effort of the U.S. military establishment was behind South Vietnam and that we could have practically anything we wanted short of combat troops."[48]

Kennedy's decision against U.S. ground forces, of course, did not settle the issue of what Air Force combat operations might be permissible, whether incidental to training missions, or direct air combat in support of Vietnamese ground and air operations. In fact, the decision against U.S. ground combat forces tended to heighten the importance of U.S. air operations, as they were the principal means left for directly harnessing U.S. firepower to South Vietnamese military operations. McNamara apparently viewed the need for U.S. air combat operations as crucial enough to approve them himself at the conference, prior to having resolved with Rusk and Kennedy the new command structure required for such operations.

Prior to the SECDEF conference the combat role of Farm Gate had been contentious. To begin with, the Jungle Jim personnel, known as "air commandos" at their home (Elgin) air base in Florida, had been specially selected after intense physical training and psychiatric screening. The result, however, according to Futrell's Air Force history, was a group not "mentally attuned to teaching members of other cultures or in fact to perform a training mission—they were combat-oriented."[49] Their air commando uniforms—an Australian bush hat, fatigues, and combat boots—had been personally picked by General LeMay. Many proved unable to work with Asian officers, says Furtrell, and this did not lend itself well to the training part of their mission.

Secondly, the controversy over their mission and lack of combat had lowered morale, says Futrell. Consequently, when Admiral Felt had ordered PACAF's General O'Donnell to "ready" plans for operations on December 4, O'Donnell went beyond this and immediately authorized Farm Gate to fly combat missions as long as one South Vietnamese was on board the aircraft being used.[50] Two days later, the JCS approved combat missions under the same restriction.[51] On December 8, Felt had approved the activation of a tactical air control system, paving the way for the start of the operation. The draft plan of the 13th Air Force submitted on December 10 makes it clear that both "advisory and training" and "combat actions" in support of the South Vietnamese were to be conducted. Nolting, however, put a damper on these plans by issuing an order on December 15 that no combat missions of any kind could be flown without his prior consent.

Thus by the time of the SECDEF conference the issue of air combat had been boiling for some time. Felt was obviously unhappy with Nolting's constraints, and he argued at the conference that Farm Gate should not wait for "tailor-made" jobs. Although Felt was careful to frame his argument in terms of training, his point seems to have been that combat incidental to training missions could not, in any practical sense, be cleared with Nolting before the missions occurred. Discussion on agenda item number four, "The status of plans to achieve United States objectives in Vietnam," resulted in the go-ahead for U.S. air combat in the war on the basis of a verbal statement by McNamara. Jungle Jim (Farm Gate), he said, "is to be used for *training and operational missions* in South Vietnam with Vietnamese riding in the rear seats" [emphasis added].[52]

McNamara's decree made Felt's discourse on incidental combat academic: the Secretary reiterated his approval of combat missions with a Vietnamese aboard, and directed Felt to monitor such flights closely and use them only for "important jobs." Nolting's order was thus obsolete less than twenty-four hours after he had rendered it. Four days after the conference, Felt informed PACAF that, besides training Vietnamese, they could conduct "all kinds of conventional combat and combat support flights" as long as a Vietnamese was along for the ride.[53]

The next incident in the history of U.S. air combat in the war episode deserves special attention. Although McNamara took it upon himself to approve U.S. air combat operations in the war, thought still had to be given on how to approach the President on this matter. A plan was developed—by whom it is not clear—to be carried out by a combination of State Department status reports and General Taylor. We know about this from a December 19 memo to Taylor from his Military Assistant, Worth Bagley. An obscure footnote in the official State Department history describes the contents of the Bagley memo to Taylor:

> the Embassy in Saigon was being told to delay the start of Jungle Jim operations with US-[South Vietnamese government] crews until December 22. In the meantime the Department of State, in transmitting the December 21 status report on Vietnam to the President, would inform him that the combined crew operations in Jungle Jim aircraft would begin soon. According to Bagley, "If there is no reaction from the White House, Saigon will be given an affirmative answer. Mr. Bundy is aware of this procedure which I gather is an agreed approach to avoid pinning down the President."[54]

The plan was executed on December 21: Taylor sent the State Department weekly status report to the President in Bermuda, where he was meeting with British Prime Minister Macmillan.[55] Taylor's cover memo informed Kennedy that among the units soon to enter into active operations were "Jungle Jim aircraft on combat missions with combined U.S.-[South Vietnamese government] crews aboard as part of combat crew training requirements. The aircraft will bear [South Vietnamese government] markings." The President did not react. U.S. air combat in Vietnam could now proceed.

It is interesting to see how this policy was actually implemented in Vietnam itself. Prior to the conference, U.S. crews were flying combat missions alone under the proviso that these missions were only those the Vietnamese were unable to perform. Farm Gate detachment Commander Colonel King had secured pure combat missions—that is, not training associated—by proving the American T-28s and B-26s could fly night missions, missions that, for a variety of reasons, the South Vietnamese were not able to perform. Since the Viet Cong operated mostly at night in any case, the need for such flights was obvious. The new rear seat rule "surprised and disappointed" Colonel King. He later admitted he had resisted the new instructions, received from the 2d ADVON commander, General Anthis, and questioned defiantly whether the backseat training was a "cover for combat or the primary mission."[56] This requirement was "grudgingly" implemented, and the Vietnamese liked riding in the rear seats even less than the Americans liked having them there. "Backseat combat training," according to the Air Force history, "was more political than practical."[57]

Taylor's December 21 cover memo to Kennedy also pointed out that the two U.S. helicopter companies, which had just arrived in Vietnam on December 11, would be "operational on December 25 and January 5." The President did not react to this either, but one may wonder what his reaction might have been if instead he had been reading the memo that Martin, Felt's Political Advisor, sent to State's Cottrell; that memo said: "U.S. transport aircraft such as the C-123s and the helicopter companies are being sent to SVN for combat support activities, not for 'taxi service.' "[58] Actually, the source of this comment was McNamara himself, and he had made it to underscore that his single objective was "to win the battle."[59] Both Lemnitzer and McNamara "brought a sense of immediacy to the conference," said Martin; "they wanted concrete actions that would begin to show results in 30 days. They were not interested in projects to be completed in 1963."[60]

On December 19, at a meeting of the National Security Council, General Lemnitzer gave a brief report to Kennedy on the first SECDEF conference. The only surviving record of his remarks are notes prepared by Vice President Johnson's military assistant, Air Force Colonel Howard Burris.[61] Burris wrote that "Lemnitzer reported certain details of the meeting which he and Secretary McNamara had at Honolulu with Nolting, McGarr and Felt." Burris' choice of the words "certain details" was an allusive way of telling the Vice President that Lemnitzer had not told the President other important details about the conference. To make sure Johnson knew what "details" Lemnitzer had not disclosed to the President, Burris added the following parenthetical sentence:

> (He did not mention Secretary McNamara's principal statement at the meeting to the effect that the United States had made the decision to pursue the Vietnam affair with vigor and that all reasonable amounts of resources could be placed at the disposal of the commanders in the area.)

It was a curious omission by Lemnitzer, almost as though he didn't want the President to know what they were actually doing. Obviously Burris thought it was significant enough to point out to Johnson. What Kennedy did not know about he did not have to disapprove.

LEMAY'S LAMENT

In retrospect, it is worth noting that McNamara's position inherently denied the basic argument the JCS had been making all along, namely, that in order to win, U.S. combat troops were necessary. McNamara was saying, in effect, that the U.S. was going to win without sending combat troops. On this point Martin's memo is particularly incisive: "In closing the conference [McNamara] said our job was to win in South Viet Nam, and if we weren't winning to tell him what was needed to win."

Many in the U.S. military felt Kennedy's program would not be sufficient to defeat the Viet Cong. General LeMay was particularly upset. He later claimed that none of the Joint Chiefs at the time believed the program was "anything except some diplomatic fiddling around" with a little more aid.[62] On December 5, the Joint Chiefs met to discuss the situation. LeMay described both the proposals of McNamara and Rusk and the measures finally approved by Kennedy as inadequate.[63] He argued the Secretaries of State and Defense had obscured, played down, or otherwise delayed the decisive actions necessary to combat the communist threat to the United States. LeMay was anxious to defeat the communists in Southeast Asia, which in his view was the best place for a showdown. He reasoned that "U.S. military intervention in Southeast Asia, *including the use of nuclear weapons*, could be followed by many layers of escalation before the ultimate confrontation would occur" [emphasis added].[64]

The December 5 JCS meeting itself, as well as LeMay's indignation, appear curiously out of place in retrospect. After all, the President had listened to interventionist proposals for the previous eight months, not just on Vietnam, but on Cuba and Laos as well. His answer on Vietnam was no, an answer he cast in concrete on November 22 and followed up with key personnel changes at State to enforce it. Nevertheless, LeMay apparently did not regard the matter as finished. At the December 5 meeting he urged the Joint Chiefs to pressure the President again to deploy substantial U.S. forces in Vietnam. LeMay wanted the Chiefs to press for a "high-level" accord that would produce a "clear statement of U.S. objectives," and to tell McNamara "timely, positive military actions are essential." The forces he had in mind included an Army brigade task force, a Marine division accompanied by an air wing, and three tactical Air Force units: a fighter squadron, a bomber squadron, and a reconnaissance task force. Nothing less than these forces, he argued, would prevent the loss of South Vietnam and "ultimately of Southeast Asia."

The upshot of the meeting was a decision by the Joint Chiefs to have the Joint Strategic Survey Council examine the rationale for deploying

U.S. troops to South Vietnam. This council was composed of senior officers free from the constraints of daily decisions and supposedly capable of taking a detached view of politicomilitary issues.[65] Their dispassionate conclusions were rendered in just forty-eight hours. Their report argued that the deteriorating military situation and "tenuous character" of South Vietnam's government made it "imperative that the United States government take the initiative." They urged the dispatch of combat forces by the United States and its Asian allies, and a "military command and modus operandi in South Vietnam which will assure loyalty and maximum combat effectiveness in the campaign against the communists." The Joint Strategic Council report also had this to say about Kennedy's advisory program: "The recently authorized measures, even when implemented, will prove to be inadequate."

On January 13, 1962, the Joint Chiefs sent to the President their most strongly worded memo yet on the strategic importance of Southeast Asia, and Vietnam in particular.[66] Ostensibly written by Lemnitzer for McNamara, the Chiefs asked McNamara to send it on to Kennedy. This McNamara did, along with his own comment that he did not endorse it.[67] The memo was extraordinary. In it the Chiefs described the stakes in Vietnam as incredibly high, and said they had done all they could under the restraints of the President's program. They then offered their views, in emphatic and foreboding language, as to what should be done should his program fail. Their solution, of course, was to send U.S. combat troops to Vietnam, and since it was their last discourse on this subject until after Kennedy's death, it will be examined in detail.

Since the prevention of communist domination in South Vietnam was an "unalterable objective" of the United States, the Chiefs began, the military objective "must be to take expeditiously all actions necessary to defeat communist aggression" there. The Chiefs stated categorically that "the fall of South Vietnam to communist control would mean the eventual communist domination of all of the Southeast Asian mainland." Air access to 5,300 miles of mainland coastline would be "lost to us," they said, U.S. allies and neutral India would be "outflanked," and the last significant British military strength in Asia would be "eliminated" with the loss of Singapore and Malaya. Then all of the Indonesian archipelago could come under Soviet "domination," and "would become a communist base posing a threat against Australia and New Zealand." The "Sino-Soviet Bloc" would get control of the eastern access to the Indian Ocean, and the Philippines and Japan could be pressured to assume "at best, a neutralist role," eliminating "two of our major bases of defense in the Western Pacific." After painting this grim picture of the long chain of dominoes that would fall if Vietnam were lost, the Chiefs said they wished to "reaffirm their position" that the U.S. "must prevent" the loss of all these areas and extend its influence "in such a manner as to negate the possibility of any future communist encroachment."

The Chiefs then turned to the problems with the President's program, pointing out that they had already implemented or authorized all of the recommended courses of action in keeping with his decision that "we must advise and support South Vietnam but not at this time engage unilaterally in combat." Unfortunately, they said, U.S. aid was "not being properly employed by the South Vietnamese government and major portions of the agreement have either not been carried out or are being delayed by Diem." One thing the Chiefs did not recommend, however, was to get rid of Diem. They said achieving U.S. objectives would be more difficult without him than with him, and argued that a "strong approach" be made to Diem to establish a "satisfactory basis for cooperation." Otherwise, they predicted the "failure of our joint efforts to save Vietnam from communist conquest."

Their point was not to ask what to do if Vietnam fell to the communists because of Diem. What they really wanted to talk about was what to do if Diem cooperated and Kennedy's plan still failed. The Chiefs granted, in one brief sentence, that "vigorous prosecution of the campaign with current and planned assets could reverse the current trend." But what if this failed? Their comments were both lengthy and pointed. If Diem cooperated fully and South Vietnam's armed forces were used effectively, they said, and the Viet Cong was still not brought under control, then they saw "no alternative to the introduction of U.S. military combat forces along with those forces of the free Asian nations that can be persuaded to participate." In any consideration arising from unacceptable results obtained despite Diem's full cooperation, the Chiefs asked that:

> you again consider the recommendation provided you by JCSM-320-61, dated 10 May 1961, that a decision be made to deploy suitable U.S. forces to South Vietnam. . . . We are of the opinion that failure to do so under such circumstances will merely extend the date when such action must be taken and will make our ultimate task proportionately more difficult.

The Chiefs' position boiled down to this: if Diem didn't cooperate the program *would* fail; if Diem did cooperate the program *could* succeed; but it might not, in which case the U.S. *must* commit combat troops. The very idea of the Chiefs sending the President a memo saying they wanted to send combat troops if Diem cooperated and the program still failed was audacious and even presumptuous. The Chiefs were not asking for a decision. Their only purpose seems to have been to register a curious sort of protest for the record, saying: Vietnam is a vital U.S. interest; we told you a year ago to send combat troops, but you didn't listen; we've done everything you asked for in your program and if it falls apart we still want to send in combat troops; and if you fail to do it then, it will only make our job more difficult when we have to do it anyway.

NOTES

1. *State History*, 1961, Document 285 and n., pp. 675–76. Lemnitzer's notes (Document 285) indicate the President skipped the early part of the meeting. Lemnitzer's notes are all that remain of the meeting, a meeting that the President's log indicates was off the record.

2. Lansdale letter to Williams, Hoover Institution, Williams Papers, Box 20.

3. A report was being prepared by William Jorden to document North Vietnamese aggression and to use this report to justify the new U.S. moves under consideration.

4. Memorandum from Taylor to participants, Subject: Meeting on Southeast Asia, 5:30 P.M., November 27, 1961, JFK Library, Newman Papers and NSF Regional Security File, SEA, Box 231A.

5. Henry Graff, *The Tuesday Cabinet: Deliberation and Decision on Peace and War Under Lyndon B. Johnson* (Englewood Cliffs, NJ: Prentice-Hall, 1970), p. 35. This particular interview of McNamara by Graff took place in June 1965.

6. Embassy Saigon telegram to Department of State, November 22, 1961, in *State History*, 1961, Document 270, pp. 649–52.

7. Ibid.

8. *Air Force History*, p. 93.

9. State cable to Saigon, No. 683, November 25, 1961, JFK Library, NSF, Country File, Vietnam, Box 195.

10. The ICC was a watchdog organization looking for violations of the 1954 Geneva Accords.

11. Telegram From the Department of State to the Embassy in Vietnam, No. 693, November 27, 1961, pp. 676–77, in *State History*, 1961, Document 286.

12. *Air Force History*, p. 81.

13. Ibid., p. 82.

14. Ibid., p. 95.

15. *State History*, 1961, Document 277, pp. 665–66.

16. *Air Force History*, p. 95.

17. Ibid., p. 96.

18. Saigon cable to State, No. 722, November 28, 1961. JFK Library, Newman Papers and NSF Country File, Vietnam, Box 195.

19. Telegram From the Department of State to the Embassy in Vietnam, November 27, 1961, p. 678, in *State History*, 1961 Document 287.

20. Embassy, Saigon, cable to State, No. 723, November 28, 1961. JFK Library, NSF, Country File, Vietnam, Box 195.

21. State cable to Saigon, No. 698, November 28, 1961. JFK Library, NSF, Country File, Vietnam, Box 195.

22. The things Diem had apparently agreed to were contained in a Memorandum of Understanding Nolting transmitted back to State on December 4 (see *State History*, 1961, pp. 714–16, Document 307). Other than innocuous things like reactivating a GVN Internal Security Council, doing "joint" provincial surveys, making a Border Ranger Force, coordinating military activities involving U.S. personnel, and accepting U.S. advisors in government organs on a "case-by-case" basis, the memo was vague. The provision for reorganization of the Vietnamese military command only stated that the GVN saw this move as necessary and would "consult" with the U.S. about it. The provisions for reforms to win public support at home and abroad simply listed several past actions and some "prompt measures" it would undertake that were either vague or very minor.

23. State cable to Embassy, Saigon, No. 725, December 4, 1961, in *State History*, 1961, pp. 712–13, Document 306.

24. For full texts of both, see Department of State *Bulletin*, January 1, 1962, in *State History*, 1962, pp. 13–14.

25. It had been sent to the Embassy in Saigon on November 15, 1961, See *State History*, 1961, Document 257, pp. 615–18.

26. Nolting cable to State, November 21, 1961, in *State History*, 1961, Document 268, pp. 645–46.

27. State cable, to Embassy, Saigon, No. 729, December 5, 1961, in *State History*, 1961, Document 310, pp. 718–19.

28. Department of State *Bulletin*, December 25, 1961, in *State History* 1961, pp. 1053–59. This was also known as the "Jorden Report," Jorden (a member of the State Department's Policy Planning Council) having authored it.

29. *PP*, DOD ed., Book 11, p. 420.

30. *PP*, DOD ed., Book 11, pp. 359–67; see specifically p. 364, paragraph 3(f).

31. Memorandum From the Secretary of Defense (McNamara) to the Chairman of the Joint Chiefs of Staff (Lemnitzer), November 13, 1961, in *State History*, Document 246, p. 590.

32. Ibid. All ten of these actions appeared in identical language as the ten actions the U.S. was to carry out under the terms of NSAM-111.

33. Memorandum From the Secretary of Defense (McNamara) to the Chairman of the Joint Chiefs of Staff (Lemnitzer), November 13, 1961, in *State History*, 1961, Document 245, pp. 589–90.

34. Memorandum From the Joint Chiefs of Staff to the Secretary of Defense (McNamara), November 22, 1961, in *State History*, 1961, Document 271, pp. 652–55.

35. For example, the first copy of Beef-Up reports (see below), authored by the J-3 of the Joint Chiefs, is still extant and available in the JFK Library (NSF, Country File, Vietnam, Box 195), and was thus obviously sent to the White House through

Taylor's office. With respect to the command issue, it said that the JCS "have submitted recommendations" for a new subordinate unified commander. It is likely that Taylor knew most of the details.

36. Telegram From the Secretary of Defense (McNamara) to the Commander-in-Chief, Pacific (Felt), and the Chief of the Military Advisory Assistance Group in Vietnam (McGarr), November 28, 1961, in *State History*, 1961, Document 289, pp. 679–80.

37. PROJECT "BEEF-UP," Status Reports of the Military Actions Resulting from the NSC Meeting, November 11, 1961; Operations Directorate, J-3, Joint Chiefs of Staff, November 27, 1961, JFK Library, NSF Country File, Vietnam, Box 195. This was the first status report on Beef-Up, and has been "sanitized" for use by scholars, but its eleven pages are mostly intact and provide a fairly comprehensive list of actions taken by November 27 and those seen as required in the near future. The deletions occur in three places: 1) p. 4: a few words deleted in a passage related to improving signals intelligence (SIGINT) capabilities in South Vietnam; 2) p. 8: a six-line paragraph deleted in a section dealing with improvements in military intelligence; and 3) pp. 10–11: a few words (which from analyzing the context and using a ruler appear to be "combat," "for combat operations," and "combat" on page 11) in the section on Jungle Jim operations. The following account is taken entirely from that report.

38. Two actions still required with respect to these units were: a presidential decision prior to December 1 to off-load the *Core* in South Vietnam, and a decision by the Defense Secretary by the same date to deploy the third company.

39. For this a presidential decision was required for deployment.

40. In this regard, future anticipated actions were a JCS TACS feasibility study, and ultimately a decision to deploy personnel and equipment by the Defense Secretary.

41. Plans were also made to strengthen the U.S Intelligence Committee by increased participation by several agencies, but it is not clear whether the paragraph that was deleted next to the passage covering this was related to the Intelligence Committee or an additional action that had been taken. Three additional required intelligence actions were identified: agreement by the Vietnamese to allow U.S. participation in their intelligence operations, JCS approval for more U.S. intelligence personnel, and JCS recommendations on all of this to be furnished to McNamara by November 30.

42. An additional required action was seen as establishing an effective Vietnamese military command structure that could make better use of the CG and SDC.

43. CINCPAC had requested another 331 personnel be sent to MAAG by the end of September 1962, which would raise the MAAG total to 1,905. Actions required in order for these efforts to proceed were: agreement from Diem that he would keep his part of the bargain, and "determination of clearly defined US objectives to be pursued in South Viet Nam."

44. These aircraft were being held at Clark Air Base pending a decision to implement the defoliation program.

45. *State History*, 1961, Document 324, p. 739.

46. A copy of the 920-word draft State reply to McNamara was produced, and Nolting generally agreed with its thrust while criticizing the USFV concept. He launched into the by then familiar politics versus military question, arguing that the creation of a USFV would encourage the South Vietnamese to overemphasize the military side of the war and tempt them to play off the new commander against himself. (See Letter From the Political Advisor [Martin] of the Commander-in-Chief, Pacific, to the Director of the Vietnam Task Force, Cottrell, December 18, 1961, in *State History*, 1961, Document 326, pp. 743–44.) Nolting proposed sticking with the old task force concept. This referred to JTF (Joint Task Force) 116, a CINCPAC contingency plan for deployment to Vietnam that did not envision a USFV command. Admiral Felt took issue with Nolting. He supported the JCS-sponsored unified subordinate command concept "in light of an enlarged MAAG, PACAF units deployed into Vietnam, and the arrival of Army helicopter companies." (*Air Force History*, p. 94.) Felt produced a detailed table of personnel distribution, and recommended an Army general as the commander, and Air Force officers as the Chief of Staff, the J-2 (intelligence), and the J-5 (plans). In the end, the discussion produced no satisfactory resolution of the command problem. Felt's Political Advisor, Ed Martin, wrote to State's Cottrell afterward, "As far as I am aware this is the only agenda subject upon which there was a significant divergence of views between the Ambassador and the military side."

This divergence had to be resolved quickly. Some new form of command had to be established to avoid the development of an illegal operation in Vietnam. The United States Army Pacific (USARPAC), which, incidentally, desired a separate theater of operations in Vietnam removed from CINCPAC control, had acquiesced in the dual hatting of the MAAG Chief as the concurrent commander of U.S. forces. This had led to McGarr's assumption of operational control over Farm Gate training missions, but he could not legally command the U.S. Air Force combat missions being contemplated at the time. The sudden appearance and disappearance of 2d ADVON as an advanced command of the U.S. 13th Air Force in Saigon during November provided a rather dramatic symptom of this command problem.

47. Memorandum From the Chairman of the Joint Chiefs of Staff's Special Assistant (Parker) to the Chairman (Lemnitzer), December 18, 1961, in *State History*, 1961, Document 325, pp. 740–41.

48. *State History*, 1961, Document 326, p. 742.

49. *Air Force History*, p. 79.

50. Ibid., p. 82.

51. Ibid., pp. 82–83, cites JCS message to CINCPAC, December 6, 1961.

52. *Air Force History*, 1961, p. 83.

53. *Air Force History*, p. 83. cites CINCPAC message to PACAF of December 20, 1961.

54. *State History*, 1961, Document 334, p. 754, n. 3.

55. Telegram From the President's Military Representative (Taylor) to the President, at Bermuda, December 21, 1961, in *State History*, Document 334, p. 754.

56. *Air Force History*, p. 127.

57. Ibid.

58. *State History*, 1961, Document 326, p. 744.

59. *Air Force History*, p. 119, cites item 8-1 of the CINCPAC record of the conference.

60. *State History*, 1961, Document 326, p. 742.

61. LBJ Library, VP Security File, National Security Council II; see also *State History*, Document 329, 1961, pp. 746–47.

62. LeMay interview with Belden, March 29, 1972, in *Air Force History*, p. 91.

63. *Air Force History*, p. 90.

64. Ibid. *Air Force History* cites a November 13 Talking Paper on Determination of Effective U.S. Policy toward South Vietnam.

65. *Air Force History*, pp. 90–91.

66. *PP*, DOD ed., Book 12, pp. 448–54.

67. Ibid., p. 447.

PART III

THE DECEIVERS
AND THE DECEIVED

CHAPTER NINE

THE CREATION OF MACV

"VIETNAM'S YEAR OF DECISION IS 1962"

As things stood in January 1962, still one month before the creation of the Military Assistance Command, Vietnam (MACV), the reporting from the MAAG, the Joint Chiefs, and U.S. national intelligence estimates all agreed: the war was going badly. The reports emanating from the intelligence section of the United States Army Pacific Command (USARPAC) agreed too. Then an odd and important change occurred. To comprehend it, one must understand the way in which military information flowed. That means a brief word about the operational and intelligence chains of command in the Pacific theater is in order.

In military parlance, the Commander-in-Chief of the Pacific (CINCPAC), who rules from his roost in Honolulu, is in charge of a "unified command," meaning that unified under his authority are other commands. These other commands are from each branch of the Armed Forces, and are called "component commands," meaning that each one is a component, whether the Army, Navy, or Air Force component, under the parent—in this case Pacific—"unified command." For example, the Army component command under CINCPAC is USARPAC. So much for Honolulu, what about Saigon? After many arguments over who should be the parent organization for the new MACV, it was decided to put it under CINC-

PAC. Since MACV is under CINCPAC, it was called a "subordinate command."

All three organizations, CINCPAC, USARPAC, and MACV, had their own intelligence sections. MACV and USARPAC could talk to each other "laterally," so to speak, but both reported directly to CINCPAC. USARPAC's intelligence section, like MACV's, analyzed and reported on the battlefield situation in Vietnam. That it did so independently of MACV was fortunate, for, as shall be seen, a comparison of the reporting from these two intelligence elements yields invaluable insights into the history of the Vietnam War during 1962. MACV's intelligence section, however, would provide the key assessments of the battlefield relayed by CINCPAC to be read by all of official Washington. The USARPAC assessments, on the other hand, presented a completely different view of the war than MACV's, but they were rarely seen outside of Hawaii. The USARPAC Intelligence Bulletins, published on the first day of each month, were high-quality reports, based in part on raw data received directly from Army Security Agency units in Vietnam. That these reports were so different from MACV's is revealed for the first time in this work; *why* they were is a matter that will be returned to later.

Again, as the year opened, there was little doubt as to the moribund state of the war effort. The January 1 USARPAC Intelligence Bulletin said that, statistical ups and downs aside, Viet Cong operations were continuing at a "very high rate," and added "nothing indicates this trend might be reversed."[1] The report described a captured document taken from a Viet Cong agent on the outskirts of Saigon that suggested a recent slackening in large-scale communist attacks was "a lull before the storm." An apparent "guide to future Viet Cong policy," the captured document instructed all Viet Cong units in South Vietnam to anticipate "a large-scale operation in the near future." The USARPAC article added its view that the Viet Cong had "the power to launch such an operation."

The USARPAC intelligence analysts saw this upcoming operation as part of the enemy's long-range strategy, and said the communists were in no hurry. Things were already going well for the Viet Cong, and no significant changes in the pattern of their activity over the next six months was envisioned, except, perhaps, a gradual increase "in scope and tempo." The Bulletin predicted the certainty of "several large-scale attacks" to dramatize Diem's weaknesses and lower morale; it concluded, gloomily: "The year of 1961 decided the fate of Laos, and perhaps of all Indochina; Vietnam's year of decision is 1962."

The title of the lead article in the February 1 Bulletin continued to reflect unqualified pessimism about the battlefield situation: "Next Few Months May Determine South Vietnam's Fate," it announced.[2] "The war continues to drag on," the article said, and added, "the nation's fate is precarious." A review of the casualty figures for all of 1961 was ominous: Viet Cong casualties were set at 19,000, up 50 percent from 1960, while government casualties were set at 12,000, up 100 percent from 1960. Communist military activity in January was surging. Except for one large-scale operation against a Self Defense Corps outpost, Viet Cong activity had been a multitude of company-level attacks—of about eighty guerrillas each—against predominantly paramilitary units, isolated outposts, and convoys. Although the full statistics were not yet available, the article estimated that "total Viet Cong incidents for January will exceed the previous all-time high, recorded in October 1961."

The situation around the capital was becoming increasingly precarious. Noting "growing Viet Cong control in the provinces surrounding Saigon," the article said, "this may indicate a strategic effort to isolate the capital." The first six months of 1962 "are extremely critical," the article warned, and forecast that the communist military and political campaign "will increase unless the national counterinsurgency effort becomes more effective than is now indicated." It would have been going too far for the author to say bluntly what he really meant: the administration's Vietnam policy had been a flop so far, and the insurgency was out of control. Indeed, the deteriorating battlefield situation and what to do about it was the focus of McNamara's second conference on the war.

JANUARY 15—THE SECOND SECDEF CONFERENCE

The first item on the agenda of the second SECDEF conference was a review of the enemy situation. On this subject, Major Von Romberg, from CINCPAC, gave an alarming presentation.[3] Hard-core Viet Cong strength was up to 20,000 to 25,000, Romberg said, and growing at a rate of 1,000 per month—after combat losses. That very month Walt Rostow addressed a key tenet of counterinsurgency theory that bore directly on the enemy statistics Romberg presented to McNamara. In the January 1962 edition of the *Marine Corps Gazette*, a respected and widely read military journal, Rostow opined that a ten-to-one superiority on the part of the counterinsurgent force was the minimum requirement for success.[4] "As you know, it takes somewhere between 10 and 20 soldiers to control one guerrilla in an organized operation," Rostow said. Taking even the low end of this formulation, a ten-to-one ratio in forces, and the low end of Romberg's enemy strength estimate, 20,000 enemy troops, a regular South Vietnamese force of 200,000 was required. Diem was having trouble building his army up to 170,000, let alone 200,000. Moreover, with a Viet Cong expansion of 1,000 men per month, the South Vietnamese Army would have to expand at 10,000 men per month just to keep pace, a clearly impossible task. What the enemy statistics meant was that the insurgency was fast careening out of control, and McNamara did not forget them.

Recent reporting, Romberg said, showed increased Viet Cong strength in Tay Ninh, Binh Duong, and Long An provinces, all three astride or near Saigon. This meant the communists could conduct large-scale operations in the Saigon area, he said, implying that not only the capital was threatened, but the U.S. Air Force and intelligence facilities at nearby Bien Hoa as well. The usual pattern of small attacks was continuing "at a fairly high level," and he attributed the decrease in large-scale attacks to the possibility that the three Viet Cong interprovincial zone commanders were attending a "strategy conference" in Hanoi. The conclusion that the Viet Cong could attack "in force strengths of 1,000 to 1,500 at places and times of their own choosing," Romberg said, "remains valid."

In light of this situation, there was naturally a great urgency in McNamara's comments and orders at the conference.[5] He was anxious to speed up the arrival of U.S. advisors, and said he wanted to "get them out to Vietnam as fast as they could be processed in Washington, even though the Vietnamese units to which they were to be assigned were not yet ready to receive them." Romberg told McNamara that the SDC was absorbing most of the casualties—over 1,000 in the previous month alone. This could indicate that the Viet Cong recognized that the SDC was a threat to their influence at the village level, Romberg said, and also that the VC saw the SDC as a "softer" target and better source of weapons than the South Vietnamese Army. This touched off "considerable discussion," which ended with McNamara declaring that the order of priority for the expansion and training of forces should be the Civil Guard, the Self Defense Corps, and then the South Vietnamese Army. He then told those present that he wanted their recommendations "by the next meeting."

McNamara's impatience led to a key flaw in his judgment. In Romberg's brief on the enemy situation he had noted that the largest enemy operation of the month involved the capture of a fifty-one-man SDC outpost. He pointed out in his brief on the second agenda item, South Vietnam government actions, that the Viet Cong saw the SDC as an easy source of weapons. Yet McNamara was determined "to get carbines into the hands of the SDC as soon as possible." So he removed the requirement for a twelve-week training course before such weapons could be issued to an SDC unit, and directed instead that the weapons be issued following a "preliminary training phase just sufficient" to teach them how to use them. In addition, McNamara authorized the immediate shipment of 40,000 more carbines to Vietnam, over and above the 37,000 already on hand, to be used by any military or paramilitary units that could properly use them. In this unusual manner, the quick arming of the vulnerable and inexperienced SDC outposts was decided upon in less than five minutes at a SECDEF conference. Before the end of the year, U.S. advisors would be referring to these SDC outposts as "VC supply points."

McNamara wanted fast results. As he had at the first SECDEF conference, he pressed for a clearing and holding operation in a single province. The concept behind a "clear and hold operation" was to first clear a populated area with the regular army and then hold it with the local civic action teams and paramilitary forces. McGarr outlined his plan for Zone D, a traditional communist stronghold in Phuoc Thanh Province, but McNamara objected because this province, being heavily forested and sparsely populated, had little in it to hold. McGarr's plan appeared to be a purely conventional military action, lacking the important paramilitary and political components of the clear-and-hold concept. McGarr was focused on killing the enemy: he would take two South Vietnamese divisions and "clean them out."[6] William Bundy, who was watching McGarr's performance in disbelief, recalls it this way: "He presented a sort of arrowed here they are dug in . . . and here's where we go and swing around them and we go clobbety-clobber to here and there and everywhere" kind of briefing.[7] Bundy passed McNamara a note saying, "This man is insane."[8] While McGarr delivered this "WWII map exercise," McNamara read Bundy's note, nodded, and whispered, "Burn that." McNamara sent McGarr back to the drawing board with instructions to come up with a plan "where permanent results can be achieved."

Admiral Felt's Political Advisor, Edward Martin, attended the conference and wrote afterward about the inability of the South Vietnamese Army to do what McNamara was asking:

> It does not yet appear capable of clearing and holding a substantial key area (such as the province of Binh Duong) without drawing off military forces from other areas to an unacceptable degree. It must reach at least this level of capability before the tide will turn.

McNamara's plans for the South Vietnamese Army were beyond its means to carry them out, and while Martin's notes indicate an awareness of that fact, there is no record of anyone telling McNamara this, either verbally or in memoranda. Nor were any objections voiced by the experts and commanders in attendance when McNamara ordered the flow of U.S. weapons to the very point where the Viet Cong were collecting them with the most success. How do we account for this breakdown in communication? Did those present fail to understand the SDC problem at this point? Or is it possible that the style of the Secretary of Defense was too domineering to encourage the give-and-take necessary?

Whatever the reason, the strategy for arming and utilizing the available military forces in South Vietnam that emerged from the second SECDEF conference was woefully misguided because basic questions were not asked. Moreover, once again, no one posed the most fundamental questions of all about the nature of the insurgency: Why were the Viet Cong winning? And, had the size of the insurgency already moved beyond the means of the South Vietnamese Army to cope with it?

DISUNITY OF EFFORT

While McNamara was personally leading the war-planning effort in Honolulu, in Washington Kennedy was trying to unify the diverse elements—which he had helped to create—that had a potential role in counterinsurgency. On January 18, he issued NSAM-124, which created a new organization, whose purpose he spelled out in the first sentence:

> To assure unity of effort and the use of all available resources
> with maximum effectiveness in preventing and resisting subversive
> insurgency and related forms of indirect aggression in friendly
> countries, a Special Group (Counter-Insurgency) is estab-
> lished . . . .[9]

In an annex to this NSAM Kennedy added, "I hereby assign to the cognizance of the Special Group (Counter-Insurgency) the following countries: Laos, South Vietnam, and Thailand." Kennedy named Taylor as the Special Group's chairman, then listed the other members, beginning with his brother, Robert Kennedy, and including Lemnitzer and McCone.[10]

The Special Group's charter was so broad that it was almost impossible to achieve. Kennedy assigned the group four major functions: 1) to insure that counterinsurgency was given the same recognition as conventional warfare; 2) to insure that this was reflected in doctrine, strategy, and tactics; 3) to review the adequacy of U.S. resources to deal with insurgencies; and 4) to insure the development of adequate interdepartmental programs to deal with them. The military did not take counterinsurgency seriously and the administration's effort in Vietnam was anything but unified. In his incisive work *The Army and Vietnam*, Andrew Krepinevich captures the essence of the Army's problem with counterinsurgency: this type of conflict challenged the very foundations upon which the Army's approach to war rested.[11] When the Army's advisors discovered this in the field and revolted against the old methods, their efforts were no match for the deep-seated conventional mind-set of the leadership. This subject still provokes lively discussion in the classrooms of the Army's Command and Staff College, and likely will for some time.

In January 1961 the measures in NSAM-124 seemed reasonable to Kennedy, but the fact is that his call was itself a little too late in the game. His final decision on an approach to the war—NSAM-111 of November 22, 1961—should have been the result of the ambitious process he was now attempting to put in place. This group, created by NSAM-124, should have been hard at work *months before* he decided on a final course of action, not two months afterward. NSAM-111 was fundamentally a compromise born of division, an escalation of the advisory commitment carried out under severe pressure to respond with conventional U.S. forces. As such, Kennedy's policy was more of a reaction against using combat troops than a well-coordinated political, economic, and social response to the problems in Vietnam. Although he sometimes talked about these problems, the "full blast ahead" approach being implemented by McNamara was not a thoughtful or effective response based on a clear-cut analysis of the nature and scope of the insurgency. In short, it was not the kind of response that NSAM-124 was supposed to bring about.

The unity of effort Kennedy sought to achieve by issuing NSAMs like 124 was a sorely needed but elusive goal. The Vietnam Task Force, officials in the State Department and the Pentagon, and General McGarr in Saigon each pushed their own viewpoints and programs. This problem of disjointed programs was apparent to some officials. In a January 11 memo to Rostow, Robert Johnson (both men were now at State) complained about the disparate character of Vietnam planning. He said that despite pressure from many people, "Washington still did not, as of last week, have a clear picture of what kind of economic programs are planned . . . to complement the new military and political effort."[12] "Somehow," he said, "the Task Force needs to get hold of the economic program and attempt to make some sense of it."

In fact the Vietnam Task Force had just issued an "Outline Plan of Counterinsurgency Operations" two days earlier,[13] and it was a model of vagary and generalization. The "overall concept" was to preserve South Vietnamese government control where it existed, designated in the report as "white" areas, and to restore it where it had broken down, designated as "pink" and "red" areas. For "military counterinsurgency operations" the reader was simply referred to a MAAG document. "Political, socio-economic and psychological counterinsurgency measures at the local and village level," the report stated in a blinding flash of the obvious, "will vary in nature depending upon the degree of security in a given area." Political measures listed included "steps" (unspecified) to improve compensation, selection, and training of local officials; a continued training program (unspecified) for district officials; and the establishment of "advisory councils of notables" at the village level. "These steps appear practical only in white and pink areas," the report said, "and can be extended to red areas only as they are made whiter."

In the socioeconomic field, the report continued, expansion and acceleration of "regular" village-level programs (unspecified) in areas now white or "light pink" should be "conducted" (unspecified as to how) so the people would see that the government offered the hope of improved living standards. In addition, there should be "special programs" in areas where "regular programs" would not "operate." These would include "rural reconstruction teams" (no program specified); "special military task forces consisting of military civic action and psychological warfare teams and protecting teams" (no specified program); "similar 'hit-and-run' civic action operations" (unspecified); and a "special impact" (unspecified) "flying-doctor program."

Needless to say, the red-pink-white approach to counterinsurgency did not win many converts in Washington or Saigon. In a major demarche in early February, Roger Hilsman, Director of State's Bureau of Intelligence and Research (INR), argued there was an "immediate" need for a better understanding of "the strategic concept for counterinsurgency war" among working-level Americans in Washington and Saigon.[14] The "top United States leadership," he said, "is rapidly developing knowledge of the strategic concepts" for guerrilla warfare. The problem, he said, was to communicate it to the working-level people, people who "do not always work as a team." Hilsman's report seems to have been aimed at the leadership, using the rather transparent tactic of praising them while blaming minor officials. Furthermore, his references to the recommendations "in the Taylor report" and to what "General Taylor says" were designed to massage the ego of the second most powerful person in the White House.

What Hilsman's strategic concept boiled down to was cutting off the Viet Cong from the people by securing strategic villages. Once a village was defended, the adjacent village would be added, and these expanded into zones especially selected to protect the more populated areas in the country. A strategic village would be created by "a regroupment of village hamlets into one compact, easily defended area." In addition, a line of "defended villages," similar to strategic villages (i.e., a regroupment of hamlets), would be created on the periphery of Viet Cong–controlled areas. Local forces would do the defending, freeing the regular army forces for operations against Viet Cong main forces. The concept of defending villages with local forces was not new. The essence of Hilsman's plan was to string these together in densely populated areas in order to push the Viet Cong away from the majority of the population.

Hilsman had no idea that Diem and McGarr had already decided on a plan to build an infrastructure of "defended" villages, a plan that would undercut Hilsman's ideas completely. A memorandum for record detailing the Diem-McGarr discussion of the plan, which took place on January 12, was given to Ambassador Nolting;[15] but he never cabled its contents to Washington, and, if it went at all, it was hand-carried on some later trip. Whether the memo got to Washington or not, Hilsman never saw it and he would not learn of the Diem-McGarr plan until he traveled to Saigon in March.

The record of the lengthy January 12 Diem-McGarr meeting is revealing.[16] Diem remarked that the best way to successfully create a "defended" village infrastructure was to set up a village defense system in conjunction with "forced resettlement of the people to strategic or more densely populated areas," an "act of surgery," he said, that would "require a sizable military force." Such a resettlement was necessary, Diem said, to prevent the people from returning to the "bush." Diem felt strongly enough about resettling the peasants that he said this twice to Harkins. It was precisely this aspect of the subsequent Strategic Hamlet Program—forcing peasants off of their ancestral lands and into camps where their social fabric disintegrated—that contributed in a major way to its ultimate failure.

Hilsman's "Strategic Concept" was far more sophisticated than the Vietnam Task Force's red-pink-white plan, and Kennedy would soon approve it. At the same time, on February 3, the government of Vietnam proclaimed the Strategic Hamlet Program as national policy.[17] The spectacle of all these new plans being formulated in different places at this late stage is indicative of how far behind and out of step the administration was with the reality of the war. The fact that Diem and McGarr were busy negotiating measures that would undercut Hilsman's plan illustrates the disunity and lack of synchronization in the joint U.S.–South Vietnamese war effort. This problem of disunity proved to be intractable, and even the Special Group for Counterinsurgency was incapable of solving it. Yet this incoherence at the policy level drew only perfunctory attention because the bureaucracy was engaged in erecting an entirely new structure in Saigon, and doing so at breakneck speed. This effort too was disjointed and plagued by petty turf-oriented battles, and consequently took a full two months to complete. One of the issues in this effort was who would command the new structure.

"WHAT WE NEED IS A YOUNG VAN FLEET"

The record does not indicate when Taylor first told Kennedy that Harkins was the best man to be the first commander of MACV. What we do know is that Taylor all but promised the job to Harkins back in October at the end of Taylor's trip to Vietnam. Harkins recalled the conversation:

> we had [Taylor] out to dinner, as a matter of fact, and he didn't do too much discussing. That was on his way out [to Vietnam]. On the way back, he stopped and he called me from the airport [in Honolulu], I think. He said, "Get ready to put your finger in the dike." . . . Those were his words, and I said, "Thank you very much."[18]

Clearly, from the very beginning, Harkins was Taylor's man.

The record suggests that Kennedy was gradually being prepared for the recommendation of Harkins for the job. On November 27 Taylor presented to Kennedy a memo outlining his ideas for command arrangements in Vietnam. His analysis was itself a model of the infamous "goldilocks" principal of government memo writing in which the author offers his own view along with two others that are clearly unacceptable. Taylor had used this same tactic the first time he framed the options in Southeast Asia for President Kennedy in July 1961.[19]

Taylor's memo described five "kinds of business"—Embassy; USOM [United States Operations Mission]; MAAG; military headquarters (to include operational U.S. forces); and intelligence "for U.S. purposes"—and laid out three models for handling them. Two of these, the Korean model and the Berlin model, both conjured up the specter of a "showdown," meaning war.[20] Taylor recommended what he called the "normal" model. Under it, "the present command relationship could be retained with [a] rather simple modification." However, Taylor's modification was anything but simple and his model far from normal. In essence, he proposed the MAAG charter be expanded to cover unspecified "additional functions beyond those presently assigned," and that the MAAG Chief would *concurrently* serve as "Commander of the U.S. units assigned to Vietnam." In other words, the person in charge of MAAG, under a separate but concurrent hat, would have *operational* command of any new U.S. forces.

If Taylor had succeeded in getting the President to accept his command plan and Harkins for the job, Harkins would have been the only MAAG Chief ever to have had concurrent command of operational U.S. military forces in the same country. The truth is that Taylor's goldilocks memo was not designed to enlighten the President but to give his old friend Harkins total control of the situation in Vietnam.

Rostow also seems to have been on board the Harkins bandwagon. A December 6 memo from Rostow to the President[21] tied the effectiveness of Kennedy's entire Vietnam program to this appointment and seemed designed to head off any thought of keeping McGarr:

> I do not believe that all the choppers and other gadgetry we can supply South Viet-Nam will buy time and render their resources effective if we do not get a first class man out there to replace McGarr. McGarr is an excellent officer, but he lacks the critical qualities to make this partnership move. . . . In my view . . . what we need is a young Van Fleet.

While Rostow didn't actually name the "first class man" he had in mind, the reference to this celebrated general was no coincidence. For Van Fleet's son-in-law was none other than General Paul D. Harkins.

McGarr was worried about the situation. On December 20 he cabled Lemnitzer complaining about the deletion of the SECDEF conference agenda item on command issues.[22] He spoke of how his "value might be depreciated" should a senior officer be brought in "to take over [the] top spot." The truth was, of course, that McGarr wanted the job himself and he asked Lemnitzer for any "straws in the wind" he could give him on the matter. Ambassador Nolting was also concerned about the new arrangements and on December 19 cabled State opposing fundamental changes in "U.S. organizational arrangements" to accommodate the "additional U.S. military personnel."[23] Adding another commander to the roster would dilute Nolting's clout; he wanted to remain the top man, not be a coequal.

The straws were already in the wind. On December 20 McNamara and Rusk agreed on the new command concept for Vietnam: the new "Commander, U.S. Military Assistance Command, Vietnam" would have direct responsibility for all U.S. military operations and direct access to CINCPAC and through CINCPAC to the JCS.[24] Two days later, McNamara sent a memorandum to Kennedy asking that Harkins be given the job and appointed a four-star general.[25] On December 23, Lemnitzer broke the bad news to McGarr, telling him everything except the name of the new commander.[26]

Not everyone was enthusiastic about Harkins. In a December 27 memo to the President, McGeorge Bundy noted "with some alarm that Secretary McNamara does not have a personal judgement of General Harkins" and argued it was "of critical importance to get the right man on the first try" in cases like this one. Bundy advised it would be "wise for you or Secretary

McNamara, or perhaps both, to have a careful talk with Harkins, before this appointment is made."[27]

On December 31, 1961, Kennedy's Military Assistant, General Taylor, called Lieutenant General Paul D. Harkins, Deputy Commander of the U.S. Army, Pacific (USARPAC), in Hawaii and directed him to report to Washington on January 2. Harkins later claimed Taylor would not reveal the nature of the summons, but by this time Harkins surely knew what it was about. He arrived in Washington and was immediately sent to see the President at his Palm Beach, Florida, home. According to Harkins, the President told him he "was going to be the commander in Vietnam" and that he was made "a four-star general as of that date." The President said it would probably be a month before he left but to "be ready to go." Harkins arrived at his new assignment in February.[28] The details of Taylor's goldilocks memo—expanding the MAAG—had not been approved, but the result he sought had nevertheless been achieved: his man Harkins was going to Saigon, and Harkins would be in real control of the war.

THE STRUGGLE OVER COMMAND RELATIONS

On January 12, Nolting complained to Kennedy about the powers Harkins would have as the new MACV commander. He claimed that in his meeting with Kennedy, the President agreed with him that "the Ambassador should have overall authority in Vietnam and that the military commander's terms of reference should reflect this relationship."[29] According to Nolting, during the course of this meeting Kennedy directed Taylor to revise the draft terms of reference outlining the job along these lines. The revision, written by Taylor on January 12, did state that "the various U.S. agencies in Saigon will continue to operate as a unified Task Force under the chairmanship and overall direction of the Ambassador."[30]

On January 13, Taylor wrote a memo for record stating that while McNamara agreed the Ambassador was the senior U.S. representative, he "does not agree to placing the commander under the over-all direction of the Ambassador as a member of the Country Team."[31] On the same day, Taylor sent a memo to Kennedy saying McNamara did not wish to reopen the issue anymore and would recommend to Kennedy—with Rusk's concurrence—that they stick with the original plan and review it after "a short test period."[32] Taylor added: "I do not think there are any great issues at stake, provided Ambassador Nolting and General Harkins behave like the sensible people I believe them to be." One cannot help but wonder if Taylor's objective was unstated, and that his memo to the President skillfully underscored comments by McNamara in order to preserve Harkins' authority in Vietnam.

Nolting had several discussions about this issue with Rusk before leaving for the second SECDEF conference. On board the plane en route to Honolulu, McNamara told Nolting "his hands were tied on the terms of reference" because of "JCS opposition to placing a four-star general in a position subordinate to an Ambassador."[33] In Honolulu Nolting met in vain with McNamara in a continuing effort to straighten out the problem. On his way back to Saigon, he drafted a letter to Kennedy complaining that "we have been unable to clarify the matter to our mutual satisfaction." What Nolting was after was a piece of paper. As his letter to Kennedy said: "Mr. McNamara and I achieved at Honolulu what is perhaps an agreement on words," adding, "but, I am afraid, not of minds, which is more important."[34] Nolting delivered a passionate defense of his position and offered to resign if Kennedy did not agree with his views. He sent the letter to State for delivery to the President. In the meantime, Nolting used his position to delay getting a final agreement from Diem on the new command arrangement for MACV.[35]

Rusk put a stop to Nolting's foot dragging as well as his letter writing to Kennedy. In a letter of his own to Nolting,[36] Rusk said he was disappointed with Nolting's January 17 letter. He also said there was no doubt that Nolting was in charge, but that he was not willing to produce "a piece of paper" in the absence of any actual misunderstanding. "Unless I hear from you again, I do not plan to submit your letter to the President," Rusk concluded. Ball added two short sentences: "Imperative that Harkins assume duty soonest. Expect you will promptly clear matter with Diem."

Nolting gave up, and two days later, on February 3, he cabled State that he had obtained Diem's "complete concurrence" on the new MACV arrangements.[37] On February 8, CINCPAC established MACV as a subordinate command, and Felt cabled Harkins' Terms of Reference to McGarr. Those terms did not establish Harkins as a subordinate of the Ambassador.

THE STRUGGLE OVER MACV'S INTELLIGENCE JOB

On February 13, 1962, General Harkins assumed command of MACV, and Air Force Colonel James Winterbottom became MACV's Intelligence Chief. At the request of General Taylor, the intelligence effort in Vietnam would be supplemented by an all-source Joint Evaluation Center (JEC) in Saigon. The JEC was to be jointly staffed by MACV, CIA station analysts, and Embassy staff, and would report directly to the Ambassador. The objective was the development and dissemination of assessments free of institutional or service biases. In February, at the urging of Winterbottom's deputy, Army Colonel Robert Delaney, MACV requested that DIA's top expert on Vietnam, George Allen, be provided to assist in establishing the JEC.[38]

The JEC, however, quickly fell victim to bureaucratic politics. For the first ten weeks only lip service was paid to the basic concept of a bias-free organization, and neither the CIA station nor the Embassy were serious in their assignment of resources to the center. By May the purpose for which the JEC was created had been totally forgotten, and it was relocated from the Embassy to MACV, where it became an adjunct of Winterbottom's intelligence section.[39]

Winterbottom's appointment to the MACV intelligence job did not occur without a struggle.[40] Major General Alva Fitch, the Army Assistant Chief of Staff for Intelligence (ACSI), objected to the appointment of Winterbottom. Fitch wrote on January 9 that he did not concur with the designation of the intelligence (J-2) position as "an Air Force Colonel space."[41] Fitch invoked the Taylor report's comments that the South Vietnamese had been "fighting blind" and that a sophisticated intelligence effort was required intimately linked to operations at every level, from the villages to the planners. The war in Vietnam was "basically a ground war," argued Fitch, and the intelligence required was "ground combat intelligence." The top intelligence officers in MACV had to be properly qualified by rank, experience, and service background in ground intelligence operations, Fitch said, and recommended the J-2 be designated as "an Army Brigadier General space."

Fitch's argument did not get very far, which was not unusual in joint service commands like CINCPAC and MACV. One reason for this, recalls William Benedict, who was in ACSI at the time, was that in such joint commands the Army was more interested in the operations side of the house, and so the intelligence jobs tended to go to the Air Force. "The Army missed the boat for years," because "they'd sell their soul" for the operations job, he states, while the Air Force went after the intelligence jobs "because they realized what we didn't know, which is that the J-2 really drives everything."[42] That ended up being the case in the Pacific, where the Intelligence Chief at CINCPAC was Air Force Brigadier General Patterson, USAF, who was, "of course," says Benedict, "Winterbottom's rabbi."

Fitch's efforts were in vain, and on March 2 McNamara approved a

MACV organization confirming that the intelligence job would go to the Air Force. Winterbottom would be staying. This meant that Air Force officers were in direct control of intelligence operations both in Vietnam and at the Pacific theater level. Meanwhile, back in Washington, both the commander and deputy of the newly created Defense Intelligence Agency were Air Force officers as well. The Air Force had gained control of military intelligence on the war from the battlefield to the decision-makers in Washington; except, of course, for the Army's little intelligence unit at USARPAC, in Honolulu.

NOTES

1. See USARPAC Intelligence Bulletin, January 1962, JFK Library, Newman Papers.
2. See USARPAC Intelligence Bulletin, February 1962, JFK Library, Newman Papers.
3. See extract from second SECDEF conference, January 15, 1962, JFK Library, Newman Papers.
4. Rostow, "Guerrilla Warfare in Underdeveloped Areas," *Marine Corps Gazette*, January 1962, p. 49.
5. An excellent account of McNamara's comments was written by Edwin W. Martin, Admiral Felt's Political Advisor, in a January 19, 1962, memo to Cottrell. See *State History*, 1962, Document 29, pp. 52–54.
6. Henry Trewhitt, *McNamara* (New York: Harper and Row, 1971), p. 193.
7. William Bundy, interview with the author, July 11, 1991.
8. See Trewhitt's account; in an interview with the author, Bundy explained that he did not mean to say "insane" about McGarr personally, but that "this is a crazy way of conducting the war."
9. NSAM-124, January 18, 1962, in *State History*, 1962, Document 26, pp. 48–50.
10. Kennedy's National Security Advisor, McGeorge Bundy, perhaps realizing the crucial role of Taylor, sent Taylor a note asking that his staff keep Bundy's assistant, Bob Komer, "clued as to what is going on" so that Bundy could "participate effectively" in the Special Group. See Bundy memo to Taylor, February 6, 1962. See *Declassified Documents*, 1989, 585.
11. Krepinevich, *The Army and Vietnam*; see especially Part 1, "The Advisory Years."
12. Robert Johnson memo to Walt Rostow, January 11, 1962, in *State History*, 1962, Document 12, pp. 21–23.

13. *State History*, 1962, Document 11, pp. 17–21.

14. Roger Hilsman, "A Strategic Concept for South Vietnam," *State History*, 1962, pp. 73–90.

15. The only record of the Diem-McGarr meeting is this memo for record, and it comes from U.S. Embassy, Saigon, files; see Memo for Record, Diem-McGarr Meeting, January 12, 1962, in *State History*, 1962 Document 13, pp. 23–30.

16. McGarr, who wanted a major attack in Zone D (north of Saigon), and had given McNamara a brief review of his plan at the first SECDEF conference, lobbied Diem and apparently got a tentative agreement for it. The really important part of the discussion concerned Diem's ideas on creating a "defended" village infrastructure. Diem made the remarks in response to McGarr's prodding for clearing a "test" province, an idea suggested by McNamara at the first SECDEF conference.

17. *State History*, 1962, Document 46, p. 96.

18. Harkins, interview with Ted Gittinger, November 10, 1981, LBJ Library, Oral History Collection, p. I-5.

19. Taylor/Rostow memo to JFK, July 27, 1961, JFK Library, NSF, Regional Security, SEA, Box 231A.

20. The Berlin model would have seen a four-star general representing both the State and Defense departments, while the Korean model would involve a "pattern of relationships appropriate to an active or potential theater of war."

21. Memorandum From the President's Deputy Assistant for National Security Affairs (Rostow) to the President, December 6, 1961, in *State History*, 1961, Document 311, p. 719.

22. Telegram From the Commander of the Military Assistance Advisory Group in Vietnam (McGarr) to the Chairman of the Joint Chiefs of Staff (Lemnitzer), December 20, 1961, in *State History*, 1961, Document 331, pp. 749–50.

23. Embassy, Saigon Cable, to State, 819, December 19, 1961, in *State History*, 1961, Document 330, pp. 747–49.

24. See Documents 327 and 328 (December 20, 1961, letters between Rusk and McNamara), in *State History*, 1961, pp. 745–46.

25. Memorandum From the Secretary of Defense (McNamara) to the President, December 22, 1961, in *State History*, 1961, Document 336, p. 756.

26. Telegram From the Chairman of the Joint Chiefs of Staff (Lemnitzer) to the Chief of the Military Assistance Advisory Group in Vietnam (McGarr), December 23, 1961, in *State History*, 1961, Document 38, pp. 758–60.

27. Memorandum From the President's Special Assistant for National Security Affairs (Bundy) to the President, November 27, 1961, in *State History*, 1961, Document 342, p. 766.

28. Harkins, interview with Gittinger, November 10, 1981, p. 6.

29. *State History*, 1962, p. 31, n. 2.

30. Terms of Reference for the Senior United States Military Commander in Vietnam, January 12, 1962, in *State History*, 1962, Document 17, pp. 35–36.

31. Taylor memo, January 13, 1962, in *State History*, 1962, Document 18, p. 37.

32. Taylor memo to Kennedy, January 13, 1962, in *State History*, 1962, Document 19, p. 38.

33. *State History*, 1962, p. 47, n. 3.

34. Nolting cable to State, January 17, 1962, in *State History*, 1962, Document 25, pp. 46–48.

35. This was obvious from the contents of Nolting's January 24 cable to State. Thuan had asked Nolting what the relationship between the Ambassador and the MACV commander would be and Nolting replied, "This remained to be worked out in precise terms." When Thuan said he would take up the matter with Diem, Nolting said Harkins could come to Saigon "as soon as necessary preparatory arrangements had been completed." See Nolting cable to State, January 24, 1962, in *State History*, 1962, Document 33, pp. 58–59.

36. A February 1 cable sent by Under Secretary of State Ball to Nolting contained the text of the letter from Rusk. See State cable to Nolting, February 1, 1962, in *State History*, 1962, Document 40, p. 70.

37. Nolting cable to State, February 3, 1962, in *State History*, 1962, Document 45, p. 95.

38. George Allen, *The Indochina Wars: 1950–1975*, unpublished manuscript, p. 174. This manuscript is now part of the public record; see Exhibit No. 1829 of the documents in *Westmoreland* vs. *CBS*.

39. Ibid., p. 177.

40. There was, in fact, a struggle over all of the senior MACV slots. The Air Force history of the war states that Admiral Felt had recommended the Air Force be given the Chief of Staff, J-2 (intelligence) and J-5 (plans) positions, while General Harkins instead picked a Marine (Major General Richard G. Weede) for his Chief of Staff and advocated Air Force officers for the J-2, J-3 (operations), and J-5 positions. (See *Air Force History*, p. 97.) If true, this looks like Harkins was more interested in an air war than counterinsurgency. The Air Force history contends that Secretary McNamara wanted the Army to have the J-3 positon, but because Admiral Felt believed this would unbalance the MACV staff, he proposed upgrading the J-5 to a brigadier general slot and giving it, along with the Deputy J-3, to the Air Force. Air Force Chief of Staff General Curtis LeMay "tried in vain to persuade McNamara to change his mind" on the Chief of Staff and J-3 positions and give the slots to the Air Force.

41. ACSI memo to DCSPER, January 9, 1962, JFK Library, Newman Papers.

42. Benedict, interview with the author, June 9, 1988.

CHAPTER TEN

"THIS INTELLIGENCE PROBLEM MUST BE SOLVED"

FEBRUARY 19—THE THIRD SECDEF CONFERENCE

On February 20 George Allen landed at the Honolulu airport. Allen was on his way to Saigon and had stopped off in Hawaii to touch base with the intelligence staffs at CINCPAC and USARPAC on the procedures for setting up the Joint Evaluation Center in Saigon, an intelligence organization that General Taylor had suggested be established. During these discussions, someone told him that his "mission might be altered" as a result of a disturbing situation that had developed right there in Honolulu the previous day.[1] Allen was told his expertise might be needed for a study on the Viet Cong that the Secretary of Defense had ordered. Did he know of anyone else who could help? There was an Army major at the Pentagon with the right kind of experience, Allen replied, and gave them the name— William Benedict. But what was this all about? Allen's intelligence colleagues explained that it was a highly sensitive and extremely urgent matter: the third SECDEF conference had ended in a cloud of controversy over the size of the enemy—a problem that could not wait.

The third SECDEF conference was a most unusual meeting in more ways than one. Present were the normal Defense and military officials from Washington and the Ambassador and others from Vietnam, but they were joined for the first time by the new MACV commander, General Harkins, and some of his subordinates. One of them was Harkins' Intelligence Chief, Colonel Winterbottom. It was during an exchange between McNamara and Winterbottom that the altercation over the size of the enemy—and the capability of U.S. intelligence to report on it—erupted. From the start of the discussion, however, this conference was not like those before it: in front of the huge gathering assembled at Admiral Felt's command center, Harkins opened the session up on a surprisingly bright note. He told the group his initial exposure to the situation in Vietnam revealed "a spirit of optimism and growing confidence within Vietnamese and U.S. military and civilian circles."[2] Optimism? Confidence? Why? Could the new American aid be working already? All eyes turned to Ambassador Nolting, who had been in country for ten months. Harkins was indeed correct, Nolting assured them, and added, a "spirit of movement is discernable in the land."[3]

Two documentary accounts of what followed are available, but the best by far is the CINCPAC record of the conference proceedings.[4] It reports that during Colonel Winterbottom's briefing on "the status of US-GVN intelligence efforts," Secretary McNamara made the following inquiries:

> what happened to the VC; in July [1961] they were reported to have a strength of 12,300, in Dec 17,000, in January 20–25,000. Have they increased or have we been miscounting?

McNamara was obviously concerned over the reported doubling of the enemy main forces within a six-month period, and he had saved this question for the right man—the new MACV Intelligence Chief. Winterbottom responded by showing McNamara several graphs depicting an array of different figures on the size of the Viet Cong main forces, ranging from 18,500 to 27,007.[5]

Though Winterbottom had *not* answered the Secretary's question, he apparently thought this barrage of numbers had satisfied McNamara, because Winterbottom then changed the subject. He proceeded on to figures covering the enemy militia and local self-defense forces: there were 100,000 of these types, he told the Secretary. McNamara, however, was not finished with the issue of the main forces, and he was not about to let Winterbottom off the hook. But since Winterbottom had brought up the size of the enemy's paramilitary forces, McNamara also had a question about them: "Do they participate in attacks too?" McNamara asked. The answer drifted in from someone in the back: "They do."

Ambassador Nolting then blurted out that he thought the estimate of 100,000 "VC sympathizers" was too low, and that "there are millions of people in VC controlled areas." This moment must have been uncomfortable for General Harkins, who had begun the discussion on such an optimistic note. At this point the Chairman of the Joint Chiefs, General Lemnitzer, apparently upset with the course of this discussion, interrupted to say he was "not concerned with general figures," but wanted "the numbers of hard core VC operators." Lemnitzer then made a comment that left a profound impression on those present, especially General Harkins. He said "the apparent *growing strength of the VC makes it look like we are losing*" [emphasis added].

For the new commander of American forces in Vietnam, the message from the Chairman of the Joint Chiefs was clear: growth of the enemy's main forces was very bad news. Part of the problem was the tenet of the counterinsurgency doctrine then under development on Kennedy's orders that a force many times larger than the insurgents was required to defeat them. The President believed forces had to be committed according to such a ratio: "You need 10 to 1 or 11 to 1, especially in terrain as difficult as Vietnam."[6] Thus even the lowest Viet Cong figure Winterbottom had referred to—18,500 from the Joint Evaluation Center—would require South Vietnamese main forces of 180,000 to 200,000, which was just barely within their capability. The MAAG figure—27,007—would require an ARVN main force of 270,000 to 300,000. Aside from the problem of another enormous increase in U.S. funds that such a force increase would require, it is doubtful that South Vietnam could have recruited, trained, and maintained that many men quickly and effectively enough to counter the growing enemy threat.

The discussion on figures at the third SECDEF conference turned into a circus. Admiral Felt "closed the subject," the CINCPAC record states. "We are dealing," the Admiral proclaimed, "with a real guesstimate." The subject was far from closed, however, for a troubling fact had reared its head: the U.S. did not know the size of the force that its national resources were being marshaled to defeat. And McNamara wanted to know why. This moment *should* have been embarrassing for Winterbottom, since he was the one in the hot seat trying to explain to the Secretary of Defense why he didn't know the size of the enemy. Remarkably, however, Winterbottom's comments indicate no awareness on his part of the seriousness or magnitude of the problem. McNamara asked why there were such discrepancies in the figures. Winterbottom responded limply that they resulted from "different methods of evaluation and estimating unknowns." McNamara was not impressed. The differences must be resolved, he told his commanders. "If we don't have a firm Order of Battle today," we will not be able to "determine what the changes have been." (An order of battle is a comprehensive listing of military forces, including the history, location, size, composition, weapons, and equipment of each unit.)

Winterbottom then resorted to a purely defensive maneuver. Only seven of his twenty-seven people, he complained, were "engaged in estab-lishing a valid basic Order of Battle." Winterbottom added that he had already requested "five expert analysts with Special Intelligence clearances" on a temporary-duty basis. Winterbottom was doing a credible job of saying none of this was his fault—after all, MACV had only just been created. Then he made another mistake by announcing that "few of the analysis personnel have had prerequisite training and experience in the [order of battle] area."

This comment upset both McNamara and Lemnitzer. McNamara asked Winterbottom whether or not the U.S. had "the necessary people." Win-terbottom, an Air Force colonel whose only experience was with the Strategic Air Command, dodged the Secretary's question with another unwise com-ment. "They are all in essential jobs," he answered. This nearly brought Lemnitzer out of his seat. The Joint Chiefs Chairman said he did not understand what the Colonel was talking about, and objected that "the Army has plenty of specialists in this field." Here McNamara's patience had come to an end. He ordered that a "specific statement of requirements" be given to him to take back to Washington that night. *"This intelligence problem,"* the Secretary ordered, *"must be solved"* [emphasis added].

Now even Ambassador Nolting realized a problem had developed. Trying to be helpful, he changed the subject and began to talk about the area controlled by the government of South Vietnam. McNamara, now didactic and rapid, "said he wanted to know what it was and how it is changing." He also "asked if it was planned to lay out an intelligence plan and picture" for these areas, and was told that a province-by-province analysis of both government and communist control was under way.[7] Winterbottom's portion of the briefing was over, and he must have been relieved to sit down. It was an inauspicious way to meet the Secretary of Defense and the Chairman of the JCS for the first time, and news of his ordeal quickly spread all over the Pacific theater and Washington. Winterbottom's fumbling and incompetent performance led to the princi-pal result of the conference, which was, as George Allen later observed, that "the Viet Cong order of battle had become the top intelligence priority for the military's command in Saigon."[8]

For the previous six months, the Pentagon, along with much of official Washington, had advertised the deteriorating situation in South Vietnam. Many officials, military and civilian, had argued that the war was going so poorly that six U.S. divisions had to be sent quickly to stem the communist tide. In fact, in the previous weeks a National Intelligence Estimate (NIE) had been written that confirmed the steady growth of Viet Cong forces and reiterated the bleak picture that had been the norm for some time. However, something strange had happened, something that caused U.S. intelligence on the enemy to suddenly become the subject of attention at high levels in the Pentagon and elsewhere. The intelligence process was about to be turned upside down, and for those accustomed to flying right side up, life was about to become difficult.

THE SUDDEN REVERSAL IN MILITARY REPORTING

In mid-February 1962, before most of the new American advisors had arrived and certainly long before the new Kennedy program had any chance to affect the tide of battle, U.S. military reporting on the war suddenly became optimistic. That was not the case, however, for the U.S. intelligence community, which published an NIE on February 21, right after the third SECDEF conference. The estimate concluded that communist control was advancing in South Vietnam and would continue to do so. The NIE sharply contradicted the optimistic picture advanced by Harkins at the conference, which suggests that his cheerful outlook on the war was prompted not by new information from the battlefield, but by a political decision from Washington.

A quick review of the sequence of events relating to this turnabout is startling. In late December the Joint Chiefs still argued that nothing short of several U.S. divisions could save off defeat in Vietnam. On February 19 Harkins presented this new picture of optimism and growing confidence. These rosy reflections were passed on to the Vietnam Task Force, and on February 23, member Chalmers Wood reported to his Senate Foreign Relations Committee contact, John Newhouse, that "developments in Vietnam were encouraging."[9] A few weeks later, McNamara, apparently won over by MACV's reporting, testified to the House Appropriations Committee that the end of the war was in sight.[10] The abruptness of this turnabout left the lower echelons of the national intelligence and defense bureaucracies unprepared and out of step with the change.

The new optimism contrasted starkly with the conclusions of the U.S. intelligence community at that time. Its February 21 NIE 10–62, entitled "Communist Objectives, Capabilities, and Intentions in Southeast Asia,"[11] continued to paint the same gloomy picture. It discerned "a clear pattern of increasing Communist military, paramilitary and political capabilities for pursuing Communist objectives," and observed that "the development of these capabilities is particularly advanced in Laos and South Vietnam."[12] The estimate addressed the size of enemy forces directly and in considerable detail, and did not waffle the way Winterbottom did. It said there were "on full-time anti-government operations at least

25,000 Viet Cong organized into 22 battalions, 109 separate companies, and 210 separate platoons," supported by "100,000 part-time, partially armed, trained local militia who serve as village self-defense forces." The estimate went on to note the presence of 50,000 "combat-experienced" North Vietnamese soldiers in the southern part of North Vietnam who "could be made available for guerrilla operations in South Vietnam," and that 800 North Vietnamese officers and soldiers were serving as cadres in the Viet Cong battalions and companies in South Vietnam.

In sum, the estimate painted a strikingly different picture than the one described by Harkins. The intelligence community felt that the communist objective was to establish control in South Vietnam, that communist military and political capabilities for doing so—which included 25,000 hard-core regulars—were "particularly advanced," and that current guerrilla activity would increase. Moreover, the figure it gave for the size of the Viet Cong main forces was identical to that which Lemnitzer had said made it look like the war was being lost. This point deserves emphasis: on February 21 the U.S. intelligence community delivered a straightforward answer to the question that McNamara had posed to Winterbottom two days earlier—the Viet Cong main force units had indeed doubled in size in just six short months.

THE FORMATION OF MACV'S INTELLIGENCE STAFF

It was February 23, 1962. As Bill Benedict drove home from the hospital that Friday evening with his wife and newborn son, his thoughts were far from the Pentagon and the Office of the Army Assistant Chief of Staff for Intelligence, where he worked. He was surprised when the moment he walked in the door the phone rang and a Navy officer from the Joint Chiefs of Staff told him he was going to Saigon. "Somebody in Honolulu" had requested him by name.[13] The trip would consume the next three months and embroil him in an extraordinary chain of events. Twenty-five years later, Bill Benedict was surprised to learn that George Allen was the "somebody in Honolulu" who had mentioned his name.[14]

In the fallout from Winterbottom's stumbling at the third SECDEF conference, people like Bill Benedict were literally yanked out of their positions to go to Saigon to work on this new intelligence problem. Benedict, however, had no idea that any intelligence problem had developed. Indeed he was not even told why he was going to Saigon. His mission, and his military orders, were classified. As he packed his bags, he could only wonder why the sudden rush to get him to Vietnam. That soon changed when he linked up with his old friend George Allen in Saigon: the two of them were there to bolster MACV's first order of battle study.

It fact it was MACV's first major intelligence effort. At the third SECDEF conference Winterbottom had said that without outside help the order of battle effort would take eighteen weeks to complete, as opposed to just eight with the help of five outside experts. As it turned out, he got his experts and it took a little over six weeks: the order of battle was presented on May 11 to McNamara at the fifth SECDEF conference in Saigon.

A master sergeant from the National Military Command Center accompanied Benedict and Allen from Washington to participate in the study. From USARPAC came Major Lou Tixier and a senior NCO. MACV assigned several people to the project, including Captain Jim Harris from the intelligence section and Major Sam Dowling from the Staff Security Office (SSO). So Harkins thus had at his disposal an impressive team of U.S. military intelligence experts to assess the size of the enemy.

The selection of Colonel Winterbottom as Harkins' Intelligence Chief (J-2), however, was an odd and unfortunate choice. His Air Force career had been devoted to Strategic Air Command reconnaissance programs, while the critical position he was chosen for demanded the intelligence skills necessary to support a counterinsurgency program. Nonetheless, the Air Force had been given the J-2 position and Winterbottom filled it. According to Blascak, Allen, Benedict, Dowling, Harris, and many others, the MACV intelligence effort languished under Winterbottom. His professional incompetence was a serious detriment to the command, says Allen, and his behavior "would have caused any junior officer to be sent home in disgrace."[15]

The raucous beginning to the formation of MACV's intelligence staff was unforgettable for those who saw it. "We were having dinner at the Rex, a club in Saigon, when a body, having just received a heavy punch, careened across our table," remembers a co-worker. It was Winterbottom's deputy, Colonel Delaney, and the person who had thrown the punch was his boss, Winterbottom. "They'd pummel each other," another co-worker recalls. "Oh, they used to get into fistfights, real knock-down drag-out fights, all the time," says another. Still another colleague recounts one of the J-2's many indiscretions, this one taking place at an official social function: "Winterbottom was massaging the buns of the wife of some major general or brigadier general. And they nearly sent him home right then and there, because she complained to her husband and he raised hell."

Colonel Winterbottom reportedly attempted to subvert the correct procedures for handling the sensitive message traffic for which SSO Army Major Sam Dowling was responsible. The SSO shop, while attached to the J-2, was autonomous and independent of MACV, reporting directly to the Army G-2 in Washington. Winterbottom so disliked this arrangement that it was a continuous source of contention throughout his tenure.[16] In late February, in front of Allen and Delaney, he ordered that Dowling first show him any messages coming through SSO channels—including the commanding general's private ones—before sending them to the proper addresses. When Major Dowling protested, Winterbottom threatened that the next time Dowling failed to conform with his wishes "would be the last."[17]

Winterbottom lost no time in clipping George Allen's wings as well. It was only a matter of days after arriving in country when Allen joined Winterbottom and Delaney in a meeting with the Vietnamese Army J-2, Colonel Phuoc. The purpose of the meeting was to make arrangements for acquiring raw data from the Vietnamese and to set up procedures for coordinating American intelligence findings with Vietnamese holdings. Phuoc was apparently overjoyed that his old friend Allen was heading up the American effort, and made the mistake of praising him as the only American he knew who understood the situation in Vietnam, and begging Winterbottom to allow Allen to tutor his Vietnamese analysts. Allen recalls:

> Colonel W. was noncommittal in Colonel Phuoc's presence, but was quick to warn me after we left that I should return to my office and had better damned well remember my place and not get any inflated ideas of my importance; my job was to break my butt for Colonel W., and he would see to it that I had no time for anything else.[18]

And so the order of battle work began under the watchful eye of Colonel Winterbottom. Despite his boorish behavior, he was extended as the MACV Intelligence Chief beyond the then normal one-year tour of duty. His many faults did not immediately suggest to those involved in the order of battle project that their work and its results would be tampered with. Six weeks later, they would be rudely awakened.

HILSMAN: "A LITTLE UNEASY" IN SAIGON

While George Allen, Bill Benedict, and the rest of their team were about three weeks into their order of battle project, the chief of the State Department's intelligence organization visited Vietnam. At the direction of President Kennedy, the Director of the Bureau of Intelligence and Research (INR), Roger Hilsman, arrived in Saigon for a meeting with Harkins and

Nolting on March 17. In Washington Hilsman had briefed those the President had asked him to on the "strategic concept" for Vietnam, but he had not yet done so with Harkins, who, by this time, had been in Saigon for over a month. This new "strategic concept," which Kennedy had clearly endorsed, required careful integration of its political, economic, military, and psychological components. When Hilsman arrived in Saigon, he discovered that this concept had been stillborn.

Hilsman learned that the MAAG had come up with a program, backed by Diem and Nhu, called Operation Sunrise, supposedly to implement the strategic hamlet concept. Hilsman felt Sunrise "represented a total misunderstanding of what the program should try to do." It envisioned building a belt of strategic hamlets on the key road from Saigon through Ben Cat in Binh Duong Province to Tay Ninh Province. Along this road most of the South Vietnamese recruits traveled for their training in War Zone D, a communist jungle base area. According to William Bundy, the story behind Sunrise began at the first SECDEF conference in December when General McGarr presented a plan to make a major attack on War Zone D.[19] When McNamara refused to support this plan, Diem and McGarr came up with Sunrise—a thrust into the provinces east of Saigon.

Hilsman was also worried because Sunrise required "all the hamlets in the region be moved bodily to new locations," which meant not only severe dislocation of the peasants, but also violating "the absolutely fundamental principle that the program should proceed outward from a secure base, like a spreading oil blot."[20] Hilsman was concerned because this area was flanked by heavy concentrations of Viet Cong forces—from Zone D on one side and from Tay Ninh on the other—and was also a major route along which Viet Cong troops and supplies flowed. He told Harkins and Nolting that the strategic hamlet concept was designed to begin in less dangerous areas and fan outward, and of his fear "that the Viet Cong would try to make an example of these villages and so discredit the strategic village concept throughout South Vietnam."[21]

In a memorandum to General Taylor after his return, Hilsman reported that Harkins too was "very disturbed" about Operation Sunrise, fearing "the troops guarding these exposed villages would be called away to meet some other threat, giving the Viet Cong precisely the opportunity they seek." Both Harkins and Nolting, he said, "were pressing Diem to cancel this operation, but they were handicapped by the fact that it was the MAAG that originally urged it."[22] Diem had not yet approved the overall hamlet program, but Hilsman reported this "delay was apparently occasioned not by any reluctance concerning the plan itself but by doubts as to who among the Vietnamese would be in charge of it."

Sunrise was not the only matter Hilsman found to worry about. He learned from the Deputy Chief of Mission that Diem's brother Nhu wanted to "blanket the whole country" with hamlets, apparently for his own political purposes and without regard for the oil blot strategy or the strength of the individual hamlets themselves.[23] Nolting told Hilsman that Nhu had personally assured him he was "aware of the danger of a blanket approach," and advised, "it would be most unwise to raise with President Diem any question about Brother Nhu at this time."[24] Diem's approval of the Strategic Hamlet Program came on March 19, the day Hilsman departed Saigon. Concerned by what he had seen, Hilsman, while remaining confident that the concept was correct, returned to Washington with a pessimistic report on how the program was being implemented. Sunrise, however, was a particular problem, as Hilsman later recalled:

> All we could do was to try to see that enough troops were assigned to guard duty to deter the Viet Cong from making an example of these four hamlets [then being planned] and then hope. We could not, of course, tell the press that we had been trying to get Sunrise called off. But they saw its flaws immediately and the whole thing cost us heavily in adverse publicity.[25]

The four hamlets were eventually built along the road to Tay Ninh, and all four were lost to the communists by 1964.

Hilsman did not grasp the extent to which the hamlet program and his entire "strategic concept" was in trouble. Part, if not most, of the reason for this was Harkins, who gave Hilsman a rosy rundown of his hamlet inspection tours. This news Hilsman happily relayed in a memo to Taylor, and singled out some newly organized strategic hamlets Harkins had spoken of in central South Vietnam. In a footnote to this sentence Hilsman included the following comment:

> The value of the strategic village approach is illustrated by two recent cables. The first is an intelligence report indicating that the arming of a very few villages in the Montagnard district along the infiltration routes has forced the infiltrating Viet Cong to change their routes drastically.[26]

The evidence for Hilsman's claim that his "strategic concept" had been implemented with the Montagnards was twofold: assurances orally furnished him by Harkins, and a MACV intelligence report.

In fact, the Montagnard program—which was viewed a success by people other than Hilsman—was already in serious trouble. To understand the problem, however, one had to actually visit the villages and find out what was going on. George Allen, traveling the countryside on the order of battle project, happened to visit the "model" Montagnard village of Buon Enao at the very time the Hilsman memo to Taylor claimed this "strategic concept" had been successfully implemented there.

The Montagnards were an ethnic minority from whom the CIA and U.S. Special Forces were trying to elicit cooperation in defending the area around their villages from the communists. At this time, the "Buon Enao experiment," as it was called, was nearing the end of its first phase of expansion in Darlac Province, a province located in the center of the II Corps area. Buon Enao was at the very center of Darlac, and the Special Forces found the surrounding villages eager to have their own weapons too. When Allen arrived in Buon Enao in March, the establishment of village defense systems in forty close-by villages was nearing completion.[27]

While the military component of the program—the establishment and training of Citizens' Irregular Defense Groups (CIDGs)—was rapidly expanding, Allen detected a curious absence of any *political* component. During a briefing he was given in Buon Enao, Allen noticed that the portions of the briefing charts marked "political action" were blank. When he inquired about the lack of political content to the program, he was told "it was necessary to tread lightly on the subject," and that Diem was suspicious of American intentions with the Montagnards. It is Allen's conclusion that the American program to integrate Montagnards into the South Vietnamese war effort was, therefore, flawed from the outset; and, furthermore, that this inattention to the political aspect of the problem would "plague" the American pacification effort for the rest of the war. At the time, Allen recalls, "I remarked that without a political base, the [Montagnard] program seemed unlikely to prosper over the long run."[28] He was right; later in the war the Montagnards in this area turned against the government.

Had Hilsman known what Allen discovered in March, he undoubtedly would have added it to the other concerns he wrote about after his return to Washington. For example, he reported that the military was proceeding "to fight the 'shooting war' quite independently, with little or no attention paid to coordination of the military effort with the 'oil blot' principle of establishing hamlets." Further, he noted military pressure for the use of "devices which had political disadvantages—such as napalm and defoliants," which could destroy rice used by the peasants as well as the Viet Cong. Hilsman also worried that the "interdiction bombing" by American T-28s and B-26s, given the questionable intelligence reporting and problems with indiscriminate or careless bombing, would turn the people toward the Viet Cong.[29]

In a separate March 19 memorandum for the record to his staff at INR,

Hilsman bluntly stated, "I find that I am a little uneasy about the way things are going in South Vietnam."[30] He was "not impressed" with John Richardson, who was replacing Colby as the CIA Station Chief. "What bothered me most . . . was his seeming failure to understand the strategic concept we had put forward." This impression, Hilsman noted, "is something we had better keep in mind." The new CIA Station Chief would be removed just fifteen months later.

Finally, this memo is noteworthy because of Hilsman's comments about the secret U.S. air war that was escalating at the time. Much of the memo was devoted to his worries about the ongoing U.S. Farm Gate air strikes: "I'm uneasy about the tendency in Washington to keep Farm Gate operations secret." He argued this was impossible because of the large numbers of Americans and Vietnamese involved. In his view, "The solution lies not in trying to keep it hidden but in using Farm Gate correctly." It was "perfectly clear," he said, that Farm Gate was "still being used on what they call 'interdiction' roles." He said Brigadier General Harvey Jablonsky, the MACV J-4 (logistics) and a West Point colleague of Hilsman's, had told Nolting that after these air strikes the Viet Cong would remove their dead soldiers and lay the bodies of any women and children who had been killed out in the middle of the street "so that the villagers on returning would find only women and children dead rather than Viet Cong." Nolting, said Hilsman, now reported growing doubts among many Americans in Saigon about the "utility" of these air strikes. However, he added:

> Diem and the South Vietnamese think it is great stuff and are continually calling for strikes on the basis of the flimsiest kind of intelligence. Our joint air control center has been screening these very carefully but there is still a very large amount of what cannot help but be indiscriminate bombing. The whole business could blow up in any number of horrendous ways.
>
> I would like all of you to give some thought to this and how we might intervene either at the White House with Bobby Kennedy or in some other way.

It all boiled down to the fact that the February SECDEF conference had not adequately covered the problems associated with U.S. air operations in the war. They would be high on the agenda of the next, fourth, SECDEF conference, which, after Hilsman's departure from Saigon, was just two days away. A surprising new development occurred in these two days that set the stage for the conference and an important presidential decision reached after it.

NOTES

1. Allen, *The Indochina Wars*, p. 175.

2. Rossen Memorandum for Record, "Trip to Hawaii—Third Secretary of Defense Conference on Vietnam, February 19, 1962, Headquarters, CINCPAC." Vietnam Files, February 1962, Military History Institute, Washington, D.C. Dated: February 23, 1962, p. 1. Rossen was the Special Assistant to the Army Chief of Staff, General Decker.

3. Ibid.

4. For the declassified portion of this record, see the JFK Library, Newman Papers, CINCPAC Summary of the Third SECDEF Conference, 19 February 1962. The other documentary record is the February 23 Rossen memorandum for record. The Rossen MFR indicates MACV briefed it "was undertaking a major effort to improve intelligence collection and evaluation." It was estimated eight weeks were required to do so. The memo also noted MACV stated "a major difficulty lies in obtaining experienced, area qualified OB [order of the battle] analysts," which prompted General Lemnitzer to say he could not understand why this was a problem. McNamara, the memo continues, "instructed" Harkins to "submit through channels" his requirements for such intelligence specialists. Rossen's memorandum indicates that responsibility within the JCS was assigned to an office under the Office of the Deputy Chief of Staff for Operations: "Action initiated by the Special Warfare Directorate, ODCSOPS, 21 February 1962." It was probably this office that called Bill Benedict on February 23. Benedict, an Army major working in the Directorate of Foreign Intelligence (DFI) under the Office of the Assistant Chief of Staff for Intelligence (OACSI), was well acquainted with order of battle work, and was the DFI's top expert on Vietnam and all of Indochina.

The Rossen memo contains only a brief account of the controversy that then erupted over the enemy order of battle. It says McNamara "requested an explanation for recent increases in the reported size of VC regular and regional forces," and that the "response" was a presentation of "conflicting estimates" due to the use of "different arbitrary factors," which in turn led to the decree that MACV "will undertake to utilize the best material available to consolidate all current estimates." Even a casual observer of this terse account would have reason to marvel over the military's confused answer to McNamara's question on the size of the enemy.

5. Winterbottom showed at least three sets of figures on the size of the Viet Cong: 18,500 held by the Evaluation Center, 22,943 held by the Vietnamese Joint General Staff, and 27,007 held by the U.S. MAAG.

6. Kennedy, December 12, 1962, news conference, cited by William Bundy, unpublished manuscript, p. 8-24.

7. The CINCPAC conference summary records that MACV was tasked to "submit (a) report to [the] SECDEF on the areas controlled by the GVN and the VC and how this area is changing." P. 34.

8. Allen, *The Indochina Wars*, p. 175.

9. Gibbons, *The U.S. Government and the Vietnam War*, vol. 2, p. 121; he cites the University of Texas, Fulbright Papers, series 48.

10. House Committee on Appropriations, *Foreign Operations Appropriations for 1963*, 87th Cong. 2nd sess (Washington, D.C.: U.S. Government Printing Office, 1962), p. 370; cited in Gibbons, *The U.S. Government and the Vietnam War*, vol. 2, p. 122.

11. NIE 10-62, February 21, 1962, was declassified in toto on April 12, 1976. Because most of the documentary studies on Vietnam were done before this date, it can only be found presently in Gareth Porter, ed., *Vietnam: The Definitive Documentation of Human Decisions* (Stanfordville, NY:, Earl M. Coleman Enterprises, 1979), vol. 2, pp. 150–56. The thorough researcher will discover, however, that an editorial error exists in Porter's work, because the annex is missing, in spite of being referenced in the text, n. 3. The full estimate, including the annex, was declassified in 1976; see JFK Library, Newman Papers.

12. A Viet Cong progression to conventional warfare "if it occurs," the estimate said, "will probably vary in different areas and will depend on a number of factors," such as lowering the morale of ARVN, strengthening their hold in rural areas, and introducing new weapons and material. The NIE concluded that in the short run there would be no significant change in the pattern of Viet Cong activity, "although the scope and tempo of the military and political campaigns will probably be increased."

13. Benedict, interview with the author, June 6, 1988.

14. Allen and Benedict, joint interview with the author, July 21, 1988.

15. Allen, *The Indochina Wars*, pp. 176–77. All of those persons interviewed by the present author who worked under Winterbottom report he had a very serious drinking problem, as did his deputy, Lieutenant Colonel Delaney. The two of them reportedly brawled regularly.

16. Don Blascak, interview with the author, April 30, 1988.

17. Allen, *The Indochina Wars*, p. 176.

18. Ibid., p. 179.

19. William Bundy, unpublished manuscript, Chap. 5, pp. 7–8.

20. Hilsman, *To Move a Nation*, p. 440.

21. Hilsman memo to Taylor, March 31, 1962, JFK Library, Hilsman Papers, Box 3, Vietnam (folder: 3/1/62–7/27/62).

22. Ibid.

23. Hilsman, *To Move a Nation*, p. 441.

24. Hilsman memo to Taylor, March 31, 1962.

25. Hilsman, *To Move a Nation*, p. 441.

26. Hilsman memo to Taylor, March 31, 1962, JFK Library, Hilsman Papers, Box 3, Vietnam (folder 3/1/62–7/27/62).

27. Kelly, *Vietnam Studies*, pp. 27–28.

28. Allen, *The Indochina Wars*, pp. 181–82.

29. Hilsman, *To Move a Nation*, pp. 442–43.

30. Hilsman memo, March 19, 1962, JFK Library, Hilsman Papers, Box 3, Vietnam (folder: 3/1/62–7/27/62).

CHAPTER ELEVEN

"WE ALL REMAIN SILENT"

ACROSS THE RUBICON

On December 22, 1961, Specialist Fourth Class James T. "Tom" Davis exited through the gate of the Army Security Agency's 3rd Radio Research Unit (RRU), a heavily guarded fenced-in compound at Tan Son Nhut air base in South Vietnam.[1] Davis, a specialist in radio direction finding (RDF), climbed into the front seat of a two-and-a-half-ton truck carrying a South Vietnamese Army RDF team in the back. The truck left the air base and was heading for a small village when a Viet Cong unit hiding on the side of the road detonated a land mine under the tailgate. The truck swerved, and Davis leapt out, managing only to fire four or five rounds before a shot fired by a Viet Cong soldier took his life. Davis was the first American to die in open combat with the Viet Cong.

On January 21, 1962, an American Farm Gate mission accidentally bombed a Cambodian border village killing many innocent civilians, and on February 2, 1962, a C-130 on a low-level training mission crashed, killing all three American crewmen aboard. The plane was apparently hit by enemy ground fire but that was never proven. These three were the first U.S. Air Force fatalities of the war.[2] At a February 26 press conference, the U.S. Air Force Pacific (PACAF) Commander, General O'Donnell, told newsmen that American pilots were in Vietnam to train the Vietnamese, not fight the war themselves.[3] He said American pilots only accompanied the Vietnamese pilots into battle to advise them.

American secrecy became a story in itself, explained Embassy Chief of Mission John Mecklin, creating the paradox where secrecy now generated more publicity than the U.S. actions themselves would have.[4] Mecklin, who became the Embassy's Public Affairs Officer in 1962, recalled the "memorable absurdities" to which this campaign was carried:

> When the aircraft carrier *Core* tied up at the dock in the Saigon River, for example, newsmen at the rooftop bar of the Majestic Hotel could almost flick a cigarette down among the helicopters cluttering her flight deck. Yet if one of them asked if that was an aircraft carrier across the street, the official reply was supposed to be "no comment."[5]

Kennedy did not want the details of increasing American involvement in the war to find their way into newspapers and other media accounts, and his angry reactions, when these stories did appear, encouraged his subordinates to keep the war—particularly the air war—a secret.

The inevitable results of stepped-up American involvement in the war included American deaths and American ordnance killing innocent Vietnamese civilians. These incidents made secrecy an enormous political liability, leaving the administration vulnerable to the charge that it was covering up atrocities and a policy that was costing American lives. Despite this risk, a discussion on how to control press coverage of the war was carried out at high levels in the government. On January 4 Deputy Secretary of Defense Gilpatric had put the wheels in motion by recommending to Lemnitzer that whenever a planned action would have "public affairs" implications the Chairman of the Joint Chiefs himself should lead an effort to develop "a suitable cover story, or stories, a public explanation, a statement of no comment or an appropriate combination thereof, for approval by the Secretary of Defense."[6] More discussion, plans, and intricate cover stories lay ahead. The administration was sinking slowly but surely into a policy of deliberate deception known and approved of by the President himself.

SECRECY AND THE AMERICAN AIR WAR

Contrary to the official claim that U.S. pilots were not flying combat missions in Vietnam, the U.S. Air Force had already flown hundreds of such missions by late February. Very often the only Vietnamese person in the backseat was not a pilot in training at all but "a low-ranking enlisted man who sat to the side while the Americans did the work."[7] The ability of reporters in Vietnam to find out what was really going on annoyed Kennedy and McNamara. The news stories were embarrassing and contradicted the administration's publicly stated policy of noninvolvement in combat actions.

This problem with the press had become a major issue by the time of the third SECDEF conference in February. At that meeting McNamara ordered the elimination of references to U.S. activities as combat operations.[8] At the same time, the State Department, in cable number 1006 on February 21, instructed the Saigon Embassy that it was not in the U.S. interest "to have stories indicating that Americans are leading and directing combat missions against the Viet Cong."[9] The cable's convoluted history is a monument to the confusing conundrum of official secrecy about the war that took place during the Kennedy administration. It began on February 17 when Carl Rowan saw a proposed State cable banning newsmen from helicopter flights in Vietnam.[10] He succeeded in getting to the President and persuading him to kill the ban. Kennedy told Rowan to rewrite the press guidelines, but after Rowan's rewrite had passed through the bureaucratic obstacle course of interdepartmental coordination in Washington, the result was the ambiguous and infamous cable number 1006 to Saigon. It left too much discretion to officials in Vietnam, and even included a provision for banning newsmen from missions whose nature was deemed to be such that "undesirable dispatches would be highly probable"—a restriction that clearly contradicted the advice Rowan had given the President. Consequently, the new guidelines in cable number 1006, which were originally intended to "liberalize" policy, says Mecklin, were "little more than codification of the errors the mission was already committing."[11]

The undermining of this attempt to come clean with the press occurred at a particularly bad time. Reports had been surfacing from U.S. advisors that the Viet Cong were using accidental American bombings of civilians for propaganda. The issue of indiscriminate bombing had been simmering for some time. Despite South Vietnamese claims that the American Farm Gate bombings were timely and accurate, the record of the February SECDEF conference indicates top American officials "had nagging doubts about the validity of the targets selected by the Vietnamese."[12] As early as March 4, General Jablonsky aired serious concerns about the bombing in a meeting with his own boss, General Harkins, and Ambassador Nolting.[13] As previously noted, Jablonsky reported the Viet Cong tactic of lining up the corpses of any dead women and children killed by the bombings in the streets of peasant villages. When Nolting appeared ready to curtail the bombings, the Air Force objected, and Jablonsky failed to cite specific examples to support his claims. Harkins sided with the Air Force, arguing tighter curbs would merely benefit the Viet Cong. The meeting resolved nothing.

Five days later, the American press blew the cover off the secret American Farm Gate missions. One story reported that for the first time since the Korean War, "American combat forces in limited numbers are once again in action."[14] These reports argued that, in essence, South Vietnam did not have enough trained fliers, and so the U.S. had committed a small number of American piloted fighters and bombers to actual combat, and that they were "carrying much of the brunt of the air war against the guerrillas."

The State Department and the Pentagon reacted immediately. On March 9 State informed the Saigon Embassy that "General Harkins is being instructed" through "military channels" on how to handle "military aspects [of] public relations."[15] The channels turned out to be Assistant Secretary of Defense for Public Affairs Arthur Sylvester, who on that same day cabled Admiral Felt not to "instruct" but to warn Harkins that these news stories had upset the President and the Joint Chiefs.[16]

Sylvester suggested that Felt, using a discreet strategy, tell Harkins to begin subtly moving away from the "present policy which results in stories indicating combat participation." He said Harkins should be urged to implement restrictions on information given to the press about combat operations gradually, "rather than an abrupt shutdown." Sylvester explained that he realized this was "a delicate operation," but something had to be done about the stories emphasizing the U.S. role and involvement in combat. He asked Harkins to "discourage" American officers involved in these missions from making any direct statements that gave the impression that Americans were "leading the combat missions against the Viet Cong." Sylvester seemed to presume that such discouragement would actually lead to less attention to American combat operations in Vietnam. This presumption was wrong. It was this sort of covering up that inevitably brought more attention to these operations.

Admiral Felt wanted to come clean with the press. In his reply to the Joint Chiefs on March 11, he said he thought Harkins *should* be authorized to state that American pilots were flying in two-seater T-28s and RB-26s to train Vietnamese pilots, and that on some of these missions ordnance was being delivered on actual Viet Cong targets.[17] Felt's reply also said: "We note State waffles and evades." A March 13 message from the U.S. Air Force Commander of 2d ADVON, General Anthis, bluntly complained that it was "extremely difficult to maintain the secrecy of this operation" due to its joint (American-Vietnamese) nature and the large number of people involved. These complaints fell on deaf ears and, like the problem of bombing indiscriminate targets, the issue of concealing the American role in it remained unresolved. The newsmen on the ground dealt with these two issues as part of the same problem, which indeed they were. The U.S. policy apparatus failed to do likewise, a flaw that Kennedy's fears of public disclosure only made worse.

While the policy apparatus in Saigon and Washington was wrestling—and failing to resolve—the dilemmas posed by these interrelated issues, Diem suddenly asked Kennedy to authorize a major new increase in American air operations. In the second week of March Diem charged that Soviet planes—flown by Chinese and Vietnamese pilots—were supplying the Viet Cong, and requested that U.S. interceptors be used to shoot them down.[18] The request led to disagreement over how to respond. General Harkins and Admiral Felt recommended approval, but Secretary of State Rusk, concerned about provoking the Chinese, opposed it. Diem's request was leaked to the press, who then badgered the White House about what Kennedy would do, but Kennedy's aides gave no hint of any presidential decision, saying only that he was calling an NSC meeting. In fact, Diem's charge was true, and as the time for the NSC meeting and another SECDEF conference (the fourth) approached, American radar sites inside South Vietnam detected a major new communist resupply effort from the air.

"PUT ON MORE SPEED AND GET OUT OF HERE"

It was very early on Monday morning, March 20, 1962. At a little after two o'clock, it was still pitch black outside the Vietnamese light radar station near Pleiku in the northern highlands of South Vietnam. The tiny site was perfectly placed to overlook the valley of the Ia Drang River, which flowed into Ratanakiri Province in Cambodia, just forty miles to the west. A strategic province in the northeast corner of Cambodia, Ratanakiri's eastern boundary straddled Kontum and Pleiku provinces in South Vietnam, while its northern boundary ran along Attopeu Province, the southernmost province of Laos. In this area was a major nexus of the Ho Chi Minh Trail, from which trails fanned out toward Thailand, Cambodia, and South Vietnam.

The personnel on duty at the radar station were far from lethargic, however. The previous morning, just before light, another unit had reported a possible airdrop to communist forces in their vicinity. Ground troops had been immediately dispatched to investigate, but were unable to locate or confirm the activity. In fact, since early that year there had been rumors that the Viet Cong were receiving secret air resupply drops in the central highlands. The Pleiku radar, as well as the radars at Tan Son Nhut and Da Nang, had repeatedly picked up unidentified tracks. Sometimes these tracks turned out to be tricks of the atmosphere or U.S. Army flights they knew nothing about.[19]

There were no tricks on Monday morning. At 2:40, the Pleiku light radar picked up two unidentified targets flying near the Cambodian border inside Vietnam.[20] By pure coincidence, communications difficulties prevented a quick attempt by the Americans to investigate. The communist air supply forces, apparently confident their efforts were going undetected in the dark of night, continued the operation. Forty-five minutes later, four more targets showed up on the Pleiku radar in the same general area. There was no doubt about it: a communist air drop was underway.

At five minutes after five, a lone U.S. B-26 scrambled to investigate. The pilot found the targets all right, but the enemy pilots were experienced, and did not allow him to make definite visual contact with his high-speed plane. Flying at extremely low altitude (900–2,600 feet) and slow speeds (80–120 knots), the communist planes maneuvered continuously and hugged the terrain to avoid intercept. The target aircraft were suspected to be either Soviet AN-2 Colt or YAK-12 Creek series aircraft with a YAK series escort of some kind. A U.S. MAAG advisor, described as a USAF captain "and qualified radar man," observed the tracks and opined they were in fact the targets suspected.

The B-26 tried in vain to get closer to the intruders, who attempted unsuccessfully to jam the B-26 communications frequency by constantly clicking a microphone. VHF radio intercept on 142.74 megacycles picked up the voices of pilots. The senior American advisor of II Corps (an area northeast of Saigon) reported that the initial words of the intercepted transmission were in Chinese. They then "immediately broke into Vietnamese." One pilot inquired what he should do, and the answer came back, "Put on more speed and get out of here."[21]

At 6:32 two South Vietnamese AD-6s scrambled to help in the intercept, but radar contact with the targets was lost as they disappeared into Cambodian territory just before seven o'clock. The B-26 pilot reported seeing position lights—either exhaust flame or fire on the ground. Road blocks were set up around Pleiku and all civilian vehicles near the drop zone were checked. By 8:10, a light aircraft found small bundles still hanging in trees only twenty-nine miles away from Pleiku. South Vietnamese Rangers were sent in H-21 helicopters to investigate, but the Viet Cong were long gone.

Beginning at 11:30 that same evening and continuing until 3:15 the following morning, twenty more tracks were picked up by the radars operating at both Tan Son Nhut and Pleiku.[22] An airdrop even larger than the night before was in progress. First Tan Son Nhut picked up unknown tracks leading out of Cambodia, but after two Farm Gate T-28s were scrambled, the tracks faded. The T-28s were recalled, but then Pleiku reported up to fifteen new low-altitude tracks emerging from Cambodia. The result was the same: one SC-47 was sent to disperse flares for two RB-26s that searched in vain.

There could no longer be any doubt about external aerial resupply of the Viet Cong. What was different about these events was the large number of intruding aircraft and the breaking of radio silence. It was as if the communists wanted the Americans to know. If so, their timing could not have been better. As the twenty-plus communist aircraft were dropping their loads inside South Vietnam, Kennedy was about to convene the NSC, and Secretary McNamara and his staff were airborne, on their way to Honolulu. There, the following morning, the Secretary convened the fourth SECDEF conference.

THE FOURTH SECDEF CONFERENCE—
AIR ISSUES

The newly discovered aerial resupply of the Viet Cong was one of several important air issues discussed at the March 22 conference. Two others, the size of the U.S. bomber force in Vietnam and its targets, had been under discussion for weeks. While the conference would put some restrictions on targets, the outcome of the conference was a major expansion of the secret American air war in Vietnam.

At the conference General Anthis used a sudden jump in Viet Cong attacks in March to win approval for adding four more B-26s and four more T-28s to the Farm Gate forces already in Vietnam.[23] He argued that the B-26s were the best aircraft for counterinsurgency, and that the T-28s were needed for detachments at smaller airfields. Nolting and Harkins endorsed the Anthis proposal, but McNamara appeared reluctant on the grounds that the Vietnamese 2d Fighter Squadron was nearly operational. He asked how much longer the American pilots would have to fly with the Vietnamese. General Anthis parried this nicely, replying that Farm Gate would have to "serve as a demonstration force" and "check the state of Vietnamese training and standardization for quite a while." This worked, and McNamara approved their request to add eight more aircraft to the U.S. Farm Gate forces.

The Air Force history of the war has subsequently revealed that McNamara was not told of the "glaring deficiencies" that impeded the Vietnamese Air Force.[24] Not only were there far too few pilots, but those flying were in dire need of more training. Their two fighter squadrons had fewer than twelve qualified flight leaders, and their ground personnel were "generally inefficient." They lacked proficiency in night and all-weather flying; mission turnaround and scramble times were miserably slow; and their planes were not equipped with the full array of ordnance they were cleared to operate with. These were the true reasons why Farm Gate aircraft needed to be increased, and, of course, the reason why Farm Gate operations had reached new high levels.

During the conference General Jablonsky again raised the issue of Farm Gate bombing targets selected—often in an apparently arbitrary manner—by the South Vietnamese.[25] Nolting urged closer scrutiny of bombing operations, while the Defense Secretary, apparently well prepared on the issue, agreed to allow the operations to continue but only under strict controls and stringent intelligence criteria. Air Force Chief of Staff Curtis LeMay—who would visit Vietnam a few weeks later—was pressuring for a far more active American role. The Air Force history summarized his arguments:

> Because Farm Gate was flying less than it could, LeMay wanted crews to log more missions. This would allow American airmen rotating through Vietnam to attain valued experience that might well be needed elsewhere. He suggested relaxing the restrictions calling for a Vietnamese crewman to be aboard Farm Gate planes and confining Farm Gate to offensive missions beyond the competence of the Vietnamese.[26]

McNamara, however, while prepared to expand the American role in the air war, was not about to remove the secrecy surrounding it. By taking the Vietnamese out of the backseat, LeMay's suggestion would remove the training cover for these air strikes, and was consequently unacceptable to the Secretary.

The big news at the conference, of course, was the events of the preceding two nights. The use of Soviet aircraft in large numbers to resupply the Viet Cong inside Vietnam could not go unchecked. With the Chairman of the Joint Chiefs, Lemnitzer, at the conference, General LeMay filled in as the acting chief at the Pentagon. LeMay cabled the President's decision authorizing shoot-down of hostile aircraft to Honolulu while the conference was in session. The reaction in Washington had been favorable, he said, clearance from both the White House and State Department had been received. Only a final plan was needed, and LeMay had four guidelines for it: 1) shoot-downs could not occur in the "Saigon area"; 2) they had to be handled sensitively to "avoid leaks" to the press; 3) they had to "avoid" Cambodian territory; and 4) the final plan had to be approved by the Joint Chiefs. "Request your plan soonest to facilitate approval," LeMay signed off.[27]

The situation presented Kennedy with little choice but to agree to Diem's request for U.S. interceptors. The Viet Cong could not be allowed uninterrupted logistical support from the air. Given the President's imposition of a secrecy blanket on U.S. air combat, however, this new authorization required elaborate planning to conceal from reporters any potential evidence of aerial dogfights. It did not work of course and, as is usually the case with cover stories, the cover turned out to be more interesting than the story.

DEVISING A PLAUSIBLE COVER STORY

The Air Force could not be accused of responding slowly to the President's authorization for air-to-air combat. On Thursday morning, March 22, only hours after Kennedy approved shooting down the Soviet aircraft, three single-seat F-102s and one twin-seat (side-by-side) TF-102 roared down the runway of Clark Air Base in the Philippines and took off out over the East China Sea. They were a detachment of the 509th Interceptor Squadron, 405th Tactical Fighter Wing, and were deploying to Tan Son Nhut, South Vietnam, where they would arrive by nightfall. Their mission was to intercept and destroy communist supply aircraft flown by Chinese and North Vietnamese pilots.[28]

The Washington bureaucracy needed a little more time to catch up. On March 24 Secretary of State Rusk withdrew his opposition to shooting down the Soviet planes in a cable from Geneva. He stated it was of the utmost importance that the "other side" not be permitted to establish this resupply as a precedent and said he hoped "arrangements are being made to see that hostile aircraft over South Vietnam are shot down."[29] On March 26, Under Secretary of State Ball cabled Rusk that Kennedy had approved the rules of engagement for U.S. interdiction of communist aircraft over South Vietnam. Public posture would be discreet he said, and the Air Force had been asked to "work it out" so that if a U.S.-marked plane actually destroyed a communist plane, "public handling will be simply that Communist plane crashed."[30] This lie sprang from the same old dilemma: how to avoid revealing the problem of the "degree to which Americans [are] engaged in active hostilities" in Vietnam.

The next day, March 27, the Joint Chiefs sent a priority message to

CINCPAC authorizing U.S. aircraft to destroy hostile aircraft over South Vietnam.[31] The message made it clear, however, that "declaration of aircraft as hostile will be tempered with judgment and discretion." A Pentagon draft of this message still extant has handwriting on the upper-right-hand corner that clearly reads: "approved by Pres, and State and DOD notified." The Pentagon communications center sent it at 9:52 P.M. Seven minutes later, the center sent another JCS message to CINCPAC with the precedence of "OPS IMMEDIATE." The second message from the Joint Chiefs contained a direct order to Admiral Felt saying it was "mandatory" that he devise "ways and means to ensure maximum discretion and minimum publicity." The Chiefs then gave amplifying instructions to the order: "This effort must be kept in [the] lowest possible key. In the event of loss of U.S. aircraft a plausible cover story or covering action must be ready." The Chiefs even spelled out specific guidelines for the cover: if an enemy aircraft was shot down, the South Vietnamese Air Force (RVNAF) would be credited with the kill; if there was no South Vietnamese aircraft operating in the area, then the loss would be falsely attributed to a crash. Obtaining the cooperation and coordination of the South Vietnamese government was "essential," the Chiefs said. They also made it clear that the order was to be carried out immediately, saying, "Your plans to achieve the above desired as soon as feasible."[32]

It is not every day that a theater CINC receives direct orders from the Joint Chiefs to fabricate false stories, particularly with such clarity and details. Within hours Felt was polishing the plan he would recommend, and the following morning he cabled it to Harkins for coordination.[33] Of course Felt had opposed keeping the air war secret, but once given the task, he did his job well, and the expressions he used for the degrees of deception are an illustration of how deeply mired in its own mesh of secrecy the U.S. government had become. Felt told Harkins that instead of the Joint Chiefs' proposal to keep the operation in *"lowest possible key,"* he preferred to give it the *"usual low key treatment."*

Felt then explained the amusing recipe for a cover story that he had cooked up. If an enemy plane was shot down, he said, the best thing to do was keep silent. This was so, he reasoned, because publicity would have little psychological benefit for "our side" while silence would create "fears of uncertainty in minds of other side." In order to enhance the plausibility of crediting the Vietnamese Air Force with the kills, Felt advised that Vietnamese T-28s should be sent up each time the U.S. F102s were scrambled on a mission. Failing this, "You must resort to story that intruder must have crashed due to accidental causes such as mechanical failure or pilot error."

In the event a U.S. aircraft was lost on an interdiction mission, Felt offered this concoction: "Accident while engaged in routine orientation flight is being investigated in normal manner to determine whether due to mechanical failure, weather or pilot error." In the event an intruder was shot down by a U.S. aircraft, Felt had yet another fabrication in store, and the press had already been set up for it:

> The story is clean-cut to the effect that while on routine training flight [aircraft] investigated unidentified plane which initiated hostile action and was thereupon destroyed. We tend toward opinion that GVN should be encouraged to exploit successful actions against intruders violating GVN airspace. *Groundwork has already been laid by UPI story datelined Saigon 25 Mar by Morton Perry* stating VNAF has begun efforts to intercept unidentified [aircraft] between Pleiku and frontier. [emphasis added]

Felt gave one final instruction to Harkins: commanding officers and officers in charge of those "having knowledge of these things" were to be "instructed and rehearsed." Felt then told Harkins to come up with ways and means and consult with Nolting about it, and then to cable back their ideas so that a fully coordinated plan could be sent to the Joint Chiefs for final approval.

Harkins and Nolting barely had time to digest the contents of this cable from Felt before the Admiral was back on the wire with another one to MACV the following day. In the new cable Felt commented on a State Department cable (number 1144) that has still not been declassified. From the text of Felt's cable, however, we know that the State cable discussed the problem of replying to press questions about the deployment on March 21 of the F-102s that were to be used for shooting down Soviet aircraft. From Felt's message it is clear that State advocated spinning a yarn "to the effect that" night interceptors had been requested by the South Vietnamese government to fill a gap in its Air Force "arsenal," and that "this kind" of a reply might be given by Kennedy at his scheduled press conference the following morning. Kennedy, however, did not mention it.[34]

Two more days of messages went back and forth sculpting and resculpting what was daily becoming an ever more elaborate lie. Finally, on March 29, Admiral Felt sent the Joint Chiefs the final coordinated plan from the Pacific. He began: "Following is my plan for assuring maximum discretion, minimum publicity U.S. air operations in [South Vietnam] in response to Ref A [the Joint Chiefs' order]."[35] This plan deserves to be reproduced here:

> 2. In event an enemy aircraft is destroyed by U.S. air action, *we all remain silent*. No results [of] U.S. missions will be passed via air-

ground radio. If leak develops, VNAF will claim credit through GVN information channels. Plausibility will be reinforced by scheduling VNAF aircraft in air at time and in general area of action.

3. In event hostile aircraft are destroyed by Farm Gate aircraft the VNAF will exploit incident as being VNAF operation through GVN information channels to prov[e] intrusion [into] SVN airspace. Explanation will be that while on routine training flight, aircraft investigated unidentified plane which initiated hostile action and was thereupon destroyed.

4. In event a U.S. aircraft is lost on an operational mission from any cause whatsoever, the explanation in reply to press query is that accident occurred while aircraft [was] engaged in routine orientation flight, [and] that accident [is] being investigated in normal manner to determine cause.

5. [Commander] MACV will take appropriate measures to insure all personnel having knowledge [of] these operations are *instructed and rehearsed* by commanding officers of all units concerned on need for strict observance [of] these ground rules.

6. [Commander] MACV advises that command[er] VNAF agrees to claim credit for any hostile aircraft destroyed and that confirmation higher level and full GVN cooperation [is] being obtained. [emphasis added][36]

This plan was quickly approved by the Joint Chiefs of Staff. An internal NSC memo of March 28 confirmed the order: "All U.S. air units with an interceptor capability [words classified] have been given orders to shoot down any Communist bloc aircraft over South Vietnamese territory in accordance with specified 'rules of engagement.' "[37]

This, then, is how the intricate cover story to hide the order authorizing U.S. aircraft to shoot down Soviet planes over Vietnam was put together. It seems tragic, somehow, that the disparate bureaucracy in Washington, Honolulu, and Saigon could come together with such efficiency, coordination, and energy to fine-tune a false cover story, and yet work with the agility and pace of a turtle on the true problems of the war. Unfortunately, controlling the public impression of the war consumed an inordinate amount of command attention.

"ERRONEOUS" IMPRESSIONS OF U.S. INVOLVEMENT

Large numbers of Viet Cong attackers came out of their mountain hideouts in late March and early April to attack the coastal plains repeatedly, from Da Nang down to Qui Nhon. Some of these attacks were designed to sever the coastal railroad network, but the overall message was as unmistakable as it was in the Delta: no place was safe, and regular government forces were no longer immune. One of these attacks aroused special attention in the press and in Washington. On April 8, a South Vietnamese platoon was overrun by a Viet Cong company-sized force. Two of the four American advisors accompanying the platoon were killed and the other two were captured.

The four Americans were all enlisted men, and had been stationed at the U.S. Special Forces Detachment at Da Nang. On the morning of April 8, they departed with a platoon of South Vietnamese civic action trainees for an exercise near the town of An Chau, in Quang Nam Province. Some of the largest Viet Cong attacks in the northern part of the country had taken place in the previous days. On the 2d, a Viet Cong battalion conducted an operation in Binh Dinh Province to the south, while on the same day another Viet Cong force attacked the railroad further north in Quang Ngai Province. Two days later, a Viet Cong force attacked a Self Defense Corps company in Quang Ngai. On the 6th, a *regimental-sized* Viet Cong operation occurred in Quang Ngai. Two Viet Cong battalions reinforced by a heavy weapons company assaulted a regular South Vietnamese Army installation while, in a coordinated move, more guerrillas overran a Civil Guard post a few miles to the west.[38] The next morning, the Viet Cong were already in their ambush positions near An Chau as the four American advisors set out with the tiny Vietnamese force for a training exercise. At 8:00 A.M., the team radioed it was under attack and asked for help. Three minutes later, they radioed that their position was being overrun.[39]

The response was too slow. Thirty minutes after the call for help, helicopters airlifted twenty U.S. Special Forces personnel and twenty Vietnamese civilian trainees to the ambush area, while additional civic action platoons were dispatched by truck. When they arrived, only a handful of stragglers could be found. Since only one Vietnamese had been killed and only four wounded, it was obvious that most of the platoon had either run away or been captured.[40] At 8:50 a U.S. helicopter spotted the bodies of Staff Sergeant Wayne Marchand and Specialist Five James Gabriel on the side of the road just three kilometers away from where the attack occurred. Both had been shot in the face at close range. This suggested that all four Americans had been alive when the fighting was over, but that these two had been wounded and then presumably murdered because they could not keep up with the Viet Cong withdrawal.[41] According to the report that evening from Da Nang, Gabriel was married, and his wife, in Okinawa, was pregnant. The report warned the Chief MAAG that "Rheinstein [of] NBC was on mission which found US dead. Understand he has sent news release by cable and has newsreel films of this."[42] The report indicated that a U.S. officer by the name of "Jinkins" had "coordinated" a message from the South Vietnamese I Corps Commander to the Vietnamese Joint Chiefs "approving" the use of his two Ranger companies that were down in Saigon for a mission to rescue the two missing Americans. The Da Nang report also requested a "Colonel Dayton" in Saigon to "coordinate" this rescue plan with his Vietnamese counterpart.

Only fragments of all of this reached CINCPAC in the first reports from Saigon. Two, one from MAAG and the other from the Embassy, are still not available, but we know that their contents worried Admiral Felt. His message seven hours later clearly demonstrates the cause of his concern. The message mistakenly informed the JCS that there was "no repeat no information as to press knowledge and/or reaction [about] this incident," but directed MACV to "advise on press handling of U.S. personnel participating in this action." Felt's cable complained that the Embassy message implied that the follow-up action was all U.S. controlled. "Need clearer explanation," the cable demanded.[43] MACV responded by retransmitting the Da Nang message, which CINCPAC in turn relayed to the JCS in Washington. Seven minutes later, CINCPAC passed on to the Joint Chiefs the gist of a telephone call from its own Public Information Officer (PIO), a Lieutenant Colonel Griscti, who had apparently been rushed to Saigon:

> [Public Information Officer] has no knowledge of how Rheinstein NBC handled [it]. Report is he took 500 feet of film of incident, and is sending out unprocessed. Griscti on top of this. He is trying to find out how NBC played story. Will do his best *to get it cleaned up from this end.* Appears now NBC team has already filed story from Da Nang. It will probably be necessary soon to confirm incident to Saigon press stressing Vietnamese training exercise in which US advisors [were] participating in training problem." [emphasis added][44]

What had to be "cleaned up"? The impression that American soldiers were participating in combat.

American soldiers could not avoid combat if they were to do their jobs. Yet even this seemed difficult for the administration to be forthright about. The U.S. commanders on the scene, at least, cared more for the lives of the two captive men, and rushed twenty U.S. Special Forces soldiers to the site in an attempt to rescue them.[45] These Americans arrived well ahead of the Vietnamese reinforcements, and there is no doubt that they would have justifiably gone straight into action to save their comrades had the Viet Cong been within reach. Given the press attention already generated by the incident, this could have led to a much larger problem to "clean up." The Viet Cong, however, along with their American prisoners, were long gone.

The Vietnamese rescue effort to find the two Americans was terminated on April 17 without success. However, they did manage to find the Viet Cong force that had captured them, although it would be more accurate to say the Viet Cong found the rescue team. On April 12, more than 100 Viet Cong ambushed the relief force, and were driven off only by American air strikes.

At a press conference on April 11, a reporter asked the President this question: "Sir, what are you going to do about the American soldiers getting killed in Vietnam?"[46] Kennedy replied, "Well, I'm extremely concerned about American soldiers who are in a great many areas in hazard." He reiterated that U.S. policy was to help Vietnam maintain its independence. He acknowledged the seriousness of its hazards were comparable to World War I, World War II, and Korea, saying, "These four sergeants are in that long roll. But we cannot desist in Vietnam." It must have been an awkward and embarrassing moment for the President. It would have demeaned the lives of the two dead servicemen to have offered anything less than a strong defense of the U.S. presence in Vietnam.

Although the two captured Americans were released by the Viet Cong three weeks later, the incident and the press coverage it generated buffeted a nervous Washington bureaucracy caught in the vise of a deteriorating war and the pressures for expanding U.S. involvement. Three days after the attack, the State Department enjoined all its diplomatic missions to use more caution in discussing the war.[47] The cable opened:

> Department seriously concerned by impression created by some press reports that the war in Viet-Nam is a U.S. war, and which imply that it is a war in which U.S. is directing, in which U.S. is participating and for which U.S. is responsible. Critics of our present policy emphasize "growing U.S. involvement," "U.S. moral responsibilities," and similar concepts, as well as role of U.S. military personnel.

This "erroneous" impression, it continued, was dangerous because of adverse international reaction, and because the Viet Cong might paint the U.S. as assuming the former French colonial role. The growing U.S. involvement in, and moral commitment to, the fate of South Vietnam, however, simply could not be denied or downplayed, particularly if the overseas missions were to retain any credibility at all with the press. The story of the growing U.S. involvement and the concomitant effort to deny it was to become one of the principal failures of the Kennedy administration. The denial did not work then, and has confounded study of Kennedy's Vietnam policies ever since.

Each act taken to cover up the truth served only to draw more attention to it. When the April 18 periodic report of the Vietnam Task Force was forwarded to Kennedy, Harriman singled out publicity and leaks to the press as the top two items most worthy of the President's attention.[48] When the *Princeton* arrived in South Vietnam on April 15, a new U.S. Marine helicopter force, "Shufly," flew directly from the ship to Soc Trang. This was done to avoid the publicity of off-loading in Saigon, and "to avoid a possible citation by the [International Control Commission]."[49] It was a silly idea to try to hide a U.S. Marine helicopter company, the fourth to be deployed and second to be used in III Corps— South Vietnam's Delta region. The press immediately found out about it anyway, which led to another expression of State Department jitters and a request to Saigon to trace the leak. No lesson was learned from this, however. The cover memo to the April 18 Task Force Vietnam report contained the following item:

> The Department learned on 18 April that the USNS *Croatan* is due to arrive Saigon April 20 to unload five jet helicopters (HU-1A's) and 18 H-21 helicopters. The Department has asked [Department of Defense] to arrange for the *Croatan* not to unload in Saigon and to avoid publicity when the helicopters do arrive.

It was a never-ending story of never-ending headaches. In fact, the official lies about American involvement had become so numerous that the reporters became used to them and knew how to account for them in the stories they filed.

The deception had become integral to the routine, so much a part of the way business was carried on in Saigon that no one seemed to notice when a fiction of a different sort emerged, a deception *within* the deception. This story was not told to newspaper reporters. It appears to have been directed at the President himself.

NOTES

1. This account of Davis' death is based exclusively on the story recounted by Ray A. Bows, *Vietnam Military Lore, 1959–1973*, vol. 1 (Hanover, MA: Bowes and Sons, 1988), pp. 21–23.

2. *Air Force History*, p. 116.

3. William Hammond, *U.S. Army in Vietnam: The Military and the Media, 1962–1968* (Washington, D.C.: Center for Military History, U.S. Army, 1980), p. 17.

4. John Mecklin, *Mission in Torment* (Garden City, NY: Doubleday, 1975), p. 110.

5. Ibid.

6. Gilpatric memo to Lemnitzer, January 4, 1962, in *State History*, 1962, Document 3, pp. 4–5.

7. Hammond, *U.S. Army in Vietnam*, p. 17.

8. *Air Force History*, p. 123.

9. *State History*, 1962, Document 76, pp. 158–60.

10. Rowan, *Breaking Barriers*, pp. 211–14.

11. Mecklin, *Mission in Torment*, p. 111.

12. *Air Force History*, p. 136.

13. Ibid., pp. 137–38.

14. David Hudson (Saigon) report on NBC News. For a verbatim text of the salient portion of the report, see State cable to Saigon, No. 1083, March 9, 1962, JFK Library, Newman Papers.

15. State cable to Saigon, No. 1084, March 9, 1962, JFK Library, Newman Papers.

16. OSD, WASH DC cable to CINCPAC, Exclusive for ADM Felt from ASD (PA) SGD Sylvester, March 9, 1962, JFK Library, Newman Papers.

17. CINCPAC cable to JCS, 110740Z MAR 62, JFK Library, Newman Papers and NSF, Country File, Vietnam, Box 196. Note: the first paragraph of this message is confusing, containing references to coordination with Harriman, and State Department statements of "9 or 19" March. The message serial, a standard military date-time group, confirms the March 11 date for its transmittal.

18. Robert S. Allen and Paul Scott, *Los Angeles Times*, March 13, 1962, p. 20.

19. *Air Force History*, pp. 128–29.

20. MACV cable No. 210531Z MAR 62, JFK Library, NSF, Country File, Vietnam, Box 196. A shorter version can be found in *Air Force History*, p. 129.

21. MACV cable No. 210531Z MAR 62, JFK Library, NSF, Country File, Vietnam, Box 196.

22. Ibid.

23. *Air Force History*, p. 131.

24. Ibid., p. 132.

25. The reason he did so was probably because Nolting had passed on to Hilsman a few days earlier the discussion of March 3 (see above), and since Hilsman was to report to the President, it could be assumed that the charge of civilian deaths and their propaganda value to the Viet Cong would thus reach the President. MACV likely had been provided a copy of McNamara's briefing book for the conference, which contained an account of the conversation to include the fact that Jablonsky had surfaced the issue in the first place.

26. *Air Force History*, pp. 131–32.

27. JCS cable to CINCPAC, 211425Z MAR 62, JFK Library, Newman Papers.

28. *Air Force History*, pp. 130–31.

29. Rusk cable to State, March 24, 1962, in *State History*, 1962, Document 128, p. 273.

30. State cable to Geneva, No. 150, March 26, 1962, JFK Library, Newman Papers and NSF Country File, Vietnam, Box 196.

31. JCS cable to CINCPAC, 3796, 270300z MAR 62, JFK Library, NSF, Vietnam, Box 196. The message stated:

> The JCS authorize the destruction of hostile aircraft which may appear over South Vietnam by U.S. aircraft operating in South Vietnam in accordance with the following rules of combat:
>
> "1. United States aircraft, operating in South Vietnam at the invitation of the Government of South Vietnam and in consonance with existing instructions, may, where means of deviating or bringing the aircraft under control are not practically possible, engage and destroy hostile aircraft within the geographical limits of South Vietnam to include territorial waters."

32. JCS cable to CINCPAC, 3797, March 26, 1962, 2159 hours, JFK Library, Newman Papers and NSF Country File, Vietnam, Box 196.

33. CINCPAC cable to MACV, 272041z MAR 62, JFK Library, Newman Papers and NSF Country File, Vietnam, Box 196.

34. Kennedy, *Public Papers*, 1962, pp. 254–61.

35. The CINCPAC message was to the JCS, with the White House, "ATTN COL Bagley/GEN Taylor Office," as an info addressee. Handwriting on the White House copy of this message, probably Bagley's, and directed to McGeorge Bundy, states: "Mr. Bundy, this is latest on SVN aircraft rules of engagement cover plan. Seems entirely adequate. You may be called by State or Defense. Do you concur in this approach? Nolting concurs." Someone crossed out the sentence "Do you concur in this approach?," but it is still clearly legible. Colonel Bagley, or whoever wrote on this message, also drew an arrow pointing to the words "my plan" and wrote "actually COMUSMACV [Harkins] plan." In other words, Admiral Felt's plan was simply a reiteration of a plan submitted to him by General Harkins.

36. CINCPAC cable to JCS, 290138Z MAR 62, JFK Library, Newman Papers and NSF Country File, Vietnam, Box 196.

37. Memo from NSC Executive Secretary Lucius D. Battle to McGeorge Bundy, "Subject: Status of Actions With Respect to South Vietnam," March 28, 1962, JFK Library, Newman Papers and NSF Country File, Vietnam, Box 202/203.

38. Ibid.

39. Senior Advisor, Da Nang, cable to Chief MAAG Saigon and MACV, 080955Z April, 1962, JFK Library, Newman Papers and NSF Country File, Vietnam, Box 196.

40. MACV cable to JCS, 091007Z, April 1962, JFK Library, Newman Papers and NSF Country File, Vietnam, Box 196.

41. Senior Advisor, Da Nang, cable to Chief MAAG Saigon and MACV, 080955Z, April 1962, p. 2, JFK Library, Newman Papers.

42. Ibid.

43. CINCPAC cable to JCS and MACV, 082003Z April 1962. JFK Library, Newman Papers and NSF Country File, Vietnam, Box 196.

44. CINCPAC cable to JCS, 090455Z April 1962. JFK Library, Newman Papers and NSF Country File, Vietnam, Box 196.

45. USARPAC Intelligence Bulletin, May 1962, p. 7, JFK Library, Newman Papers.

46. Kennedy, *Public Papers*, 1962, p. 322.

47. State cable no. 1730, April 11, 1962, JFK Library, Newman Papers.

48. L.D. Battle (NSC Executive Secretary) memo for McGeorge Bundy, Subject: Status of Actions With Respect to South Vietnam, April 18, 1962, JFK Library, Newman Papers.

49. Ibid.; Vietnam Task Force Status Report, April 18, 1962, p. 1.

CHAPTER TWELVE

WEBS OF DECEPTION

"O what a tangled web we weave, when first we practice to deceive."
—Sir Walter Scott,
Marmion, 1808

One afternoon in March 1962 an American H-21 helicopter lifted off from Saigon and headed for Bac Lieu Province.[1] Three passengers were on board, all from MACV. The ranking man was the MACV Intelligence (J-2) Chief, Colonel Winterbottom. Army Captain Don Blascak carried Winterbottom's duffel bag, which contained the Colonel's lunch and his Swedish K machine gun. Blascak worked primarily in the Special Operations section of the J-2 in MACV, but he accompanied Winterbottom on trips like these. On this occasion Winterbottom was also accompanied by the civilian head of his order of battle team, George Allen. Winterbottom was conducting a survey of U.S. intelligence advisors in the III Corps area in the Delta, and on this day his objective was to exchange information with the U.S. intelligence advisor to South Vietnam's 21st Division, Army Major Jonathan Ladd.

The plan had been to call first on the division commander, and so the helicopter headed for the division command post. When the Americans arrived, however, they discovered that the commander and Major Ladd were out on an operation. The Vietnamese volunteered the location of it and the three intelligence officers reboarded the H-21 and flew to the site. Allen found the division intelligence (G-2) chief, and during their discussions, reports suddenly came in that a Viet Cong platoon had just run into a tree line so close to them they could see it. As was the case so often in situations like these, the South Vietnamese commander did not send in troops to flush out the communists. He called in a U.S. air strike.

During the next forty long minutes there was no activity from the Viet Cong, no sniper fire, nothing. Finally the American B-26s arrived, and flew "right down the tree-line, napalm all over the goddamned place." When this was over, the division commander boldly ordered a company in to check out the situation. The minutes rolled by as Allen and the other advisors waited impatiently for word of the outcome. Still no activity, no shots, no movement. Eventually the time to depart arrived. Allen and the others were naturally still curious, so they asked the Vietnamese what had happened. The reply was disappointingly short: "Well, no sign of any bodies or anything."

The ride back to Saigon was more eventful. Allen recalls:

> Winterbottom, as usual, is sitting in the open door of the chopper, with one cheek hanging out, and his back up against the door. Blascak is sitting up in the same side of the chopper as the door is on, and I'm across the way, and Blascak looks over at me and gets my eye. . . .

With a playful look on his face, Blascak motioned with his hands for Allen to push Winterbottom out of the chopper. Allen couldn't help but laugh at the thought of Winterbottom screaming on his way down. "I didn't have the guts to do it," Allen jokes about it now. "Geez, it would have been a service to the country. It really would." To this day, whenever they meet, Blascak greets him with: "You should have done it, George."

It did not take long for Winterbottom to do something that would remind Allen why he disliked him so much:

> [Winterbottom is] stewing, and just after we land in Saigon on our return, he says, "How many guys in a platoon, George?" And I say "Oh, about thirty-six. That would be standard." And he said, "Okay." And so the next day, when that incident is reported, the MACV report says thirty-six KIA [killed in action]. And I went in to him and I said, "Where'd they get this? When we left they had no body count at all. They didn't see anything that they knew were the bodies." And he said, "Well, ah, it was a platoon that ran into the goddamned tree-line wasn't it?" I said, "Yeah." And he said, "Well Christ, they, you know, they napalmed the goddamned place! They must have killed them all."

Winterbottom had put the 36 KIAs in the MACV report himself. "It was crazy," Allen said later, "just crazy."

Crazy yes, but not unusual for the MACV Intelligence Chief. As Allen and the others involved in MACV's ongoing intelligence work would soon find out, an incident like this was only the tip of the iceberg. When they submitted their order of battle findings to Winterbottom, a great deal more than a platoon of Viet Cong disappeared in the jungle.

BACK CHANNEL TO THE VICE PRESIDENT

At the third SECDEF conference in February, General Harkins had painted the war effort in very optimistic terms. His rosy accounts provided to McNamara at this and subsequent SECDEF conferences were exactly the opposite of the bleak situation being detailed by his own intelligence analysts and those at USARPAC as well. Yet McNamara's view of the war effort was based principally on the accounts of his field commanders. Consequently, his testimony on March 16 to the House Appropriations Committee reflected their confident and hopeful statements. The Defense Secretary told the congressmen he was optimistic about the war; that he believed that the U.S. would attain its objectives; and that the end appeared to be in sight. He said: "I would say definitely we are approaching it from the point of view of trying to clean it up and *terminating* subversion, covert aggression and combat operations" [emphasis added].[2]

The same day McNamara was telling Congress how the U.S. was winning the war, Lyndon Johnson was in his office reading about how the war was being lost. By the middle of March 1962 one's view of the war depended entirely on who gave you your information. Why the Vice President was reading an opposite and, as shall be seen, true account of the battlefield situation is one of the great mysteries of the Vietnam War during the Kennedy years. There is incontrovertible proof, however, that accurate details of the failing war effort were provided to Johnson through a privileged intelligence back channel.

Ironically, the first documentary evidence of this back channel bears the same date as McNamara's optimistic testimony to Congress. In a March 16 memorandum to Johnson, his Military Aide, Air Force Colonel Howard Burris, flatly proclaimed that "the U.S. program in South Vietnam still has not reversed the level nor intensity of Viet Cong operations."[3] Whereas communist attacks were formerly made by small groups of men, he said, attacks were now executed by company- and battalion-sized units. In other words, while Burris was telling Johnson that the U.S. program had not made a dent in Viet Cong operations—which, on the contrary, he said, were becoming even larger—McNamara was telling Congress the end of the war was in sight.

Were McNamara's comments a reflection of the policy of official optimism? According to the U.S. Army's *The Military and the Media,
1962–1968*, steering the press away from South Vietnam's defeats on the
battlefield "toward other areas of progress" *was* official policy.[4] Occasion-
ally, when the newspapers cooperated, this policy did produce optimistic
press accounts. For example: "McNamara Off on Trip," read a March 21
headline in the *Baltimore Sun*, "for another of his periodic visits to the
Pacific command relative to the extremely fluid situation in South Vietnam."[5] The article was upbeat, and printed the military's assurances that a
"slow improvement" of South Vietnam's position was taking place due to
a number of "successful actions." These included the growing skills of
South Vietnam's government forces, improved equipment, the breaking
up of several guerrilla strongholds, and, not least, the "influential" activities of the U.S. "military assistance group." Singled out for particular praise
was the new U.S. equipment provided to Vietnam, the value of which, the
press was told, had been clearly demonstrated since McNamara's last visit
in February. Precisely because steering the press *was* official policy, however, such newspaper stories are not the best indicators of what McNamara
was told nor what he believed was happening on the battlefield.

To unravel the twisted story of who knew what, and, more importantly,
what McNamara knew or was told, we must first understand what MACV
was reporting to him at his SECDEF conferences. These were top secret
meetings, where the most sensitive classified intelligence from the battlefield was shown to the Secretary and the top Pentagon brass, information
which did *not* find its way into the newspapers. It was behind these closed
doors that General Harkins and his MACV staff presented the facts,
statistics, and analyses upon which McNamara based his view of the war.
What did it mean when the Secretary emerged from these conferences
and made optimistic remarks? Was he holding back anything significant
he had heard in these meetings? The record suggests he was not: like the
third SECDEF conference before it, the news MACV gave McNamara
in March at the fourth SECDEF conference was an account of great
progress, and McNamara honestly reported to the press the gist of what
he heard.

Why, then, was the Vice President's information so different? Consider,
for example, the Burris memo to Johnson on March 30.[6] In it he delivered
to LBJ an even more lurid account of the failing war effort than he had
on the 16th. Intensification of Viet Cong activity "on an increasingly
broader spectrum" was under way, Burris said, and had now crossed the
threshold of direct attacks against units of South Vietnam's regular forces.
What is particularly arresting about this March 30 memo is the raw data
Burris included in it, data that was explicitly and forcefully contradicted
at the March conference. The memo stated:

In the face of this increased activity, South Viet Nam statistics, in one area in particular, are somewhat alarming. Desertions from the regular forces have increased to 1,000 a month. Even this does not include the figures among the para-military forces. When the battle casualties are added the total losses are expected to increase to the point where an overall increase in the effectiveness of the South Viet Nam armed forces is doubtful.

Where was the Vice President's information coming from? Burris says he "got a lot of raw information."[7] When pressed for his exact sources he replied, "We got it from everywhere." In a more revealing explanation on another occasion he said: "They'd hand you a copy of a memo. You'd get stuff from the boys in the woodwork. Later McCone put a stop to what I was getting."

Burris says that "the figures, facts, and circumstances were tailored to make them look good," and it was being done, he says, to support a "point of view" and prevent the "top people" from looking at "all sides" of the situation; but, he explains, "I had other ways to get the information—I could get the McNamara memos too."[8] By this he means material from the McNamara conferences and "what Harkins was telling him." Did the Vice President talk to Burris about this? "Oh sure," Burris states. "We talked about it a lot." The Vice President told Burris to "find out what the hell was going on." Johnson felt McGeorge Bundy and McNamara were "working hand in hand"; Burris claims LBJ did not like them, and told him: "Keep me posted on what they're doing and what they're up to."

So Burris went forth to gather and report as honestly as he could the inside scoop for the Vice President on the battlefield and on who was saying what about it and to whom in Washington. In his March 16 memo Burris delivered an illuminating summary of whom he had talked with about the fact that the war was going badly. He had *not*, he said, brought the matter to the attention of McNamara, but had kept track of what the "commanders of the Pacific" were telling him. He also indicated he was talking with people in General Taylor's "office" and on the "staff" of the Joint Chiefs. They had confirmed the grim battlefield news and talking with them had failed to produce any estimate as to when the negative trend "might be reversed." Before long, he had put together the following general information:

> Taylor and Harkins had one view. Then there was the JCS, and there were the professionals. Then there was also this Colonel [meaning himself] telling the Vice President something else. [McGeorge] Bundy didn't like the memos I was sending to LBJ.

While it is unclear why McGeorge Bundy would have disliked Burris' memos to LBJ, Burris' claim that Taylor and Harkins held the same view on the war would be borne out by later events. As for where the details of the failing war effort came from, an exhaustive search to find documents that match the Burris memos by date and content has produced only one source: the USARPAC Intelligence Bulletins in Hawaii.[9]

These USARPAC bulletins were at odds with MACV reporting from the very start. While General Harkins talked optimistically about the war at the February SECDEF conference, USARPAC analysts, in an office not very far from where the conference was taking place, were busy putting together a far different account of the war. The results of their work would shortly be published as the feature item in the March 1 edition of the USARPAC Intelligence Bulletin. The headline bluntly read: "Guerrilla War Drags On in South Vietnam."[10] The article explained that the South Vietnamese government was making no substantial headway in regaining effective control, and lamented that "the sapping of Government strength and authority continues." Its author complained of the growing monotony of weekly reports on friendly operations conducted "without significant results," and said flatly, "The Communists are more than holding their own." Hard-core Viet Cong forces had risen to 20,000–22,000, up from the 16,000–20,000 USARPAC had reported in February. This "powerful enemy force" was slowly growing in size and influence despite heavy casualties, the article concluded, and warned that "it appears certain that enemy capability for large-scale action has in no way diminished."

The disparity between the USARPAC and MACV reporting was even more pronounced by the time of the fifth SECDEF conference in May. So was the difference between what the President heard from McNamara and what the Vice President heard from Burris. These dissimilarities are unsettling. The fact that General Taylor knew the truth is as arresting as the fact that the Vice President knew. Taylor was the President's Military Representative. Did Taylor pass what he knew on to Kennedy? There is nothing in the record or in Taylor's writings that suggests he did so.

If the Vice President knew the truth, and if members of the Joint Staff knew the truth, why didn't any of them tell McNamara? The answer is elusive. There is no evidence that he knew or suspected what was going on in March; but there is evidence that he was worried. Scrawled in handwriting at the end of the March 16 Burris memo is the following postscript: "This same question of 'where are we in [South] Vietnam' still disturbs Mr. McNamara. He is leaving today, Mar[ch] 20, for meetings in Honolulu, where he hopes to obtain some answers." He got answers all right, but not an accurate picture of the battlefield. When the March

22 conference was over McNamara told reporters that the discussions were the most encouraging he had heard thus far. He stated:

> I am pleased to learn that the armed forces of Vietnam are taking the offensive throughout the country, carrying the war to the Viet Cong, inflicting higher casualty rates, and capturing Viet Cong weapons and supplies in greater numbers.[11]

Unknown to McNamara, what happened at the conference went well beyond the subtle slanting of figures.

A DECEPTION WITHIN THE DECEPTION

The highly selective use of statistics by MACV at the fourth SECDEF conference effectively concealed the failure of the war, and the point bears emphasizing that this was carried out *inside* the U.S. government. This effort had nothing to do with the official optimism inherent in press releases to the public; rather, it was an illusion created in top secret briefings to convince the Secretary of Defense and, through him, the President, that the war was being won. The withholding from the public of the details of the American role in the war was a broader deception within which this deeper subterfuge was executed. It was, in effect, a deception *within* a deception.

It is important at the outset to define clearly what is meant by this *inside* deception. The target has already been stated: the President; the objective was to hide the failure of the war effort from him; the story was that the enemy's size and area of control were manageable, and that the South Vietnamese Army was winning on the battlefield. Not all of the elements of this deception story were used at the fourth SECDEF conference: *hiding* some key facts or presenting them *out of context* was sufficient to permit a story of battlefield success to be told. By the time of the fifth SECDEF conference in May, the stakes in both Saigon and Washington had risen, and it would become necessary to include other elements in the story that would require the *falsification* of intelligence information.

McNamara's statement to the press after the March 22 conference— that the South Vietnamese Army was taking the offensive—resulted from critical data being hidden from him. Again, the true facts of the failing war effort were being documented and prepared for publication by intelligence analysts at USARPAC. The work of these analysts, which appeared in the

April 1 edition of the USARPAC Intelligence Bulletin, strongly suggests that any claim of a South Vietnamese offensive against the Viet Cong was baseless. The title of the April 1 feature article was itself instructive: "Pace of Viet Cong War in South Vietnam Slowly Accelerating."[12] In other words, the pace of the Viet Cong offensive, *not* South Vietnamese operations, was picking up. The government's operations would not significantly increase in tempo until later in the year.

It so happened that this USARPAC report contained the riveting news of the significant numbers of Soviet aircraft being used to resupply the Viet Cong. It stated, "The presence of the planes probably was the most significant development in last month's Communist operations in South Vietnam." It also revealed what the briefers at the conference did *not* tell McNamara: the reason for this large and sudden aerial resupply effort. In the weeks immediately before the March SECDEF conference, the Viet Cong had undertaken their biggest operations in the war to date. Consequently, more weapons and equipment were necessary to support their offensive, and the airdrops were the most effective way to maintain its tempo. The USARPAC report left no doubt that a major change in Viet Cong operations was under way. It recapitulated the earlier pattern of enemy attacks through late February: small in scale, directed against isolated outposts of South Vietnamese paramilitary forces, and accompanied by intensive political and military organizing in the countryside. As March began, however, the pattern changed markedly: larger in scale, more aggressive and better armed forces, and directed against the regular South Vietnamese Army.

Let us consider another statement McNamara made right after the conference: that South Vietnamese forces were inflicting higher casualties on the Viet Cong. This statement resulted from the way in which facts were presented out of context to him during the conference. What the briefers *failed* to tell him was the reason why Viet Cong casualty rates were up. Here are the facts: Viet Cong casualties had been running a little over 400 a week since October 1961, and were up 25 percent to 500 a week only during the mid-February to mid-March time frame, and only then because during this period the Viet Cong undertook a large-scale offensive. Government casualties showed an identical rise and fall, with both sides declining at the end of March when Viet Cong attacks again abated.[13]

In other words, Viet Cong casualties were already back down to their normal level by the time McNamara listened to the MACV briefing. The facts, in their true context—a Viet Cong offensive—were known to MACV intelligence before the conference. Statistics, however, can easily be made to tell a different story, and McNamara's weakness for statistics was by then lengendary. In hindsight, one can only wonder what McNa-

mara's reaction would have been if the briefer had told him not only
what the casualty statistics actually meant, but also what U.S. military
intelligence had recently discovered about them. This revelation had already been published in the March 1 USARPAC Intelligence Bulletin: "a
recent, reliable report states President Diem's military psywar [psychologi-
cal warfare] chief has ordered government casualty figures to be slashed
by 30% and enemy losses augmented by the same amount."[14] This would
mean that government casualties were actually running consistently 20 to
30 percent *above* those of the Viet Cong.

A final example of critical information on the war that was not shown
to McNamara at the conference was the unhappy news that the South
Vietnamese Army was hemorrhaging worse off the battlefield than it was
on it. No one told McNamara at the conference what U.S. military
intelligence had learned about the statistics on desertions and defections.
(When a Viet Cong soldier bolted ranks it was a "defection," but when a
South Vietnamese soldier did it was a "desertion.") The monthly Viet
Cong defection rate was running around 200 a month, compared to
around 1,200 a month for South Vietnam's regular armed forces alone.
This was a dramatic increase from the 1961 figure of 450 a month, and
did not include the estimated 250 a month deserting from the Self Defense
Corps. These facts were reported in the April 1 USARPAC Intelligence
Bulletin, *and* in the office of the Vice President. These statistics were
identical to those, discussed previously, that appeared in Burris' March
30 memo to LBJ.[15]

The SECDEF conferences had become the vehicle through which a
fictionalized account of the war was being funneled to the President—
through his principal advisor on Vietnam, Robert McNamara. *Why* this
was being done will become apparent later when the events that unfolded
off the battlefield during April in Washington and Saigon are examined.
Those events, however, began as a consequence of what the Viet Cong
were doing on the battlefield, and they were doing a great deal.

THE BATTLEFIELD SITUATION

The Chairman of the Joint Chiefs of staff, General Lemnitzer, who had
attended the fourth SECDEF conference with McNamara, proceeded to
Vietnam for an "intensive" two-day inspection of the battlefield to see
the supposed South Vietnamese offensive firsthand.[16] On March 30 the
General sent a glowing report to McNamara summarizing his trip. The
highlight was a helicopter ride to a "rich farming community" in northern

I Corps where, he was told, a two-battalion South Vietnamese Army operation against the Viet Cong was "in progress." Using helicopters, he said enthusiastically, he and Harkins had visited the commander conducting the operation. Lemnitzer was "impressed" by the way the operation was handled. "By the time I arrived," he said, the Viet Cong had withdrawn to nearby mountains "where operations were being pressed against them." In other words, the General had not really *seen* anything!

The Chairman's trip was just one more brick in the facade of progress put together by General Harkins. Lemnitzer, a professional military man, was no less susceptible to eyewash than his civilian boss, McNamara. The true battlefield situation continued to be disturbing. U.S. Army intelligence showed that the pace of the war's deterioration was increasing. Viet Cong expansion was more marked in the southern Delta area of III Corps, but the enemy was also making considerable gains in the northern area, where Lemnitzer had just been.

As already mentioned, early March saw the Viet Cong launch their largest attacks of the war, in many cases taking their offensive directly to the regular South Vietnamese Army. The initial, almost daily, wave of attacks ended on March 15–16, with large concentrations of Viet Cong forces attacking in An Xuyen and Chuong Thien provinces in the south of the III Corps sector. After a brief respite, the Viet Cong offensive began again in earnest on March 19 and 20. Moreover, on these dates, the Viet Cong went after *new kinds* of targets, temporarily seizing the Cape Varella lighthouse to confiscate its radio equipment, and employing an entire battalion in an operation against the shipyards in Go Cong Province south of Saigon. On the 25th, the Go Cong shipyards were attacked by another battalion-sized force, while from the 26th through the 31st, the Viet Cong conducted six different raids within a small area against the coastal railroad network near Phan Thiet (just outside the III Corps sector in Binh Thuan Province). In these and subsequent attacks, the Viet Cong crippled the railroad network, dealing a severe blow to the economy and slowing delivery of U.S. weapons and other supplies to South Vietnamese forces.

The momentum of Viet Cong assaults in the Delta continued to build during late March and blossomed into a crescendo during April. On April 1, a Viet Cong battalion struck in An Xuyen Province on the Ca Mau Peninsula, a few miles east of where a large Viet Cong force had attacked only three days earlier. On the 2d another large concentration attacked in Phong Dinh Province just a few miles from Can Tho, the main city in the Delta. On the 4th, another Viet Cong battalion carried out an operation a few miles northeast of Saigon in Hau Nghia Province, while on the 6th yet another battalion attacked again to the southwest of Can Tho. The

Viet Cong had thus conducted five battalion-level attacks in just nine days in the III Corps sector alone.

The developing April offensive in the Delta displayed creative tactics and underscored an ominous new trend. On April 9 a large force of Viet Cong attacked an outpost defended by 102 South Vietnamese Civil Guard troops in Vinh Binh Province, while the same day another battalion attacked just to the west of My Tho, the seat of the 7th Division headquarters. The Vinh Binh operation was typical of the menacing new trend that saw ever larger quantities of new American weapons and equipment falling into the hands of the Viet Cong.[17] U.S. advisors in the Delta now viewed these Civil Guard and SDC outposts as "VC supply points," and their elimination became an early American priority.[18] On April 13, the Viet Cong delivered a convincing demonstration of an ingenious tactic, used only sparingly in 1961, east of Can Tho, in Vinh Binh Province. A Viet Cong battalion raided a paramilitary outpost for weapons, while another enemy force ambushed and trapped the South Vietnamese forces attempting to rush to the scene of the attack. This tactic was successful in several more operations in April and soon became a standard technique.

The May 1 USARPAC Intelligence Bulletin's feature article was titled: "Enemy Presses Hard on Shaky South Vietnam Regime."[19] The analysis was the most pessimistic to date. "Despite friendly pressure on the Viet Cong," it said, "the Communists appear to be moving steadily ahead with plans." The article stated frankly that none of the war's major statistical indices reflected an improvement in the capabilities of the South Vietnamese Army that should have occurred as a result of the level of U.S. aid, advice, and equipment. On the contrary, the unabridged statistics showed the Viet Cong were gaining steadily. The gloomy USARPAC report concluded that the actual situation was even worse than the statistics indicated. The *record* number (an all-time monthly high of 1,861) of Viet Cong attacks in March, the bulletin said, "does not tell the whole story." The real point, according to the bulletin, was the fact that these attacks were increasing in both scale and in distribution in time and locale.

All of this boiled down to the fact that the Kennedy program was flat on its back in Vietnam. The Viet Cong had taken measure of the new program and were expanding as quickly as they had been in 1961 before it started. They had been quick to alter their tactics to counter the effectiveness of the helicopter: quick strikes followed by withdrawal in fifteen minutes to avoid rapid reaction pursuit by heliborne government troops.[20] Were the facts of the failing battlefield placed before the national leadership and command authority charged with responsibility for decision making? The answer is no. Once again, the headline and the detailed information wound up *not* in Kennedy's office, but in Johnson's.

On April 16 LBJ sat in his office pondering the latest intelligence on the failing effort in Vietnam. A memo from Burris of that date[21] provided Johnson with the precise raw data that ended up in the May 1 USARPAC Intelligence Bulletin two weeks later. Burris informed Johnson that Viet Cong operations in the month of March had reached an all-time high of 1,861 incidents. He passed on a similarly gloomy assessment of the war's progress: "The activities and effectiveness of South Vietnam forces were not sufficient to show a net gain or effectiveness in the struggle." On the other hand, Burris noted "increasing effectiveness" of the Viet Cong, particularly as reflected in communications and supply, and pointed out "apparently a portion of the supplies for the rebels comes across the border from Laos where air transport activity reached new levels last week."

DIFFERENT LENS, SAME PICTURE

In addition to McNamara there was another lens through which the President saw top secret details about the war: the biweekly Vietnam Task Force reports authored by Cottrell at the State Department. The President read them regularly. While the task force meetings considered inputs from all national agencies in its deliberations, the crucial input on the battlefield situation for its reports came *directly* from MACV. In this way, MACV battlefield assessments took a short, unfiltered route to Kennedy's desk. Their content, of course, was identical to the optimistic line given to McNamara at the SECDEF conferences.

Take for example the April 18 Vietnam Task Force report, which included MACV's assessment of the war for April 4–11. A short cover memo summarized the MACV assessment as "moderately optimistic," and said, "Despite many complications arising from the nature of the war, the situation is far from being unmanageable."[22] The only realism added to this predictable pabulum were the comments that too many South Vietnamese troops were employed in static security missions and that much of the rural population was still "unenthusiastic" about the regime. Most of the MACV input to the task force report, however, was a distortion.

MACV excluded the details of the ongoing Viet Cong offensive from its input to the task force report, entitled "General Evaluation of Security Situation."[23] Instead it highlighted South Vietnamese–initiated actions, improved reaction time to Viet Cong attacks, and significant Viet Cong losses resulting from counteraction by government forces. The truth, however, was that Viet Cong weekly losses during April 2–9 had increased only slightly, from 505 to 540; more importantly, they had *fallen* significantly during April 9–16, from 540 to 393, while government casualties had increased from 260 to 307. This news, reported in the May 1 USARPAC bulletin, was based on information held by MACV.[24] The question arises as to why MACV chose to report on casualties from April 4–11 for an April 18 task force report. This was a Tuesday-to-Tuesday period, instead of the Sunday-to-Sunday period normally used (such as April 9–16). The reason appears, again, to have been the manipulative use of statistics to paint a positive picture of the war.

The MACV input went on to note the addition of 3,000 men to the Vietnamese Air Force as well as an increase in the number of South Vietnamese and U.S. Farm Gate missions flown. These statistics, standing alone, gave the positive impression of an improving Vietnamese Air Force capability. This is the same artificial impression delivered to McNamara at the fourth SECDEF conference in March, which was dealt with earlier. The MACV input also noted a 3,000-man increase to South Vietnam's Self Defense Corps. Again, the truth about the strength of the SDC was alarming. Consider the South Vietnamese Government's own reporting[25] on SDC casualties—over 1,000 a month—and U.S. Army intelligence estimates of SDC defections—about 200 a month.[26] These figures even taken at face value would indicate over 3,600 losses to the ranks of the SDC for the first three months of 1962. Since U.S. Army intelligence knew that South Vietnam was underreporting its own casualties by 30 percent, the real losses were substantially higher.

The glowing bottom line of the April 4–11 MACV input to the task force report was as follows:

> The Country Team's relations with the GVN are good, and the framework for successful prosecution of the war exists now. While the situation is complicated by many considerations which do not exist in a conventional war, it is far from unmanageable and the overall outlook is optimistic.

The fact is, however, that this MACV input distorted Viet Cong losses, provided statistics on the air force and the SDC out of their true context, and generally corrupted the true picture of the war. Yet the Vietnam Task Force report dutifully transmitted this artfully embellished snapshot of military accomplishments to the President. The President, however, had just thrown a wrench into the gears of U.S. military involvement in the war.

A STRUGGLE ERUPTS OVER "REVERSAL OF U.S. POLICY"

On Sunday, April 1, Ambassador (to India) John Kenneth Galbraith met with the President at the latter's private retreat in Glen Ora, near Middleburg, Virginia. Galbraith was greatly concerned about the growing U.S. commitment to Vietnam and confronted Kennedy over the wisdom of it. Only a month earlier he had written the President and asked: "Incidentally, who is the man in your administration who decides what countries are strategic? I would like to have his name and address and ask him what is so important about this real estate in the space age."[27] He urged the President to keep open the possibility of a neutralist political solution along the lines then being pursued in Laos, and warned of the political dangers of such a highly visible U.S. presence.[28]

Kennedy, says Galbraith, "was immediately interested," and directed him to talk with Harriman and McNamara about it.[29] Kennedy also asked him to put his ideas in writing, which he did in a memorandum dated April 4. In it Galbraith suggested that "U.S. policy keep open the door for a political solution," and also that "we should measurably reduce our commitment to the particular present leadership of South Viet-Nam." Galbraith even went so far as to recommend that those U.S. forces already in South Vietnam not be involved in "combat action" and be kept out of "actual combat commitment," and that "their various roles should be as invisible as the situation permits."[30]

Two days later the President met with Harriman and Michael Forrestal to discuss the Galbraith memo.[31] Harriman disagreed with the idea of a neutral solution in Vietnam, and said that although Diem was a "losing horse" in the long run, "we should not actively work against him" because there was no one to replace him. He did agree that it was important that "overt association of the U.S. with military operations in Vietnam be reduced to absolute minimum." The President, on the other hand, made a comment that had profound implications: "he wished us to be prepared to *seize upon any favorable moment to reduce our commitment*, recognizing that the moment might yet be some time away" [emphasis added]. This comment, which exposed the President's true feelings against deepening involvement in the war, wound its unwelcome way around Washington.

The Joint Chiefs argued vehemently against the Galbraith proposal. They warned McNamara on April 13 that "any *reversal of U.S. policy* could have disastrous effects, not only on our relationship with South Vietnam, but with the rest of our Asian and other allies as well" [emphasis added].[32] They reminded the Secretary of Kennedy's public commitments to support South Vietnam "to whatever extent may be necessary to eliminate the Viet Cong threat" and of the President's communications to Diem along the same lines. They urged "that the present U.S. policy toward South Vietnam, as announced by the President, should be pursued vigorously to a successful conclusion."

In just five months the central issue in Vietnam policy had changed from whether or not to send in combat forces to whether or not to reduce the level of advisors. Understanding this contextual change in the policy debate is crucial in order to appreciate the extraordinary events that would shortly take place in the military's Vietnam intelligence operations and in high-level meetings in Honolulu and Saigon during the spring of 1962. American pilots were already flying combat missions and ferrying South Vietnamese units into battle, and these battles were being directed as much as possible by American advisors attached to these units. Although presidential approval for U.S. ground combat forces had not been given, it is clear that the envelope was being pushed to its extremity. After all, had not McNamara promised them in December they could have anything they wanted *except* combat troops? Yet reducing American involvement was precisely what Kennedy and McNamara would shortly direct the military to plan for and implement.[33]

It would be a difficult situation to turn around. American advisors, full of confidence that they could help the South Vietnamese Army capture the initiative on the battlefield, were still pouring in. Whole units were still arriving. On April 9, U.S. Marine KC-130s began a five-day airlift out of Futemma, Okinawa, to deploy an element of Marine Air Base Squadron 16 to Soc Trang in the Delta region of South Vietnam. Meanwhile, U.S. Marine Medium Helicopter Squadron 362 left Okinawa aboard the *Princeton*. They arrived off the Mekong Delta at dawn on Palm Sunday, April 15.[34] This Marine helicopter squadron, which would be known as Shufly, joined the three Marine helicopter companies already in Vietnam. Their mission was to provide troop and cargo lift for South Vietnamese combat units, and their first operation was a week later, on Easter Sunday.

The intensity with which the Joint Chiefs argued against the Galbraith proposal, and the energy with which they advocated taking the fight against the Viet Cong to a successful conclusion, effectively torpedoed any idea of a political settlement. When Harriman and Hilsman also spoke against it in a May 1 NSC meeting, the idea met its end.[35] Nevertheless the swirl of controversy surrounding the Galbraith proposal foreshadowed events to come. For Kennedy's intention was to get out of Vietnam when he could find a way. Indeed, the episode was the seed for what would develop shortly thereafter into the Kennedy withdrawal plan. The first concrete step in this direction McNamara would announce to a surprised Harkins at the upcoming fifth SECDEF conference in early May.

NOTES

1. Allen and Benedict, joint interview with the author, July 21, 1988.
2. See House Committee on Appropriations, *Foreign Operations Appropriations for 1963*, 87th Cong., 2d sess. (Washington, D.C.: U.S. Government Printing Office, 1962), p. 370. See also Gibbons' analysis in *The U.S. Government and the Vietnam War*, vol. 2, pp. 121–22, particularly n. 124 and the associated text on p. 122. During his testimony to the House committee, McNamara said that U.S. combat forces should not be used in Vietnam, but Gibbons, in one of his finer pieces of research, uncovered the fact that this remark was deleted from the printed text of the hearing by the Defense Department. However, perhaps because the remark reappears in the Gravel edition of *The Pentagon Papers* (vol. 2, p. 173), Gibbons failed to pose the question as to whether this deletion is collateral evidence that someone in the Pentagon did not want McNamara to go on the public record against U.S. combat troops in Vietnam.
3. Burris memo to Lyndon Johnson, March 16, 1962, pp. 1–2, LBJ Library, VP Security File, Box 5, Item 190.
4. Hammond, *The Military and the Media*, pp. 17–18.
5. "McNamara Off on Trip," *Baltimore Sun* (Washington Bureau), March 21, 1962, pp. 1–2.
6. Burris memo to Lyndon Johnson, March 20, 1962, LBJ Library, VP Security File, Box 5. The date is incorrect: the contents make it obvious the date is March 30 instead of the 20th; the State Department historians also drew this conclusion; see *State History*, 1962, p. 284, n. 2.
7. Burris, interview with the author, May 8, 1991.
8. Burris, interview with the author, June 29, 1991.
9. These Intelligence Bulletins were declassified at the author's request in 1988. They can all be located at JFK Library, Newman Papers. Exactly how it went from USARPAC to Colonel Burris is another matter. Since USARPAC was subordinate to CINCPAC, formal distribution of the bulletins outside of CINCPAC was probably limited to Army channels in the Pentagon or nonexistent. The CINCPAC Intelligence (J-2) Chief, Colonel Anderson, like the MACV J-2 and Johnson's Military Aide, was an Air Force officer, and one possibility is that this intelligence conduit to the Vice President was handled through Air Force channels. Burris says he knew of both Anderson and Winterbottom, but does not suggest they played any personal role in giving raw data.
10. "Guerrilla War Drags On in South Vietnam," USARPAC Intelligence Bulletin, March 1962.
11. Trewhitt, *McNamara*, pp. 199–200.
12. "Pace of Viet Cong War in South Vietnam Slowly Accelerating," USARPAC Intelligence Bulletin, April 1962.
13. USARPAC Intelligence Bulletin, April 1962, p. 14.
14. USARPAC Intelligence Bulletin, March 1962, p. 15.
15. Note to researchers: again, the date on this memo, which reads "March 20," should read March 30.

16. See Lemnitzer's trip summary, dated March 30, 1962, *Declassified Documents*, 1976, 331.

17. An April 9 MACV OPSUM (Operations Summary) reported the following equipment captured by the VC in the Vinh Binh operation: "4 BAR, 15 SMG, 63 rifles, 2 pistols and 1 radio." See MACV OPSUM 32, 091007Z, April 1962, JFK Library, Newman Papers and NSF Country File, Vietnam, Box 196, p. 6.

18. Neil Sheehan, *A Bright Shining Lie* (New York, Random House: 1988), pp. 99–100. Of course, these outposts were never eliminated. At the time, there were 776 in the Delta alone. The priorities were set by Colonel Daniel Boone Porter, the senior American advisor in the III Corps Tactical Zone, and Major John Paul Vann, the senior American advisor with the ARVN 7th Division, which operated in the III Corps area.

19. USARPAC Intelligence Bulletin, May 1962.

20. From a Marine Corps study of helicopter operations in 1962, as cited in Krepinevich, *The Army in Vietnam*, p. 76.

21. Burris memo to Lyndon Johnson, "RE: Viet-Cong Activities," April 16, 1962, LBJ Library, VP Security File, Box 5.

22. Vietnam Task Force Status Report, April 18, 1962, and cover memo by Lucius D. Battle, same date, JFK Library, NSF, Country File, Vietnam, Box 202/203.

23. The task force report did note in the next section, "Internal Security," paragraph 2(b), "Incidents," that there were 108 VC attacks for the period April 3–9. Although the text said this was a "meaningful indicator," it meant absolutely nothing to the President or anyone else who did not know whether an attack was a platoon-level action or a coordinated multiple battalion operation. Moreover, it also said that this number, 108, was down from the 114 attacks recorded in each of the previous two weeks, giving the impression that the "meaning" to be inferred here was that VC attacks were on the decline. The point is that if Kennedy did read this sentence, which he probably did not, he would figure VC activity was declining instead of what was really happening.

24. See USARPAC Intelligence Bulletin, May 1962, p. 6, for table showing VC casualty rates from April 3–16, 1962. These statistics were compiled from data provided by MACV.

25. USARPAC Intelligence Bulletin, March 1962, pp. 14–15.

26. USARPAC Intelligence Bulletin, April 1962, p. 17.

27. Rust, *Kennedy in Vietnam*, p. 70.

28. Gibbons, *The U.S. Government and the Vietnam War*, vol. 2, pp. 119–20.

29. John Kenneth Galbraith, *A Life in Our Times* (Boston: Houghton Mifflin, 1981), p. 477; cited in Gibbons, *The U.S. Government and the Vietnam War*, vol. 2, p. 120.

30. Ibid.

31. Memorandum of Conversation, JFK, Harriman, and Forrestal, April 6, 1962, signed by Forrestal. U.S. Army, MHI, Washington D.C.

32. *PP*, DOD ed., Book 12, pp. 464–65.

33. McNamara would first raise the issue with Harkins in May 1962 and announce it formally in July.

34. *USN and the Vietnam Conflict*, p. 76.

35. *State History*, 1962, Document 176, pp. 366–67.

CHAPTER THIRTEEN

SECRETS IN SAIGON

THE ORDER OF BATTLE TEAM AND ITS WORK

The size of the enemy and the area they controlled were critical indicators of whether the Washington-backed regime in Saigon was winning or losing the war. This is why Winterbottom's waffling on the size of the enemy caused such consternation at the third SECDEF conference in February; and why, afterward, the Defense Department assigned some of its best experts to Saigon to formulate an order of battle—a definitive enemy profile.

Under the leadership of George Allen, temporarily transferred to Saigon for this project, the team worked for six weeks to sort out the disparate and often fragmentary evidence of the elusive Viet Cong. Allen, along with Bill Benedict from the Pentagon and Lou Tixier from USARPAC in Honolulu, joined Jimmy Harris, Sam Dowling, and other intelligence analysts at MACV. They began their work inside the Embassy, in a tiny room with a secure vaulted door, and eventually moved into more adequate spaces in MACV. Because their initial office was small and cramped, they formed two working shifts to reduce congestion, and mounted large-scale maps on sliding panels that graphically depicted the enemy units they added to the emerging enemy profile. They established meticulous and extensive working files on each one of them.

Their work was demanding because the evidence was often spotty or inflated by the South Vietnamese. Each piece of data had to be painstakingly checked, rechecked and evaluated. It was collated and cross-filed with other available data, and then, if possible, plotted on one of the maps. Paying careful attention to the source of each piece of information, the team built a well-documented "all-source data base" covering all known Viet Cong activity over the previous two years.

The amount of information on each Viet Cong unit varied, as did the sources, so they developed a methodology for accepting units as "valid" before entering them into the official order of battle. Allen decided early on to err on the conservative side, since units could always be added later if more convincing evidence became available. The acceptance criteria were strict: first, two prisoners or one prisoner and a number of documents were necessary, a formula which General Joseph McChristian (Westmoreland's intelligence chief) later used.[1] This first requirement thus ensured that at least two reports from reliable sources were used. In addition, Allen required evidence of activity in an area commensurate with the size of the unit reported.[2] Using this data, the analysts "confirmed" tactical units and identified their strengths and ultimately combined them into a "minimum" assessment of the enemy's main, regional, and local forces. In this manner, day by day, the order of battle team "recovered" pieces of the Viet Cong puzzle, of parent and subordinate units and their areas of operations. Slowly but surely, they built an accurate countrywide picture.

As part of this effort, the team decided it was necessary to personally see as much of the country as possible, and to meet and interview Vietnamese intelligence personnel at every opportunity. Their adventures into the countryside provided valuable information, and exposed the sketchy nature of South Vietnamese intelligence on the enemy. Benedict and Harris recall this was particularly so in the areas they visited, which included Quang Tri, Thua Thien, Quang Nam, Quang Tin, and Quang Ngai provinces in the north, and a few provinces in the central highlands.

On one of these trips Harris recalls taking along an enlisted soldier from MACV's intelligence section who was fluent in Vietnamese. They soon discovered he could eavesdrop during their discussions, which were all in English. The linguist sat in the back row during these briefings and gave no indication he could speak Vietnamese. When Harris and Benedict would ask about the size of the enemy forces, the briefers would talk to each other in Vietnamese and then reply in English that the figures were such and such. On one such occasion Harris asked their linguist, during a coffee break, what the Vietnamese had actually said to each other, and he responded that they had simply made up the figures.[3]

The serious purpose of these trips and the deadly nature of the targets

they gathered information on sometimes faded, and often seemed secondary or even surrealistic against the vivid richness of the tropical forests
and jungles, the ethnic tribes, and the friendly Vietnamese in their little
villages. The "enemy" was colored swathes on a map in their Saigon office;
once out in the countryside the experience was something to be enjoyed
and absorbed to the limit. Harris recalls:

> I remember we went to Da Nang and drove to Quang Tri, and
> even drove over to Lao Bao on the Laos border; and having several
> drinks with the consul in Hue and playing croquet at two o'clock
> in the morning on his lawn—things, that if we had known what
> we were doing and any degree of the threat, we wouldn't have done
> half of them, particularly driving over to Laos on the Lao Bao
> border. The Laotians had a battalion over there right on the border
> of Vietnam, and it was cut off and stayed cut off the whole war.
> The 33rd BV was over there and it worked for everybody. It worked
> for the communists, it worked for the Lao army, and it worked for
> the G-2 of I Corps. Those sort of things—after we had completed
> our study—we never would have done. But we weren't that smart
> at the time.[4]

Indeed, by the time their study was complete in mid-April they would be
a lot smarter, about the enemy and a great deal more.

"WE CAN'T TELL MCNAMARA"

As the middle of April neared, the order of battle team "had a figure which
we were fairly firm on," Benedict reports; "the local force battalions and
recognizable guerrilla units were over 40,000." This figure simply "blew
away" Winterbottom. He "flat said that was unacceptable."[5] To their
amazement, Winterbottom ordered them to come up with a lower one.
The men were stunned—command pressure was the last problem they had
anticipated. Just how much lower they were supposed to go was unclear.
The order was verbal and transmitted through one or more intermediaries,
but all the members of the team are sure that the order at that time came
from the MACV Intelligence Chief, Colonel Winterbottom.
     The team leaders groped for a solution. In an attempt to keep peace
in-house and still preserve the integrity of their work, they attempted to
strike a compromise. Rather than cutting the figures, they added new and
even more rigid criteria for accepting an enemy unit as valid. Whereas

previously a unit was either accepted or rejected according to the initial methodology, they now devised three categories of enemy units: "confirmed," "probable," or "possible." Although their recollections today are insufficient to permit a reconstruction of how much each of these discriminators was toughened or softened, the new formula obviously resulted in a much smaller "confirmed" figure than the 40,000 they began with.

Subdividing the enemy force in this way was nothing new to order of battle work, but to do it because of Winterbottom's pressure made it, in this instance, distinctly distasteful. This unsavory aspect of that act remains with these men to this day, and it still evokes emotion when they discuss it. At the time, however, something had to be done besides blindly caving in to Winterbottom's arbitrary demand for lower figures. Benedict recounts what happened:

> George and Lou and I sat down over a bottle of bourbon and we tried to come up with some way. . . . We wanted a figure of 20,000 main force, roughly speaking, as I recall, and so that's how we came up with the probable and possible units, feeling that . . . a reasonable commander would look [at this] and say okay, if there's 20,000 confirmed, and there's 10,000 probable, and 5,000 possible, why there's a hell of a lot of bad guys out there.[6]

In this way, the team reconciled the command pressure with their need to maintain some sort of objective criteria.[7] While there is no record of the "confirmed" figure reached after the addition of the "probable" and "possible" discriminators, the consensus is that it was between 20,000 and 25,000.

A "confirmed" Viet Cong main force of this magnitude was still unacceptable to Winterbottom, who was after a much lower number. He had a plan to bring this about, and was clever enough not to force it on the team while the representatives from Washington were still involved. The feisty Allen was his biggest problem, not only because his scruples would not permit him to make wholesale cuts in the figures but, more importantly, because he was a civilian and therefore more difficult to control. Benedict too was a problem: he worked in the Pentagon, in the offices of the Army Assistant Chief of Staff for Intelligence (ACSI). Winterbottom could not take the chance that Benedict would tell the ACSI, General Fitch, or, worse, Fitch's boss—the Army Chief of Staff, General George Decker—about the brazen act he was planning to carry out. Consequently, Winterbottom took Allen and Benedict off the order of battle study and assigned them to other duties.[8]

Winterbottom completed the study using the two remaining officers who worked for him personally: Jimmy Harris and Sam Dowling. Significantly, it was at this point that Harkins' name became involved. Dowling, the Staff Security Officer, recalls, "we had to go back and come up with additional figures—less than what we had."[9] He remembers the problem being that Harkins said *"we can't tell McNamara* that there's that many [Viet Cong] in the country" [emphasis added]. Dowling's recollection of the next round of cutting is vivid:

> The first figure . . . was something like 20,000–25,000 hard-core. . . . And I remember General Harkins saying he would not buy a figure that high. It had to be around 15,000 to 18,000. So we went back and applied that criteria again, and of course there's always some judgment factors, and we dropped a few, and I think we got in the neighborhood of 19,000, and he still wouldn't accept it. And I think the first, very first order of battle figure was something in the neighborhood of 17,500, and that's the figure he would allow us to publish.

Whereas Benedict and Allen had felt the pressure from Winterbottom, Harris and Dowling both recall the involvement of General Harkins, though they did not mention it to Allen and Benedict, an omission which would be important later.

Captain Harris confirms that the initial estimate of 20,000–25,000 hard-core Viet Cong was not acceptable to Harkins, and that the figure was then scaled back to 17,500.[10] "We felt awful about it, just terrible," Dowling says. "We didn't like it," Harris agrees, "but we did it because we were ordered to." Harkins and Winterbottom had their way, and on April 15, 1962, MACV's first official enemy order of battle was published.[11] It listed 18 battalions, 79 companies, and 137 platoons and a total of 16,305 regular troops.[12] It appears that Harris and Dowling were not privy to the final figure because it was 1,195 less than the lowest figure that both men recall. Their colleagues, Allen, Benedict, and Tixier, would soon have a more compelling reason to be unhappy, for Winterbottom's plan was far from complete.

"IF YOU TWO GUYS GO IN AND TALK TO HARKINS . . . YOU GUYS ARE DEAD"

As the time for the fifth SECDEF conference approached, Allen and Benedict were due to rotate back to Washington, but Winterbottom would not let them go. Benedict recalls: "I was held, out in Saigon, literally against my will for six weeks . . . there was no doubt in our minds, they wouldn't release us."[13] Though he does not remember the "specifics of it," Captain Harris also recalls that Benedict encountered "some problems" in "getting out of there."[14] At one point Winterbottom called Allen into his office and threw a memorandum down in front him canceling his return to Washington. "What do you think of that," Winterbottom asked, as Allen read it. "I guess it means that you must like the work that I am doing here very much," Allen replied, sarcastically. "I just wanted to show you I can do it," Winterbottom snapped back.[15] In effect, Winterbottom had placed Allen, Benedict, and Tixier under virtual house arrest because of what they knew.

McNamara was due in Saigon in three weeks to be briefed on the order of battle, and Winterbottom had no intention of permitting Allen and Benedict to return to Washington and blow the whistle before that briefing. This "house arrest" was imposed until McNamara had come and gone. Understandably these men were angry at being held in Saigon against their will. It only added to their malaise about everything else that was going on. As Benedict explained:

> We were just so frustrated and we felt that there was so much more—there were other things going on out there too that were bad. It wasn't a good operation at all . . . all kinds of phony reporting was going on.

There was seemingly no way around being cooped up in Saigon, however, and the men resigned themselves, for the time being, to their unfortunate fate.

One evening during the latter part of April, Benedict and Tixier were walking through the stands of the small Algerian marketplace in Saigon, not far from their apartment, where they often went to buy their wine and steaks.[16] Tixier caught sight of an old and familiar face, a fellow classmate from West Point, class of 1946. It was Lieutenant Colonel Amos Jordan, a professor at the Military Academy at West Point. "This guy was high level," recalls Benedict, "one of the few people I ever knew that went from captain [skipping over major] to lieutenant colonel."

On this trip to Saigon, however, Jordan was the Executive Officer for Allen Dulles and Karl Bendetsen, a former Under Secretary of the Army. These two were part of a group the Kennedy administration sent to visit U.S. forces around the globe to emphasize the proper military code of conduct, following the questionable behavior of General Edwin Walker in Europe. (Walker, a vocal supporter of the John Birch Society, overstepped the ethical limits of the code of conduct by indoctrinating troops with his own extreme ideology. Lee Harvey Oswald would allegedly fire shots at this same Edwin Walker in 1963.) Vietnam had been included in Dulles' trip itinerary, and the Algerian marketplace in Saigon provided the scene for this coincidental reunion with Jordan.

After some preliminary conversation, the three men decided to go to a bar for a drink. Before long, Tixier and Benedict dumped their troubles on Jordan. No details were spared, says Benedict. They told Jordan every-thing, not just about cutting the figures and being held incommunicado, but also about the falsification of operations reports as well.[17] Benedict recalls: "We unloaded this on Jordan, and Jordan says, well, hell, I've got Allen Dulles." Dulles and Bendetsen were staying at the Hotel Caravelle, so Jordan set up a meeting in the hotel for the next night.

The following evening they went to Dulles' room. "We went in," says Benedict, but "Dulles was sick. He had a case of diarrhea." Benedict and Tixier talked to Bendetsen while Jordan looked on and Dulles listened from the bathroom. Benedict recounts:

> We told old Bendetsen what we not only knew, but what we suspected as well. I mean, you know, we told him that we were being held out there and that they were manipulating the figures and everything like that. . . . Bendetsen didn't really fully appreciate what we were telling him. But he was no dummy. And he turned to Jordan, and he says, "Well obviously there's nothing that I can do," but he says, "I can get you in touch with some people . . . but"—pointing at Tixier and I—he says, "if you two guys go in and talk to Harkins . . . you guys are dead. They'll drum you right out of the corps."

Suddenly Benedict was acutely aware of the dangerous ground they were treading on. Then he came up with an idea: why not have George Allen talk to Harkins? Since Allen, a civilian, was not in the corps, he could not be drummed out. Bendetsen agreed with the idea and volunteered to make the appointment. So, says Benedict, "that's how Allen got called up to see Harkins." The meeting, however, did not take place until after McNamara's visit (May 8–11).[18]

Benedict did not tell Allen he and Tixier had "fingered" him for the job that night in Dulles' room, and Harkins did not tell Allen that Dulles and Bendetsen reported this attempt to jump the chain of command to him. Allen already had a meeting scheduled with Harkins, and so he went into it blind on both counts; his remarks were highly combative. While Allen did not specifically accuse Winterbottom of faking the figures, he charged that Winterbottom had no comprehension of the real situation in Vietnam:

> I laid it on the line. . . . I told him his biggest problem was . . . "You don't understand the situation, sir, and the reason you don't is because your J-2 [Winterbottom] isn't informing you; and the reason he's not informing you is he doesn't understand it, and he's not the kind of guy who will ever understand it. He just does not comprehend."

Allen felt good about his performance but his efforts were in vain. Harkins reacted calmly during the discussion, even offering to cooperate to fix the problem. He fixed things all right, as Allen found out later, so that Allen would not be making trouble anymore.

Since Allen, Benedict, and Tixier did not yet know what Harris and Dowling did—that Harkins was involved in the cutting of the order of battle—neither of them realized that when Allen entered Harkins' office he was like an unsuspecting fly walking into the web of a spider. Benedict and Tixier had hoped that Allen's meeting with Harkins would expose Winterbottom's activities, but instead the meeting alerted Harkins to the threat Allen and Benedict posed. Consequently—as Allen found out to his dismay—Harkins made phone calls to Honolulu to control the damage these men might do after leaving Vietnam. Benedict and Tixier had miscalculated badly, acting precipitously without any appreciation of how high up the chain of command the pressure originated. "We tried to take an end run really, to get to Harkins. We thought—we didn't realize, that it was him." When nothing happened to Winterbottom, Benedict finally began to understand who was behind it all. "This is why I'm so damned sure that Harkins *was* in on it," he says now.

"WE'RE NOT SHOWING THAT TO MCNAMARA"

Meanwhile, between Benedict's tryst in Dulles' room and Allen's tirade in Harkins' office, the climax to the unfolding drama of Secretary McNamara's visit took place. Benedict had left the Caravelle confident the problem with Winterbottom would soon be fixed. Neither he nor Allen knew about the final order of battle cuts nor the figure of 16,305 that would be shown to McNamara at the conference. Allen was still on his special project, and Winterbottom now assigned Benedict the task of helping on certain parts of the intelligence report that would be presented to the Secretary.

Benedict quickly made a nuisance of himself again. His part of the report covered enemy and friendly intelligence capabilities, and he concluded both sides were improving. He explains:

> The thrust of the damned thing said . . . "ARVN has made great strides in . . . improving their intelligence operation. But at the same time the VC have continued to grow in sophistication" . . . so you had a balanced approach.

Benedict's input was most unwelcome. "They cut out everything I wrote about the VC," he states. He is still not sure who was behind it, but, of course, he suspects it was Winterbottom. He still remembers how he got the news:

> This was Delaney [who] told me. He says, "We can't tell that to the Secretary, he's not interested in that bullshit. Cut that VC out." So, so far as I know . . . it's the only intelligence briefing that was ever presented to a senior official where they never mentioned the enemy. . . . There was no section in the briefing which dealt with the VC and their improvement.

Despite Benedict's efforts, once again, pertinent—indeed vital—facts on the enemy were suppressed and withheld from McNamara.

Something else about the briefing angered Benedict. An item was inserted into his part of the estimate that he did not write and that he claims was a lie. The process of getting U.S. intelligence advisors into position with Vietnamese units was not going well. Great numbers of these advisors were still living in tents at the Saigon airport or at more remote locations. Allen recalls that these advisors did not take kindly to being cooped up, and that several "raised hell" in the central highlands (II Corps), leading to problems between MACV and the American Embassy. Many who had arrived at their destinations had not been integrated into the Vietnamese units they were sent to support. Benedict had made no reference to this problem, but it had been identified by McNamara himself at previous SECDEF conferences as a high priority. Consequently, after Delaney and Winterbottom received Benedict's input, they inserted language claiming that 92 percent of these intelligence advisors were in place.[19] This figure was far from the truth. Benedict explains why: "They didn't want McNamara to know" that the South Vietnamese Army "wasn't accepting them."

There remained one final dramatic scene before the conference. Winterbottom was responsible for preparing the first graphic battlefield assessment of the enemy forces and their areas of control, which Harkins would present to McNamara. McNamara had specifically ordered this to be done at the third SECDEF conference in February. This graphic assessment ended up being the very map that the order of battle team had prepared as a result of their study.[20] It was huge—six feet by three feet—and illustrated, using a color code, government- and Viet Cong–controlled areas on a province-by-province basis. Red acetate depicted "VC in ascendancy," red with blue stripes depicted "VC controlled" areas, yellow depicted "GVN [Government of Vietnam] in ascendancy," blue depicted "GVN controlled," and white depicted "neither VC or GVN control." Due to the large number of red splotches on it, this chart acquired the name "the measles map."

Harkins apparently assumed that since he had cut the enemy hard-core forces to just over 15,000, the map would reflect this figure, and he never actually looked at it until the night before McNamara's arrival. That evening he presided over a rehearsal of the briefing he would give to the Secretary the next morning. Harkins and his entourage entered the room and took their seats. "Oh my God!" Harkins blurted out, spotting the map, "We're not showing that to McNamara!" The map got "edited" then and there. Winterbottom stripped off large portions of acetate depicting enemy areas, and replaced it with acetate depicting neutral or government areas.[21] Allen, who witnessed the entire event, recounts that General Harkins directed while Colonel Winterbottom physically removed and changed "large chunks" of the acetate overlays. By "large chunks" Allen means sixty-by-forty kilometer-square areas. In all, Harkins and Winterbottom removed about one-third of the "enemy-controlled" areas, and converted about half of the "neutral" areas to "government" control.[22] (The falsified "measles map" was declassified at the author's request in 1988.) When Bill Colby, who in 1962 was the CIA's Director of the Far East Division, looked at it in 1988, this was his reaction:

> I don't believe a word of it, because it gives you a totally false picture of Vietnam. . . . I think there was a lot of red; there was very little blue—that's for sure. Now VC control—I would give a lot more VC control . . . and I think the communists were much stronger in the Delta.[23]

Shortly after this map-changing incident occurred, Dr. Thomas Glenn III, a Department of Defense Special Representative in Saigon at the time, learned about it. He recalls hearing the story from officers angry about it, and in particular Major Charles Thomann, asking, "Why do I have to brief this if it's not true?"[24]

THE FIFTH SECDEF CONFERENCE

At 11:00 A.M. on May 8, McNamara convened his fifth SECDEF conference, not in Honolulu but Saigon. He was joined by Admiral Felt, Ambassador Nolting, General Harkins, and other officials in MACV
headquarters, an old French villa on Pasteur Street. This conference was
one of the most bizarre meetings of the entire Vietnam War. There were
eleven major agenda items, as well as a twelfth at the very end that was
attended only by the principals and a few DOD civilians and MACV J-2
officers. Lasting until two in the afternoon, McNamara listened to one
briefing after another describing a story of unadulterated progress and
success. The record itself remained classified until its salient portions were
opened at the author's request in 1988.[25] It was subsequently published
in the State Department history in 1990.

The first two items on the agenda were reviews of Viet Cong and
government military activities, separately but back-to-back, like individual
recapitulations of the scoring by two teams that had just played a football
game. However, something about the periods they covered was odd: the
briefing on government operations covered the fifty days prior to the
conference, while the briefing on Viet Cong operations covered twenty-
six. Thus the Viet Cong review began with the date April 14, and the
government review began with the date March 21. This would be analogous to a sports announcer reporting the score of a football game by
giving the points of one team for the entire game and only the second
half's points for the other team. Something else about these briefings
was odd: McNamara was only told about the major communist actions,
whereas he was given major *and* minor government actions. This would
be analogous to reporting only touchdowns for one football team while
reporting the touchdowns and field goals for the other team.

When talking about Viet Cong operations, the briefer told McNamara
that, since April 14, there had been no operations of battalion size
(300–500 men), the largest involving about fifty men; the briefer gave
no figure at all for how many of these fifty-men operations had occurred.
When talking about government operations the briefer said that, since
March 21, there had been over forty operations of battalion size along
with 400 minor offensive efforts. In our football analogy, this would
make it look like one team virtually shut out its opponent. The problem
is that the Viet Cong score for the first half of the game as well as their
field goals for the entire game had been dropped.

Why did MACV drop the Viet Cong score for the first half? Because
they had scored touchdowns of their own during that part of the game:
the Viet Cong carried out seven known and possibly as many ten battalion-

level attacks between March 29 and April 9. (See map #3 in insert.) Moreover, they had conducted seventeen large-scale attacks involving 100 or more troops between March 15 and April 15.[26] True, these attacks were companies, not battalions, but they were not platoons (fifty men) either. Why did MACV drop the Viet Cong field goals from the entire game? Because they added up to a lot of points: the Viet Cong conducted over 200 minor offensive efforts between March 21 and the SECDEF conference, and over 3,000 armed incidents during the same period. These Viet Cong statistics are from the same time period that MACV was reporting on government operations. When all of the points for both teams are tallied for the whole game, the score looks closer to a draw. Even this would depend on the figures supplied by the South Vietnamese about their own operations being true. As we will see, this was hardly ever the case.

The Viet Cong attacks had been coming in waves all year long, punctuated by periods in which they regrouped to replace their dead and refit their battalions with new weapons. MACV deliberately chose to report statistics taken from one of the lulls in Viet Cong activity, and at the same time to report South Vietnamese Army activities during a period nearly twice as long. What made this sordid sleight of hand all the more reprehensible was the fact that the excised communist data also happened to be the largest and most concentrated Viet Cong attacks of the war up to that point. A true comparison of large- and small-scale Viet Cong and government operations for the same time period would have been alarming if briefed to the Secretary. The level and extent of Viet Cong operations was a truly amazing achievement for a force as small—and beleaguered by government attacks—as MACV was reporting.

McNamara finally got his answer from Harkins on the size of the enemy. In the briefing the figure was rounded off to 16,500 men. Aware that McNamara might be curious about the number being lower than even the lowest of the figures briefed in February, the conference record states:

> While this is a reduced estimate, the reduction was described as being more a matter of accurate reporting than of lesser numbers. . . . With regard to these facts, it is likely that we shall be getting better information in the future, inasmuch as there are now intelligence advisors down to section level.

The 16,500 figure was very good news indeed, for even with the caveat that it had resulted from more "accurate" reporting, it implied there had been no significant expansion of communist forces since the stepped-up American assistance had begun in late 1961. It thus appeared the program was working very well. One can only wonder what McNamara's reaction would have been if he had been told what the order of battle team originally concluded: that there were 40,000 regular Viet Cong soldiers in South Vietnam.

Items three and four, on clear-and-hold operations and weapons issue to the Civil Guard (CG) and Self Defense Corps (SDC), contained little new information because they had been "discussed earlier."[27] The fifth agenda item described the problem of relieving South Vietnamese units, tied down in static defense tasks, with CG and SDC units. McNamara was told that the difficulty was training: as SDC and CG units were trained, they were being sent to relieve untrained SDC and CG units rather than the regular army units tied down at airfields, supply depots, and hamlets. This explanation was only partly true, and it was not the *real* problem. The real problem was Diem. Diem was reluctant to risk casualties in regular army units by sending them into combat. He regarded these troops as his own personal protection against coup attempts, and was afraid that sending them into combat would lower their morale and their support of him. Diem's idea was to grind down the Viet Cong with long-range artillery and American air strikes.

As a result Diem forced the SDC to shoulder the brunt of the casualty burden, hanging them out like sacrificial lambs in thousands of isolated tiny outposts all over the countryside. When one of these outposts was overrun and its SDC defenders killed, it was quickly rebuilt and again manned by more paramilitary personnel. Diem considered the outposts as an important *symbol* of the extension of his rule in the countryside. In fact, Diem had no intention of using anything but regular army units to guard his most vital supply points and airfields. Control over these facilities was necessary, not to deny them to the communists, but to insure they could not fall into the hands of coup plotters. For these reasons, the SDC were dying almost as fast as they could be replaced. So SDC training, per se, was not the problem—the problem was Diem's priority for keeping the outposts manned and doing so with the SDC, who suffered such a tragic number of casualties in the process that they were never available to relieve regular army units.

The sixth item on the agenda was the "Establishment of the Intelligence Net." Identified as a high priority back at the February conference (when McNamara had directed that U.S. intelligence advisors be assigned to each corps area and major army units), the briefer now unveiled statistics showing that 92 percent of the people and 98 percent of the equipment for the intelligence network were in place and "substantially" operational. Benedict recalls:

> and so here comes McNamara, and they get up and brief that the intelligence advisors—they didn't exactly say "in place," but they

wangled it, they didn't want McNamara to know . . . that ARVN wasn't accepting them. . . . And yet they . . . flatly briefed McNamara that all the intelligence sector coordinators were in position.[28]

This, too, was as disturbing to Benedict as the cutting of the order of battle.

The seventh item, on communications in the countryside, was skipped because it too had been "discussed earlier." The eighth item, on infiltration, is interesting because it *did* present a problem to the Secretary. The summary stated: "Infiltration, which has been at a low level for the past few months, is estimated to be on the increase, using routes through Laos." With the fall of Nam Tha in Laos having occurred the day before McNamara arrived in Thailand (a few days before the conference), the effect of this report could be expected to cause the Secretary to approve a strong U.S. response in Laos. The truth about infiltration, however, was far worse than what was shown to McNamara. As will be seen in more detail later, if the truth had been told, it would have compromised the effort to hold down the number of hard-core Viet Cong troops on the battlefield.

The ninth item covered desertion rates in the South Vietnamese forces. It appears that only two statistics were given. First, that the army rate had dropped from 6 per 1,000 per month to 4 per 1,000 per month and, second, that "there is no desertion problem in the Air Force or Navy." At first glance this seems to be a decrease in an already low figure. In fact, as has been seen, government defections were running at about 1,200 a month (not including the Civil Guard), compared to 200 a month for the Viet Cong, a very alarming situation. However, even the reported figures were cause for alarm: 4 desertions per 1,000 per month for the regular army forces, which numbered around 170,000, would mean 680 desertions per month, more than three times the Viet Cong desertion rate, and certainly enough to offset recruitment. The army was, in effect, running to stand still. When the SDC and CG defections were added, the total government losses to desertion were a staggering 1,000 men per month. Moreover, there was good reason to be suspicious of the reported drop in desertions. U.S. Army intelligence had learned in April that reported defections to the Viet Cong were being wrongly reported as terrorist kidnappings.[29] Real desertion rates were, in all probability, much higher, if not at a critical level.

During the MACV conference the falsified "measles map" was shown to McNamara. The reader will recall Allen's account of how Harkins and Winterbottom had removed about a third of the enemy-controlled area and increased the government-controlled area by about as much. Yet even this was not sufficient to satisfy Harkins: he now told McNamara that the map was overly generous to the enemy and an underestimation of government control.[30] Captain Blascak, who worked for Winterbottom at the time, believes the reason Harkins ordered the map to be altered was to prevent McNamara from going back to Washington with news so bad that the administration would not keep up even its advisory effort.[31] This is the same impression that Benedict, Dowling, and Harris had. In this author's view, their interpretation is correct; given Kennedy's decision not to intervene in Vietnam, the true extent of the Viet Cong's size and area of control would have called into question the viability of the advisory program itself.

Agenda item ten concerned defoliation, which was described as a favorable report, but McNamara asked to submit further, more specific recommendations. Item eleven concerned how much of the land and rural population was controlled by whom; land was said to be split about half and half between the government and the Viet Cong, while the government fared slightly better in terms of the rural population.

Toward the end of the conference, the room was cleared of most people in preparation for a special briefing (item twelve). However, "when the door shut behind the last staffers to depart, McNamara waved aside reference to our agenda item," says Allen, and launched into a discussion of Laos.[32] It was during this portion of the conference, and in apparent reaction to a comment on the growth of MACV, that the Secretary interjected that it was not the job of the U.S. to assume responsibility for the war but to develop the South Vietnamese capability to do so, and asked when that point could be reached. Allen recalls that "Harkins' chin nearly hit the table."[33] Harkins responded that MACV had scarcely thought about this, and that they had been too busy expanding their structure to think about how it might all be dismantled. McNamara then ordered MACV to devise a plan for turning full responsibility over to South Vietnam and reducing the size of our military command, and to submit this plan at the next conference.[34]

The authors of *The Pentagon Papers* were unaware of this early McNamara order to Harkins, an order that he gave again in July that they did report in their twelve-volume study of the war.[35] Yet this order in May is the institutional origin of the Kennedy withdrawal plan, a controversial and little understood program to remove the American advisors from Vietnam.

The May 1962 SECDEF conference, then, was a watershed event in more ways than one. Above all else, however, it is a monument to the first arbitrary reduction of the Viet Cong order of battle—and it would not be the last. Benedict reports a great deal of frustration among those who had worked so hard to develop the intelligence, which was then corrupted and delivered to McNamara in this conference. Captain Blascak recalls: "That is when the big lie started."[36]

The Secretary of Defense was purposely misled on nearly all of the crucial aspects of the war: the size of the enemy; the number and quality of enemy operations versus the number and quality of friendly operations; the territory controlled by the enemy versus the territory controlled by friendly forces; the number of desertions from South Vietnam's armed forces; the success of the placement of U.S. intelligence advisors; and the problems with the Self Defense Corps. The maps, statistics, and briefings he was given led him to remark at a press conference after the meeting that "every quantitative measurement . . . shows that we are winning the war."[37] He was quoted in the *New York Times* as saying he was "tremendously encouraged" by the military developments in South Vietnam.[38]

In a rare comment made in response to questions posed by the author, McNamara stated: "1. I did not know; 2. did not suspect; have no indication now that I was deceived."[39]

NOTES

1. Benedict, interview with the author, June 6, 1988.

2. Allen, *The Indochina Wars*, p. 180.

3. Harris, interview with the author, June 4, 1988.

4. Ibid., June 7, 1988.

5. Benedict, interview with the author, June 6, 1988.

6. Ibid.

7. Ibid.

8. Winterbottom did not have to worry about Benedict for a while, as he had become seriously ill.

9. Dowling, interview with the author, June 2, 1988.

10. Harris, interview with the author, June 4, 1988.

11. *Air Force History*, p. 139.

12. Allen, in *The Indochina Wars*, uses a figure of 20,000 for regular forces; see p. 180. However, in a recent interview, June 4, 1988, he recalls that the figure Harris remembers is probably right.

13. Benedict, interview with the author, July 21, 1988.

14. Harris, interview with the author, June 7, 1988.

15. Allen and Benedict, joint interview with the author, July 21, 1988.

16. The following story was reconstructed from the author's interviews with Bill Benedict, especially the June 6, 1988, interview and the joint interview with him and Allen on July 21, 1988.

17. It should be noted here that in a June 26, 1988, telephone conversation the author had with General Jordan, he denied having any recollection of this episode involving Benedict, Tixier, and Allen.

18. As it turned out, Allen already had a calling card to see Harkins. Allen met him soon after his arrival in February and had agreed to another meeting before his departure.

19. "Visit to Southeast Asia by the Secretary of Defense, 8–11 May, 1962," JFK Library, Newman Papers; see also *State History*, 1962, Document 187, pp. 379–87, especially p. 385.

20. Allen, interview with the author, August 10, 1987.

21. Allen, *The Indochina Wars*, p. 184.

22. Allen, interview with the author, August 10, 1987.

23. Colby, interview with the author, July 21, 1988.

24. Glenn, interview with the author, December 21, 1987.

25. "Visit to Southeast Asia by the Secretary of Defense, 8–11 May, 1962," JFK Library, Newman Papers. An identical copy of the portion (Part III, South Vietnam), declassified at my request, was published in June 1990 in *State History*, 1962, Document 187, pp. 379–87.

26. USARPAC Intelligence Bulletin, May 1962.

27. The third agenda item, on "The status of Clear and Hold operations," said only there was no time schedule set for the approved Delta plan and that the Vietnamese preferred to divide the clear-and-hold "scheme" into three phases according to ascending difficulty and each to be accomplished in three months. Item four was titled "Progress in Gaining GVN Acceptance of Issue of Weapons to the CG and SDC." Little was new in this brief either, except for a short discussion of Saigon's preference to issue the weapons at SOC training centers instead of at home stations as an inducement to attendance at these centers. The very title of this item would have looked like a misnomer to senior advisors like Colonel Porter and Lieutenant Colonel Vann who were trying to stop the flow of weapons to the SDC, because these weapons had become the richest source of supply for the Viet Cong. But for Harkins, who was pushing Diem to issue the weapons because McNamara had urged this in an earlier SECDEF conference, more guns in the hands of more friendly forces was a good statistic, and McNamara liked statistics. A more relevant statistic would have been the number of American weapons captured from these SDC outposts as a percentage of those issued. For this statistic would have gone a long way in explaining another that was not shown to McNamara: the increase in friendly casualties—especially CG and SDC casualties.

28. Benedict, interview with the author, June 6, 1988.

29. This important discovery is easy to miss, because when it was reported in the May edition of the USARPAC Intelligence Bulletin, an editorial error occurred: "Viet Cong defections" was printed when "defections to the Viet Cong" was the intended meaning. However, the intended meaning can be derived by looking at the whole paragraph, and the extant copy at CMH (Army Center for Military History) and in my papers has a question mark in the margin left by someone who realized the printed version didn't make sense. Just to be sure, I talked with the USARPAC analysts who were there at the time, and defections to the Viet Cong were routinely being reported as terrorist kidnappings.

30. Allen, *The Indochina Wars*, pp. 184–85.

31. Colonel Don Blascak, from an interview with the author, April 30, 1988.

32. Allen, *The Indochina Wars*, p. 188.

33. Allen, interview with the author, August 10, 1987.

34. Allen, *The Indochina Wars*, p. 192. It was only during the August 10, 1987, interview with Allen that he clearly explained that the discussion of withdrawal occurred during that portion of the conference when the room had been cleared in preparation for the special brief.

35. *PP*, Gravel ed. vol. 2, p. 175.

36. Blascak, interview with the author, January 6, 1988.

37. Karnow, *Vietnam* p. 254.

38. Homer Bigart, "McNamara Says Aid to Saigon Is at Peak and Will Level Off," *New York Times*, May 12, 1962.

39. Robert McNamara, marginalia to letter to McNamara from the author dated May 23, 1991.

PART IV

DARKNESS AT
THE END OF THE TUNNEL

CHAPTER FOURTEEN

THE PRICE OF LAOS

LAOS: PHOUMI AND CIA "RENEGADES"

Throughout February and March, Kennedy became increasingly concerned over Laos because of resurgent communist activity and new military moves by General Phoumi that threatened to undermine American attempts to forge a coalition government. Phoumi had begun using the airstrip near Nam Tha to reinforce his garrison there—against American advice.[1] He simply ignored this advice, and Harriman's protestations in particular, adding paratroopers in February and continuing to do so throughout March until they totaled 5,000 men. Phoumi's supporters claimed this was necessary because the North Vietnamese were backing Pathet Lao probes in the area. "On the other hand," says William Bundy, it remained unclear "whether Phoumi's posture was excessive and provocative."[2]

While it's true that Phoumi was unhappy with the U.S. decision to back the neutralist Souvanna Phouma for Prime Minister, the brazen character of his actions suggested something more was involved: encouragement by recalcitrant American officials opposed to Kennedy's neutralist policy in Laos. Harriman was convinced the CIA was behind Phoumi's reinforcement at Nam Tha.[3] If he is correct, it would suggest that renegade CIA elements were bent on scuttling the coalition negotiations then at a crucial stage. They probably would have been motivated by the belief that the administration's policy was leading to the collapse of the American position in Vietnam and perhaps all of Southeast Asia. There was certainly no longer any doubt that the communists were using the negotiations as a cover for expanding their control over infiltration routes to Vietnam. Whatever the reasoning might have been for sabotaging the negotiations, it was too late to stop them unless the communists attempted to grab all of the ground down to the Thai border. This was not about to happen and, for Kennedy, Phoumi's interference was a serious, but manageable, problem.

Right or wrong in his suspicions about CIA involvement in Phoumi's pernicious behavior, Harriman won the transfer of Phoumi's closest CIA advisor, Jack Hazey, and the cancellation of February's aid payment to the general. The question of continuing CIA attempts to undermine the Kennedy administration's neutralist policy continued to be murky and controversial, with some sources in Laos denying it, and reports surfacing in the news media that Hazey and other CIA operatives continued, without authorization from Washington, to lobby Phoumi against agreeing to a coalition government. These reports also alleged that the CIA countered the cutoff of aid to Phoumi by supplying CIA funds to his forces.[4]

Harriman eventually displayed consummate skill in successfully orchestrating the purge of every American official in the agencies and departments represented in Laos who was a personal friend of Phoumi. Hilsman recalls: "There were some unforgettable battles about 'interference in other agencies,' but Harriman won."[5] Harriman was less successful in his handling of Phoumi himself. Their conflict had become too personal; Hilsman, in his memoir, entitled this period on Laos "Phoumi Versus Harriman."[6] The U.S. tried to compel Phoumi to drop his opposition to the coalition at a conference on March 24 at Nong Khay, Thailand. The meeting began well enough, with Thai Premier Sarit Thanarat personally pledging support of the U.S. position. This was followed by some negative comments from Phoumi designed, says Bundy, as "the face-saving prelude to his acceptance."[7] Hilsman states that some who were present felt Phoumi would have agreed "if given time and suitable opportunities for saving face. But Harriman lost patience."[8] Bundy wrote that "Harriman then intervened forcefully, Phoumi's back went up, and no agreement was reached." The meeting fell apart and William Sullivan was dispatched to the Plain of Jars to assure Souvanna Phouma of continued U.S. support. Thus, "the issue still hung fire."[9]

Kennedy decided to increase the pressure on Phoumi and was considering another suspension of military aid, withdrawal of U.S. advisory teams, or both. When the Laotian Ambassador delivered a letter from the King to Kennedy on April 9, Kennedy took the opportunity to send one back assuring the King the U.S. would not intervene and promising the withdrawal of the American White Star teams (CIA-controlled Special Forces teams). Harriman's design for neutrality in Laos may have worried some in the CIA and the military, but this move by the President worried even Harriman and Hilsman. They felt that the communists would inevitably learn of Kennedy's letter and interpret it as evidence of an American decision to withdraw "no matter what."[10] Harriman and Hilsman were less concerned with an all-out communist offensive that might result from this than they were with an "ambiguous" use of force by the communists and loss of more government-controlled territory.

Kennedy was not dissuaded, although he did soften the plan as a result of Harriman's arguments. (Harriman had recently been promoted from Ambassador-at-Large status to the position of Assistant Secretary of State for Far Eastern Affairs.) The President issued NSAM-149 on April 18, approving the withdrawal of "7 or 8" White Star teams.[11] The NSAM stated the teams "would be withdrawn to the rear echelon and would remain in Laos until their normal tour of duty expired. Their replacement will be decided upon subsequently." It stated further that the timing would be at the discretion of the Secretary of State, but that "it is not presently contemplated that this would occur before May 7th, 1962." Finally, it directed the Secretary of State to make an "appropriate" public announcement at the time of the withdrawal, while requiring secrecy until then. Hilsman was not pleased, and he reiterated his concerns in a memo to Harriman, which he also asked Forrestal to pass to Kennedy on April 24.[12] The gist of the memo was cabled to Vientiane, and "still another attempt was made to persuade Phoumi to withdraw from the trap, but without success."

One week later, on May 2, the much anticipated attack on Nam Tha began. Pathet Lao forces supported by at least seven North Vietnamese battalions had little difficulty in routing Phoumi's forces. By the following day, the airfield—the last remaining one in northern Laos—had been captured, and the outpost adjacent to Nam Tha fell on May 4. Nam Tha itself fell on May 6, with the White Star team at the site being evacuated by helicopter ninety minutes before it was all over. William Bundy's account contains a curious footnote on the episode:

> Some close observers at the time say that Phoumi's generals on the spot simply abandoned the village, under Phoumi's orders. Thus, it is argued, Phoumi was trying to create a situation in which Communist power reached the banks of the Mekong and compelled U.S. intervention.[13]

Bundy reports that even for those in the U.S. government who lay the blame with Phoumi, the consequences seemed so ominous that "it was clear the U.S. had to act to stabilize the situation."[14]

In Hilsman's view the communist action had been a large-scale probe to discredit Phoumi and test the limits of U.S. resolve. He argued that unless the U.S. responded, the communists would nibble away, at a rate just below that which would seem to justify an American intervention, until the whole country had been taken over. "It was the Laos crisis of 1961 all over again—only worse."[15]

Was Bundy's observation—that Phoumi might have deliberately withdrawn in the hope of forcing the Americans in—correct? Was Hilsman's argument—that the communists would nibble until they had the whole country—correct? While both views differed somewhat on why Nam Tha fell, they both hinted at large-scale American intervention down the line. What were the communists up to? What did McNamara and his subordinates think? It happened that both McNamara and Lemnitzer were in northern Thailand less than 200 miles from Nam Tha when it fell, and this defeat was fresh in their minds when they arrived in Saigon for the fifth SECDEF conference.

LAOS—THE MAY SECDEF CONFERENCE

"Somebody had just yelled 'boo' at the Lao Army," George Allen recalls, "and it was swimming across the Mekong."[16] He was close to the mark: Royal Laotian soldiers were frantically paying their way across the Mekong, after which they were interned by Thai police. Allen was at the fifth SECDEF conference two days later in Saigon, and, even though Laos was not on the agenda, recalls that McNamara was keenly interested in how the U.S. should respond to the fall of Nam Tha. The Secretary waited until the room was cleared for a special briefing before bringing up the issue. Aside from McNamara, Lemnitzer, Felt, Harkins, and Ambassador Nolting, George Allen was one of the few people left in the room.

McNamara motioned aside the briefing and immediately began talking about what the communists were up to in Laos. "Let's assume that the enemy is going all of the way to the Mekong," he began. "What do you think we should do? I'd like to hear from each of you." Tension immediately filled the room—everyone at the table was looking at their notes for the briefing, which had, with a wave of McNamara's hand, just vanished. No one was prepared. "What do you think, Lem?" the Secretary asked the JCS Chairman. "Well, ah . . ." Lemnitzer began stammering as he thumbed through his loose-leaf booklet looking for the item on Laos. But there was no item on Laos. "Well sir," he said tentatively, "I think we ought to implement SEATO Plan Five, and go in and seize the key points along the Mekong."

That was all that Lemnitzer could muster for an answer, Allen recalls, so McNamara turned to Admiral Felt. "What do you think, Don?" Felt's name was Harry, but McNamara had a habit of forgetting it. While Lemnitzer had been on the hot seat, Felt had time to prepare this answer:

> Well, sir, we have two carrier task forces in the Gulf of Tonkin right now, and we can launch air strikes immediately, and in forty-eight hours, for example, we could wipe the town of Tchepone right off the face of the map.

Thus McNamara's Chairman of the Joint Chiefs, Lemnitzer, had just advocated massive American intervention, and Felt, his Pacific commander, had just urged the destruction of Tchepone by air. Neither was a suggestion McNamara would be passing on to the President anytime soon.

It was General Harkins' turn next. "Well Paul, what do you think we ought to do?" Harkins was out of his league but had had the time, while his superiors were speaking, to come up with an answer. After stammering a few "ahs" he said:

> I think whatever we do has got to make it clear to the enemy that we are serious and that we're going to make a stand. But on the other hand it's got to be within our capabilities to do so.

He had managed to say something without proposing anything. "What do you think?" the Secretary then asked the Ambassador. Nolting, coming last, had more time to work on his answer than anyone else and had erected the following architectural analogy:

> Well as I see it, Mr. Secretary, there are two pillars to our policy in Southeast Asia, Thailand and Vietnam, and Laos is the keystone, and if the keystone falls, the columns will collapse.

According to Allen, McNamara was "wincing" at each one of these responses. He probably had already received word that a final decision on any deployments had been postponed until his return, and was using this group as a sounding board.

"That's all very good, but let me play the devil's advocate," McNamara said, preparing to give his subordinates a few lessons. Turning to the JCS

Chairman, he delivered this lecture in geography: "Lem, you say we ought to implement SEATO Plan 5. That means we've got to occupy Luang Prabang, Vientiane, Pak Sane, Savannakhet, and Pakse," he said, naming the towns in descending order from north to south. He followed that with this soliloquy on strategy and tactics:

> Okay, so we do that. We put our forces in there. [Then] what do we do? Do we *sit*? Or do we *move out*? And if we're going to move out, what's our objective? Are we going to move out to destroy the enemy? Or just to occupy a larger perimeter, and if that's the case, what's that going to do to our force requirements? You know if we just implement SEATO 5, the forces won't be enough to move very far.

Felt must have guessed, as the Secretary turned toward him, that his answer would fare no better than Lemnitzer's had. McNamara tore it up with this argument:

> Okay, you say we can launch air strikes and take out Tchepone. What's the North Vietnamese reaction going to be? Don't they have a fighter regiment up at Yunnan [China] somewhere, and isn't it likely they'll bring that in? And won't they contest this with us? And what are going to be the rules of air engagement? Will we strike their bases if they . . . bring this outfit in?

After a brief remark on Harkins' and Nolting's insubstantial comments, the lecture was over, but not the ordeal.

McNamara, having demonstrated an extraordinary and detailed grasp of the situation, sat back calmly in his seat. "Okay fellows, I've played the devil's advocate, let's have at it. Let's arm wrestle on this." Allen recalls what happened then:

> And they all sit there . . . some of them looking for the goddamned Laos thing in the book. There's no agenda item on Laos! There's no background in there. And after this painful silence—Jesus I wanted to shrink up and crawl out under the door—McNamara says, "Well, we don't have much time for discussion here I guess."

"I was so disappointed in Lemnitzer," Allen recalls, "and even in Harry Felt. I wasn't disappointed in Harkins because I didn't expect anything from him." It was a poor showing by McNamara's subordinates, but a good lesson for the Secretary. At least he knew several proposals he would not be making to the President when he returned.

LAOS: A DECISION IN WASHINGTON

The fall of Nam Tha galvanized Washington into action because it appeared to directly challenge not only the cease-fire but also American
hopes for a negotiated withdrawal from Laos.[17] It also appeared to present
a serious threat to the security of Thailand, which asked for new U.S.
assurances. When a White Star patrol probed the Nam Tha area afterward,
however, no North Vietnamese troops were in evidence, and the team
reported seeing only local Pathet Lao guerrillas.[18] Like Harriman's reaction to the communist attack on Padong a year earlier, the Kennedy
administration reacted more to what Nam Tha seemed to symbolize—
a move by Hanoi toward the Mekong—than to reality: another poor
performance by the Royal Laotian Army.

At a press conference on May 9, Kennedy said there were only two
options: restore the cease-fire through negotiations, or restore it through
the introduction of U.S. forces. He said:

> we've got . . . to try to move ahead in our political negotiations.
> Now I agree it's a very hazardous course, but introducing American
> forces which is the other one—*let's not think there is some great third
> course*—that also is a hazardous course, and we want to attempt to
> see if we can work out a peaceful solution, which has been our
> object for many months. [emphasis added][19]

The next day at an NSC meeting Harriman and Hilsman recommended
a naval show of force and a limited troop deployment to Thailand, a plan
that Kennedy had rejected a year before and was still skeptical about now.
The Chiefs agreed with this naval maneuver but not with the troop
deployment unless they could use whatever force necessary to meet any
potential communist reaction.[20] This, of course, was out of the question
as far as the President was concerned. Since Rusk, McNamara, and Lemnitzer were all traveling in Asia and scheduled to return in two days,
Kennedy decided to delay a final decision on the Thailand troop deployment until then, and, at the same time, to seek Eisenhower's advice. He
did, however, authorize the naval action that day, and American warships
headed for the South China Sea. After the meeting Harriman and Hilsman
approached Kennedy and argued that, without the troop deployment, the
ship movement was too weak and should be stopped; Kennedy agreed,
but then changed his mind one hour later.[21] His vacillation would appear
to indicate how difficult this decision was to make.

The President's wavering ended at the May 12 NSC meeting.[22] Eisenhower had recommended the same thing he told Kennedy in January

1961: send American combat troops into Laos. In the meeting McNamara recommended the limited troop deployment to Thailand and logistical preparations for a possible large-scale intervention in Laos. McNamara's position was apparently sufficient to persuade Kennedy, and he approved a plan to send 3,000 combat troops to Thailand as a signal that a communist move on the Mekong would mean fighting American forces.

Hanoi's objective in Laos, however, was not to move to the Mekong. The goal was to secure the infiltration trails into South Vietnam, and the strategy was to hamstring the Americans with a diplomatic commitment that would freeze the status quo on the ground. Kennedy's move to defend the Mekong was no real threat to this plan; on the contrary, the communists could now negotiate under what *appeared* to be American military pressure, and then Washington would declare victory and go home. The victory on the ground, however, would belong to the communists, and the agreement would be nothing more than a face-saving device for Washington.

SETTLEMENT ON LAOS

On June 7 the princes in Laos began meetings in the Plain of Jars, and four days later arrived at an agreement to form a government of national union. On June 14 American financial aid to Laos was resumed, and on June 23 the new government was officially formed. Souvanna Phouma became Prime Minister, while General Phoumi and Prince Souphanouvong were named Deputy Prime Ministers, with any important action requiring the agreement of all three men. Their first act was a proclamation of a cease-fire throughout Laos. Next they renounced SEATO protection, declared Laos neutral, and objected to the presence of U.S. forces—which were already returning to the U.S.—across the border in Thailand. Laos presented its declaration of neutrality to the Geneva conference on July 6, which served as the basis for the Geneva Declaration on the Neutrality of Laos and the Protocol signed by all of the delegates on July 23.[23]

Beginning in June and continuing through October, the 3,000 American troops in Thailand were gradually reduced to a small residual force. At a White House meeting on September 28 Kennedy issued NSAM-189, which directed the withdrawal of all American military forces from Laos by October 7 and the retention of the remaining U.S. combat forces in Thailand "pending a further review of developments in Laos."[24] The International Control Commission counted all 666 American military personnel, and the 403 Filipino technicians, as they departed Laos through the ICC's checkpoints; but only *forty* of the estimated 10,000 North Vietnamese troops in Laos passed through ICC checkpoints.[25] Some of these forces may have withdrawn, but nobody knew for sure. Communist secrecy and obstructive tactics by the Polish contingent of the ICC prevented the organization from formally registering what was a blatant violation of the Geneva provisions for troop withdrawals.

Arthur Dommen, a respected observer of this period, later said this about the North Vietnamese troops:

> The United States . . . did not make the issue a *casus belli*. The acceptance of these forces was *part of the price* to be paid for neutralizing Laos without committing American troops. [emphasis added][26]

The price turned out to be high, especially for the South Vietnamese Army and the American advisors in the field with them. It was a price no one in Washington, especially in the State Department, was anxious to acknowledge; in fact, for the next several months there would be a concerted attempt to deny that the settlement had produced any increase in infiltration to Vietnam. Someone in MACV's intelligence office, however, was busy writing a report that would contradict this claim, and upset General Harkins as well.

AN INFILTRATION REPORT IS SUPPRESSED

Toward the end of the third week in July, Captain Jimmy Harris was hard at work one afternoon in his office in Saigon when he noticed someone in brown khaki trousers standing beside his desk.[27] He looked up and immediately recognized General Harkins, the MACV Commander, glowering at him. Jimmy had never been visited at his desk before by a four-star general and this one had a foreboding look in his eye. It was obvious he was about to catch hell.

"Captain Harris," the General snapped, loud enough for others in the office to hear, "I have just one question for you. How many communists have you actually seen come across the border?" That was easy: "None sir," Harris replied, not getting what Harkins was driving at. "And that's how many I'll accept," Harkins said defiantly, and then departed, leaving the startled captain wondering what might happen next. A few moments later Delaney explained what the problem was. Harkins was angry over Harris' infiltration report and had recalled all copies of it.

Captain Harris was the section's expert on infiltration and he had released a major study on the subject only a week before. He had worked on it for over two months and was quite proud of it. It showed a sizable increase in communist infiltration into Vietnam over the previous months, and a more recent acceleration through the trails in Laos. "It was a hard copy," Harris recalled, "a documented study rather than a message. It wasn't electrical; it went out as a mimeographed paper." What Harris was most proud of, however, was the congratulatory message that MACV had received from CINCPAC over the report. Just two days before this unnerving visit by Harkins, the kudos had come in from Hawaii. Such pats on the back were rare and naturally had generated cheers and compliments from his colleagues in the office.

Harkins, Delaney explained, had issued a message to CINCPAC canceling it and discrediting Harris' assertion of a recent major increase in infiltration. "I never forgot that day for the rest of my life," Harris later remarked.

INFILTRATION THROUGH LAOS

General Harkins *knew* how serious the infiltration problem had become. In a later interview he admitted: "It was bad when I got there, and it got worse and worse."[28] The infiltration issue became entangled in a number of other problems over the course of 1962: it had implications—up to the end of June—for the renewed call for American intervention in Laos; after July it posed an embarrassing problem for American backing of the Laos neutralization settlement; and, beginning in the summer and continuing afterward, it posed a grave problem for the effort to keep low the number of Viet Cong in South Vietnam. In short, infiltration through Laos had become a multifaceted political football.

During the fifth SECDEF conference it had been described this way: "Infiltration, which has been at a low level for the past few months, is estimated to be on the increase, using routes through Laos."[29] That was in early May, however, when, in the wake of Nam Tha's fall to the communists, the decision facing the President was whether to introduce U.S. combat forces into Laos. The June 1 USARPAC Intelligence Bulletin reported that infiltration through Laos "is on the increase," and that "varied evidence has led U.S. officials in Saigon to conclude that the monthly infiltration rate that had fallen to 100–200 persons between Dec 61 and Apr 62 may shortly reach last summer's high of 500 to 1,000."[30]

With American combat troops poised on the Thai banks of the Mekong

Vice President Lyndon Johnson among crowds of South Vietnamese,
May 1961 *(Courtesy of Howard Burris)*

LBJ, with President Diem
and Ambassador Nolting,
during his visit to South
Vietnam *(Courtesy of
Howard Burris)*

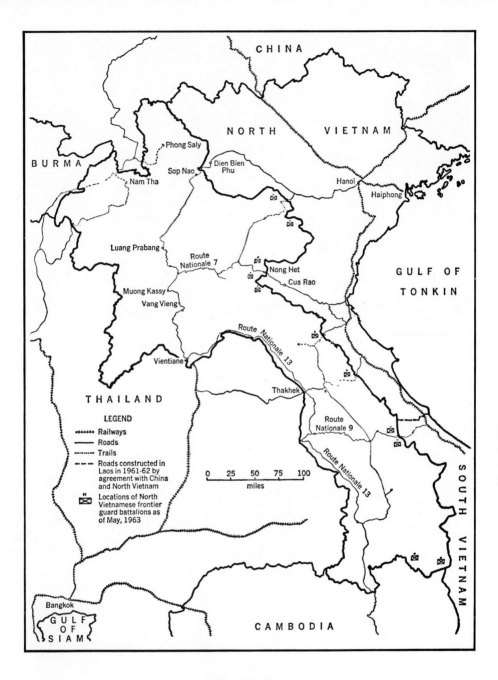

Map #1, Laos

A short break for a soda in a South Vietnamese village in III Corps.
Left to right: Captain Blascak, Major Young, and Jim Drummond.
(Courtesy of Jim Drummond)

U.S. helicopter downed by ground fire. Two were destroyed by fire on
this operation in III Corps, South Vietnam, 1962.
(Courtesy of Jim Drummond)

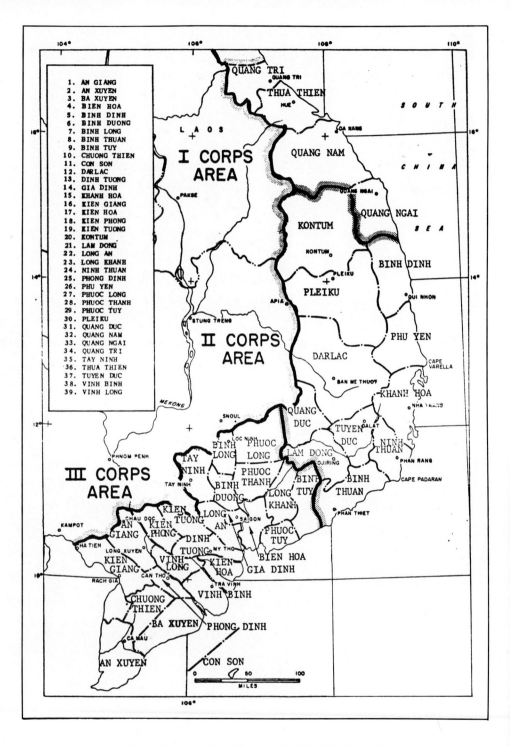

Map #2, South Vietnam, 1962 *(USARPAC)*

Major General Edward Lansdale, 1963
(Official U.S. Air Force Photograph)

Laotian government soldiers providing supporting fire east of Huong
Phalane, in Southern Laos, 1962 *(Courtesy of Jerry King)*

Viet Cong dead; South Vietnam, 1962 *(Courtesy of Jim Drummond)*

December, 1962, in Palm Beach, Florida. Left to right: General David
Shoup, Marines, General Earl G. Wheeler, Army, Admiral George
Anderson, Navy, Secretary of Defense Robert S. McNamara, Presi-
dent John F. Kennedy, General Maxwell Taylor, Chairman of the
Joint Chiefs of Staff, Deputy Secretary of Defense Roswell Gilpatric,
and General Curtis LeMay, Air Force *(Photo. No. ST-C73-2-62*
In the John F. Kennedy Library)

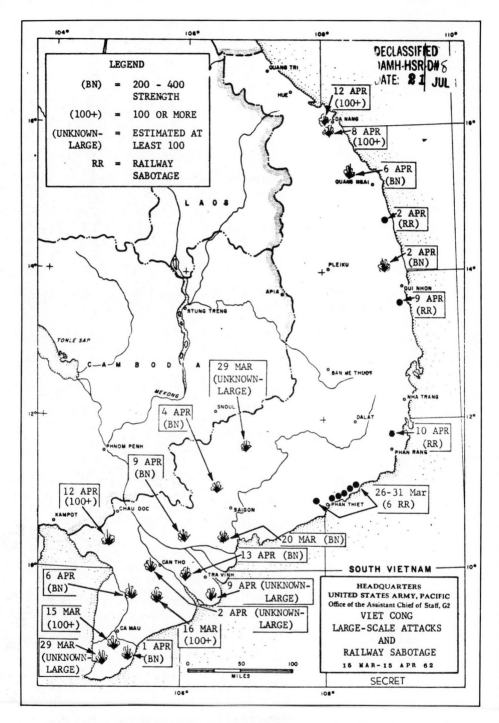

Map #3, declassified map of South Vietnam, showing Viet Cong attacks
in the spring of 1962 *(USARPAC)* (See page 251)

and the issue of a larger American intervention still up in the air, MACV's reporting continued to reflect higher infiltration: a June 29 report said "800 to 1,000 Viet Cong infiltrated during May 1962 and about 800 in the first three weeks of June."[31] The report also forecast that the "formation of [a] new coalition government in Laos may lead North Vietnam to expedite infiltration into South Vietnam." The effect of underscoring infiltration from Laos to Vietnam was to buttress the case for a strong U.S. military response in Laos. Just one month later the situation had changed completely: the U.S. troops sent to Thailand were packing their duffel bags to leave and preparations were under way to endorse the Laotian declaration of neutrality. The communists, knowing there was nothing the Americans would do about it, stepped up their use of the trails through Laos even more. In Washington and Saigon, however, infiltration was not a popular subject.

On July 27 another MACV report said that, according to "unconfirmed" reports, "on July 3 three Viet Cong battalions crossed from Laos" into Kontum Province and proceeded southward toward War Zone D.[32] Three Viet Cong battalions would include about 1,500 to 2,000 men, and would most likely have comprised one Viet Cong regiment. These were some of the units described in the hard-copy Harris report that Harkins recalled and destroyed, and use of the word "unconfirmed" by the July 27 report—issued four days after the Laos settlement at Geneva—was part of the new effort by MACV to reverse its reporting on infiltration through Laos. This became more obvious seven days later when MACV issued another report, this time criticizing "South Vietnamese estimates" that at least 2,000 Viet Cong had "infiltrated into Kontum province just opposite Laos."[33] MACV, the report said, "discounts" this information, as well as information indicating there were five more Viet Cong battalions "stationed in Laos along South Vietnam's Kontum and Quang Nam provinces."

The effects of information like the analysis contained in Jimmy Harris' report were twofold. It was publicly embarrassing for the administration because it advertised the high price that was being paid for its neutralization policy: that is, a much greater threat to South Vietnam, Cambodia, and Thailand. At the top secret level the impact was even more profound and complicated by the ongoing attempt to hide the truth about the failure of the war effort. Harris' infiltration report directly undermined the attempt to suppress the facts about the size of the Viet Cong force. MACV, the July 27 report said, "holds to infiltration figures of 1,600–1,800 since May from all routes." This would be a monthly rate of 500 to 600 men, well below the 800 to 1,000 figure used by MACV in June along with its prediction that it would go up after the Laos settlement.

Harris had failed to consider that his report on infiltration might pose a problem in Saigon, and he did not understand the political sensitivity of the matter in Washington. On the contrary, he thought it would be well received there:

> Really it was patterned after the State Department "Threat to the Peace" paper in 1961, and what I tried to do was to take that as a basic document and bring it up to date with any additional [information] and everything that had been captured after that through somewhere in July.

In fact, Harris' report came at the very moment that Hilsman, at Rusk's direction, was examining infiltration through Laos. The State Department was interested in showing, if possible, that the Geneva agreement had not led to an increase. The reversal of MACV's reporting at the end of July dovetailed perfectly with this desire, while Harris' analysis did not.

Despite Harkins' efforts to recall it, word about "a MACV report on infiltration" managed to get to Hilsman by the end of August. For the next two weeks he had been trying, "without success," to get a copy of it when he received a call from Forrestal in the White House reporting the upshot of a disquieting Tuesday luncheon meeting. Forrestal said that "Bill Bundy, the Joint Staff representative, Mac Bundy and Walt Rostow were all talking as if there had been a marked increase on infiltration into South Vietnam."[34] Hilsman replied that there was a MACV study he had been trying to get hold of, and that he would give Forrestal the cable reference so that Forrestal could "attempt to obtain the MACV report for us."

It seems unlikely that Hilsman suspected that this MACV report contained Harris' revelations about increased infiltration. It is more likely he thought the report would be consistent with the MACV material he had been collecting since late July discounting the earlier claim of increased infiltration through Laos.[35] It is clear Hilsman knew that MACV had changed its tune.[36] It is unlikely that Forrestal or Hilsman ever saw Jimmy Harris' report; on September 28 Hilsman summarized MACV's reporting in these words:

> No information [is] available to confirm specific instances of Viet Cong infiltration from Laos. Indeed, some of the reports are from low-level sources and appear highly exaggerated.[37]

Hilsman said he agreed with this, and he said it again in another paper he wrote three weeks later.[38]

For Kennedy, who was being fed the corrupted data depicting tenuous success on the battlefield in South Vietnam,[39] the infiltration problem seemed the one component most likely to derail this success, and he worried that this would buttress the argument for U.S. retaliation against the source: North Vietnam. That Kennedy worried about the problem in these precise terms—although he did not want to take U.S. military action against the North—is evident from a conversation he had with Roger Hilsman. He recalls the President made a comment "that turned out to be painfully prophetic for both himself and his successor." Referring to Hilsman's argument that it was impossible to completely cut off infiltration no matter what "draconian measures" were taken, Kennedy said that it was "really worse than that." Even if the flow were reduced to a trickle there would always be a "political burden." Kennedy added this prediction:

> No matter what goes wrong or whose fault it really is, the argument will be that the communists have stepped up their infiltration and we can't win unless we hit the north. Those trails are a built-in excuse for failure, and a built-in argument for escalation.[40]

Kennedy said he did not think people "would actually lie," but that every time things went badly there would be reports "about increased use of the trails, and people in Saigon and Washington would take them more seriously."

For those directly involved in perpetrating the inside deception, as well as the few in Washington who knew about it, the increase in infiltration through Laos meant something different. The cutting and "freezing" of the size of the enemy on the battlefield was the crucial element in their deception story, for when the numbers were crunched the final line always had to read the same: the policy was on track and only a little more time was needed to win. An enormous slice of the hard-core Viet Cong force had already been dropped from the books, and Winterbottom's intelligence analysts were now besieged by new sightings of those units that the order of battle team had originally identified. It was hard enough for Harkins to restrain estimates on the size of the Viet Cong—and thereby keep his success story intact—without adding into the equation new battalions and regiments fresh from North Vietnam. To have done so would have brought down the entire house of cards upon which the continuing presence of the advisory force depended: the appearance of a winnable war.

It was not that the war's decline was producing, as Kennedy predicted, more infiltration reports, but rather that the war was deteriorating *and* infiltration was increasing. In other words, increased infiltration was making a bad situation even worse. MACV had succeeded in suppressing the true figures on communist infiltration through Laos, and the State Department was happy because there appeared to be no hard evidence the agreement reached at Geneva was a serious threat to Vietnam. The tragedy is that concealing intelligence on the enemy makes life far riskier for the soldiers who have to carry the burden of battle.

American advisors were being killed in increasing numbers by the burgeoning communist army in South Vietnam. Harkins had told Harris he would not accept the North Vietnamese battalions in his report because he had not personally seen them. There *were* Americans who saw these battalions—*as they were infiltrating through Laos into South Vietnam*. We are fortunate to have the recollections of the American commander, Army Captain Jerry King, of the Special Forces team that patrolled the key Tchepone portion of the Ho Chi Minh Trail at the precise time Harris' report was destroyed. His recapitulation of what happened on the Trail in July 1962 allows us, thirty years later, to understand how it felt to run smack into the middle of one of these "unconfirmed" North Vietnamese battalions.[41]

ON THE TRAIL

Dusk was descending on the Ho Chi Minh Trail as six men entered a small clump of trees and prepared to bed down on another steamy mid-July night. A Laotian sergeant guarded the perimeter while his two Laotian privates, a Thai Ranger, and two U.S. Army Special Forces advisors moved deeper into the trees to find a suitable sleeping site. It had been a long day on the Trail, and the slope had been mostly uphill as the men had made their way back from a patrol that had taken them to within ten kilometers of the communist stronghold at Tchepone. Captain King, commander of the only U.S. Special Forces A Team operating in this critical zone of the Trail (there were fewer than twenty such teams in all of Laos), often led small patrols like this one to oversee the training of the American and Laotian soldiers under his command.

It would take all of the following day to return to their base camp at Savannakhet, located near the Thai border on the western side of the Laotian panhandle across from Tchepone. The three days of patrolling had been uneventful and the men were tired. The sweltering July heat and high humidity during the trek back up from Tchepone had drained their body fluids, so the last thing they did before finding a camp site was to fill their canteens with fresh water. With a sense of relief they threw down their rucksacks, feeling secure in the relative safety of the trees and the approaching darkness. King, and his Special Forces sergeant, Frank Helms, sat motionless, listening to the tropical insects and birds with whom they would share the night, content just to let their limbs rest for a while. A half hour went by, shadows began to hug the trees, and some of the men finally stirred to make a spot on the ground comfortable.

Suddenly the calm was broken by the sound of hurried footsteps pounding through the underbrush. All eyes riveted on the path that led to their recess. The diminutive figure of the Laotian sergeant came running toward them. He stopped in the middle of the group, looked at King with frightened eyes and whispered loudly, "Viet Minh!" King jumped up, motioning to the others to pick up their things, and headed for the spot where the Laotian sergeant had been. Within seconds he was peering out from the trees into the rice paddies; there was still enough light to make out what had so frightened the Laotian sergeant. Sure enough, there they were, all over the place, more than 300 of them. The distinctive green uniforms and black straw hats covered with plastic left no doubt in Captain King's mind what he was looking at.

It was the main body of a North Vietnamese regular army infantry battalion. They were less than 100 yards away and closing. King had to think fast. It appeared that the advance guard had already gone past his own position in the trees. Based on the approaching angle of the main body, which was heading straight for him, he estimated the lead element had passed behind the clump of trees his men were in. North Vietnamese squads protecting the flanks of the main element could be anywhere. He decided immediately there was no chance to run for it, and returned swiftly and stealthily to his men.

Only a few yards from where they were standing was a thorny thicket of bushes. Time was up. King motioned at the bushes and everyone scrambled for them except one of the two Laotian privates. He gestured frantically that he wanted to get out of there but stern looks from King and the others left him no alternative, and all six men crawled into the bushes on their bellies. They spread out in a circle on their stomachs, with their feet on the inside and their shoulders an arm's length away on the outside. They checked their weapons, set the safety switches to the off position, and concentrated on breathing evenly as they waited for the moment of truth.

One minute passed, then two, but it seemed like an eternity. Suddenly Viet Cong squads were sweeping the area all around their bushes, poking here and there and, fortunately for King's patrol, not taking their job very seriously. A North Vietnamese soldier walked by the bushes and King could see the familiar shape of his AK-47 rifle. The Laotian private, the one who had wanted to bolt, aimed his weapon but the other men quickly and silently stopped him from opening fire. The communist soldier moved on and King passed the order to hold fire until the very moment they were discovered. The sweeper units disappeared and, as he peered out through the leaves of the bushes, King could see North Vietnamese officers assigning spots for squads to bed down right where he and his men had been only moments before. Luckily they had left no evidence of their presence.

With the sweat dripping from their bodies, King's men began to quietly apply mud to the exposed areas of their skin for camouflage. They began to realize that, for the moment at least, they would not be discovered. King knew they would be tortured and killed if they were found. The tension mounted. A North Vietnamese soldier walked right up to the bushes, dropped his trousers and squatted. Their nostrils rebelled at the putrid scent. Others came to relieve themselves by the bushes in the hours that followed. Finally, the Viet Cong went to sleep.

King and his men did not sleep. Every few moments one man would touch the man to his left on his shoulder to help ward off the drowsiness. When the urge to urinate finally became overwhelming, there was nothing to do but just let it happen in place. The major problem of the night was drinking water from their metal canteens, but drink they had to, for the humidity was still very high, and that, along with their anxiety, caused them to sweat all night. King estimated their water would be gone before noon the next day, and that they would not be able to last in their present position if the Viet Cong decided to stay another night.

To the patrol's relief, the infantry battalion began moving out at daybreak. It was about 9:30 when the last of them disappeared from view. Just to be safe, King made his men hold their positions for one more hour. King and Helms then crept out of the bushes and scouted around the immediate area. The Viet Cong were nowhere in evidence. King decided to move out on an angle away from where he thought the Vietnamese were headed—into South Vietnam. The Laotian sergeant led the others in a line formation. Jerry King did not have to motivate his men to move fast.

When he returned to base, he immediately reported the movement of this North Vietnamese battalion through the Tchepone area. As he did so, he had no idea that Laos had just declared itself neutral and that this political breakthrough, for which Washington had labored for the previous fifteen months, was about to be sealed by the delegations at Geneva. Although he didn't realize it at the time, Jerry King's experience in the Laotian bush had just given him a firsthand view of what the political solution meant on the battlefield. The price of neutralization was a large North Vietnamese presence on the ground in Laos, and unrestricted use of the trails King was patrolling. It is not surprising, then, that reports like the one King made that day were both militarily alarming and politically controversial; but King did not know that either: he never got feedback on his reports.

NOTES

1. Hilsman, *To Move a Nation*, p. 140.
2. William Bundy, unpublished manuscript, p. 5-21.
3. Stevenson, *The End of Nowhere*, p. 170.
4. Ibid.
5. Hilsman, *To Move a Nation*, p. 139.
6. Ibid., p. 138.
7. William Bundy, unpublished manuscript, p. 5-21.
8. Hilsman, *To Move a Nation*, pp. 139–40.
9. William Bundy, unpublished manuscript, p. 5-20.
10. Hilsman, *To Move a Nation*, pp. 140–41.
11. NSAM-149, April 19, 1962. JFK Library, Newman Papers.
12. Hilsman, *To Move a Nation*, p. 141.
13. William Bundy, unpublished manuscript, p. 5-21.
14. Ibid.
15. Hilsman, *To Move a Nation*, p. 141.
16. Allen, joint interview, Allen and Benedict with the author on July 21, 1988. The following reconstruction is based on Allen's recollections in this interview.
17. Stevenson, *The End of Nowhere*, pp. 174–75.
18. Arthur Dommen, *Conflict in Laos* (New York: Praeger, 1971), p. 218.
19. Kennedy, *Public Papers*, 1962, p. 378.
20. Stevenson, *The End of Nowhere*, p. 175; and Hilsman, *To Move a Nation*, p. 143.
21. Stevenson, *The End of Nowhere*, p. 176.
22. Ibid.
23. For a copy of both see Appendix V in Dommen, *Conflict in Laos*, pp. 415–23.
24. NSAM-189, September 28, 1962, Army Center for Military History, Southeast Asia files, declassified October 8, 1980; see also JFK Library, Newman Papers.
25. Stevenson, *The End of Nowhere*, pp. 178–79.
26. Dommen, *Conflict in Laos*, p. 241.
27. This section is based upon Harris' recollection, given in a June 7, 1988, interview with the author.
28. Harkins, interview with Ted Gittinger, November 10, 1981, LBJ Library, Oral History Collection, p. 11.

29. Conference record, in *State History*, 1962, Document 187, p. 386.

30. USARPAC Intelligence Bulletin, June 1962.

31. See account of "COMUSMACV, Headway Addenda to OPSUM 112, June 29, 1962," in "Summary of Back-Up Material" to a Hilsman "Talking Paper: Communist Infiltration Into South Vietnam From Laos," September 28, 1962; JFK Library, Hilsman Papers, Country File, Laos, Box 2.

32. See account of "COMUSMACV, Headway Addenda to OPSUM 140, July 27, 1962," in "Summary of Back-Up Material" to a Hilsman "Talking Paper: Communist Infiltration Into South Vietnam From Laos," September 28, 1962; JFK Library, Hilsman Papers, Country File, Laos, Box 2.

33. See account of "COMUSMACV, Headway Addenda to OPSUM 147, August 3, 1962," in "Summary of Back-Up Material" to a Hilsman "Talking Paper: Communist Infiltration Into South Vietnam From Laos," September 28, 1962; JFK Library, Hilsman Papers, Country File, Laos, Box 2.

34. Hilsman memo to Allen Whiting, September 12, 1962, JFK Library, Hilsman Papers, Country File, Laos, Box 6.

35. A list of the MACV Headway Addenda in Hilsman's possession at the time can be found in "Summary of Back-Up Material" to a Hilsman "Talking Paper: Communist Infiltration Into South Vietnam From Laos," September 28, 1962; JFK Library, Hilsman Papers, Country File, Laos, Box 2.

36. This is evident from Hilsman's earlier comments on July 16: he said MACV was reporting that infiltration had "increased significantly" and that the Laos agreement might prompt a further "step up" of it. At that time Hilsman had added that, despite the Saigon Embassy's July 5 claim that "the MACV assessment was based largely on unconfirmed information," it nevertheless appeared to him that MACV's assessment "remains valid." He denied, however, that it was related to "recent developments in Laos." See Hilsman, "Research Memorandum RFE-30," July 16, 1962, JFK Library, Hilsman Papers, Country File, Laos, Box 2.

37. Hilsman "Talking Paper: Communist Infiltration Into South Vietnam From Laos," September 28, 1962, JFK Library, Hilsman Papers, Country File, Laos, Box 2.

38. Hilsman's "Research Memorandum RFE-49," October 19, 1962, JFK Library, Hilsman Papers, Country File, Laos, Box 2.

39. See, for example, the June 27, 1962, "Status Report on Southeast Asia, Prepared by the South East Asia Task Force," in *State History*, 1962, Document 230, pp. 478–81. It began: "The GVN is making progress against the VC, but it is still too early to predict assured success in the counterinsurgency effort."

40. Hilsman, *To Move a Nation*, p. 439.

41. King, interviews with the author, May 25 and June 22, 1991.

CHAPTER FIFTEEN

FAILURE IN VIETNAM

When Bill Benedict finally got back to Washington he tried to sound the alarm about what was happening in Saigon. He recalls what happened:

> I went in, and I told [General] Fitch what the story was, how they'd manipulated the figures, you know, the pressure we'd had to hold the point down. He tried to call the [Army] Chief of Staff, but that was just at the time when Decker was checking out of the net, and he wasn't available. . . . So what happened is, Fitch sent me over to the [CIA] National Board of Estimates. . . . I went over and gave a two-hour talk to those guys where I leveled with them, and they all said, "Hey, the suspicion is confirmed, but what are you going to do?" By then the whole thing had reached a point where there was a political implication overpowering us.[1]

The "old gray beards" at the CIA's Board of Estimates seemed to have taken Benedict's charges with uncharacteristic calm. It was as if they already knew what he was going to say and had made up their minds to do nothing about it.

George Allen did not have any better luck telling the truth after he left Saigon than Benedict did. On his way back to the Defense Intelligence Agency (DIA) in Washington, Allen stopped off in Honolulu for discussions with CINCPAC's intelligence organization, headed by Air Force

Brigadier General Patterson. After listening to Allen's criticism of the state of MACV's intelligence effort, the General, recalls Allen, "pressed me for details . . . and what I thought ought to be done."[2] Allen said Winterbottom had to be replaced by someone "better qualified," a suggestion to which Patterson "evinced no great shock." Allen recounts, however, what Patterson did afterward:

> I later learned that after our meeting, he sent a "back channel" message both to Col. W. [Winterbottom] in Saigon and to Air Force intelligence in Washington advising that I was "out to get" Col. W.

Later in the day after the meeting Allen received word from Washington "that I should report to the office of General Carroll, the director of DIA, the first thing Monday morning." At that time, Allen did not know about Patterson's back-channel warning to Washington.

Allen dutifully reported at 8:00 A.M. to Carroll's office. Allen recalls that he was asked about the situation in Vietnam and that he told them the truth, "candidly expressing myself as I had done at CINCPAC." Carroll asked him what should be done, and Allen recalls what happened then:

> I began, after taking a deep breath, with the suggestion that J-2 [Winterbottom] be replaced, again, outlining his unsuitability for the assignment. General Carroll asked what service the J-2 belonged to; when I replied that he was an Air Force colonel, the general flushed, but then continued questioning me on other matters for another 15 minutes or so. Finally he thanked me, and dismissed me. After the door closed behind me, one of those who remained later told me, the general asked the assembled colonels and brigadier generals who the hell that civilian thought he was to call into judgment the competence of an Air Force colonel.

Still, Carroll had paid attention to Allen's depressing news about the situation in Vietnam because McNamara had ordered the DIA director to do something about improving MACV's intelligence operations.

Shortly after the encounter with Allen, General Carroll left with a task force to investigate the matter. Allen says this is what happened to Carroll's mission:

> the wind was taken out of his sails when he made the required courtesy call [at CINCPAC] en route to Saigon. Admiral Felt chose to remind General Carroll that Vietnam was on CINCPAC's turf,

and that as the theater commander, he was responsible for intelligence in Vietnam; that he reported directly to the Joint Chiefs, that DIA was not in his chain of command and therefore had no authority over intelligence in Admiral Felt's theater, and that he trusted General Carroll understood this and would conduct himself accordingly.

General Carroll returned to his plane and told his task force "that they would not conduct a *review* of intelligence in Vietnam."

Somehow Walt Rostow, at this time Chairman of the Policy Planning Council at the State Department, learned—from whom it is not clear—that some specialists had returned from Vietnam with views critical of the situation there. This prompted Rostow to request a personal briefing by George Allen. Allen recalls the buildup to that meeting:

> This caused quite a stir throughout DIA, which finally agreed to Rostow's request, provided that he come to the Pentagon for the briefing. It was also decided that a DIA general officer (an Air Force Brigadier) should attend the briefing session as "moderator." I was warned to refrain from criticizing MACV's intelligence competence. While I could offer my own views on the enemy situation, I would not do it in ways that might suggest any shortcomings in MACV's intelligence effort.

Rostow left the meeting no better informed than before it, Allen says. He tried writing some reports that called MACV's "overly optimistic views" into question, but this only resulted in a new gag order: "We were instructed to refrain from any analytical remarks which could not be directly attributed to the military command in Vietnam."

Allen, an old intelligence pro himself, then resorted to some back-channel techniques of his own. He used them to send a query to people on Winterbottom's staff asking whether there had been any changes in the enemy order of battle. After a brief delay, Allen recalls, they sent back word that a number of additional combat units, "numbering several thousand men," now met the criteria for "acceptance," and that Winterbottom "would be announcing this after clearing the matter with General Harkins." What happened next was predictable:

> Shortly thereafter, they advised that Harkins had rejected the notion that the enemy forces could be increasing while suffering the kind of losses being inflicted on them by friendly operations, and the J-2 had therefore decided not to change the order of battle holding

at this time, despite the evidence of continued growth in enemy capabilities.

Allen says he was "astonished" that "a field commander's subjective views could lead to the suppression of hard intelligence of mounting enemy capabilities," but his attempts to do something about it failed.

The efforts of Allen and Benedict to tell the truth about MACV in Washington were not the only ones. Army Brigadier General W.B. Rossen, Special Assistant to Army Chief of Staff Decker, went out to examine the situation in Vietnam and returned in May 1962 with a disturbing report. He had found "almost universal skepticism" that the Viet Cong could be defeated "expeditiously," and he outlined the differences of opinion between MACV and the American advisors. Somewhat to his surprise, says historian Andrew Krepinevich, "the Army Staff generally ignored his report."[3] Krepinevich explains:

> The negative reports given Rossen by advisors in the field were symptoms of an emerging revolt by many Army advisors against the Army hierarchy's view of how well the war was going and how well suited the methods of the Concept were against insurgents.

By "Concept," Krepinevich means the old World War II conventional approach to war. The advisors' arguments were "doomed to failure," he notes, because this unwelcome message challenged the very foundations upon which the Army had constructed its approach to the war.

That Harkins did not listen to his advisors in the field, that the Army Staff did not listen to General Rossen, that DIA did not listen to George Allen, and that the old gray beards at the CIA did not pay attention to Benedict was most unfortunate indeed. For their old and inappropriate approach to the war was about to be tested in battle—against a far larger and more determined enemy than MACV was willing to admit existed.

SUMMER 1962: THE BATTLE IS JOINED

With the onset of the rainy season in May the communists' spring offensive came to an end and, from the middle of the month through the end of June, the level of large-scale attacks declined. The Viet Cong concentrated on consolidating their power in the regions into which they had expanded, and launched a series of small-scale attacks into the adjacent government-controlled areas to cripple the economy and divert attention there, and to tie up the South Vietnamese Army. In May, these attacks, mostly comprised of 100 to 200 men, struck farm projects and Civil Guard outposts in Kien Phong Province along the Mekong (on the 4th and 6th), in Phuoc Thanh Province just north of Saigon (on the 5th), and in Quang Ngai Province along the central coast (on the 9th). To the north of this area on the next day, attacks in Quang Nam and Thua Thien provinces temporarily crippled the railway line and led to a government decision to suspend night railway traffic there. On May 12, the Viet Cong attacked three separate SDC outposts in An Xuyen Province in the southern Ca Mau Peninsula, while in Darlac Province in the central highlands they attacked a district headquarters manned by three government paramilitary platoons. In the Darlac attack government forces sustained seventy casualties and the VC just sixteen, while collecting all of the government weapons before a U.S. air strike forced them to withdraw.

At the same time that the communist spring offensive came to an end, South Vietnamese actions finally began to pick up momentum. Many of these attacks were concentrated within a 100-mile radius of the air bases near Saigon, where most of the American helicopters were located. On April 24 a government air-mobile operation in Phong Dinh Province claimed fifty-three Viet Cong killed, while two South Vietnamese battalions reported forty-four enemy dead in Long An Province on the same day. A May 9 heliborne operation in Ba Xuyen Province reported sixty-one Viet Cong killed in action (KIA), and on May 23 a large South Vietnamese Army force, supported by the U.S. 57th Helicopter Company, counterattacked the new Viet Cong operation going on in Kien Phong Province, claiming 100 enemy KIAs.

Because of these and other government operations, it appeared that the high death toll being exacted from the Viet Cong might begin to cripple their operations. The question was: were these claims accurate? U.S. advisors in the Kien Phong battle, two of whom were wounded, confirmed those Viet Cong kills. The June 1 USARPAC Intelligence Bulletin did not openly deny the other South Vietnamese body counts, but the author's subtle choice of words sometimes revealed his skepticism.[4] For example, his description of the May 23 heliborne operation, which was also supported by U.S. air strikes, said 100 Viet Cong had "supposedly" been killed. Moreover, the article reminded its readers that, in general, casualty statistics were "known to be grossly inflated," and disclosed that "this fact has been determined from evaluation of many reports over the past six months and from actual on-the-spot observation."

Still, there could be no doubt about the fact that U.S. air strikes were killing a lot of people. That many of the dead were in fact innocent civilians had been the source of General Jablonsky's concern, shared by many advisors and officials in Washington like Hilsman. The only justification for continuing the air strikes, however ill-advised it appears in retrospect, was the belief that these air strikes *must* have been killing large numbers of Viet Cong forces, which, after all, was the principal military objective of the war effort. The problem was that these forces were still growing. Despite losses, the June bulletin noted, "Their military units have demonstrated remarkable regenerative capabilities." Equally significant was the fact that the firepower of American high-tech weapons systems had not sapped the will of the Viet Cong to fight. While the advisors, helicopters, and B-26s did motivate, for a while, the South Vietnamese Army to attack more often and deeper into Viet Cong territory, they did not succeed in weakening the enemy's motivation. "Despite Government pressure," the June bulletin said, "the Viet Cong are losing no aggressiveness."

The June USARPAC Intelligence Bulletin was noteworthy for another reason: it directly addressed the prevalent beliefs inside the U.S. Embassy on the course of the war. The article summarized the Embassy's view in this way: although the tide had not turned, government operations in the last six months had arrested some of the unfavorable trends, and U.S. advice and matériel would produce further dividends. The USARPAC bulletin cautioned, however, that during the same six months Viet Cong strength and determination had also increased, and added, "It now seems clear that the communists are not going to back down or voluntarily retard their timetable for conquest as a result of increased U.S. aid." What had been achieved "at best," the article said, "is a military standoff . . . with no real indication that the government is competing successfully with the Viet Cong for control of the countryside and support of the population." It was precisely "on this level," the article said forebodingly, "that the Viet Cong have proved themselves most adept, and it is *where the battle for South Vietnam will ultimately be fought*" (emphasis added).

The war in South Vietnam heated up during June and July. Urged into battle by U.S. advisors, the South Vietnamese Army conducted its largest operations to date. On July 20–21 they conducted a successful attack deep into Viet Cong territory in the Kien Tuong Province, located on the border with Cambodia, which included an unprecedented night heliborne lift. Operations of the 7th Division in the Mekong Delta during that same week claimed 400 Viet Cong casualties. The Viet Cong launched large operations as well, and their attacks were every bit as deadly as the government's. On July 14, a battalion-sized force ambushed two South Vietnamese airborne companies in Binh Duong Province just north of Saigon, killing twenty-four—including a U.S. advisor—and wounding twenty-nine. Six Viet Cong attacks in the first week of July alone in the III Corps Delta area resulted in 180 South Vietnamese dead, and "considerable" losses of arms and equipment. A particularly disturbing development was the Viet Cong's new use of a technique known in military intelligence parlance as "imitative deception." They broke into South Vietnamese radio nets and mimicked South Vietnamese communications, steering a Ranger company to a point where a Viet Cong force ambushed it.[5]

The war had truly been joined by both sides, but the Viet Cong withstood the best that the South Vietnamese Army could muster. The August 1 USARPAC Intelligence Bulletin reported the outcome in these words:

> Enemy capabilities have not been significantly reduced by GVN offensives; communist vigor remains undiminished, and the rainy season, now in full force, is not expected to slow down guerrilla attacks appreciably. Despite continuing high casualties in July, the Viet Cong many times showed that they are still able to strike in strength effectively.[6]

The will of the Viet Cong still remained unshaken by the test of battle. "Despite all the GVN can do," said the bulletin, "Viet Cong strength and determination to fight have not been weakened." The question was: how much longer would it be before the will of the South Vietnamese forces cracked? When the smoke cleared from the battles of July, the Viet Cong had not been beaten, and, if anything, had come out on top. The August bulletin concluded gloomily that the Viet Cong "undoubtedly still retain the initiative and are free to set the pattern of military action."

Of course this was not the view of the war that had come to dominate the U.S. leadership. The official optimism begun earlier in the year seemed to have justified itself because of what Harkins' top secret briefings showed: the military situation had turned the corner and now looked bright. The American approach seemed sound, and the continuing favorable developments held out the promise of eventual success. As *The Pentagon Papers* later noted, "to many the end of the insurgency seemed in sight. . . . In some quarters, even a measure of euphoria obtained."[7] At Kennedy's behest, McNamara now focused on bringing the Vietnam problem "to a successful conclusion within a reasonable time." The first evidence of this bidding was McNamara's instruction to Harkins during the fifth SECDEF conference that he come up with a plan to wrap things up and come home. On July 23, the same day that the Laos Accords were signed, McNamara made this decision official during the sixth SECDEF conference on the war. The Americans were ready to declare victory and come home.

JULY 23—THE SIXTH SECDEF CONFERENCE

General Harkins opened the discussion with the comment that "there is no doubt we are on the winning side. If our programs continue, we can expect VC actions to decline."[8] He said 2,400 strategic hamlets had been built, and the total would reach 6,000 by the end of the year; in certain areas, he said, "the reception of the Hamlet program has been very good." The programs for the South Vietnamese Army, the Civil Guard, and the Self Defense Corps were "coming along well and in most cases are ahead of schedule." All of this pleased McNamara, who, the conference record indicates, "noted that six months ago we had practically nothing and we have made tremendous progress to date." The Secretary declared that it was time to move beyond "short term crash-type actions" to a carefully conceived long-range program for training and equipping South Vietnamese forces and a "phase out of major U.S. combat, advisory and logistics support activities."

McNamara turned to Harkins and asked how long it would take before the Viet Cong could be "eliminated as a disturbing force." One year, Harkins replied, "from the time we are able to get [Vietnamese forces] fully operational and really pressing the VC in all areas." Apparently unimpressed by this claim, McNamara ordered that the long-range program to wrap up the war be laid out assuming that it would take three years to bring the Viet Cong under control. McNamara then added:

> we are behind schedule in our Defended Hamlet-Strategic Village program and the key to the problem is wresting areas from VC control and protecting the population. We must take a conservative view and assume it will take three years instead of one year. We must line up our long range program as it may become difficult to retain public support for our operations in Vietnam. *The political pressure will build up as U.S. losses continue to occur.* In other words we must assume the worst and make our plans accordingly. [emphasis added]

As if to defend his one-year scenario, Harkins said that government control was better in some places than others, but that it had increased in the Delta area "from 40% to 70% in the past year." He added that some of the attacks there were not VC-initiated but the acts of "bandits" that had been operating in South Vietnam "for thousands of years."

McNamara mentioned a "pessimistic report of the Washington teams on the hamlet program," and added, "perhaps Washington was uninformed" about the progress Harkins had mentioned. McNamara directed his Assistant Secretary of Defense for Public Affairs, Arthur Sylvester, to look into this with CINCPAC and MACV in order to "get good material into the press." After this, however, the conversation went downhill. Ambassador Nolting said he thought it was necessary to develop the "will of the villagers to resist." This drew a reaction from Rufus Phillips, a Lansdale protégé working in the Embassy who would shortly become the Assistant Director of Rural Affairs. Phillips said that the hamlets that demonstrated the will to resist were the ones that the Viet Cong attacked. This comment, predictably, disturbed McNamara: what arms do the villagers have? he asked. Shotguns, grenades, and French rifles, Phillips replied.

McNamara, who had directed several times at previous conferences that better weapons be put into the hands of the Self Defense Corps, seemed irritated by the news that the villagers had poor weapons. The conference record indicates:

> [McNamara] then said not to let the shortage of arms keep us from arming the villagers properly. Requisition the carbines if they can do the job better. We should indicate the number of people in the villages that should be armed with the carbine.

It was the same mistake the Secretary had made by impatiently arming the SDC, only worse: who was to say which villagers were Viet Cong? Many of the areas Harkins claimed were sympathetic to the government were Viet Cong strongholds; they would be only too grateful to receive brand-new American weapons without having to fight for them.

The top secret briefings and reports of progress at the conference, though completely at odds with the reality of the villages and the battlefield, justified the prophecy of victory and McNamara's order to plan for an eventual American withdrawal. Two days after the conference the Joint Chiefs formally directed CINCPAC to develop a Comprehensive Plan for South Vietnam (CPSVN) to carry out this withdrawal, and by August 14 CINCPAC relayed, along with its own additional guidance, the order to MACV to develop the plan.[9] The plan was to be based on three assumptions: that the insurgency would be under control within three years; that "extensive" U.S. support would be necessary during that time; and that the current funding ceilings[10] could be raised. "Program those items [that are] essential," CINCPAC ordered, "to do this job." Thus began the lengthy paper trail on the Kennedy withdrawal plan for Vietnam. That it was based on a wholly unrealistic view of the war at the creation was unfortunate, but that view continued to be fed by a steady stream of good news.

McNamara did not question Harkins' view that the war was being won, but did question the suggestion that it could be over in one year. Harkins' claim seems so incredibly naive that one may ask with justification: how could the American commander be so out of touch with reality? If Harkins knew that the order of battle carried well under half of the actual communist forces; if he knew—as he later admitted but would not let Jimmy Harris report outside MACV—that the infiltration problem was serious and getting worse; if he knew the casualty figures were 30 percent too high for the Viet Cong and 30 percent too low for the government; if he knew that the SDC were defecting as fast as the government was trying to replace them—how could he possibly think that victory could be achieved in just twelve months? We do not know what motivated Harkins, but whatever it was, it surely defies a sound military explanation.

Optimism, as a justification for battlefield predictions, has its limits. When soldiers are dying in combat there is little room for inaccurate assessments of the enemy's strength and will. Unfortunately, in Washington and Saigon, there was all too much room for precisely such assessments.

"THE GREATEST VICTORY OF THE WAR"

"The parade was held on a Saturday," Neil Sheehan, a news correspondent at the time, later wrote of it, "so that as many civil servants and their families as possible could be recruited to fill the crowds."[11] It was the South Vietnamese Army's "greatest victory of the war," the Saigon newspapers boasted about the July 20 operation the 7th Division had concluded against the Viet Cong. This division was the best in the South Vietnamese Army, and its Commander, Colonel Huynh Van Cao, rode triumphantly through the cheering crowds, Patton style, sporting his swagger stick and his Colt .45. After marching in front of his soldiers past the National Assembly building, he was decorated by Diem for gallantry. Cao's troops had killed ninety Viet Cong in this battle, and in six subsequent operations in August and September they claimed 100 or more VC kills each time.

The senior American advisor for that area (III Corps), Army Colonel Daniel Boone Porter, said later that he and Cao's advisor, Army Lieutenant Colonel John Paul Vann, "doubted" Cao's claims "very much," but that they "nevertheless reported in most instances what the old colonel said he had killed."[12] Cao's claimed figure of 131 dead VC as a result of the July 20 operation was typical of the way the South Vietnamese inflated figures to exaggerate success, but behind this little lie lurked a deeper and more troubling truth about the battle on that summer day. The ninety bullet-riddled Viet Cong bodies left floating in the open rice paddies, across which they had been fleeing for the safety of the Cambodian border just four miles away, were casualties of rounds from a supporting Farm Gate mission. Sheehan's work *A Bright Shining Lie* poignantly describes how Colonel Cao, who held in his grasp the opportunity to annihilate the entire Viet Cong 504th Main Force Battalion, gave up—out of fear the Viet Cong would fight if backed into a corner—and let them go.[13]

Cao refused Vann's pleas not to let the communists "escape like this to fight another day." Cao had already lost two dead and a dozen wounded when his forces landed next to the VC force, which foolishly fled into the sights of American aircraft. The only major ground kills made by the 7th Division that day occurred when some of its soldiers found and shot seven guerrillas hiding underwater and breathing through hollowed reeds. Vann was incredulous at Cao's apparent cowardice, but subsequent operations revealed a common pattern: Cao always refused to commit his reserve and complete the encirclement of the enemy. The reason, Sheehan explains, was this: once trapped, the Viet Cong would fight and Cao would take casualties too; then he would "get into trouble" with Diem, not be promoted, and might even be dismissed.

That Vann had managed to prod Cao into large operations was an accomplishment, and he continued them because they brought him more kills than any other division commander. In so doing, however, Cao was gambling with his own career; consequently, after bagging several Viet Cong, he would always let the rest escape. This convenient arrangement did wonders for Cao's career, but it also let large concentrations of Viet Cong loose in the Delta when he should have been trying to root them out. This chance would not come again, for Cao's game came to a crashing halt on October 5, when Rangers from his division staged an operation into the Plain of Reeds and ran into the Viet Cong 514th Ranger Battalion. The 514th stood and fought, stayed in their foxholes when the air strikes came, and then retreated in an orderly manner. Cao lost twenty dead and forty wounded, was summoned to the palace, called on the carpet and browbeat by Diem for listening to his American advisors and taking casualties. Diem threatened to deny Cao his promotion to general and a corps command. That brought an end to any effective operations for the 7th Division: it suffered only three dead for the rest of 1962. Cao, however, got his promotion.

THE MYTH IS SHAKEN

On August 8, National Security Council member Michael Forrestal wrote to McGeorge Bundy predicting that when the rains stopped in November the following six months would determine the success or failure of the U.S. program in Vietnam.[14] The truth, of course, was that the program had already failed and that the indices of this failure had been blocked and replaced with statistics showing success. Forrestal's memo is interesting because it borders on the negative. It ended with the recommendation that the U.S. step up "pressures" on Diem, adding—with a hint of desperation—"even at some risk." The lying about the success of the war demanded a psychology of success, but Forrestal's memo was symptomatic of the developing cracks in this psychology.

In Vietnam, closer to the reality of the failing war effort, an institutionalized schizophrenia was necessary for the psychology of winning to exist. Ambassador Nolting reported to State on August 16 that he had discussed the attitudes of "various" governments, presumably including that of the U.S., "in relation to the psychology of the Vietnamese people."[15] To signal that these talks were based on reality instead of the fiction of official optimism, Nolting said they were held "in context"—a creative code word meaning the true situation. Nolting reported his view that because "war-weariness" in Diem's army was a factor in the Viet Cong's success, "a definite shift in GVN psychological line should be made." The new line he proposed was "light at the end of [the] tunnel," which might also be close at hand. "This line can be made credible," he added, saying Secretary of State Thuan agreed it should be "injected" into Diem's speeches.

Two officials at State who understood the difference between "in context" and optimistic assessments were Chester Bowles, at this time an Ambassador-at-Large, and Joseph Mendenhall, who had recently returned from the post of Political Counsel in the American Embassy in Saigon. Bowles wrote to Rusk that "although our military authorities appear hopeful about the outcome, qualified *outside* observers place the odds for a clear-cut victory at less than fifty-fifty."[16] Bowles then bluntly added that if the situation continued to deteriorate it would force a decision within the next year to choose between committing more troops "to what the President's political opponents will call 'another Democratic war' or withdrawing in embarrassed frustration." He then issued this warning: "For the U.S. Government to adopt the classic 'let's wait and see' posture under such circumstances strikes me as not only sterile but foolhardy."

Mendenhall, just back from Vietnam, was graphically pessimistic. He argued that even though American aid had stopped the "rapid" deterioration of 1961, "the present overall security trend continues against us. In the Central Vietnam lowlands provinces security has seriously deteriorated in 1962."[17] Mendenhall finally posed the basic question: "Why are we losing?" His answer was simple: "President Diem and his weaknesses represent the basic underlying reason for the trend against us in the war." His solution was frank and blunt:

> *Conclusion:* That we cannot win the war with the Diem-Nhu methods, and we cannot change those methods no matter how much pressure we put on them.

> *Recommendation:* Get rid of Diem, Mr. and Mrs. Nhu and the rest of the Ngo family.

This was a drastic recommendation and it was based on an observation that directly contradicted the false notion that the tide of battle favored the government.

Although Mendenhall's analysis did not go higher than the Deputy Assistant Secretary of State for Far Eastern Affairs, Ed Rice, this memo and Bowles' comments make it clear that MACV's attempt to hide the failure of the war effort was being undercut by communications between the Embassy and the State Department. LBJ's aide, Colonel Burris, reported to him on August 17 that there was "concern" over just what U.S. "measures have contributed toward winning the war," and added that "it is virtually impossible to elicit specific replies" from the State or Defense departments "as to the degree of success or failure, particularly in the military field."[18] Burris then spoke about "eventual" victory being "generally" accepted, but in this regard he revealed that "only General Harkins has said that "we are on the winning side." (These were the precise words that Harkins had used at the sixth SECDEF conference in July.) Burris added that the director of State's Vietnam working group, Chalmers Wood, had said "an upward trend in our favor is not clearly in sight."

McNamara was still an important topic in the memoranda of the Vice President's aide. On the all-important question of McNamara's opinion of the war effort, Burris reported it was the Secretary's view that "we appear to be just about turning the corner." Burris also noted McNamara was moving with "a great sense of urgency" and had set a time limit for how long the U.S. effort in Vietnam would be maintained. The news from Burris boiled down to the fact that the myth of victory was in trouble. Help, however, was on the way.

TAYLOR'S TRIP REASSURES

"General Taylor would be pleased with the progress which has been made since his visit to Vietnam in October last year," Diem told Harkins.[19] Taylor, who was scheduled to arrive in Vietnam four days later, was on a worldwide trip examining things in preparation for his new job as the Chairman of the Joint Chiefs of Staff. Harkins responded that "this progress was not restricted to the III Corps area but was evident throughout the country." Harkins had put the finishing touches on his own strategy for defeating the Viet Cong, a plan that would become known as the "explosion" plan because Harkins intended to attack the Viet Cong everywhere at once. Harkins presented this strategy in detail to Diem, hoping to get Diem's approval before Taylor's arrival. Diem asked Harkins how long the plan would take. In a long-winded answer, Harkins said he was convinced that victory could be achieved in one year. He conceded, however, that McNamara did not agree with him and that "it was somewhat difficult to find others who would."

The sight of Harkins, with his charts, his notebooks, and his situation maps, talking of victory in a year, must have been an intriguing picture to Diem. Had Harkins gone off the deep end? Could he actually believe what he was saying? Harkins did admit to being optimistic—he always was, he told Diem during this meeting—but something beyond optimism was responsible for this uncanny briefing. Before presenting his explosion plan Harkins had pulled out a chart, depicting VC strength in each province, to which Diem had taken exception:

> On examination of the figures the President protested that those indicated for the I Corps and II Corps regions were too low and said that his national intelligence people had much higher holdings in those areas. . . .

Harkins had replied that his figures were based on Vietnamese and American information, which showed there was just over 20,000 hard-core VC in the entire country. Diem knew there were more than 30,000 hard-core VC,[20] and did not bother to argue the point anymore. He told Harkins his plan was good "in principle," but added, "one had better look to three years instead of one." Interestingly, McNamara said the same thing at the July SECDEF conference.

Harkins was not the only one preparing for Taylor's visit. So was Vann. He had been invited to represent the division-level advisors at a lunch with Taylor on September 11, and understood that he was to give Taylor a frank appraisal of the situation. Vann "was thrilled with this opportunity to state his worries to a man who had the power to influence high policy and set matters right."[21] Vann intended to convey a balanced message at the luncheon, "encouraged and worried," writes Neal Sheehan, who studied Vann's life for sixteen years. He hoped to raise issues such as the loss of American weapons to the Viet Cong via the SDC outposts, indiscriminate bombing, and the problem of the army not fighting. At the luncheon, however, Harkins monopolized the conversation and overrode the key points that Vann tried to make.[22] Sheehan's account makes it clear that Vann had misjudged both Harkins' invitation and Taylor's desire to know the truth about the war; Vann had been invited "to sit at the table . . . as an animated exhibit for General Taylor of how General Harkins was killing Communists in Vietnam."[23]

Taylor's call on Diem was generally uneventful except for a brief moment when Diem brought up the subject of Laos.[24] Diem, in another unsubtle display of his dissatisfaction with American policy in Laos, said the Viet Cong had been building up in the Tchepone area, and, alluding to the appeasement that had preceded World War II, he warned that a Hitler-type "folly" should not be overlooked. Taylor did not respond and Diem let the matter drop, which was just as well given Diem's ire on this point. At his meeting with Harkins the day before, however, Diem had been less diplomatic: "he was not happy" with the position the U.S. had adopted on Laos; the U.S. could have said it favored a coalition but supported one side of it; and further, there should have been a U.S. statement against "neutralism." This was a biting criticism of Kennedy and Diem did not repeat it to Taylor.

That Taylor took seriously the importance of the ratio between the number of guerrillas and the number required to defeat them was evident from his meeting with Diem's brother Nhu on September 11.[25] During a discussion on the Strategic Hamlet Program Taylor commented that "the Viet Cong would be expelled from the villages and they would then be compelled to wage a counter-guerrilla war." Taylor then made this remark: "if the accepted average of 20 to 1 is true it would certainly be better to be the guerrilla instead of the person obliged to fight against him." This comment was unrealistic only in the sense that Taylor had in mind a reversed scenario in which South Vietnamese peasants were waging a guerrilla-style war against the communists. But if he accepted this enormous force disparity in this fantasy war, he must also have accepted its compelling implications in the real war in Vietnam. It would mean every additional 10,000 hard-core Viet Cong soldiers required 200,000 more South Vietnamese troops.[26] The point is that Taylor not only accepted the concept of a ratio, but used a far more alarming one—twenty-to-one—than most.

Taylor's view of force ratios meant a regular South Vietnamese Army of 800,000 men was required *if* the true size of the Viet Cong had been known. His point man Harkins, however, had taken care of this, and seemingly had everything in order for his boss's visit. On the morning of his departure Taylor talked to reporters. The *New York Times* relayed his comments:

> "One has to be here personally," he said, "to sense the growing national character, the resistance of the Vietnamese people to the subversive insurgency threat. My overall impression is of a great national movement, assisted to some extent, of course, by Americans, but essentially a movement by Vietnamese to defend Vietnam against a dangerous and cruel enemy." He said he was particularly pleased with the progress in building "strategic hamlets". . . . This plan, he said, "has grown far beyond our hopes of a few months ago."[27]

He later wrote of his conclusions after this trip: "In spite of this problem of quantifying progress, my general conclusion was that we were achieving qualitative progress in the military and economic fields but that the socio-political programs continued to lag."[28] The myth of "qualitative" military progress was the centerpiece of the *inside* deception, and it was that story that Taylor took back with him to Kennedy.

Taylor's comments were backed up by the Deputy Chief of Mission (American Embassy), William Trueheart, who traveled to Washington and presented his views before a September 19 meeting of the Southeast Asia Task Force.[29] "The military progress has been little short of sensational," he told the group. Trueheart said there was only one problem:

> The one gloomy spot in the picture, he noted, was the mission's relations with the U.S. press corps. He asked for suggestions on how to deal with this problem. The press, he said, believes the situation is going to pieces and we have been unable to convince them otherwise.

Taylor wrapped up his own impressions for Kennedy in a memo on September 20.[30] Taylor told Kennedy, "Much progress has been accomplished since my last visit in October 1961." The Strategic Hamlet Program, military training, resistance of the Montagnard ethnic minority to communist domination, and statistics on the war were all evidence of progress. Taylor said:

> the statistics—for what they are worth—indicate improvement in comparative casualties, in the reduced loss of weapons to the enemy,

and in the freeing of a larger segment of the population and of the
national territory from VC domination.

Taylor's use of the phrase "for what they are worth" was odd. If their
worth was questionable, why cite them? The answer lies in the fact that
there was nothing other than the statistics generated by MACV to sustain
the myth of qualitative military progress.

Taylor's "for what they are worth" had been necessary because he
knew Harkins' statistics were under attack in Washington. Consider, for
example, the criticism of them delivered to Kennedy by Mike Forrestal
two days earlier.[31] The U.S. statistic on Viet Cong casualties for the first
eight months of 1962 was 19,404, of which 12,791 were killed in action.
This figure was almost identical to the size of the hard-core Viet Cong
force that Harkins said existed in South Vietnam. Since MACV would
only admit to 500 to 600 infiltrators per month, the implication of this
casualty statistic was that the Viet Cong had successfully recruited a force
nearly equal to its own size. "I do not believe that one can rely on these
figures," Forrestal said, but added, "I am assured by the State Department
that there has been considerable improvement both in the accuracy of
casualty reports and the degree of checking by our own people."

The sheer logic of these figures, when combined with Taylor's claim
of a great outpouring of popular support in the countryside for the
government, just did not add up. How could the Viet Cong recruit and
train 20,000 new soldiers in just eight months if popular support for the
government was on such an upswing? The answer, known to the U.S.
advisors, was twofold: many of the dead were not Viet Cong, and major
flaws in the military campaign were driving many peasants to support the
communists. The "net result" of all artillery and air strikes in the critical
Delta area was negative, recalled Vann, and added, "We did more damage
with airplanes and artillery than we did good."[32] Guerrilla warfare involves
"fleeting targets," he argued, and only the rifle had the discrimination
necessary to kill the guerrilla without harming innocent bystanders. "But,
in our zone the primary kills were made by air, artillery and mortar. As a
result of this a great many innocent people were killed, and by innocent,
I mean women and children."

Such views did not surface during Taylor's trip, and only glitter was
on display for the new Chairman of the Joint Chiefs of Staff. Taylor's trip
checked, for the moment, the rumblings begun by Bowles and Mendenhall. In response to a request by Kennedy, in the first week of October,
the State Department prepared a paper on the developments in Vietnam
between General Taylor's visits in 1961 and 1962.[33] There had been a
"dramatic" change in morale, the report said, and South Vietnam "and
its military are confident and anxious to get on with the job." The political

climate had improved, the government was gaining popular support in the key rural countryside for the war effort, and military progress was "encouraging." The Viet Cong were winning in October 1961, it said, but, "Now a year later, the Viet Cong are not winning the war." Communist casualties were high and going up, the guerrillas were troubled by shortages of food and medicine, and morale was low. "In short, the momentum of the VC attack has been lost."

The false facade of progress was back intact, but it would not be long before the myth was embattled again. In the meantime, Harkins had to deal with McNamara once more, and Harkins had a foolproof plan for winning the war to present to him.

OCTOBER 8—THE SEVENTH SECDEF CONFERENCE

The best available record of the proceedings are the notes taken by Chalmers Wood, director of the Vietnam working group at the time.[34] They show clearly that General Harkins again painted a picture of progress to McNamara. Viet Cong battalion-sized operations had declined steadily, he said, while South Vietnamese battalion-sized operations had increased. The South Vietnamese troops were staying out longer; one had even stayed out for three weeks, he said. There were some difficulties in their staff planning, he noted, but it was improving. Some of the troops were not as fit as they should be and recently one group had eaten up all of their food too soon and gotten their feet wet, and so had to be pulled back. Aside from these glitches, Harkins did not indicate to McNamara that there were any other problems within the South Vietnamese Army. The rest of his briefing was a story of success: the 9th Division was now operational; the 26th Division would be in January; two new airborne battalions were ready; there was a new airfield at Pleiku and helicopter training was under way; the Civilian Irregular Defense Groups (CIDG) had made good progress; and defoliation operations in the Delta were "very" successful—six target areas would soon be "finished."

In short, Harkins was confident that the South Vietnamese forces were now ready to do what he had said at the previous SECDEF conference— defeat the Viet Cong. His concept for doing this had been approved by Secretary Thuan, he said. Harkins then presented his plan: it would be "an explosive type operation," a "nation-wide offensive to exert sudden and continuing pressure on known areas of VC concentration." The whole thing would begin with a "preparatory phase," he explained, which would include "saturation bombing against VC installations, especially in Zone D." This sort of recommendation seems so mindless, so inappropriate to the struggle being waged then in the countryside, that it leads one to question how he could possibly justify the carnage that might result. Obviously, Harkins' thinking was little improvement over McGarr's similar World War II style of planning for counterinsurgency operations.

"Theoretically," Harkins explained, "the *explosive* phase would consist of full-scale coordinated operations *exploding* at every level from the rice roots to the national level and finally follow-up operations" (emphasis added). Such an operation, he said, "might have to be repeated several times." Beyond detailing how the chain of command for his operation would eliminate the field commanders, how the Vietnamese troops would be deployed, how equipment would be prepositioned, how intelligence and training would be approved, "etc," Wood's notes give us no clues as to *how* these forces were to "explode" the Viet Cong insurgency.

There is no indication of how McNamara reacted in the conference to Harkins' plan, but when news of it reached Washington, a worried Harriman immediately wrote to Ambassador Nolting to oppose it.[35] "I am frankly concerned by General Harkins' presentation of the 'Explosion' operation," Harriman said, because the Viet Cong would "make themselves scarce," and the operation "would lead to chaos and the loss of many innocent lives." Harriman feared that when it was over the Viet Cong "could slip back into their positions easily." The political implications of such a plan "are so important," Harriman said, "that it should not be approved without full consultation with the Department of State."

One point of conflict did arise at the seventh SECDEF conference when Harkins and Anthis asked for yet another increase in American Farm Gate aircraft. American pilots were flying 100 hours of operations per month and this could not be maintained, they said, and "more planes were needed now." Surprisingly, the Ambassador supported them this time: "evidence from the VC showed that these operations were hurting," he chimed in. Furthermore, Nolting flatly rejected the claim made by General Jablonsky and many U.S. advisors at earlier conferences and meetings about the value of these bombing missions to the Viet Cong; he said "there was no evidence" that the Viet Cong thought they were getting any propaganda advantages from the air strikes.

McNamara was not pleased with the direction of this discussion. He interrupted to say that it was *not* the U.S. objective to "carry the burden of the combat." He told Harkins and Anthis to "get a B-26 unit flown by South Vietnamese pilots as soon as possible." One wonders whether McNamara realized he had never been told the real problems of the Vietnamese Air Force and why they still did not have B-26 units of their own. Regardless, he told Harkins and Anthis to expand the Vietnamese

Air Force "as fast as possible," and added, "if you really want more U.S. pilots, then make recommendations, but they will be received coolly." Then he reiterated that "our objectives are to help the Vietnamese fight their war and to reduce, not increase, our own combat role."

The plans for withdrawing U.S. forces from the conflict, however, did not receive much attention at this conference. We know from Wood's notes only that "General Harkins did not have time to present his plan for phasing out U.S. personnel in Vietnam within three years." It was a strange conference—the request to expand Farm Gate again, American saturation bombing, and "explosions" down at the "rice roots." There was no discussion of the continuing growth of the Viet Cong, the expanding area under their control, and the increase in infiltration through Laos. The facts relating to these, the truly significant problems with the war effort, had long since been pushed aside by MACV's vision of victory. Could it be that Harkins failed to understand the importance of these facts? Did he really believe he could "explode" the insurgency? There would soon be an "explosion" all right, but not the one Harkins briefed to McNamara. The American story of success in Vietnam was sailing into a head-on collision with reality.

BREAKDOWN ON THE BATTLEFIELD

Despite the problems faced by the Viet Cong, said the November USAR-PAC Intelligence Bulletin, "the Viet Cong military force continues to grow . . . in the past few months, not only in numbers but in organization."[36] One of the reasons for this, particularly in the southern Delta, was that the government's 7th Division, the one that had inflicted the most casualties on the Viet Cong during the summer, virtually ceased to function on the battlefield in the fall. In planning his operations, the division commander, Cao, did not consult the Americans, and now used their intelligence to go where he knew there would be no Viet Cong. Cao planned fourteen operations in November and December 1962, Vann recalls, with "great care to avoid any contact with the enemy."[37] Cao's scheme of maneuver was designed to cover the eventuality of meeting the enemy by mistake by always leaving a hole through which the communists could safely exit. As for the problem of his division's purpose for being— to kill Viet Cong—"Cao solved that by inventing even larger kills from air strikes than he had in the past."[38] Consequently, the 7th Division received only three casualties for the rest of the year. Diem, pleased, promoted Cao to General and gave him a Corps command.

Vann discovered Diem had issued a secret verbal order to his command-
ers not to conduct offensive operations that resulted in serious casualties.[39]
Vann told Colonel Porter and General Harkins, and Harkins confronted
Diem. Diem simply lied; Sheehan explains:

> It was certainly not true, Diem said. On the contrary, he had
> lectured the ARVN commanders and his province chiefs to be
> aggressive. He had ordered them to attack the Viet Cong without
> hesitation wherever they could be found. Harkins did not question
> Diem further. He began to accept Cao's faked body counts and to
> pass these reports on Communist losses on to Washington with no
> warnings attached.[40]

Diem's order had disastrous consequences on the battlefield. Even though
the claims of victory had been false, the body counts inflated, and the
government's operations had not stopped the overall growth of Viet
Cong forces, some communist units had been hurt in the Delta and these
government operations disrupted their growth. After Diem's secret order
the Viet Cong expansion gathered unprecedented speed, proceeding unhindered by the South Vietnamese Army.

The secret order helped to destroy the confidence the American advisors
had tried so hard to build in the army, the kind of confidence that comes
from the bonding between soldiers that occurs from the stress and trials of
combat. The soldiers knew they were not seeking engagements with the
Viet Cong and before long this undermined their self-confidence. "They
were so frightened, so afraid," says Colonel Porter, the senior American
advisor in Vietnam. "The Viet Cong appeared fifteen feet tall to most of
them."[41] When this process set in, it slowly fed upon itself and destroyed
the soul of Diem's army. On patrols or when setting ambushes for the Viet
Cong, Porter recalls, "someone 'inadvertently' fired a round or coughed or
made a noise of some sort, and it was so obvious that they did it deliberately." When small units set up night ambushes, the soldiers often clicked
the bolts on their rifles to warn the Viet Cong of their presence.

Vann's intelligence officer, Major Jim Drummond, soon discovered
that the Viet Cong units the 7th Division had not fought had increased
in size and that the local guerrilla forces were much larger than earlier
thought.[42] The fact was that government operations failed to check the
growth of Viet Cong forces *and* the area under their control. "We didn't
inflict enough casualties on the Viet Cong for it even to be noticeable,"
recalls Porter. "I've always been very doubtful that we hurt them materially
at all."[43] Most of the army's success stories were based on phony operations, he says, and Diem "knew quite well that most of this was fraudulent."

What began, in the summer of 1962, as an attempt to meet the Viet Cong in battle had broken down completely three months later. Artillery shells continued to rain on hamlets in the countryside, and bombs from American aircraft found the targets supplied by the South Vietnamese. Enormous amounts of American money and matériel were being pumped into a losing war, much of it finding its way into the hands of the rapidly expanding military forces of the Viet Cong. On the battlefield, by the end of 1962, the Viet Cong no longer feared the South Vietnamese Army. The situation was rather the reverse. As the new year opened, the Viet Cong would make this point undeniably clear.

NOTES

1. Benedict, interview with the author, June 6, 1988.
2. The material in this section is based upon Allen, *The Indochina Wars*, pp. 199–207.
3. Krepinevich, *The Army in Vietnam*, p. 76.
4. USARPAC Intelligence Bulletin, June 1962.
5. USARPAC Intelligence Bulletin, August 1962.
6. USARPAC Intelligence Bulletin, August 1962.
7. *PP*, Gravel ed., vol. 2, p. 174.
8. "Record of the Sixth Secretary of Defense Conference, Camp Smith, Hawaii, July 23, 1962," in *State History*, 1962, Document 248, pp. 546–56.
9. *PP*, Gravel ed., vol. 2, p. 176.
10. In the Military Assistance Program.
11. See Sheehan, *A Bright Shining Lie*, pp. 90–93. For a thorough account of the July 20 operation see especially pp. 79–90.
12. Porter, interview with the author, July 2, 1988.
13. Sheehan, *A Bright Shining Lie*, p. 87.
14. Forrestal memo to McGeorge Bundy, August 8, 1962, in *State History*, 1962, Document 261, pp. 583–84.
15. Nolting cable to State, August 16, 1961, in *State History*, 1962, Document 265, pp. 588–89.
16. Bowles memo to Rusk, August 16, 1962, in *State History*, 1962, Document 267, pp. 591–95.
17. Mendenhall memo, August 16, 1962, in *State History*, 1962, Document 268, pp. 596–601.
18. Burris memo to LBJ, August 17, 1962, in *State History*, 1962, Document 269, pp. 601–3.

19. Memorandum for the Record, dated September 10, 1962, Subject: Meeting at Gia Long Palace, September 7, 1962, in *State History*, 1962, Document 277, pp. 622–33.

20. In October Harkins told McNamara that 30,000 was the South Vietnamese estimate. See *State History*, 1962, Document 298, p. 690.

21. Sheehan, *A Bright Shining Lie*, p. 96.

22. Ibid., p. 99.

23. Ibid., p. 117.

24. Nolting cable to State, September 22, 1962, in *State History*, 1962, Document 280, pp. 642–43.

25. The record of this meeting is in *State History*, 1962, Document 279, pp. 636–41.

26. The U.S. had struggled for the previous two years to build up ARVN from 150,000 to 200,000. A VC force of 30,000–40,000 would demand 600,000–800,000 ARVN soldiers. As discussed previously, even using Rostow's ten-to-one ratio, when considering the true size of the rapidly growing Viet Cong, these figures showed that the insurgency had long since surged past ARVN's ability to cope with it. Whether Taylor's ratio was better or worse than Rostow's is irrelevant.

27. David Halberstam, "Taylor Hopeful on Vietnam Fight," *New York Times*, September 14, 1962.

28. Maxwell Taylor, *Swords and Plowshares*, p. 258.

29. For the minutes of the September 19, 1991, meeting of the Southeast Asia Task Force, see *State History*, 1962, Document 286, pp. 655–57.

30. Taylor memo to Kennedy, September 20, 1962, in *State History*, 1962, Document 288, pp. 660–63.

31. Forrestal memo to Kennedy, September 18, 1962, in *State History*, 1962, Document 283, pp. 649–50.

32. John Paul Vann, interview with Charles V.P. von Littichau, July 22, 1963, U.S. Army Center for Military History, Vietnam files, p. 25. See also JFK Library, Newman Papers.

33. *State History*, 1962, Document 297, pp. 679–87.

34. Vietnam Working Group Director Wood's summary record of the Conference, in *State History*, 1962, Document 298, pp. 688–91.

35. Harriman letter to Nolting, October 4, 1962, in *State History*, 1962, Document 300, pp. 693–96.

36. USARPAC Intelligence Bulletin, November 1962.

37. Vann, interview with von Littichau, p. 10.

38. Sheehan, *A Bright Shining Lie*, pp. 120–21.

39. Ibid., p. 122.

40. Ibid., pp. 122–25.

41. Porter, interview with the author, June 7, 1989.

42. Sheehan, *A Bright Shining Lie*, p. 98.

43. Porter, interview with the author, July 6, 1988.

CHAPTER SIXTEEN

ALL HELL BREAKS LOOSE

THE BATTLE OF AP BAC[1]

Despite the fact that the South Vietnamese Joint General Staff had diverted fighter air support to other operations and reduced from sixteen to ten the number of (H-21) helicopters planned for the assault on the Viet Cong force near Tan Thoi, a few miles north of the Mekong River in Dinh Tuong Province, the operation proceeded anyway. There was still complete artillery coverage of the area and a great preponderance of friendly forces. On January 2 ten helicopters began discharging a battalion of the 7th Division into an arc around the northern side of the enemy force—a company of the Viet Cong 261st Main Force Battalion and a company of the 514th Regional Battalion. The initial wave of three H-21 landings north of Tan Thoi prompted the Viet Cong commander to immediately retreat to the south. This move had been anticipated and a South Vietnamese Civil Guard battalion was already moving up from the south to block the way. The Viet Cong ran into this force and, after a brief firefight, began withdrawing westward only to encounter another Civil Guard battalion with an armored personnel carrier (M113) company that had moved into the area from the southwest.

It was foggy, a factor that may have helped many of the Viet Cong slip into Ap Bac unnoticed; after that things began to fall apart. The battle of

Ap Bac started as a series of fluid skirmishes, and the fact that there were two South Vietnamese commanders giving orders and directing traffic— the new 7th Division commander, Lieutenant Colonel Bui Dinh Dam, and the province chief, Major Tho—doomed the operation from the start. This absence of unity of command characterized many of South Vietnam's military operations. Diem had designed the dual nature of South Vietnam's military structure to guard against coup plotting but it hamstrung military operations and, in the end, did not prevent a coup.

In the absence of effective command, the American advisors, which included Vann, could only hop about hopelessly trying to influence the battle in piecemeal fashion. Coordination of fire and maneuver, without which an offensive military operation is a dubious proposition at best, was awful. An American advisor with the Civil Guard warned the province chief by radio that the artillery fire was faulty, but Tho took no corrective action. Maneuver was stopped while the various unit commanders argued over whose job it was to go in and dig out the Viet Cong. The M113 task force stopped at a canal and a long argument ensued about where to cross. The 50-caliber machine guns mounted on the M113s could have wreaked devastation on the Viet Cong if used quickly and correctly. When they finally closed in at 2:00 P.M., their attack was uncoordinated and the Viet Cong picked off the gunners and left their foxholes to hurl grenades at the approaching 113s. The 113 company, after absorbing heavy casualties, was finished by 2:30.

What air attacks there were occurred later in the afternoon instead of being synchronized to suppress the Viet Cong while the 113s moved in. Similarly, the Civil Guards did not inch to within rifle range until 5:00, and a reinforcement of paratroopers did not begin their jumps until after 6:00. By this time the corps commander, Cao, had already begun to shape the battle so that the Viet Cong could escape. Once night fell, the remaining troops of the 261st and the 514th Viet Cong battalions withdrew safely. Cao made sure of this by refusing Vann's request to illuminate the battlefield with flares, and by sharply curtailing the number of artillery rounds that could be fired. Government losses were eighty dead and more than 100 wounded; this included three dead and eight wounded Americans. Five American helicopters were lost. The Viet Cong lost eighteen dead and thirty-nine wounded. Two Viet Cong companies had pulled off a stunning victory over three South Vietnamese battalions with an M113 company task force.

Admiral Felt arrived in Saigon two days after the battle and called it a government victory because the Viet Cong had left their positions.[2] When Associated Press reporter Peter Arnett asked a question that challenged this, Admiral Felt, angered by it, snapped back, "Get on the team."[3] The Viet Cong had done more than defeat the South Vietnamese Army at Ap

Bac. They had lifted the veil from the elaborate lie of progress in the war effort.

THE GATHERING STORM

"I am concerned over recent allegations," Harkins said in a January 10 news release, "critical of the valor and courage of the Vietnamese soldier."[4] The defeat at Ap Bac had led to a flood of unfavorable news stories critical of the South Vietnamese Army's fighting ability, some quoting U.S. military officers as saying, "It was a miserable damn performance."[5] Harkins felt the press coverage was bad enough without U.S. officers adding to the problem. "I believe that anyone who criticizes the fighting qualities of the Armed Forces of the Republic of Vietnam," Harkins said pointedly, "is doing a disservice to the thousands of gallant and courageous men who are fighting so well in defense of their country." Then he added this, which can only make one shudder at the ghastly reality of Vietnam: "Approximately ten thousand Vietnamese soldiers have been killed in action in the past year. Almost thirty thousand dead Viet Cong attest to their courage."

He was proud of the South Vietnamese Army, he said; and, in an oblique reference to Ap Bac, added, "There are always lessons to be learned from any action." Then came the boilerplate:

> This past year has seen the Vietnamese take the initiative away from the Viet Cong. I think the coming year will bring even greater efforts and I have all confidence that the Vietnamese Armed Forces will attain even greater success.

The truth, however, was that the South Vietnamese had *never* taken the initiative away from the Viet Cong, and the fiction of progress fabricated by Harkins was in real trouble.

The CIA's latest assessment on the war effort, issued the day after Harkins made this statement, stated bluntly that "the tide has not yet turned."[6] The CIA impugned the very statistics used by Harkins, and said they were "misleading as a basis for a consideration on who is winning." If VC strength had increased, as MACV claimed, from 17,600 in their revised June 1962 estimate to the current 22,000–24,000, while at the same time suffering—as Harkins now boasted—30,000 casualties, a reasonable person would be justified in asking, "Just who are we fighting out there?" The logic underpinning Harkins' story was simply breaking down. These statistics suggested, said the CIA report, "that the casualty figures are exaggerated or that the Viet Cong have a remarkable capability—or both."

Hilsman, who was traveling in Vietnam with Forrestal on a fact-finding mission for Kennedy, had raised precisely the same question two days earlier with William Trueheart, the Embassy's Deputy Chief of Mission.[7] "Trueheart scoffed at this and said that the explanation was only that the statistics were more accurate, meaning that last year there were considerably more than 18,000." Hilsman, who had no knowledge that MACV had cut the VC strength from 40,000 to 16,500 was stunned because he realized, after doing some quick addition, that this would have meant there had been 42,000 regular Viet Cong "last year," and he simply could not believe that U.S. military intelligence had been that bad.

Unfortunately for Harkins, the Hilsman-Forrestal team had arrived forty-eight hours before Ap Bac and were now fishing around for some answers. The good news for Harkins was that Taylor, who could anticipate that the Hilsman-Forrestal report to Kennedy would be damaging, had decided on January 7 to dispatch a team of his own, headed by Army Chief of Staff General Wheeler, to get a current assessment. If Taylor could not control what Hilsman and Forrestal had to say, he could at least counter with Wheeler. Also, Taylor had adroitly added to the team Marine Major General Victor Krulak, whom Kennedy had installed in the Pentagon as the Special Assistant for Counterinsurgency and Special Activities (SACSA) to the JCS.

It was right at the crucial point of the Wheeler assessment, when he was preparing a very rosy report for the President in the first week of February in Washington, that a startling new development occurred in Saigon. Harkins was confronted with new American intelligence that showed the pace of Viet Cong growth and the area under their control in the crucial Delta region was accelerating, and that the reason for the acceleration was the false nature of South Vietnamese military offensives there. All hell was breaking loose for Harkins as the flimsy foundation upon which the story of progress was built began to collapse around him.

BLOWING THE WHISTLE IN SAIGON

In Washington, senior officials worried that the defeat at Ap Bac would undermine support for the war in Congress. From the standpoint of South Vietnamese combat operations, however, Ap Bac was a strategic defeat for one ominous reason. The new 7th Division commander had represented an opportunity to get away from false operations and begin genuine attacks on the rapidly growing Viet Cong forces in the Delta. The result of Ap Bac removed whatever sliver of hope there might have been for such a change. It was business as usual again, except that it was carried out on an even grander scale. Now South Vietnamese forces began mounting false attacks with up to 3,000 men, who would be sent, Vann stated, "to an area which everyone knew was clear of Viet Cong, or at the very maximum, [where] we could anticipate finding a local guerrilla platoon."[8] The Americans tried in vain to press for real operations, but Dam "did not approve a single operation in an area where we suggested."

It was all the more frustrating because intelligence had long since located the enemy's battalions. "We were doing this at a time when we knew where the 514th Viet Cong Battalion was located," Vann recalled, which simply "sat in there" and boasted to the people that the South Vietnamese Army was afraid to fight. This pattern continued throughout the spring:

> we had not mounted an offensive operation as of 1 April which was designed to go in and get the enemy. On two occasions, again, as a result of pressure by General Harkins on General Cao to go in and get the 514th Battalion, General Cao came up with two plans. We did one one week and the next one the following week in the same area the 514 Battalion was. However, the plans were designed to alert the 514th that we were having an operation. They kicked off with a so-called diversionary operation in the vicinity, the day before. The plans were designed to leave open areas for the Viet Cong to escape.

While Washington received glowing accounts via MACV's regular "Headway Reports" on the success of these operations, the Viet Cong was rapidly expanding their forces, their political infrastructure, and the area under their control.

Jim Drummond, the intelligence advisor in the 7th Division zone, sent monthly, weekly, and sometimes daily reports to MACV's intelligence organization, detailing the steady growth of the Viet Cong in his area. During the summer of 1962, "we were faced with platoons and poorly organized company units," Drummond recalls.[9] Their growth "continued to escalate," he explains, "so that by the time I left [in March 1963] we were facing battalions and regiments." The lack of any true South Vietnamese offensive action against the Viet Cong in his sector since the previous October—nearly four months—had resulted in an acceleration of the growth of communist forces. Drummond explains:

There's no question in my mind. If General Cao had taken action on all the information that was presented to him in a timely manner then I think we could have interdicted the growth of the Viet Cong structure there. . . . Unfortunately every time Cao would take casualties on his side, he became afraid. Because he was afraid of what the President [Diem] would say, and it always came back to that point. So we did not take action in a number of cases after Ap Bac.[10]

When Drummond reported this in February to the intelligence section in MACV, it was such a bombshell that a major effort was launched to "investigate" his findings.

Initially Harkins tried to fix the problem by getting Drummond to simply reissue his report. It began with a telephone call from MACV. Neal Sheehan recaptured this important detail:

A couple of days later a major on Harkins' intelligence staff called and said that Drummond had too much red [enemy] on his map overlay. Other information available to the headquarters, the major said, claimed that a number of the areas Drummond had colored in red were still controlled by the Saigon authorities. The major told Drummond to review his information and submit a new report.[11]

Drummond had already had trouble with previous reports showing that MACV was listing areas as secure for the government that the Viet Cong really controlled. Drummond had found out through his own acquaintances on Harkins' staff that "because he had refused to dilute his previous report, it had been suppressed."[12]

Now, at the precise time Harkins and officials in the Pentagon were saying that the Viet Cong had lost the initiative, Drummond's unsettling and unwelcome news arrived. Drummond remains firm to this day about his facts. When pinned down specifically to the question of whether Viet Cong growth was accelerating at that time, Drummond's answer remains resolute:

That's correct. They were getting better organized, their recruitment methods were much better, they were getting better trained, and they were getting more cadres from the north.[13]

The real problem posed by his findings was in Saigon and Washington:

unfortunately there was a lot of misinformation . . . going back to Washington on the basis of telling them what they wanted to hear rather than telling them what the situation was. I think the Saigon staff was under pressure to do that.

Where did he hear this from? Did Vann or someone else tell him?

Well, that came up. John [Vann] and I discussed it, especially after the one [February] report I sent up there was investigated by the team coming down. . . . He said, "You can send up what you want but that's not going back to Washington."

Harkins sent a team to investigate after he read Drummond's revised report. He had indeed rechecked his facts and issued a new report, but the revision had more enemy in it than the original.[14] Adding insult to injury, Vann decided the time had come to act precipitously. On February 8 he sent a telegram to Porter with an information copy to MACV so Harkins would see it.[15] Vann bluntly exposed the false nature of South Vietnamese operations. He said that despite good intelligence on the enemy, "the division commander and the corps commander were approving operations where we knew there were no Viet Cong." Harkins sent a team to search for discrepancies he could use as a pretext to fire Vann.[16] "It was a Harkins effort to get one John Paul Vann," states Don Blascak, who flew down with the team.[17]

Colonel Winterbottom; his deputy, Colonel Delaney; another aide, Major Grinder, and Captain Blascak strode into the briefing room at the 7th Division headquarters. "It wasn't a friendly 'let's look over the situation together,' " says Blascak. Drummond and Vann were thoroughly prepared for this inquisition.

Blascak's presence was a source of comfort to Drummond. He knew that Blascak was honest and that Winterbottom would not be able to lie about the investigation:

Blascak came down with Winterbottom when they checked my information. . . . Blascak knew that what I had in that report was 100 percent correct, and if they didn't believe it I'd take them out and take them over to the area and let them get shot at and show them it was.[18]

There was no way around it: the Viet Cong expansion was accelerating and Drummond had the photos, the prisoner reports, and all of the other intelligence sources to confirm his reports. "I showed them the same information and proved to them that what I had sent up in my reports was correct," Drummond says. "It was very formal," Blascak recalls, "but they did a hell of a good job."

When it was over, Winterbottom had little to say. Drummond recalls, "The statement by Winterbottom was that 'You have proved your position to us.' So he went back to Saigon." Winterbottom did the only thing he could do: he told Harkins that Drummond's report was correct. The investigation, however, had not been to get the truth about the enemy, but to get at Vann. What Winterbottom had to say about Drummond's facts mattered little to Harkins. Drummond found out through his contacts at MACV that his findings had been suppressed. After the final report went out to Washington, Drummond states, "I got the word from Saigon. . . . I was told this is the way it was, and this is what Washington wanted to see and this is what they were going to get."

Washington got another bill of goods on the war, but that was nothing new. All hell was breaking loose in Vietnam, the MACV story of success was in tatters, and the debate was just starting to heat up.

THE TRUTH EMBATTLED

As noted earlier, the defeat at Ap Bac—and the press coverage it received—threatened to undermine support for the war effort in Washington. At a January 17 meeting of the Special Group for Counterinsurgency, attended by U. Alexis Johnson, Taylor, McCone, and others, Ralph Dungan, Special Assistant to the President, said that should episodes like Ap Bac be repeated, "It could result in difficulties with Congress."[19] There followed a discussion "at length" on the "predilection" for negative press coverage and the question of "relating" press coverage "to the positive side"—an unsubtle euphemism for controlling the press. The group decided to notify Wheeler to be prepared for a public appearance upon his return, and to arrange "background briefings for key members of Congress in the hope of heading off adverse reaction to the newspaper articles."

After this meeting, U. Alexis Johnson met with Rusk and told him about the Special Group's discussion of the press problem. Rusk had his own suggestion on how to fix it: he told Johnson to look into the possibility of "keeping a book" on the correspondents.[20] Rusk wanted them to be given "offers" to cover successful operations, and the "book" would keep track of the numbers of those accepted versus the numbers of those they accepted "when they sensed" less-successful operations. Depending on how the record turned out, Rusk said, "We could then decide what use could best be made of it." That the Secretary of State had become so personally involved in the press coverage that he would make such a suggestion is a powerful testimonial to the level of energy being expended at high levels to manage information about the war.

General Wheeler, the Army Chief of Staff, was not being asked, but simply put on notice, that he would be making some sort of public statement when he returned to Washington. His boss, Taylor, Chairman of the Joint Chiefs, was not leaving him any choice in the matter. Wheeler stopped off in Hawaii to write his report, and returned to the Pentagon on January 30. His written report as well as his public statement clashed head-on with the report of Hilsman and Forrestal, who had returned before him. At the same time a struggle over the upcoming National Intelligence Estimate on the war effort had erupted in the State Department and in the CIA. It was so serious that the Ambassador in Saigon and the Director of the CIA had become entangled in a series of skirmishes during the drafting process. The truth about the war had itself become embattled, and most of official Washington was involved.

"There can be no more profound index to the progress of the battle in Vietnam than the measure of changes in the level and quality of information coming to the Vietnamese forces,"[21] read Wheeler's predictably optimistic report after his return to Washington. "The more good intelligence that is forthcoming," the report said, "the greater the number of successful operations that can be undertaken." Presumably, Harkins did not allow Wheeler and Krulak to hear that many of these so-called successful operations were fraudulent. The report admitted that the continued or "slightly" increased Viet Cong strength was "disquieting," yet it announced that "the intelligence tide has begun to run toward the government." The report contained all sorts of "intelligence indicators" and statistics to show how the Viet Cong offensive capability had "diminished," including hunger, sickness, shortage of medical supplies and munitions, defections, number of incidents, and last but not least, the old standby—and most corrupt statistic of all—the increasing number of dead bodies.

The Hilsman-Forrestal report, which Kennedy saw *before* he heard personally from Wheeler on February 1, said that no one really knew how many of the 20,000 so-called Viet Cong killed in 1962 were merely innocent villagers.[22] Although their report did say that it was clear the war was going better than it had been a year earlier, Hilsman and Forrestal said "the negative side of the ledger is still awesome." They said that the strength of the Viet Cong—now listed as 23,000 hard-core soldiers— in the face of increased government pressure was "ominous," and that 3,000–4,000 had infiltrated via the Ho Chi Minh Trail the previous year. Then came a red flag: "Thus the conclusion seems inescapable that the Viet Cong could continue the war effort at the present level," they predicted, "or perhaps increase it, even if infiltration routes were completely closed."

Such negative statements moved them to alter the winning formula in this way: "We are probably winning, but certainly more slowly than we had hoped." Then came an even more conspicuous warning:

> At the rate it is now going the war will last longer than we would like, cost more in terms of both lives and money than we anticipated, and prolong the period in which a sudden and dramatic event would upset the gains already made.

These were some of the most critical comments yet made directly to Kennedy by anyone, and coming from two of his own advisors, the news must have been troubling. Wheeler, however, had not yet had his turn.

In his meeting with Kennedy on February 1, Wheeler repeated the claims he made in his report. In his public statement General Wheeler proclaimed that "politically, economically and militarily the tide is beginning to turn in our favor."[23] The South Vietnamese Army was on the offensive, he said, "drawing [the enemy] into combat and inflicting major losses both in personnel and equipment." In a February 4 memo to Kennedy, Forrestal made this statement:

> The meeting with General Wheeler on Friday was a complete waste of your time for which I apologize. It was intended to provide you an opportunity to initiate action on some of the problems in South Vietnam described in the Eyes Only Annex to Hilsman's and my report. The rosy euphoria generated by General Wheeler's report made this device unworkable.[24]

The contradiction between Wheeler's statements and the Hilsman-Forrestal report, as well as Forrestal's attack on the "rosy euphoria" about the war, led to a flurry of cable traffic from both MACV and CINCPAC attempting to blunt the effect of what Hilsman and Forrestal were saying. MACV called the Hilsman-Forrestal remarks on overall planning "not relevant to the military situation," and said the report was reasonable but "less encouraging than we view affairs locally." It was necessary to "correct some impressions and conclusions of the report which [are] due to the short time the authors could devote to their investigation," Harkins added. "My overall comment," he said, "is that improvement is a daily fact, thanks to the combined efforts of [Vietnam] and the U.S. The success of the counterinsurgency is attainable and we are confident of the outcome."[25]

It was at this point that a new person in the Pentagon, Marine General

Victor Krulak, began to have a heavy influence on Vietnam policy. In his February 7 report to the Special Group for Counterinsurgency (SGCI) Krulak said he believed "real progress has been made in the struggle against the Viet Cong since the occasion of his last visit during the summer of 1962."[26] There had been continuous improvement in intelligence; modest gains in the economy; the morale of the South Vietnamese people was "good" while the Viet Cong's was "deteriorating"; and "Vietnamese military operations were moving in the right direction," he said, "although more urging is required by U.S. advisors to maintain this momentum."

Krulak was not in a press conference, but a top secret meeting in Washington, D.C., and these statements suggested that he might cast his lot with Harkins and Taylor. However, Krulak did tick off some items that, in his opinion, needed improvement: the MAAG and MACV should be "drawn closer together"; reaction time for air support reduced; greater rapport established with the Vietnamese; and, he said, "Rules of engagement should be modified to permit U.S. helicopters to fire upon the Viet Cong without having to wait to be fired upon." This left no doubt that Krulak was in favor of U.S. crews initiating combat at their own discretion. Attorney General Robert Kennedy suggested "an early decision should be sought as to whether or not this would be desirable." It was decided that Krulak would follow up on the issue.

At his March 14 presentation to the SGCI, Krulak "observed that Viet Cong activities during the last six months have been at a level 50% less than last year."[27] It looked like Krulak was getting ready to rubber-stamp MACV's story again until he followed with this further comment: "It is not known whether this means they are regrouping for a greater effort, or if their capability has been reduced." This comment was remarkable in that it allowed for the possibility that a statistical indicator of Viet Cong operations, whatever it was, said something about Viet Cong intentions instead of the increasingly successful job that MACV was doing with the South Vietnamese Army. Was Krulak trying to distance himself from Harkins and Taylor? Whatever the answer, there seems to be a hint that by the middle of March some change, however subtle, was at hand.

David Halberstam offers an intriguing analysis: at this point not just Krulak but even Harkins began to have doubts, but Taylor was firmly in control. Taylor had put Harkins in Vietnam, says Halberstam, "not because Harkins was the ablest general around, but because, far more important, he was Taylor's man and Taylor could control him."[28] Halberstam maintains that, as despair developed over the conduct of the war, the following took place:

> Taylor wanted to hold the line, to keep up the appearances, to keep
> from failing at what they were trying. As the struggle continued he

kept Krulak in line, and he slowed McNamara's own tendency to
swing over.

In this struggle, Halberstam says, the debate over information also mounted,
and Taylor was a formidable "bureaucratic player" who was "determined to
keep as much control as possible over military assessments."

APRIL 17—A NEW NATIONAL INTELLIGENCE ESTIMATE ON VIETNAM

By the time the intelligence community released NIE 53-63, entitled
"Prospects in Vietnam," the estimate had been substantially revised. "I initiated the estimate in the fall of 1962," recalls Hal Ford, then the head of
the Far East staff in the CIA's Office of National Estimates (ONE).[29]
"There was a lot of reluctance in the upper policy-making levels to do it,"
he says. " 'Why do we need one?' " senior officials wanted to know. "I and
other analysts contended," Ford says, "that both the political and military
situation was worsening." A working-level document was available by
February 1962, Ford recalls, "and the message was very grim." The director of ONE, Sherman Kent, got a nasty surprise when he delivered the draft
to the United States Intelligence Board (USIB), the body of intelligence
agency directors that gave final approval to estimates before publication.
    Kent, a historian of French history with a Ph.D. from Yale, had not
anticipated the reaction of CIA Director McCone. Ford explains:

> McCone may have had doubts about ONE because the previous
> fall they had felt that the Soviets were not putting missiles into
> Cuba. This may have influenced him, in this instance, four months
> later, to challenge ONE's analysis. Ironically, in the end, McCone
> would come to agree with the ONE staffers.

In the USIB meeting, however, McCone did not agree. "The upper-level
policy folks were putting the best face on things," says Ford, and
McCone's suspicions of ONE's analytic capabilities led him to intervene
in the outcome of this estimate.
    Ford's recollections accurately reflect the storm of opposition the unfor-
tunate drafters met with. In January 1963 the State Department input to
the estimate was sent to the American Embassy in Saigon for coordination. Both Nolting and Trueheart "took exception," Hilsman wrote in a

memo for record, "to several of the cautious, general statements" provided by the department's intelligence organization, INR.[30] Hilsman thought "it was hard to see exactly what specific basis there is for the Embassy's optimism." As noted earlier, CIA's own analysis in January indicated that "the tide has not yet turned" in the war against the Viet Cong.[31] The discussion "dragged on for several weeks," says Ford, during which "Krulak, Forrestal, and Rostow gave us the snow job."

"McCone ate up Sherman Kent in the USIB meeting," Ford recounts, "and said the NIE was overly pessimistic; this was a surprise, and it was embarrassing for Kent." Willard Matthias, who was in charge of this NIE, "protested," Ford says, but to no avail. McCone ruled against them and "remanded the estimate," meaning he sent it back to the drawing board. Ford recalls that McCone directed them to "check with those who know best." Since the drafters had already checked with their best experts in the CIA and the State Department, this presumably meant that they were to bring the estimate into line with MACV's reporting.

The NIE that finally emerged on April 17[32] was optimistic and only its main conclusions need to be reproduced here: although the communists had not been "grievously hurt," their progress had been blunted; the open U.S. commitment made it unlikely that North Vietnam would attack or introduce "military units into the South in an effort to win a quick victory"; the Viet Cong could be contained and further progress made in expanding government control and security in the countryside; and there was "some promise of resolving political weaknesses." This political forecast was tempered by the statement that the regime's capacity to bring this about was "questionable," and the optimistic military forecast was restrained by the comment that decisive battles lay ahead and that the situation "remains fragile."

When the Vietnamese political situation exploded—a week after the publication of this estimate—and the truth about the war effort eventually bubbled to the surface, McCone was the one who was embarrassed. He "said he was wrong," recalls Ford, "and apologized; he said he wouldn't intervene like that again." For the time being, however, the fiction of a winnable war remained precariously perched on the untenable foundation of MACV's reporting and Harkins' scintillating presentations to McNamara.

MAY 6—THE EIGHTH SECDEF CONFERENCE

The briefing reports at this conference once again "confirmed gratifying progress in the military situation."[33] The minutes indicate Harkins "discussed the over-all progress that had been made since the last meeting and conveyed the feeling of optimism that all elements of the Country Team now have."[34] This time he did not offer a date for when the insurgency would be broken and said the struggle would be protracted; but "we are certainly on the right track and . . . we are winning the war in Vietnam," he declared.

After a discussion of several topics concerning weapons, the medical program, and loudspeakers used to encourage Viet Cong defections, Trueheart reported on the Strategic Hamlet Program. He said the program was going "very well" except in the IV Corps—southern Delta—area. In that area he identified these problems: the people were more spread out; some hamlets were one house wide and five miles long beside canals; there were more Viet Cong in the area; and the people were more generally hostile to the government. No one seemed to have much to add to this; to have done so would have moved into distinctly unpleasant realities.

The conference minutes contain the following single sentence on how Harkins dispensed with "border problems": "General Harkins stated that as long as we have Laos and Cambodia there will be border problems." With that, Harkins moved on to the outlook for the future. On this topic he had just two things to say. First was "his opinion that some of our recent setbacks had been due to people dropping their guard." This was undoubtedly his vague way of referring to the defeat at Ap Bac, implying that the South Vietnamese Army had simply been standing in the middle of the boxing ring and hadn't heard the bell when it rang for the next round. This was "natural," Harkins said, "when things are going well, and it is something we have to watch." Incredibly, what Harkins was saying about the military problem was this: the government was so far ahead of the communists that vigilance against overconfidence was now necessary.

The discussion turned to the Comprehensive Plan for South Vietnam (CPSVN), which McNamara had directed at the sixth SECDEF conference in July 1962. In general, the Secretary felt the plan assumed an unrealistically high force level for the South Vietnamese armed forces and assigned them overly expensive equipment that was too complicated to operate and maintain.[35] McNamara then said that the plan's phaseout of U.S. forces was "too slow" and he wanted it revised. He directed the plan to reflect a faster American withdrawal from Vietnam and toward this end to accelerate training programs in order to speed up replacement of U.S. units by South Vietnamese units "as fast as possible." The conference record indicates the following then ensued:

> The Secretary stated that we should have a plan for phasing out
> U.S. personnel; as the situation improves we should phase down

our effort. The Secretary also stated that the last category of personnel he would take out would be advisors. He still desires that we
lay down a plan to have the [South Vietnamese military] take
over some functions this year so that we can take out 1,000 or so
personnel late this year if the situation allows.

McNamara then asked that "concrete plans" be drawn up for the 1,000-
man withdrawal.[36] The 1,000-man withdrawal would turn into a contentious issue in October, and ultimately would become a point of considerable controversy after it was later leaked to the *New York Times* by Daniel
Ellsberg.

There was a brief but fascinating discussion of press relations. The
conference record states: "It was pointed out that we have a problem
either if U.S. personnel talk too much or refuse to talk to the press at all."
Then a decision was rendered: the "only" way to improve this was "better
indoctrination"—presumably of U.S. personnel, not reporters. (The use
of the word "indoctrination" here did not signify being briefed for access
to classified information—a common usage of the term in the government.) It is most unpleasant today to realize how alien and intricate
MACV's story of the war had become by the summer of 1963; so complex
and so far removed from reality that a person espousing it required intense
indoctrination in order to conduct a problem-free conversation with a
member of the press.

BLOWING THE WHISTLE IN WASHINGTON

"Harkins threw him out of the theater," Westmoreland later said of John
Vann's departure from Vietnam in April 1963.[37] Westmoreland said Vann
had been too critical of Harkins' optimistic assessments of Dinh Tuong
Province in the Delta, which was "about 90 percent Viet Cong controlled." Vann had been critical of much more in his April 1 "Senior
Advisor's Final Report."[38] His charges against the Strategic Hamlet Program were serious: where hamlets had been built there had been a failure
to adhere to the "oil spot" principle—putting them in a "priority area"
cleared by the army and then turned over to the paramilitary forces so the
regular army could expand the area; this failure had already caused a
"marked reduction" in offensive army operations in areas where hamlets
were being built; and therefore the planned construction of 2,400 new
hamlets might "precipitate a communist victory" because it would "so
fragment our effort as to lose an offensive capability, and eventually have

2,400 islands of resistance, no one of which will be able to resist an attack by the regular Viet Cong."

Operations in his zone, when conducted, Vann said, were no more than "walks in the sun" or "safari operations," in which "troops and helicopter support have been wasted"; plans were either inadequate tactically or deliberately rigged with "advanced knowledge that the operational area was devoid of Viet Cong; and this had gone on for the previous six months "while highly reliable intelligence and lucrative Viet Cong areas were ignored." Vann revealed a percentage breakdown for the previous six months of how three mobile battalions in his zone had spent their time: training, 3 percent; combat, 13 percent; preparation for or cleanup after operations, 10 percent; and other activities "(Primarily Resting)," 74 percent.

Vann should not have been too surprised, then, to find out in June, when he arrived in Washington, that his report had been "pigeonholed by MACV."[39] The same fate befell Porter's less devastating but nevertheless critical final end-of-tour report. Undeterred, Vann came up with a plan to blow the whistle on Harkins. He would put together a briefing, complete with slides and charts, that would exceed even his Final Report in its assault on Harkins. Vann's new job in the Pentagon, devising financing and procurement procedures for Special Forces counterinsurgency missions, left him plenty of spare time to put his briefing together. He began, in late May, to talk with and interview hundreds of Army officers, and by the end of June had polished the spear he intended to thrust into the heart of the false story of the war emanating from MACV.

Vann's briefing[40] was extremely damaging to MACV and to Harkins personally because it exposed how far from reality Harkins' performances for McNamara had been. In it, Vann charged that the numbers of enemy reported killed were "highly misleading," and he provided an estimate made by "over 200 advisors in the field" to back up this charge:

> We estimate . . . that the total number of people killed was less than two-thirds of those claimed. Additionally, we estimate from 30 to 40% of the personnel killed were merely bystanders who were unfortunate enough to be in the vicinity of combat action.

This meant, roughly, that for every three Viet Cong soldiers MACV claimed had been killed in action, one was really a Viet Cong, one did not exist, and the third was an innocent bystander.

The cause of these horrific circumstances was even worse: the South Vietnamese Army was not being sent into combat. "The fact is," said Vann, that "these figures point out the major combat deficiency" of the refusal "on the part of Vietnamese commanders to have their troops close with and kill the enemy." Casualties in South Vietnamese Army units

were low, Vann declared, only because their commanders used "air, artillery, and long range crew served weapons to kill the enemy rather than
rifles." This practice was unjustified by the available intelligence, Vann
said, adding, "Guerilla warfare requires the utmost discrimination in killing. Every time we killed an innocent person we lost ground in our battle
to win the people." It was a frank and biting report of wasteful and
fraudulent South Vietnamese operations while the carnage in the countryside slowly frittered away the support of the peasants to the communists.

Vann took his case to Army Lieutenant General Barksdale Hamlett,
the Deputy Chief of Staff for Operations (DCSOPS). Hamlett was sympathetic and open-minded. He already felt that "the people that were going
over there from the JCS staff" were "really looking through rose tinted
glasses," and consequently "we . . . weren't getting the story that we
should have been getting about some of the things that happened over
there."[41] He realized that "Vann had a lot to say about what was going
on inside Vietnam which was completely counter to the reports we were
receiving through JCS channels." What Vann had to say was "so different," Hamlett recalls, "that I wanted him to brief the Chiefs." Hamlett
recounts what happened next:

> I asked [Vann] if he would and he said he would love to, and so I
> went to General Taylor who was the Chairman and talked to him
> about Vann and some of the things that he was talking about. And
> Taylor sort of pooh-poohed the whole idea. . . .

Apparently Taylor agreed to see Vann alone, but Hamlett set up a Vann
briefing for the Chiefs on July 8 anyway. Hamlett's insistence that the
Chiefs hear Vann's presentation "almost got me into trouble" with Taylor,
he claims.

The day of the briefing arrived, and General Krulak—the person in
charge of guerrilla warfare on the JCS staff—requested a copy of Vann's
briefing. Krulak had just returned from Vietnam and his trip report parroted the rosy picture of the war touted by Harkins and Taylor. Vann,
correctly surmising that Krulak would intercede with Taylor, stalled for
as long as possible—until just four hours before his scheduled brief to
the Joint Chiefs—before giving Krulak a copy of his report.[42] In this
particular case, however, that was all the time in the world. Krulak was
waiting; and so was Taylor: he canceled Vann's JCS briefing one hour
later. The Army Chief of Staff, General Wheeler, was disappointed at the
cancellation, and contacted Lansdale (now working on South American
affairs) to see if an end run could be made around Taylor to Gilpatric or
McNamara.

Lansdale said that "if a Chief couldn't get a debrief on the JCS agenda" he didn't see how he could, but he agreed to try anyway. In a letter to Hangin' Sam Williams, Lansdale recalled what happened then:

> I got the military assistants to McNamara and Gilpatric, along with Jim Kent and my own staff, in for a private session with Vann. I told him that he should stick to things he knew first-hand, and delete his gossip about what he'd heard was going on in Saigon. Then we all tried to crash the barriers of getting him in for even ten minutes with the top folks. No dice.[43]

Lansdale then explained to Williams what he thought was behind Taylor's suppression of the Vann report. Lansdale explained that "this sort of censorship" had also been applied to "messages" from Vietnam, meaning that officers who had tried to send reports from Vietnam that did not conform with the cover erected by Harkins found their messages similarly blocked. Lansdale then offered this revealing insight:

> The only inference I can draw is that one hell of a lot was being covered up by a handful of US officials by the summer of 1963. Taylor, Alex Johnson, and Sullivan, the team now in Saigon, were all in on this cover-up. I figure they made the bed they are now lying in, and it is costing our national security sorely.

Lansdale's view complements nicely the outline Burris gave LBJ about the Taylor-Harkins link and the "tailoring" of facts and figures in Saigon. "If there ever is a witch-hunt over the loss of [Vietnam]," Lansdale concluded, "I think there are some of us who would welcome the battle."

THE DEEPENING WEB OF DECEPTION

By the spring of 1963, Taylor had become progressively more involved in helping Harkins maintain the fiction of battlefield success. The question is: in this effort whose purpose did he serve? There is hard evidence that by this time Kennedy knew his earlier confidence in this success story "was misplaced," and had become aware that the intelligence on which the optimistic judgments were based was "not very sound."[44] There is also evidence that he felt that the deepening American commitment was a mistake. At the end of 1962 Kennedy had invited Senator Mike Mansfield to go to Vietnam and assess the situation. The Senator returned with a gloomy report and charged that Kennedy's military commitment was leading to the unenviable position the French had been in; Mansfield recommended withdrawing U.S. troops. White House aide Kenneth O'Donnell recalls Kennedy's reaction:

> The President was too disturbed by the Senator's unexpected argu-
> ment to reply to it. He said to me later when we talked about the
> discussion, "I got angry with Mike for disagreeing with our policy
> so completely, and I got angry with myself because I found myself
> agreeing with him."[45]

Moreover, by March 1963 a new pattern of contradiction emerged in which the President's public comments began to conflict with the statements he made in confidence to a few trusted friends.

When those to whom the President had confided in privately went on record years later to tell the public what Kennedy had said, it was clear that he had excluded his Secretary of State, Dean Rusk, from this privileged circle. McNamara remains an enigma because of his silence on the war, but collateral evidence—discussed later—suggests he was *included*. Taylor, however, did not keep silent. The fact is that not one word in his subsequent book and in all of his public comments suggests that the President confided his ultimate plans to him.

In the view of this author, by March 1963 Kennedy had figured out— exactly when is unclear—that the success story was a deception. The reader will recall the dark picture of the war that his advisors had painted at the end of 1961; its replacement with the success story in early 1962; and then the uproar that ensued, in April of that year, when Kennedy let slip (in a White House meeting) the comment about seizing a favorable moment to reduce the American commitment. The context of that debate, sparked by Galbraith's suggestion for a political solution in Vietnam, led the Joint Chiefs to charge that such action would amount to a "reversal of policy." At that time the picture of the war MACV presented to McNamara was one of gradual success *but one in which more aircraft, equipment, and men were always needed to get the job done*. The success story both forestalled the notion that the situation was desperate enough to warrant a Laotian-type political solution, and justified the further expansion and intensification of the "winning" U.S. effort.

By the fall of 1962 the deception was working, and Kennedy, like McNamara, had come to believe the perception delivered by the uninterrupted string of false reports emanating from Vietnam. Kennedy, however, had to notice when the military myth was shaken by Bowles and Mendenhall in late 1962,[46] and Mansfield's critical comments about the deepening vortex of military commitments at the end of the year surely nurtured the seeds of doubt about MACV's reporting. When the drama of the Wheeler versus Hilsman-Forrestal match ended up in his office in February 1963, the implication that the story of success was untrue could no longer be overlooked.

Just how unreal the myth of success was can be seen from this remarkable tabulation of the figures MACV itself had developed for 1962:[47]

TOTAL LOSSES FOR 1962:
GOVERNMENT VERSUS VIET CONG

	Killed	Wounded	Captured	Deserted	Total
Government:	4,561	7,278	1,401	21,036	*34,276*
Viet Cong:	20,919	4,236	5,518	1,596	*32,269*

The government forces actually experienced greater total losses than the Viet Cong. Moreover, as Burris had told Vice President Johnson, the desertion problem in Diem's army was deeply troubling. Such a disturbing presentation, of course, was never made at a SECDEF conference, and these figures were not put together until June 1964. When Harkins claimed in January 1963 that more than 30,000 Viet Cong had been killed during the previous year, however, the shocking revelation that their forces had grown anyway—which was discovered by Hilsman and Forrestal and concurred in by the CIA—destroyed the statistical illusion of success.

Kennedy's program was a failure—in his heart he must have known that. Hearing it put so bluntly by Mansfield angered him, but may have helped him face up to the fact that he was trapped. Kennedy decided, apparently, as we will see, in February or March 1963, to get out of Vietnam even if it meant the war would be lost. At this time a new element emerged in the withdrawal plan McNamara had been working on since the previous year: pulling out 1,000 men during the election campaign of 1964.

When McNamara began talking about a 1,000-man withdrawal in April, it is most likely that a secret agreement he had made with Kennedy was already in effect. That agreement—which McNamara did not reveal until he told a trusted subordinate about it in the spring of 1964—was that they would get out of Vietnam after 1964, according to Daniel Ellsberg.[48] A remark made by McGeorge Bundy in an interview with the author seems to support Ellsberg's claim. Bundy said this about the 1,000-man withdrawal:

> I remember it as very much coming out of a conversation that was quite closely held between Kennedy and McNamara. And what

they meant by it beyond what they said, which was not very much,
I honestly don't know.[49]

Kennedy did not make the mistake he had made in April 1962: talking
too freely about his real intentions with respect to the war.

It would appear that Taylor was not, at this point, involved in what
Kennedy and McNamara were planning. Why was this so? Kennedy
realized that the story of success was a deception and had decided to
engage in a deception of his own. The reader will recall that Kennedy
planted bogus stories in the newspapers before the 1961 Taylor trip and
afterward to counter the troop recommendation that Taylor delivered. By
the spring of 1963 Taylor had become an integral part of maintaining the
fiction of success, and it would appear that Kennedy decided not to
interfere with the General's efforts but to use them to his own advantage.
Kennedy decided to use Taylor's and Harkins' reports of battlefield success
to justify the beginning of the withdrawal he was planning.

Kennedy kept his plan a closely guarded secret, but by March he was
determined not only to withdraw—come what may—after 1964, but, if
possible, to take a clear step in that direction during the presidential
campaign as well: the 1,000-man withdrawal. One of the few people he
did confide in at this time, Senator Mansfield—a critic of Kennedy's
Vietnam policy—found out *why* it had to be kept a secret. Kennedy's
aide, O'Donnell, recounts what Kennedy told Mansfield:

> Later the President asked me to invite Mansfield to his office for a
> private talk on the problem. I sat in on part of the discussion. The
> President told Mansfield that he had been having second thoughts
> about Mansfield's argument and that he now agreed with the Sena-
> tor's thinking on the need for a complete military withdrawal from
> Vietnam. "But I can't do it until 1965—after I'm reelected," Ken-
> nedy told Mansfield. President Kennedy explained, and Mansfield
> agreed with him, that if he announced a withdrawal of American
> military personnel from Vietnam before the 1964 election, there
> would be a wild conservative outcry against returning him to the
> Presidency for a second term.[50]

It is obvious from this that Kennedy feared the political repercussions
that would ensue if his real intentions became known to the wrong people.
That he had no illusions about the consequences of a withdrawal is evident
from what he told O'Donnell later:

> After Mansfield left the office, the President said to me, "In 1965,
> I'll become one of the most unpopular Presidents in history. I'll be

damned everywhere as a Communist appeaser. But I don't care. If I tried to pull out completely now from Vietnam, we would have another Joe McCarthy scare on our hands, but I can do it after I'm reelected. So we had better make damned sure that I *am* reelected."[51]

This makes it abundantly clear that Kennedy knew the war was a lost cause, and that his problem was how to disguise his intentions until after the election.

How did Kennedy do that? The answer is evident from his March 6 press conference. A reporter noted that Senator Mansfield had recommended a reduction in U.S. aid to the Far East and asked the President to comment. This is what he said:

> I don't see how we are going to be able, unless we are going to pull out of Southeast Asia and turn it over to the Communists, how we are going to be able to reduce very much our economic programs and military programs in South Vietnam, in Cambodia, in Thailand.
>
> I think that unless you want to withdraw from the field and decide that it is in the national interest to permit that area to collapse, I would think that it would be impossible to substantially change it particularly as we are in a very intensive struggle in those areas.
>
> So I think we ought to judge the economic burden it places upon us as opposed to having the Communists control all of Southeast Asia, with the inevitable effect this would have on the security of India and, therefore, really begin to run perhaps all the way toward the Middle East. So I think that while we would all like to lighten the burden, I don't see any real prospect of the burden being lightened for the U.S. in Southeast Asia in the next year if we are going to do the job and meet what I think are very clear national needs.[52]

To the advocates of intervention and Kennedy's political opponents alike, this sounded like a forceful statement against withdrawal.

In the nearly thirty years since Kennedy made those public remarks, and in private disclosed his true intent to Mansfield and O'Donnell, no major work on the war has attempted to analyze both of them and explain the contradiction between the two. Some seize on the Mansfield exchange to defend Kennedy against the charge that he would have done what Johnson did later, while others seize on this and subsequent press conference statements to make the opposite case. The fact that what Kennedy said at the press conference is so diametrically opposed to what he told

Mansfield in secret makes it reasonable to ask: is there a possibility that O'Donnell was wrong—that he somehow misunderstood what was said?

In 1975 Mansfield confirmed the story to Jack Anderson, saying that Kennedy had "definitely and unequivocally" made the decision, and that the withdrawal would be gradual.[53] In 1978 he provided even more details, which confirmed O'Donnell's account:

> [Kennedy] called me down and said he had changed his mind and that he wanted to begin withdrawing troops beginning the first of the following year, that would be in January 1964. He was unhappy about the situation which had developed there and felt that even then with 16,000 troops we were in too deep. . . . He was very concerned, I believe, mortified at how far we'd gone in.[54]

Since there is no doubt that Kennedy made these confidential remarks, his public and private comments must therefore be considered side by side. Neither one, by itself, is the key to the puzzle. Only when both pieces are put into place does the purpose for his remarks at these press conferences become clear: they were calculated to throw off his political opponents and the supporters of massive U.S. intervention.

It is significant that Kennedy confided in McNamara, Mansfield, and O'Donnell, but not in his Secretary of State. "I had hundreds of talks with President Kennedy," Rusk recalled later, "and on no single occasion did he ever express to me any ideas on that line."[55] Rusk apparently never considered the unflattering possibility that Kennedy did not trust him enough to tell him the truth. When Rusk found out about the Mansfield conversation years later, he refused to accept its validity, adding, "And I am not suggesting at all that Senator Mansfield was untruthful." Kennedy liked to "chew the fat and gossip," Rusk offered, and said the implication of the Mansfield story was that Kennedy would "leave Americans in uniform in a combat situation for domestic political purposes, and no President can do that." Rusk was wrong about Kennedy's intent to withdraw because Rusk was simply out of the loop. His comment that such a plan would have been playing politics with the war found support from Ellsberg, who believed Kennedy intended to withdraw and charged that he had been willing to keep on bombing "for a couple of more years in order to get through the election."[56]

Arthur Schlesinger defended Kennedy's decision to hide his plans in this way:

> In any event, would it have been better to have lost in 1964 to a presidential candidate who agreed with General Curtis LeMay that North Vietnam should be bombed back to the Stone Age?[57]

Whether or not one agrees with Schlesinger's justification, there is no doubt in this author's mind that Kennedy had decided to withdraw from what he knew to be a losing situation and to keep this decision a secret so that he could get reelected.

What is particularly striking about Kennedy's behavior is the length to which he went to disguise his intent, and the way in which he used the story of success—a fiction for which he had been the target—against its perpetrators. Until this point the deception had functioned this way: the deepening American involvement had led to greater success in the war, but there was still no light as yet at the end of the tunnel. Kennedy parroted *exactly that line* on March 6, and began planning his disengagement based on that same deception of success. He assumed this position would enable him to start the limited withdrawal he needed during the campaign, while if and when the battlefield deterioration could no longer remain hidden he could claim he had been misled by incorrect reports on the war.

This was a risky game to play, for it depended on keeping his opponents off guard by talking only of withdrawal in the context of victory while simultaneously laying the groundwork for withdrawal in a losing scenario. As risky and duplicitous as the President's plan was, he must have believed it was the only way to extricate the United States from the quagmire in Vietnam. In March 1963 it appeared that he might be able to steer this tricky course and that his problem would not arise until after the election. Unfortunately for the President's plan, the situation in Vietnam would not hold until the next American election, for it was about to take a sudden and violent turn for the worse.

NOTES

1. This account of the battle is based primarily upon Vann's interview with Charles V.P. von Littichau, July 22, 1963, and Sheehan's comprehensive account in *A Bright Shining Lie*, pp. 203–65.

2. Karnow, *Vietnam*, p. 262.

3. Ibid.

4. Harkins message to Taylor on January 10, 1963, press release, JFK Library, NSF, Country File, Vietnam, Box 197.

5. See Harriman letter to Nolting, January 30, 1963, in *State History*, 1963, vol. 3, Document 24, pp. 67–69.

6. CIA Intelligence Memorandum, January 11, 1963, in *State History*, 1963, vol. 3, Document 11, pp. 19–22.

7. Hilsman memo for record, Saigon, 1963, in *State History*, 1963, vol. 3, Document 3, pp. 5–7.

8. Vann, interview with von Littichau, p. 11.

9. Drummond, interview with the author, June 9, 1989.

10. Ibid., June 14, 1989.

11. Sheehan, *A Bright Shining Lie*, p. 323.

12. Ibid., p. 324.

13. Drummond, interview with the author, June 9, 1989.

14. Sheehan, *A Bright Shining Lie*, pp. 324–25.

15. Vann, interview with von Littichau, July 22, 1963, pp. 10–11.

16. Sheehan, *A Bright Shining Lie*, p. 325.

17. Blascak, interview with the author, July 4, 1991.

18. Drummond, interview with the author, June 4, 1989.

19. See the minutes of the Special Group's January 17, 1963, meeting, in *State History*, 1963, vol. 3, Document 14, pp. 28–30.

20. See U. Alexis Johnson's account of the discussion, in *State History*, 1963, vol. 3, pp. 28–29, n. 3.

21. "Report of Visit by Joint Chiefs of Staff Team to South Vietnam, January 1963," JFK Library, NSF, Country File, Vietnam, Box 197.

22. Hilsman-Forrestal report to Kennedy, January 25, 1963, in *State History*, 1963, vol. 3, Document 19, pp. 49–62. The President had read this report by at least January 28; see Document 21, pp. 63–64.

23. See the recapitulation of the Wheeler Statement in State Cable CA-8776, February 15, 1963, JFK Library, NSF, Country File, Vietnam, Box 197.

24. Forrestal memo to JFK, February 4, 1963, in *State History*, 1963, vol. 3, Document 29, pp. 97–98.

25. MACV cable to CINCPAC, relayed to JCS on February 14, 1963, JFK Library, NSF, Country File, Vietnam, Box 197.

26. Minutes of a Meeting of the Special Group for Counterinsurgency, February, 7, 1963, in *State History*, 1963, vol. 3, Document 32, pp. 103–5.

27. Minutes of a Meeting of the Special Group for Counterinsurgency, March 14, 1963, in *State History*, 1963, vol. 3, Document 59, pp. 150–51.

28. Halberstam, *The Best and the Brightest*, p. 270.

29. Ford, interview with the author, July 22, 1988.

30. Hilsman memo for record, dated "January 1963," in *State History*, 1963, vol. 3, Document 3, pp. 5–7.

31. CIA Current Intelligence Memorandum, January 11, 1963, in *State History*, 1963, vol. 3, Document 11, pp. 19–22.

32. NIE 53–63, "Prospects in South Vietnam," April 17, 1963, in *State History*, 1963, vol. 3, Document 94, pp. 232–35; and *PP*, DOD ed., Book 12, pp. 522–24.

33. *PP*, Gravel ed., vol. 2, p. 180.

34. Memo for record of the Secretary of Defense Conference, Honolulu, May 6 1963, in *State History*, 1963, vol. 3, Document 107, pp. 265–70. This record is signed by Rear Admiral Heinz, Regional Director of the Far East, Office of the Assistant Secretary of Defense for International Security Affairs.

35. McNamara "questioned the need for more Vietnamese forces in FY 68 (224.4

thousand) than the present level of 215 thousand. His reasoning was that a poor nation of 12 million like Vietnam could not support that many men under arms. Qualitatively, furthermore, the planned evolution of VNAF seemed over-ambitious in terms of sophisticated weaponry such as fighter aircraft." See *PP*, Gravel ed., vol. 2, p. 180.

36. *PP*, Gravel ed., vol. 2, p. 180.

37. Westmoreland, interview with Paul Miles, March 6, 1971, Army Center for Military History.

38. Vann, Senior Advisor's Final Report, April 1, 1963, Army Center for Military History; see also JFK Library, Newman Papers.

39. Westmoreland, interview with Paul L. Miles, March 6, 1971; see also Krepinevich, *The Army in Vietnam*, p. 83.

40. See excerpts from John Paul Vann's "JCS Briefing, Observations of the Senior Advisor to the South Vietnamese Seventh Infantry Division, 8 July 1963," as quoted in Krepinevich, *The Army and Vietnam*, pp. 83–84.

41. Hamlett, interview with Jacob Couch, Jr., January 23, 1976, U.S. Army Military History Research Collection, Carlisle Pennysylvania.

42. Sheehan, *A Bright Shining Lie*, pp. 340–41.

43. Lansdale letter to Williams, October 24, 1964, Hoover Institution, Williams Papers, Box 20.

44. NBC White Paper, "Death of Diem."

45. Kenneth O'Donnell, *Johnny, We Hardly Knew Ye* (Boston: Little Brown, 1976), p. 15.

46. Mansfield visited Vietnam December 1–3, 1962, and submitted a report on December 18; see *State History*, 1962, Document 330, pp. 779–87. He went again in February 1963, and submitted a report on February 25; see *State History*, 1963, vol. 3, Document 42, pp. 122–23.

47. These figures were not shown until June 1964; see "Report, Summary of U.S. Aid to Vietnam," June 15, 1965, Vietnam files, U.S. Army Center for Military History. This fifty-one-page study was declassified on March 19, 1973, but to the author's knowledge has never been cited in any work on the war.

48. Ellsberg, interview with the author, August 8, 1991. Ellsberg says he learned this from McNamara's subordinate, McNaughton.

49. McGeorge Bundy, interview with the author, July 16, 1991.

50. O'Donnell, *Johnny, We Hardly Knew Ye*, p. 16.

51. Ibid.

52. Kennedy, *Public Papers*, 1963, pp. 243–44.

53. Jack Anderson, *Washington Post*, May 4, 1975; see also Arthur Schlesinger, *Robert Kennedy and His Times* (Boston: Houghton Mifflin, 1978), p. 712.

54. Mansfield, quoted in Michael Charlton and Anthony Moncrieff, *Many Reasons Why* (New York: Hill and Wang, 1978), p. 81.

55. Rusk, quoted in Charlton and Moncrieff, *Many Reasons Why*, p. 82.

56. Ellsberg, *Rolling Stone*, December 6, 1973, cited in Schlesinger, *Robert Kennedy and His Times*, p. 711.

57. Schlesinger, *Robert Kennedy and His Times*, p. 711.

CHAPTER SEVENTEEN

BROTHERS AND BUDDHISTS

THE STRATEGIC FAILURE OF THE HAMLET PROGRAM

The Strategic Hamlet Program was "spottily" continuing, the June 1962 USARPAC Intelligence Bulletin said, and was "poorly coordinated."[1] The CIA reported on July 13 that a "major weakness" of the program was its "hit-and-miss construction" and "insufficient integration [of] hamlet defenses into overall district and provincial security plans."[2] Intelligence in December began to accumulate bearing out these early pessimistic observations. "Despite some of the glowing strategic hamlet progress reports," said the December USARPAC Intelligence Bulletin, "there is evidence that all is not well."[3] U.S. intelligence sources had gained possession of a report from a "high provincial figure" that suggested the program was largely fraudulent. The official indicated that provincial officials from central Vietnam had reported in September that they had completed over 250 strategic hamlets, but only four actually existed and only one of those met most of the requirements for a strategic hamlet. The other hamlets listed, he said, met only one or more of the requirements, such as a fenced perimeter. The official added, "It was not difficult to prevent the government from finding out the true situation as provincial officials would protect one another," and visitors were only shown what local officials wanted them to see.

The same problems existed in the Delta, where most of South Vietnam's population lived. For example, as of March 1, in the seven provinces which comprised the 41st Division Tactical Area, the Vietnamese reported 950 of the planned 2,424 strategic hamlets had been completed. Vann stated:

> The Americans did not agree with this figure. We considered only 250 of the hamlets as meeting the criteria for being complete. So the first deficiency that existed were the people who were measuring progress by the degree of completion of the Strategic Hamlet Program accepting the Vietnamese statistics.[4]

There were far greater deficiencies than false statistics. One was corruption, and Vann had pretty strong views on that subject:

> we have documented evidence of graft and corruption and have sent them in to MACV. [I] have presented briefings on them. I know that one of them even resulted in a letter from General Harkins asking that a province chief be investigated. . . . I believe the Ambassador attempted to get this province chief removed.[5]

This province chief, said Vann, was selling promotions and had a nonexistent Self Defense Corps troop on his payroll whose money went into the chief's pocket. There were just "countless things along this line," Vann said, that were well known.

Even worse than the corruption was the fact that, in many areas, there were no provisions to clear the area of Viet Cong before proceeding with hamlet construction. Hamlets were built willy-nilly, instead of starting in one area and gradually expanding—which had been the original "strategic" concept of growing "ink blots" in the first place. "So in our zone . . . we were establishing . . . islands of resistance and not clearing any single area, and not clearing the area between hamlets," Vann explained.[6]

Since troops had to be used to defend the hamlets, the scattershot pattern of their construction, besides drawing off troops which were already in short supply, weakened the disposition of military power in the countryside. In one province, Vann recalled, offensive operations had been curtailed by 75 percent before the program was one-fourth complete because "troops which had been available for offensive actions had been placed into the strategic hamlets as they were built in order to establish security for them." This left the Viet Cong free, as Vann pointed out, to "pick out any hamlet they want and gobble it up any time they want to."[7]

"We recently bombed a strategic hamlet by mistake," Chalmers Wood, director of the Vietnam working group, wrote in a February 28 memo to Harriman.[8] Five thousand of these hamlets had been built and almost 60 percent of South Vietnam's rural population put inside of them. The Viet Cong had attacked nine and entered five during the week of February 13–20, Wood added. These attacks were mild, however, compared to the terror the Viet Cong would shortly unleash—as John Vann had predicted—on these vulnerable little camps. On March 14, Colonel Serong, the senior Australian advisor in Vietnam, wrote this to General Harkins:

> the presently successful Strategic Hamlet Program, if continued on current lines (and there is no suggestion to the contrary), will unbalance our overall strategy, and create a situation favorable to the VC, who are now preparing for a long war. . . . The strategic aim is in jeopardy. A modification of the plan is necessary.[9]

The haphazard construction of these hamlets and the problems of defending and administering them, which had been pointed out by the CIA the previous summer and since then by nearly everyone who saw them, still had not been rectified as the summer of 1963 approached. Even a State Department paper written at the unclassified level to publicly praise the program's success said, "The physical defenses of strategic hamlets admittedly vary in quality and, in some cases, leave much to be desired."[10]

Meanwhile, at the secret level, there was a much darker side to the story. According to the Director of the American Operations Mission in Vietnam at the time, Joseph Brent, the local officials who were in charge of the program felt unable to carry it out "without using methods sure to alienate the population whose support is its real objective."[11] Brent related this experience:

> I have accompanied the Minister of Interior, for instance, on visits to hamlets where he praised the Province Chief for having moved the population without expense to the government, but where I found out later the Province Chief was obliged, because of popular discontent, to use two companies of Civil Guard to keep the people in the hamlets. This continues up to the present to be the main approach of the central government.

This had to be changed, said Brent, otherwise the province chiefs were forced into "actions surely destructive to the program."

This picture was pretty well papered over by Krulak, who went to Vietnam in late June and returned in early July to report, "The people have come willingly—in some cases having sent deputies to request the development of a hamlet."[12] However, even Colby, who believed that if the hamlet program had been properly implemented the war might have turned out differently, concedes there were gross errors, and that many people were involuntarily displaced—especially in the Delta region.[13] Colby, in this author's view, is probably right, but there can be no doubt that moving the peasants was an unmitigated disaster and a fatal flaw in the program. As noted earlier Diem was adamant about resettling the peasants, and it is therefore doubtful whether the program could have succeeded under his regime.

The forced resettlement of the peasants was another significant factor, like indiscriminate bombing and artillery shelling, which helped turn the population against the government. For centuries the village had been the basic political unit in Vietnam, and each village was tied to a physical location due to the cultural and religious nature of the society. The vast majority of South Vietnamese peasants were devout ancestor worshippers, and the most fundamental aspect of their creed and the rites they practiced was the land where their ancestors were buried. Moving these peasants to new locations destroyed the political order and stability of the country-side and the very basis of the peasant's values along with it. The destruction of the peasant's identity and value system was the first—and most diffi-cult—prerequisite for extending communist control among the billions of peasants in China. The failures of the Strategic Hamlet Program repre-sent one more of the war's great ironies—that American money and power made the Vietnamese countryside ripe for revolution, and at a pace much faster than the Viet Cong, if left to their own devices, could ever have dreamed of.

While Diem's brother Nhu presided over this misguided tragedy in the countryside, two more brothers of Diem unleashed a tidal wave that swept through Vietnam's major cities and destroyed all vestiges of support for the government there. The calamity that resulted was truly a family affair.

TWO BROTHERS IN HUE

When Diem returned to Vietnam in 1954, the only people who showed up to greet him at the airport were Catholics.[14] When one million, pre-dominantly Catholic, refugees fled from North to South Vietnam after the French defeat that same year, Diem, also a Catholic, gave these refugees preferential treatment. Diem saw in them a quick way to insert people loyal to himself into all key civilian and military positions as he built South Vietnam's central and provincial power structures.[15] In other areas, especially land redistribution, export-import licenses, and government employment, these northern Catholics profited at the expense of the majority Buddhist population. The Catholic Church enjoyed a special legal status and its primate, Archbishop of Hue Ngo Dinh Thuc, was another of Diem's brothers. In April 1963 Thuc indulged in officially encouraged celebrations commemorating the twenty-fifth anniversary of his own ordination, and Papal flags were flying everywhere. Then the Hue government, the personal fiefdom of another of Diem's brothers, Ngo Dinh Can, ordered the enforcement of an obsolete law against the public display of religious flags—just days before the festival for Buddha's birthday. Such religious discrimination, which was not new in Vietnam, was sufficiently distasteful this time to backfire. This, in turn, ignited an explosion that even Harkins could not help but notice.

When the Buddhists flew their flags anyway, held a rally to commemorate Buddha's birthday, and then defied a request to disperse, the Catholic deputy province chief ordered his troops to fire on the crowd (on May 8). When the smoke cleared the next morning, the U.S. Consul in Hue, John Helble, reported seven dead, including two children crushed by armored vehicles, and fifteen injured.[16] The Diem government's lies that a Viet Cong agent had thrown a grenade into the crowd and that the victims had been crushed in a stampede were issued as an official report, which fooled Nolting, who, to this day, says it was "objective, accurate and fair."[17] Nolting says that, at the time, he felt "the immediate crisis had passed" and so he left with his family for a sailing vacation near Greece.

The government's report, however, was undermined after Nolting left, when neutral observers produced films showing government troops firing on the crowd.[18] Within the U.S. administration it was no secret that Diem's regime was lying: a June 3 CIA report confirmed "the weight of evidence indicating that government cannon-fire caused the deaths" at the Hue rally.[19] Saving face, a central characteristic of the mandarin psyche, led Diem to cling to his false story and further inflame the crisis. Thousands of Buddhists swarmed into the streets to demonstrate; the Buddhist clergy quickly organized, levied a list of demands on Diem, including the right to fly Buddhist flags and legal equality with the Catholic Church. Despite U.S. urging to make peace, Diem stubbornly dragged his feet, and the CIA concluded that his "inept" handling of the situation had "permitted a localized incident in Hue to grow into a potential political crisis."

Hunger strikes and mass demonstrations grew toward the end of May, and events during the first three days of June in Quang Tri and Hue escalated the crisis to new heights. Government soldiers used tear gas on the Buddhist demonstrators in Quang Tri all three days; on June 4 MACV filed this report of what happened in Hue the previous day:

> soldiers threw glass ampoules at people; ampoule approximately 2 inches in diameter, 4½ inches long; liquid contents brownish red color. Incident resulted in 63 casualties hospitalized with blisters. Rumors of deaths, however, not repeat not confirmed by hospital. Tear gas (CN) was also used in this incident. Two ampoules containing agent have been recovered and are being flown to Saigon.[20]

On June 3 MACV estimated 1,000 people, "mixed men, women and children," were gassed, and reported three "unconfirmed" deaths.[21] Consul Helble "had himself observed blistering on victims" and the "fact that some appeared [to] be having respiratory difficulties," said a June 4 cable from Deputy Chief of Mission Trueheart, adding, "These were symptoms which could be associated with mustard gas."[22]

Although it is not clear what happened to the two glass ampoules, later tests conducted by U.S. Army chemists in Maryland reported—"from samples supplied"—that the substance was "a tear gas of the type used by the French during World War I."[23] Whether mustard or ancient tear gas, however, the repression at Hue created an enormous problem for American policy in Vietnam. Trueheart immediately approached Thuan and told him that U.S. support for the government "could not be maintained in [the] face of bloody repressive action at Hue."[24]

BATTLE OF THE BONZES

On June 4 an interministerial committee headed by Vice President Nguyen Ngol Tho was formed to resolve the religious issue, but this government gesture was too little and too late, as large portions of the population had already rallied to the Buddhists. Madame Nhu (outspoken wife of Diem's brother Nhu) was apparently enjoying the Buddhist ordeal, and seemed to delight at poking around sadistically in the festering wound that had opened. She exacerbated the problem on June 8 by claiming that the Buddhists had been infiltrated by communists. On June 11, when Thich Quang Duc shocked the world and electrified South Vietnam by becoming the first monk to burn himself to death, Madame Nhu, "with seeming glee,"[25] described the immolation as a "barbecue," and said if the

Buddhists wanted to have another one, "I will be glad to supply the gasoline."[26] "Let them burn, and we shall clap our hands," she said.[27]

The U.S. intensified its already considerable pressure on the government to mollify the Buddhists. "In our judgment the Buddhist situation is dangerously near the breaking point," said a June 11 State cable to Trueheart, who was acting in Nolting's absence.[28] The cable was extraordinary because it told Trueheart to demand that Diem "fully and unequivocally" meet the Buddhist's demands. This had to "be done in a public and dramatic fashion," the cable said, "if confidence is to be restored." The cable ended with these words:

> FYI—If Diem does not take prompt and effective steps to reestablish Buddhist confidence in him we will have to reexamine our entire relationship with his regime. End FYI.

Trueheart, who Nolting later said, disparagingly, "carried out his instructions with a vengeance,"[29] lost no time in delivering this message to Diem. The next day he showed Diem a "paper" based on the June 11 State Department cable. Trueheart reported afterward that it was "very strong medicine and will be hard for Diem to take. I would not care to predict the outcome."[30]

Unaware that this action had been taken, Kennedy read about it for the first time the following morning in the daily CIA President's Intelligence Checklist. A memorandum for the record prepared in the White House that day states:

> The President noticed that Diem has been threatened with a formal statement of disassociation. He wants to be absolutely sure no further threats are made and no formal statement is made without his own personal approval.[31]

The President was upset that events in Vietnam had so suddenly and unexpectedly careened out of control. Nothing Kennedy had been told by his advisors had prepared him for this breakdown in Vietnam. "How could this have happened?" he asked Forrestal. "Who are these people?" he inquired of the Buddhists in apparent bewilderment and irritation. "Why didn't we know about them before?"[32]

Because Nolting had been too soft with Diem, and so out of touch that he had taken an extended vacation in the middle of this crisis, Kennedy decided that week to replace him with Henry Cabot Lodge.[33] In the meantime, on June 14, with Nolting still sailing in the Aegean, the State Department sent a message to Trueheart.[34] The cable, drafted by Wood and cleared by Hilsman and Harriman, made reference to a plan drafted

by Vietnam Working Group Director Chalmers Wood, approved by
Nolting on the day he left on vacation—May 23—and by Kennedy on
June 6, for a contingency in case there was a change of government in
Saigon.[35] The cable said that if Diem could not continue as President due
to "internal political circumstances (in which the U.S. would play no
part)" then Vice President Tho would be the constitutional successor.
The cable said the Department wanted Tho to know this and also that "we
would assume he would need military support." The "present precarious
situation," it said, seemed to make it "worthwhile to run the risk" of
telling Tho, and Trueheart was also given permission to say this "directly
to Diem." Trueheart was then given these instructions:

> Suggest you consider steps [to] gradually increase covert and overt
> contacts with non-supporters of GVN. In present situation this
> should only be done if you feel our (overt or covert) contacts with
> those who might play major roles in [the] event of [a] coup are
> now inadequate.

This was far from an instruction to encourage a coup—that would come
in August—but it serves as a useful baseline for when the State Department began seriously looking for coup prospects. On June 16 Trueheart
replied, "We have all the lines out that we know how to put out and have
had for some days."[36]

On June 14 Trueheart had cabled Washington that an accommodation
with the Buddhists was imminent.[37] On the 16th, however, when a joint
government-Buddhist communiqué was released outlining the elements
of a settlement, no responsibility for the May 8 incident was affixed.
Violent government suppression of rioting the next day made it clear that
the agreement was not meant as a genuine gesture of conciliation by
Diem, but instead was an effort to mollify the U.S. by papering over the
widening political fissure in Vietnam. The June 17 suppression had another important consequence: it discredited the conciliatory policy of the
moderate Buddhist leadership. They were replaced in late June by a more
radical set of monks who made skillful political use of their popular
support—and of the American news media. This only led to even more
severe government suppression of Buddhist activities and to acrimonious
criticism and threats to the American newsmen. When Vice President
Tho's committee announced in early July that the May 8 deaths at Hue
were the result of Viet Cong terrorism, any pretense of conciliation evapo-
rated. The Buddhists used this mistake to intensify popular support for
their protests. A June 28 CIA assessment of the situation concluded that
a significant "shift" in the South Vietnamese population had occurred
"from apparent apathy to active opposition."[38]

After discussing the spiraling deterioration in Vietnam at a July 1 meeting, Harriman, Hilsman, and Forrestal sent a cable to McGeorge Bundy, who was traveling with Kennedy in Rome, predicting this chain of events: "We all believe one more burning Bonze [Buddhist monk] will cause domestic U.S. reaction which will require strong public statement despite danger that this might precipitate coup in Saigon."[39] By this time Nolting had arrived in Washington and had learned on his way there—over the commercial radio—that he was to be replaced as Ambassador by Lodge.[40] Nolting met with Hilsman and Harriman, and he later claimed he confronted them for not having notified him during his vacation about the crisis that had developed in Vietnam. Harriman was "testy and uncommunicative," Nolting says, and he suspects they deliberately connived to keep him away because they wanted the crisis "to come to a head, to make a change in the government inevitable."

It is almost axiomatic that when coup talk inside the government becomes more pronounced, the record of the discussion begins to get murky; at least this was so in 1963. A cable was sent from State to Trueheart doing exactly what Kennedy had forbade: telling Trueheart to threaten Diem that the U.S. might "have to make a public statement" if he did not make a "forthright effort" to reconcile with the bonzes.[41] The cable went out on July 1 while Kennedy was still in Rome and, curiously, was sent, "From Hilsman and Nolting to Trueheart." Perhaps Nolting had not seen Kennedy's prohibition on threats to Diem, but since he later said he did not agree with the policy anyway, his name at the top of the cable is odd. Hilsman definitely should have known better, and his involvement is troubling. A July 3 memo written for Kennedy by Forrestal suggests that Nolting's name should not have been on the cable. After describing its contents, Forrestal said this about Nolting:

> Ambassador Nolting does not agree with this approach and argues that it will succeed only in destroying the last vestiges of Diem's confidence in us. Secretary Ball, Governor Harriman, Roger Hilsman and I feel that the political problem has come to such a point in the United States that we could not avoid public comment in the face of another bonze suicide. . . .[42]

In view of this evidence, it appears likely that Nolting's name was added to the July 1 cable to give Trueheart the impression of unity in Washington when, in fact, a division was in the making.

Kennedy returned to Washington and met with his advisors on July 4 to discuss the crisis.[43] They told him about the new pressure that had been applied to Diem; that Diem had agreed to make a speech; and, further, that Diem had been told if he did not make the speech and the demonstrations resumed, then the U.S. would make a public statement opposing his Buddhist policy. Kennedy apparently did not react to this. Hilsman told the President that no matter what Diem did there would still be coup attempts against him "over the next four months." Hilsman took issue with Nolting's claim that a coup against Diem would lead to civil war; this was possible, but not likely, said Hilsman, and the chances for post-coup chaos were less than they had been before. Forrestal then said it was Krulak's view that even if there was chaos, the South Vietnamese Army would continue its military actions against the communists. The idea of "getting rid of the Nhus"—just how is not clear from the record— was discussed and rejected.

Once again coincidence crept into another watershed moment of the war's history. As Kennedy listened to his advisors in Washington talk— for the first time—seriously about coup possibilities, that same day in Saigon Lucien Conein, a veteran CIA agent and old colleague of Lansdale, was contacted by General Tran Van Don. Don was the Acting Chief of Staff of the Vietnamese armed forces, and he wanted to make a coup against Diem. His plan appears to have been described in a July 8 CIA cable from Saigon, which was extensively sanitized upon its release in 1985.[44] There was a "military plan for the overthrow of the government," Don reported to Conein and "except for one or two general officers, all were in agreement." Don explained:

> The reason for the military takeover was that President Diem had failed to act in the best interests of Vietnam on the occasion of the 8 May Buddhist incident in Hue. The government should have admitted its mistake and made amends to the people involved; the government had unfortunately failed to do this and permitted the incident to become a national issue. The military must act in order to prevent the Viet Cong from taking full advantage of the continuing Buddhist problem.

After the coup, Don said, elections would be announced immediately, to be held three to six months hence.

Nolting returned to Saigon on July 10, upset and feeling betrayed by Trueheart, whom he had personally selected to be his deputy. Embittered at being abandoned by his own colleagues, Nolting embraced General Harkins, with whom he now agreed that "it looks like the State Department thinks Diem is the enemy, rather than the Viet Cong."[45] His analysis of the Buddhists lined up with Madame Nhu's: "It was contrived in my opinion, strictly by the VC. It was a political rather than religious outbreak with political rather than religious motives."[46] In his memoir Nolting says he believes "the crisis was a Viet Cong conspiracy."[47] There was a "dump

Diem" movement headed by Harriman, Hilsman, and "others" in the White House, says Nolting, who were glad that he had been on vacation so they could give Diem "a lot of rope to hang himself."[48] Nolting spent his last days in Saigon trying to patch things up with Diem.

A U.S. Special National Intelligence Estimate on July 10, entitled "The Situation in South Vietnam," concluded that if the Diem regime failed to appease the Buddhists, more demonstrations would result along with the strong possibility of a coup attempt.[49] Evidently, brother Nhu had come to the same conclusion. On July 11, he proposed to some army general officers "that they stage a *coup d'etat* as soon as possible," a CIA cable the next day reported.[50] Nhu said no progress was being made in the war, that general officers had been "continually humiliated in the eyes of the people," and that they had to engineer a coup in order to regain popular respect. Nhu told them "he would support the coup"; that he was not "in accord" with Diem; that fast action was necessary because the new U.S. Ambassador "would bring about changes"; that the coup had to be staged at night and be "lightning fast"; and that all general officers should cooperate. On July 13, after a ceremony opening a course on the Strategic Hamlet Program for general officers, Nhu called all of the officers aside and criticized the government's handling of the Buddhists. The CIA cable recounting the event attributed these remarks to Nhu: "If the army was thinking of a coup d'etat, he did not blame the officers and would be with them. Nhu added that the Buddhist problem might then be solved."[51]

These reports and others caused a stir in Washington. What did they mean? The Deputy Assistant Secretary of State for Far Eastern Affairs, Ed Rice, wrote a memo to Rusk on July 15 saying that although two or three reports indicated Nhu was planning a coup, it was "not unlikely" that he was in fact seeking to "confuse and divide" the generals, "smoke out their intentions," and improve his personal position with them in case they mounted a successful coup.[52] Rice's analysis paralleled the American Embassy's view, which Nolting later described in this way: "Nhu was testing the generals' loyalty, trying to draw out the dissenters."[53] The authors of *The Pentagon Papers* conclude that Nhu's gambit was "a bold move designed to frighten coup plotters, and to throw them off guard"; they also claim the CIA reported rumors that Nhu was planning a "false coup" to "draw out and then crush the Buddhists."[54] It seems that Nhu was playing both ends against the middle: his ploy was a warning that the Ngo brothers were aware of coup plotting *and* an attempt to protect his own neck if a coup succeeded. Since coup plans were still at such an early stage, however, the timing of Nhu's slippery proposition seems out of place—unless it was connected to something else he had up his sleeve. As it turns out, he was indeed lying in the grass, waiting for the opportunity, between Nolting's departure on August 15 and Lodge's arrival on the 22nd, to strike.

On July 19 Diem had delivered a two-minute radio address, ostensibly to express conciliation to the Buddhists, but had spoken so coldly and made such minor concessions that it only inflamed the situation. Consequently, in August Buddhist militancy intensified: American television viewers were treated to more grisly bonze burnings on the 5th, 15th, and 18th; eventually seven monks and one nun put the match to themselves. The escalating tension in mid-August should have suggested that a showdown was coming, but when it happened on August 21, the American Embassy "was apparently caught almost completely off guard."[55] At midnight Diem placed South Vietnam under martial law and throughout the day Nhu had the Combat Police, his own shock Special Forces, carry out raids on pagodas, arresting over 1,400 Buddhists. Nhu used the cover of martial law to make it appear the raids had been ordered by army generals.

It immediately became obvious that Nhu had masterminded the entire affair and American–South Vietnamese relations went into a deep freeze. The State Department condemned the pagoda raids with these words:

> On the basis of information from Saigon, it appears that the Government of the Republic of Vietnam has instituted serious repressive measures against Vietnamese Buddhist leaders. The action represents a direct violation by the Vietnamese Government of assurances that it was pursuing a policy of conciliation with the Buddhists. The United States deplores repressive actions of this nature.[56]

Nhu ordered the American Embassy's phone lines cut. Angry Vietnamese generals went to the Embassy and asked if the U.S. would support a coup.

Nolting, in Hawaii with Lodge and Hilsman at the time, was stunned. He immediately sent Diem a personal telegram saying, "This is the first time you've ever gone back on your word to me."[57] Hilsman recalls the moment he and Nolting watched the news coming in over the teletype:

> I remember someone cursing softly as we read the tickers. The assault, timed for the period between ambassadors, was a deliberate affront. Diem had callously broken his word. He had made no gesture to salvage the dignity of the United States. He was presenting us with a *fait accompli* that he knew violated our deepest sense of decency and fair play, and he was doing it with a disdainful arrogance, contemptuously confident that we would swallow this

just as we had swallowed so much in the past. There was a stricken look on Nolting's face.[58]

This bitter pill would not be swallowed, however; Hilsman would make sure of that.

NOTES

1. USARPAC Intelligence Bulletin, June 1962.
2. Memo from Lieutenant General Marshall Carter, Acting Director, CIA, to McNamara, July 13, 1962, *PP*, Gravel ed., vol. 2, p. 686.
3. USARPAC Intelligence Bulletin, December 1962.
4. Vann, interview with von Littichau, July 22, 1963, p. 33.
5. Ibid., p. 21.
6. Ibid., p. 34.
7. Ibid., p. 34.
8. Wood, memo to Harriman, February 28, 1963, in *State History*, 1963, vol. 3, Document 48, pp. 130–31.
9. Serong Paper to Harkins, March 14, 1963, LBJ Library, Westmoreland Papers, Box 1.
10. Research memorandum RFE-58, July 1, 1963, JFK Library, Thomson Papers, Southeast Asia, Box 23.
11. Brent memo to Rufus Phillips, May 1, 1963, in *State History*, 1963, vol. 3, Document 102, pp. 256–58.
12. Report of the Joint Chiefs of Staff's Special Assistant for Counterinsurgency and Special Warfare, (Krulak), (undated but from July 1963), in *State History*, 1963, vol. 3, Document 207, pp. 455–65.
13. Colby, interview with the author, August 9, 1991.
14. Karnow, *Vietnam*, p. 218.
15. *PP*, Gravel ed., vol. 2, p. 226.
16. Helble cable to State, May 9, 1963, in *State History*, 1963, vol. 3, Document 112, pp. 277–78.
17. Nolting, *From Trust to Tragedy*, p. 108.
18. *PP*, Gravel ed., vol. 2, p. 226.
19. CIA Current Intelligence Memorandum, June 3, 1963, JFK Library, NSF, Country File, Vietnam, Box 197.
20. MACV message to CINCPAC, 041350Z, June 1963, JFK Library, NSF, Country File, Vietnam, Box 197.
21. MACV message to CINCPAC, 031726Z, June 1963, JFK Library, NSF, Country File, Vietnam, Box 197.

22. Trueheart cable to State, No. 1100, June 4, 1963, JFK Library, NSF, Country File, Vietnam, Box 197.

23. *State History*, 1963, vol. 3, pp. 352–53, n. 3.

24. Trueheart cable to State, No. 1100, June 4, 1963, JFK Library, NSF, Country File, Vietnam, Box 197.

25. Richard Lewy, *America in Vietnam* (New York: Oxford University Press, 1981), p. 96.

26. Thomas Boettcher, *Vietnam: The Valor and the Sorrow* (Toronto: Little, Brown 1985), p. 192.

27. Karnow, *Vietnam*, p. 281.

28. State cable to Saigon No. 1207, June 11, 1963, in *State History*, 1963, vol. 3, Document 167, pp. 381–83.

29. Nolting, *From Trust to Tragedy*, p. 112.

30. Trueheart cable to State, No. 1168, June 12, 1963, in *State History*, 1963, Document 169, pp. 385–87.

31. *State History*, 1963, vol. 3, pp. 386–87, n. 5.

32. Rust, *Kennedy in Vietnam*, p. 102.

33. State cable to Saigon No. 1250, June 19, 1963, JFK Library, NSF, Country File, Vietnam, Box 197.

34. State cable to Saigon, No. 1219, June 14, 1963, in *State History*, 1963, vol. 3, Document 175, pp. 394–95.

35. For Nolting's approval see *State History*, 1963, vol. 3, Document 133, pp. 316–17; see n. 1 for JFK's approval.

36. Trueheart cable to State No. 1195, June 16, 1963, in *State History*, 1963, vol. 3, Document 179, pp. 398–99.

37. Trueheart cable to State No. 1182, June 14, 1963, in *State History*, 1963, vol. 3, Document 172, p. 391.

38. CIA Information Report, June 28, 1963, in *State History*, 1963, vol. 3, Document 190, pp. 423–25.

39. Forrestal cable to McGeorge Bundy, July 1, 1963, in *State History*, 1963, vol. 3, Document 195, p. 432.

40. Nolting, *From Trust to Tragedy*, p. 111.

41. State cable to Saigon No. 196, July 1, 1963, in *State History*, 1963, vol. 3, Document 196, pp. 433–34.

42. Forrestal memo to Kennedy, July 3, 1963, in *State History*, 1963, vol. 3, Document 202, pp. 447–48.

43. Memorandum of Conversation, White House, July 4, 1963, 11–11:50 A.M., in *State History*, 1963, vol. 3, Document 205, pp. 451–53.

44. CIA cable, TDCS-3/552, 822, SUBJECT: "Military Plan for Overthrow of the Diem Regime," July 8, 1963, JFK Library, NSF, Country File, Vietnam, Box 198/199.

45. Nolting, *From Trust to Tragedy*, p. 116.

46. Michael Maclear, *The 10,000 Day War: Vietnam, 1945–1975* (New York: Avon, 1981), p. 64.

47. Nolting, *From Trust to Tragedy*, p. 115.

48. Maclear, *The 10,000 Day War*, p. 64.

49. SNIE 52-2-63, "The Situation in South Vietnam," July 10, 1963, in *State History*, 1963, vol. 3, Document 217, pp. 483–85.

50. CIA cable, TDCS DB-3/655,517, July 12, 1963, JFK Library, NSF, Country File, Vietnam, Box 198/199.

51. CIA cable, TDCS DB-3/655, 523, July 13, 1963, *Declassified Documents*, 1985, 2470.

52. Rice memo to Rusk, July 15, 1963, in *State History*, 1963, vol. 3, Document 220, pp. 488–91.

53. Nolting, *From Trust to Tragedy*, p. 117.

54. *PP*, Gravel ed., vol. 2, p. 228. The authors do not give any date or other identification for these CIA reports, and they have not been found.

55. Ibid.

56. State cable to Saigon No. 226/449, August 21, 1963, Army Center for Military History, Washington D.C.; see also JFK Library, Newman Papers.

57. Nolting, *From Trust to Tragedy*, p. 121.

58. Hilsman, *To Move a Nation*, p. 482.

PART V

THE TRAGIC
CROSSROADS

CHAPTER EIGHTEEN

"COPS AND ROBBERS"

THE SATURDAY NIGHT SPECIAL

Hilsman returned to Washington and conferred with Colby, Forrestal, and Krulak on August 21. The four decided the most important order of business was to find out who was in control in Saigon.[1] Accordingly, Colby asked the CIA for data, Hilsman cabled Lodge asking for the latest information on the situation there,[2] and Taylor cabled Harkins with a similar request.[3] Lodge, who had been diverted that night from a planned trip to Hong Kong by a presidential message,[4] arrived at Tan Son Nhut Airport at 9:30 P.M. on the evening of the 22nd. Harkins said that the war was still going well and that, although operations against the Viet Cong might drop until "things settle down," that the "present situation might be a blessing in disguise"; a "few bones were bruised" in the pagodas, but military authority had been established "without firing a shot," and this had "precluded a lot of bloodshed which would have spilled if rival factions had tried to take over."[5]

On Saturday, August 24, Kennedy was at Hyannis Port, Rusk in New York, McNamara mountain climbing in Wyoming, and McCone vacationing in California when news from the new American Ambassador began arriving in Washington. Rusk's Under Secretary, Ball, was playing golf at the Chevy Chase Club, as was Krulak, while McNamara's Deputy

345

Secretary, Gilpatric, was at his farm in Maryland. Lodge's first cable reported that Secretary of State Thuan was firmly backing Diem but advocating that the U.S. "split the Nhus off" from him.[6] His second cable reported that a key South Vietnamese general had said that retaining Diem was preferable "providing all Ngo family influence could be permanently and effectively eradicated."[7] The Saigon CIA Station's answer to Colby's query came in at this point, reporting that General Don had invited a CIA operative, Lucien Conein,[8] to the General Staff headquarters and informed him that the army had nothing to do with the Buddhist crackdown. When Conein probed for the generals' intentions, Don demurred; he said the U.S. should make its position known and said martial law was a first step, and then added, cryptically, "the secret of what is going to happen is not mine to give."[9] In Lodge's third cable, still on the 24th, he said that in further conversations with South Vietnamese officers the suggestion had been made that the U.S. had only to indicate to the generals that it "would be happy to see Diem and/or Nhus go, and [the] deed would be done."[10] Lodge said he felt it was not that simple and that U.S. action under the circumstances would be "a shot in the dark."

Hilsman, with Harriman's support, then drafted the single most controversial cable of the Vietnam War. Known as the "Saturday Night Special" or simply the "August 24 cable," it mired Kennedy in a plot to overthrow Diem and created an irreversible division in the administration. The cable instructed Lodge to demand the removal of Nhu, and added that, if this ultimatum was unacceptable, "We must face the possibility that Diem himself cannot be preserved."[11] Lodge was instructed to tell "key military leaders" that the U.S. would not support Vietnam militarily and economically unless these steps were taken immediately. Diem was to be given a chance to oust Nhu, the cable said, and added:

> but if he remains obdurate, then we are prepared to accept the obvious implication that we can no longer support Diem. You may also tell appropriate military commanders we will give them direct support in any interim period of breakdown [of the] central government mechanism.

Forrestal participated at various points in the drafting of this cable. The role of Rusk is shrouded in controversy, as is the entire saga of its coordination.

That saga begins on a bad note: it would appear that someone has had a serious failure of memory or is simply not telling the truth. Hilsman claims that he sent Rusk—who was at the U.N. in New York—a copy of the cable and that the Secretary *strengthened* it by adding "the important provision for continuing to furnish the Vietnamese war supplies if there were a breakdown in central government communications for any reason."[12] Rusk, of course, flatly denies Hilsman's story, and told author William Rust that he was "absolutely certain" he had not put this sentence in the cable.[13] The fact that Rusk never kept a diary or organized record, refused to set aside his own personal papers when he left the State Department, and "systematically destroyed records of confidential conversations with Presidents Kennedy and Johnson,"[14] has made it difficult to substantiate crucial details such as this.

Forrestal claims Kennedy participated in the early part of the coordination process. In a 1981 interview with Rust he described it in the following way. On Saturday afternoon he called Kennedy in Hyannis Port, read him the cable, and said that so far the coordination had only occurred in the State Department. When Kennedy asked why it could not wait until Monday when everyone was back, Forrestal said it was because Harriman and Hilsman "really want to get this thing out right away." Kennedy replied: "Well, go and see what you can do to get it cleared."[15] He specifically asked that McCone be consulted.

The next step, involving the Joint Chiefs, is problematical—the precise role they played is still unclear. Forrestal called Krulak at the Chevy Chase Club. Krulak claimed, in a 1981 interview with Rust, that he refused to "touch" it, saying it would need approval at higher levels in the Pentagon, and that he set out in search of Taylor.[16] This much of Krulak's claim might be true; the problem arises because he did not actually take a copy of the cable to Taylor until around midnight that evening, and did so then only because Taylor, apparently upset after learning about the cable from *Gilpatric*, had ordered a copy be sent to him at his quarters.

By this time Harriman had shown the cable to Under Secretary Ball at his house, and Ball called Kennedy to read him its key passages. Ball reports that the President's position was this: if both Rusk and Gilpatric agreed, then Ball could send the cable.[17] Ball then called Rusk. Ball reports the Secretary's position was this: if Ball, Harriman, and Kennedy were on board, so was he. In other words, at this point Kennedy would approve it if Rusk would approve it and vice versa, while neither had actually done so or even talked to each other.

The story of the coordination of the Saturday Night Special to Saigon ends the same way it started: with two accounts that flatly contradict each other. Whereas the first conflicting testimony was between Hilsman and Rusk, this one is between Forrestal and Krulak. The Joint Chiefs needed to be advised about such a major decision too, and Forrestal claims that Krulak called and said Taylor did not like the cable but would "raise no objections" to it. Krulak denies this, and says he played no role whatsoever after informing Taylor about the cable.[18] Taylor claims he did not learn about the cable until Gilpatric's call that evening, at which time he immediately ordered that a copy be sent to him at his home. By then it was too late to stop the cable. *The Pentagon Papers* indicates Taylor approved the cable for the JCS,[19] and Hilsman at first claimed Taylor "approved the cable without question,"[20] but, if Taylor is right about when he first saw it, he could not have approved it. As it turns out, Hilsman later admitted Taylor was right.[21]

Since Taylor *was* right, either Krulak made up the story he told Forrestal about Taylor's approval, or Forrestal concocted the story himself. It appears that Forrestal's account, not Krulak's, is inaccurate on this point. An August 24 memorandum for the record written by Krulak—which was included in the State Department history (volume 3) released in May 1991—clarifies the matter of the Krulak telephone call to Forrestal and the matter of Krulak's search for Taylor.[22] For one thing, Krulak had not been searching for Taylor at all that day. Krulak did call Forrestal all right, but not to tell him Taylor had approved the cable; he could not have for the simple reason that Krulak had not spoken to Taylor at all. This is what actually took place: at 6:00 P.M. Krulak received a call about the situation from Vice Admiral Riley, Director of the Joint Staff, and the two placed a conference call to Forrestal. He told them that the cable had been sent to Kennedy and that clearance from the Defense Department was not desired. Forrestal said he was only "seeking to advise Mr. Gilpatric of the message." This remark was meant to deceive, since Kennedy had specifically asked that the cable be cleared by Gilpatric. Forrestal then asked Krulak if he would show the cable to Taylor, and, when Krulak agreed, asked him to come to the White House situation room and get a copy. While Krulak was on his way, Forrestal called Gilpatric.

Forrestal knew he had to get Gilpatric's concurrence, otherwise he would be directly contravening the President's express instructions. How the matter was presented to Gilpatric, of course, was the key to what he would say. Forrestal made the call just before 7:00 P.M. and put it to Gilpatric this way: the President, the Secretary of State, and the Under Secretary of State all "favored" sending the cable.[23] Gilpatric did not like it, but he cleared it; how could he do otherwise after what Forrestal had said? The truth was, of course, that both Kennedy and Rusk had given only an if-you-will-then-I-will answer. To say that Kennedy and Rusk "favored" sending the cable was Forrestal's second indiscretion within an hour. Gilpatric had been deceived, but he was still worried, and he called Taylor to tell him what was going on. Everyone that Kennedy had specifically asked to be consulted had been contacted, with the exception of McCone. McCone was known to think Diem was the best person to lead the government in Vietnam; consequently, when Richard Helms cleared the cable for the CIA the matter of consulting McCone was dropped.

Helms apparently agreed that Diem should go; he reportedly said: "It's about time we bit this bullet."[24]

It was just after 7:00 P.M. when Krulak showed up in the White House situation room. After he read all the messages that had come in during the day, Forrestal showed him a copy of the proposed cable. At this time Forrestal reiterated that it had been sent to Kennedy for approval, and then "stated he had just finished discussing it with Mr. Gilpatric by telephone, and that Mr. Gilpatric was in accord with its content." Forrestal did not ask Krulak for his views, but Krulak said it appeared "we must start with Diem and not foreclose him." He also said that the South Vietnamese Army was not "homogeneous."[25] Forrestal, of course, picked no argument with either of these comments and sent Krulak on his way with a copy for Taylor.

Taylor, however, could not be found. Krulak called Taylor's home shortly before 7:30 P.M. and left a message to be notified when he returned. As soon as Krulak had gone, Forrestal called Kennedy and told him that everyone had concurred. This too was stretching the truth; and there was no justification for being anything other than 100 percent accurate on what the President's top advisors had said about such a momentous decision. Forrestal's story led the President to agree that the cable could be sent. Forrestal called Krulak and told him to add, in his report to Taylor, the fact that Kennedy had approved the cable. Krulak immediately called Taylor's home again, but to no avail, and so he then "made specific arrangements" for Taylor to call when he returned. The cable to Saigon went out at 9:36 P.M., and Taylor returned to his quarters soon afterward. Taylor, however, either did not receive Krulak's message or he ignored it: at 11:45 P.M. Krulak called and found Taylor at home. Krulak then delivered the cable.

It was around midnight, then, when Krulak showed up on Taylor's doorstep. Taylor describes his thoughts then:

> On reading the cable, my first reaction was that the anti-Diem group centered in State had taken advantage of the absence of the principal officials to get out instructions which would never have been approved as written under normal circumstances.[26]

Taylor, however, did nothing about it that night or all of the next day. Taylor's actions that night are problematical: since he admits to being called by Gilpatric, which could only have occurred between 7:00 and 7:30 P.M.—unless he was purposely evading all of Krulak's calls—what was he doing in the interval between then and midnight? After all, once he got Gilpatric's call, he knew a major problem was brewing. Why did he make no further attempt to find out what was going on? The answers to these questions are elusive, but his inaction the following day is even more troubling.

If Taylor is telling the truth about his initial reaction to the cable, why didn't he call Kennedy? This question seems justified if the Chairman of the Joint Chiefs of Staff indeed believed that the President had just been taken advantage of regarding an extremely serious and far-reaching decision. Taylor describes his inaction with the following paltry sentence: "In the absence of senior officials from Washington, I had all of the following Sunday to meditate on the situation and the probable consequences of the cable." Krulak's August 24 memorandum for record bears out Taylor's reaction. Taylor told Krulak this about the cable:

> It reflects the well-known compulsion of Hilsman and Forrestal to depose Diem and, had McGeorge Bundy been present, he would not have approved the message. Finally, he stated that the message had not been given the quality of interdepartmental staffing it deserved, and that he would be prepared to say so at a proper time.[27]

Why wait? When *is* the proper time to tell the President he has just been misinformed about the unity of his government with respect to U.S. encouragement of a coup d'etat in a foreign country?

The next day, while Taylor was meditating, the following events took place. Ambassador Lodge, amazed, interpreted the cable as a direct order to prepare for a coup against Diem: "They were asking me to overthrow a government I hadn't even presented my credentials to."[28] Lodge immediately convened the Country Team to decide on how to proceed in implementing it. They decided that Diem would never agree to remove Nhu, and so they quickly sent a cable to the State Department saying the "risk" of following the plan as sent "was not worth taking, with Nhu in control of combat forces in Saigon." Lodge proposed to change the plan as follows: they would not approach Diem, but "go straight to the generals" instead.[29] "Agree to [the] modification proposed," the State Department replied the same day.[30] Since Rusk was still away, Ball was in charge, but this approval was not signed; there is no time of transmission or receipt of it; and it appears to have been sent through CIA channels. In other words, this crucial change in the plan does not appear to have been authorized by anyone higher than Ball. A few hours later a Voice of America broadcast in Saigon declared that officials in Washington:

> say the [pagoda] raids were made by police under the control of President Diem's brother, Ngo Dinh Nhu. They say America may

cut its aid to Vietnam if President Diem does not get rid of the police officials responsible.[31]

An irritated Lodge immediately dashed off a cable saying this broadcast had complicated an "already difficult problem" by eliminating the possibility that an effort by the generals could achieve surprise.[32]

When Kennedy met his advisors on Monday morning, he discovered the uncertainty and lack of unanimity of views among his advisors. It was a most disturbing situation. They quarreled over the cable and the events that had led up to it.[33] Taylor took issue with Hilsman's comment that Admiral Felt had called personally to counsel "against delay." Hilsman's comment was not true, but Taylor was "visibly shaken" in the meeting to find out that Felt had been making phone calls to Hilsman during the coordination on the 24th. The next day Taylor sent a telegram reprimanding the Commander-in-Chief of the Pacific for "expressing his views on a substantive issue outside of proper channels."[34] During the meeting on the 26th, Hilsman stuck to his guns that the Nhus had to go, and Kennedy, unimpressed with this meeting, declared another would be held the next day. Taylor suggested that Nolting should attend. Hilsman argued against this, saying Nolting's views were "colored," to which the President quickly remarked, "Maybe properly [so]."

McCone was upset that he wasn't consulted, and the President was furious with Forrestal over it. Had he not specifically asked for this? Forrestal offered his resignation, but Kennedy refused, saying, "You're not worth firing. You owe me something, so you stick around."[35] The quarreling got worse that week and continued to escalate.

"WE THOUGHT HE WAS FOR THE COUP PLAN"

What would happen if "we find we are faced with having to live with Diem and Nhu," the President asked at the August 26 White House meeting.[36] It would be "horrible to contemplate," Hilsman replied. Secretary Rusk then interjected that unless a major change in South Vietnam's policy could be "engineered," it appeared "we must actually decide whether to move our resources out or to move our troops in." With simple clarity Rusk had just described the fork in the road toward which the administration's Vietnam policy appeared headed: withdrawal while losing or massive American intervention.

That no consensus was reached—*before* the August 24 coup cable was sent—on whether intervention or withdrawal were, in fact, the only alternatives to a coup, is a major indictment of the way the administration was functioning. Unfortunately, Rusk's question that day did not produce the definitive answers necessary to generate such a consensus. On the contrary, as the momentous decisions approached, the most basic questions remained unanswered: Can we still win with Diem? Can we win without him? And why are the reports about the battlefield situation so conflicting? The discussion of these issues was muted by the sometimes personal or even vitriolic arguments they engendered, and also, for a few days, by the apparent momentum for a coup that the cable itself had generated. For example, an August 27 cable from the CIA Station in Saigon reported a meeting between Conein and General Tran Thien Khiem, an influential member of the Joint General Staff who also exercised some control over the secret police.[37] Khiem told Conein that a "committee" of generals headed by Doung Van "Big" Minh had "agreed a coup will take place within one week."

The apparent likelihood of a coup should have prompted an examination of the fundamental questions involved but, instead, the administration was consumed that day with finding out who would be carrying it out and what actions the U.S. might have to take in response. Harkins reported emergency evacuation planning and identified who might be among the coup plotters;[38] Harriman wondered "if some people were getting cold feet," while Hilsman said "he could bring Nolting around" but was "afraid of Maxwell Taylor";[39] and Forrestal arranged for Hilsman and Colby to brief Kennedy on the "latest developments and progress in planning."[40] During these presentations, however, something other than the coup was troubling the President. How were the civil disturbances affecting the war effort? Only slightly, replied Krulak: "There had been no dramatic degradation of South Vietnamese military capability." There hadn't been enough time for the Viet Cong to react yet anyway, Rusk added, while Nolting pitched in that "the unrest was limited to the cities and had not yet affected the countryside."

As the discussion dragged on about various matters—whether Diem had lied to Nolting; whether the unrest had changed Diem's mind; Madame Nhu's unstoppable mouth; Nhu's relationship to Diem; how much military support there was for a coup—the more basic question of whether the coup was necessary to win the war irresistibly impressed itself on the President. Finally Kennedy asked Nolting this: would Diem's actions of the last few months prevent Diem from carrying on the war? It was a question that should have been posed prior to sending the cable on August 24. Nolting's answer was vague. He "called attention to the fact that [CIA] agents had already told some generals to undertake a coup." Even Nolting, who had been dead set against a coup, could not now envision turning it off: "If we go back on these generals now," he said, "we will lose them."

Suddenly the context changed, and for a brief moment the fear of being trapped in the wrong place became manifest. Was it too late to turn back? Kennedy offered what was no more than a desperate hope: the situation hadn't gone "so far we can't delay." Hilsman helped out: had not Harkins reported that the generals said they would need a few days? McNamara had the answer: we need to ask both Lodge and Harkins if this coup can succeed, and if it can't we "caution the generals not to move." Kennedy wanted to know right then what Harkins' position was, and the minutes of the meeting indicate the following: "General Taylor responded that General Harkins had never been asked for his views—that he merely got orders."

The discussion then drifted to something else, but the President interrupted and returned to the views of Harkins and Lodge. The minutes state:

> The President said we should send a cable to Ambassador Lodge and General Harkins asking for their estimate of the prospects of a coup by the generals. They should also be asked to recommend whether we should proceed with the generals or wait. He also wanted their views on what we should do if the situation deteriorates.

The State Department cable to Lodge that evening asked the questions posed by the President and said Washington would "give you all possible support" in developing the best possible course.[41] This properly gave Lodge the freedom to speak his own mind. Taylor's cable to Harkins left the MACV commander little latitude for how he should respond.[42] Taylor ended his cable by saying that the August 24 coup cable had been prepared without the participation of the Department of Defense or the Joint Chiefs of Staff, and further, that "authorities are now having second thoughts."

There followed a lengthy, confused, and argumentative White House meeting that began at noon on August 28.[43] Nolting's comment that only Diem could hold South Vietnam together threw the session into an uproar and led to an acrimonious and heated argument in which Ball, Harriman, and Hilsman ganged up on Nolting. McNamara began expressing strong doubts about the prospects that the coup could proceed, and Robert Kennedy began asking tough questions, such as, "What we would do if Diem acted to destroy the coup before the generals were ready to pull it off." The President finally adjourned the meeting and asked everyone to

return at 6:00 P.M. Harriman was so angry with Nolting that he refused
to ride in the same limousine with him afterward. The widening breach
among Kennedy's advisors deeply troubled him and he confided to a
friend: "My god, my government is coming apart."[44]

As in the meeting on the previous day, Kennedy had again been preoccupied with Harkins during this midday session, referring to him several
times. For example:

> The President commented that we had asked General Harkins twice
> if he approved of our going ahead in support of a coup. Both
> Ambassador Lodge and General Harkins say we should support
> the rebel generals.

This was only partly true; Harkins had not, as Taylor had pointed out,
been asked for his views; but Harkins had, as Kennedy was saying, supported the move. When Harkins' response to Taylor's message arrived
shortly after the noon meeting, however, it appeared that Harkins was
now against the coup.[45] He said because he had presumed the coup cable
represented the U.S. government's position, "I had no choice but to go
along." He also said that although the "die is cast" the generals would
still not do it "unless we give the final say so." He argued that the military
"could live with Diem if the Nhus were out of the picture." He concluded
that there was insufficient reason for a "crash approval on our part at this
time."

When the 6:00 P.M. meeting convened, Kennedy asked Rusk, McNamara, McGeorge Bundy, and Taylor to step into another room with
him.[46] Kennedy told them he was in doubt as to General Harkins' views.
"We thought he was for the coup plan," Kennedy said, "but General
Harkins apparently thought that a decision had been made in Washington
to back a coup and that his task was to carry out a decision communicated
to him." Kennedy said he wanted Harkins' views on "what we should do,
not his reaction to what he thought was the decision here." The four men
returned to the other room and Kennedy announced that three messages
would be sent to Saigon: Taylor would again ask for Harkins' views;
Kennedy would ask Lodge for his, and also direct that there must be "full
coordination" between Washington and Saigon; and a third "general"
cable covering the earlier noon meeting, this to be drafted by McNamara,
Harriman, Bundy, Forrestal, and Hilsman. The minutes indicate the meeting ended this way:

> The meeting broke up with Mr. Harriman's saying "Mr. President,
> I was very puzzled by the cable from General Harkins until I read
> the outgoing from General Taylor." (The President had some diffi-

culty containing himself until everyone left the room, whereupon he burst into laughter and said, "Averell Harriman is one sharp cookie.")

The truth, of course, is that Taylor did not have to twist Harkins' arm to get him to oppose the coup. Harkins was indeed against it, while the Ambassador was for it. The Americans were as divided in Saigon as they were in Washington.

When the answers from Lodge[47] and Harkins arrived,[48] the illusion of unity was over. Lodge complained that Harkins wanted him to first try and wean Diem away from Nhu. Lodge said this would be regarded by the generals as a "sign of American indecision and delay." The following day he added that Diem would oppose getting rid of Nhu anyway: "He wishes more Nhus, not less."[49] Lodge's views would only harden further as the days went by; on September 5 he would send Washington this observation about Diem's government:

> They are essentially a medieval, Oriental despotism of the classic family type, who understand few, if any, of the arts of popular government. They cannot talk to the people; they cannot cultivate the press; they cannot delegate authority or inspire trust; they cannot comprehend the idea of government as the servant of the people. They are interested in physical security and survival against any threat whatsoever—Communist or non-Communist.[50]

By the time Lodge wrote these words, however, the generals had balked, and the chance to topple Diem, for the moment, had passed.

"This particular coup is finished," began an August 31 cable from the CIA Station in Saigon.[51] In a crucial meeting with General Khiem, it said, Harkins' judgment was that the generals "were not ready and could not achieve [a] balance of forces favorable to them." Consequently, Harkins had declined to give any American assurances. This led to a charge by Paul Kattenburg, a State Department official, in an August 31 meeting of high-level officials at State, that Harkins had not carried out his instructions. Both Rusk and McNamara jumped to Harkins' defense, saying that in light of General Khiem's wavering remarks Harkins had done the right thing.[52] It did not make much sense to quibble about it anyway: the coup was off.

Kennedy was not at this White House meeting—he was resting at Hyannis Port, where he would give an important interview to Walter Cronkite two days later. Someone who had attended hardly any of these meetings happened to be on hand, however: Vice President Johnson. He complained that he had not known—until the following Tuesday evening—about the actions taken the previous Saturday. Notes taken by Bromley Smith, the NSC Executive Secretary, indicate that Johnson made the following remarks:

> He had never been sympathetic with our proposal to produce a change of government in Vietnam by means of plotting with Vietnamese generals. Now that the generals had failed to organize a coup, he thought we ought to reestablish ties to the Diem government as quickly as possible and get forward with the war against the Viet Cong.[53]

Johnson was obviously not only upset at having been cut out, but also completely opposed to what had been going on. That these harsh and aggressive remarks had a chilling effect on those present is attested to by the fact that no one said anything in reply. LBJ also said he recognized the "evils" of Diem but there was no alternative, and that there was certainly no way to pull out. "We must establish ourselves," Johnson announced, "and stop playing cops and robbers."

NOTES

1. Krulak, memo for record, August 21, 1963, in *State History*, 1963, vol. 3, Document 265, pp. 601–2.

2. Hilsman cable to Lodge No. 235, August 22, 1963, in *State History*, 1963, vol. 3, Document 268, pp. 604–5.

3. Taylor memo to Rusk, August 23, 1963, with Harkins' reply, in *State History*, 1963, vol. 3, Document 270, pp. 606–7.

4. *State History*, 1963, vol. 3, p. 606, n. 3.

5. Harkins telegram to Taylor, No. 1,495, August 22, 1963, in *State History*, 1963, vol. 3, Document 270 (attachment), pp. 607–10.

6. Lodge cable to State No. 324, August 24, 1963, in *State History*, 1963, vol. 3, Document 273, pp. 611–12.

7. Lodge cable to State No. 320, August 24, 1963, in *State History*, 1963, vol. 3, Document 274, pp. 613–14.

8. Conein's name is still missing from the cable, but Don himself revealed it was Conein in his book *Our Endless War: Inside Vietnam* (Novato, CA: Presidio Press, 1978), p. 91.

9. CIA telegram from Saigon No. 0265, August 24, 1963, in *State History*, 1963, vol. 3, Document 275, pp. 614–20.

10. Lodge cable to State No. 329, August 24, 1963, in *State History*, 1963, vol. 3, Document 276, pp. 620–21.

11. State cable to Lodge, August 24, 1963, in *State History*, 1963, vol. 3, Document 281, pp. 628–29.

12. Hilsman, *To Move a Nation*, p. 488.

13. Rust, *Kennedy in Vietnam*, p. 112.

14. Thomas Schoenbaum, *Waging Peace and War: Dean Rusk in the Truman, Kennedy, and Johnson Years* (New York: Simon and Schuster, 1988), p. 12.

15. Rust, *Kennedy in Vietnam*, p. 114.

16. Ibid.

17. NBC News White Paper, "Death of Diem," December 22, 1971, Part 2, Section 8, p. 8; and Rust, *Kennedy in Vietnam*, p. 115.

18. Krulak's version of this conflict comes from an interview he gave to Rust on December 2, 1981 (see *Kennedy in Vietnam*, p. 116), while Forrestal's comes from the NBC News White Paper.

19. *PP*, Gravel ed., vol. 2, p. 235.

20. Hilsman, *To Move a Nation*, p. 488.

21. Excerpt from Krulak, memo for record, August 28, 1963, in *State History*, 1963, vol. 3, p. 675, n. 1.

22. *State History*, 1963, vol. 3, Document 282, pp. 630–31.

23. NBC News White Paper, "Death of Diem," December 22, 1971, Part 2, Section 8, p. 8; and Rust, *Kennedy in Vietnam*, p. 115.

24. Thomas Powers, *The Man Who Kept the Secrets* (New York: Knopf, 1979), p. 164; and Rust, *Kennedy in Vietnam*, p. 115.

25. *State History*, 1963, vol. 3, Document 282, p. 630.

26. Maxwell Taylor, *Swords and Plowshares*, p. 292.

27. Krulak Memorandum for Record, August 24, 1963, *State History*, 1963, vol. 3, Document 282, pp. 630–31.

28. *International Herald Tribune*, July 26, 1975.

29. "Lodge's Reply to Washington," *PP*, Gravel ed., vol. 2, p. 735.

30. Ball cable to Lodge, August 25, 1963, in *State History*, 1963, vol. 3, Document 286, p. 635. The cable was from "Acting Secretary of State."

31. VOA broadcast in Saigon, August 24, 1963, in *State History*, 1963, vol. 3, Document 287, p. 636.

32. Lodge cable to State, August 26, 1963, *State History*, 1963, vol. 3, Document 288, pp. 636–37.

33. Memorandum for the Record, White House meeting, noon, August 26, 1963, in *State History*, 1963, vol. 3, Document 289, pp. 638–41. It was written by Krulak.

34. *State History*, 1963, vol. 3, p. 639, n. 7.

35. These comments are according to Forrestal, in an interview he gave to William Rust on September 2, 1981; see *Kennedy in Vietnam*, p. 119.

36. Minutes of the noon, August 26, 1963, White House meeting, in *State History*, 1963, vol. 3, Document 289, pp. 638–41.

37. Saigon Station telegram to CIA, August 27, 1963, in *State History*, 1963, vol. 3, Document 299, pp. 653–55.

38. Harkins telegram to Taylor, August 27, 1963, in *State History*, 1963, vol. 3, Document 300, pp. 655–57.

39. Memo of telephone conversation between Harriman and Hilsman, 1:50 P.M., August 27, 1963, in *State History*, 1963, vol. 3, Document 301, pp. 657–58.

40. Forrestal memo to Kennedy, August 27, 1963, in *State History*, 1963, vol. 3, Document 302, pp. 658–59.

41. State cable to Lodge No. 256, August 27, 1963, in State History, 1963, vol. 3, Document 305, pp. 667–68.

42. Taylor telegram to Harkins, August 28, 1963, in *State History*, 1963, vol. 3, Document 309, p. 675.

43. Memorandum of the Conference in the White House, noon, August 28, 1963, in *State History*, 1963, vol. 4, Document 1, pp. 1–6, and Document 2, pp. 6–9.

44. Karnow, *Vietnam*, p. 288.

45. Harkins' telegram to Taylor, August 29, 1963, in *State History*, 1963, vol. 4, Document 4, pp. 10–11.

46. Memorandum of White House Conversation, 6:00 P.M., August 28, 1963, in *State History*, 1963, vol. 4, Document 6, pp. 12–14; for the restricted meeting see n. 2 on p. 13.

47. Lodge telegrams to Kennedy (No. 373) and to State (No. 375), August 29, 1963, in *State History*, 1963, vol. 4, Documents 11, p. 20, and 12, pp. 20–22, respectively.

48. Harkins telegram to Taylor, August 29, 1963, in *State History*, 1963, vol. 4, Document 13, pp. 23–24.

49. Lodge cable to State No. 383, August 30, 1963, in *State History*, 1963, vol. 4, Document 20, pp. 38–39.

50. Lodge cable to State No. 417, September 5, 1963, in *State History*, 1963, vol. 4, Document 60, pp. 109–110.

51. Saigon Station cable to CIA, August 31, 1963, in *State History*, 1963, vol. 4, Document 32, p. 64.

52. Memorandum of a Conversation, Department of State, 11:00 A.M., August 31, 1963, in *State History*, 1963, vol. 3, Document 37, pp. 69–74.

53. *State History*, 1963, vol. 3, p. 74, n. 7.

CHAPTER NINETEEN

A CITY OF TWO TALES

GENESIS OF THE KENNEDY WITHDRAWAL PLAN

The origin of the withdrawal plan dates back to April 6, 1962, when Kennedy commented that the U.S. should be prepared to seize upon any favorable moment to reduce its commitment to Vietnam. McNamara carried it a step further a month later at the May 8 SECDEF conference when he asked a surprised Harkins when the South Vietnamese would be ready to take over the war effort. At the sixth conference on July 23 McNamara made the intent to withdraw official. Nevertheless, at the next conference, on October 8, Harkins, preoccupied with presenting his "explosion" operation, "did not have time" to discuss the withdrawal plans. Finally, McNamara cast the idea in concrete at the May 6, 1963, conference, at which time he also introduced the 1,000-man withdrawal to be accomplished by the end of the year.

Actually the idea of pulling out 1,000 men predates the May meeting, and was already shrouded in mystery and intrigue. Vietnam Working Group Director Wood reported to Hilsman on April 18, 1963, that McNamara would tell the Pentagon "to cut their forces by 1,000 at the end of this year," and advised Hilsman that if he tried to get the Defense Department to put a ceiling on forces *before* they were asked to make this cut, it would only add "one more emotional element to an already tight situation."[1] If State insisted on a ceiling and the war suddenly took "a turn for the worse," Wood predicted, "we would then have to approve a break in the ceiling and DOD would have to rush in additional men." Wood said that State could achieve a ceiling simply by vetoing "any further requests for increases," and he recommended that they "quietly support McNamara's intention to achieve a significant reduction by the end of the year, *provided things go well*" [emphasis added].

The situation was a lot tighter than Wood knew, for he was unaware, of course, that Kennedy had decided to withdraw from Vietnam after the 1964 elections knowing things would *not* go well and fully aware that, in some quarters, he would be damned "as a Communist appeaser." A conservative backlash was only part of Kennedy's concern. He also had to worry about rising congressional criticism from liberals opposed to the deepening American presence in Vietnam, which is why he confided his plan to Mansfield—one of the most vocal critics; and also why he decided to *begin* the pullout *before* the election. The Mansfield discussions and the Wood memo to Hilsman make it clear that Kennedy and McNamara had agreed to start the withdrawal at the beginning of 1964, the intent being to restrain such criticism by trickling Americans home from Vietnam over the course of the election campaign.

What made the 1,000-man withdrawal particularly risky was the criticism from conservatives that would be unleashed if it were carried out against the backdrop of a collapsing battlefield situation. The deception of progress begun in 1962—which had justified the continuation and expansion of the American effort—was now seized on by the President and used as the *reason* for the 1,000-man withdrawal. This meant that Kennedy, despite his realization that the intelligence underpinning the success story was unsound, would have to pretend that he believed it, otherwise his willingness to withdraw while losing would become obvious. This pretense was as dangerous as the idea of the 1,000-man withdrawal itself, but Kennedy apparently felt he had no other choice, other than to abandon the idea altogether. At the outset he delivered a convincing performance, as evidenced by Wood's memo: everyone assumed the withdrawal was tied to success on the battlefield. The Buddhist crisis that followed underscored the fragility of the course Kennedy was pursuing, making optimistic public comments by him unwise.

The military too, for the time being, did not understand—any more than the State Department did—that Kennedy had reconciled himself to withdraw, in a losing battlefield situation, after the election. They also believed the withdrawal was to be tied to the success of the war effort, and were planning to allocate the resources they thought necessary to win. Withdrawal planning was interwoven with the discussion of the Comprehensive Plan for South Vietnam (CPSVN) and the Military Assistance Program (MAP). In these discussions, there were disagreements about how much money should be spent on the future war effort. For example, in May 1963, William Bundy thought more would be necessary for the 1965–69 MAP for Vietnam than McNamara did.[2] In this debate too, the notion of battlefield progress was useful in heading off high spending and in influencing the pullout schedule. When McNamara called for a review of the CPSVN at the May 6 SECDEF conference, he used the prevailing optimism over the war to argue that the plan's assistance was too costly and that its schedule for the planned withdrawal of U.S. forces too slow. He followed this up on May 8 with two memos to his staff: the first directing development of plans to replace U.S. with South Vietnamese forces, as soon as possible, to permit the withdrawal of 1,000 U.S. troops by the end of 1963; and the second requesting a complete overhaul, by September 1, of the MAP recommended in the CPSVN.

On May 9, the JCS formally directed CINCPAC to take the necessary actions resulting from that week's Honolulu conference and revise the CPSVN, and singled out the requirement for a U.S. force withdrawal. The JCS directive read:

> As a matter of urgency a plan for the withdrawal of about 1,000 U.S. troops before the end of the year should be developed based upon the assumption that the progress of the counterinsurgency campaign would warrant such a move. Plans should be based upon withdrawal of US units (as opposed to individuals) by replacing them with selected and specially trained RVNAF [South Vietnamese] units.[3]

General withdrawal plans were to be contingent upon continued progress in the counterinsurgency campaign. MACV in turn was tasked to draft the revised CPSVN and prepare a plan for the 1,000-man reduction.

The JCS proposal to remove the first increment of U.S. forces complied with McNamara's instructions to emphasize units rather than individuals, but the list of so-called units contained elements that were all smaller than company size. The plan also complied with the guidance that most of the personnel selected were to be those with service support and logistics skills in order to minimize the effect on operations. The total came to 1,003 U.S. military personnel to be withdrawn, by units rather than individuals, from South Vietnam by the end of December 1963. All services were represented. CINCPAC provided MACV with a suggested list identifying where the reductions could take place with the least impact. CINCPAC received MACV's response and, after some changes and revisions, concurred and forwarded the plan to the JCS on May 11.

As the paper trail on the pullout proceeded, so did the record of the

President's public statements about the state of the war and withdrawal. With the 1,000-man pullout beginning to take shape, Kennedy did his best to steer through the tricky waters by trying to convince the conservatives he would stay the course, while starting the withdrawal, without making comments that might turn out to be overly optimistic. Nhu had commented that too many American troops were in Vietnam, and a reporter asked for the President's views on this and on the state of the war at a May 22 press conference. Kennedy said, of course, that if asked, the U.S. would be happy to leave immediately, and also made these remarks:

> we are hopeful that the situation in Vietnam would permit some withdrawal in any case by the end of the year, but we can't possibly make that judgment at the present time. There is still a long, hard struggle to go. . . . I couldn't say that today the situation is such that we could look for a brightening in the skies that would permit us to withdraw troops or begin to by the end of this year. . . . As of today we would hope we could begin to perhaps do it at the end of the year, but we couldn't make any final judgment at all until we see the course of the struggle the next few months.[4]

He said that part of the problem was the effect of the Laos situation on Vietnam; he could also have added that the unfolding Buddhist crisis had complicated matters even more.

Had the Buddhist crisis affected the war effort? Kennedy was asked at a July 17 press conference. "Yes I think it has," he replied, adding, "I think it is unfortunate that this dispute has arisen at the very time when the military struggle has been going better than it has been going in many months."[5] No one had told Kennedy that the Buddhist crisis had affected the war effort. On the contrary, at the July 4 White House meeting he was told that it had not.[6] Forrestal was the one who brought the subject up, referring to Krulak's assessment after his recent trip to Vietnam. Krulak had said that the nearer one got to the battle "the less gravely the problem was regarded," and concluded that military operations were becoming "more effective."[7] Furthermore, the U.S. intelligence community had just issued, on July 10, a new Special National Intelligence Estimate on "The Situation in South Vietnam," which concluded that the Buddhist issue did not "appear to have had any appreciable effect on the counterinsurgency effort."[8] Why, then, did Kennedy go against what he was being told?

Kennedy's statement that the Buddhist problem *had* affected the war effort appears to have been part of the groundwork he was laying for the eventuality that the withdrawal might have to take place in a losing situation—in that case the repressive actions of the Diem regime could be fingered in assessing the blame. Once again, however, Kennedy covered himself by adding that the U.S. would not pull out. He added: "In my opinion, for us to withdraw from that effort would mean a collapse not only of South Vietnam, but Southeast Asia. So we are going to stay there."[9]

An interesting aside to Krulak's contention that the military operations were becoming more effective occurred at this time when he requested a map from DIA showing the enemy and friendly forces in the Saigon area. When George Allen, who prepared the map, showed up with it, Krulak noticed Allen's attire and inquired if he was a civilian. Allen recalls what happened:

> His jaw fell when I replied affirmatively. He asked if any military officers had helped me put the map together. I replied that none had, but that I would personally vouch for the accuracy of the data, since I had obtained it from the appropriate analysts. He was dismayed, paused, and then said maybe he could get along without the map after all, that perhaps it wasn't really necessary, thanked me for my efforts, and asked me to take the map with me on my way out.[10]

Allen was not part of the progress story, and his map undoubtedly reflected that. Krulak was not taking any chances.

In his July report, Krulak said that the "shooting part of this war is moving to its climax," but the training effort "has passed its climax." This meant that not much of a reduction in U.S. logistical and tactical support was possible, but that a reduction in the advisory effort was "a logical prospect." Harkins, he said, "considers that a reduction of 1,000 men could be accomplished now, without affecting adversely the conduct of the war."

Meanwhile, Admiral Felt, responding to a JCS request for more details on the 1,000-man withdrawal, responded on July 21 with his final plan.[11] Withdrawal "will be ordered if progress in the counterinsurgency campaign warrants such action," he began. The objective was to withdraw units rather than individuals "to the extent practicable to gain maximum psychological impact rather than reach a predetermined in-country strength" by the end of the year, he continued, and recommended that the final decision be made between October 1 and October 31 because, among other things, the "highly volatile situation in Laos makes it prudent to delay [the] decision as long as possible."

In his previous plan Felt noted that "half of the personnel to be withdrawn were not units at all and were to have been absorbed in[to] units for [the] purpose of withdrawal." He had changed his mind because "an alert press would readily ascertain the facts with resultant unfavorable publicity," and he now proposed to simply list these men as "individuals" instead of pretending they had been in the units all along. The news media would be told that the Vietnamese "counterpart" for each individual "has been brought up to a level of self-sufficiency." This was a tricky point, however, because "individuals" could be withdrawn through the simple manipulation of the personnel pipeline—by not sending a replacement for someone who was due to rotate back to the U.S. or who had become ill or for other administrative reasons. The pipeline could be turned back on as fast as it was turned off, so the only real teeth in his 1,000-man withdrawal were the 500 men in units.

Finally, on August 20, Taylor sent the JCS recommendation on the 1,000-man withdrawal to McNamara, saying he should approve the MACV-CINCPAC proposed plan "in three to four increments for planning purpose only," and urged that the final decision on the withdrawal plan "be delayed until October."[12] On August 30 McNamara's staff recommended he approve this JCS proposal but pointed out that many of the "units" to be withdrawn were ad hoc creations of expendable support personnel, and cautioned that public reaction to "phony" withdrawal would be damaging.[13] They also suggested that actual strength and authorized ceiling levels be publicized and closely monitored. McNamara took their advice, and on September 3 he approved the JCS recommendation but warned against creating special units as a means to cut back unnecessary personnel; he also requested the projected U.S. strength figures for the remainder of 1963.[14]

Did Secretary McNamara understand that the fine print in the plan he approved meant that only half of the 1,000-man withdrawal would actually be units? Did he know and approve of Felt's argument that "the withdrawal of individual advisors is as newsworthy as units"? The record is not clear. On September 6, 1963, the JCS notified CINCPAC of McNamara's final decision.[15] The plan, said the Chiefs, had been approved "for planning purposes pending final decision on or about 31 Oct." McNamara, "in reviewing your plan," the Chiefs said, "questioned the advisability of creating special holding units if their only purpose is for withdrawing individual advisors and headquarters personnel." In other words, a patently phony withdrawal plan would not fly in Washington. But since this particular aspect had already been addressed by Felt's July 21 message, it leaves open the question as to whether the JCS passed on the solution: simply list half of the withdrawal as individuals.

The Joint Chiefs asked CINCPAC to develop and forward a detailed public affairs plan "treating the withdrawal as a package operation." This plan, said the notice, should impress on both the American and foreign public the following: that the government "is making progress against the VC"; that, in a short time, Vietnam would be able to successfully assume the functions of certain U.S. units, thereby permitting their withdrawal; and, now that South Vietnamese units have been trained to conduct the war on their own against the communists, a portion of the U.S. forces were to be withdrawn. In their response to McNamara's request for the U.S. military strength figures, the Chiefs said that the 1,000-man reduction would be counted against the peak October strength of 16,732 men. The first increment was scheduled to leave Vietnam in November, and the rest in December.[16]

McNamara's September 3 green light for the withdrawal came on the heels of an important interview Kennedy gave the day before in Hyannis Port.[17] His remarks to Walter Cronkite included this often quoted passage:

> I don't think that unless a greater effort is made by the [South Vietnamese] government to win popular support that the war can be won out there. In the final analysis, it is their war. They are the ones who have to win it or lose it. We can help them, we can give them equipment, we can send our men out there as advisors, but they have to win it, the people of Vietnam, against the Communists.

These remarks are usually cited in the perennial debate over whether Kennedy would have committed U.S. combat troops to the war later, as Lyndon Johnson did, a debate which will be returned to later. Kennedy also told Cronkite this: "I don't think that the war can be won unless the people support the effort and, in my opinion, in the last two months, the government has gotten out of touch with the people." With his advisors embroiled at the time in a secret debate over a coup against Diem, Kennedy was saying, in effect, that the ability to win the war had slipped from Diem's grasp. He was also talking, for the first time, about the possibility of *losing* the war. Again, Kennedy was laying the groundwork to blame the failure of the war on Diem.

The President, of course, did not miss the opportunity to deliver his pat statement against withdrawal:

> I don't agree with those who say we should withdraw. That would be a great mistake. I know people don't like Americans to be engaged in this kind of an effort. Forty-seven Americans have been killed in combat with the enemy, but this is a very important struggle even though it is far away.

Again, it is important to remember that Kennedy was not opposing a withdrawal if the war was being won. He made these remarks in order to give the impression he was opposed to withdrawing from a *losing* situation. This was not true, but very few people knew that in September. More hints of his intentions would emerge later as the likelihood of losing appeared to increase. By September 1963, the basic question—which should have been squarely addressed at the beginning of 1961—could no longer be avoided.

"CAN WE WIN IN VIETNAM?"

Just as Taylor and McNamara were putting the finishing touches on the withdrawal plan, shocking news of the war's failure began bypassing the barrier built by Taylor and reaching the President and his top advisors. This occurred partly because, during the fog of coup planning in Washington, Kennedy had demanded unfiltered access to the views of officials in Saigon. For example, Secretary of State Thuan—who now feared for his life—had decided to tell the truth to the Americans as a means of buying safe passage out of Vietnam. Negative reports like Thuan's were supplemented by others as the discussion began to vet the true battlefield situation. The question of "whether we can win with Nhu and Diem" began to look more like "can we win in Vietnam at all?"

When Harkins had been pressed to answer how he could help Lodge put pressure on Diem, he answered, "by indicating how [the] present state of affairs [is] so detrimental to [the] war effort which has been going so well."[18] Then, to leave no doubt in Kennedy's mind as to Harkin's precise reading of the war situation, Harkins added, "In all corps the war against the VC is progressing, although at a somewhat diminished rate." Even this delicate description of *slowing success* could not soften the impact on Kennedy: if the trend continued, a withdrawal tied to success was in jeopardy. That Kennedy was looking hard at each little indicator of potential battlefield success is attested to by the following episode. On September 2, Nhu tried to trick Lodge into believing three Viet Cong battalions were waiting for Nhu's permission to let them "desert." Nhu claimed this was the reason he could not leave Vietnam.[19] Nhu's assertion went *unfiltered* to Kennedy; at the White House meeting the next day the President, hopeful at the prospect, asked if there was "any information" on this report. McCone explained to Kennedy that Nhu's claim was bogus.

Just as the screws holding down the facts of failure were beginning to loosen, Taylor intervened to keep the lid on tight. Only moments before the September 3 White House meeting, he personally hand-carried to the President a memorandum from himself devoted almost exclusively to the battlefield situation.[20] In that memo, Taylor assured Kennedy that, despite the political unrest there, "military operations in Vietnam for the month of August indicate favorable trends in all military activities." To back this claim up he presented statistics on how many offensive operations had been conducted. He added that "progress continues with the strategic hamlet program," explaining how many hamlets existed and the fact that 76 percent of the rural population had been put in them.

Taylor's use of statistics was selective and highly misleading. "Not surprisingly," Andrew Krepinevich points out in his study of this period, the figures Taylor used from MACV on the offensive operations failed to say how many of them "had actually resulted in contact with enemy forces."[21] The true picture, of course, differed widely from that painted by Taylor. Field reporting began to reflect a deterioration of the war situation by August 1963, says George Allen, who had been reading the reports received by DIA and CIA.[22] One of these reports contained a conversation between Ambassador Lodge and a provincial-level U.S. Information Agency representative. When Lodge asked how the Strategic Hamlet Program was going in the provinces, the man replied it was going terribly, adding that three-quarters of the hamlets were "torn up."

That things were declining on the home front as well became evident on September 5, when hearings held by the Senate Foreign Relations Committee revealed far-reaching doubts not only about the leadership of Diem but also about the advisability of continued American participation in the war. Senator Frank Church introduced a Senate resolution calling for a suspension of American aid to Vietnam unless Diem undertook drastic reforms. Hilsman sent this congressional "storm-warning" to Lodge, who replied that it might be "helpful" in his effort to dislodge Nhu and open the way for a "showdown conference" with Diem.[23]

Taylor's story of battlefield success came at a time when Kennedy's entire program was particularly vulnerable. Taylor's September 3 memo stood in stark contrast to Rusk's opening comment at the September 6 White House meeting, which began before the President arrived.[24] Rusk said:

> if the situation continues to deteriorate in Vietnam, if our relations with Diem continue to deteriorate, and if U.S. domestic opinion becomes strongly anti-Diem, we will be faced with no alternative short of a massive U.S. military effort.

This remark is revealing not only because it is evidence that Rusk felt the war was deteriorating, but also because it demonstrates that his answer to that was large-scale American intervention. This is precisely the reason that Rusk could not say, twenty years later, that—like McNamara and Mansfield—Kennedy had taken him into his confidence and told him the truth.

The discussion soon turned to press accounts that quoted Harkins as saying that the South Vietnamese military efforts had been reduced by 50 percent. Bundy said he doubted Harkins had said this, and Krulak pointed out that Harkins had said "the military effort had been affected but not seriously." At some point later it "developed" that the press accounts had "misrepresented" Harkins, but the spectacle of so much discussion in the White House on what Harkins was saying about the war's *slowing success*—and what others were saying about what he said— illustrates how highly charged the issue of the battlefield situation had become.

Robert Kennedy asked pointedly "whether we could win the war with Nhu and Diem." Rusk said the answer was no, as long as the Nhus continued their present actions. The Attorney General and Rusk began to spar with each other about press stories, and then Robert Kennedy made this statement:

> We have to be tough. Ambassador Lodge has to do more than say our President is unhappy. We have to tell Diem that he must do the things that we demand or we will have to cut down our effort as forced by the U.S. public.

Moreover: "If we have concluded that we are going to lose with Diem, why do we not grasp the nettle now?" he asked. Rusk countered with this little lecture: "Our actions should be taken in two or three bites. It is very serious to threaten to pull out of Vietnam. If the Viet Cong takes over in Vietnam we are in real trouble."

Once again, the discussion seemed to be heading to a juncture where the words "withdraw" and "losing" were about to be uttered in the same breath. Here, not surprisingly, Taylor offered this positive comment: "Three weeks ago we still believed that we could win the war with Diem. The Joint Chiefs of Staff shared that view." He then asked whether "recent events had changed our judgment." Robert Kennedy was obviously not interested in framing the question that way. The minutes of the meeting indicate he "asked again what we should do if we have concluded that we can't win with Diem." McNamara replied that this question could not be answered because there was not enough information in Washington, but Rusk said he agreed that a "reassessment" was necessary. Robert Kennedy then asked if it was possible to "get the views promptly of U.S. officers working with Vietnamese military units." McNamara said he would have Harkins do this "today." Taylor immediately countered this proposal with one of his own: why not have General Krulak go to Vietnam? Taylor got his way: McNamara agreed, and said Krulak should return within three days. McNamara then ordered Krulak to leave in ninety minutes. The State Department wanted to balance Krulak with their man, Mendenhall. Hilsman later claimed that he had to delay the departure of the plane until Mendenhall could get to the airport.[25]

Rusk's final comments before President Kennedy entered the meeting are again revealing. The real questions, he said, were: "Can we win in Vietnam? Can we contain criticism in the U.S.?" The minutes also include this interesting paragraph:

> Secretary Rusk described our present position as being stage one. There may be no stage two if we decide to pull out. If we pull out, we might tell Diem that we wish him well. Diem may be able to win the war without us, but this is unlikely. Prior to actually pulling out, we might want to consider promoting a coup.

This cryptic comment deserves scrutiny. Since he had already described the war effort as deteriorating, we know what he meant by "stage one," but what did Rusk mean by "stage two"? It obviously did not mean withdrawal because he said pulling out would *preclude* stage two. The answer is found in the remark he made at the beginning of the meeting— that if things continued to deteriorate it would leave no alternative to "a massive U.S. military effort." The conclusion seems unavoidable that the Secretary of State's stage two was massive intervention with U.S. combat troops.

THE KRULAK-MENDENHALL TRIP

While Krulak and Mendenhall were scurrying around in Vietnam, some important news from South Vietnamese leaders arrived in Washington. The last decision made at the September 6 White House meeting was to contact Thuan to see if he still felt Nhu had to be removed. Later that day the State Department also instructed Lodge to get a move on in setting up his overdue dialogue with Diem.[26] When the news of Lodge's showdown with Diem came back, it was predictable.[27] No, Nhu could not go, Diem said: "Why it would be out of the question for him to go away when he could do so much for the Strategic Hamlets." No, Nhu was not responsible for the pagoda raids. "He has been very unjustly accused." Finally, despite all the trouble he had been having, Diem claimed "the war was going very well."

While Lodge was meeting with Diem, Rufus Phillips was talking with Thuan, and Phillips' account of what Thuan said was shocking indeed.[28] Thuan reported the following: Nhu had accused Thuan of being "bought" by the Americans and threatened to "certainly kill him" if he tried to resign; Nhu was in effective control of the country; both Nhu and Diem were "completely unrealistic about the progress of the war"; a senior official of the hamlet program reported the war would be lost by 1965; this same official felt—and Thuan agreed—that the government "is losing the war in the Delta now"; the Americans should cut off aid to show they mean business; and all of the Vietnamese military officers were looking to the Americans for leadership and most would follow the American lead. Despite Nhu's threat to kill him, Thuan wanted to quit anyway and asked if the Americans could get him out of the country.

Thuan's comments, of course, went straight to Kennedy and everyone else. A cable to counter Thuan's claim that the war was being lost also went to Kennedy—but *not* to everyone else. It was a preliminary report by Krulak on the Delta area, where he had talked with thirty-five U.S. advisors.[29] Krulak reported these advisors held the following "uniform" attitudes:

> They are attentive to fighting the war, certain that steady progress is being made, convinced that [the] present thrust will ultimately bring victory, assured that their units are worrying about the Viet Cong and not about politics or religion, generally unwilling to say categorically that [the] war effort has slowed, but anxious to illus-trate that the change has been small.

Almost as soon as this telegram came off the wire, "someone" at a White House meeting on the test ban treaty pulled it out and showed it to Kennedy, explained McGeorge Bundy's assistant, Bob Komer, in a memo immediately afterward.[30] Hilsman and Harriman were "sore as hell" over this tactic, Komer said, which they called "dirty pool" by the Pentagon. The State Department had not been given a copy of the telegram and had called the National Security Council and asked Komer to "spring it."

Apparently there had been an agreement to wait until Krulak and Mendenhall returned before passing their comments to the President, and the move in the test ban session subverted this. Mendenhall had in fact already cabled a preliminary report of his own to the State Department the same day—September 9.[31] Fear "pervades" South Vietnam's major cities, Mendenhall said, which "have been living under a reign of terror which continues." In these "cities of hate," he stated, "Vietnamese fear to be seen with Americans." The army situation in the northern provinces was a "mixed picture," he said, with the top commanders predictably loyal and an undetermined degree of dissatisfaction below them. In some of the northern provinces the war "appears to be taking [a] downturn," he said, and the Viet Cong were regaining coastal areas they had been pushed out of earlier.

Krulak and Mendenhall arrived in Saigon at 6:00 A.M. on September 8, parted company and agreed to meet thirty-six hours later to return home. Krulak interviewed more than eighty American military advisors, while Mendenhall talked to Vietnamese and American civilian officials in the central coastal provinces. No love was lost between Krulak and Mendenhall, but there was even worse blood between Krulak and John Mecklin, Counselor for Public Affairs in Vietnam, who had been invited, along with Phillips, to return with Krulak and Mendenhall and deliver his view to the President. During the flight back to Washington Krulak noticed that Mecklin was bringing home some evidence of the Diem government's misdeeds: several cans of television film they had tried to censor. Krulak angrily protested that South Vietnam was a sovereign nation and that its laws had to be respected. He told Mecklin it was wrong to "smuggle," and ordered the film removed from the plane. In a later interview with William Rust, Krulak said he had "suggested that Mecklin needn't leave the film unattended—he could always remain with it in Alaska."[32]

The plane carrying the party from Saigon landed in Washington at 5:00 A.M. on September 10. Five and a half hours later the group was in the White House meeting, which began with Krulak briefing the President on his main conclusions.[33] He said: "The shooting war is still going ahead at an impressive pace. It has been affected adversely by the political crisis, but the impact is not great." The Viet Cong were still strong in the Delta, so "there was plenty of war left to fight" in that region. The U.S.-Vietnamese military relationship had not been damaged by the political crisis, and while some officers would like to see Nhu go, few would "extend" their necks to bring it about. Krulak's bottom line was this: "The Viet Cong war will be won if the current U.S. military and sociological programs are pursued, irrespective of the grave defects in the ruling regime." Then it was Mendenhall's turn. He said he had found "a virtual breakdown" of the civil government in Saigon and a pervasive atmosphere of fear and hate. He argued that "the war against the Viet Cong has become secondary to the 'war' against the regime." He concluded by saying that "the war against the Viet Cong could not be won if Nhu remains in Vietnam." Incredulous, Kennedy asked: "The two of you did visit the same country, didn't you?"

Nolting, ever the defender of Diem, began to pick on Mendenhall, arguing that "the present government will bear the weight of our program." The President, however, still amazed, interrupted: how could it be that "two people who had observed the same area could have such divergent reactions?" Hilsman says he responded that "it was the difference between a military and a political view."[34] Krulak, seemingly always at odds with Hilsman, recalls it this way:

> After a period of silence, when it became evident that no one else was going to respond, I suggested to the President that the answer was plain—that Mr. Mendenhall had given him a metropolitan viewpoint on Vietnam; and that I had given him a national viewpoint.[35]

It was obvious the two men had very different views about what the U.S. should do in Vietnam. What no one told Kennedy during the meeting, however, was that Krulak and Mendenhall disliked each other intensely, and on the entire trip back, when they should have been coordinating their reports, "They spoke to each other only when it was unavoidable."[36]

It was Phillips' turn next. He reported that there was a crisis of confidence in Vietnam "not only between the Vietnamese people and their government but between the Vietnamese and the Americans." He said no one would run any great risk until the U.S. took a real stand, and he added: "The Vietnamese do not lack the guts to move against the government once they are sure of the U.S. position." Nhu had to go, he asserted, and most Vietnamese he knew "have come reluctantly to this conclusion." Phillips had a plan:

> we need a man to guide and operate a campaign to isolate the Nhus and to convince the government and people that the U.S. will not support a government with Nhu in it, thus encouraging them to do the job if Diem won't come around.

There is "one man," Phillips said, "who could guide and operate this campaign as a special assistant to the Ambassador" and that man "was Ed Lansdale."

Phillips went on to say that "we are indeed losing the war," and that things were in a "tragic state" in the Delta. Phillips delivered a devastating blow to the account Krulak had given. Armed with data from Harkins, Krulak had claimed the Delta province of Long An had witnessed a 300 percent increase in the number of strategic hamlets since January 1963, and that the huge increase in hamlet construction countrywide had seen a corresponding decline in Viet Cong incidents. Moreover, Krulak had also relied on MACV's figures when he claimed that only 0.2 percent of the strategic hamlets had been overrun by the Viet Cong.[37] By coincidence or design, Phillips was prepared to discuss Long An, having had access through a colleague in that province (Earl Young) to a recent report written by a U.S. Army major about the situation there. Armed with the information from that report, Phillips countered that "60 of the strategic hamlets had been overrun" in Long An; and with all due respect to General Krulak, "the military campaign was not going forward satisfactorily." The hamlets in the Delta were being "chewed to pieces," he added—with fifty of them recently overrun.

Phillips' facts so thoroughly demolished Krulak that Kennedy made a point of offering the general a chance to recoup. Krulak later described how he defended himself to the President:

> I told him that my statement respecting military progress had its origin in a reservoir of many advisors who were doing nothing other than observe the prosecution of the war; that their view was shared and expressed officially by General Harkins and, as between General Harkins and Mr. Phillips, I would take General Harkins' assessment.[38]

At this point Harriman, who had been quiet the entire time, went after Krulak with all the venom he could muster. Halberstam provides this account:

> Harriman said he was not surprised that Krulak was taking Harkins' side—indeed he would be upset if he did not. Harriman said that he had known Krulak for several years and had always known him to be wrong, and was sorry to say it, but he considered Krulak a damn fool.[39]

Phillips came out on top in the meeting and in the brouhaha that followed, but the Army major who had written the Long An report did not. According to Halberstam, General Richard Stillwell led a subsequent investigation to find out how Phillips got the report; there was thought of charging him with a security violation until Ambassador Lodge intervened; the major, however, was reprimanded, given a bad efficiency report and transferred.[40]

Finally it was Mecklin's turn. He had written a report on the plane ride back.[41] It included the following main conclusions: a new Vietnamese government is essential; real power must go to a new man; the odds are heavily against ousting the Ngo Dinhs without considerable bloodshed; an unlimited U.S. commitment in Vietnam is justified; U.S. forces could be used against Asian communist guerrillas and win—and the stakes are so high that, if unavoidable, we must take the risk anyway; and the U.S. must accept the risks of covertly organizing a coup if necessary.

This was a strongly worded prescription for direct U.S. intervention. Mecklin said it would be "vastly wiser—and more effective—to make this unpalatable decision now." If diplomatic pressure and selective suspension of aid failed to remove Diem and Nhu, then the U.S. should covertly plan a coup and suspend all aid. If the coup ran into trouble, "there would be plenty of excuses to bring in U.S. forces," he said, "making it possible now for the U.S. to have its way by simply presenting the Ngo Dinhs with an ultimatum." He ended his memo with this comment:

> And once U.S. forces had been introduced into Vietnam, it would be relatively simple—on the invitation of the new regime—to keep them on hand to help, if needed, in the final destruction of the Viet Cong.

Mecklin later wrote this about that period:

> Events in the months that followed reinforced my belief that we should be ready to use American forces as a last resort to save South Vietnam from the Communists. In the context of American domestic politics in 1963, however, such a suggestion apparently was unthinkable, like a Sunday school pupil asking the teacher to talk about sex.[42]

The analogy was a fitting one and reflected what happened in the meeting. Mecklin got up and said he agreed with Phillips' pessimistic conclusions about the deleterious effect of Diem's government on the war effort, but that U.S. combat troops—not a suspension of aid—was the answer. Kennedy simply ignored the suggestion and instructed his advisors to prepare papers on specific steps that might be taken for a gradual and selective cut in aid. "As far as I could make out," Mecklin wrote later, "President Kennedy was wholly undecided but profoundly uncomfortable about the suggestion that the U.S. should apply sanctions against a non-Communist, sovereign regime, much less try to unseat it."[43]

The President then lectured those present about how disturbed he was that officials in both Washington and Saigon were fighting "our own battles" in the newspapers, and said he wanted these different views "fought out at this table" instead. According to Forrestal, however, the

President was, in fact, alarmed and irritated by the divisions that were deepening among his advisors. "This is impossible," Kennedy said afterward. "We can't run a policy when there are such divergent views on the same set of facts."[44]

The group reconvened—away from the President—at 5:45 P.M. in the State Department.[45] The meeting was futile and grew contentious when McNamara and Harriman squared off. McNamara said the U.S. should try to change Diem, and that "our present policy," meaning getting rid of him, "was not viable." He knew of no alternative to Diem, he said, and by trying to overthrow him the U.S. was "making it impossible" to continue working with him. McNamara therefore proposed going back to where they had been three weeks earlier, and, in effect, "start with a clean slate."

The record shows that "Harriman stated his flat disagreement" with McNamara's remarks. Starting with a clean slate was "not permissible," he said, and added:

> we have to operate within the public statements already made by the President; that we cannot begin afresh, overlooking the fact that Diem had gravely offended the world community.

Diem had created a situation "where we cannot back him," Harriman said. McCone defended McNamara's position, and expressed "doubt that alternative leadership existed in Vietnam." The President's advisors were hopelessly split and becoming more so each day. This dichotomy was paralleled in military planning: the withdrawal plan ran counter to another, more secret plan, this one being developed by CINCPAC.

THE GENESIS OF OPLAN 34A

At the May 6, 1963, SECDEF conference, item five on the agenda concerned South Vietnamese operations against North Vietnam, and the record of the meeting parenthetically indicates that this item was "(Being reported separately by Gen. Krulak)."[46] A brief footnote to this record in the Department of State History tells us only that "no such report has been found." It is likely that the discussion of agenda item five planted the seed for what later became CINCPAC OPLAN 34A and the secret American actions that led to the Gulf of Tonkin incidents in August 1964. "The covert program was spawned," says *The Pentagon Papers*, in May of 1963, when the JCS directed CINCPAC to prepare a plan for South Vietnamese "hit and run" operations against North Vietnam.[47] The work that went into this plan was eventually honed further by an interdepartmental committee formed by President Johnson on December 21, 1963, and chaired by Krulak. Prior to this time, 34A had a hazy history, beginning with the disappearance of Krulak's presentation to the May SECDEF meeting.

What began as CINCPAC OPLAN 34-63 was the first major comprehensive American plan for covert operations against North Vietnam. In keeping with the tenets laid down by Kennedy's post Bay of Pigs directive—NSAM-55—large covert operations were controlled by the Department of Defense. Taylor's order to Felt after the SECDEF meeting to prepare the plan said the hit-and-run operations were to be "non-attributable,"[48] presumably in the same manner as the U.S. Farm Gate missions then being flown inside South Vietnam. Although described as South Vietnamese operations against the North, they were to be carried out "with U.S. military material, training and advisory assistance." Admiral Felt had been pushing for such an action against North Vietnam anyway, and his staff completed work on the plan and sent it to the JCS on June 17.[49] We know that Taylor "approved" it twelve weeks later on September 9, apparently without any changes, but what happened to it in the interim is still unclear.

The Navy history of the war suggests an attempt was made to get the operations moving right away, but due to "various difficulties" this was unsuccessful.[50] Delays in the operational employment to the Pacific of two fast patrol boats, to be used in the maritime phase of the plan, "prevented quick approval and implementing of the proposed program." Further, Diem's government, "preoccupied with internal political troubles, evinced little enthusiasm for these extraterritorial actions." Taylor did not send the plan he had approved to McNamara, so neither the Secretary nor the White House was informed. Taylor sat on the plan for two and a half months before allowing it to be shown to McNamara—at the November 20 Honolulu meeting.

The three-day period of September 9–11, then, presents a memorable sequence of events. On the first day Taylor, acting on his own, approved the plan for covert actions against North Vietnam, which would lead eventually to the Tonkin Gulf incidents, the congressional resolution in their wake, and, ultimately, to full-scale American intervention. On the second day Krulak and Mendenhall presented President Kennedy with nearly opposite accounts of what was going on in Vietnam and what to do about it. On the third day Taylor, responding to a request from McNamara, scheduled the first increment of the 1,000-man withdrawal from Vietnam to begin in November. In retrospect, the escalatory nature of the covert program seems as antithetical to the de-escalatory nature of the withdrawal as Krulak's and Mendenhall's proposals were to each other.

The meaning behind this pattern of contradictions is clear: the Kennedy administration was deeply divided not only over what to do about Diem, but about staying in Vietnam at all. Until Kennedy's death, the withdrawal plan was hotly debated while OPLAN 34A remained hidden; after his death, the withdrawal plan withered while OPLAN 34A blossomed. Was Kennedy himself planning this reversal? Or was this just one more—perhaps the most profound—coincidence of the Vietnam War?

NOTES

1. Wood memo to Hilsman, April 18, 1963, in *State History*, 1963, vol. 3, Document 97, pp. 243–45, especially p. 245.
2. *State History*, 1963, vol. 3, p. 275, n. 3. William Bundy proposed a 1965–69 MAP of \$450 million, while McNamara wanted a figure of \$390 million.
3. *PP*, Gravel ed., vol. 2, p. 181.
4. Kennedy, *Public Papers*, 1963, p. 421.
5. Ibid., p. 569.
6. Memorandum of a Conversation, White House, 11–11:50 A.M., July 4, 1963, in *State History*, 1963, vol. 3, Document 205, pp. 451–53.
7. Report by the Joint Chiefs of Staff's Special Assistant for Counterinsurgency and Special Activities (Krulak), (undated but from July), in *State History*, 1963, vol. 3, Document 207, pp. 455–65.
8. SNIE 53-2-63, "The Situation in South Vietnam," July 10, 1963, in *State History*, 1963, vol. 3, Document 217, pp. 483–85.
9. Kennedy, *Public Papers*, 1963, p. 569.
10. Allen, *The Indochina Wars*, p. 209.
11. CINCPAC 212210Z July 1963 to the JCS, in *Declassified Documents*, RC, 83E.
12. *PP*, Gravel ed., vol. 2, p. 168.
13. Ibid.
14. Ibid.
15. Message to CINCPAC from JCS, JCS 2388, ref: CINCPAC DTG 212210Z Jul 63, sub: Withdrawal of 1,000 U.S. military from Vietnam. U.S. Army files, MHI; see also JFK Library, Newman Papers.
16. *PP*, Gravel ed., vol. 2, p. 168.
17. Kennedy, *Public Papers*, 1963, pp. 650–53.
18. Harkins telegram to Taylor, August 29, 1963, in *State History*, 1963, vol. 4, Document 13, p. 24.
19. Lodge cable to State No. 403, September 2, 1963, in *State History*, 1963, vol. 4, Document 44, p. 85.

20. Taylor memo to Kennedy, undated but signed by Taylor and apparently delivered on September 3, in *State History*, 1963, vol. 4, Document 53, pp. 98–99, and n. 1.

21. Krepinevich, *The Army and Vietnam*, p. 88.

22. Allen, interview with the author, August 10, 1987.

23. Hilsman cable No. 335 to Lodge, September 6, 1963, and Lodge cable to State No. 431, September 6, 1963, in *State History*, 1963, vol. 4, Document 63 and n. 2, both on p. 113.

24. Minutes of the 10:30 A.M., September 6, 1963, White House meeting, in *State History*, 1963, vol. 4, Document 66, pp. 117–20.

25. Hilsman, *To Move a Nation*, p. 501.

26. State cable to Saigon No. 70, September 6, 1963, in *State History*, 1963, vol. 4, Document 70, pp. 128–29.

27. Lodge cable to State No. 455, September 9, in *State History*, 1963, vol. 4, Document 77, pp. 140–43.

28. Saigon Embassy cable to State No. 447, September 9, 1963, in *State History*, 1963, vol. 4, Document 76, pp. 137–38.

29. *State History*, 1963, vol. 4, p. 146, n. 2.

30. Komer memo to McGeorge Bundy, September 9, 1963, in *State History*, 1963, vol. 4, Document 79, p. 146.

31. Saigon Embassy cable to State No. 453, September 9, 1963, in *State History*, 1963, vol. 4, Document 78, pp. 144–45.

32. Rust, *Kennedy in Vietnam*, p. 135.

33. Memorandum of Conversation, White House, September 10, 1963, 10:30 A.M., in *State History*, 1963, vol. 4, Document 83, pp. 161–67.

34. Ibid.

35. Ibid.

36. Mecklin, *Mission in Torment*, pp. 206–7.

37. Krepinevich, *The Army and Vietnam*, p. 87.

38. Memorandum of Conversation, White House, September 10, 1963, 10:30 A.M., in *State History*, 1963, vol. 4, Document 83, pp. 161–67.

39. Halberstam, *The Best and the Brightest*, p. 279.

40. Ibid.

41. Memo, Mecklin, September 10, 1963, in *State History*, 1963, vol. 4, Document 81, pp. 149–53.

42. Mecklin, *Mission in Torment*, p. 211.

43. Ibid., p. 209.

44. Forrestal in a September 2, 1981, interview with William Rust, cited in *Kennedy in Vietnam*, p. 137.

45. Memorandum of Conversation, Department of State, 5:45 P.M., September 10, 1963, in *State History*, 1963, vol. 4, Document 85, pp. 169–71.

46. *State History*, 1963, vol. 3, Document 107, p. 270.

47. *PP*, Gravel ed., vol. 3, p. 150.

48. Ibid.

49. *USN and the Vietnam Conflict*, p. 334.

50. Ibid.

CHAPTER TWENTY

FORK IN THE ROAD

THE LATEST LODGE REPORT

"The time has come for the U.S. to use what effective sanctions it has to bring about the fall of the existing government,"[1] wrote Ambassador Lodge about the Diem regime—just eighteen days after his arrival in Vietnam. His call, in a September 11 cable, to overthrow Diem precipitated a new round of debate in the Kennedy administration that only the President could resolve. Have you "seen the latest Lodge report from Vietnam?" Bundy asked Forrestal at a meeting the next morning—it "was one of his best."[2] Surely, Bundy added, this would lead Kennedy to call a meeting on Vietnam today. When someone remarked that Diem's brother Archbishop Thuc was coming to the U.S. to make arrangements for the visit of Madame Nhu, Bundy said, "This was the first time the world has been faced with collective madness in a ruling family since the days of the czars."

Bundy was right: Kennedy, after reading Lodge's cable, called a meeting of his top advisors; the group was to assemble at 6:00 P.M. and the President would join them after they had discussed the cable. Bundy called Rusk at 11:35 A.M., and told the Secretary that the President felt Lodge's assessment was "the most powerful he has seen on this situation."[3] Would the Secretary be going to the balance of payments meeting at 5:00? Bundy wanted to know. Rusk said he "understood only Ken Galbraith would be there." Well, it's your choice, but there won't be any decisions made, Bundy said, to which Rusk replied he "had better stay with Vietnam." That was what Bundy wanted. He had been working hard with Harriman, Hilsman, Forrestal, and Lodge to get U.S. policy off the fence and get rid of Nhu, and the Secretary of State—up to that point—appeared to be supporting their view.

Rusk's last definitive comment on this matter was at the end of the September 6 discussion right before the President had entered the room. At that time Rusk seemed to be saying that if the war could not be won with Diem then a coup against him should be considered. He had been fairly quiet at the September 10 Krulak-Mendenhall presidential briefing, emerging only toward the end to say that all the reports needed to be digested to figure out "what it was" that "has changed all our views that the war could be won with the Diem government." Rusk had been absent from the stormy meeting later that same day where McNamara and Harriman squared off and split the group into two distinct camps on the issue. In his telephone call to Rusk, Bundy confided his personal view about that meeting: it "was difficult," he said, "McNamara and Taylor just don't buy the assessment this is going to get worse and something serious must be done." Bundy told Rusk that both McNamara and Taylor disagreed with Lodge's cable; Bundy also reported, however, that McNamara was prepared to "mobilize" the Defense Department to "do this"—meaning bring down Diem's government—"if the Pres[ident] decides to."

Bundy further divulged his personal opinion that it was easier for McNamara to do this than for the Defense Department as a whole. As for the State Department, Bundy said, "Harriman just says the decision has been made and this is the way we want it." Rusk said he would spend the rest of the day on this matter, and added that what bothered him was that Lodge had not really confronted Diem yet. This comment was certainly valid, but did it mean that the Secretary had second thoughts about forcing the issue over Nhu? There had been no chance to lay it out before Diem, Bundy said, defending Lodge; he referred Rusk to what the Ambassador had said in his cable, and added, "Hilsman knows the rest of the details." The "details" were the two papers[4] Bundy had asked Hilsman to prepare on U.S. objectives in Vietnam and on pressures that could force Diem to "meet our demands," and two other papers[5] that Hilsman had drafted. One of these was a plan for reconciliation with Diem, and the second a proposal to pressure and persuade him. All four would be shown to those attending the 6:00 P.M. meeting.

When the meeting began, Rusk, not Bundy, was presiding, reading excerpts from cables, and announcing his opinions about what was "important"; what "we ought to try to define"; under what conditions we "should leave" Vietnam; what we "don't know"; what he "doubted"; and what "the next step" should be.[6] As the other men sat and listened to this long soliloquy from the Secretary of State, they may have wondered, with some justification, why his comments in previous meetings had been so much briefer. What Harriman, Hilsman, and Forrestal gradually began to see, as Rusk droned on, line after line, was that the Secretary was *not* on their side anymore—if, indeed, he ever had been.

Rusk said, "Nhu probably has to go, but this did not mean that we had to turn against Diem." He said it was possible to work with Diem and maybe even persuade him to "separate from Nhu"; Lodge, he said, had been unable to "break through to Diem and conduct meaningful conversations." He made clear his opposition to cutting back aid that benefited the war effort *or* the Vietnamese people. What had to be done now was for Lodge to "wrestle" with Diem to "get him to make changes in the government we feel are essential if the war effort is to succeed." The degree of urgency should be measured in weeks, and he added, "We are not in a hurry in terms of the coming days." Those present were then treated to a Rusk lecture on Chinese history and how the U.S. had made the mistake of not backing Chiang Kai-shek and thus letting Mao take over. "Perhaps we could assist Diem," Rusk said, returning to the present day, "in finding out whether the Viet Cong was responsible for instigating the student riots."

The Secretary's extraordinary speech was over, and Taylor immediately struck while the iron was hot. He liked the idea of examining what was happening in Vietnam against the perspective of the loss of China, and who, he asked, would possibly think of organizing religious and political opposition to an existing government that was engaged in a civil war?, implying that the communists were behind the unrest. Lincoln, he added, would never have given into religious and political protest in the American Civil War. Irritated with the way things were going, Hilsman interrupted, saying that "we had never accused the Vietnamese of religious persecution, but only religious oppression." Taylor was on a roll, however, and again suggested that the government's actions should be evaluated in the context of a civil war; he advocated avoiding "pin pricks which serve to annoy Diem."

Bundy eventually got the other side going by saying "we should start pressures against Diem." Hilsman managed to present, in piecemeal fashion, his plan to pressure Diem, but ran into trouble with Taylor and McCone on a point or two, and then Taylor stated flatly that Hilsman's idea would not succeed if Nhu chose to resist. What would we do if it fails? Taylor asked. Bundy defended it: "We need not look at the plan in such black and white terms." There could be an "interim target" and then a later decision if more "drastic action" was necessary. Rusk reiterated that the next step was to explain the American position to Diem. Rusk had clearly prepared for this meeting and had thrown his weight successfully against the idea of a coup.

The men then adjourned to the cabinet room and were joined by Kennedy.[7] Rusk reviewed what had been said so far; Hilsman summarized his plan to pressure Diem; and Bundy pointed out that Lodge wanted a suspension of aid. Gilpatric countered that this would hurt the war effort. Why not just evacuate dependents instead? he asked. Any reference to the battlefield could always be expected to draw Kennedy out and this was no exception. Kennedy asked "whether deterioration has set in and whether the situation was serious." McCone said it might become serious in three months, but McNamara said this could not be estimated, and that there had been as yet "no serious effect on the war effort."

It soon became evident that Rusk and Kennedy had probably coordinated their strategy that afternoon. Had the letter he asked to be prepared for Diem been done? the President inquired. No, Bundy said. He explained that "it was felt" a letter from the President to Diem asking him to silence Madame Nhu was too difficult to write because this was a "family matter." It would be better to have Lodge handle this "orally." Clearly, Bundy hadn't gotten the drift of what was happening. Kennedy then made his point crystal clear:

> The President said his idea of a letter was to spell out our general view toward the situation faced by Diem. This is one method of getting Ambassador Lodge going on his conversations with Diem. The letter would not be released to the press. He asked that a draft of our concerns and our complaints be prepared for him.

Kennedy said instructions needed to be sent to Lodge that would include a request he "hush up the press in Saigon." Lodge should be told "we are considering his cable." He should also be told to express "our concerns to Diem and get a response from him."[8]

Once again the advocates for a coup had failed to get strong presidential action, as neither Hilsman's plan to pressure Diem nor Lodge's call to overthrow him were approved. They did not come away entirely empty-handed, however, because Kennedy did agree that, for the next few days, all aid decisions should be held up.

PRESIDENTIAL GUIDANCE REQUIRED

The rift between the Defense and State departments had so deepened over the 10th and 11th of September that one of the few ideas that had not produced an argument was Gilpatric's suggestion to evacuate American dependents as a way of indicating to Diem how strongly the U.S. felt about the changes they wanted him to make. That is, until Harkins heard about it. Krulak, who had cabled Harkins right after the September 11 White House meeting, received an angry response the following day.[9] "It's all right to plan evacuation of U.S. dependents," Harkins began, "but let's stop there unless we're going to give up [Southeast Asia], and we must never do that." The Buddhist protest, of course, was "another well organized covertly led Communist trick. And a tough one to handle—but another must." He added this passionate plea:

> We have chosen to fight Communist aggression here in Southeast Asia; and we must be prepared to meet every form at every cross-road. . . . No we haven't lost this one by a long shot and we must not take counsel in our fears. Perhaps some of the tools are tired and worn—having been practically at war since 1945 they must be. So it's another must for us to sharpen the cutting edges of the old or come up with some new, and get on with the offensive. "Amen."

It would be quite a while before his prayer was answered in Washington. For the time being, discord and dissent reigned there.

Another large meeting of administration officials—minus the President—took place on the evening of September 12.[10] McGeorge Bundy, not Rusk, presided over this meeting, and he opened with the Harkins invocation from Saigon, drawing attention to the comment "that the Communists had deeply infiltrated the Buddhists and students." McCone said the CIA had "little specific information" on this claim, and there followed an inconclusive discussion of the matter.

The group spent most of its time discussing a draft telegram to Lodge written by Rusk.[11] In it Rusk had said:

> The key question is what has gone wrong to block or reverse the favorable developments of the first six months of this year when we were beginning to feel that a corner had been turned and that we could anticipate a successful conclusion.

Rusk had also added this bit of doublespeak: "I agree fully with your sense of urgency which I am inclined to measure in weeks rather than days." Rusk's draft, in essence, soft-pedaled what should be done about Diem. The minutes of the meeting state that the group then engaged in a "considerable discussion" about the impact on Lodge of the proposed cable. A considerable *argument* would probably have been a more appropriate description: Bundy charged, "It would convey a major change in policy, from one of urgent action to one of restrained sequential steps." At length Bundy won his point that Rusk's draft did exhibit a major change in Washington's thinking, and the Secretary's draft was rejected. From here, however, the meeting degenerated into several points of disagreement.

The next five days did absolutely nothing to break the impasse or reduce the building confusion in the administration: Lodge warned that someone had better be thinking about what to do if Nhu negotiated with Hanoi and asked the U.S. to withdraw;[12] Lodge also asked that the CIA Station Chief, John Richardson, be replaced by Lansdale;[13] McCone called Rusk and refused the Lansdale appointment;[14] McCone forwarded a Saigon CIA assessment that argued against a go-slow approach;[15] Harriman sent a letter to Lodge telling him that his divergence with Harkins was causing "confusion" and asked Lodge to explain the differences;[16] and the September 16 daily White House staff meeting found McGeorge Bundy back-pedaling somewhat, Forrestal trying to follow suit but nonetheless unable to hide his eagerness to dump Diem, and the CIA growing impatient with the Pentagon's gradualism.[17]

That same morning a group of administration officials convened at the State Department to hear what some CIA experts had to say about the situation in Saigon. This gathering managed to avoid discussions and further arguing. Rusk, however, could not help but say that of the two latest Hilsman papers—one outlining a conciliation "track" and the other a pressures "track"—he preferred conciliation.[18] In a memo written to Rusk immediately after the meeting, explaining his papers, Hilsman said point-blank: "My own judgment is that the 'Reconciliation Track' will not work."[19] One interesting detail in the answers provided by the CIA experts was the fact that the coup plots in Saigon generally pivoted around a quick, violent attack on the palace *and* assassination.

The Kennedy administration had come to a full stop as far as Vietnam policy was concerned. The mood in the White House was glum. "I am trying this memorandum," said Forrestal to Bundy on September 16, "mainly as an exercise in relieving some of my own frustrations."[20] He continued:

> I think we have come to a position of stall in our attempts to develop a Washington consensus. For a week now the fundamental

attitudes of the principal officers in the Government have remained unchanged.

He complained that Harriman saw the solution as a change of government in Saigon, while McNamara viewed the problem in terms of how many of the enemy could be killed. "Each fundamentally views the other's position as an impractical one." New information, Forrestal said, would not lead either to change their position. "This leads me to the conclusion that the governmental situation here requires Presidential guidance."

It is possible that Bundy sent this memo to the President, who made a major decision the next day. This decision, however, was not the one Forrestal wanted and it did not break the impasse or provide any guidance. At 4:20 P.M. Harriman, who had just read a draft of a cable the President was getting ready to send to Lodge, called Forrestal to say he and Hilsman were "very much disappointed" with it.[21] Kennedy was sending to Vietnam "two men opposed to our policy," Harriman complained, "plus one who wouldn't stand up to carry out policy." McNamara and Taylor were two of those Harriman was talking about, and the President's idea of sending them to Vietnam was "a disaster," he said. Forrestal agreed, and explained the trip had been added after he had seen the draft, meaning that he had not anticipated it.

The cable, which was sent on the 17th, boiled down to an instruction for Lodge to again talk to Diem and report back before any decision would be reached in Washington.[22] "We see no good opportunity," the cable said, for action to remove Diem "in the immediate future." Bundy explained to Rusk, McNamara, and others that the cable was "a final effort of persuasion and pressure short of a decision to dump the regime no matter what." The cable noted Lodge's "reluctance" to talk with Diem, but said, "We ourselves can see much virtue in [an] effort to reason even with an unreasonable man when he is on a collision course." The cable then explained the rationale for the McNamara-Taylor trip in this way:

> Meanwhile, there is increasing concern here with [the] strictly military aspects of the problem, both in terms of actual progress of operations and of [the] need to make [an] effective case with Congress for continued prosecution of the effort. To meet these needs, [the] President has decided to send [the] Secretary of Defense and General Taylor to Vietnam, arriving early next week.

In other words, the story of winning in Vietnam had been so critically wounded that the President was putting his two top military advisors on the line, and they would have to report not only to him but also to the Congress on the true battlefield situation.

Lodge immediately cabled the President directly that such a trip "would certainly put a wet blanket on those working for a change of government."[23] They would all have to call on Diem, Lodge complained, just at the time when Lodge's "policy of silence" was beginning to get "the family into the mood to make a few concessions." This advantage would "obviously be lost," Lodge concluded, "if we make such a dramatic demonstration as that of having the Secretary of Defense and General Taylor come out here." Kennedy sent a cable straight back to Lodge saying he appreciated the Ambassador's views, but that "my need for this visit is very great indeed."[24]

What were these "very great" needs? One of them, argues Andrew Krepinevich, was to keep the military "on board" with his program, since Kennedy's fear was that the Joint Chiefs "might seek congressional support to widen the war."[25] Krepinevich's analysis is certainly borne out by the sort of operations that were being contemplated in the still developing OPLAN 34-63. His needs, however, involved more than that.

THE PRESIDENT'S NEEDS

Another of the President's great needs was to keep his plan to extricate himself from the quicksand of Vietnam, a task made vastly more complex by the political collapse of the regime in Saigon. On September 9, newsman David Brinkley had astutely asked Kennedy if the U.S. was "locked into a policy" that was difficult to change. The President responded this way:

> Yes that is true. . . . We have felt for the last two years that the struggle against the Communists was going better. Since June however, [because of] the difficulties with the Buddhists, we have been concerned about a deterioration, particularly in the Saigon area. . . . So we are faced with the problem with wanting to protect the area against the Communists. On the other hand, we have to deal with the government there. That produces a kind of ambivalence in our efforts which exposes us to some criticism.[26]

Again, no one had told the President that the political crisis had caused the war to deteriorate, yet his comment that this was especially true around

Saigon suggests that he was familiar with—and concerned about—the true extent of communist control there.

Brinkley asked the President if he doubted the domino theory, and specifically, "That if South Vietnam falls, the rest of Southeast Asia will go behind it?" Kennedy's answer makes clear the extent to which he was prepared to go to deny his opponents from both sides of the aisle political ammunition:

> No, I believe it. I believe it. I think that the struggle is close enough. China is so large, looms so high just beyond the frontiers that if South Vietnam went, it would not only give them an improved geographic position for a guerrilla assault on Malaya, but would also give the impression that the wave of the future in Southeast Asia was China and the Communists. So I believe it. . . . What I am concerned about is that Americans will get impatient and say because they don't like events in Southeast Asia or they don't like the government in Saigon, that we should withdraw. That only makes it easy for the Communists. I think we should stay. We should use our influence in as effective a way as we can, but we should not withdraw.

There seems little use in pondering whether this affirmation of the domino theory was feigned; he might well have believed it. It only highlights the desperation of his dilemma and the poignancy of that moment: the President was erecting an alibi—creating a record that showed he was on the side of sticking it out while, in fact, he was planning a retreat.

The fact that Kennedy had stuck it out for two and a half years may attenuate his pretense somewhat, but he had already delivered his defense to O'Donnell: getting out of Vietnam depended on his getting reelected. Schlesinger's contention, that a LeMay-type President who would bomb Vietnam "back to the Stone Age" was the only alternative, poses the classic moral and philosophical problem: does the end justify the means? In his duplicity, was the President acting for a higher, nobler cause? Or simply trying to get himself reelected? Or, perhaps, both?

Consider the remarks that Kennedy made at his September 12 press conference:

> I think I have stated what my view is and we are for those things and those policies which help win the war there. That is why some 25,000 Americans have travelled 10,000 miles to participate in that struggle. What helps win the war, we support; what interferes with the war effort, we oppose. I have already made it clear that any action by either government which may handicap the winning of

the war is inconsistent with our policy objectives. . . . We have a
very simple policy in that area, I think. In some ways I think the
Vietnamese people and ourselves agree: we want the war to be
won, the Communists to be contained, and the Americans to go
home. That is our policy. I am sure it is the policy of the people of
Vietnam. But we are not there to see a war lost, and we will follow
the policy which I have indicated today of advancing those causes
and issues which help win the war.[27]

All the elements of a dilemma are here: American advisors in a combat
situation and a President committed to winning the war and bringing
them home. Winning and bringing them home, however, as Kennedy
well knew, would be like having his cake and eating it too; and the truth
was, in Kennedy's view, that bringing them home required winning not
the war in Vietnam but the upcoming presidential election in the U.S.
    The fiction of continued success had become more necessary than ever
to justify the beginning of the withdrawal. At this same press conference,
a reporter asked the President whether he had been "operating on the
basis of incorrect and inadequate information." Kennedy replied:

I am operating on the basis of, really, the unanimous views and
opinions expressed by the most experienced Americans there—in
the military, diplomatic, AID agency, the Voice of America, and
others—who have only one interest, and that is to see the war
successful as quickly as possible.

Of course, the battlefield information had been incorrect since early 1962,
and the spectacle of Kennedy telling a press conference that his administration was unanimous in its views underlines how "very great" his needs
had become. He needed unity, progress on the battlefield, and a recommendation from his top advisors that the withdrawal could proceed. Save
for unity, this was precisely what he was about to get.

THE MCNAMARA-TAYLOR TRIP

As the weather cooled down in Washington, which it normally does
toward the end of September, the increasing frictions in U.S. Vietnam
policy gave the administration no break from the heat. As the Taylor-
McNamara departure date approached, the needle on everyone's stress
meter stayed pegged on maximum while fragments of news from Sai-

gon—some disturbing, others tantalizing—found their way to the nation's capital. On the 19th there was a new zinger from Lodge, recapping
his impressions during a dinner the previous evening with Nhu:

> Nhu is always a striking figure. He has a handsome, cruel face and is
> obviously very intelligent. His talk last night was like a phonograph
> record and, in spite of his obvious ruthlessness and cruelty, one
> feels sorry for him. He is wound up as tight as a wire. He appears
> to be a lost soul, a haunted man who is caught in a vicious circle.
> The Furies are after him.[28]

Then there was ex-Ambassador Tran Van Chuong, who called on Taylor
the same day. Taylor, busy preparing for his trip, wrote this about
Choung's visit:

> The purpose was to warn me against the optimistic reports on the
> military situation coming from military officials in South Vietnam.
> He is convinced that the basic facts are quite different.[29]

There was an even more startling report the next day in a Saigon cable
on what General "Big" Minh had just said of the situation in Vietnam:

> Minh thought [the] VC were gaining steadily in strength and 80
> percent of the population now have no basis for choice between
> [the government] and VC. . . . Lifting of martial law was simply
> eyewash for the Americans. The situation remains the same. Arrests
> were continuing, and Minh remarked that the two guardhouses
> outside his headquarters were full of prisoners. . . . In hypothetical
> terms, he said that [a] coup would have to be carried out suddenly
> and with complete success, so as to leave no opportunity for Viet
> Cong exploitation and to avoid risk of civil war.[30]

There seemed no point to have any more large meetings in the White
House to hash out what all of the indicators meant. The next big session
would not take place until September 23—the day McNamara and Taylor
would leave for Saigon—so the news just continued piling up in a giant
heap, waiting for the two men to return from the battlefield, wave their
magic wand, and sort it all out.

On the 21st, however, Kennedy did put pen to paper to explain, as he
had done for Taylor in 1961, the purpose of this trip.[31] He began: "I am
asking you to go because of my desire to have the best possible on-the-
spot appraisal of the military and paramilitary effort to defeat the Viet

Cong." The program had brought heartening results, he said, "at least until recently." Kennedy continued:

> The events in South Vietnam since May have now raised serious questions both about the present prospects for success against the Viet Cong and still more about the future effectiveness of this effort unless there can be important political improvement in the country. It is in this context that I now need your appraisal of the situation.

The "question of the progress of the contest" was of the first importance, the President concluded, and "you should take as much time as is necessary for a thorough examination both in Saigon and in the field."

At a meeting in the White House the morning of McNamara's and Taylor's departure, the President added additional comments to his written instructions.[32] He said that during visits with Diem the two men should press reforms on him "as a pragmatic necessity and not as a moral judgment." Kennedy also "emphasized" to McNamara "the importance of getting to the bottom of differences in reporting from U.S. representatives in Vietnam." McNamara agreed this was a "major element in his mission," and said he thought more and more that this resulted from Lodge's focus on the future, in light of the regime's present behavior, while Harkins' focus was on the recent military situation without accounting for the possible impact of political events on future operations. The minutes state parenthetically that this estimate had been "precisely" what Kennedy had said a few days earlier. The minutes show the meeting concluded this way:

> General Taylor thought it would be useful to work out a time schedule within which we expect to get this job done and to say plainly to Diem that we were not going to be able to stay beyond such and such a time with such and such forces, and that the war must be won in this time period. The President did not say "yes" or "no" to this proposal.

Taylor's suggestion was undoubtedly an invitation for Kennedy to use the withdrawal timetable as leverage to extract concessions from Diem. The fact that the President did not respond is important, for it bears on a controversy that is still raging about the withdrawal plan thirty years later.

Taylor's suggestion is sometimes taken as Kennedy's position and cited as proof that Kennedy was not serious about withdrawing from Vietnam. The opposite was true, of course, and Kennedy's 1,000-man withdrawal was not intended as leverage to be used against Diem but meant to convince critics in Congress that Kennedy *was* serious about getting out. His dilemma, as always, was to convince the conservatives on the other side of the aisle that the troops could come home because the war was being won. That *Taylor* did not take the withdrawal seriously is another matter, and his suggestion may indicate he did not.

The September 24 arrival of the McNamara-Taylor mission in Saigon was memorable. Since one of McNamara's primary objectives was to assess the state of the war, John Mecklin wrote later, it was therefore a fitting beginning to the trip when "a Viet Cong sniper knocked out an engine of a Pan American 707 jet coming in to land on that same day."[33] The situation got even more interesting after McNamara's plane landed. According to Halberstam, Lodge had assigned two staff members to block General Harkins so that Lodge could be the first to greet the Secretary: the plan worked like a charm, leaving an irate Harkins struggling to crash through this "human barrier" while shouting, "Please, gentlemen, please let me through to the Secretary."[34]

The airport scene foreshadowed what was to come: before long McNamara and Taylor were listening to briefings that made it clear that the civilian versus military division in Washington was mirrored in Vietnam. Unlike his previous visits, however, McNamara treated his hosts differently this time. Embassy Counselor Mecklin recalls of the Secretary:

> McNamara waded boldly into the argument, harassing each briefing officer with pointed questions, challenging undocumented assertions, and otherwise making life miserable for supposed experts who had not done their homework.[35]

While Taylor initially remained in Saigon, says Mecklin, the "remarkable McNamara set out to see how things were going in the field":

> Wearing an open-necked, short-sleeved shirt and GI boots, he traveled for the better part of a week all over the country, by jeep and limousine, helicopter and flivver plane, interrogating scores of Vietnamese and American officials at every level.[36]

The exercise was nevertheless superfluous, says Mecklin, because it would have been unnatural for the young captains and majors to whom McNamara spoke to express their minds freely, especially because "they knew what Harkins believed and Harkins was often present."[37]

The eyewash was hardly necessary for Taylor, the architect of the war-winning deception on the Washington end. The military field briefings for McNamara, however, were carefully countered by the civilians. According to Krepinevich:

McNamara, meanwhile, had been targeted by the American Ambassador, Henry Cabot Lodge, for a number of briefings to reinforce the picture of a Vietnam in trouble as presented by Mendenhall, Phillips, and Mecklin in the NSC meetings. The effect of these briefings was to place some doubts in McNamara's mind that things were going as well as MACV claimed.[38]

In the end, says Mecklin, the civilian side "could not conclusively prove" their case, while Harkins' staff "had impressive, correlated evidence . . . which seemed to prove that the military situation had not yet seriously deteriorated."[39]

The statements most damaging to the fiction of battlefield success were delivered not by American civilians but by the top South Vietnamese generals themselves. The trip had not been under way two days before General Khiem requested a meeting with an American, presumably a CIA agent, whose name is still classified.[40] There is little doubt that McNamara, before he left Vietnam, was shown a copy of the cable regarding the Khiem meeting, which the Saigon CIA Station sent to Washington, if for no reason other than the startling nature of Khiem's remarks. The general said the Viet Cong were now making a "show of strength in [the] battlefield," and that, for the first time, the South Vietnamese Army's dead were "almost as heavy as the Viet Cong's." The U.S. military, which resisted this view at that time, would reverse itself in early November and then say almost the same thing at the November 20 Honolulu meeting.

In the meantime, Khiem had even more disturbing news. The CIA cable went on to mention that Khiem had referred to certain operations mounted by the head of the South Vietnamese military intelligence, Colonel Phuoc (the same Phuoc who had asked Winterbottom to loan him George Allen). The CIA added this fragment about Phuoc's operations: "(*Comment:* From other sources known to have been in progress for [the] past few weeks)." In other words, the CIA had independent intelligence corroborating the ongoing nature of these intelligence operations. What did they reveal? The cable continues: "Evidence is mounting steadily that VC are very strong, have thoroughly completed [a] plan and have assets in place for [a] takeover attempt in Saigon should any major disturbance occur."

Naturally, McNamara was given a totally opposite—and obviously false—account of the war effort by Diem.[41] Diem treated McNamara and Taylor to the normal two-hour speech, for which their memo for record appropriately used a major subheading entitled "THE MONOLOGUE." The war was going well, said Diem, "thanks to the strategic hamlets program." This program, he said, had made it increasingly difficult for the Viet Cong to get food and new recruits. One cannot help but wonder if McNamara remembered MACV's own figures for what the Viet Cong was recruiting: nearly 30,000 men a year. Diem droned on, extolling the virtues of the hamlets: never mind that the program "was overextended" or that some hamlets were built before the defenders were "properly trained or armed"; on balance, Diem said, "both the risks and the losses were acceptable."

Either Diem was doing his best to deceive his guests or his mind was not in the real world. This is how he explained his concept of "acceptable" lost hamlets:

> he could push ahead rapidly with the establishment of ten substandard strategic hamlets. The Viet Cong would attack these and overwhelm, say, two of them. But if two fell, eight others would survive and grow stronger, and the area in which the Viet Cong could operate with impunity would shrink faster than otherwise would have been the case.

Surely it was news to the Secretary of Defense—and alarming news at that—that the Strategic Hamlet Program as implemented by the South Vietnamese was based on the presumption that 20 percent of the hamlets would be overrun in the early stages of construction.

When McNamara made his case that the "political deficiencies" in Diem's government would damage the war effort, and presented the "tangible evidence" of the seriousness of the crisis, "Diem rebutted these points in some detail and displayed no interest in seeking solutions or mending his ways." When McNamara counterattacked by shifting to Madame Nhu's outbursts, Diem's "glances and manner suggested that perhaps for the first time in the whole conversation" he understood the point, "especially when the Ambassador remarked that Mme. Chiang Kai-shek had played a decisive part in losing China to the Communists." Nevertheless Diem mustered his wits and rose to Madame Nhu's defense, after which McNamara removed the gloves and hit hard:

> The Secretary indicated that this was not satisfactory and that the problems of which he spoke were real and serious and would have to be solved before the war could be won or before Vietnam could be sure of continued American support that he sincerely hoped it would merit and receive.

Diem seemed to care little, and the meeting was simply a necessary going-through-the-motions that all were relieved to have behind them. Especially Secretary of State Thuan. He was present too and, throughout the entire meeting, did not utter a single word.

Thuan's predicament had deepened when the August plans for a coup were aborted. He had made the mistake of throwing in his lot with the Americans too early, asking for safe passage out of Vietnam, and even joining in the exposure to Washington of the truth about the twin failures on the battlefield and in the hamlet program. Thuan realized the tightrope on which he was wobbling when Harkins—the chief American architect of the battlefield success story in Saigon—had confronted him about his desire to resign a week earlier.[42] What Harkins was doing, of course, was replaying to Thuan what he had confided to the CIA's Phillips; since Thuan knew Harkins was close to Diem and did not favor a coup, Harkins' crude probing sent Thuan's paranoia spiraling to unprecedented heights. Thuan squirmed under the pressure and lied outright to Harkins: he categorically denied it, said "it was fantastic," and pleaded that "any such rumor that could be spread around deeply endangered his life." During the meeting with Diem on the 29th, McNamara had good reason to sympathize with Thuan's desperation—two days earlier CIA Station Chief Richardson had told McNamara that Thuan was on the government's assassination list.[43]

So far the Diem-Harkins fiction of battlefield success had been rebutted not only by General Khiem but also by Diem's military advisor, "Big" Minh, and his Secretary of State, Thuan. Now it was South Vietnamese Vice President Tho's turn to answer McNamara's questions about the war, and it was perhaps fitting that this happened the day after the meeting with Diem.[44] The "police state methods" being used, Tho said, were causing deep discontent and he had been unable to do anything about it. He apologized for speaking so frankly, but said the situation was "very serious." Wasn't it true, however, that "all the dissatisfaction" was only in the cities and not in the villages at all, asked one of the Americans. (It is not known which American made the inquiry, but only McNamara, Taylor, and Lodge were present.) Not true, said Tho: there was serious discontent in the villages too, "but not because of the police state methods being used in the cities." When the villager, who feels he is already overtaxed by the government, Tho said, "leaves his hamlet to go out to work in the field, he meets the Viet Cong who forces him to pay another set of taxes."

What happened next was extraordinary. "This should not happen in a well fortified hamlet," General Taylor butted in. It *doesn't* happen in the hamlet, Tho snapped as if irritated that Taylor wasn't listening carefully, it happens when the villager *steps out* of the hamlet and goes into the field. Taylor's ego would not allow this to go by. "In a properly defended hamlet this should not happen," he shot right back, as if it were Tho who hadn't been listening well. Tho and Taylor were now ready to face off. "Why, General Taylor," Tho said sardonically, "there are not more than

20 to 30 properly defended hamlets in the whole country." Then, talking to all three Americans, Tho said, "Why do you gentlemen think that the Viet Cong is still so popular?" He now had a captive audience. "Two years ago there were between 20–30,000 in the Viet Cong army; for the last two years we have been killing a thousand a month; and yet the Viet Cong is even larger today. Why is this true?"

Tho had just thrust the spear directly into the heart of the darkest secret concealed behind the deception of success: the unrestrained growth of the Viet Cong and the vibrancy of their success with the villagers. Both McNamara and Taylor protested that the cause for Viet Cong success with the villagers "might be intimidation," but Tho refused to give his American guests any room for comfort: "Intimidation can make them join," he said, "but it cannot stop them from running away. While some of them do run away, there are many who stay. Why is this?" The Americans had no explanation for such startling accounts of the Viet Cong's popularity, for this was one of those basic questions that never seemed to get asked in Washington. "It might be the promises that the Viet Cong make," McNamara tried. "They cannot promise a thing," Tho immediately contradicted the Secretary, and to underscore his point he added, "neither food nor shelter nor security." Tho was finished playing with his guests and decided to finish it then and there: "The answer is that they stay in the Viet Cong army because they want to, and the reason they want to is their extreme discontent with the government of Vietnam." Needless to say, Tho's perspective did not make it into the final McNamara-Taylor report.

One final episode that occurred during the trip deserves mention. There was a second, and again unproductive, meeting over dinner with Diem, during which both McNamara and Taylor said they were confident the Viet Cong could be defeated by 1965 as long as Diem made the reforms they had asked him to make. "Altogether it was a depressing evening," Taylor recalled, "the refusal of this stalwart, stubborn patriot to recognize the realities which threatened to overwhelm him, his family, and his country."[45] Diem did ask Taylor for his "professional comments" on the military situation, and Taylor supplied them in a letter to Diem that was delivered on October 2.

This letter reveals much of what Taylor truly thought about the battlefield.[46] It was not until the political disturbances between May and August, Taylor wrote, "that I personally had any doubt as to the ultimate success of our campaign against the Viet Cong." So, Taylor *did* have doubts after all. The war could still be won, he said, providing there were no further political setbacks and that Diem undertake some military actions necessary for an improvement. The situation in I, II, and III Corps was "generally" good, he said, but added, "The record of one of the divisions in the III Corps falls notably short of the minimum standard for mobile actions in the field set by your High Command—twenty days out of every thirty." There is no doubt that Taylor was referring to the 7th Division. So, he *had* paid attention to news from Porter, Vann, and Drummond after all. "As a result," Taylor continued, "some of the hard core war zones of the Viet Cong remain virtually untouched. In my opinion, the full potential of the military units in this area is not being exploited." So, Taylor *knew* about the significant tracts of Viet Cong strongholds in III Corps. He added, however, that "your principal military problems are now in the Delta." This was IV Corps. So Taylor *realized* the situation was even worse in IV Corps than III Corps. If there were large concentrations of unmolested Viet Cong forces in III Corps, what could have been so much worse in IV Corps?

The concentration of effort in II Corps (to the north) during 1962, said Taylor, came "at the expense of the campaign in the south where the Viet Cong have always had their principal sources of strength." Now it was time to "regroup our forces and place the center of gravity" in IV Corps, he said, an acknowledgment that he *had* been genuinely disturbed by what he had seen on his trip. He stated:

> The kind of war we are fighting in the Delta is a small unit war, fought principally by small infantry-type organizations. . . . Yet I found in my recent visit that the infantry companies in the Delta and elsewhere are often less than two-thirds of authorized strength—a hundred men for duty out of a company of an authorized strength of about 150 men. . . . Headquarters soldiers do not hurt the Viet Cong—infantrymen with rifles in the jungle do.

Though Taylor then went into the usual pabulum about winning in two years, most of this letter sounds almost as though it could have been written by John Vann. It was precisely this kind of information that Taylor had been blocking from view in Washington.

The upshot of the trip was a peculiar blend between battlefield optimism and political pessimism; a compromise, as Krepinevich points out, that would lead to a report to the President that recommended "pressure and persuasion" to get Diem to ease government repression, but it also maintained that "the tactics and techniques employed by the Vietnamese under U.S. monitorship are sound and give promise of ultimate victory."[47] Quite aside from the fact that MACV's military statistics were inaccurate, in this curious political-military mixture lay the crucial flaw that McNamara and Taylor incorporated in their report. The war could be won by 1965 *if* the political situation could be righted. Yet at no point during the trip did they see any indication or hear any report that such a righting was likely.

Deputy Assistant Secretary of Defense William Bundy was a member of the McNamara-Taylor team and assisted in the process of writing the lengthy report. In his memoir he has this to say about it:

> there is a clear internal inconsistency that I myself missed in the flight across the Pacific, that the *immediate readers of the report in Washington* did not see or perhaps feel confident enough to highlight, and that simply got through in the stress and pressure of the time. If the medical profession needs examples of the effect on judgment of long flights across twelve hours of time zones, or of the workings of the mind immediately after such trips, I would myself offer the military conclusion of the McNamara-Taylor report on October 2, and above all the press release resulting from it, as a first exhibit. The words of the release on the military situation were extraordinarily unwise—and extraordinarily haunting for the future. [emphasis added][48]

Since the report was already written by the time the group returned, who were these "immediate readers of the report in Washington"? Of one thing we may be sure: *they* were not suffering from jet lag.

NOTES

1. Lodge cable to State, No. 478, September 11, 1963, in *State History*, 1963, vol. 4, Document 86, pp. 171–74.

2. Memorandum for Record of the daily White House staff meeting, September 11, 1963, in *State History*, 1963, vol. 4, Document 87, p. 174.

3. Record of McGeorge Bundy's call to Rusk, 11:35 A.M., September 11, 1963, in *State History*, 1963, vol. 4 Document 88, p. 176.

4. Hilsman papers, "U.S. Objectives in Current Vietnam Situation," and "Possible Political Pressure Weapons for Use Against Diem and Nhu," both dated September 11, 1963, in *State History*, 1963, vol. 4, Document 89, pp. 177–80, and Document 90, pp. 180–81, respectively.

5. Attachments to Document 114, in *State History*, 1963, vol. 4, pp. 221–30.

6. Memorandum of Conversation, the White House, 6:00, P.M., September 11, 1963, in *State History*, 1963, vol. 4, Document 93, pp. 185–90.

7. Memorandum of the Conference, the White House, 7:00 P.M., September 11, 1963, in *State History*, 1963, vol. 4, Document 94, pp. 190–93.

8. The instructions went out the next day; see State cable to Lodge No. 391, September 12, 1963, in *State History*, 1963, vol. 4, Document 97, pp. 195–96.

9. Harkins cable to Krulak, September 12, 1963, in *State History*, 1963, vol. 4, Document 96, pp. 194–95.

10. Memorandum for the Record of a meeting, White House, 6:00 P.M., September 12, 1963, in *State History*, 1963, vol. 4, Document 99, pp. 199–201.

11. Draft telegram from Rusk to Lodge, September 12, 1963, in *State History*, 1963, vol. 4, Document 98, pp. 196–98.

12. Lodge cable to State No. 505 September 13, 1963, in *State History*, 1963, vol. 4, Document 102, p. 203.

13. Lodge letter to Rusk, September 13, 1963, in *State History*, 1963, vol. 4, Document 104, pp. 205–6. Lodge thus endorsed Phillips' praise of Lansdale (during the Krulak-Mendenhall meeting).

14. Record of telephone conversation between McCone and Rusk, 12:01 P.M., September 17, 1963, in *State History*, 1963, vol. 4, Document 120, p. 240–41.

15. McCone, memo for record, September 13, 1963, in *State History*, vol. 4, Document 105, pp. 206–7.

16. Harriman letter to Lodge, September 14, 1963, in *State History*, 1963, vol. 4, Document 107, p. 209.

17. Memorandum for the Record, daily White House staff meeting, 8:00 A.M., September 16, 1963, in *State History*, 1963, vol. 4, Document 112, pp. 216–217. The CIA's concern was reflected in this meeting in remarks by Chester Cooper, Assistant for Policy Support to the CIA Deputy Director for Intelligence (Ray Kline).

18. Memorandum for the Record of a meeting at the Department of State, 11:00 A.M., September 16, 1963, in *State History*, 1963, vol. 4, Document 113, pp. 217–20.

19. Hilsman memo to Rusk, September 16, 1963, in *State History*, 1963, vol. 4, Document 114, pp. 221–30.

20. Forrestal memo to McGeorge Bundy, September 16, 1963, in *State History*, 1963, vol. 4, Document 116, pp. 235–36.

21. Memorandum of Conversation between Harriman and Forrestal, 4:20 P.M., September 17, 1963, in *State History*, 1963, vol. 4, Document 124, p. 251.

22. White House cable to Lodge, September 17, 1963, in *State History*, 1963, vol. 4, Document 125, pp. 252–54.

23. Lodge cable to Kennedy, September 18, 1963, in *State History*, 1963, vol. 4, Document 126, p. 255.

24. Kennedy cable to Lodge, September 18, 1963, in *State History*, 1963, vol. 4, Document 128, pp. 256–57.

25. Krepinevich, *The Army and Vietnam*, p. 88.

26. Kennedy, *Public Papers*, 1963, pp. 658–60.

27. Ibid., pp. 673–77.

28. Lodge cable to State No. 541, September 19, 1963, in *State History*, 1963, vol. 4, Document 129, pp. 258–59.

29. Maxwell Taylor, Memorandum for the Record, September 19, 1963, in *State History*, 1963, vol. 4, Document 135, pp. 268–69.

30. Lodge cable to State, September 20, 1963, in *State History*, 1963, vol. 4, Document 138, pp. 272–73.

31. Kennedy memo to McNamara, September 21, 1963, in *State History*, 1963, vol. 4, Document 142, pp. 278–79.

32. Memorandum for the Record of a meeting, the White House, 10:00 A.M., September 23, 1963, in *State History*, 1963, vol. 4, Document 143, pp. 280–82.

33. Mecklin, *Mission in Torment*, p. 213.

34. Halberstam, *The Best and the Brightest*, p. 283.

35. Mecklin, *Mission in Torment*, p. 214.

36. Ibid.

37. Ibid.

38. Krepinevich, *The Army and Vietnam*, p. 89.

39. Mecklin, *Mission in Torment*, p. 215.

40. Saigon CIA Station cable to CIA, September 26, 1963, in *State History*, 1963, vol. 4, Document 149, pp. 291–92.

41. Memorandum of Conversation, Gia Long Palace, September 29, 1963, in *State History*, 1963, vol. 4, Document 158, pp. 310–21.

42. Harkins cable to Felt, September 20, 1963, in *State History*, 1963, vol. 4, Document 139, pp. 274–75.

43. Report of McNamara's September 27, 1963, interview with Richardson, in *State History*, 1963, vol. 4, Document 154, pp. 301–3.

44. Memorandum of Conversation by McNamara, September 30, 1963, in *State History*, 1963, vol. 4, Document 160, pp. 323–25.

45. Maxwell Taylor, *Swords and Plowshares*, pp. 298–99.

46. Maxwell Taylor letter to Diem, October 1, 1963, in *State History*, 1963, vol. 4, Document 163, pp. 328–29.

47. Krepinevich, *The Army and Vietnam*, p. 89; see also *PP*, Gravel ed., vol. 2, p. 187.

48. William Bundy, unpublished manuscript, p. 9-26.

CHAPTER TWENTY-ONE

"WE HAVE A POLICY"

OCTOBER 2—THE MCNAMARA-TAYLOR REPORT

The documentary record indicates that on board the aircraft on the way to Saigon, McNamara handed out assignments to the five deputies: William Bundy to edit the report; Forrestal to help Bundy edit; Colby to evaluate the intelligence; William Sullivan (from the State Department) to evaluate conflicting views of U.S. personnel in South Vietnam; and General Krulak to determine the attitudes of the South Vietnamese and U.S. military.[1] Each of these five men was also given a list of people to contact and specific questions to answer for the report. The outline of the report had already been worked out by Krulak, and the master list of questions was to be consolidated by Bundy. To the maximum extent possible, McNamara said, the report should be worked out in Saigon; there would be a layover in Honolulu to finish it, and it must be complete before the return to Washington.

William Bundy's recollection that there were "immediate readers of the report in Washington" needs an explanation. The report, as it was put together, was transmitted back and forth electrically between Washington and Saigon. Where was the nerve center for this operation in Washington?

Who was in charge of it? The person in charge, it turns out, was General Krulak. Although his name is included on the trip's passenger list, along with his assignment from McNamara and the people he was to contact, Krulak was not on board the aircraft after all. A close look at who he was supposed to contact reveals he could reach them from Washington: the British and Australian missions, Colonel Serong (the senior Australian advisor), and "cable questions to Thompson [a veteran British counterinsurgency expert] through Serong." Not just Thompson, but all of these could easily be handled by cable. Colby does not remember Krulak being on the trip,[2] and William Bundy does not even bother to include Krulak in his lengthy account of the trip;[3] the simple reason, of course, was that Krulak was not on the mission.

He was back in Washington at the Pentagon, in charge of a round-the-clock operation to help write and edit the report that he had outlined before the party left. Cots were brought in for teams of secretaries who worked in shifts, while Krulak and an ad hoc staff toiled nearly eighteen hours a day to keep up with the flow of information.[4] During the trip Krulak traveled—almost daily—to the White House where Robert Kennedy pored over the material coming in from Saigon and advised Krulak of the President's reactions and any instructions he had for him. The coordination of the McNamara-Taylor report was probably the classic back-channel operation of its time.

This enabled the President himself to play a key role in the report that he received on October 2. McNamara and Taylor did not bring back a recommendation for a coup because Kennedy did not want such a recommendation. This explains the "inconsistency" that William Bundy noted was so clearly a part of the report, and why, when all the political indicators pointed to disaster with Diem, McNamara could not propose a coup. Why did Kennedy oppose such a recommendation? Just as he had told McNamara to impress on Diem that the U.S. wanted his policies changed for practical not moral reasons, similarly, Kennedy's reasons for opposing a coup were also practical: such an act would only force the United States into assuming more responsibility for South Vietnam's fate. That was precisely what Kennedy did not want to do. On the contrary, at this point he was planning to extricate himself from the mess in Vietnam. By the time of this trip, wrote Henry Brandon, then a reporter for the *London Sunday Times*, "He seemed sick of it, and frequently asked how to be rid of the commitment."[5] The McNamara-Taylor trip was part of his effort to do just that.

Of all the questions that McNamara parceled out to the members of his delegation, one, in particular, overshadowed the others. William Bundy recalls:

All through the Saigon briefings and in the field, the question at the top of McNamara's mind had been testing the hypothesis dating from May: Could the U.S. look forward to a reduction in its military advisors by the end of 1965? The insistence on this question shows the degree to which the planning of May had survived intervening events.[6]

The answer Kennedy wanted, of course, was that the phased withdrawal could be carried out; and, because he wanted it, that is the answer he got.

The first conclusion of the final report stated: "The military campaign has made great progress and continues to progress."[7] The first recommendation of the report was this:

> 1. General Harkins review with Diem the military changes necessary to complete the military campaign in the Northern and Central areas (I, II, and III Corps) by the end of 1964, and in the Delta (IV Corps) by the end of 1965.

There followed some steps necessary to achieve this, and then the second and third recommendations:

> 2. A program be established to train Vietnamese so that essential functions now performed by U.S. military personnel can be carried out by Vietnamese *by the end of 1965*. It should be possible to *withdraw the bulk of U.S. personnel by that time*.

> 3. In accordance with the program to train progressively Vietnamese to take over military functions, the Defense Department should announce in the very near future presently prepared plans to *withdraw 1,000 U.S. military personnel by the end of 1963*. This action should be explained in low key as an initial step in a long-term program to replace U.S. personnel with trained Vietnamese without impairment of the war effort. [emphasis added]

This last sentence makes it clear that Kennedy had decided against Taylor's suggestion of using the 1,000-man withdrawal simply as a device to extract concessions from Diem.

The history of the recommendation on withdrawing 1,000 men from Vietnam reveals that, during the McNamara-Taylor trip, a deep split in the administration erupted over this issue. While the McNamara-Taylor group was finishing their work in the offices of MACV in Saigon, William Sullivan was shocked when he saw the chapter (the first) McNamara had been working on.[8] He immediately went to the Secretary and said, "I just can't buy this. This is totally unrealistic. We're not going to get troops out in 1965. We mustn't submit anything as phony as this to the President." He threatened to write a dissenting report. Sullivan claims that McNamara concurred and that Taylor then agreed to "scrub it." What McNamara and Taylor agreed to excise from the report in Saigon later became the final report's third recommendation: to pull out 1,000 U.S. advisors by the end of 1963. The version of the report as it stood by the time they reached Honolulu is preserved at the Kennedy Library, and the 1,000-man troop withdrawal is clearly missing.[9]

On the plane trip home the subject of withdrawal came up again between Sullivan and Taylor. Sullivan later said "we talked about it a bit," and he described the conversation:

> Max [Taylor] said "Well, goddammit, we've got to make these people put their noses to the wheel—or grindstone or whatever. If we don't give them some indication that we're going to get out sometime, they're just going to be leaning on us forever. So that's why I had it in there." I said, "Well, I can understand that. But if this becomes a matter of public record, it would be considered a phony and a fraud and an effort to *mollify the American public* and just not be considered honest. [emphasis added]

We already know that Kennedy planned to withdraw gradually and that his 1,000-man pullout was indeed meant to mollify congressional critics. What this extraordinary little conversation tells us is that Maxwell Taylor considered the withdrawal phony, and the reason that *he* wanted it in the report was to pressure Diem.

On the morning of October 2 the mission members had their first meeting with Kennedy. He listened to a one-hour oral briefing summarizing the report's findings, evaluations, and recommendations. Kennedy then took McNamara and Taylor into the Oval Office for a private discussion; when they emerged McNamara ordered the recommendation on the 1,000-man withdrawal be put back into the report.[10] Both Forrestal and Harriman recall that many in the room immediately objected, and that the President, after listening impatiently to their remonstrations, "turned on his heel and left the room."[11] The statement on the 1,000-man withdrawal stayed in the report.

In the meantime, a final draft of a White House public statement on the McNamara-Taylor trip was prepared, and another White House meeting scheduled for 6:00 P.M. But that meeting was several stormy hours away.

"WE MUST ALL SIGN ON"

The way Kennedy steamrolled his opposition that morning left some hard feelings. Sullivan later recalled:

> I felt it would be misleading to suggest that the job could be done by 1965 and that we could start withdrawing people by the end of 1963. . . . It looked to me as though it was going to be just the opposite: We were going to be putting more people in by the end of 1963.[12]

An Assistant for Policy Support from the CIA, Chester Cooper, was working in the West Basement of the White House when Kennedy walked out of the morning meeting. Shortly afterward the two Bundy brothers brought Cooper the final draft of the White House public statement. Cooper reports that he "was surprised and outraged" that the statement would say McNamara and Taylor had reported the American military task in Vietnam could be finished by 1965.[13] Cooper says a reference in the statement to military progress did not bother him because "such statements were now part of the liturgy"; in other words, for Cooper, reading statements about military progress was like going to church and observing the rites prescribed for public worship.

Cooper felt the "Bring-the-boys-home-by-1965" sentence was gratuitous, loaded with "booby traps," and would destroy whatever credibility the statement had. He recalls what happened:

> Both Bundys agreed, but Bill had little elbow room. Finally, in utter exasperation Bill said, "Look, I'm under instructions!" In Washington that closes any argument, unless recourse is taken by tackling the Instructor. Mac called Secretary McNamara, but was unable to persuade him to change his mind. McNamara seemed to have been trapped too; the sentence may have been worked out privately with Kennedy and therefore imbedded in concrete.

From this reaction it is clear we can include both Bundys and Cooper with Sullivan: all four were opposed to the bring-the-boys-home sentence. When Sullivan found out about the proposed White House statement he too was angered. He called McNamara as well, and said, "Why in hell is it back in public print again?" The reply, says Sullivan, "was not all that convincing at the time."[14] The words "remained," Cooper laments, "and McNamara and the Administration were to pay a heavy price for them."

Emotions were running high when everyone assembled for the meeting at 6:00 P.M. with the President.[15] Kennedy opened the session himself, and began, somewhat defensively, by saying that most everyone was in agreement and that "we are not papering over our differences." They had agreed, he said, not to cut off all U.S. aid to Vietnam but that it was necessary to bring about changes there. He then delivered a powerful statement demanding unity among his advisors and support for his policy:

> Reports of disagreements do not help the war effort in Vietnam and do no good to the government as a whole. We must all sign on and with good heart set out to implement the actions decided upon. Here and in Saigon we must get ahead by carrying out the agreed policy. Because we are agreed, we should convey our agreement to our subordinates. There are no differences between Washington and Ambassador Lodge or among the State and Defense Departments and the CIA.

It was a poignant moment: a President demanding unity from a cabinet more divided than ever before, demanding support from advisors, most of whom, in their hearts, did not believe in his policy.

Kennedy then opened discussion on the draft public statement. He said attacking Diem publicly was not as effective as taking actions quietly, and that in any case U.S. Vietnam policy should be based not "on our moral opposition to the kind of government Diem is running," but on the harm his actions were causing to the effort against the Viet Cong. Both Rusk and Ball said moral emphasis would have a beneficial effect on world public opinion, but Kennedy replied the problem was *U.S. public opinion*, and he reiterated that "we should stress the harm Diem's policies are doing to the war effort against the Communists." McGeorge Bundy, perhaps forgetting that Kennedy had just said there were no differences between the State and Defense departments, remarked that McNamara and Taylor wanted to emphasize winning the war, but the State Department "wanted something more than an objective of merely winning the war." Harriman shrewdly defused Bundy's blooper by saying he was "prepared to accept the language proposed."

The discussion then turned to the language regarding the 1,000-man withdrawal. The minutes record that this took place:

> The President objected to the phrase "by the end of this year" in the sentence "The U.S. program for training Vietnamese should have progressed to the point where 1,000 U.S. military personnel assigned to South Vietnam could be withdrawn." He believed that if we were not able to take this action by the end of this year, we would be accused of being over optimistic.

This passage once again makes clear that Kennedy did not view the 1,000-man withdrawal as a way of tricking Diem into reforms or the South Vietnamese Army into fighting. He wanted the withdrawal to be tied to an improving situation, and apparently his concern here was how he would look if he personally embraced the optimistic schedule proposed in the White House statement. Kennedy's remark also demonstrates his fear that the battlefield reporting could change at any moment.

McNamara, apparently afraid that Kennedy might be considering dropping the sentence entirely, interjected his view:

> Secretary McNamara said he saw great value in this sentence in order to meet the view of Senator Fulbright and others that we are bogged down forever in Vietnam. He said the sentence reveals that we have a withdrawal plan. Furthermore, it commits *us* to emphasize the training of Vietnamese, which is something we must do in order to replace U.S. personnel with Vietnamese. [emphasis added]

This statement is enlightening. What does it mean for Sullivan's story that McNamara agreed, while in Saigon, to the deletion of this same sentence from the trip report? In view of McNamara's position at the NSC meeting, three possible explanations come to mind: that Sullivan invented this part of his story; that the Secretary had changed his mind during the seventy-two-hour interval; or that, in order to prevent Sullivan from carrying through on his threat[16] to write a minority report, McNamara agreed to excise the passage, hiding from Sullivan the fact that these words had already been approved by President Kennedy and would be put back in later. Of the three, the last is probably closest to the mark.

McNamara's statement in the NSC meeting is revealing for another reason. Whereas Taylor wanted to use the withdrawal to pressure Diem or the South Vietnamese Army, McNamara wanted to use it to reassure senators like Fulbright and to motivate the U.S. Army to get serious about training Vietnamese instead of fighting the war for them. It is a subtle but profound difference. While Sullivan claimed that on the plane ride back Taylor had agreed the withdrawal timetable was really "phony," Sullivan made no such claim about McNamara, and well he should not. The reader will recall that when McNamara's staff had informed him a month earlier that the 1,000-man withdrawal plan forwarded by MACV and CINCPAC—and approved by Taylor—looked "phony," the Secretary had cautioned Taylor against "creating special units as a means" of carrying out this withdrawal. McNamara's warning to Taylor then, and his comments to Kennedy in the evening NSC meeting, indicate that the Secretary of Defense was determined to execute the Commander-in-Chief's intent: a genuine withdrawal from Vietnam.

If McNamara was concerned that his boss was wavering on retaining the sentence, he need not have been. What Kennedy worried about was appearing personally unduly optimistic. The minutes indicate the matter was resolved this way:

> The draft announcement was changed to make both of the time predictions in paragraph 3 [1,000 in 1963 and all out by 1965] a part of the McNamara-Taylor report rather than a prediction of the President.

In other words, the President had been adamant that McNamara and Taylor recommend a withdrawal from Vietnam and was now publicly accepting it, while making clear that the optimistic timetable was theirs alone. In so doing the President left himself the option of implementing the schedule as he personally saw fit.

The President then asked what measures should be taken to bring pressure on Diem. McNamara requested that a working group would have to be formed to tackle this problem, and said that it would propose recommendations for the President "at a later date." Kennedy agreed to this, but forbade any talking to the press until he had received these measures and all were approved. Friday, October 4, was set for briefing them to the President.

"As of tonight," Kennedy declared, "we have a policy and a report endorsed by all the members of the National Security Council." He then left the room. Those present might have thought to themselves, with some justification, that Kennedy should have added the words "whether they like it or not." The group discussed preparations for the Friday meeting and then broke up. McNamara headed for some waiting reporters to announce his recommended timetable for the withdrawal of American forces from Vietnam.[17] Kennedy reemerged and yelled to the Secretary as he left: "And tell them that means all of the helicopter pilots too."[18]

NSAM-263 AND THE SECRET IMPLEMENTATION OF THE 1,000-MAN WITHDRAWAL

"To many of us in Saigon," Mecklin recalls of the White House press release, "this was sickening news," and its contention that discontent with

Diem might hurt the war effort "was made meaningless by the business about withdrawing one thousand Americans in 1963 (a long-standing plan designed for its propaganda value) and the reckless implication that the war would be won by 1965."[19] Mecklin recalls:

> Kennedy seemed to have chosen this moment of blackest crisis to permit the Pentagon once again to indulge its obsession with excessive optimism, which so long had dogged our efforts to establish a degree of credibility for the U.S. Mission.

"Not long thereafter, we began to realize in Saigon that the White House statement was only part of a plan that was brilliantly realistic and imaginative," says Mecklin. In the President's view, of course, his plan was far more than propaganda: it was the beginning of a genuine withdrawal and an integral part of his reelection campaign.

As Kennedy's advisors struggled to develop measures to use in pressuring Diem, it was inevitable that Taylor's idea of using the withdrawal timetable as a weapon would come up in the discussion. On October 4, during the second day of these talks in the White House—neither of which the President attended—Robert Kennedy questioned "the logic of making known the plan to withdraw U.S. soldiers."[20] It seemed pretty obvious, from the way the Attorney General asked this question, that his point was this: making the withdrawal known to Diem would not work as a pressure device. The minutes indicate the following response by McNamara:

> Mr. McNamara rationalized this course of action to him in terms of there being no wisdom in leaving our forces in Vietnam, when their presence is no longer required, either by virtue of the Vietnamese having been trained to assume the function, or the function having been fulfilled.

McNamara's answer, of course, once again made clear his view that the withdrawal of U.S. forces was not part of the plan to pressure Diem; forces were to be withdrawn because they were not needed. The Secretary had not, however, addressed the Attorney General's specific question: why make the withdrawal known? and the one implied: why make it known to Diem?

At the earlier October 2 evening meeting with the President, McNamara had answered the first of these questions: the withdrawal should be made known in order to relieve congressional pressure and to force the U.S. military to de-Americanize the war. At an October 5 White House meeting, the President himself addressed the issue of making the plan known to Diem.[21] The minutes indicate that Kennedy brought it up during the discussion on the McNamara-Taylor report:

> The President also said that our decision to remove 1,000 U.S. advisors by December of this year should not be raised formally with Diem. Instead the action should be carried out routinely as part of our general posture of withdrawing people when they are no longer needed.

That made it unequivocal: the 1,000-man withdrawal was not a device, but a policy objective in its own right. This particular passage, however, contains more significant news: it uses the words "our decision" to remove the 1,000 men. Did Kennedy actually *decide* to implement the 1,000-man withdrawal that day?

The fact is that he did. That McGeorge Bundy forgot to mention this detail in the minutes of the meeting that he drafted two days later is only a minor nuisance for historians. When Forrestal drafted the final NSAM—which was not officially signed as NSAM-263 until October 11—he did not forget to describe the President's historic actions on October 5.[22] That was Judgment Day for the McNamara-Taylor report. Here is the President's decision on the military aspects of that report as set forth in the NSAM:

> The President approved the military recommendations contained in Section I B (1–3) of the report, but directed that *no formal announcement be made* of the implementation of plans to withdraw 1,000 U.S. military personnel by the end of 1963. [emphasis added]

He also decided that no active covert encouragement should be given to a coup, a subject which will be shortly returned to. The military recommendations in Section I B (1–3) of the McNamara-Taylor report were these: 1) that MACV and Diem come up with what had to be done to complete the military campaign in I, II, and III Corps by the end of 1964 and IV Corps by the end of 1965; 2) that a training program be established so that the South Vietnamese could take over essential functions and permit the bulk of American forces to be withdrawn by that time; and 3) that the Defense Department should announce "in the very near future" the 1,000-man withdrawal.

The President, however, made some changes on the third provision. The McNamara-Taylor report had said the Defense Department should announce it soon and explain it "in low key" as an initial step in the long-term withdrawal of U.S. forces. First Kennedy actually implemented the plan, directing that 1,000 men be withdrawn before the end of the year, and that "no further reductions in U.S. strength would be made until the requirements of the 1964 [military] campaign were clear."[23] Furthermore, in directing that no formal announcement of the implementation be made, the President jettisoned the idea that the Pentagon make any statement or explanation. The question is: why did the President slap a secrecy order on the withdrawal?

For several reasons. In the first place, the moment he implemented the withdrawal plan he was exceeding the White House statement issued three days earlier. At that time the public had been told only that McNamara and Taylor had reported that "the U.S. program for training Vietnamese *should* have progressed to the point" where the 1,000 men could be withdrawn by the end of the year [emphasis added]. It would have been awkward, having disassociated himself from this timetable, to suddenly embrace it publicly three days later. Also, as already mentioned, Kennedy specifically ordered that the subject not be brought up with Diem; Kennedy did not want his approval of the plan to be construed by anyone in Saigon or Washington as part of the pressures package he also approved on October 5. Finally, and most important, was the fact that Kennedy had not yet decided how *he* was going to publicly justify his withdrawal plan.

So far, it had been couched in terms of battlefield success. The irony of the elaborate deception story, begun in early 1962, was this: it was originally designed to forestall Kennedy from a precipitous withdrawal, but he was now using it—judo style—to justify just that. The original architects of the deception had feared a collapse on the battlefield would bring about a U.S. pullout, but they had been careful to paint a picture of "cautious" success to prevent a claim of victory and a bring-the-boys-home routine to justify increased U.S. military participation in the war. Kennedy's plan was indeed more imaginative and brilliant than Mecklin first realized—and duplicitous. He was using the McNamara-Taylor trip to hold the fiction of success in place while he engineered a withdrawal.

The one big risk associated with his plan was the possibility that the battlefield might fall apart during the 1964 election campaign. What would he do then? He had disassociated himself from the optimistic McNamara-Taylor timetable because he could not yet know whether his withdrawal would be conducted under a winning or a losing battlefield situation. Winning was obviously better than losing, but the worst case would be American boys coming home in body bags after the President himself said the war was being won. Kennedy had always been cautious in making positive public assessments of the battlefield—it was he who had said the Buddhist crisis had affected the war negatively—because he knew how tricky the issue might prove to be in the campaign. The primaries were just around the corner, and he would have to make up his mind soon.

That he decided to implement the withdrawal plan on October 5 and keep it secret indicates that he was still in the process of doing just that.

"FULLY DENIABLE"

When Kennedy's advisors met on October 2 to consider what to do about Diem, McNamara's first comment was: "We cannot stay in the middle much longer."[24] The program in his report, he said, "will push us toward reconciliation with Diem or toward a coup to overthrow Diem." What did he mean by this? Of the three alternatives—reconciliation, pressure, and promoting a coup—the McNamara-Taylor report had chosen pressure, and specifically recommended cutting off any aid that would not be essential to the war effort. In other words, work with the Diem government only to the extent required to keep up the war effort, but, otherwise, withdraw support.

This hostility could not remain permanent; Diem's actions would either lead to moderation and reconciliation, or to a complete rupture: "we would have to decide in two to four months," said the report, "whether to move to more drastic action or try to carry on with Diem even if he had not taken significant steps." Under Secretary Ball hit the nail on the head when he posed the problem this way: "It will become known that we are using our aid as pressure on Diem. What position will we be in if we cut off aid, Diem does not do what we want him to do, and then we face a decision to resume aid because, if we do not, the effort against the Viet Cong will cease?" The alternatives appeared to be: lose credibility and the war, or promote a coup. Feeling was running strong that Diem would not change for the better. He and Nhu wanted to make Vietnam a "totalitarian state," said Sullivan to Hilsman that same day.[25] Moreover, at a meeting of essentially the same group the next afternoon, Robert Kennedy said, "We are so deeply committed to the support of the effort in Vietnam that Diem will not be greatly influenced by the steps contemplated in this program."[26]

When the group met with President Kennedy to make a final decision on October 5, two important events had just taken place in Saigon. The CIA Station Chief, John Richardson, who had been close to Nhu, was transferred to Washington, and this in itself was a powerful signal that the U.S. was backing away from the regime. The big news of the day from Saigon, however, was that General Don had called Conein in again and said this to him: "Action to change the government must be taken or the war will be lost to the Viet Cong because the government no longer has the support of the people."[27] NSAM-263 records what happened in the White House meeting that day after a discussion of the recommendations on Diem: "The President approved an instruction to Ambassador Lodge which is set forth in State Department telegram No. 534 to Saigon."[28]

The instructions to Lodge[29] were spelled out in great length, but were further boiled down in a short accompanying message from McGeorge Bundy.[30] Bundy explained to Lodge:

> President today approved recommendation that no initiative should now be taken to give any active covert encouragement to a coup. There should, however, be urgent covert effort with closest security under broad guidance of Ambassador to identify and build contacts with possible alternative leadership as and when it appears. Essential that this effort be totally secure and *fully deniable*. . . . We repeat that this effort is not to be aimed at active promotion of coup but only at *surveillance and readiness*. [emphasis added]

A strong case can be made, however, that simply by not talking with the generals and not discouraging them, the United States was tacitly encouraging a coup. At the very least, as Mecklin points out, the United States had not turned off the "green light" it had given the generals in August.[31]

Lodge's reaction, cabled back to Rusk on October 7, made clear his view that a coup was the logical outcome of the pressures track the U.S. had taken.[32] An analysis of the situation, Lodge said, "leads me to the conclusion that we cannot remove the Nhus by non-violent means against their will." His conclusions, he added, "make it hard to see today a good future" for the U.S.–South Vietnamese relationship, "because the only thing which the U.S. really wants—the removal of or restriction on the Nhus—is out of the question." Diem and Nhu saw the U.S. demanding things "which they are absolutely sure they cannot give" and therefore, Lodge concluded, "we should consider a request [from them] to withdraw as a growing possibility." He ended with this prediction: "The beginning of withdrawal might trigger off a coup."

Lodge asked that Bundy come to Saigon to discuss the situation, but this idea would eventually be turned down in favor of a Lodge trip to Washington.[33] In the meantime, the CIA sent a cable to Lodge passing on "additional general thoughts" that, it said, "had been discussed with the President."[34] Those "thoughts" were as follows:

> While we do not wish to stimulate coup, we also do not wish to leave impression that U.S. would thwart a change of government or deny economic and military assistance to a new regime if it

appeared capable of increasing effectiveness of [the] military effort, ensuring popular support to win war and improving working relations with U.S.

The generals needed to hear no more to finalize their plans, but Harkins, ever out of step, tried to thwart them. On October 23 General Don called in Conein to complain about it.[35] Don explained that the "coup committee" had decided to take advantage of its own presence in Saigon for the October 26 national holiday to "stage a coup within a week." Don said that his staff member Colonel Khuong, however, had contacted MACV seeking support, and that Harkins had approached Don the day before saying, "It was the wrong time to stage a coup because the war against the Viet Cong was progressing well."

Don told Conein that Diem had learned of Khuong's approach to Harkins, meaning, of course, that Harkins had blown the generals' cover by warning Diem of the impending coup. The consequence of this had been an order by Diem extending the assignment of two key army divisions outside Saigon—two divisions that the coup leaders had planned on supporting the coup. Don reprimanded Khuong and said "he would be disciplined by the coup committee." Khuong's only mistake was his failure to realize that Harkins was on Diem's side—a most unfortunate error for Khuong. When Lodge found out about Harkins' interference, he became irate, confronted Harkins, and fired off a cable to Washington relating Harkins' indiscretion.[36] Lodge said he had explained to Harkins that, while it was true the U.S. did not desire to initiate a coup, "we had instructions from the highest levels not to thwart" one. "Harkins expressed regret if he had inadvertently upset any delicate arrangements in progress," Lodge said. He also noted that Conein had "assured Don that Harkins' remarks had been inadvertent and were actually contrary to Presidential guidance from Washington."

In a White House meeting on October 29, Colby briefed the status of the coup forces and plans.[37] General Don had asked Lodge to stick with his arrangement to leave Vietnam, and Kennedy agreed with this because a delay would tip off Diem that "we are aware of coup plans." It would be best to have Lodge out of the country when a coup takes place, he said. Robert Kennedy questioned whether a coup could succeed, and did not support sending a cable to Lodge that appeared to favor a coup and just asked for more information. He believed a failed coup "risks so much"—perhaps the fate of all Southeast Asia, a view that he acknowledged was "the minority view." Rusk countered that "if a major part of the Vietnamese leadership feels that the war against the Viet Cong could not be won with the Diem Government then it is a major risk for the U.S. in continuing with this government."

At another White House meeting that same evening, Kennedy said that the "burden of proof should be on the coup promoters to show that they can overthrow the Diem government and not create a situation in which there would be a draw."[38] The resulting cable to Lodge said this:

> believe Conein should find earliest opportunity [to] express to Don that we do not find presently revealed plans give clear prospect of quick results. . . . We reiterate burden of proof must be on coup group to show a substantial possibility of quick success; otherwise, we should discourage them from proceeding since a miscalculation could result in jeopardizing U.S. position in Southeast Asia.[39]

This cable seems odd in retrospect. How could the generals possibly be expected to *prove* their coup would succeed? The fact is that a question like this—as well as how fast it would happen—could not reasonably be expected to discourage the generals. They could now only think that if these were the only concerns in Washington, there was no reason *not* to proceed with their plans.

Those plans were quite ingenious, as interviews with Conein and others later showed.[40] Nhu, who was well aware of the coup planning by the end of October, had engineered a "last ditch ploy" to save the regime by showing Washington that he and his brother were the "saviors" of Vietnam. He had instructed the Saigon Military District Commander, General Dinh, to stage a fake Viet Cong uprising in Saigon, including the assassination of "key U.S. officials," whereupon Nhu would send in troops "loyal" to Dinh to "put down the revolt, restore order, and save Vietnam." What Nhu did not know was that Dinh had all along been on the side of the coup committee, and they used Nhu's plan as part of their own in order to, as Conein described it, "double bump" Nhu. Consequently, when the generals launched their coup Nhu thought it was the uprising he had planned.

At the November 1 daily White House staff meeting—the President did not attend these sessions—McGeorge Bundy presided and summarized the situation. Notes made by Taylor's aide, Major William Smith, indicate Bundy opened with the comment that he "had spent quite a night watching the cables from Vietnam."[41] It had been a "well executed coup," Forrestal said, "better than anyone would have thought possible." Smith's notes state: "Bundy then commented that Diem was still holding out in the palace, adding that no one wanted to go in for the kill." (An unfortunate choice of words under the circumstances.) "They preferred that Diem leave the country." The Lodge trip, Bundy said, was "obviously" off.

The following morning the President held an off-the-record meeting with his advisors.[42] The meeting began at 9:35 A.M., while the fate of

Diem and Nhu was still up in the air. A few moments later, Forrestal entered the room with a cable, which claimed both men had committed suicide, and handed it to Kennedy. As he read the message Kennedy, himself a Catholic, had to realize that as practicing Catholics the brothers would not have taken their own lives. In fact two days later it was confirmed by an "unimpeachable source" who examined the bodies that both men had been "shot in the nape of the neck and that Diem's body in particular showed signs of having been beaten up."[43] Taylor's description of Kennedy's face and reactions to the cable are poignant:

> Kennedy leaped to his feet and rushed from the room with a look of shock and dismay on his face which I had never seen before. He had always insisted that Diem must never suffer more than exile . . . .[44]

"He was somber and shaken," said Schlesinger. "I had not seen him so depressed since the Bay of Pigs."[45] Kennedy said that "Diem had fought for his country for twenty years and it should not have ended like this."

After regaining his composure, Kennedy called his advisors back to the White House at 4:30 P.M. to discuss what should be done. The record of that meeting was never declassified, and now cannot be found.[46] We know from the President's log book that Rusk, McNamara, McCone, Krulak, both Bundys, Hilsman, Cooper, Bell, Salinger, and a few others attended.[47] We also know that the meeting ended at 5:35 P.M.; and two cables sent by Rusk, one at 5:49 P.M. and the other at 6:52 P.M., suggest something about the meeting's discussion. In the first cable, which went to all diplomatic posts, Rusk said, "We now expect to recognize [the] new regime in Saigon early next week."[48] The decision to recognize the new regime, then, appears to have been made only eight hours after news of Diem's death reached Washington.

The other cable was sent to Ambassador Lodge. In it Rusk said this:

> Our present belief is that there will be so much to do in organizing effective relations with [the] new regime that you should not plan to come to Washington on November 10. Instead we propose [a] conference in Honolulu with McNamara and me about November 20 since I will be en route to Tokyo, following which you may wish [to] proceed [to] Washington.[49]

He also said Kennedy had asked Colby to go out to Vietnam to observe the situation and "talk with you and others" and to develop a current and accurate report on the "immediate prospects." It appears that the decision to have a major Vietnam conference in Honolulu—as well as the November 20 date for this meeting—was also made in the immediate wake of Diem's murder. This Honolulu meeting on Vietnam would be special: for the first time both the Secretary of State and the President's Special Assistant for National Security Affairs, McGeorge Bundy, would attend.

NOTES

1. Memorandum for the Record by Lieutenant Colonel Sidney Berry, Jr., "en Route to Saigon, September 23, 1963," Subject: Secretary McNamara's Instructions to Party Delivered Aboard Plane, 1230–1330 (EDST) 23 September 1963, in *State History*, 1963, vol. 4, Document 146, pp. 146, 284–87.
2. Colby, interview with the author, August 9, 1991.
3. William Bundy, unpublished manuscript, pp. 9-17–9-28.
4. One person on Krulak's staff was Air Force Colonel Fletcher Prouty (the same colonel who had worked with Lansdale in 1961); Prouty, interview with the author, August 2, 1991. Prouty worked with Krulak every day and long into the night sending the cables back and forth to Saigon. He recalls that Krulak worked with Robert Kennedy in the White House, and perhaps with Ed Sorensen as well.
5. Henry Brandon, *Anatomy of Error*, p. 30. At the time, Brandon always seemed to get the inside story from the White House where other reporters did not.
6. William Bundy, unpublished manuscript, p. 9-23.
7. McNamara-Taylor Memorandum to the President, October 2, 1963, in *State History*, 1963, vol. 4, Document 167, pp. 336–46.
8. The material in this paragraph is based on William Sullivan's recollection as given in his Second Oral History, JFK Library.
9. For the October 1, 1963, version of the entire trip report see "Report of the McNamara-Taylor Mission to South Vietnam, 24 September–1 October 1963," JFK Library, Hilsman Papers, Vietnam, McNamara & Taylor Trip, Box 4/6.
10. Schlesinger, *Robert Kennedy and His Times*, p. 716.
11. Forrestal interview with Schlesinger, July 13, 1977, and Harriman interview with Schlesinger, June 6, 1965, as quoted in *Robert Kennedy and His Times*, p. 716.
12. Sullivan interview with William Rust, January 25, 1982, in *Kennedy in Vietnam*, p. 141.
13. Cooper, *The Lost Crusade*, pp. 215–16.
14. Sullivan Second Oral History, JFK Library.
15. Summary Record of the 519th Meeting of the National Security Council, White House, 6:00 P.M., October 2, 1963, in *State History*, 1963, vol. 4, Document 169, pp. 350–52.
16. Sullivan reportedly made such a threat; see Schlesinger, *Robert Kennedy and His Times*, p. 716.

17. For a complete text of the White House statement see *State History*, 1963, vol. 4, Document 170, pp. 353–54.

18. O'Donnell, *Johnny, We Hardly Knew Ye*, p. 17.

19. Mecklin, *Mission in Torment*, pp. 216–17.

20. Memorandum for the Record of a Meeting of the Executive Committee, the White House, 4:00 P.M., October 4, 1963, in *State History*, 1963, vol. 4, Document 174, pp. 358–59.

21. Memorandum for the Files of a Conference With the President, White House, 9:30 A.M., October 5, 1963, in *State History*, 1963, vol. 4, Document 179, pp. 368–69.

22. For NSAM-263, see *PP*, DOD ed., Book 12, p. 578; and *State History*, 1963, vol. 4, Document 194, pp. 395–96.

23. *PP*, Gravel ed., vol. 2, p. 169. Researchers beware that the date in this chronology in *The Pentagon Papers* is mistaken: it has this meeting taking place on October 3; the correct date, however, is given in the narrative portion of the same volume on p. 251.

24. Memorandum of a Meeting, White House, 6:00 P.M., October 3, 1963, in *State History*, 1963, vol. 4, Document 172, pp. 356–57.

25. Sullivan memo to Hilsman, October 3, 1963, in *State History*, 1963, vol. 4, Document 173, pp. 357–58.

26. Memorandum for the Record of a Meeting of the Executive Committee, White House, 4:00 P.M., October 4, 1963, in *State History*, 1963, vol. 4, Document 174, pp. 358–60.

27. Saigon CIA Station cable to CIA, October 5, 1963, in *State History*, 1963, vol. 4, Document 177, pp. 365–67.

28. For the meeting, see Memorandum for the Files of a Conference with the President, 9:30 A.M., October 5, 1963, in *State History*, 1963, vol. 4, Document 179, pp. 368–70; for NSAM-263 see Document 194, pp. 395–96.

29. State cable to Lodge No. 534, October 5, 1963, in *State History*, 1963, vol. 4, Document 181, pp. 371–79.

30. McGeorge Bundy cable to Lodge CAP 63650, October 5, 1963, in *State History*, 1963, vol. 4, Document 182, p. 379.

31. Mecklin, *Mission in Torment*, p. 219.

32. Lodge cable to Rusk No. 652, October 7, 1963, in *State History*, 1963, vol. 4, Document 186, pp. 385–86.

33. *State History*, 1963, vol. 4, p. 397, n. 3.

34. CIA cable to Lodge, October 9, 1963, in *State History*, 1963, vol. 4, Document 192, p. 393.

35. Summary of Saigon CIA Station cable to CIA, October 23, 1963, in *State History*, 1963, vol. 4, p. 423, n. 5.

36. Excerpt from Saigon CIA Station cable to CIA, October 23, 1963, in *State History*, 1963, vol. 4, Document 209, pp. 427–28.

37. Memorandum of a Conference With the President, 4:20 P.M., October 29, 1963, in *State History*, 1963, vol. 4, Document 234, pp. 468–71.

38. Memorandum of a Conference With the President, 6:00 P.M., October 29, 1963, in *State History*, 1963, vol. 4, Document 235, pp. 427–73.

39. McGeorge Bundy cable to Lodge, October 29, 1963, in *State History*, 1963, vol. 4, Document 236, pp. 473–75.

40. See the recapitulation of the generals' "double bump" plan in *State History*, 1963, vol. 4, p. 506, n. 3.

41. Memorandum for the Record of Discussion at the Daily White House Staff Meeting, 8:00 A.M., November 1, 1963, in *State History*, 1963, vol. 4, Document 263, p. 518.

42. *State History*, 1963, vol. 4, Document 274, p. 533.

43. Lodge cable to State No. 913, November 4, 1963, in *State History*, 1963, vol. 4, Document 290, pp. 559–60.

44. Maxwell Taylor, *Swords and Plowshares*, p. 301.

45. Schlesinger, *A Thousand Days*, pp. 909–10.

46. *State History*, 1963, vol. 4, p. 533.

47. See comprehensive list of meeting attendees, August 27, 1963 through November 2, 1963, JFK Library, NSF, Meeting, Box 317.

48. State cable to All Diplomatic Posts, November 2, 1963, in *State History*, 1963, vol. 4, Document 277, p. 536.

49. Rusk cable to Lodge No. 694, November 2, 1963, *Declassified Documents*, RC, 829G.

CHAPTER TWENTY-TWO

THE HONOLULU AGENDA

END OF THE OPTIMISTIC INTERLUDE

Midway between Kennedy's implementation of the withdrawal plan and the assassination of Diem, the State Department led a frontal attack on the fiction of battlefield success in Vietnam. The assault was launched with a major study by the State Department's Bureau of Intelligence and Research (INR)—RFE-90, entitled "Statistics on the War Effort in South Vietnam Show Unfavorable Trends."[1] The report, signed by INR Director Thomas Hughes on October 22, caused a sensation in Washington because it made the case for a deteriorating battlefield situation using statistics from MACV. Of course such conclusions would not have been the least bit surprising to USARPAC intelligence analysts, who had been doing this since MACV's creation in early 1962. The USARPAC Intelligence Bulletins, however, had not been landing on the desk of the President—even though we know that the Vice President was aware of their substance all along.

The timing of RFE-90 was no accident. The State Department did not suddenly figure out, in late October 1963, that something was wrong with the war effort. Nine days after the instructions that flowed from NSAM-263 were sent to Lodge, Kennedy followed up with a personal cable on October 14, in which he asked the Ambassador to "send personal reports at least weekly for my attention."[2] The President asked that Lodge address himself to a series of questions, and at the top of the list was this one: "Are we gaining or losing on balance and day by day in the contest with the Viet Cong?" Having already implemented the withdrawal plan, the answer to this question would ultimately determine both the justification and the fate of that plan. Lodge's first answer, sent to Kennedy on October 16, stated:

> We appear to me to be doing little more than holding our own. This looks like a long, smoldering struggle, with political and military aspects intertwined, each of which is stubborn in its own way.[3]

This was not an encouraging answer to the President, whose secret implementation of the first withdrawal increment had already left him casting a wary eye toward the battlefield. It was precisely at this time that a major effort was launched to document the war's failure and expose MACV's statistical charade.

The Hughes report said that "since July 1963, the trend in Viet Cong casualties, weapons losses, and defections has been downward while the number of Viet Cong armed attacks and other incidents has been upward." The report then added this numbing news:

> Comparison with earlier periods suggests that the military position of the government of Vietnam may have been set back to the point it occupied six months to a year ago. These trends coincide with the sharp deterioration of the political situation.

Even without the Buddhist crisis, the report went on, it was possible that the regime would not have been able to "maintain the favorable trends of previous periods in the face of accelerated Viet Cong effort."

The same day RFE-90 was issued, the U.S. Army attaché in Saigon sent a cable to the Pentagon about the approach of Colonel Khuong—the same approach that led to Harkins' attempt to thwart the coup—which confirmed the dreary interpretation of the battlefield held by the Vietnamese Joint General Staff where Khuong worked.[4] Did the U.S. really believe the military reports that the war would be won by 1965? Khuong asked. It was clear *he* did not. Why does the South Vietnamese Army fail to attack and press their advantage and kill more Viet Cong? Khuong asked the surprised Americans. The army could win, he said, but would not "so long as the present government remains in power." If things went unchanged, he said, the *Viet Cong* would win by 1965.

On October 23 Lodge sent Kennedy his second update.[5] The Ambassador said: "There appears to have been no significant change in the last week on a day-to-day basis." He concluded with the comment that the government was more preoccupied with protecting its own internal power structure than with attaining victory over the Viet Cong, adding darkly, "And the Viet Cong is developing." Two Lodge reports and RFE-90 were sufficient to get Taylor into the act. On October 29 he sent a cable to Harkins calling attention to "the divergent reporting on the military situation arriving through the MACV and Ambassadorial channels."[6] Taylor complained about Lodge's last battlefield report in this way:

> Saigon 768 contains statements on the progress of the campaign at variance with those which we have received from you and with the impressions which Secretary McNamara and I received in Saigon. Are we correct in believing that the Ambassador is forwarding military reports and evaluations without consulting you?

An embittered Harkins cabled back on October 30 that Lodge's "methods of operations" were entirely different than Nolting's had been where military reporting was concerned.[7] He said he disagreed with the Ambassador's assessment that "we are just holding our own." The government was "way ahead in I, II and part of III Corps," he said, "and making progress in the Delta." Harkins concluded with this reassuring sentence: "Nothing has happened in October to change the assessment you and Secretary McNamara made after your visit here."

That same day came Ambassador Lodge's next battlefield update for the President. It read:

> No major change in military situation since last week. Most noteworthy event which happened to me personally is highly secret statement by Gen[eral] Don, Acting Chief, Joint General Staff, that he did not think the war could be won [with] the present government in power before the Americans left and certainly could not be won after that.[8]

Lodge said it could be won but that it would take "more than is now being done" by the government. That evening Harkins sent another cable to Taylor showing inputs submitted to Lodge on October 16, 23, and 30, all saying, of course, that the government was winning the war.[9] Harkins said he never knew if Lodge used them because he was not allowed to see the cables the Ambassador sent to the President.

Back in Washington the battle over the battlefield began heating up. McGeorge Bundy called Harriman on October 30 to say McNamara was "indignant" that Harkins was not asked about Lodge's military assessments.[10] Harriman replied that Harkins' assessments were inaccurate and that Bundy should keep that in mind in connection with what Harkins might say. Harriman added that "he had a great deal of misgivings about the competence of Harkins' staff."

Not surprisingly, when the coup was over Lodge changed his tune. On November 5 he sent his next battlefield assessment to Kennedy.[11] It passed on this optimistic view: "I believe prospects of victory are much improved provided the generals stay united." Lodge took a jab at Harkins for saying the coup committee had been "greatly preoccupied" with the coup. "They did not," said Lodge, "lose sight of the necessity to keep a weather eye out for the counterinsurgency effort."

Meanwhile Krulak prepared a talking paper for a November 6 meeting that attacked RFE-90.[12] While the State paper used statistics from the defense agencies, he said, "Neither the memorandum itself nor its conclusions were coordinated with the Defense Department." The report had used "a few select statistical indicators over a short period of time, while ignoring many others, to form an extrapolated military judgment." Krulak said the report itself was of "little importance," but it could lead to interpretations of disagreements between the Departments of State and Defense that could only lead to the "embarrassment of both Departments and of the Government." He said the subject had been made more sensitive by "recent events" in Saigon—presumably the coup—and recommended McNamara be asked to bring up the matter with Rusk.

This is indeed what happened. On November 7 McNamara sent a copy of RFE-90, along with disparaging comments by the JCS, to Rusk.[13] In his cover memo McNamara said wryly: "If you were to tell me that it is not the policy of the State Department to issue military appraisals without seeking the views of the Defense Department the matter will die." Rusk sent McNamara a memo agreeing to this but he also included a memo by Hughes that said that in this case close "contact" had been effected both with the Defense Intelligence Agency and with Krulak's office.[14] In his memo Hughes pointed out that some of the statistics cited by the Defense Department in rebuttal of his study were wrong or had been made possible only because MACV had simply changed the reporting criteria on the Viet Cong. Finally, he said, the CIA had just released an independent study that "concurred with our findings using essentially the same statistical indicators and the same time period."[15]

At the end of October and early November then, overlaying the drama of Diem's death in Saigon was a sudden convergence of effort to show that the war was failing—using MACV's statistics. As Krepinevich states in his trenchant analysis of the war, the State Department assessment clearly struck a nerve among the Joint Chiefs, "questioning as it did the basic foundations upon which MACV had set its counterinsurgency program."[16] This was especially true for Taylor, whose influence over

Harkins had been prevalent since MACV's beginning. His incitement to Harkins to attack Lodge and Krulak's quibbling with the coordination of RFE-90, however, were remnants of a lost cause.

The final gasp was a Krulak study forwarded directly to McNamara at this time, which, in a once-over-the-world manner, delivered a broad retrospective evaluation of the war from 1960 through October 1963. *The Pentagon Papers* offers this comment on it:

> The [Krulak] report presented nothing less than a glowing account of steady progress across the board in the military situation. Significantly, it contained no hint that the rate of progress possibly might have temporarily slowed somewhat in the second half of 1963, despite the fact that it expressly treated events as late as October. Yet by this time, other evaluations giving quite a different picture were already asserting themselves.[17]

As Krepinevich points out, in December the Army staff would switch its view of the war from optimism to pessimism and "MACV would fall in line once General Harkins was removed."[18] It was in early November, however, that the last vestiges of support for the fiction that Harkins and Taylor had been clinging to finally fell away. As the Honolulu meeting approached the tide turned toward pessimism as suddenly and as swiftly as the optimistic interlude had begun in early 1962.

"TO BRING AMERICANS HOME"

It was November 12, just ten days before the assassination, when Senator Wayne Morse had a riveting talk with President Kennedy.[19] "I went down to the White House," Morse recalls, "and handed him his education bills, which I was handling on the Senate floor." Morse remembers making "two to five speeches a week against Kennedy on Vietnam." The Senator says his colleagues used to kid him, saying, "Wayne, haven't you covered that subject?" He would respond: "Apparently not. We teachers know the value of repetition in the learning process." Morse described what happened with Kennedy that day:

> I'd gone into President Kennedy's office to discuss education bills, but he said, "Wayne, I want you to know you're absolutely right in your criticism of my Vietnam policy. Keep this in mind. I'm in the midst of an intensive study which substantiates your position

on Vietnam. When I'm finished I want you to give me half a day
and come over and analyze it point by point."

Surprised, Morse asked if Kennedy understood his objections. Kennedy
replied, "If I don't understand your objections by now, I never will."

What was this "intensive study" on Vietnam that Kennedy was in the
midst of? Since early in the year his plan had been to wait until after the
1964 election to pull out. He had agreed with Mansfield that announcing
the withdrawal would lead to "a wild conservative outcry against returning
him to the Presidency for a second term."[20] Morse is not the only person
who knew Kennedy was reconsidering his Vietnam policy: so did Forrestal, who found out about it nine days later. Forrestal, of course, knew
something Wayne Morse did not: that Kennedy had already given the
order to withdraw 1,000 Americans from Vietnam by the end of the year.
Kennedy's rethinking appears to have been prompted by the sudden
shift in reporting on the battlefield situation in early November and
his nervousness about what this might mean for the upcoming election
campaign.

The shift in Kennedy's thinking led him to modify his public position
on the withdrawal and to make a far clearer commitment to carrying it
out. A brief review demonstrates how this came about. By waiting until
after the election to fully withdraw he could steer clear of a conservative
backlash; and, by beginning to bring a few men home, supposedly because
of the success on the battlefield, he could fend off the liberals, like Fulbright, who argued that Kennedy was bogging the U.S. down in a hope-
less quagmire. The crux of his public position was to stay in the middle
while letting his military advisors emphasize that they were winning the
war. Consequently, he had distanced himself from the optimistic withdrawal timetable announced publicly by McNamara on October 2. In
keeping with this plan, Kennedy included a requirement for secrecy when
he actually implemented the 1,000-man withdrawal with NSAM-263,
putting this secrecy requirement right in the directive itself.

In this way Kennedy moved forward as planned, well insulated from
attacks on either side as the upcoming election approached. The potential
problem, of course, was what to do if the battlefield situation made staying
on the fence untenable politically. The President's remarks at the October
2 NSC meeting[21] clearly indicate his fear that the situation could change
at any time, and his statements at an October 9 press conference demonstrate his concern that this uncertain situation could be a problem in the
election campaign. He said:

I cannot tell what our relations will be in Southeast Asia a year
from now. I know what results our policy is attempting to bring.

But I think the result ought to be judged in the summer of '64 and the fall of '64. . . . I would not want to make those judgments now, because I think we still have a long way to go before next summer. . . . I would say we are going to have a hard, close [election campaign] fight in 1964.[22]

As the moment drew nearer for the 1,000-man withdrawal, Kennedy still maintained secrecy about his decision to implement it. On October 31 Kennedy was asked point-blank whether he intended to speed up the withdrawal from Vietnam. He responded:

Well as you know, when Secretary McNamara and General Taylor came back, they announced that we would expect to withdraw a thousand men from South Vietnam before the end of the year and there has been some reference to that by General Harkins. *If* we were able to do that, that would be our schedule. I think the first unit or first contingent would be 250 men who are not involved in what might be called front-line operations. It would be our hope to lessen the number of Americans there by 1,000, as the training intensifies and is carried on in South Vietnam. [emphasis added][23]

These remarks show that the President, three weeks after the fact, was still not prepared to acknowledge that he *had* agreed to this timetable. His public position remained that the 1,000-man withdrawal was still an "if" at this point.

Then came the sudden turnaround of reporting in early November, as the CIA joined the State Department in decrying the state of the battlefield. The manner in which this reversal occurred—citing MACV's own statistics—thoroughly impugned Harkins' reporting, and any possibility of maintaining the fiction of battlefield success was dashed. It had become crystal clear to Kennedy, by this time, that the battlefield would not hold until the following summer. It was surely this unwelcome fact that forced him to reconsider his public stance on the war. This new situation was the context of the President's conversation on November 12 with Wayne Morse. In a press conference two days later someone asked Kennedy for his appraisal of Vietnam and what the purpose was for the Honolulu conference. In reply he said this:

Because we do have a *new* situation there, and a new government, we hope, an increased effort in the war. The purpose of the meeting at Honolulu—Ambassador Lodge will be there, General Harkins will be there, Secretary McNamara and others, and then, as you know, later Ambassador Lodge will come here—is to attempt to assess the situation: what American policy should be, and what our aid policy should be, how we can intensify the struggle, how we can bring Americans out of there. [emphasis added][24]

This was strange: gone from his list of American objectives was winning the war—it had been replaced by the phrase "intensify the struggle."

Earlier, at his September 12 press conference, Kennedy had said his policy was "simple" and listed three objectives: win the war, contain the communists, and bring the Americans home. That was *before* the change in reporting on the battlefield in early November. At the November 12 press conference he restated the American objectives this way:

> Now, that is our object, *to bring Americans home*, permit the South Vietnamese to maintain themselves as a free and independent country, and permit democratic forces within the country to operate—which they can of course, much more freely when the assault from the inside, and which is manipulated from the north, is ended. So the purpose of the meeting in Honolulu is how to pursue these objectives. [emphasis added]

This was a stronger emphasis on withdrawing Americans than the President had ever made publicly before: he now placed it at the head of America's objectives in Vietnam. In this statement too there was no provision for winning the war. He merely refers to permitting "democratic forces within the country to operate," a formulation that was only a step away from a political solution along the lines he had pursued in Laos.

Kennedy followed up this declaration with another substantive change: he lifted the secrecy requirement from the 1,000-man withdrawal. Two days after this press conference, the MAAG Chief in Vietnam, Major General Charles Timmes, made it official: 1,000 American soldiers would be coming home by the end of December.[25] Kennedy himself did not issue a press statement; he was at Palm Beach, Florida, at the time, where a White House spokesman would neither confirm nor deny the number of troops to be withdrawn. The spokesman did say, however, that the number "was being determined by the Department of Defense." Any high-level announcement in Washington would await the results of the Honolulu meeting.

Kennedy asked Forrestal to go along and then to proceed to Cambodia, which had been making charges of U.S. interference in its affairs. Before leaving, Forrestal met with Kennedy on November 21.[26] Forrestal reports what Kennedy said in that encounter:

He asked me to stay a bit; and he said: "When you come back, I want you to come and see me, because we have to start to plan for what we are going to do now, in South Vietnam." He said: "I want to start a complete and very profound review of how we got into this country; what we thought we were doing; and what we now think we can do." He said: "I even want to think about whether or not we should be there."

Kennedy told Forrestal that because this "was in the context of an election campaign," he could not consider a quick, "drastic change" of policy but instead how "some kind of a gradual shift in our presence in South Vietnam could occur."

Kennedy's dilemma was how to engineer this gradual shift while the battlefield situation was rapidly declining, and would perhaps do so even faster as the U.S. pulled out. His last remark about Vietnam, made in Fort Worth the morning he died, could not have stated this dilemma more clearly: "Without the United States, South Vietnam would collapse overnight."[27]

THE SITUATION SHAPES UP

It would be like one of the "periodic" sessions on Southeast Asia conducted by McNamara in Honolulu in the past, said a Defense Department official to reporters on November 12.[28] "State Department sources," said the *New York Times*, "indicated that the meeting in Honolulu would spare Ambassador Lodge the necessity of coming to Washington." This State Department tip on Lodge was certainly news, and so was the rest of what the Defense Department said about the war. In addition to being "notably cautious" in their outlook, the background briefers launched into the same sort of negative statistics that the State Department and CIA had been flagging earlier in the month. The *Times* article stated:

> In late October, according to Defense Department reports from South Vietnam, the ratio of fighting men killed, which had favored the government forces by 3 to 1, fell to barely 2 to 1. Defense officials are watching to see whether there is any improvement.

The same Defense officials said there had been "no change in plans" with respect to the 1,000-man withdrawal. "Presumably the Honolulu meeting will discuss the plans," the article said.

"From what I can gather the Honolulu Meeting is shaping up into a replica of its predecessors," Forrestal wrote to Bundy on November 13, "i.e., an eight-hour briefing conducted in the usual military manner."[29] Forrestal explained that in the past this meant that 100 people in CINC-PAC's conference room would be "treated to a dazzling display of maps and charts, punctuated with some impressive intellectual fireworks from Bob McNamara." At the daily White House staff meeting that morning, McGeorge Bundy remarked that "the agenda seemed to be full of briefings," and he asked Forrestal "if something could be done about that or whether they would have to have some dinners on the side to do some real talking."[30]

What did Bundy mean by "real talking" at dinners "on the side"? The minutes of the meeting, again made by Taylor's aide, Smith, indicate that this followed:

> Forrestal replied that the only way to break it up was to do as McNamara did, which was to interrupt loudly in the middle of any mechanical briefing. From this exchange, it became clear that at least Bundy and Forrestal plan to do most of their work outside the meetings.

What work would McGeorge Bundy be doing? He had never been to one of these conferences before. This question obviously struck someone in this staff meeting, who asked him why he was going at all. Bundy replied with the cryptic comment that "he had been instructed."

Kennedy had given Bundy his instructions. He was being sent to Honolulu to develop a new presidential directive centered on the objectives that Kennedy announced at his press conference the following day. As previously discussed, at the top of that list was "to bring Americans home." In anticipation of a possible public statement that would follow the Honolulu recommendations and subsequent presidential decisions, Kennedy also sent his Press Secretary, Pierre Salinger. Consequently, Rusk brought along his Assistant Secretary for Public Affairs, John Manning, and McNamara brought his Assistant Secretary for Public Affairs, Arthur Sylvester.

The final topic of discussion at Bundy's morning meeting was Lodge. It was decided that the State Department had misspoke about the Ambassador, who would "still have good reason to come to Washington," and this issue was to be cleared up that day. As has already been noted, the President confirmed this the next day. What was the "good reason" for Lodge to come to Washington? David Halberstam's *The Best and the Brightest* contains this passage:

On November 21 Henry Cabot Lodge flew to Honolulu on the first leg of a trip to Washington, where he planned to tell the President that the situation was much worse than they thought; even Lodge, who had been pushing the idea that the war was going badly, was shocked at just how discouraging it really was, and he planned to tell Kennedy that there was serious doubt as to whether any government could make it any more.[31]

Before the coup Lodge was pessimistic; after it he was optimistic. If Halberstam is right, Lodge had now changed his view again, the second time in just three weeks. Why so much vacillating?

The only answer could be the sudden turnabout of reporting in early November. *The Pentagon Papers* contains this description of that reversal:

> First, there was unmistakable and accumulating evidence that, in the period immediately after the coup, the situation had deteriorated in many places as a direct result of the coup. Then came increasing expression of a judgment that the deterioration was not merely an immediate and short lived phenomenon, but something, rather, that continued. . . . Finally, the impression, developed in many quarters, and eventually spread to all, that *before* the coup, the situation had been much more adverse than we had recognized officially at the time.[32]

The conference was shaping up all right, but not in the way that Kennedy, Bundy, and Forrestal had foreseen. The Secretary of Defense was about to be given—for the first time and in front of the most impressive group ever assembled on Vietnam policy—the unvarnished truth about the failing war effort.

THE HONOLULU CONFERENCE

Security was tight at Camp Smith, Hawaii, as the conferees began arriving on Wednesday the 19th. McCone had already arrived, and McNamara's plane landed at 10:00 P.M.; McGeorge Bundy and Forrestal would be on Rusk's plane, which would not arrive until moments before the conference began the following morning. "Officials Silent at Hawaiian Huddle on South Vietnam Policy," read a newspaper headline; Felt's staff told reporters: "There would most likely not be much said for publication."[33] The reporters were told they "would not be encouraged" to visit Camp Smith, where the talks would be held.

There was a reason for the secrecy, and the fact that McNamara said nothing when he left afterward. What happened in the conference was startling, and both Rusk and McNamara returned to Washington with "growing concern" about the war, especially in the Delta.[34] McGeorge Bundy returned with a draft NSAM for the President, which, if approved, would have expressed these growing concerns while maintaining his plans for withdrawing from the war. Kennedy did not approve it, of course, because he was on his way to a sniper's bullet in Dallas. The directive—NSAM-273—would be signed by his successor, Lyndon Baines Johnson. What Johnson signed, however, was not the same piece of paper that Bundy prepared for Kennedy.

When the November 20 meeting was over, McGeorge Bundy had the difficult task of trying to reconcile what had happened at Honolulu with Kennedy's Vietnam policy, a topic that will be returned to shortly. The NSAM that directly resulted from the proceedings at Honolulu has become one of the most controversial documents of the war. It is appropriate, therefore, before laying out what we do know about the meeting, to state what we still do not know about it and, in particular, the discussions that occurred "on the side."

The conference began at 8:00 A.M. with a private session in Felt's office restricted to the principals: Rusk, McNamara, Lodge, Taylor, Felt, and Harkins. There is no record of what happened at this meeting. From 8:30 to 10:15, all conference members met in the command center to listen to presentations on Agenda Items A—"Country Team Review of Situation"—and B—"Prospects and measures proposed by Country Team, for improved prosecution of the war under the new Government." For these briefings we have a record created at CINCPAC.[35] After a short break, the principals, joined this time by McGeorge Bundy, McCone, and Bell, retired to the executive conference room for another restricted session. There is no record of what happened at this meeting either, which took place from 10:35 to 12:00. While this was going on, the rest of the conferees were broken down into four groups to carry out separate discussions "of programs to produce recommendations to Principals."

Group 1 was to again discuss Agenda Items A and B; Group 2 was to discuss Items C—the MAP and Comprehensive Plan and "associated Country Team Plans"—and D—an outline of the withdrawal program; Group 3 was to discuss Item E—a new reporting system; and Group 4 was to discuss Items F—CIA-MACV "Relationships"—and G, whose subject we do not know, but which was probably North Vietnam and Laos operations if the list of subjects in an associated "Briefing Book" are any indication. No record exists of any of these discussions; but we do have a sanitized version of the Honolulu Meeting Briefing Book.[36] The briefing book has nearly all of the submissions made at the Conference.

Lodge's presentation was full of contradiction. Where he had earlier been so insistent on reforms by Diem, he seemed to have a different standard for the generals. He said he "doubted the wisdom of the U.S. making sweeping demands for democratization or for early elections at this time." He said he would "instead urge that the U.S. be patient and give the generals a chance to get on with the war." His outlook was "hopeful," he said, but certain facts in his briefing must have been upsetting for McNamara and Rusk to hear. For example, his comment that the generals wanted to drastically reduce or eliminate the population being put into "forced labor" to build the strategic hamlets was not the picture of happy little villagers secure from the Viet Cong that the Secretaries had been reading about for the past two years. Lodge said the government finally had the support of the urban population, but then added, "However, in the final analysis the war will be won or lost in the country-side and to date the rural population is still apathetic."

When Harkins got up to brief the military situation, he said there was "no difference of opinion" between him and Lodge on the situation or the conduct of the war, to which Lodge immediately agreed. This was not true, and even amusing. After all the backbiting and struggle of the previous two months, one could justifiably ask what had happened to make them now like two peas in a pod? Harkins discussed statistics, but these were inconclusive. The problem was "one of people, not statistics," he said. He too said the rural population was "apathetic."

Harkins said the support from the "man in the hamlet" would depend on whether the government could assure his security. He also said there were insufficient military forces at the village level to "make it safe for the people to report on the VC." McNamara then "asked if the reason that so many strategic hamlets were considered unsuccessful was for security, economic, or political reasons." For "all three," replied an expert on hand. In his briefing on the hamlet program, Deputy Chief of Mission Trueheart admitted that its implementation had been "faulty" under the Diem regime.

A briefing item on the "Requirements for the Delta Campaign"[37] contained some truly shocking military news. According to the briefing book:

In the summer of 1963 the Viet Cong in the Delta began to react more sharply to the growing Vietnamese pressure. While engagements were only slightly more frequent, they were much more intense on both sides. The toll against the Viet Cong was particularly heavy. During August, September, and October over

4,000 Viet Cong were killed or captured in the Delta area, yet their
strength in mid-November had not greatly diminished, remaining
at something over 7,000 hard-core plus about 25,000 irregulars.

These casualty figures were either suspect or the Viet Cong had successfully recruited 4,000 soldiers from an "apathetic" population. In any
event, this briefing indicated that the war was going downhill in the Delta,
and had been since July. It is not clear how many of these briefings
McNamara listened to before he finally made the comment that "the
situation in the Delta and [the] strategic hamlet program itself are both
serious, immediate problems."

The briefing on the withdrawal program had a surprise.[38] The overall
plan, as directed by McNamara at the July 1962 conference, according to
the written submission, was "based on the assumption" that Viet Cong
activity would be reduced to a level the government could handle by
1965. No statement followed on whether this assumption still appeared
to be valid. In truth, of course, it was not. The briefing went on to cite
some of the aspects of the Comprehensive Plan, and how the 1,000-man
withdrawal was part of that. In one of the tabbed enclosures (TAB E) to
the written report, however, was evidence that the 1,000-man withdrawal
had been gutted.

The initial plan that CINCPAC had submitted in July and McNamara
approved in September had what was called a "50-50 mix of unit and
individual personnel withdrawal." The personnel portion of this mix is
where slack could be introduced, since it was possible to show a medical
evacuee, for example, as an individual personnel withdrawal—providing
that the individual was not replaced until January. In other words, the
plan as it stood in September required true units comprising 500 men
to be withdrawn. In October, following a MACV "recommendation,"
CINCPAC changed the mix to "30 percent units and 70 percent individuals." This meant that only 300 men in real units would be withdrawn.
Taylor, according to the tabbed enclosure, approved this revision in November 1963.

The history of how true units were eviscerated from the 1,000-man
withdrawal plan can only be found in the Honolulu Meeting Briefing
Book. The nearly fifty pages of material on the withdrawal plan in *The
Pentagon Papers* do not mention this at all.[39] What follows here is, to the
author's knowledge, the first time the details of this obscure but significant
act have been fully discussed. The plan that Taylor approved removed the
following nine units from the withdrawal: an Army support unit; an
armed helicopter (HU-1B) transportation company; a Caribou (cargo)
test unit; an Air Force support unit; a defoliation C-123 detachment; an

Air Defense F-102 detachment; the 6091st Reconnaissance Detachment; a detachment of the 1964th Communications Group; and a detachment of the 5th TAC (air control) Group. These units contained a total of 538. Two new units were added to the withdrawal: a Caribou (cargo) company and the 91st Medical Detachment, which together had 157 men in them. To keep the appearance of a 1,000-man withdrawal, however, the list was padded with 513 Army and Air Force "individuals."

The only original units this left were the 560th Military Police Company, a few medical civic action teams, and a Marine security platoon, which together comprised just 134 men. When these were added to the new cargo company and the 91st Medical Detachment, the units in the final withdrawal plan contained only 284 men. In other words, the final withdrawal plan was 72 percent "individuals." It is not clear whether this was briefed orally to the principals. It is obvious from these changes that the 1,000-man withdrawal had been whittled down to the point that it was meaningless. The remaining 28 percent of the withdrawal, which were units, was nothing more than a few medics, some military police, and one solitary platoon of Marines. This was a far cry from the armed helicopters, fighter aircraft, and other combat-associated units in the plan McNamara had approved in September. *The Pentagon Papers* does tell us this about the plan's "execution" after the Honolulu meeting:

> It proved essentially an accounting exercise. Technically, more than a thousand U.S. personnel did leave, but many of these were part of the normal turnover cycle, inasmuch as rotation policy alone, not to mention medical evacuation or administrative reasons, resulted in an average rate of well over a thousand returnees per month.[40]

It was therefore a simple matter of slowing down the "replacement pipeline" temporarily.

Incredibly, after all the meetings, memos, plans, approvals, and a Presidential National Security Action Memorandum (263), the much vaunted 1,000-man withdrawal was carried out by a couple of personnel clerks who accomplished it by just delaying replacements of individuals for a few days. Even this did not work fully, and the December strength dipped by about 800 men instead of 1,000 because of "additional deployments approved since September." This was a pathetic end to the bold and determined effort that Kennedy had engineered in NSAM-263.

When Taylor approved CINCPAC's "revision" of the withdrawal plan he did not send it to McNamara's office. Instead, it just showed up quietly as a little tabbed enclosure to a written document in a briefing book at the Honolulu meeting. Why was this? The answer might be that Taylor did not want McNamara to know about it. McNamara had asked for real units to be put in the 1,000-man withdrawal, and, in fact, they had been; that they were gutted from the plan Taylor approved in early November, which was itself placed in an obscure corner of a briefing book, indicates, at the least, that Taylor played a key role in rendering the 1,000-man withdrawal inconsequential.

Taylor had approved something else that had not been sent to McNamara's office: CINCPAC OPLAN 34-63, plans for covert operations against North Vietnam. This plan Taylor had approved on September 9, and it too showed up at the Honolulu meeting—more than ten weeks later. It, however, was not buried in the back of a briefing book, and was discussed in detail by the principals.

The OPLAN that emerged from the Honolulu meeting contained provisions for the following covert actions against North Vietnam:

> (1) harassment; (2) diversion; (3) political pressure; (4) capture of prisoners; (5) physical destruction; (6) acquisition of intelligence; (7) generation of intelligence; and (8) diversion of [North Vietnamese] resources.[41]

In addition, the plan included "selected actions of graduated scope and intensity to include commando type coastal raids." It was such raids that produced the Tonkin Gulf incidents the following August—along with a congressional blank check to escalate the war.

The issue of operations against North Vietnam was part of the larger Switchback program, dating from the investigation into the failure of the Bay of Pigs, which was meant to transfer large paramilitary covert operations from the CIA to the military. Up to this point in the war, operations had been conducted against North Vietnam, but these were small CIA actions, and the military's attitude at the Honolulu meeting, says Colby, was that "the CIA was not vigorous or large enough" to have enough military effect.[42] Colby contends the military wanted to take over operations against the north, and argued this:

> we were running a sort of hand-to-mouth operation—a few tired old airplanes and a fairly small number of teams dropped in—and if the military could get hold of it they'd put a critical mass of bulk in it and it would begin to have an effect.

The failure of these small operations had led Colby to lose confidence in the entire idea of covert operations against North Vietnam. Consequently, he says, this happened:

So in the middle of the conference, when they were talking about how they were going to build up to make bigger operations, finally, at one point, I said, "Mr. Secretary, it isn't gonna work. It's just not gonna work."

In his memoir, Colby says: McNamara "listened to me with a cold look and then rejected my advice."[43]

The CINCPAC OPLAN was discussed, he says, and "all these operations," and the military felt that "if the CIA, and personally me, didn't think that they could run it, that was because we just diddled at it instead of putting a massive effort into it." The military was confident that a "full-fledged effort"—as opposed to the sort of small operation that failed at the Bay of Pigs—"could work." Colby later wrote that McNamara was sure the larger scale that was possible for the military could wreak "serious damage" to North Vietnam's military effort. In the end the decision was made to go ahead with the operations. Both MACV and Colby, says the Navy history of the war, "were ordered to prepare a twelve-month, three-phase plan for actions against North Vietnam in a campaign of graduated intensity."[44] The CIA was asked, Colby wrote, to contribute to the military's effort in the political and propaganda fields, and several CIA officers were attached to the military program for this purpose.[45]

"The desire to put pressure on North Vietnam prevailed," Colby recalls, "and there and then the United States military started the planning and activity that would escalate finally to full-scale air attacks."[46] Did the discussion include direct U.S. actions against North Vietnam? "Oh sure, that was the idea in turning it over to the military." He says that he never thought this would work or "that we would be able to succeed in paramilitary operations into North Vietnam." There was one occasion, three or four months after the conference, when a team got off a boat in North Vietnam, went in and shot up a convoy, and got out in the boat. "McNamara thought that was the greatest thing since sliced bread," Colby said, but added, "I've been on those operations. I know. I've blown up railroads. The enemy fixes them the next day."

The upshot of the Honolulu meeting, then, was that the shocking deterioration of the war effort was presented in detail to those assembled, along with a plan to widen the war, while the 1,000-man withdrawal was turned into a meaningless paper drill. The phony withdrawal remained buried in the fine print; the widening of the war against North Vietnam, however, would require presidential approval.

NOTES

1. *PP*, DOD ed., Book 12, pp. 579–82.
2. Kennedy cable to Lodge, October 14, 1963, in *State History*, 1963, vol. 4, Document 195, pp. 396–97.
3. Lodge cable to Kennedy No. 712, October 16, 1963, in *State History*, 1963, vol. 4, Document 197, pp. 401–3.
4. Jones cable to the ACSI, Department of the Army, October 22, 1963, in *State History*, 1963, vol. 4, Document 206, pp. 419–20.
5. Lodge cable to Kennedy No. 768, October 23, 1963, in *State History*, 1963, vol. 4, Document 207, pp. 421–24.
6. Taylor cable to Harkins, October 29, 1963, in *State History*, 1963, vol. 4, Document 227, pp. 455–56.
7. Harkins cable to Taylor, October 30, 1963, in *State History*, 1963, vol. 4, Document 240, pp. 479–82.
8. Lodge cable to Kennedy No. 821, October 30, 1963, in *State History*, 1963, vol. 4, Document 245, pp. 493–95.
9. Harkins cable to Taylor, October 30, 1963, in *State History*, 1963, vol. 4, Document 246, pp. 496–98.
10. Memo of Harriman-McGeorge Bundy telephone conversation, October 30, 1963, in *State History*, 1963, vol. 4, Document 248, p. 500.
11. Lodge cable to Kennedy No. 302, November 6, 1963, in *State History*, 1963, vol. 4, Document 302, pp. 575–78.
12. SACSA-T11-63, November 4, 1963, JFK Library, Hilsman Papers, Far East, Box 4/6.
13. Memo from McNamara to Rusk, November 7, 1963, with attachments, JFK Library, Hilsman Papers, Far East, Box 4/6.
14. Memo from Hughes to Rusk, November 8, 1963, in *State History*, 1963, vol. 4, Document 306, pp. 582–86.
15. This document has not been found; *State History* (1963, vol. 4, p. 584, n. 5) says only that it was "Not further identified."
16. Krepinevich, *The Army and Vietnam*, p. 89.
17. *PP*, Gravel ed., vol. 2, p. 192.
18. Krepinevich, *The Army and Vietnam*, p. 91.
19. See comments by Wayne Morse, in David Nyhan, "We've Been a Police State a Long Time," *Boston Globe*, June 24, 1973.
20. O'Donnell, *Johnny, We Hardly Knew Ye*, p. 16.
21. *State History*, 1963, vol. 4, p. 351.
22. Kennedy, *Public Papers*, 1963, pp. 774–75.
23. Ibid., p. 828.
24. Ibid., p. 846.
25. Associated Press, "1,000 Troops to Leave Vietnam," *New York Times*, November 16, 1963.
26. See the NBC White Paper on Vietnam, December 1971. For a shorter treat-

ment of this Kennedy-Forrestal exchange, see Schlesinger, *Robert Kennedy and His Times*, p. 722.

27. He made these remarks at the Forth Worth Chamber of Commerce, and was assassinated a few hours later in Dallas; Kennedy, *Public Papers*, 1963.

28. *New York Times*, November 13, 1963.

29. Forrestal memo to McGeorge Bundy, November 13, 1963, JFK Library, NSF, Country File, Vietnam, Box 204.

30. Memorandum for the Record of Discussion at the Daily White House Staff Meeting, 8:00 A.M., November 13, 1963, in *State History*, 1963, vol. 4, Document 312, pp. 593–94.

31. Halberstam, *The Best and the Brightest*, p. 298.

32. *PP*, Gravel ed., vol. 3, pp. 22–23.

33. Charles Bernard, "U.S. Officials Silent at Hawaii Huddle on S. Vietnam Policy," *Philadelphia Enquirer*, November 20, 1963.

34. Cooper, *The Lost Crusade*, p. 225.

35. Memorandum of Discussion at the Special Meeting on Vietnam, Honolulu, November 20, 1963, in *State History*, 1963, vol. 4, Document 321, pp. 608–24.

36. JFK Library, NSF, Country File, Vietnam, Box 204. Researchers beware: the extant copy is scrambled, and it took the author some time to put his own copy in correct order—this may be found in JFK Library, Newman Papers.

37. Honolulu Meeting Briefing Book, Item 12.

38. Ibid., Item 15.

39. It is interesting that this particular part of the story is missing from *The Pentagon Papers*, which has an otherwise useful account of withdrawal planning. For example, see the Gravel ed., vol. 2, pp. 165–73, for a chronology of the paper trail: the July submission (mentioned in the Honolulu Meeting Briefing Book) appears to be the CINCPAC MAP program proposed to the JCS on July 18; however, the October MACV "recommendation" and CINCPAC "revision," as well as Taylor's November approval, are all missing. The narrative, on pp. 182–83, is no more enlightening on this point.

40. *PP*, Gravel ed., vol. 2, pp. 191–92.

41. *PP*, DOD ed., Book 3, Section IV.C.2(a), p. 2.

42. Colby, interview with the author, July 21, 1988.

43. William Colby, *Honorable Men* (New York: Simon and Schuster, 1978), p. 220.

44. *USN and the Vietnam Conflict*, p. 335.

45. Colby, *Honorable Men*, pp. 220–21.

46. Colby, interview with the author, August 9, 1991.

CHAPTER TWENTY-THREE

THE DRUMS AFTER DALLAS

NOVEMBER 21—DRAFT NSAM-273

"Defense Secretary McNamara left here last night for Washington," read an Associated Press dispatch from Hawaii on November 21, "to report to President Kennedy on his top-level meeting with experts on South Vietnam's new regime."[1] McGeorge Bundy was on board McNamara's plane, but Rusk and others stayed behind waiting for their departure to Tokyo on the morning of November 22. Rusk's public affairs chief, Robert Manning, made a brief announcement on November 21 about the Honolulu conference. He described it as "more of a discussion than an arrival at a full set of finished decisions," and further explained that the meeting had produced "the raw material for recommendations" to be made to the President.

These materials were indeed put into recommendations for Kennedy, which were themselves put into a draft NSAM by McGeorge Bundy, which was prepared in the White House on November 21. Asked nearly thirty years later to examine the document and comment about its authorship, Bundy stated, "The typewriter appears to have been mine, and while some of the sentences were submitted by others, yes, I probably was the drafter."[2] After examining this and other documents pertaining to his participation at the Honolulu meeting, Bundy recalled the experience and the fact that he was surprised by the pessimism of the military briefings there. With respect to the recommendations, including the planned widening of the war against North Vietnam, Bundy explained that, in drafting the NSAM, "I tried to bring them in line with the words that Kennedy might want to say."

The first four paragraphs were general, and did not necessarily proceed from the Honolulu meeting. The first paragraph reiterated the essence of Kennedy's policy: "It remains the central object of the United States in South Vietnam to *assist* the people and government of that country to win *their* contest against the externally directed and supported Communist conspiracy" [emphasis added].[3] The test of all decisions and actions was to be how effectively they contributed to "this purpose."

The second paragraph, which addressed the withdrawal, was ambiguous. It was one sentence: "The objectives of the United States with respect to the withdrawal of U.S. military personnel remain as stated in the White House statement of October 2, 1963." That statement, however, had spoken only of McNamara's and Taylor's "judgment" that the "major part" of the U.S. military task could be finished by the end of 1965, and that the training program "should have progressed to the point" where 1,000 men could be withdrawn. What was implied in the draft NSAM, then, was that the 1963 and 1965 benchmarks were valid only if the McNamara-Taylor judgment held up. Since the October 2 statement had been purposely designed to separate Kennedy from that judgment, the reference to this unclassified statement—instead of the top secret NSAM (263) that implemented the first part of the withdrawal—was a tacit step backward from NSAM-263.

The third paragraph was an innocuous slap on the wrist to "U.S. officers," reminding them to "conduct themselves" in a way to help the new government "consolidate itself" and increase its popularity. The fourth paragraph, however, was a strongly worded order to "all senior officers of the government" to steer clear of any "public recrimination" and to "take energetic steps to ensure that they and their subordinates go out of their way to maintain and to defend the unity of the United States Government both here and in the field." This problem had been bothering Kennedy, who had issued similar stern warnings for the past several weeks.

The next six paragraphs were described as "lines of action developed in the discussions of the Honolulu meeting of November 20." Paragraph five called for a concentration of American and South Vietnamese effort "on the *critical* situation in the Delta" [emphasis added]. It mentioned a full panoply of military and nonmilitary efforts and referred to turning the tide not just of battle but also of "belief." That the tide of popular support was against the government was something Kennedy had begun to publicly acknowledge in the summer—beginning with the Cronkite interview. What made this paragraph unusual and important was that Kennedy, if he approved it, would be admitting for the first time that the battlefield situation in the most populous and rich area of the country—the Delta—was failing.

Paragraph six was technical—unusually so for a presidential NSAM. It was essentially a call to *maintain* military and economic assistance at the same levels as during the time of Diem's government. It contained the curious provision that these levels should not decline in "their magnitude and effectiveness in the eyes of the Vietnamese government," raising the possibility that this might not be the case in the eyes of someone else—such as the U.S. The call was further complicated by a provision that meant, in essence, that there could be no economizing within the Military Assistance Program (MAP) for ammunition and no readjustments whatsoever between the MAP and "other U.S. defense resources." Without getting into the nitty-gritty of financing, the real question is whether this paragraph was really aimed at restoring assistance to what it had been before some of the cuts were made to pressure Diem, or whether it was in fact a subtle attempt to forestall any future cutback in U.S. assistance. In this author's opinion, it included strands of both, and it is the sort of wording that could lead people to justify contradictory actions.

Paragraph seven addressed actions against North Vietnam and watered down considerably the measures—under OPLAN 34-63—that Colby and Harkins had been told to develop. It stated:

> With respect to action against North Vietnam, there should be a detailed plan for the development of additional Government of Vietnam resources, especially for sea-going activity, and such planning should indicate the time and investment necessary to achieve a wholly new level of effectiveness in this field of action.

Not one word about U.S. resources was mentioned. South Vietnamese covert actions against the North was something that Kennedy had urged since the first days of his administration.[4] Escalating the war to include unilateral American actions against North Vietnam, however, was something Kennedy had been against from the beginning, and had told Hilsman in 1962 that he feared there would be calls for such action. Moreover, such an escalation was not the direction in which the President wished to move U.S. policy, and that is the reason why Bundy confined the words in this paragraph to "Government of Vietnam resources."

Paragraph eight called for South Vietnamese "military operations up to a line [of] 50 [k]ilometers inside Laos, together with political plans for minimizing the international hazards of such an enterprise." This meant that U.S. advisors might be going inside Laos with Vietnamese units and that a plan for plausible denial was needed. It also said that since operational responsibility for these kinds of actions should pass from the CIA to MACV—part of the Switchback program—an alternative method of "political liaison" was necessary, meaning coordination between MACV and the Embassies in Vietnam and Laos and perhaps other organizations as well.

Paragraph nine dealt with Cambodia, which had been making charges against the U.S., including CIA–Chinese Nationalist collusion to assassinate Sihanouk and communist officials; U.S. smuggling of arms into the country under diplomatic immunity; and infiltration of Cambodian antigovernment forces by the CIA.[5] The draft NSAM said this:

> measures should be taken to satisfy ourselves completely that the recent charges from Cambodia are groundless, and we should put ourselves in a position to offer the Cambodians a full opportunity to satisfy themselves on this same point.

Paragraph nine, referring back to the paragraphs on operations against North Vietnam and inside Laos, said that another version of the Jordan report was necessary—an updated demonstration of how the insurgency in the south was controlled from the north and supplied through Laos.

All in all, the draft NSAM was an effort to produce—from the news of defeat on the battlefield and recommendations to step up the war—a directive that Kennedy could live with. Kennedy, after all, could be expected to approve measures which would "intensify"—a word he used in his press conferences—the struggle, so long as they contributed toward the overall objective of de-Americanizing the war.

In the daily White House staff meeting on November 22, held at 8:00 A.M., Bundy explained that briefings of McNamara "tend to be sessions where people try to fool him, and he tries to convince them they cannot."[6] At the Honolulu meeting, however, Bundy said, someone had told him that "for the first time" the military reporting was realistic about the situation in the Delta. Bundy added he was not sure whether this had resulted from the U.S. military feeling it could criticize the war effort without fear of criticizing the government, "or whether it was something more fundamental."

Was there some more fundamental reason why the truth was finally told at Honolulu? In this author's opinion there was. It is the same reason that the reporting changed so swiftly in November—*backdated* to July. Kennedy had engineered a public recommendation from McNamara and Taylor on withdrawal that he had secretly implemented. The timing of the change in reporting was apparently an immediate reaction to this move by Kennedy, and an attempt to create political circumstances during the upcoming campaign that would make it difficult to carry through with the withdrawal spelled out in NSAM-263.

At 12:30 P.M., on November 22, the shots rang out in Dealey Plaza that took the President's life. His Vietnam policy died with him. On the surface, the shift in the war effort seemed gradual: it was fifteen months before the first American Marines waded ashore at Da Nang, South Vietnam. Some aspects of the reversal, however, were more sudden— almost instantaneous. The underlying reason why the larger change took as long as it did was that Johnson faced the same problem Kennedy had: the 1964 presidential election. The key to understanding how this campaign problem differed for these two men is this: Kennedy had to disguise a withdrawal; Johnson had to disguise intervention.

NOVEMBER 24—THE FIRST VIETNAM MEETING

On November 23 McGeorge Bundy wrote President Johnson a memo advising him on how to handle his cabinet members during the meeting scheduled for that day.

> A number of them—and perhaps still more some of the others who regularly attend Cabinet [meetings]—are quite numb with personal grief, and in keeping with your own instinct of last night you will wish to avoid any suggestion of over-assertiveness.[7]

Johnson heeded this advice. At a 3:00 P.M. meeting the following day, however, he was his usual assertive self. Rusk, McNamara, Ball, McGeorge Bundy, McCone, and Lodge were all on hand for Johnson's first Vietnam meeting as President.

Some accounts of the meeting say Lodge gave a pessimistic briefing, others that he was hopeful.[8] Most, however, agree that Johnson made some startlingly strong remarks. "I am not going to lose Vietnam," Johnson said, and added, "I am not going to be the President who saw Southeast Asia go the way that China went."[9] He ordered Lodge to "tell those generals in Saigon that Lyndon Johnson intends to stand by our word."[10]

McCone's notes of the meeting suggest the *he*, not Lodge, gave a dire description of the war effort.[11] McCone's notes show that Lodge exerted great effort to assure Johnson that "we were in no way responsible" for the deaths of Diem and Nhu. This was just as well for Lodge, because the President said he was "not at all sure we took the right course in upsetting the Diem regime," and implied, according to McCone, that, "left to his own devices, he would *not* have supported the courses of action which led to the coup." McCone's recollections of that meeting contain this passage:

> *Note:* I received in this meeting the first "President Johnson tone" for action as contrasted with the "Kennedy tone." Johnson definitely feels that we place too much emphasis on social reforms; he has very little tolerance with our spending so much time being "do-gooders"; and he has no tolerance whatsoever with bickering and quarreling of the type that has gone on in South Vietnam.

Johnson's words were apparently quite threatening. He said he had *"never been happy with our operations in Vietnam"* [emphasis added]. There had been "serious dissension and divisions" and he told Lodge he "wanted the situation cleaned up." LBJ said he wanted "no more divisions of opinion, no more bickering and any person that did not conform to policy should be removed."

McCone says he told Johnson that there had been a continuing increase in Viet Cong activity; that enemy communications possibly reflected preparations for sustained communist pressure; the military were getting little help from the civilians in completing the political reorganization of the government; and that he could not give an optimistic appraisal of the future.

According to Johnson's own account, after the talk with Lodge (who apparently left at this point), the conversation shifted to what had transpired at the Honolulu meeting.[12] Johnson says he understood the conference to have been a "modestly encouraging assessment," but that Rusk and McNamara "expressed some reservations." Most agreed, Johnson said, that "we could begin withdrawing some of our military advisors by the end of the year and a majority of them by the end of 1965." This statement needs clarification, since "some advisors" was not the same as the units originally intended to be in the withdrawal.

Although there is no account indicating that the composition of the units to be included in the withdrawal was discussed at the November 24 meeting, a message sent to CINCPAC from the JCS two days later—after Johnson signed NSAM-273—directed Felt to "make specific recommendations on [the] extension of the USMC helicopter squadron in [Vietnam] beyond [the] currently contemplated withdrawal date.[13] The message, however, had been drafted by Krulak on November 23 and sent to both McNamara and William Bundy. This helicopter squadron undoubtedly included the armed helicopter company that had been excised from the withdrawal by the revision Taylor had approved before the

Honolulu conference. It was also probably the same unit Kennedy had in mind when he told McNamara, regarding the withdrawal, to tell the reporters "that means the helicopter pilots too."

The "Honolulu report," Johnson's account says, "originally prepared for President Kennedy," emphasized three problems: the new government needed "strong support" from the U.S.; the enormous South Vietnamese deficit could undermine everything; and the divisiveness in the American Mission in Saigon had to be eliminated. No such Honolulu report has ever been seen or commented on by anyone in the nearly thirty years since then. Johnson may have been referring to the two memoranda, one from McNamara[14] and the other from Rusk,[15] he received before the meeting, as these two memoranda do stress the need for "teamwork" and dealing with the deficit problem. Johnson's memoir, however, does not do justice to the troubling picture he received of the war effort at the White House meeting on November 24.

When it was over, Johnson, alone with his aide, Bill Moyers, tilted back in his chair, propped his feet up on the wastebasket, and began "clinking the ice cubes in his pale-colored glass."[16] What did Lodge say? Moyers asked. "He says it's going to hell in a handbasket out there," Johnson replied. "He says the army won't fight. . . . Says the people don't know whose side to be on. If we don't do something, he says, it'll go under—any day."

This contradicts the statement in Johnson's memoir that Lodge gave a "hopeful" presentation. Since Moyers was with the President right after the meeting, the weight of the evidence appears to support what Halberstam said about the pessimistic report Lodge intended to bring back to Kennedy. The rest of LBJ's conversation with Moyers was extraordinary. "So?" said Moyers, in response to the possibility of Vietnam going under. Johnson stared in his glass, and said, "So they'll think with Kennedy dead we've lost heart. So they'll think we're yellow and we don't mean what we say."

"Who?" asked Moyers, apparently uncertain what people Johnson had in mind. "The Chinese," Johnson said. "The fellas in the Kremlin. They'll be taking the measure of us. They'll be wondering just how far they can go." "What are you going to do?" Moyers inquired. "I'm going to give those fellas out there the money they want," LBJ said. "This crowd today says a hundred or so million will make the difference." "What did you say?" Moyers asked. Johnson replied:

> I told them they got it—more if they need it. I told them I'm not
> going to let Vietnam go the way of China. I told them to go back
> and tell those generals in Saigon that Lyndon Johnson intends to
> stand by our word, but by God, I want 'em to get off their butts

and get out in those jungles and whip hell out of some Communists. And I want 'em to leave me alone, because I've got some bigger things to do right here at home.

"I hope they will," Moyers replied.

In fact, Johnson did more than authorize additional money for the war in Vietnam. As a result of the conversations he had with his advisors that day, a new presidential directive on Vietnam was prepared, and Johnson signed it the day after Kennedy was buried.

NSAM-273—THE DAM BREAKS

Johnson claimed that he and "Kennedy's principal foreign affairs advisors" agreed that it was important to show that Johnson was continuing Kennedy's Vietnam policy, and that, with this in mind, he approved NSAM-273 on November 26. There are two reasons why this claim is extremely misleading. In the first place, while McGeorge Bundy had originally drafted the NSAM expecting that Kennedy would be alive to examine it, it had *not*, of course, been approved by Kennedy, and it contained some items he might have changed. The most important reason Johnson's claim is invalid is that the NSAM he approved on November 26 had been altered—*significantly*—from the November 21 draft. These revisions were uniformly escalatory, and were based, according to Bundy, upon the directives that Johnson gave on Sunday, November 24.[17] Johnson, recalls Bundy, "held stronger views on the war than Kennedy did," and this was the reason that the final NSAM was stronger.

The first change in the final version of NSAM-273 was paragraph four, which strengthened the requirement that officials avoid public recriminations by adding this sentence:

> It is of particular importance that express or implied criticism of officers or of other branches be scrupulously avoided in all contacts with the Vietnamese Government and with the press.

The effect was to amplify this requirement and to specify the press and the Saigon regime as areas were expression of dissent was particularly to be avoided. This change should not be considered a reversal of Kennedy's views.

A tiny change was made to paragraph five,[18] but the next substantive change was to paragraph seven, on operations against North Vietnam.

This revision was the most significant of all the changes made to Bundy's first draft. The entire first part of the sentence from the draft NSAM—which mentioned who the operations were against, as well as the specific wording that the plan would be to develop South Vietnamese resources—was missing. The paragraph now read as follows:

> 7. Planning should include different levels of possible increased activity, and in each instance there should be estimates of such factors as:
> A. Resulting damage to North Vietnam;
> B. The plausibility of denial;
> C. Possible North Vietnamese retaliation;
> D. Other international reaction.
> Plans should be submitted promptly for approval by higher authority.

This revision opened the door to direct U.S. attacks against North Vietnam, and CINCPAC OPLAN 34-63, which became OPLAN 34A, was promptly submitted to the White House less than a month later. This provision of NSAM-273 was a significant escalation of the war that went way beyond the dropping of South Vietnamese commandos into the North that Kennedy had approved.

A December memorandum for the President, prepared by Hilsman, detailing actions that had "been taken pursuant to NSAM-273," contained this passage:

> A joint CIA-Defense plan for intensified operations against North Vietnam, providing for selective actions of graduated scope and intensity, is being prepared in Saigon and is due in Washington by December 20.[19]

In the first weeks of December the plan was developed, and McNamara approved it at a SECDEF conference in Saigon on December 20. During this process, "provisions for expanded U.S. support or the commitment of U.S. forces to counter Communist escalation were incorporated into the final plan, which was then carried back to Washington."[20]

McNamara sent President Johnson a memo on December 21 stating:

> *Plans for Covert Action into North Vietnam* were prepared as we had requested and were an excellent job. They present a wide variety of sabotage and psychological operations against North Vietnam from which I believe we should aim to select those that provide maximum pressure with minimum risk. In accordance with your direction at the meeting, General Krulak of the JCS is chairing a group that

will lay out a program in the next ten days for your consideration. [emphasis in original][21]

Krulak submitted his report on January 2 and Johnson approved it on January 16, directing that the initial four-month Phase I—of the 2,062 separate operations listed as possible in the plan—be implemented on February 1.[22]

A Special Operations Group was established under MACV on January 24 to exercise operational control over 34A activities, which included maritime DE SOTO[23] "patrols" by U.S. destroyers in the Gulf of Tonkin to "acquire visual, electronic and photographic intelligence on infiltration activities and coastal navigation from North to South Vietnam."[24] The first DE SOTO patrol began on February 28 and lasted until March 10, during which the *Craig* was authorized to come within four nautical miles of the North Vietnamese mainland. The second patrol began on July 31, during which the *Maddox* was authorized to go within eight nautical miles of the coast, leading to the incident with North Vietnam on August 2— the match that lit the tinder box—and led to the Gulf of Tonkin Resolution by the American Congress, and, eventually, full-scale American intervention in the war.

While the seeds had been planted by the summer of 1963, Kennedy had never been shown 34A (then 34-63); they sprouted in the November 20 Honolulu meeting. Still, Bundy's draft NSAM had scaled back the proposed operations to keep them in line with Kennedy's concept of strictly South Vietnamese operations against the North. The dam broke when NSAM-273 was rewritten four days after Kennedy's assassination.

Two other provisions of the final NSAM-273 deserve comment. Paragraph eight, on operations in Laos, was also changed—in a subtle yet intriguing way. The sentence in question flowed from the requirements of Operation Switchback, the transfer of certain CIA covert paramilitary operations to MACV. The draft had said this would require a different method of political "liaison"—meaning MACV coordination with both Ambassador Lodge in Vietnam and Ambassador Leonard Unger in Laos. The revised NSAM said a redefined method of political "guidance" was required. What did this change signify?

That the word "liaison" was replaced by "guidance" might make it appear that the final NSAM was enhancing Embassy control over these operations, but this is not exactly what was going on. The draft NSAM said that MACV could conduct operations inside Laos up to fifty kilometers and required that they had to be coordinated, presumably with the Embassy and perhaps the local CIA Station. After Kennedy's death however, it is clear from the December State Department memo to Johnson mentioned above, that *the proposal for operations into Laos changed signifi-*

cantly. MACV would be able to run operations up to fifty kilometers inside Laos without any clearance at all, and could run operations deeper into Laos and would only be required to "inform" the Embassies in Vietnam and Laos.

All of this was acceptable to the Defense Department, the CIA, MACV, and CINCPAC, but not to the State Department. Hilsman insisted that *all* cross-border operations first be cleared in Washington by the Assistant Secretary of State for Far Eastern Affairs—himself—and the insertion of the word "guidance" was probably his idea. The fate of NSAM-273's provision for cross-border operations into Laos was ignominious. A November 1964 memo prepared in the State Department stated:

> Earlier this year several eight-man reconnaissance teams were parachuted into Laos as part of Operation Leaping Lena. All of these teams were located by the enemy and only four survivors returned to [South Vietnam].[25]

After this, of course, Operation Leeping Lena was suspended.

The final change between the draft NSAM and the final version occurred in paragraph nine, on investigating Cambodian charges against U.S. clandestine operations in that country. This was another subtle, but interesting revision. The draft had said the U.S. should undertake "measures" to "satisfy ourselves completely" that the charges were groundless—meaning, presumably, that if the charges were true the actions should be stopped—so that Cambodia could be given a "full opportunity to satisfy themselves on this same point." The final NSAM replaced all that with these words: "A plan should be developed using all available evidence and methods of persuasion for showing the Cambodians that the recent charges against us are groundless." Gone were the measures to "satisfy ourselves," and whatever actions would have been taken to verify the Cambodian charges.

The truly important change in NSAM-273, beyond dropping the investigation into the Cambodian charges and the attempt to widen operations into Laos, was the authorization for plans to widen the war against North Vietnam. McGeorge Bundy states that the difference between the draft and final versions of NSAM-273, the "strengthening" of its provisions for stepping up the war effort, "tracks with my memory of the directions Johnson issued on Sunday the 24th, and my clear recollection of the change that had taken place in the Oval Office."[26] Those changes were immediate, but the larger change between the two Presidents—the willingness to send U.S. ground combat forces to Vietnam—was still to come.

The reversal of intent with respect to combat troops, however, was as sudden as the emergence of OPLAN 34A. A comment that Lyndon Johnson made in December underlines the far-reaching and profound nature of this reversal and demonstrates how the tragedy of Dallas affected the course of the Vietnam War. While Kennedy had told O'Donnell in the spring of 1963 that he could not pull out of Vietnam until he was reelected, "So we had better make damned sure I *am* reelected," at a White House reception on Christmas eve, a month after he succeeded to the presidency, Lyndon Johnson told the Joint Chiefs: "Just let me get elected, and then you can have your war."[27]

Four agonizing years later, Johnson was pondering what his mistake in Vietnam had been. The way Johnson thought about it then seems odd today, for what he wondered about was whether he had waited *too long* to commit American ground troops. "He questions only whether the judgment of history will be," wrote Ted Sell in the *New York Times*, "that the United States acted too late—not whether American should have acted at all."[28] Whether this was in fact his mistake, and in this author's opinion it was not, that certainly did not turn out to be the judgment of history.

NOTES

1. AP release, November 21, 1963; see *New York Post*, November 21, 1963.

2. McGeorge Bundy, interview with the author, August 5, 1991.

3. Draft NSAM, 11/21/63, JFK Library, NSF, Meetings and Memoranda Files, Box 342.

4. For example, a February 24, 1961, memo for file of a JFK meeting with the JCS the day before said that Kennedy "wishes to have the matter of operations in Vietminh territory pressed." See Claflin, *Kennedy Wants to Know*, p. 52.

5. See, for example, Prince Norodon Sihanouk, *My War With the CIA* (New York: Random House, 1972), p. 269; see especially Chapter Eight, pp. 112–21.

6. Memorandum for the Record of Discussion at the Daily White House Staff Meeting, 8:00 A.M., November 22, 1963, in *State History*, 1963, vol. 4, Document 322, pp. 625–26.

7. McGeorge Bundy memo to Johnson, November 23, 1963, LBJ Library, NSF, Country File, Vietnam, Box 1.

8. Bill Moyers (who talked to LBJ right afterward), Tom Wicker, and David Halberstam all say Lodge was pessimistic. McCone and Johnson himself say Lodge was hopeful.

9. Tom Wicker, *JFK and LBJ: The Influence of Personality Upon Politics* (Baltimore,

MD: Penguin, 1968), p. 205; Karnow, *Vietnam*, p. 323; Halberstam, *The Best and the Brightest*, p. 298; and Schlesinger, *Robert Kennedy and His Times*, p. 726 (Schlesinger cites Wicker).

10. Karnow, *Vietnam*, p. 323.

11. Memorandum for the Record of a Meeting, Executive Office Building, 3:00 P.M., November 24, 1963, in *State History*, 1963, vol. 4, Document 330, pp. 635–37.

12. Lyndon Johnson, *The Vantage Point*, pp. 44–46.

13. JCS message No. 3698, 261755Z November 1963; LBJ Library, NSF, Country File, Vietnam, Box 1.

14. McNamara memo to Johnson, November 23, 1963, LBJ Library, NSF, Country File, Vietnam, Box 1.

15. Memo from Rusk to Johnson, November 24, 1963, with two enclosures: (1) a situation report on Vietnam, and (2) a briefing paper for LBJ's talk with Lodge; LBJ Library, NSF, Country File, Vietnam, Box 1.

16. This account is taken entirely from Bill Moyers, "Flashbacks," *Newsweek*, February 10, 1975.

17. McGeorge Bundy, interview with the author, August 5, 1991.

18. The word "hamlet" was replaced by "land," and the effect was not significant.

19. Hilsman memo to LBJ Library, NSF, Country File, Vietnam, Box 1, Document 76b; also see *Declassified Documents*, 1990, 3598.

20. *USN and the Vietnam Conflict*, p. 337.

21. *PP*, Gravel ed., vol. 3, Document 156, pp. 494–96.

22. Ibid., vol. 3, p. 151.

23. DE SOTO was the code name for covert U.S. Navy operations.

24. Ibid., vol. 5, p. 321.

25. Ibid., vol. 3, p. 610.

26. McGeorge Bundy, interview with the author, August 5, 1991.

27. Karnow, *Vietnam*, p. 326.

28. Ted Sell, *New York Times*, November 15, 1968.

CONCLUSION

THE WAR AND THE STRUGGLE FOR POWER

CAMELOT LOST

The first phase of the Vietnam War during the Kennedy administration lasted from the inauguration until the first days of May 1961. Overshadowed by the debacle in Cuba and the failure in Laos, Vietnam policy languished as the bureaucracy in Washington charged with developing it paid more attention to turf battles than those waged by the Viet Cong. The program produced—the Counterinsurgency Plan (CIP)—made the desperately needed new American aid dependent on reforms by Diem, a man whose record demonstrated that he would not implement them. The attempt to force him to do so turned into an ugly parody of intrigue in Saigon, wasting three precious months in the process. By the time the linkage between aid and reform was dropped and the Vice President sent out to patch things up, the Viet Cong had expanded their operations in Vietnam and captured most of the key terrain in Laos that would later become known as the Ho Chi Minh Trail.

The options, which the administration ended up facing in the summer of 1963, were already apparent by this stage: get out of Vietnam; instigate a coup against Diem; or say three Hail Marys and hope for the best with him. These choices were not clearly posed to the President, but he did not provide clear leadership either. The policy that emerged by default was the Hail Mary option. It was a sloppy, sluggish American slide into deeper commitment, more aid, and acquiescence to Diem.

What was painfully lacking in Washington was a concerted effort to define the nature of Vietnamese society; the insurgency raging there; and the nature of Diem's policies to cope with it. What would such an effort have revealed? At the minimum: a rural society whose political engine was driven by the simple aims of freedom from foreign bondage and government interference; a ferocious runaway insurgency that had long since ruthlessly harnessed this engine to its goal of a unified communist country; and a repressive and authoritarian regime in Saigon that stood in the path not only of the communist insurgency in the countryside, but also of the educated, noncommunist urban element of the population seeking a more democratic alternative for the country. By this time the autocratic nature of Diem's regime was simply one more unsavory aspect of his naked struggle for political power.

Even if such a systematic examination had been undertaken, it is doubtful that these sobering conclusions would have been accepted at the decision-making level in Washington. For the United States was already too deeply entrenched in Vietnam. The situation was well out of hand by the time Kennedy was elected, and the hope, enthusiasm, and vigor he symbolized only helped to forestall serious consideration of the true nature of the problem and the long odds America faced in Vietnam. The President began to understand, in those first three months, that the intrigues that had preoccupied both Saigon and Washington had not served U.S. policy well. Above all else he learned this: that his advisors—including the Vice President—wanted to intervene in Southeast Asia and that he did not.

TAKING CHARGE

The second phase of the war during the Kennedy years begins with NSAM-52 in early May 1961, and runs through the initial implementation of NSAM-111 at the end of the year. During the period between these two directives, three elements were on the rise: the success of the communist insurgency, the American commitment, and the resultant discord in Washington over what to do. NSAM-52 committed U.S. policy to preventing communist domination in Vietnam and dispatched 400 U.S. Special Forces advisors, while NSAM-80 in October dispatched the first Air Force Jungle Jim unit to participate in the war. In both instances the President, in making these decisions, had resisted a recommendation to send in combat troops, pushed mainly by the military in May, but largely supported by civilian advisors as well in October. The pressure for combat troops continued to build, especially when Taylor too, after his trip in late October, joined the chorus.

Kennedy's final decision—NSAM-111, issued on November 22, 1961—against intervention, was arrived at after all the arguments for it that could be made had been mustered: when the intelligence unequivocally showed the battlefield situation was desperate, when all his top advisors agreed that the fate of Vietnam hung in the balance, and when most of them believed that vital U.S. interests in the region and the world were at stake. Clearly, then, it was the major Vietnam decision of his presidency, drawing, as it did, a line that he never crossed. One of the principal theses of this work, derived from that decision, is that Kennedy would never have placed American combat troops in Vietnam. He did, nevertheless, make a commitment short of that, giving in to the urgency of the situation and to the pressure from his advisors, for NSAM-111 unleashed a flood of advisors, helicopters, and other equipment into Vietnam in the hope that American technology and know-how might somehow work a miracle.

Yet here, again, this momentous decision was made without the benefit of answers to the most basic questions: Why were the Viet Cong winning? Why wouldn't Diem mend his ways? At what point and under what conditions would the U.S. have to withdraw? The Hail Mary solution prevailed: a long shot with time running out. More advisors, more airplanes, and more helicopters were sent but the Viet Cong kept on growing. Kennedy had not faced the music; he had only taken the "bucket of slop," as Bissell called paramilitary operations, from the CIA and handed it to the military. The irony was that by the time Kennedy ruled out American combat troops, once and for all, the size of the Viet Cong had grown to the point where there was little hope that the South Vietnamese Army could contain it.

Kennedy had cleaned house in Washington and firmly taken charge, and the policy that emerged was his alone. Although he would not accept the recommendations of his advisors for combat troops—an act of great moral courage—neither would he accept defeat. Here was where the President became more personally entangled in the agony that his decision helped to prolong, and where his purpose became blurred by his own need to retain political power.

THE DECEIVERS AND THE DECEIVED

The third phase of the war during the Kennedy presidency, which lasted for the first half of 1962, was marked by the continued and dramatic growth of the Viet Cong and a sudden reversal toward optimism in the U.S. military's reporting on the war. Since this change occurred well before the new Kennedy program had any chance to influence the situation, it was suspicious—all the more so considering the military's long record of dire reports on the state of the battlefield. One of the theses of this work is that this reversal in reporting went well beyond the deception of official optimism and the denial of the true extent of U.S. involvement that the administration was engaging in. Rather, it was conducted at the top secret level and went so far as to eliminate from the order of battle more than half of the hard-core Viet Cong forces.

Because the President was cognizant of—and encouraged—the first level of this deception, and was, at the same time, the target of the second, the phrases "deception within a deception" or "inside deception" have been used to characterize the deepening web of intrigue that followed Kennedy's refusal to put combat troops into Vietnam. That refusal was the baseline from which all planning had to proceed. The Viet Cong's explosion, in the spring of 1962, beyond the ability of the South Vietnamese Army's ability to cope with them meant that the advisory effort was not working. The reason this was hidden from the President probably was because, of the two military choices available, withdrawal or intervention, his bar against combat troops would have meant withdrawal.

Prompted in April by Galbraith, Kennedy appeared to entertain the thought of a neutralist solution in Vietnam but was dissuaded by a consensus of his military and civilian advisors. Here the deception of progress looms large in building the case for a lengthier American presence and in encouraging hope for victory. Although Kennedy decided to pursue that course, McNamara made clear—probably at the President's urging—that there was still a limit to how long U.S. participation could last because the public would not accept American casualties indefinitely.

DARKNESS AT THE END OF THE TUNNEL

The fourth phase of the war in the Kennedy years extends from the summer of 1962 to the spring of 1963. This phase began while the false story of success continued to build the hopes of Kennedy and McNamara in ultimate victory. At this point, consumed by the Cuban Missile Crisis, they let Vietnam policy run its course. Too little attention was paid to the fact that the illusion of success somehow always seemed to require more men, more planes, more helicopters and other equipment to sustain it. Eventually, Kennedy and McNamara found themselves trapped in a deepening vortex of military escalation in which victory seemed ever more elusive. By the spring of 1963 the involvement had become so deep that the failure unfolding on the battlefield began to have foreboding implications for Kennedy's chances at a second term as President.

It was not that the American military had not done its job in Vietnam. It had. The advisors had counseled the South Vietnamese Army, and the intelligence specialists had been accurate and honest in reporting on the enemy. In retrospect, these men are the real heroes of the early stages of the war; but they were up against impossible odds. The South Vietnamese Army was too small and Diem was reluctant to let them fight anyway. The organization and training of South Vietnamese forces in general was wholly inappropriate to counterinsurgency operations, and MACV failed to pass on to Washington the observations of American advisors about the resulting problems. The harsh judgment of history on the American military performance in Vietnam during the Kennedy years should not fall on the privates, sergeants, lieutenants, and captains; it should fall on the command level and the senior leadership in Washington.

THE TRAGIC CROSSROADS

The final phase of Kennedy's developing dilemma in Vietnam, then, began in the spring of 1963. The Buddhist crisis and subsequent political collapse of the Saigon regime in the summer transformed his predicament into a nightmare. The President reconciled himself to pulling the U.S. out of the war and to the unpopularity he was sure this decision would bring. Perhaps a sense of guilt over his own role clouded his vision and helped move him to conclude that *only* his reelection could extricate America from the mess in Vietnam. The elements of his plan to accomplish this became increasingly desperate as the situation continued to deteriorate into the fall and Diem met his grim fate.

Kennedy's plan to pull out contained four components, three of which were present by the time the design was firmly put into place in the spring.

First and foremost was his belief that the bulk of the withdrawal could not take place before the election without sparking another Joe McCarthy–style red scare that might dash the chance for extrication. Unfortunately, this part of the plan required that Kennedy project an image to the conservatives that did not reflect his true views on the war. The second element of the plan was to trickle out some of the Americans *during* the campaign in order to neutralize the growing criticism from liberals who felt the U.S. was becoming bogged down in the war. To begin such a limited withdrawal without provoking the conservative backlash he feared was difficult to do. The key to accomplishing it was the third ingredient of the plan: linking the 1,000-man withdrawal to the MACV success story emanating from Saigon.

If, by this time, Kennedy had not given up entirely on the notion of winning, he at least had deep suspicions about MACV's reporting. In hindsight, his willingness to tie the 1,000-man pullout to the story of success is indicative of the desperation that began creeping into his actions, and it raises the more fundamental issues of candor and presidential prerogative. At the time, however, this tie-in to success was so vital to his plan that the veracity of the success story probably seemed minor compared to the goal he sought: resolution of the seemingly intractable American problem in Vietnam.

The fourth and final component to his plan resulted from the political collapse in Saigon. That both the military and political sides of the struggle there were collapsing threatened the tie-in to success. Kennedy would be vulnerable to attacks from *both* sides of the aisle if he publicly justified the 1,000-man withdrawal by a presumption of battlefield success and that "success" then turned into a failure (especially if this occurred during an election campaign). Therefore, the last girder he put into place in the fall was the arrangement for his top military advisors to publicly make the case for this linkage (1,000-man withdrawal linked to success on the battlefield) while he remained at a safe political distance from any potentially damaging implications.

There seems little doubt that Kennedy was headed for a total withdrawal—come what may—from Vietnam when he left for Texas. Whether the comments he made to Senator Morse and Mike Forrestal indicate he was thinking of accelerating his plan is an intriguing idea but one that remains unproven. Any such modification, as well as the plan itself, were snuffed out on November 22, 1963. The vague sentence in NSAM-273 on withdrawal—however much we contrast its nuances with the clear-cut words of NSAM-263—became a fig leaf of continuity in the hands of the new President. The tragedy in Texas, in the end, brought about the outcome that Kennedy had opposed throughout his presidency: full-scale American intervention in Vietnam.

KENNEDY AND COMBAT TROOPS

Many unanswered questions remain about Kennedy and Vietnam. For example, just what was the new study he was in the midst of when he died? Would he have been willing to face the consequences of accelerating the pullout and seeking a neutral South Vietnam during an election year? Why did his last press conferences no longer include winning the war as an American objective? These questions may not be answered with authority, but one question can be: would Kennedy have sent in the combat troops as Johnson did? The answer to that is no. That perennial question has been the focus of debate for nearly thirty years, but its politicization has obscured the more fundamental questions raised by the *way* he dealt with this issue. These questions strike at the very heart of the American presidency and processes of government and have great relevance for the study of the subsequent administrations.

Kennedy's public duplicity on the issue of American intervention has made it all too easy for Johnson apologists to seize on Kennedy's statements as proof that he too would have sent in the troops. The speech he would have delivered at the Trade Mart in Dallas, had he lived, was the last example of this questionable pretense. The speech contained this passage:

> Our assistance to these nations can be painful, risky and costly, as is true in Southeast Asia today. But we dare not weary of the task. For our assistance makes possible the stationing of 3.5 million allied troops along the Communist frontier at one-tenth the cost of maintaining a comparable number of American soldiers. A successful Communist breakthrough in these areas [like Southeast Asia], *necessitating direct United States intervention*, would cost us several times as much as our entire foreign aid program, and might cost us heavily in American lives as well. [emphasis added][1]

The Kennedy apologists who ignore such statements are no more helpful than his critics who rely on them exclusively. Disregarding them only subverts the truth. The fact is that he made them, and did so continuously, up to the day he died. However high or noble his larger purpose may have been, in so doing he besmirched his own reputation and that of the office he held.

There is no need to restate here the evidence that Kennedy would not have sent in combat troops; it is sufficient to say that the top secret NSC meetings of 1961 more than resolve the question. There is also no need to revisit the sad litany of his misleading public statements. Both of these subjects have been dealt with in detail and at length in this work. The real questions posed by the Janus-like nature of his public and private postures go to the core of the American political system: What is the legitimate national interest? Who shall decide this? When is it permissible for the President to mislead the public about his intentions with respect to war? With respect to anything? Is there a higher end that justifies these means? If one President may deceive to stay out of a war, cannot another do likewise to go into one?

Kennedy concluded that a retreat from Vietnam could not happen unless he was reelected. Although subsequent events appear to have justified such a conclusion, the fact is that he had the option to withdraw when he realized that failure was inevitable and to fight honestly for his beliefs in the campaign, relying on strong leadership and example. To do so meant rising above the personal goal of political power, and attempting to inspire and unify friends and foes alike as he did in his inaugural address. This course would have been risky, but so was the one he was pursuing. By taking his case directly to the people the onus would have been placed upon those arguing for intervention.

The Dallas Trade Mart speech contains another passage that merits attention:

> We in this country, in this generation, are—by destiny rather than choice—the watchmen on the walls of freedom. We ask, therefore, that we may be worthy of our strength with wisdom and restraint, and that we may achieve in our time and for all time the ancient vision of "peace on earth, good will toward men." That must always be our goal, and the righteousness of our cause must always underlie our strength. For as was written long ago: *except the Lord keep the city, the watchman waketh in vain.* [emphasis in original]

Perhaps lying veiled in this old parable is Kennedy's recognition and his acceptance of the fact that his efforts at one place along that long wall had met defeat: Vietnam. Still, speaking about policy in parables, however eloquent, was no way to take his case to the people.

In raising these questions, the intent is not to demean Kennedy and his many accomplishments; but failing to raise them would demean both. We can no longer afford to look at just one side of Camelot, to do so trivializes Kennedy's life and the price the nation paid for his death. We can still admire him for the great courage he showed in ruling out the use of American combat troops in Vietnam, and point out that he had been deceived, for a time, about the state of the war effort, understanding that that deception was instrumental in the choices he made. Had he lived, he still would have had time to take his case truthfully to the American people in 1964, and he might have done so. That he never had the chance was his misfortune and the nation's as well. Finally, it must be pointed out that Kennedy was not the President who sent in the troops. As a highly decorated U.S. Army General said in 1968: "Let us not lay on the dead the blame for our own failures."[2]

WHAT ABOUT THE ASSASSINATION AND THE WAR?

Clearly the most tragic consequence of Kennedy's death was the subsequent escalation of the war. One may argue about which aspect of war policy was altered, changed, or reversed, and how suddenly or gradually it happened, but the fact is that it did happen. Scholars with august reputations steer clear of looking seriously at this question in part because it is so politically charged and, like Kennedy's war policies, it raises basic and alarming questions about American democratic institutions.

The American people have never been satisfied with the official explanation of the Kennedy assassination, nor has the Congress for that matter. Nevertheless, it is psychologically less troubling to believe that Johnson carried on Kennedy's Vietnam policy than to acknowledge the reverse. If that premise, and the Warren Commission's conclusion that Lee Harvey Oswald acted alone, are dispelled, where, then, does honest inquiry lead? Until now, such inquiry has been off-limits for serious political scientists and historians because of the conspiratorial presumptions that appear inherent in the material. The implication seems to be that any study that dares examine the possibility of a recent conspiracy is somehow un-American. Yet, in fact, it is *that* idea that is un-American. That we the people have not only the right but the duty to examine such questions is a basic assumption of our most treasured political institutions.

Hopefully the passage of time has begun to erode fears of looking critically at the role of the assassination in the subsequent escalation of the war. Unfortunately, appropriate educational background and rigorous analytical methodology is virtually absent among those few who have tackled the subject. The one exception that comes to mind is Professor Peter Dale Scott, a serious early researcher who was stigmatized for his effort; in 1972 he persuasively argued that the assassination played a major role in the escalation of the war.[3] The problem that Scott faced in the six years he had spent researching the subject was a lack of adequate documentation, not the least of which is the gaping documentary hole in *The Pentagon Papers* between the end of October 1963 and the assassination. Scott's chapter in volume 5 of the Senator Gravel edition of *The Pentagon Papers* was a monumental effort to unlock the mysteries of NSAM-273—without actually having seen the document—an effort that even Sherlock Holmes would have admired.

The final version of NSAM-273 was declassified a few years later but it was not until 1991, when an early draft of it and many of the secret documents from the last half of 1963 were declassified, that a more robust foundation for analyzing and interpreting that period was established. Perhaps the present work will encourage further examination of this subject as well as the broader political issues involved. How the war progressed after Kennedy's death, and the assassination itself, are subjects beyond the scope of this work. One lesson the author learned in the process of researching and writing this book is that preconceived and simplistic ideas most often do not hold up under careful scrutiny. For that reason no effort will be made here to offer quick answers to these profound questions. It is hoped, however, that this work will help to establish the respectability of this subject matter as a legitimate field of inquiry.

Finally, the sometimes startling nature of the events detailed and the preliminary interpretations in this work should be considered no more than a first attempt to reopen this lost chapter of American history and to draw the lessons we must from its mistakes. The issues at stake go beyond the Kennedy administration and the Vietnam War: they touch upon the entire spectrum of our political institutions and Western moral and ethical traditions.

NOTES

1. Kennedy, *Public Papers*, 1963, p. 893.
2. General James Gavin, "We Can Get Out of Vietnam," *Saturday Evening Post*, February 24, 1968.
3. *PP*, Gravel ed., vol. 5, pp. 211–32; see also Peter Dale Scott, *The War Conspiracy: The Secret Road to the Second Indochina War* (New York: Bobbs-Merrill, 1972).

ACRONYMS

ACSI: Army Assistant Chief of Staff for Intelligence
ADVON: Advance Echelon
AF: Air Force
AFB: Air Force Base
AID: Agency for International Development
ARVN: Army of the Republic of Vietnam [South]
ASA: U.S. Army Security Agency
ASAP: as soon as possible
CAS: Saigon office for CIA
CDC: Combat Development Command
CG: Civil Guard
CHMAAG: Chief, Military Assistance Advisory Group
CHMAAG SVN: Chief, Military Assistance Advisory Group, South Vietnam
CI: counterinsurgency
CIA: Central Intelligence Agency
CIDG: Citizens Irregular Defense Groups
CINC: Commander-in-Chief
CINCPAC: Commander-in-Chief, Pacific
CINCPACAF: Commander-in-Chief, Pacific Air Force
CINCPACFLT: Commander-in-Chief, Pacific Fleet
CIP: Counterinsurgency Plan

CO: Commanding Officer
Col: Colonel
COMUS: Vietnam, Commander of U.S. Forces, Vietnam
CONUS: Continental United States
COSMUSMACV: Commander, U.S. Military Assistance Command, Vietnam
COSVN: Central Office of South Vietnam
CPSVN: Comprehensive Plan for South Vietnam
CT: Country Team
CY: calender year
DCM: Deputy Chief of Mission
DCSOPS: Deputy Chief of Staff for Operations
DIA: Defense Intelligence Agency
DMZ: demilitarized zone
DOD: Department of Defense
DRV: Democratic Republic of Vietnam [North]
FSO: Foreign Service Officer
FY: fiscal year
FYI: for your information
GEN: General
GVN: Government of South Vietnam
Hq: Headquarters
Hq Det: Headquarters Detachment
ICA: International Cooperation Administration
ICC: International Control Commission
INR: Bureau of Intelligence and Research, Department of State
ISA: Office of International Security Affairs, Department of Defense
ISC: International Security Council
JCS: Joint Chiefs of Staff
JCSM: Joint Chiefs of Staff memorandum
JEC: Joint Evaluation Center
JGS: Joint General Staff (South Vietnamese counterpart of the JCS)
JIG: Joint Intelligence Group
KIA: killed in action
LTG: Lieutenant General
MAAG: Military Assistance Advisory Group
MACV: Military Assistance Command, Vietnam
MAP: Military Assistance Program
MilAd: Military Advisor
msg: message
MSTS: Military Sea Transport Service
NATO: North Atlantic Treaty Organization
NCO: Noncommissioned Officer

NEA: Bureau of Near Eastern and South Asian Affairs, Department of State
NIE: National Intelligence Estimate
NSAM: National Security Action Memorandum
NSC: National Security Council
NVA: North Vietnamese Army
NVN: North Vietnam
OASD/ISA: Office of the Assistant Secretary of Defense for International Security Affairs
OB: order of battle
ONE: Office of National Estimates, CIA
Opcon: Operational control
OPLAN: Operation Plan
OPS: Operations
OSA: Office of Special Assistant to the Ambassador in Vietnam, Office of the Secretary of the Army
OSD: Office of Secretary of Defense
PACAF: Pacific Air Force
PACFLT: Pacific Fleet
PACOM: Pacific Command
PAO: Public Affairs Officer
PAVN: People's Army of Vietnam [North]
PIO: Public Information Officer
PL: Pathet Lao
PolAd: Political Advisor
POW: prisoner of war
PsyOps: Psychological Operations
PsyWar: Psychological Warfare
RAdm: Rear Admiral
RDF: radio direction finding
RKG: Royal Khmer Government
RLA: Royal Laotian Army
RLG: Royal Laotian Government
ROK: Republic of Korea
RRU: Radio Research Unit
RVN: Republic of Vietnam [South]
RVNAF: Republic of Vietnam Armed Forces
SAC: Strategic Air Command
SACSA: Special Assistant of Counterinsurgency and Special Activities
SDC: Self Defense Corps
SEA: Southeast Asia
SEATO: Southeast Asian Treaty Organization
SECDEF: Secretary of Defense
SF: U.S. Army Special Forces

SI: Special Intelligence
SIGINT: signals intelligence
SNIE: Special National Intelligence Estimate
SSO: Staff Security Office
SVN: South Vietnam
TAC: Tactical Air Command
TACS: Tactical Air Control System
TF: Task Force
TF (Vn): Task Force (on Vietnam)
TS: top secret
U: unclassified
UN: United Nations
USA: U.S. Army, United States of America
USAID: U.S. Agency for International Development
USAF: U.S. Air Force
USARPAC: U.S. Army, Pacific
USARV: U.S. Army, Vietnam
USFV: U.S. Forces, Vietnam
USG: U.S. Government
USIA: U.S. Information Agency
USIB: United States Intelligence Board
USIS: U.S. Information Service
USN: U.S. Navy
USOM: U.S. Operations Mission
VNAF: (South) Vietnamese Air Force
VOA: Voice of America
VC: Viet Cong
VN: Vietnam, Vietnamese
XO: Executive Officer, second in command to Senior Officer
Z: Greenwich Mean Time
Zone D: Viet Cong jungle base area northeast of Saigon

LIST OF PERSONS

Allen, George: Analyst for DIA, from 1962 to 1963

Anthis, Brigadier General Roland H.: Commander of the U.S. Second Air Division; Chief, U.S. Air Force Advisory Group, Vietnam, from 1962

Ball, George W.: Under Secretary of State for Economic Affairs, February 1 to December 3, 1961; Under Secretary of State from January 1, 1962

Bao Dai: exiled Emperor of Vietnam

Battle, Lucius D.: Special Assistant to the Secretary of State and Executive Secretary of the Department of State

Benedict, William: Analyst for Assistant Chief of Staff, Intelligence, Army, Directorate of Foreign Intelligence from 1961 to 1962

Blascak, Don: Officer in MACV J-2, Special Operations, from 1962 to 1963

Bohlen, Charles E.: Special Assistant to the Secretary of State until 1963; thereafter Ambassador to France

Bowles, Chester: Under Secretary of State, January 25 to December 3, 1961; Ambassador-at-Large until July 19, 1963; thereafter Ambassador to India

Bundy, McGeorge: Special Assistant to the President for National Security Affairs

Bundy, William P.: Deputy Assistant Secretary of Defense for International Security Affairs; Defense Representative on the Task Force on Southeast Asia

Burke, Admiral Arleigh A.: Chief of Naval Operations until August 1, 1961

Burris, Colonel Howard L.: Vice President Johnson's Military Aide

Carroll, Lieutenant General Joseph F.: Director, Defense Intelligence Agency

Chiang Kai-shek: President of the Republic of China

Colby, William E.: CIA Station Chief in Saigon, 1959–1962; Chief of CIA's Far East Division, 1962–1968.

Conein, Lucien: Army Lieutenant Colonel, assigned to the Interior Ministry; maintained CIA contacts with Vietnamese generals, 1962–1963

Cooper, Chester L.: Assistant for Policy Support to the Deputy Director for Intelligence, Central Intelligence Agency, until November 1963; thereafter Assistant Deputy Director for Policy Support

Cottrell, Sterling J.: Political Advisor to the Commander in Chief, Pacific, until April 1961; Director, Interdepartmental Task Force on Vietnam, from May 1961 to June 1962; thereafter Deputy Director and Chairman of the Task Force on Southeast Asia

Dam, Bat Dinh: Commander of ARVN 7th Division from late 1962

Decker, General George H.: Army Chief of Staff

De Gaulle, Charles: President of France

Dowling, Sam: Staff Security Officer, MACV, from 1962 to 1963

Drummond, James: Intelligence Advisor, 7th ARVN Division, from 1962 to 1963

Dulles, Allen W.: Director of Central Intelligence until November 1961

Duong Van "Big" Minh, Major General (after November 4, 1963, Lieutenant General): Commander of the Army Field Command, Republic of Vietnam Army, until December 1962; Military Advisor to President Diem until November 1, 1963; thereafter Chairman of the Executive Committee of the Revolutionary Council; President of the Provincial Government of the Republic of Vietnam after November 4, 1963

Durbrow, Elbridge: Ambassador to Vietnam until May 3, 1961

Dutton, Roland: Commander, Special Forces A-Team, Laos, in 1962; Commander, Special Forces A-Team, Vietnam, in 1963

Eisenhower, Dwight D.: President of the United States until January 20, 1961

Felt, Admiral Harry D.: Commander-in-Chief, Pacific

Forrestal, Michael V.: National Security Council staff member

Galbraith, John Kenneth: Ambassador to India from April 18, 1961

Gilpatric, Roswell L.: Deputy Secretary of Defense from January 24, 1961; Chairman of the Presidential Task Force on Vietnam, April to May 1961; member of the Counterinsurgency Group in 1963

Glenn, Dr. Thomas L., III: Department of Defense Special Representative, Saigon, in 1962

Halberstam, David: Reporter for the *New York Times* in 1962 and 1963

Harkins, General Paul D.: Commander of the Military Advisory Command, Vietnam, from February 8, 1962

Harriman, W. Averell: Ambassador-at-Large, February 13 to December 3, 1961; Assistant Secretary of State for Far Eastern Affairs and Chairman of the Task Force on Southeast Asia until April 13, 1963; thereafter Under Secretary of State for Political Affairs and Chairman of the Special Group for Counterinsurgency

Harris, Jim: Intelligence Analyst, MACV J-2, from 1962 to 1963

Helble, John J.: Consul in Hue

Hilsman, Roger: Director of the Bureau of Intelligence and Research, Department of State, from February 19, 1961, until April 25, 1963; thereafter Assistant Secretary of State for Far Eastern Affairs

Ho Chi Minh: President of the Democratic Republic of Vietnam

Hughes, Thomas L.: Deputy Director of the Bureau of Intelligence and Research until April 28, 1963; thereafter Director

Johnson, Lyndon B.: Vice President of the United States from January 20, 1961, until November 22, 1963; thereafter President

Johnson, Robert: Member of the National Security Council Staff and Alternate Member of the Interdepartmental Task Force on Vietnam, 1961; member of the Policy Planning Council in 1962

Johnson, U. Alexis: Member of the Presidential Task Force on Vietnam, April to May 1961; Deputy Under Secretary of State for Political Affairs from May 2, 1961

Kennedy, John F.: President of the United States from January 20, 1961, until November 22, 1963

Kennedy, Robert F.: Attorney General

Khrushchev, Nikita S.: Chairman of the Council of Ministers of the Soviet Union

King, Jerry: Commander, Special Forces A-Team, Laos, in 1962

Komer, Robert W.: National Security Council staff member

Krulak, Major General Victor H.: Special Assistant for Counterinsurgency and Special Activities, Joint Staff of the Joint Chiefs of Staff; JCS representative on the Task Force on Southeast Asia

Lansdale, Brigadier General Edward G.: Deputy Assistant for Special Operations to the Secretary of Defense until May 1961; thereafter Assistant for Special Operations to the Secretary of Defense; member, Presidential Task Force on Vietnam, April to May 1961

Lemnitzer, General Lyman L.: Chairman of the Joint Chiefs of Staff until October 1, 1962

Lodge, Henry Cabot, Jr.: Ambassador to South Vietnam from August 26, 1963

Mansfield, Mike: Senator from Montana and member of the Foreign Relations Committee; Majority Leader after January 3, 1961

Mao Tse-tung: Chairman of the Central Committee, People's Republic of China

McConaughy, Walter P.: Assistant Secretary of State for Far Eastern Affairs, April 24 to December 3, 1961; thereafter Special Assistant in the Office of the Deputy Under Secretary of State for Administration

McCone, John A.: Director of Central Intelligence from November 29, 1961

McGarr, Lieutenant General Lionel C.: Chief of the Military Assistance Advisory Group, Vietnam

McNamara, Robert S.: Secretary of Defense from January 21, 1961

Mecklin, John: Public Affairs Officer at the Embassy in Saigon, July 8 to September 28, 1962; thereafter Counselor for Public Affairs

Mendenhall, Joseph A.: Counselor for Political Affairs in Vietnam and Chairman of the Country Team Staff Committee until June 23, 1963; thereafter United Nations Advisor, Bureau of Far Eastern Affairs, Department of State

Morse, Wayne: Democratic Senator from Oregon and member of the Senate Foreign Relations Committee

Murrow, Edward R.: Director of the U.S. Information Agency from March 21, 1961

Nehru, Jawaharlal: Prime Minister and Minister of External Affairs and for Atomic Energy of India

Ngo Dinh Can: Brother of President Diem and unofficial governor of Central Vietnam

Ngo Dinh Diem: President and Secretary of National Defense of the Republic of Vietnam until November 1, 1963

Ngo Dinh Nhu: Brother of President Diem and Political Advisor to the President; Head of the Interministerial Committee for Strategic Hamlets until November 1, 1963

Ngo Dinh Nhu, Madame (Tran Le Xuan): Sister-in-law of President Diem and member of the Vietnamese National Assembly; official hostess for the President; daughter of Tran Van Chuong

Ngo Dinh Thuc: Brother of President Diem and Archbishop of Hue

Nguyen Ngoc Tho: Vice President of the Republic of Vietnam and Secretary of State for National Economy; after May 27, 1961, Vice President and Coordinating Secretary of State for Economic Development until November 4, 1963; thereafter Prime Minister and Minister of Finance and National Economy of the Provincial Government

Nolting, Frederick E.: Ambassador to Vietnam from May 10, 1961, until August 15, 1963

Parsons, J. Graham: Assistant Secretary of State for Far Eastern Affairs until March 30, 1961

Phillips, Rufus: Consultant at the Operations Mission in Vietnam, June 9 to September 19, 1962; thereafter Assistant Director for Rural Affairs

Phoumi, Nosavan, General: Laotian Deputy Premier and Minister of Defense

Porter, Colonel Daniel Boone: Senior U.S. Advisor, III Corps, Vietnam, from 1962 to 1963

Rice, Edward E.: Member of the Policy Planning Staff, Department of State in 1961; thereafter Deputy Assistant Secretary of State for Far Eastern Affairs

Richardson, John: CIA Station Chief in Saigon from 1962 until October 5, 1963

Rostow, Walt W.: Deputy Special Assistant to the President for National Security Affairs until December 4, 1961; thereafter Counselor of the Department of State and Chairman of the Policy Planning Council; Member of the Presidential Task Force on Vietnam, April to May 1961

Rowan, Carl T.: Deputy Assistant Secretary of State for Public Affairs from February 27, 1961; thereafter Counselor of the Department of State and Chairman of the Policy Planning Council; Member of the Presidential Task Force on Vietnam, April to May 1961

Rusk, Dean: Secretary of State from January 21, 1961

Salinger, Pierre: President Kennedy's Press Secretary

Schlesinger, Arthur M., Jr.: President Kennedy's Special Assistant

Sheehan, Neil: United Press International correspondent in Vietnam

Sihanouk, Prince Norodom: Head of State of Cambodia; also President of the Council of Ministers from January 26, 1961

Sorensen, Theodore C.: President's Special Counsel

Souphanouvong, Prince: Pathet Lao leader and representative to the Geneva Conference on Laos; Deputy Premier and Economics Minister from July 1962

Souvanna Phouma, Prince: Premier of the neutralist government of Laos

Staley, Eugene A.: Research Director of the Standford Research Institute

Sullivan, William H.: United Nations Advisor, Bureau of Far Eastern Affairs, Department of State, until April 28, 1963; thereafter Assistant to the Under Secretary of State

Sylvester, Arthur: Assistant Secretary of Defense for Public Affairs

Taylor, General Maxwell D.: President Kennedy's Military Representative from July 1, 1961, until October 1, 1962; thereafter Chairman of the Joint Chiefs of Staff

Thuan (Nguyen Dinh Thuan): Vietnamese Secretary of State for the Presidency of the Republic of Vietnam and Assistant Secretary of State for National Defense; after May 27, 1961, Secretary of State for the Presidency in Charge of Security Coordination and Assistant Secretary of State for National Defense

Timmes, Major General Charles J.: Chief of the Military Assistance Advisory Group, Vietnam, from March 6, 1962

Tixier Lou: Intelligence analyst at USARPAC, 1962

Tran Thien Khiem, General: ARVN, Chief of Staff after November 1,

1963, Military Affairs Member, Executive Committee of the Military Revolutionary Council

Tran Van Chuong: Ambassador of the Republic of Vietnam to the United States until August 22, 1963, and the father of Madame Nhu

Tran Van Don, General: I Corps Commander, Republic of Vietnam Army, until December 1962; Commander of III Corps until July 1963; thereafter Commander of the Army of the Republic of Vietnam; Acting Chief of the Joint General Staff after August 1963; First Deputy Chairman of the Executive Committee of the Military Revolutionary Council after November 1, 1963; Minister of National Defense after November 4, 1963

Tri Quang: Bonze, Buddhist opposition leader

Truehart, William C.: Counselor and Deputy Chief of Mission at the Embassy in Vietnam from October 29, 1961

Vann, John Paul: Senior Intelligence Advisor, 7th ARVN Division, 1962 to 1963

Wheeler, Lieutenant General Earl G.: Director, Joint Staff Organization, Joint Chiefs of Staff; became Army Chief of Staff in 1962

Williams, General Samuel T. "Hangin' Sam": US MAAG Chief in Vietnam, 1955–60

Winterbottom James: Chief of Intelligence (J-2) MACV, 1962–3

Wood, Chalmers B.: Officer in Charge of Vietnam Affairs in the Bureau of Far Eastern Affairs, Department of State; Member of the Interdepartmental Task Force on Vietnam from May 1961 until June; thereafter Executive Director of the Working Group on Vietnam and State Department representative on the Task Force on Southeast Asia

GLOSSARY

Agency: Central Intelligence Agency

Ap Bac: South Vietnamese hamlet near Cambodian border; site of Battle of Ap Bac in January 1963

A-Teams: Twelve-man Green Beret units

Attrition: The wearing away of enemy forces to the point where they are either unable or unwilling to continue fighting

B-52: U.S. heavy bomber

Battalion: A military organizational unit of about 900 in infantry and 500 in artillery, but usually smaller in the Vietnam War

Bonze: Buddhist monk or priest

Buddhism: Dominant organized religion of Vietnam

Chieu Hoi: "Open Arms"; program under which GVN offered amnesty to Viet Cong defectors

Company: A military organizational unit consisting of two or more platoons

Corps: A military organizational unit made up of at least two divisions

Counterinsurgency: Military, paramilitary, political, economical, psychological, and civic actions taken by a government to defeat subversive insurgency

Defense: U.S. Department of Defense

Defoliant: Herbicides used to destroy dense vegetation or jungle

Demilitarized Zone: Buffer zone of about five miles between North and South Vietnam

Division: A military organizational unit consisting of approximately 20,000 troops

Escort: Armed helicopter escort

Farm Gate: U.S. Air Force combat detachment; its mission was air operations in support of ground forces; also called Jungle Jim

Fatigues: Standard combat uniform, green in color

G-1: Military personnel staff division

G-2: Military intelligence staff division

G-3: Military operations staff division

G-4: Military logistics staff division

Green Berets: Members of Special Forces of the U.S. Army

Guerrillas: Soldiers of a resistance movement who are organized on a military or paramilitary basis

Guerrilla warfare: Military operations conducted in enemy-held or hostile territory by irregular, prominently indigenous forces

Hamlet: A small rural village

Huey: Nickname for the UH-series helicopters

Insurgency: A condition of revolt against a government

Irregulars: Armed individuals and groups not members of the regular armed forces, police, or other internal security forces

J-2: Chief, Joint Intelligence Section, MACV (highest U.S. military intelligence officer in Vietnam)

J-2, JGS: Chief, Joint Intelligence Section, JGS (senior South Vietnamese military intelligence officer)

Jungle Jim: The 4400th Combat Crew Training Squadron; see Farm Gate

Lao Dong Party: Vietnamese Workers' Party, Marxist-Leninist Party of North Vietnam

Local Force: Viet Cong combat unit subordinate to a district or province headquarters

Main Force: Viet Cong and North Vietnamese military units

Millpond: U.S. plan for graduated responses in Laos (1961)

Mission: The Embassy

Montagnards: Primitive tribespeople living in mountainous region in Vietnam

Napalm: Incendiary used in Vietnam by French and Americans both as defoliant and antipersonnel weapon

Neutrality: The state of being not aligned with a political or ideological grouping

Pacification: Several programs of the South Vietnamese and U.S. governments to destroy the Viet Cong in the villages, gain civilian support for the government of South Vietnam, and stabilize the countryside

Pathet Lao: Communist-controlled group in Laos

Platoon: Approximately forty-five men belonging to a company

Province Chief: Governor of a state-sized administrative territory in South Vietnam, usually a high-ranking military officer

Regional Forces: South Vietnamese paramilitary troops organized at the province level to protect villages and hamlets

Special Forces: U.S. soldiers, popularly known as Green Berets, trained in techniques of guerrilla warfare

State: U.S. Department of State

Strategic Hamlets: Program conceived and inaugurated by Diem's brother Nhu for the defense of rural South Vietnam against communist attacks and penetration

Sunrise: GVN clear-and-hold operation in Binh Duong Province in 1962

Tan Son Nhut: Airport in Saigon

Tonkin Gulf Incident: Encounter between U.S. destroyers and North Vietnamese torpedo boats in July 1964. As a result Congress passed a resolution authorizing President Johnson to take military action to defend U.S. forces and allies in South Vietnam

Viet Cong: Communist forces fighting the South Vietnamese government

Viet Minh: Viet Nam Doc Lap Dong Minh Hoi, or the Vietnamese Independence League

Walk in the sun: Ground troop movement free of the risk of combat

CHRONOLOGY

1961

January 6	Khrushchev speech on Soviet support of "wars of national liberation" includes Vietnam
January 19	Eisenhower tells JFK he might have to intervene in Laos
January 20	Kennedy inaugurated
January 28	First White House meeting on Vietnam: CIP approved, links U.S. aid to SVN reforms; JFK decides to replace Ambassador Durbrow with Lansdale
February 1	NSAM-2: emphasis on counterinsurgency plans
February 5	NSAM-12: JFK query to JCS if ARVN forces can be better distributed
February 7	Initial Laos Task Force plan approved, recommending neutralization of Laos, military offensive by Phoumi
February 13	Ambassador Durbrow presents CIP to Diem

February 14	Decision to appoint Lansdale as Ambassador scuttled by this date; Nolting chosen
February 23	NSC meeting: JFK unhappy with progress in developing counterinsurgency plans
March 6	Pathet Lao destroy a large part of Phoumi's army, initial JFK Laos plan fails
March 9	Laos Task Force recommends Operation Millpond
March 21–22	Two NSC meetings: argument over intervention in Laos
March 28	SNIE: Army kills argument favoring coup against Diem
March 29	SEATO Ministers Council meeting; Rusk meets with Thuan, signals support for Diem
April 4	Soviet broadcast demands Laos conference before cease-fire
April 13	Lansdale writes plan for Vietnam Task Force
April 17	Invasion of Bay of Pigs, Cuba
April 20	American military effort in Laos upgraded to MAAG; servicemen don uniforms
	Kennedy approves setting up of Vietnam Task Force
April 26	JCS alerts CINCPAC "to be prepared to undertake air strikes against NVN, possibly southern China"
April 27	Laos meeting: JCS proposes intervention; LBJ supports; JFK not convinced, defers decision
	JFK approves Vietnam Task Force plan; Lansdale will not be going to Vietnam
April 28	Laos Annex to Vietnam Task Force plan recommends U.S. troop commitment to Vietnam
April 29	JFK advisors hold brainstorming session on Laos: reach consensus on intervention
May 1	NSC Meeting: Laos intervention looks bleak
May 2	NSC Meeting: Laos intervention looks bleaker

May 2–4	Kennedy decides not to intervene in Laos
May 5	Kennedy at news conference announces Vice President Johnson will visit South Vietnam
May 6	Vietnam Task Force issues report recommending preparation for possible commitment of combat troops to Vietnam, to be decided after Johnson talks with Diem
May 10	JCS strongly recommends sending U.S. combat troops to Vietnam
	Ambassador Nolting arrives in VN
May 11	NSAM-52 issued, approving U.S. objective to prevent communist domination of South Vietnam; authorizes increase in MAAG, 400 U.S. Special Forces to South Vietnam, and JCS to study combat troops deployment to South Vietnam
	Laos conference convenes in Geneva.
May 11–13	Johnson in Vietnam, meets with Diem, commits U.S. to fund 20,000-man increase in ARVN, Diem agrees to send two letters, second with wish list; Diem agrees to U.S. combat troops for training
May 15	Diem's first letter sent to JFK
May 18	JCS reiterates support for combat troops to Vietnam
May 19	NSAM-52 reviewed: no combat troops
May 25	Johnson briefs cabinet and then testifies before Congress on Vietnam trip
May 29	Kennedy sends cable to all Embassies in the world stating the Ambassadors are in charge of the entire mission
June 14	Thuan meets with Kennedy, delivers Diem's second letter; Kennedy ignores request for "elements" of U.S. forces
June 28	NSAMs 55, 56, and 57 issued: plans to turn over large covert paramilitary operations from CIA to DOD

mid-June to mid-July	Staley mission sent to South Vietnam to help develop economic plan, returns with Joint Action Program recommending an ARVN force increase
July 18–21	Major VC–Pathet Lao operation conducted, creating "pocket at Tchepone," widening area for VC infiltration into South Vietnam and giving communists control of network of trails to the south and west
August 11	NSAM-65 issued, stating U.S. would provide equipment and training assistance for an increase in the South Vietnamese Army from 170,000 to 200,000
August 17	Rostow plan for intervention in Laos
August 24	Harriman torpedos Rostow Laos plan
August 29	NSAM-80 issued, authorizing discussion of SEATO Plan 5 with allies as contingency plan only, "intensification" of Harriman's diplomatic efforts in Geneva, and small increase in U.S. advisors in South Vietnam to level of 500
September 15	Rostow forwards General Craig's Vietnam report urging U.S. intervention in Vietnam
September 18	Large VC action in Phuoc Vinh Province
September 30	Diem requests bilateral defense treaty with the U.S.
October 5	Presidential advisor Walt Rostow to JFK: "As for Vietnam, it is agreed we must move quite radically to avoid perhaps slow but total defeat. The sense of the town is that, with Southern Laos open, Diem simply cannot cope."
	SNIE cites growth of Viet Cong
October 10	SNIE says Hanoi and Beijing will not counter SEATO intervention in Vietnam
October 11	Diem requests U.S. combat troops
	NSC meeting: U. Alexis Johnson presents plan to intervene in South Vietnam; Kennedy defers decision again and issues NSAM-104, authorizing one

Jungle Jim squadron to Vietnam, allowing U.S. advisors to go along on guerrilla operations in Laos; Taylor to go to South Vietnam

October 18   Taylor mission arrives in Saigon to assess situation

November 1–21   Various proposals for sending U.S. combat troops to South Vietnam

November 1   Taylor cable to JFK: proposes U.S. combat forces go to South Vietnam under cover of "flood relief task force"

November 2   Taylor mission returns to Washington

November 5   NIE reverses earlier judgment, now says U.S. escalation would be matched by Hanoi, air attacks against North Vietnam would not stop its support for Viet Cong, and Moscow and Peking would react strongly to such raids

November 22   NSAM-111 issued, approves significant increases in advisors and equipment, but no combat troops

November 26–29   Kennedy's "Thanksgiving Day Massacre" occurs, reorganizing top State Department and CIA jobs

November 27   McNamara given responsibility for carrying out Kennedy's Vietnam problem

                 Nolting instructed that if his discussions with Diem were "clearly not satisfactory" he should return promptly to Washington

December 4   Nolting reports Diem's substantive agreement with U.S. policy

December 8   State Department releases "A Threat to the Peace: North Vietnam's Effort to Conquer South Vietnam"

December 10   Two helicopter companies arrive in South Vietnam as U.S. advisory effort widens

December 16   First SECDEF conference convenes in Honolulu

December 22   Specialist Fourth Class James T. Davis is shot and killed by a Viet Cong soldier during an ambush, making him the first American to die in open combat with the VC

1962

January 13 — JCS memorandum: if VC are not brought under control, Chiefs see no alternative to the introduction of U.S. combat forces

January 15 — Second SECDEF conference convenes in Honolulu, situation in Vietnam reported to be going bad, training of Civil Guard and Self Defense Corps made top priority, "clear and hold" operations discussed

January 18 — NSAM-124 issued, creating special group (Counter-Insurgency) for Laos, South Vietnam, and Thailand, to be headed by Taylor

February 2 — C-130 crashes on low-level training mission, killing all three American crewmen, the first three Air Force fatalities of the war

February 8 — CINCPAC establishes MACV as subordinate command, headed by General Harkins

February 19 — Third SECDEF conference convenes in Honolulu: Harkins is optimistic about situation in Vietnam, so is Nolting; MACV unclear about size of enemy; McNamara demands "this intelligence problem must be solved"

February 21 — National Intelligence Estimate gives continued gloomy picture of situation in Vietnam

March — GVN's relations with press deteriorate

early March — First press reports of American Farm Gate missions

March 17 — Hilsman visits Saigon to brief Harkins on "strategic concept" for Vietnam, returns to Washington "very disturbed" about Operation Sunrise (protected hamlets)

March 19 — Diem approves Strategic Hamlet Program

March 20–21 — Large Viet Cong airlift using Soviet aircraft occurs near Cambodian border

March 22	Fourth SECDEF conference convenes, leading to further expansion of secret American air war in Vietnam; McNamara told the war is going well
March 24	Laos conference convenes in Thailand, Phoumi will not agree to coalition government
March 29	Admiral Felt presents Joint Chiefs with plan of various cover stories to keep U.S. air operations in Vietnam covert
April 4	Memorandum from Ambassador John Kenneth Galbraith to JFK urges neutral solution in Vietnam and measurably reducing U.S. commitment to Diem
April 6	JFK, Harriman, and Forrestal discuss Galbraith memorandum; JFK says, "Be prepared to seize upon any favorable moment to reduce our commitment"
April 8	Two Americans killed and two captured during Viet Cong ambush of South Vietnamese platoon on training mission; press coverage causes concern over American deaths in combat and whether or not Americans are fighting in the war
April 13	JCS strong rebuttal to Galbraith memo, equates it to a "reversal of U.S. policy"
April 15	MACV publishes first extensive Viet Cong order of battle of 16,305 hard-core Viet Cong
May 2–6	Pathet Lao attack Nam Tha, taking control of the last airfield in northern Laos, and Nam Tha itself
May 8–11	Fifth SECDEF conference convenes in Saigon, VC order of battle of 16,500 reported to McNamara; McNamara tells Harkins to produce plan for winning and getting out; Laos discussed; McNamara tells press he is "encouraged"
May 12	President Kennedy directs deployment of U.S. forces to Thailand due to deteriorating situation in Laos
June 11	The three princes in Laos agree to form a govern-

ment of national union, headed by Souvanna Phouma

June 23   New coalition government formed in Laos, declares Laos neutral, renounces SEATO protection, and objects to presence of U.S. forces in Thailand

Early July   Geneva conference convened to conclude Laos negotiations

July 20   South Vietnam's so-called greatest battle of the war conducted by Colonel Cao's 7th Division

July 23   Laos Conference ends; declaration of neutrality signed in Geneva

Sixth SECDEF conference convenes in Hawaii; Harkins tells McNamara, "We are on the winning side"; McNamara directs Harkins to begin planning for phaseout of U.S. forces in Vietnam by 1965

August 14   CINCPAC orders MACV to develop Comprehensive Plan for South Vietnam to carry out phased American withdrawal

September 11   Taylor, shortly to be Chairman of the JCS, leaves for South Vietnam, pleased with progress of war effort

September 28   NSAM-189 issued, directing the withdrawal of all U.S. military forces in Laos

October 8   Seventh SECDEF conference convenes in Honolulu; Harkins says war is going well, presents his "explosion" plan, requests more U.S. fighter planes; McNamara urges Harkins to get Vietnamese pilots flying operations

October 16–28   Cuban Missile Crisis

1963

January   Hilsman and Forrestal visit South Vietnam

General Wheeler visits South Vietnam, reports war is going well

January 2   Two Viet Cong companies badly defeat three

South Vietnamese battalions and an M113 company task force at battle of Ap Bac

January 4   Admiral Felt, CINCPAC, arrives in Vietnam, confers with General Harkins, sees "inevitable" defeat of Viet Cong, confident South Vietnamese will win the war

January 11   CIA Current Intelligence Memorandum: "Though the South Vietnam government probably is now holding its own against the Viet Cong and may be reducing the menace in some areas. . . . on balance, the war remains a slowly escalating stalemate"

February 7   Krulak reports on war in Vietnam, is optimistic about success

February 24   Senator Mansfield reports situation in Vietnam appears less stable than in 1955 despite U.S. aid

April 17   NIE 53-63: "We believe that Communist progress has been blunted and that the situation is improving"

May   JCS and CINCPAC to prepare plans for "nonattributable hit-and-run operations against North Vietnam." Conducted by the South Vietnamese, these operations will be carried out with "U.S. military materiel, training, and advisory assistance"

May 6   Eighth SECDEF conference convenes in Honolulu: Harkins confirms progress in military situation, presents McNamara with Comprehensive Plan for South Vietnam; McNamara directs it to be revised to reflect faster American withdrawal and acceleration of training programs, and directs "concrete plans" to be drawn up for 1,000-man withdrawal

May 8   Government troops fire on crowd in Hue celebrating Buddha's birthday, killing seven

May 9   JCS formally directs CINCPAC: "As a matter of urgency a plan for withdrawal of about 1,000 U.S. troops before the end of the year should be developed based upon the assumption that the progress of the counterinsurgency campaign would warrant such a move"

June 1–3   Government troops gas demonstrators in Quang Tri and Hue, three "unconfirmed" deaths reported

June 11   Buddhist monk Thich Quang Duc burns himself to death on busy street in Saigon

State cables Trueheart: "If Diem does not take prompt and effective steps to reestablish Buddhist confidence in him we will have to reexamine our entire relationship with his regime"

June 14   State instructs Truehart to consider steps to "gradually increase covert and overt contacts with nonsupporters of GVN"

late June   Moderate Buddhist leadership replaced with more radical monks with less conciliatory policy toward government

June 27   President Kennedy announces appointment of Henry Cabot Lodge as Ambassador

July 4   General Don contacts CIA Agent Conein seeking U.S. advice and support for coup against Diem

July 17   President Kennedy in news conference says war effort is hurt by crisis

July 21   Felt (CINCPAC) presents the JCS with final plan for the 1,000-man withdrawal

August 15   Ambassador Nolting departs from Saigon

August 20   Taylor sends JCS recommendation for 1,000-man withdrawal to McNamara, saying he should approve the MACV-CINCPAC proposed plan "in three to four increments for planning purposes only"

August 21   Diem imposes martial law; Nhu's forces raid pagodas, arresting over 1,400 Buddhists

August 22   Lodge arrives in Saigon as new Ambassador

August 24   Hilsman and Harriman send "August 24 cable" to Lodge, instructing him to demand the removal of Nhu, and if Diem does not comply they would have to "face the possibility that Diem himself cannot be preserved"

August 27   CIA Station in Saigon reports the generals, headed by "Big" Minh, "agreed a coup will take place within one week"

August 31   CIA Station in Saigon says that Harkins had decided in meeting with General Khiem that the generals did not have enough support for a coup, ending coup planning for the time being

September 2   JFK, in interview with Walter Cronkite, says South Vietnamese government "has gotten out of touch with people"

September 3   McNamara approves JCS recommendation on 1,000-man withdrawal plan but warns against creating special units as a means to cut back unnecessary personnel

September 8   Krulak and Mendenhall arrive in Saigon

September 9   JCS approves OPLAN 34-63, a program of covert action against North Vietnam

                   U.S. decides to cut aid unless government institutes reform

September 10   At White House meeting to hear reports of Krulak and Mendenhall, just back from Vietnam, Kennedy asks: "The two of you did visit the same country, didn't you?"

September 11   Lodge tells Diem that Nhu must go, Diem says that is unacceptable

September 12   JFK at press conference: "What helps win the war, we support; what interferes with the war, we oppose"

September 21   JFK sends McNamara and Taylor to South Vietnam to review military situation

September 24   McNamara and Taylor arrive in Vietnam

October 2   McNamara and Taylor report to JFK and National Security Council: say South Vietnam political situation serious, but war can be won by end of 1965

unless political crisis hampers war effort; recommend withdrawal of 1,000 men in 1963

October 5

CIA operative Lou Conein meets with General Don, who says, "Action to change the government must be taken or the war will be lost to the Viet Cong"

White House cables Lodge: "No initiative should now be taken to give any active covert encouragement to a coup," but covert action that is "secure and totally deniable" should be taken to build contacts with possible alternative leadership

October 9

White House cables Lodge: "While we do not wish to stimulate coup, we also do not wish to leave impression that U.S. would thwart a change of government"

October 11

NSAM-263 issued, directing implementation of 1,000-man withdrawal, with no formal announcement made, by the end of 1963

October 16

Lodge reports to Kennedy: "We appear to be doing little more than holding our own"

October 22

State Department's RFE-90 concludes war is going much worse than MACV reports

October 30

Lodge reports to Kennedy that General Don "did not think the war could be won [with] the present government in power before the Americans left and certainly not after that"

October 31

Kennedy says at press conference that "if" the U.S. could withdraw 1,000 men by the end of the year, "that would be our schedule"

November 1

Military coup in Saigon; Diem and Nhu assassinated; Vice President Tho and military generals take over control

November 2

Rusk cable to Lodge announcing November 20 Honolulu meeting

November 6

Lodge cables Kennedy: "I believe prospects of a victory are much improved provided the generals stay united"

November 6	Krulak authors talking paper criticizing RFE-90
November 8	U.S. recognizes new government in South Vietnam
November 12	Kennedy informs Senator Morse of his "intensive study" on Vietnam and admits Morse's criticism of his Vietnam policy was correct
November 14	Kennedy press conference lists first American objective in Vietnam policy as "to bring Americans home"
November 16	General Timmes, CHMAAG in South Vietnam, announces 1,000-man withdrawal by the end of 1963, following Kennedy's lifting of secrecy of timetable
November 20	Honolulu meeting convenes: for the first time since early 1962 MACV reports are accurate on the war situation in the Delta (it was critical); OPLAN 34-63 discussed: Colby opposes, McNamara sides with JCS
November 21	NSAM-273 drafted
	Kennedy tells Forrestal that upon Forrestal's return from his trip to Cambodia, "I want to start a complete and very profound review of how we got into this country [Vietnam]; what we thought we were doing; and what we now think we can do. . . . I even want to think about whether or not we should be there."
November 22	President Kennedy assassinated in Dallas
November 24	At White House meeting, President Johnson expresses his dissatisfaction with operations in Vietnam up to this point, and says, "I am not going to be the President who saw Southeast Asia go the way China went"
November 26	NSAM-273 signed by Johnson; final NSAM is changed from November 21 draft—change is escalatory
December	Hilsman memo to Johnson details actions taken

pursuant to NSAM-273, including a joint CIA-Defense plan for "intensified actions against North Vietnam"

December 20   At SECDEF conference, McNamara approves plan of covert actions against North Vietnam

BIBLIOGRAPHY

Adler, Renata. *Reckless Disregard: Westmoreland v. CBS et al.; Sharon v. Time.* New York: Knopf, 1986.

Allen, George. *The Indochina Wars: 1950–1975.* Unpublished manuscript.

Anson, Robert Sam. *War News.* New York: Simon and Schuster, 1989.

Atkins, James D. *The Edge of War.* Chicago: Henry Regenry, 1960.

Austin, Anthony. *The President's War: The Story of the Tonkin Gulf Resolution and How the Nation Was Trapped in Vietnam.* New York: Lippincott, 1971.

Ball, George W. *The Discipline of Power: Essentials of a Modern World Structure.* Boston: Little, Brown, 1968.

———. *The Past Has Another Pattern: Memoirs.* New York: Norton, 1973.

Berman, Larry. *Planning a Tragedy: The Americanization of the War in Vietnam.* New York: Norton, 1982.

Biu Diem with David Chanoff. *In the Jaws of History.* Boston: Houghton Mifflin, 1987.

Boettcher, Thomas D. *Vietnam: The Valor and the Sorrow.* Toronto: Little, Brown, 1985.

Bohlen, Charles E. *Witness to History, 1929–1969.* New York: Norton, 1973.

Bowles, Chester L. *Promises to Keep.* New York: Harper and Row, 1971.

Bows, Ray A. *Vietnam Military Lore, 1959–1973.* 2 vols. Hanover, MA: Bowes and Sons, 1988.

Bradlee, Benjamin C. *Conversations With Kennedy.* New York: Norton, 1975.

Brewin, Bob, and Sydney Shaw. *Vietnam on Trial: Westmoreland v. CBS.* New York, Atheneum, 1987.

Bundy, William. Untitled. Unpublished manuscript.

Charlton, Michael, and Anthony Moncrieff. *Many Reasons Why.* New York: Hill and Wang, 1978.

Claflin, Edward B. *Kennedy Wants to Know.* New York: William Morrow, 1991.

Clifford, Clark. *Counsel to the President: A Memoir.* New York: Random House, 1991.

Cohen, Steven. *Vietnam: Anthology and Guide to Television History.* New York: Knopf, 1983.

Colby, William. *Honorable Men.* New York: Simon and Schuster, 1978.

———. *Lost Victory.* Chicago: Contemporary Books, 1989.

Cooper, Chester. *The Lost Crusade.* New York: Dodd, Mead, 1970.

Currey, Cecil B. *Self-Destruction: The Disintegration and Decay of the United States Army During the Vietnam War.* New York: Norton, 1981.

Davidson, Phillip B. *Secrets of the Vietnam War.* Novato, CA: Presidio Press, 1990.

———. *Vietnam at War: The History, 1946–1957.* New York: Knopf, 1983.

Department of the Army. *Vietnam Studies: The Role of Military Intelligence, 1965–1967.* Washington, D.C.: U.S. Government Printing Office, 1974.

Department of Defense. *United States–Vietnam Relations, 1945–1967.* 12 vols. Washington, D.C.: U.S. Government Printing Office, 1971.

Department of State. *Foreign Relations of the United States, 1961–1963: Vietnam.* 4 vols. Washington, D.C.: U.S. Government Printing Office, 1988–91.

Dommen, Arthur. *Conflict in Laos.* New York: Praeger, 1971.

Facts on File. *South Vietnam: U.S.-Communist Confrontation in Southeast Asia, 1961–65.* New York: Facts on File, 1966.

Fay, Paul B., Jr. *The Pleasure of His Company.* New York: Harper and Row, 1966.

Fulbright, J. William. *The Arrogance of Power.* New York: Random House, 1966.

Futrell, Robert Frank, and Martin Blumenson. *The United States Air Force in Southeast Asia: The Advisory Years to 1965.* Washington, D.C.: U.S. Government Printing Office, 1981.

Galbraith, John Kenneth. *How to Control the Military.* Garden City, NY: Doubleday, 1969.

———. *A Life in Our Times.* Boston: Houghton Mifflin, 1981.

Galluci, Robert L. *Neither Peace Nor Honor: The Politics of American Policy in Vietnam.* Baltimore: Johns Hopkins University Press, 1975.

Gelb, Leslie H., with Richard K. Betts. *The Irony of Vietnam: The System Worked.* Washington, D.C.: The Brookings Institution, 1979.

Gibbons, William Conrad. *The U.S. Government and the Vietnam War.* 3 vols. Princeton: University Press, 1986.

Goodwin, Richard N. *Triumph or Tragedy: Reflections on Vietnam.* New York: Random House, 1976.

Graff, Henry H. *The Tuesday Cabinet: Deliberation and Decision on Peace and War Under Lyndon B. Johnson.* Englewood Cliffs, NJ: Prentice-Hall, 1970.

Grant, Zalin. *Facing the Phoenix: The CIA and Political Defeat of the United States in Vietnam.* New York: Norton, 1991.

Gulley, Bill, with Mary Ellen Reese. *Breaking Cover.* New York: Simon and Schuster, 1980.

Halberstam, David. *The Best and the Brightest.* New York: Random House, 1972.

————. *The Making of a Quagmire.* New York: Random House, 1964.

————. *The Powers That Be.* New York: Knopf, 1979.

Gravel, Senator Mike, ed. *The Pentagon Papers: History of the United States Decision Making on Vietnam.* 5 vols. Boston: Beacon Press, 1971.

Haley, J. Evetts. *A Texan Looks at Lyndon: A Study in Illegitimate Power.* Canyon, TX: Palo Duro Press, 1964.

Hallin, Daniel C. *The Uncensored War: The Media in Vietnam.* New York: Oxford University Press, 1989.

Herring, George C. *America's Longest War: The United States and Vietnam, 1950–1975.* 2d. ed. New York: Knopf, 1986.

Hammond, William. *U.S. Army in Vietnam: The Military and the Media, 1962–1968.* Washington, D.C.: Center for Military History, U.S. Army, 1988.

Hilsman, Roger. *To Move a Nation.* New York: Doubleday, 1967.

Johnson, Lyndon Baines. *A Time for Action.* New York: Pocket Books, 1964.

————. *The Vantage Point.* New York: Holt, Rinehart and Winston of Canada, 1971.

Johnson, U. Alexis. *Right Hand of Power.* Englewood Cliffs, NJ: Prentice-Hall, 1984.

Kahin, George McT. *Intervention: How America Became Involved in Vietnam.* Garden City, NY: Anchor/Doubleday, 1987.

Karnow, Stanley. *Vietnam: A History.* New York: Viking, 1983.

Kelly, Francis J. *Vietnam Studies: U.S. Army Special Forces, 1961–1971.* Washington, D.C.: U.S. Government Printing Office, 1985.

Kennedy, John F. *Profiles in Courage.* New York: Harper and Brothers, 1955.

————. *Public Papers of the Presidents of the United States: John F. Kennedy, 1961–63.* Washington, D.C.: U.S. Government Printing Office, 1962.

————. *The Strategy of Peace.* New York: Harper and Row, 1960.

Kennedy, Robert F. *In His Own Words: The Unpublished Recollections of the Kennedy Years.* New York: Bantam, 1988.

————. *Thirteen Days: A Memoir of the Cuban Missile Crisis*. New York: Norton, 1969.

————. *To Seek a Newer World*. Garden City, NY: Doubleday, 1967.

Komer, Robert W. *Bureaucracy at War: U.S. Performance in the Vietnam Conflict*. Boulder, CO: Westview Press, 1986.

Krepinevich, Andrew. *The Army and Vietnam*. Baltimore: Johns Hopkins University Press, 1986.

Krock, Arthur. *Memoirs: Sixty Years on the Firing Line*. New York: Funk and Wagnalls, 1968.

Krulak, Victor H. *First to Fight: An Inside View of the U.S. Marine Corps*. Annapolis, MD: Naval Institute Press, 1984.

Lansdale, Edward G. *In the Midst of Wars*. New York: Harper and Row, 1972.

Lewy, Richard. *America in Vietnam*. New York: Oxford University Press, 1981.

Lodge, Henry Cabot. *As It Was: An Inside View of Politics and Power in the 50's and 60's*. New York: Norton, 1976.

Maclear, Michael. *The 10,000 Day War: Vietnam, 1945–1975*. New York: Avon, 1981.

Macmillan, Harold. *Pointing the Way, 1959–1961*. New York: Harper and Row, 1972.

Mailer, Norman. *The Presidential Papers of Norman Mailer*. New York: Bantam, 1964.

Manchester, William. *Portrait of a President*. Rev. ed. Boston: Little, Brown, 1967.

Maneli, Mieczyslaw. *War of the Vanquished*. New York: Harper and Row, 1971.

Marolda, Edward J., and Oscar P. Fitzgerald. *The United States Navy and the Vietnam Conflict*. Washington, D.C.: U.S. Government Printing Office, 1986.

Martin, David C. *Wilderness of Mirrors*. New York, Harper and Row, 1980.

Martin, Ralph G. *A Hero for Our Time: An Intimate Story of the Kennedy Years*. New York: Macmillan, 1983.

Mecklin, John. *Mission in Torment*. Garden City, NY: Doubleday, 1975.

Meyer, Col. Howard J. *Hanging Sam: A Military Biography of General Samuel T. Williams*. Denton, TX: University of North Texas Press, 1990.

Moyers, Bill. *The Secret Government: The Constitution in Crisis*. Washington, D.C.: Seven Locks Press, 1988.

Nguyen Cao Ky. *How We Lost the Vietnam War*. New York: Stein and Day, 1976.

Nolting, Frederick E. *From Trust to Tragedy*. New York: Praeger, 1988.

O'Brien, Lawrence F. *No Final Victories*. New York: Ballantine, 1974.

O'Donnell, Kenneth. *Johnny, We Hardly Knew Ye.* Boston: Little, Brown, 1970.

Oglesby, Carl. *The Yankee and Cowboy War: Conspiracies From Dallas to Watergate.* Kansas City: Sheed Andrews and McMeel, 1976.

Olson, James, ed. *Dictionary of the Vietnam War.* New York: Peter Bedrick Books, 1987.

Palmer, Gen. Bruce, Jr. *The 25-Year War: America's Military Role in Vietnam.* New York: Simon and Schuster, 1984.

Palmer, Dave R. *Summons of the Trumpet: U.S.-Vietnam in Perspective.* San Rafael, CA: Presidio Press, 1978.

Parker, Charles F., IV. *Vietnam: Strategy for a Stalemate.* New York: Paragon House, 1989.

Parmet, Herbert S. *Jack: The Struggles of John F. Kennedy.* New York: Dial, 1980.

Patti, Archimedes L.A. *Why Vietnam? Prelude to America's Albatross.* Berkeley: University of California Press, 1980.

Pfeffer, Richard C., ed. *No More Vietnams?* New York: Harper and Row, 1968.

Pike, Douglas. *History of Vietnamese Communism, 1925–1976.* Stanford, CA: Hoover Institution Press, 1978.

———. *Viet Cong.* Cambridge, MA: MIT Press, 1966.

Porter, Gareth, ed. *Vietnam: The Definitive Documentation of Human Decisions.* 2 vols. Stanfordville, New York: Earl M. Coleman Enterprises, 1979.

Powers, Thomas. *The Man Who Kept the Secrets.* New York: Knopf, 1979.

Prouty, Fletcher. *The Secret Team.* Englewood Cliffs, NJ: Prentice-Hall, 1973.

Rostow, W.W. *The Diffusion of Power: An Essay in Recent History.* New York: Macmillan, 1972.

Rowan, Carl T. *Breaking Barriers.* Boston: Little, Brown, 1991.

Rusk, Dean. *As I Saw It.* New York: Norton, 1990.

———. *Winds of Freedom.* Boston: Beacon Press, 1963.

Rust, William. *Kennedy in Vietnam: American Vietnam Policy, 1960–1963.* New York: Charles Scribner's Sons, 1985.

Schlesinger, Arthur. *The Bitter Heritage: Vietnam and American Democracy, 1961–1966.* Boston: Houghton Mifflin, 1966.

———. *Robert Kennedy and His Times.* Boston: Houghton Mifflin, 1978.

———. *A Thousand Days.* New York: Fawcett, 1965.

Schoenbaum, Thomas J. *Waging Peace and War: Dean Rusk in the Truman, Kennedy, and Johnson Years.* New York: Simon and Schuster, 1988.

Scott, Peter Dale. *The War Conspiracy: The Secret Road to the Second Indochina War.* New York: Bobbs-Merrill, 1972.

Shaplen, Robert. *The Lost Revolution: The U.S. in Vietnam, 1946–1966.* Rev. ed. New York: Harper and Row, 1969.

————. *Time Out of Hand: Revolution and Reaction in Southeast Asia.* New York: Harper and Row, 1969.

Sharp, Adm. U.S.G. *Strategy in Defeat: Vietnam in Retrospect.* San Rafael, CA: Presidio Press, 1978.

———— and Gen. W.C. Westmoreland. *Report on the War in Vietnam.* Washington, D.C.: U.S. Government Printing Office, 1968.

Sheehan, Neil. *A Bright Shining Lie.* New York: Random House, 1988.

Sidey, Hugh. *John F. Kennedy, President.* New York: Atheneum, 1964.

Sihanouk, Prince Norodom. *My War With the CIA.* New York: Random House, 1972.

Snepp, Frank. *Decent Interval.* New York: Vintage, 1978.

Sorensen, Theodore. *Kennedy.* New York: Harper and Row, 1965.

Spector, Ronald H. *Advice and Support: The Early Years, the U.S. Army in Vietnam.* Washington, D.C.: U.S. Government Printing Office, 1983.

Stavins, Ralph, Richard J. Barnett, and Marcus G. Raskin. *Washington Plans an Aggressive War: A Documented Account of the United States Adventure in Indochina.* New York: Random House, 1971.

Stevenson, Charles A. *The End of Nowhere: American Policy Toward Laos Since 1954.* Boston: Beacon Press, 1972.

Summers, Col. Harry G. *On Strategy: A Critical Analysis of the Vietnam War.* Novato, CA: Presidio Press, 1982.

Taylor, John M. *General Maxwell Taylor.* New York: Doubleday, 1989.

Taylor, Gen. Maxwell D. *Responsibility and Response.* New York: Harper and Row, 1967.

————. *Swords and Plowshares.* New York: Norton, 1972.

Tilford, Earl H., Jr. *Search and Rescue in Southeast Asia, 1961–1975.* Washington, D.C.: Office of Air Force History, 1980.

Tran Van Don. *Our Endless War: Inside Vietnam.* Novato, CA: Presidio Press, 1978.

Trewhitt, Henry L. *McNamara.* New York: Harper and Row, 1971.

White, Ralph K. *Nobody Wanted War.* Garden City, NY: Anchor/Doubleday, 1970.

Wicker, Tom. *JFK and LBJ: The Influence of Personality Upon Politics.* Baltimore: Penguin, 1968.

Wyden, Peter. *Bay of Pigs.* New York: Simon and Schuster, 1979.

INTERVIEWS AND ORAL HISTORIES

Unless otherwise indicated, all interviews are with the author.

Adams, Samuel. July 6, 1987; July 7, 1987.

Allen, George. July 6, 1987; August 10, 1987; June 4, 1988; June 7, 1988; June 14, 1989.

Allen, George, and William Benedict. Joint interview. July 21, 1988.

Benedict, William. June 6, 1988; June 9, 1988; June 26, 1988; July 21, 1988; November 22, 1988; June 13, 1989.

Blascak, Don. January 6, 1988; April 30, 1988; May 29, 1988; June 13, 1989; July 4, 1991.

Bowles, Chester. Interview with Joe B. Frantz. November 11, 1969. LBJ Library, Oral History Collection.

Bundy, McGeorge. July 16, 1991; August 5, 1991.

Bundy, William. July 11, 1991.

Burke, Admiral Arleigh. Interview with Joseph E. O'Connor. January 20, 1967. JFK Library, Oral History Collection.

Burris, Howard. May 8, 1991; June 29, 1991.

Colby, William. Interview with the author. October 29, 1987; December 28, 1987; December 29, 1987; December 30, 1987; July 21, 1988; December 8, 1990; December 28, 1990; July 4, 1991.

————. Interview with Ted Gittinger. March 1, 1982. LBJ Library, Oral History Collection.

Crile, George. June 9, 1989.

Decker, General George H., Senior Officers Debriefing Program Interview with Lt. Col. Dan H. Ralls. November 3, 1972. U.S. Army Military History Research Collection, Carlisle, Pennsylvania.

Depuy, General William E. Senior Officers Debriefing Program Interview with Lt. Col. Bill Mullen and Lt. Col. Les Brownlee. March 19, 1979. U.S. Military History Research Collection, Carlisle, Pennsylvania.

Dowling, Sam. June 2, 1988; June 5, 1988; June 12, 1988; July 6, 1989.

Drummond, James. June 9, 1989; June 14, 1989; November 10, 1990.

Durbrow, Elbridge. Interview with Congressional Research Service. October 25, 1978.

Dutton, Roland. June 10, 1991.

Ellsberg, Daniel. August 8, 1991.

Ford, Hal. July 22, 1988.

Gilpatric, Roswell L. Interview with Dennis J. O'Brian. May 5, 1970. JFK Library, Oral History Collection.

Glenn, Dr. Thomas L., III. December 21, 1987.

Halberstam, David. June 18, 1988.

Hamlett, General Barksdale. Senior Officers Debriefing Program Interview with Col. Jack Ridgeway and Lt. Col. Paul Walter. January 23, 1976. U.S. Army Military History Research Collection, Carlisle, Pennsylvania.

Harkins, General Paul D. Interview with Jacob B. Couch, Jr. April 28, 1974. U.S. Army Military History Research Collection, Carlisle, Pennsylvania.

————. Interview with Ted Gittinger. November 10, 1981. LBJ Library, Oral History Collection.

Harris, Jim. June 4, 1988; June 7, 1988.

Hilsman, Roger. Interview with Paige E. Mulhollan. May 15, 1969. LBJ Library, Oral History Collection.

Johnson, General Howard K. Senior Officers Debriefing Program Interview with Col. Richard W. Jensen and Lt. Col. Rupert F. Glover. January 27, 1972. U.S. Army Military History Research Collection, Carlisle, Pennsylvania.

Jordan, Amos. June 26, 1988.

Joy, Jess. June 11, 1988.

Karnow, Stanley. January 1988.

King, Jerry. May 25, 1991; June 22, 1991.

Lemnitzer, Gen. Lyman L. Senior Officers Debriefing Program Interview with Lt. Col. Walter J. Bickson. February 17, 1972. U.S. Army Military History Research Collection, Carlisle, Pennsylvania.

McChristian, Joseph A. June 30, 1988; June 10, 1989.

McColsky, Jack. July 2, 1988.

Methvin, Gene. May 15, 1991.

Parsons, J. Graham. Interview with Dennis J. O'Brian. August 22, 1969. JFK Library, Oral History Collection.

Phillips, Rufus. April 20, 1991.

Porter, Daniel Boone. July 2, 1988; June 7, 1989.

Prouty, Fletcher. June 26, 1991.

Rostow, W.W. Interview with the author. February 4, 1988.

————. Interview with Richard Neustadt. April 11, 1964. JFK Library, Oral History Collection.

Smith, Sam. June 14, 1989.

Vann, John Paul. Interview with Charles V.P. von Littichau. July 22, 1963. Military History Institute, Oral History Collection.

Vought, Don. November 2, 1990; November 9, 1990.

Westmoreland, Gen. William C. Interview with Maj. Paul L. Miles. March 6, 1971. Army Center for Military History, Oral History Collection.

Whitson, William. April 30, 1991.

INDEX